CIVIL RIGHTS
IN THE
UNITED STATES

CIVIL RIGHTS

— IN THE —

UNITED STATES

Edited by

WALDO E. MARTIN, JR.
Department of History
University of California, Berkeley

and

PATRICIA SULLIVAN
W. E. B. Du Bois Institute
Harvard University

VOLUME 1

MACMILLAN REFERENCE USA
An Imprint of The Gale Group
NEW YORK

Macmillan Library Reference USA
1633 Broadway
New York, NY 10019

PRINTED IN THE UNITED STATES OF AMERICA

Printing Number
1 2 3 4 5 6 7 8 9 10

Library of Congress Cataloging-in-Publication Data
Civil rights in the United States / Waldo E. Martin, Jr., Patricia Sullivan, editors.
    p. cm.
   "Volume 1."
   Includes bibliographical references and index.
   ISBN 0-02-864765-3 (set)—ISBN 0-02-864763-7 (vol. 1)
   1. Minorities—Civil rights—United States—History—Encyclopedias.
2. Afro-Americans—Civil rights—History—Encyclopedias. 3. Civil rights movements—United States—History—Encyclopedias. 4. United States—Race relations—Encyclopedias. 5. United States—Ethnic relations—Encyclopedias.
I. Martin, Waldo E., 1951– II. Sullivan, Patricia.

E184.A1 C47   2000
323′.0973′03—dc21

                                           99-057548

This paper meets the requirements of ANSI-NISO Z39.48-1992 (Permanence of Paper).

Contents

Preface

The goal of *Civil Rights in the United States,* a two-volume reference compendium, is to make the latest scholarship on the subject available to a wide audience in a highly accessible format. It offers a fresh historical perspective and a forward-looking vision that sees civil rights as evolving out of many, often diverse, sources and moments. These key sources and moments include the creation of fundamental documents such as the Bill of Rights to the United States Constitution, and they also include critical developments such as the African-American civil rights movement of post–World War II America.

This approach to civil rights necessarily involves the consideration of different kinds of individuals and groups. The approach is decidedly eclectic and wide-ranging, open and flexible. It stresses the diverse, multicultural reality of the American experience. In a very important sense, the individual and group-based biographical entries in this encyclopedia provide a unifying thread: inspiring and illuminating stories of civil rights struggles. Put another way, these stories, along with all the other accounts and discussions, seek to capture the diverse and various tributaries that have flowed into and out of the mighty river of civil rights.

In addition, this reference work represents a wide and exciting variety of windows onto who we are as a nation and how we became who we are, in all of our variety and complexity. These are narratives of heralded grand victories and grand defeats. These are also narratives of unheralded small victories and small defeats. Throughout, the struggle persists.

The guiding vision of this encyclopedia is that the civil rights struggle, broadly conceived, is the driving engine behind the historical development of civil rights in this country. Equally important to this guiding vision is the argument throughout that both civil rights and struggles for civil rights are inextricably linked. Indeed, both civil rights and civil rights struggles are basic to the ongoing American experiment. In this encyclopedia, civil rights per se and struggles for civil rights merge to make up a single, contiguous narrative of *Civil Rights in the United States.*

Civil rights in the broadest sense of the term emerges out of the core American belief that Americans, as members of both a civil society and a body politic, possess a body of fundamental rights. In particular, civil rights are generally understood to be a vital expression of the legally protected right under law to one's life, liberty, and property. In light of the American commitment to both justice and the rule of law, in theory no citizen can be deprived of the right to life, liberty, or property without due process or a fair hearing.

This encyclopedia treats the theory as well as the historical reality of civil rights. On one level, it looks at civil rights as a developing body of rights to be defined, protected, and at times extended. On another level, it looks at individual and group efforts to realize civil rights for oppressed, marginalized, and excluded Americans. In other words, this encyclopedia treats both the upside and the downside of the theory and practice of civil rights in the United States since the founding of the nation.

The architects of the new nation formally excluded African Americans, women, and miscellaneous "others" from the body politic and the rights and obligations of citizenship. In spite of this, these marginalized groups organized and fought to have their membership in the body politic recognized. Out of those struggles a variety of social movements emerged that propelled the development of a tradition of civil rights struggles, spearheaded by the struggles of African Americans.

This project evolved in tandem with a series of team-led NEH Summer Institutes at Harvard University's W. E. B. Du Bois Institute on Teaching the History of the Civil Rights Movement. The primary goal of the institute was to develop a framework for conceptualizing and understanding the civil rights movement in the United States, its origins, processes, and consequences. Working in collaboration with more than one hundred college and university teachers from around the country over the past five years has generated more questions than answers. Nevertheless, several key themes have framed the approach in *Civil Rights in the United States*. During the course of the production of these volumes, this project has evolved dramatically in terms of its chronology, thematic emphasis, and guiding vision.

The initial approach was to expand the focus beyond the traditional chronological paradigm that treats the African-American civil rights movement from the 1954 *Brown* decision to the assassination of Martin Luther King, Jr., in 1968. This encyclopedia emphasizes a more long-term historical perspective. Toward this end, the history of the African-American civil rights struggle is divided into four broad periods: first, the formative years, 1790–1865; second, the revolutionary period of Reconstruction and the counterrevolution of disfranchisement and Jim Crow segregation, 1865–1909; third, the development of a national yet Southern-based movement for civil rights, 1910–1965; and fourth, the post-1965 expansion of the civil rights agenda.

The first period began with the Naturalization Law of 1790, which affirmed that only whites could become United States citizens. It concluded with the end of the Civil War (1861–1865), which solidified the abolition of slavery. Throughout this period, the problem of civil rights emerges as a series of often interrelated struggles led by those excluded from those rights, in particular African Americans and women. The overriding question in this period was who is a citizen or, even more pointedly, who possesses citizenship rights? At the end of the Civil War, these were very much unsettled issues.

Reconstruction (1865–1877) and the constitutional amendments it created initiated the second period. Attorney Oliver Hill has aptly referred to the Thirteenth, Fourteenth, and Fifteenth Amendments as "a second Bill of Rights for African Americans." The Thirteenth Amendment abolished slavery, and the Fifteenth Amendment gave black men the vote. It was the Fourteenth Amendment, however, that guaranteed the full rights of citizenship for African Americans, not only in the states where they resided but also in the nation-at-large. It also provided a legal and constitutional framework for the subsequent expansion of citizenship rights in many directions. As the federal presence diminished in the Reconstruction South, most symbolically with the withdrawal of federal troops in 1877, the meaning of black citizenship was violently challenged and legally contested. The counterrevolution often referred to as "Redemption" witnessed the triumph of white supremacy, as codified in the *Plessy v. Ferguson* decision (1896) as well as in the enactment of disfranchisement and Jim Crow.

The third period begins with the founding of the National Association for the Advancement of Colored People (NAACP) in 1909. The NAACP initiated an organized, sustained legal challenge to segregation and disfranchisement. This group became a critical vehicle for creating a national consciousness of African-American civil rights struggles. Notwithstanding the intensity of the opposition to black citizenship rights, community-based African American–led movements emerged throughout the South to assert African-American citizenship rights. National developments such as World War I, the Great Migration, New Deal reforms, the growth of organized labor, and World War II, as well as dramatic advances in mass communication technologies, invigorated these movements. An important aspect of these developments was the strengthening of the ties between civil rights struggles at the local and at the national levels. What we typically think of as the modern civil rights movement crests with the mass movements and legal victories of the 1950s and 1960s.

Since 1965 the theory and practice of civil rights has expanded formally and exponentially. In particular, the civil rights struggles and social movements of women as well as communities of color—notably Latino Americans, Asian Americans, Native Americans, and African Americans—have transformed the very idea and practice of civil rights. In addition, in the last quarter of the twentieth century, civil rights has been dramatically reshaped by the civil rights struggles of growing numbers of other individuals and groups, including prisoners, political dissidents, and immigrants. We now recognize the extraordinary range and depth of what constitutes civil rights. We also understand both the contested and shifting nature of civil rights. Rights are not only fixed, but they also change.

This broadening of our understanding of civil rights has led us in another novel direction. This encyclopedia incorporates new ways of thinking about civil rights. It seeks to enlarge the readers' understanding by making the civil rights paradigm, or framework, more inclusive and flexible. In particular, it shifts the discussion to include the civil rights struggles of other peoples of color as well as of other marginalized groups such as women, lesbians and gays, immigrants, and the differently abled.

Throughout the history of civil rights, but especially in this last phase, the tension between notions of individual rights as against group-based rights is especially telling. The current debate over the prevalence of identity politics rooted in rights-based claims attests to the historical significance of this tension. This can be seen in contemporary debates about the connections between affirmative action and civil rights.

In the end, then, the struggle for civil rights in the United States is not a separate chapter, but rather is at the very center of the American experience. The movement to realize the promise of democracy and equality has been waged across generations, and it is one that continues to engage the hopes and aspirations of those committed to a broad vision of democratic possibilities. To speak of the civil rights movement in terms of a final victory or defeat fails to acknowledge the historic and dynamic nature of the struggle. As veteran civil rights activist Robert Moses has explained, for one to challenge the practices and structures of inequity and racism in America is to come to understand that "our lot is struggle."

By providing access to the broad sweep and rich diversity of this history, it is our hope that the study of civil rights in the United States will find a central place in the teaching and learning of American history. In that way, it can also inform the ongoing struggle for civil rights and human rights—not only in the United States, but throughout the world.

Waldo E. Martin, Jr.
Patricia Sullivan

The Bill of Rights

The Bill of Rights, adopted in 1791, consists of the first ten amendments to the United States Constitution. The struggle for civil rights has been deeply connected to the Bill of Rights, which has generally protected civil liberties and personal liberties. Civil liberties and civil rights are closely connected but do not mean the same thing. Often civil liberties have been used as a vehicle for asserting civil rights, but sometimes the two kinds of liberty have been in conflict.

1791 to the Civil War

At the time of the ratification of the Bill of Rights (1791), state governments generally had the power to restrict or expand both civil rights and civil liberties. The Bill of Rights placed limitations on what the national government could do but had no effect on state powers. Some of the protections were directed at preventing the national government from interfering in the fundamental liberties of individuals, whereas other parts of the Bill of Rights protected the states themselves from an overly powerful national government.

The First Amendment, for example, guaranteed that the national government could not "abridge freedom of speech or press" or establish a national religion that would be forced on people of differing faiths. Similarly, the Fifth Amendment prohibited the government from taking private property without just compensation. Other amendments guaranteed fundamental due process in criminal cases, such as the right to a jury trial, the right of a defendant to subpoena witnesses, and the right to an attorney.

The Second Amendment guaranteed that the states would always be allowed to maintain a "well-regulated militia," thus ensuring that the states could defend against riots, insurrections, and invasion and, if necessary, against a tyrannical central government. The Tenth Amendment reminded Congress that many basic rights, which at the time would have included the regulation of civil rights, rested with the states.

In the years following their adoption, none of these provisions were seen as helpful to civil rights although some of them were used to prevent an expansion of civil rights. The Fifth Amendment, for example, prevented Congress from ending slavery because slaves were property and thus could not be taken from their owners without "just compensation." In *Dred Scott v. Sandford* (1857), the Supreme Court ruled that the Fifth Amendment prevented Congress from prohibiting slavery in the federal territories. The Tenth Amendment also prohibited Congress from regulating slavery or civil rights in the states. The Second Amendment was helpful in guaranteeing that the states could use their militias to suppress slave rebellions as, in fact, a number of states did. Virginia, for example, used its militia to help suppress the Nat Turner Rebellion in 1831; South Carolina used its militia to round up slaves and free blacks on the eve of the Denmark Vesey Rebellion in 1822, thus stopping the rebellion before it could begin.

From the 1830s until the beginning of the Civil War, opponents of slavery unsuccessfully tried to use the Bill of Rights as a tool in their struggle against human bondage. Abolitionists attempted to take advantage of the "right to petition" in the First Amendment, but the House of Representatives essentially nullified this right by refusing to accept anti-slavery petitions. Instead, the House passed a resolution, known as a "gag rule," under which that body immediately tabled all anti-slavery petitions. This response actually worked to the benefit of the anti-slavery movement, which used the issue to help convince northerners of the dangers posed by slavery to the liberty of all Americans.

Abolitionists made similar arguments when supporters of slavery tried to suppress their speech or when pro-slavery mobs attacked their newspapers. By the end of the antebellum period, the abolitionists had successfully tied their movement to the protection of freedom of expression, and most northerners, even those who did not like abolitionists, agreed that slavery threatened liberty everywhere in the nation.

Abolitionists argued that slavery in federal territories and the District of Columbia violated the Fifth Amendment, which declared that no person could be deprived of "life, liberty, or property without due process of law." However, as noted earlier, the Supreme Court rejected this theory in *Dred Scott*, instead asserting that freeing slaves would be an illegal taking of property, which the Fifth Amendment prohibited.

Abolitionists similarly argued that the Fugitive Slave Law of 1850 violated the bill of rights because it denied alleged slaves the due process protections found in the Fourth, Fifth, Sixth, and Eighth Amendments. Federal courts rejected these contentions.

Civil War, Reconstruction, and the Age of Segregation

During the Civil War, the United States government moved against slavery, through the first and second Confiscation Acts (1861, 1867) and President Abraham Lincoln's Emancipation Proclamation (1863). Both Congress and the President claimed authority to free slaves under the war powers granted by the Constitution, but both Lincoln and congressional leaders feared that the Supreme Court might nullify these actions on, at least in part, Fifth Amendment grounds. Congress failed to completely avoid this problem in the Thirteenth Amendment, which only abolished slavery. At least in theory, a master might have claimed that, in freeing the slaves, Congress had taken "private property for public use" and thus had to offer "just compensation." Congress cleared up this issue in the Fourteenth Amendment, which provided in Section 4 that no person could make "any claim for the loss or emancipation of any slave."

The Fourteenth Amendment also profoundly affected the nature of civil liberties in the United States. The amendment, ratified in 1868, declared, "No State shall make or enforce any law which shall abridge the privileges or immunities of citizens of the United States; nor shall any State deprive any person of life, liberty, or property, without due process of law." Most modern scholars believe that this clause was designed to apply the protections of the Bill of Rights to the states. Initially, the Supreme Court did not read the amendment this way and, in the *Slaughterhouse Cases* (1873), the Court denied that the "privileges and immunities" clause of the Fourteenth Amendment applied the Bill of Rights to the states.

From the end of Reconstruction until the end of World War II, the Bill of Rights had only a marginal effect on civil rights. In general, African Americans and other minorities saw few protections of their civil rights in this period. In what might be considered an early enforcement of the Sixth Amendment, the Supreme Court ruled in *Strauder v. West Virginia* (1880) that states could not prohibit blacks from serving on juries. However, this was one of the few times the Court supported black rights during this period.

In *Plessy v. Ferguson* (1896), the Supreme Court gave its blessing to legalized segregation, as long as the "separate" facilities were "equal." In fact, of course, such facilities were rarely, if ever, equal. Tied to legalized segregation was a concerted effort by the South to push African Americans out of politics and to restrict their access to public accommodations, jobs, and education.

The Bill of Rights and the Civil Rights Movement

In response to this all-out assault on black rights, black and white opponents of racism formed the National Association for the Advancement of Colored People (NAACP) in 1909. By the 1920s, the NAACP had emerged as the leading opponent of segregation and legalized racism. In the 1920s and 1930s, the NAACP challenged segregation in housing, voting, and education. Most of these challenges did not raise Bill of Rights issues, however.

Starting with *Gitlow v. New York* (1925), the Supreme Court began to interpret the "due process" clause of the Fourteenth Amendment to make some Bill of Rights protections applicable to the states. The Court said that some parts of the Bill of Rights were "incorporated" into the "due process" and "liberty" that the states could not deny to anyone. In the 1930s, the NAACP and other organizations began to defend blacks tried in southern states. A few of these cases expanded black civil rights through an application of the Bill of Rights.

In *Powell v. Alabama* (1932), a case arising out of the infamous Scottsboro trials, the Supreme Court ruled that a right to counsel in capital cases was a fundamental aspect of due process found in the Fourteenth Amendment. The Court did not specifically hold that the Sixth Amendment right to counsel was also applicable to the states as a result of the Fourteenth Amendment. Nevertheless, this was the beginning of the use of concepts found within the Bill of Rights to protect minorities from state action.

The Bill of Rights became more significant with the advent of the civil rights movement in the 1950s. The key legal event in the civil rights movement, the desegregation decision in *Brown v. Board of Education of Topeka, Kansas* (1954) did not involve the Bill of Rights but involved only the equal protection clause of the Fourteenth Amendment. However, following *Brown*, the civil rights struggle moved into the streets, even as it remained in the courts. Here the Bill of Rights soon came to matter a great deal.

Civil rights advocates used the various First Amendment liberties—speech, press, and assembly—to protest segregation. The civil rights march became the hallmark of the movement. Some were small protest marches, confined to tiny southern towns. Others were major events in the struggle to secure civil rights. The 1963 March on Washington highlighted to the nation the need for a radical change in civil rights legislation. Some marches, like the March on Washington, had the approval (if not the support) of the local government. But others, like the Selma-to-Montgomery March in 1965, met with stiff opposition. Cities and towns denied parade permits to civil rights marchers, who then relied on the courts and the First Amendment to gain access to the streets and sidewalks of the Deep South.

The movement also led to an expansion of the concept of freedom of association, which is also based on the First Amendment but touches on other amendments as well. A number of southern states attempted to undermine the civil rights movement by requiring that the NAACP and other civil rights organizations provide the state with a list of all members. In *NAACP v. Alabama* (1958), the Supreme Court struck down such laws on the grounds of freedom of association.

The Bill of Rights also protected the right of civil rights organizations to bring lawsuits to challenge existing segregation laws. In *NAACP v. Button* (1963), the Supreme Court overturned Virginia's attempt to prevent lawyers from representing organizations, such as the NAACP, in civil rights cases.

The most important modern freedom-of-press decision, *New York Times v. Sullivan* (1964), was also a civil rights case. L. B. Sullivan, a local official in Montgomery, Alabama, sued the *New York Times* for libel, after the *Times* published an advertisement criticizing the treatment of black protesters in Alabama. Some of the statements in the advertisement were factually incorrect, and Sullivan won a huge libel judgment in a local court on the basis of this "false" reporting. The case was, in fact, an attempt to intimidate the national media in their coverage of the struggle for civil rights in the South. The Supreme Court overturned the Alabama verdict and enunciated a sweeping argument in favor of a free press.

The criminal due process protections of the Bill of Rights also helped the civil rights movement. With the whole world watching, the federal courts forced southern justice to apply the protections of the Bill of Rights to civil rights marchers and, eventually, to any blacks arrested in the South. A revolution in due process took place in the 1960s, stimulated in part by the civil rights movement. Starting with *Batson v. Kentucky* (1986), the Supreme Court also moved to prevent prosecutors from arbitrarily removing blacks from jury pools, especially when black defendants were on trial. Thus the Sixth Amendment was expanded to protect civil rights of nonwhite defendants.

Modern Tensions and Limitations

Because the Bill of Rights protects the liberties of all Americans, it has not always been seen as helpful to civil rights. In the 1980s, some legal scholars and civil rights activists proposed that racist speech be proscribed under the guise of "hate speech." Similarly, when some feminists argued that their civil rights were threatened by pornography, courts universally rejected such concepts, arguing instead that the Bill of Rights protects the freedom of expression of all people within the United States. The law can make no distinction between "good" and "bad" speech. Similarly, just as the Bill of Rights protects civil rights marchers, so too does it allow the Ku Klux Klan or the American Nazi Party to march. The Bill of Rights also limits the government's ability to monitor the activities of private organizations, whether they are civil rights groups or hate groups.

The Bill of Rights, as a set of limits on governmental action, has also failed to provide equal justice for all Americans. Nonwhite minorities are incarcerated and executed at a rate far higher than that of whites. Statistics demonstrate that people who kill whites are far more likely to be executed in the United States than those who kill nonwhites. Moreover, most people executed in the United States were represented at their trials by inexperienced, court-appointed attorneys. Thus the Sixth Amendment right to counsel has not yet been expanded to provide full and fair representation for all defendants, just as the Eighth Amendment has not been interpreted to eliminate race as a factor in sentencing.

Paul Finkelman

List of Articles

List of Contributors

Ward S. Albro
Texas A & M University, Kingsville
Flores Magon, Ricardo and Enrique
Murieta, Joaquin and Tiburcio Vasquez

D. T. Alegado
University of Hawaii, Manoa
Filipino Labor Union

Arnold Alpert
American Friends Service Committee, Concord, New Hampshire
New Hampshire

Matthew Andrews
University of North Carolina, Chapel Hill
Sports

Judith Antell
University of Wyoming
Native American Rights Fund
Society of American Indians
Trail of Broken Treaties

Carl Anthony
San Francisco, California
Urban Habitat Program

Edward Phillip Zuzee Antonio
Iliff School of Theology, Denver, Colorado
King, Martin Luther, Sr.

Raymond O. Arsenault
University of South Florida
Civil Rights Act of 1866
Civil Rights Act of 1875

Katya Gibel Azoulay
Grinnell College
Iowa

Laurie Balfour
Babson College
Baldwin, James

Joann D. Ball
University of California, San Diego
Olympic Boycott (1968)
We Shall Overcome

Lucy Barber
University of California, Davis
Million Man March
Poor People's Campaign

Bernice McNair Barnett
University of Illinois, Urbana-Champaign
Black Studies
Carr, Johnnie Rebecca
Civil Rights History: 1946–1965
Clark, Septima
Cotton, Dorothy
Ethnic Studies
Freedom Schools
Motley, Constance B.
Student Nonviolent Coordinating Committee
Women and Civil Rights Struggles

Donny Barnett
Champaign, Illinois
Carmichael, Stokeley
Garvey, Marcus Mosiah
Gray, Fred D.
Sam, Alfred Charles
Southern Regional Council

John Barnhill
Yukon, Oklahoma
Dees, Morris

Harold M. Baron
Northwestern University
American Dilemma, An

Jay Barth
Hendrix College
American Association of Retired Persons
Elementary and Secondary Education Act of 1965
Gay and Lesbian Rights
Internet, Censorship and the

Bess Beatty
Oregon State University
Oregon
Reconstruction

David Blight
Amherst College
Douglass, Frederick

Joshua Bloom
University of California, Berkeley
Black Panther Party
Seale, Bobby

Frederick J. Blue
Youngstown State University
Nullification
Stevens, Thaddeus
Sumner, Charles

Bradley Bond
University of Southern Mississippi
Bilbo, Theodore G.
Eastland, James

Freedom Summer
Mississippi

Eileen Boris
Howard University
Fair Employment Practice
Committee

Wesley Brian Borucki
University of Alabama
Alabama
Busing
Connor, Eugene
Dombrowski, James
Highlander Folk School
Liuzzo, Viola Fauver Gregg
Michigan
Tuskegee Experiment

Linda Bosniak
Rutgers University
Nativism

Nan Boyd
University of Colorado, Boulder
Daughters of Bilitis
Lyon, Phyllis
Martin, Del

Kevin Boyle
University of Massachusetts, Amherst
Liberalism
Unions

John Braeman
University of Nebraska, Lincoln
Roosevelt, Franklin D.
Wallace, Henry

Leslie Brown
University of Missouri, St. Louis
Jim Crow

Lloyd L. Brown
New York City
Robeson, Paul

Wendy Brown Scott
Tulane University
Civil Rights Act of 1991
National Bar Association
Plessy v. Ferguson

W. Fitzhugh Brundage
University of Florida
Lynching

Paul Buhle
Brown University
Radicalism

Dorothy Burnham
New York City
Burnham, Louis

Stewart Burns
Stanford University
March on Washington (1963)

Kim Burton
Detroit, Michigan
Black Berets

Orville Vernon Burton
University of Illinois, Urbana-
Champaign
South Carolina Progressive
Democratic Party

Albert Camarillo
Stanford University
Congress of Spanish-Speaking
People
Mexican American Legal Defense
and Education Fund

Duane Campbell
California State University, Sacramento
Agricultural Workers Organizing
Committee

Dan Carter, Sr.
Emory University
Griffin, John

David Carter
Duke University
Bond, Julian
Young, Andrew

Maria Raquel Casas
University of Nevada, Las Vegas
Chicano Movement
Huerta, Dolores

Charles Casey-Leininger
University of Cincinnati
Children's Defense Fund
Fair Housing Act (Civil Rights
Act of 1968)
Housing

Noel A. Cazenave
University of Conneticutt
War on Poverty

John Cell
Duke University
Race
White Supremacy

Sucheng Chan
University of California, Santa Barbara
Chinese Equal Rights League
Chinese for Affirmative Action
In Re Ah Yup
Wong Kim Ark, United States v.

James S. Chase
University of Arkansas, Fayetteville
Progressive Party (1924)
Socialist Party

John Brown Childs
University of California, Santa Cruz
African Blood Brotherhood

Gabriel J. Chin
Western New England College of Law
Lau v. Nichols

Sue Fawn Chung
University of Nevada, Las Vegas
Chinese American Citizens
Alliance
Organization of Chinese
Americans

Ward L. Churchill
University of Colorado, Boulder
Bellecourt, Clyde
Cohen, Felix S.
International Indian Treaty
Council and Conferences
Mount Rushmore Protests
Thomas, Robert K.

Claude Clegg III
North Carolina A & T State University
Malcolm X
Muhammad, Elijah
Organization of Afro-American
Unity

Richard A. Cloward
New York City
National Welfare Rights
Organization

Robert Cohen
University of Georgia
Savio, Mario

David Colburn
University of Florida
Florida

Peter Cole
Boise State University
Idaho

Willi Coleman
University of Vermont
Vermont

Craig Collins
Detroit, Michigan
Black Colleges and Universities
California

Donald Collins
East Carolina University
Japanese American Citizens
League
Japanese American Internment
Cases

James H. Cone
Union Theological Seminary,
New York City
King, Martin Luther, Jr.

Daniel O. Conkle
Indiana University School of Law
Religious Freedom Restoration
Act

Delia Crutchfield Cook
Kansas City, Missouri
Missouri

Richard A. Couto
University of Richmond
Tennessee

Pamela Cowen
University of Colorado, Colorado
Springs
Colorado

Gregg Crane
University of Washington
Delany, Martin Robison

Emilye Crosby
State University of New York, Geneseo
Chaney, James; Goodman,
Andrew; Schwerner, Michael
Evers, James Charles
Moses, Robert P.

Malcolm Lee Cross
Tarleton State University
Ford, Gerald
Kennedy, John F.
Peace and Freedom Party

Eric Cummins
Boulder Creek, California
Anti-War Movements
Civil Disobedience
Conscientious Objection
Convict Labor
Jackson, George
Kunstler, William
Pacifism
Prisoners

Constance Curry
Atlanta, Georgia
Penn Center

Raymond D'Angelo
Redding, Connecticut
Public Opinion

David Daniels
McCormick Theological Seminary,
Chicago
Black Church

Roger Daniels
Cincinnati, Ohio
Chinese Exclusion Acts
Japanese American Redress and
Reparations Movement

McCarran-Walter
Immigration Act

T. J. Davis
Arizona State University
Southwest Voter Registration
Education Project
Velasquez, William C.

Michael Dawson
Detroit, Michigan
Free Speech Movement
Mothers of East Los Angeles
Movimiento Estudiantil Chicano
de Aztlan
National Congress for Puerto
Rican Rights
Nebraska
New Deal and Depression
Rainbow Coalition (Operation
PUSH)
Roosevelt, Eleanor
Williams, Robert

Michelle Donaldson Deardorff
Millikin University
Bradley, Thomas
Hopwood v. State of Texas
Milliken v. Bradley
Rehnquist, William
Voting Rights Amendment of
1970
Voting Rights Amendment of
1975
Voting Rights Amendment of
1985

Debra L. DeLaet
Drake University
Immigration and Immigrants
Naturalization

Vine Deloria, Jr.
University of Colorado, Boulder
Indian Child Welfare Act of 1978
National Indian Youth Council
Wounded Knee Massacre
Wounded Knee Occupation

Dennis C. Dickerson
Williams College
National Urban League

Leonard Dinnerstein
University of Arizona
Anti-Semitism

John Dittmer
De Pauw University
*Council of Federated
    Organizations
Evers, Medgar
Henry, Aaron*

Douglas W. Dodd
California State University, Bakersfield
*Bracero Program (Public
    Law 78)
Fierro de Bright, Josefina*

Harvey Dong
University of California, Berkeley
*International Hotel Episode
Third World Student Strikes*

Gerald Early
Washington University
*Ali, Muhammad
Multiculturalism*

Pamela Edwards
City University of New York, School of
Law at Queens College
Test Bias

Theodore Eisenberg
Cornell University
*Civil Rights Act of 1957
Civil Rights Act of 1960
Civil Rights Act of 1964*

Maureen N. Eke
Central Michigan University
*Colonialism
Hughes, Langston
Lorde, Audre*

Maureen Elgersman Lee
University of Southern Maine
Maine

Glenn Eskew
Georgia State University
*Birmingham Campaign
Birmingham Civil Rights
    Institute*

Yen Le Espiritu
University of California, San Diego
Asian American Movement

Shelly Eversley
University of Washington
Johnson, James Weldon

Hayward Farrar
Virginia Polytechnic Institute and State
University
Pan-African Congresses

Michael Ferner
Farm Labor Organizing Committee,
AFL–CIO, Toledo, Ohio
*Farm Labor Organizing
    Committee*

Paul Finkelman
University of Tulsa College of Law
*Bill of Rights
Dred Scott v. Sandford
Fourteenth Amendment
Know-Nothing Party
Liberty Party*

Peter G. Fish
Duke University
*Fifth Circuit, United States Court
    of Appeals for the
Fourth Circuit, United States
    Court of Appeals for the
Parker, John J.*

Jaime Fitzgerald
Detroit, Michigan
American G.I. Forum

Michael W. Fitzgerald
St. Olaf College
*Bureau of Refugees, Freedmen,
    and Abandoned Lands*

Sheila Flemming
Bethune-Cookman College
Bethune, Mary McLeod

Juan Flores
Hunter College
Puerto Rican Liberation

Lee W. Formwalt
Organization of American Historians,
Bloomington, Indiana
Georgia

Jimmie Franklin
Vanderbilt University
*Arrington, Richard
Oklahoma*

V. P. Franklin
Drexel University
Black Nationalism

Milton Gaither
Indiana University, Bloomington
*Emergency School Aid Act
Harding, Vincent*

Elizabeth Garcia
New York City
*Comité, El
League of United Latin American
    Citizens
Mexican American Student
    Organizations
Movement for Independence—
    Puerto Rican Socialist Party
Salt of the Earth Strike*

Ignacio Garcia
Brigham Young University
*Crusade for Justice
Raza Unida Party, La*

Juan R. Garcia
University of Arizona
Cortez Lira, Gregorio

Tim Garrison
Portland State University
*Bakke, Regents of the University
    of California v.*

Raymond Gavins
Duke University
*Alexander, Kelly M.
Double Duty Dollar Campaign
McKissick, Floyd
National Baptist Convention
North Carolina*

Carol George
Hobart and William Smith Colleges
Religion and Civil Rights

Elizabeth Gessel
University of California, Berkeley
Exodusters

Paul Gilje
University of Oklahoma
Racial Disturbances Against
Blacks

Howard F. Gillette
George Washington University
District of Columbia
Home Rule for Washington, D.C.

Jill Ginstling
University of California, Berkeley
Victim's Rights

Jon Gjerde
University of California, Berkeley
Immigration Act of 1965
Immigration Restriction League

Matt Gladue
University of Michigan, Ann Arbor
Smith, Lillian

Jacqueline Goggin
Harvard University
Woodson, Carter G.

L. Patrick Goines
Austin Community College
American Indian Religious
Freedom Act of 1978
Dawes Severalty Act
Indian Reorganization Act of
1934
Indian Self-Determination and
Education Assistance Act of
1975

James Goodman
Rutgers University
Scottsboro Case

Hugh Davis Graham
Vanderbilt University
Congress
U.S. Commission on Civil Rights

Joanne Grant
New York City
Baker, Ella

Henry T. Greely
Stanford University
Brown, John Robert
Tuttle, Elbert P.
Wisdom, John Minor

William Green
Augsburg College
Minnesota

Cheryl Greenburg
Trinity College
Black–Jewish Relations

Christina Greene
University of South Florida
Hurley, Ruby
Lampkin, Daisy

Fred Grittner
Detroit, Michigan
Civil Rights History: 1865–1918
Civil Rights Law
Ethnicity and Race

Marc Grossman
United Farm Workers of America,
Sacramento, California
United Farm Workers of America

Harlan D. Hahn
University of Southern California
Rehabilitation Act of 1973
Rehabilitation Act Protest and
Takeover of 1977

Kermit L. Hall
North Carolina State University
Hastie, William H.

Richard Hanes
Detroit, Michigan
Alaska
Alaska Native Claims
Settlement Act
Castro et al. vs. People of
California
Center for Autonomous
Social Action
Class
Movimiento de Liberacion
Nacional
Racial Disturbances Against
Native Americans
Red Power
Senior Rights
Sovereignty, Native American
Tribal
Treaty Rights
Urban Indians
Women of All Red Nations

Claude Hargrove
Fayetteville State University
Lawson, James
Nash, Diane Bevel
Racism
Trotter, William Monroe
Weaver, Robert C.

Robert L. Harris, Jr.
Cornell University
March on Washington Movement

Cynthia Harrison
George Washington University
Equal Rights Amendment,
Movement for
President's Commission on the
Status of Women

John Haskell
Drake University
Democratic Party
DePriest, Oscar
President's Committee on Civil
Rights
Progressive Party (1948)
Republican Party
Truman, Harry

Cynthia Hawkins-Leon
Syracuse University College of Law
Pan-Africanism

Stephen Haycox
University of Alaska
Native Alaskan Civil Rights

Rochelle Hayes
Duke University
Braden, Anne and Carl
Gutierrez, José Angel
Hansberry, Lorraine
Lucy Foster, Autherine
Oliphant v. Suquamish Indians
Olivares, Luis
Turner, Henry McNeal

Michael Heale
Lancaster University, England
House Un-American Activities
Committee
McCarthyism

Joseph Heathcott
Washington University
 Justice for Janitors
 Knights of Labor
 Peltier, Leonard
 Southern Poverty Law Center

Ronald Heinemann
Hampden-Sydney College
 Byrd, Harry F.
 Virginia

Rodger Henderson
Pennsylvania State University, Fayette
Campus
 Cloud, Henry Roe
 Dual Citizenship
 Indian Claims Commission Act
 Warrior, Clyde

Charles P. Henry
University of California, Berkeley
 Bunche, Ralph

Homer D. Hill
Duke University
 Black Towns
 Eyes on the Prize
 Hancock, Gordon Blaine
 Lee, Herbert
 National Afro-American League

Rickey Hill
South Carolina State University
 Deacons for Defense and Justice
 Lowndes County Black Panther
  Party

William Ho-Gonzalez
U.S. Department of Justice,
Washington, D.C.
 Puerto Rican Legal Defense and
  Education Fund

Jonathan Holloway
University of California, San Diego
 Amenia Conferences (1916 and
  1933)
 Du Bois, W. E. B.
 National Negro Congress
 Social Science

Pippa Holloway
Ohio State University
 Hay, Harry
 Homophile Movement

 Mattachine Society
 Stonewall Riot

Thomas Holm
University of Arizona
 American Indian Movement

Michael Honey
University of Washington, Tacoma
 AFL–CIO
 Memphis Sanitation Workers
  Strike
 National Civil Rights Museum

Herbert T. Hoover
University of South Dakota
 Deloria, Vine, Jr.
 Eastman, Charles Alexander
 Oglala Sioux Civil Rights
  Organization

Gerald C. Horne
University of North Carolina, Chapel Hill
 Civil Rights Congress
 Cold War
 Watts Riot

Brian Hosmer
University of Wyoming
 Bureau of Indian Affairs
 Menominee DRUMS

Timothy S. Huebner
Rhodes College
 Civil Rights History: Up to 1865
 Thirteenth Amendment

Heather Huyck
National Park Service, Lakewood,
Colorado
 National Parks

Booker T. Ingram
Presbyterian College
 Civil Liberties

Pamela B. Jackson
Duke University
 Prejudice

Shirley A. Jackson
Southern Connecticut State University
 Attica Rebellion

Stanley W. Johnson
Fayetteville State University
 Equal Opportunity

Victoria Johnson
University of North Carolina, Chapel Hill
 Television

Beverly W. Jones
North Carolina Central University
 Terrell, Mary Church

J. Wayne Jones
University of Arkansas
 National Committee to Abolish
  the Poll Tax

Tracy K'Meyer
University of Louisville
 Alabama Christian Movement for
  Human Rights
 Mays, Benjamin Elijah

Craig Kaplowitz
Vanderbilt University
 Office of Federal Contract
  Compliance Programs

Andrew Kaye
Cambridge, Massachusetts
 Dobbs, John Wesley
 Rapier, James T.

Kori Kelley
Woodrow Wilson Institute,
Washington, D.C.
 Height, Dorothy
 Ickes, Harold

Robin Kelley
New York University
 Communist Party USA

Ben Keppel
University of Oklahoma
 Philanthropy and Foundations

Todd M. Kerstetter
University of Nebraska, Kearney
 Alcatraz Occupation
 National Congress of American
  Indians
 Native American Movement

Jay P. Kesan
University of Illinois, Urbana-
Champaign
Ohio

Richard King
Woodrow Wilson International Center
for Scholars, Washington, D.C.
Conservatism
Forman, James

William M. King
University of Colorado, Boulder
Wyoming

John Kirk
University of Wales, Lampeter
Arkansas
Bates, Daisy
Branton, Wiley
Clinton, William
Faubus, Orval

Paul Kobel
Detroit, Michigan
Pennsylvania

Jeff Kolnick
Southwest State University
Labor Movement

Virginia Sanchez Korrol
Brooklyn College
Aspira
Pantoja, Antonia

Michelle Krowl
Falls Church, Virginia
Black Codes
Emancipation Proclamation
Hayden, Casey
National Organization for
*   Women*
Students for a Democratic Society

Sarah Kurian
Yorktown Heights, New York
American Woman Suffrage
*   Association*
Anthony, Susan B.
Bonnin, Gertrude
Harper, Frances E. W.
League of Women Voters
Mason, Lucy Randolph

National American Woman
*   Suffrage Association*
Stone, Lucy
Violence against Women Act of
*   1994*
Woman Suffrage Movement

Robert W. Larson
University of Northern Colorado
Gorras Blancas, Las

Peter F. Lau
Rutgers University
Double V Campaign
Jackson, Esther Cooper
Jackson, James E.
Southern Negro Youth Congress
Waring, J. Waties

Steven F. Lawson
Rutgers University
Civil Rights History: 1966 to the
*   Present*
Voting Rights
Voting Rights Act of 1965

Chuck Lee
Carnegie Mellon University
National Colored Labor Union

Karen Leong
University of California, Berkeley
Page Law
Yick Wo v. Hopkins

Johanna Lessinger
Southern Asian Institute, Brooklyn,
New York
Association of Indians in America

Jack Levin
Northeastern University
Age Discrimination (Ageism)

Alex Lichtenstein
Florida International University
Southern Tenant Farmers' Union

Peter Ling
University of Nottingham, England
Citizenship Schools
Horton, Miles and Zilphia
Robinson, Bernice

Monroe H. Little
Indiana-Purdue University at
Indianapolis
Indiana

Paul K. Longmore
San Francisco State University
Americans with Disabilities Act of
*   1990*
Independent Living Centers
Jerry Lewis Telethon Controversy
Roberts, Edward V.

Ron Lopez
University of California, Berkeley
Brown Berets
Brown Power
Community Service Organization

Marion B. Lucas
Western Kentucky University
Kentucky

Mitchell Maki
University of California, Los Angeles
Civil Liberties Act of 1988

Nancy Weiss Malkiel
Princeton University
Jordan, Vernon
Young, Whitney

Lawrence H. Mamiya
Vassar College
Farrakhan, Louis

Sue Marasco
University of Colorado, Colorado
Springs
Colorado

Gerald Markowitz
John Jay College
Clark, Kenneth and Mamie

Norman Markowitz
Rutgers University
Brown, H. Rap
Dodge Revolutionary Union
*   Movement*
Fellowship of Reconciliation
International Labor Defense
Lazarus, Julius
National Lawyers Guild
National Student Association

Frank Martinie
Palomar College
Bush, George
Kennedy, Robert
Nixon, Richard Milhous

David Maurrasse
Yale University
Cleaver, Eldridge
Newton, Huey

Matthew May
Detroit, Michigan
American Indian Citizenship Act of 1924
American Indian Civil Rights Act of 1968
Civil Rights Decision of 1883
Congressional Black Caucus
Music
Santa Clara Pueblo v. Martinez
South Carolina
West Virginia
Wisconsin

John McCoy
Detroit, Michigan
All-African People's Revolutionary Party
Civil Rights Memorial
Connecticut
National Woman's Party
Southern Christian Leadership Conference

Judith McDaniel
University of Arizona
Deming, Barbara

Micki McElya
New York City
Ames, Jessie Daniel
Citizenship
Singleton, Benjamin
Woodward, C. Vann

Phillip McGuire
Fayetteville State University
Davis, Benjamin Jefferson, Jr.
Davis, Benjamin O., Sr.
World War II

Noeleen McIlvenna
Duke University
Berry, Mary Frances
Cobb, Ned
Means, Russell
Universal Negro Improvement Association

Steve Messer
Taylor University
Gomillion, Charles
Johnson, Frank
Lynch, John Roy
Robinson, Ruby Doris
Sellers, Cleveland

Christopher Metress
Detroit, Michigan
Literature and Civil Rights

Gregg Michel
University of Virginia
Southern Student Organizing Committee

Bertha H. Miller
Fayetteville State University
National Education Association

Jake C. Miller
Daytona Beach, Florida
Moore, Harry T.

John Miller
South Dakota State University
South Dakota

Matt Millikan
Big Timber, Montana
Montana

Pablo Mitchell
University of Michigan, Ann Arbor
New Mexico

Melodie Monahan
Detroit, Michigan
Betances, Ramon Emeterio
Durham Manifesto

Rusty Monhollon
University of Missouri, Columbia
Kansas

Dan L. Monroe
Peabody Museum, Salem, Massachusetts
Native American Graves Protection and Repatriation Act of 1990

Iwan W. Morgan
London Guildhall University, England
Brownell, Herbert
Carter, James Earl
Eisenhower, Dwight D.

Jennifer Mossman
Detroit, Michigan
Abzug, Bella
Oakes, Richard

Carlos Muñoz, Jr.
University of California, Berkeley
Galarza, Ernesto

Blair Murphy
Duke University
Davis, Angela
Moore, Amzie
Parks, Rosa
Segregation

Bernard Nalty
Hyattesville, Maryland
Korean War
Vietnam War

Richard Newman
Afropedia, Cambridge, Massachusetts
Father Divine

Roger Newman
New York City
Abram, Morris B.
Black, Hugo
Censorship
Loyalty Oaths
Rives, Richard

Mae M. Ngai
Columbia University
Immigration Act of 1924

Robert W. Nill
Lehigh University
Marcantonio, Vito
Powell, Adam Clayton, Jr.
Rustin, Bayard
Vega, Bernardo

Voter Education Project
Washington, Booker T.
White Rights

Patrick O'Neil
Broome Community College
California Agricultural Strikes of
the 1930s
Pan-Tribalism
Republic of New Africa

Kenneth O'Reilly
University of Alaska
Federal Bureau of Investigation
Presidency
Presidential Politics and Civil
Rights

Aaron Oppliger
Detroit, Michigan
Abernathy, Ralph

Lorena Oropeza
University of California, Davis
Corona, Bert
Crystal City Electoral Revolt
Mora, Magdalena
Moreno, Luisa
Tijerina, Reies López

David Oshinsky
Rutgers University
Parchman Farm

Gregory Parker
Brighton, Michigan
Industrial Workers of the World
Museum of African American
History
Robinson, Jackie

Shaunda Partida
Chicago, Illinois
Anti-Apartheid Movement
Charles, Robert
Edelman, Marian Wright
National Council of Negro
Women
Richardson, Gloria

Donna Patterson
Indiana University, Bloomington
TransAfrica

Anthony A. Peacock
Utah State University
Affirmative Action
Constitutionalism
Courts
Shaw v. Reno

Stephen L. Percy
University of Wisconsin, Milwaukee
Disability Rights

Michael Perman
University of Illinois, Chicago
Radical Republicans

Paula F. Pfeffer
Loyola University, Chicago
Brotherhood of Sleeping Car
Porters
Hedgeman, Anna Arnold

Merline Pitre
Texas Southern University
Jordan, Barbara Charlene
Texas

Frances Fox Piven
Millerton, New York
National Welfare Rights
Organization

Gerald Podair
Lawrence University
New York

Kimberly K. Porter
University of North Dakota,
Grand Forks
North Dakota

Charles Postel
University of California, Berkeley
Homeless Rights
Revolutionary Action Movement

Robert Pratt
University of Georgia
Massive Resistance
School Desegregation

Patrick Rael
Bowdoin College
Colonization Movements

Karthick S. Ramakrishnan
Princeton University
Chavez, Cesar
Talmadge, Eugene

Luz Elena Ramirez
State University of New York, Oneonta
Gonzales, Rodolfo
Martinez, Elizabeth

Ann Rayson
University of Hawaii, Manoa
Hawaii

Linda Reed
University of Houston
Commission on Interracial
Cooperation
Gelders, Joseph
Hamer, Fannie Lou
Southern Conference Educational
Fund
Southern Conference for Human
Welfare

David Riddle
Detroit, Michigan
Migration
Mississippi Freedom Democratic
Party
Southern Manifesto
Southern Strategy
War Resister's League

James Riddlesperger
Texas Christian University
Johnson, Lyndon B.
Reagan, Ronald

Natalie Ring
University of California, San Diego
National Association of Colored
Women
Redemption
Republicanism

Nancy Marie Robertson
New York City
Young Men's Christian
Association and Young
Women's Christian Association

Greg Robinson
New York City
Americans for Democratic Action
Barnett, Claude
Bond, Horace Mann
Dixiecrats
Hope, John
Innis, Roy
Kameny, Franklin
Kerner Commission Report
Meier, August
Moton, Robert R.
NAACP Legal Defense and
Educational Fund
Robinson, Randall
Russell, Richard
Shuttlesworth, Fred
Smith, Howard W.
Smith v. Allwright
Thurmond, Strom
White, George

Alicia Rodriquez
California State University, Bakersfield
Bruce, Blanche K.
Doar, John
Warren, Earl
Wells, Ida B.

Renee Romano
Wesleyan University
Catt, Carrie Chapman
Chisholm, Shirley
Friedan, Betty
Paul, Alice
Sit-Ins
Stanton, Elizabeth Cady
Title VII of the 1964 Civil
Rights Act
Williams v. Mississippi

Horacio N. Roque Ramirez
University of California, Berkeley
Homophobia

Jacqueline A. Rouse
Georgia State University
Murray, Pauli

Marc Rubin
New York City
Gay Activists Alliance

Elmer Rusco
University of Nevada, Reno
Nevada

Tomás F. Sandoval, Jr.
University of California, Berkeley
Gonzalez, Pedro
Guzman, Pablo Yoruba
Guzman, Ralph
Racial Disturbances Against
Latinos
Zoot Suit Riots

Mark R. Scherer
University of Nebraska, Omaha
La Flesche, Francis

John R. Schmidhauser
University of Southern California
American Civil Liberties Union

Frederick C. Schult
New York University
Banks, Dennis

Thomas F. Schwartz
Illinois Historic Preservation Agency,
Springfield, Illinois
Illinois

Loren Schweninger
University of North Carolina,
Greensboro
Franklin, John Hope

Jason Scorza
Princeton University
New Jersey

Clifford H. Scott
Purdue-Indiana University at Fort
Wayne
East St. Louis Race Riot
Tulsa Race Riot

Basilio Serrano
State University of New York,
Old Westbury
Albizu Campos, Pedro
Lebron, Lolita
Puerto Rican Movement
Puerto Rican Student Union

Jared Sexton
University of California, Berkeley
Children's Rights Movement
Head Start, Project

Stephanie Shanks-Meile
Indiana University Northwest
American Nazi Party
Ku Klux Klan
Ku Klux Klan Act of 1871
Wallace, George
White Backlash
White Citizens' Councils

Herbert Shapiro
University of Cincinnati
Populist Party

Thomas E. Sheridan
University of Arizona
Arizona

Amy Shindler
September Films, London
Film

Elizabeth Shostak
Detroit, Michigan
Education

A. D. Simmons
Fayetteville State University
Freedom Rides
Student Movements

Joseph Slaughter
Dorchester, Massachusetts
Critical Race Theory

Helene Slessarev
Wheaton College
Equal Employment Opportunity
Commission

James Smethurst
W. E. B. Du Bois Institute, Harvard
University
Baraka, Amiri
Harlem Renaissance

Larissa Smith
Emory University
Alexander, Will Winton
Hill, Oliver
Jackson, Luther Porter
Walker, Maggie Lena

Michael T. Smith
Raleigh, North Carolina
Draft Riots

Dorothy A. Smith-Akubue
Lynchburg College
Bell, Derrick
Farmer, James
Randolph, A. Philip

Paul Spickard
University of California, Santa Barbara
Gentlemen's Agreement (1907)
Loving v. Virginia

Dianne Spriggs
National Park Service, Lakewood,
Colorado
National Parks

Stephen Steinberg
Queens College
Employment

Amy Stillman
University of California, Santa Barbara
Native Hawaiian Sovereignty
Movement

Christopher Strain
University of California, Berkeley
National Rifle Association
Right to Bear Arms

Patricia Sullivan
W. E. B. Du Bois Institute, Harvard
University
Civil Rights History: 1919–1945
Durr, Virginia
Foreman, Clark
Leadership Conference on Civil
Rights
National Association for the
Advancement of Colored
People
Niagara Movement
Weber, Palmer

Scott Tang
University of California, Berkeley
Chinese Consolidated Benevolent
Association
Ozawa v. United States
Racial Disturbances Against
Asian Americans

Reparations
Thind, United States v.

Cynthia Taylor
Graduate Theological Union, Berkeley,
California
Cleage, Albert
Reeb, James

Ula Y. Taylor
University of California, Berkeley
California Civil Rights Initiative

Donn Teal
New York City
Gay Activists Alliance

Jerry D. Thompson
Texas A & M University
Cortina, Juan Nepomuceno

Timothy Thurber
State University of New York, Oswego
Humphrey, Hubert

Bridget Travers
Detroit, Michigan
Tenayuca, Emma

Stephen Tuck
University of Cambridge, England
Albany Movement
Lewis, John

Kara Miles Turner
Virginia State University
Morgan v. Virginia

Richard Turner
DePaul University
Nation of Islam

Mark Tushnet
Georgetown University Law School
Brown v. Board of Education
Carter, Robert L.
Desegregation
Greenberg, Jack
Houston, Charles Hamilton
Integration
Marshall, Thurgood
Supreme Court

William M. Tuttle
University of Kansas
Red Summers of 1917–1921

Timothy B. Tyson
University of Wisconsin, Madison
Hill, Herbert

Thomas Upchurch
Mississippi State University
Meredith, James

William Van DeBurg
University of Wisconsin, Madison
Black Power

Lea B. Vaughn
University of Washington School of Law
Washington

Charles Vincent
Southern University
Fortune, Timothy Thomas
Louisiana
Revels, Hiram

Lori G. Waite
Trinity College
Chicago Freedom Movement
Congress of Racial Equality
Don't Buy Where You Can't Work
Campaigns
Operation Breadbasket

Christopher Waldrep
Eastern Illinois University
States' Rights

Jenny Walker
Newcastle University, England
Gandhi, Mohandas

Ronald Walters
Howard University
Jackson, Jesse

Hanes Walton, Jr.
University of Michigan, Ann Arbor
Political Parties

Xi Wang
Indiana University of Pennsylvania
Federal Election Bill of 1890

Brian Ward
Newcastle University, England
*American Friends Service
  Committee*

Michael H. Washington
Northern Kentucky University
Afrocentrism

Denton L. Watson
Freeport, New York
*Mitchell, Clarence
White, Walter Francis
Wilkins, Roy*

William Wei
University of Colorado, Boulder
Yellow Power

Robert Weisbrot
Colby College
Little Rock Nine

Ashton W. Welch
Creighton University
Emancipation

Ken Wells
Detroit, Michigan
*Freedom's People
Massachusetts
Newspapers and Magazines
Radio
Rhode Island
Utah*

Jeannie M. Whayne
University of Arkansas
Peonage

Stephen Whitfield
Brandeis University
Till, Emmett, Lynching of

Robert Wiebe
Northwestern University
Democracy

Russ Wigginton
Rhodes College
Webster, Milton P.

Randall Williams
Black Belt Press, Montgomery, Alabama
*Montgomery Bus Boycott
Montgomery Improvement
  Association
Nixon, E. D.*

Rhonda Williams
Case Western Reserve University
Maryland

William H. Williams
University of Delaware
Delaware

Clint C. Wilson, II
Howard University
*Crisis, The
Freedom (newspaper)
Freedomways*

Adrien Katherine Wing
University of Iowa College of Law
Critical Race Feminism

Barbara Winslow
Brooklyn College
*Feminism
Steinem, Gloria*

Michael Allan Wolf
University of Richmond
*Fifteenth Amendment
Nineteenth Amendment*

Christy Wood
Detroit, Michigan
*Armed Forces
Sexism*

Komozi Woodard
Sarah Lawrence College
*Black Arts Movement
Black Convention Movement,
  Modern*

Barbara A. Woods
South Carolina State University
Simkins, Modjeska

Martin Morse Wooster
Capital Research Center,
Washington, D.C.
Rosenwald, Julius

Neil Wynn
University of Glamorgan, Wales
World War I

Robert Zangrando
University of Akron
Anti-Lynching Campaign

Scott Zeman
New Mexico Institute of Mining and
Technology
*Alianza Federal de Pueblos Libres
Asociación Nacional México-
  Americana*

A

Abernathy, Ralph David

(1926–1990), clergyman, civil rights leader.

As the right-hand man for Dr. Martin Luther KING, Jr., Ralph David Abernathy was one of the most influential figures in the civil rights movement of the 1960s. Abernathy helped form such prominent civil rights groups as the Montgomery Improvement Association (MIA), the SOUTHERN CHRISTIAN LEADERSHIP CONFERENCE (SCLC), and the Foundation for Economic Enterprises Development (FEED).

Abernathy was born in Linden, Alabama, the tenth of twelve children of William Abernathy, a hardworking farmer and church deacon. Growing up on his parents' farm, Abernathy was brought up with a great respect for the church. He attended the Linden Academy, a local black high school, and, after graduation, served in the U.S. Army during the final months of WORLD WAR II. When he returned from the war, Abernathy enrolled in classes at Alabama State College. He proved to be a good student and natural leader, becoming the student council president and leading protests to obtain improved cafeteria conditions and living quarters. In 1948, Abernathy formally announced his calling as a Baptist minister, and continued taking classes at Alabama State.

After graduating from Alabama State, Abernathy enrolled at Atlanta University, where he earned a masters degree in sociology. It was during this time that Abernathy first met Martin Luther King, Jr. Abernathy had been attending church services at the Ebenezer Baptist Church, where he introduced himself to the young King. Upon receiving his masters degree, Abernathy returned to Alabama and soon became the minister at Montgomery's First Baptist Church. Three years later, King accepted a call to Montgomery's Dexter Avenue Baptist Church, and the two men began working together on many civil rights issues.

The two ministers were quickly drawn into the civil rights movement when they created the Montgomery Improvement Association (MIA) to promote equal rights in Alabama. The group led a boycott of Montgomery's segregated bus system as a response to the arrest of of Rosa PARKS, a black woman who refused to leave her bus seat to make space for a white man. King was the head of the MIA and Abernathy worked as program chief, moving people to act peacefully against the city's segregated policies. Although Abernathy and King were threatened many times, the boycott lasted over a year until the federal courts upheld an injunction against the bus company's policies of segregation.

Building on their success in Montgomery, Abernathy and King met with Southern clergymen to create the Southern Christian Leadership Conference (SCLC) in 1957. King was elected president of the SCLC and Abernathy became the secretary-treasurer. Over the next few years, Abernathy and King led many peaceful movements across the South, including marches, rallies, and sit-ins. Despite being arrested many times, the two ministers continued their protests.

Abernathy was named vice president of the SCLC in 1965 and he and King began to work on their POOR PEOPLE'S CAMPAIGN, designed to gather people of all

1

Reverend Ralph D. Abernathy arrives at the Montgomery, Alabama, courthouse on March 19, 1956, for the beginning of the bus boycott trial. Abernathy and ninety-three African-American activists were charged with conspiracy as a result of a city-wide boycott of segregated city buses. (CORBIS/Bettmann)

races for demonstrations to promote better living conditions for the poor. The campaign came to a head in 1968, but met with tragedy when King was assassinated on April 4, on the balcony of his Memphis, Tennessee, motel room.

SCLC leaders unanimously elected Abernathy as president of the organization, and he continued to work for the Poor People's Campaign, creating Resurrection City near the Lincoln Memorial in Washington, D.C. Resurrection City, the center of the campaign, drew in poor people from around the country, and led to a meeting between Abernathy and members of Congress in which Abernathy petitioned for help for the nation's unemployed.

As president of the SCLC Abernathy continued to push for stronger civil rights measures in the South.

However, after King's death, the organization began to lose its voice, and newer, more militant groups, such as the Black Panthers, became the prominent voice of the civil rights movement. Abernathy resigned from the SCLC in 1977.

After leaving the SCLC, Abernathy ran for a seat in Congress in 1977, but lost the race. He soon formed the Foundation for Economic Enterprises Development (FEED), an organization created to train blacks for better economic opportunities. In addition to heading FEED, Abernathy continued to fulfill his duties as minister at West Hunter Street Baptist Church.

Although he was troubled by occasional health problems later in life, Abernathy toured the United States lecturing at schools and for organizations. In 1989, he published his autobiography, *And The Walls Came Tumbling Down*. Some black leaders criticized the book for its detailed account of King's extramarital affairs, but many praised the book for providing a true and informative account of the civil rights movement. Abernathy died of a heart attack on April 30, 1990.

BIBLIOGRAPHY

Brown, Ray D., ed. *Contemporary Heroes and Heroines, Book I.* 1990.

Edwards, Jim, ed. *American Decades CD-ROM.* 1998.

Marion, Allison, ed. *American Law Yearbook.* 1998.

Melton, J. Gordon. *Religious Leaders of America,* 2nd ed. 1999.

Muller, Michael E. "Ralph David Abernathy." In *Contemporary Black Biography,* Vol. 1, edited by Michael L. La Blanc. 1992.

Aaron Oppliger

Abram, Morris B.

(1918–   ), lawyer and public official.

Morris B. Abram was born in Fitzgerald, Georgia, in 1918 and graduated from the University of Georgia in 1938 and the University of Chicago Law School in 1940. After service in military intelligence in World War II, for which he received the Legion of Honor, and as a member of the prosecution at the Nuremburg Trials in 1946, he attended Oxford University as a Rhodes Scholar. Abram practiced law, largely representing railroads, starting in 1948. He wrote a pamphlet for the Anti-Defamation League that led to many state and local laws aimed at the KU KLUX KLAN and ordering that marchers' faces not be covered.

Overturning Georgia's "county unit" election rule became a passion for Abram. By requiring that election results be measured by counties as a bloc, this law gave disproportionate weight to rural areas and helped perpetuate SEGREGATION. Abram felt its impact firsthand when he ran for Congress in 1954 but lost two out of three counties and, therefore, the election. Remaining in Georgia largely to help abolish it, he brought a lawsuit challenging the county unit's constitutionality; it reached the United States SUPREME COURT in 1963; "A vote is a vote is a vote," Abram told the justices. In *Gray v. Sanders* the Court ruled the county unit law unconstitutional.

In 1960, on behalf of John F. KENNEDY's campaign for president, Abram helped negotiate the release of Martin Luther KING, JR., from a Georgia jail and engineered Martin Luther KING, SR.'s, endorsement of Kennedy. Kennedy named Abram general counsel of the Peace Corps in 1961. In 1962, he moved to New York to join the law firm of Paul, Weiss, Rifkind, Wharton & Garrison, with which he was thereafter associated. Abram helped plan President Lyndon JOHNSON's WAR ON POVERTY but rejected Johnson's offer in 1964 to be the first chairman of the EQUAL EMPLOYMENT OPPORTUNITY COMMISSION.

A judgeship was long Abram's goal. "I would have given my eyeteeth," he later said, but in Georgia it was politically "impossible." There he was the "village pariah." In New York, however, he lost interest in the bench and in 1965 turned down the offer of a federal judgeship. In 1967, Abram was planning to run for the Democratic nomination for senator and had Senator Robert F. KENNEDY's support. However, operatives of President Johnson sent word that Abram's position on the conflict in VIETNAM was not acceptable and he did not run.

Abram served as president of Brandeis University from 1968 to 1970. A SIT-IN by students, faculty, and administrators who demanded a BLACK STUDIES program and unspecified racial preferences tried his patience. He permitted the protest to run its course and took no action against the protesters, but "it just disrupted the righteousness of my feelings toward university principles," Abram recalled, and he resigned in 1970.

In 1983, President Ronald REAGAN nominated Abram to the U.S. COMMISSION ON CIVIL RIGHTS. A bruising nomination battle followed. "Failure to defend a belief [is] cowardice," Abram told Congress. "I could never support racial preference," he said later. ". . . If you discriminate against a group, you are endangering all minority groups." After civil rights organizations worked against Abram's confirmation, Reagan named him in a way that did not require Senate approval. Abram was then selected as vice-chairman of the Commission and served from 1984 to 1986.

Abram was the U.S. representative to the United Nations Commission on Human Rights from 1985 to 1988. In 1989 President George BUSH appointed him U.S. Permanent Representative to the U.N. in Europe.

It was Abram's fifth appointment by a president, and he remained in the post until 1993, when he became chairman of UN Watch, one of whose purposes was the curbing of ANTI-SEMITISM in the world organization.

Abram was involved in numerous professional, civic, educational, religious, and diplomatic organizations, serving as president of the American Jewish Committee (among several other Jewish organizations) and of the Field Foundation and the United Negro College Fund. He was also chairman of an investigation of New York's nursing home industry and chairman of President Jimmy CARTER's Commission for the Study of the Ethical Problems of Medicine. This last position came after Abram contracted leukemia in 1973.

"I have tended [since college] to consider a stand-up position as a mark of good character," Abram once said. "It is personally distressing to stand by an unpopular cause, but if there were not those who do, it would be a poorer world." This creed as well as his persistence rankled opponents, but it helped Abram achieve his goals.

BIBLIOGRAPHY
Abram, Morris B. *The Day is Short: An Autobiography.* 1982.
Manfredi, P. Reston. "An American Conscience." *Lifestyles,* Spring 1998.

Roger K. Newman

Abzug, Bella Savitsky

(1920–1998), attorney, congresswoman, and civil rights activist.

Bella Abzug made a significant impact on American politics and civil rights. A congresswoman and women's rights activist, Abzug was an outspoken figure on the political scene in the United States for decades, and dedicated the bulk of her professional life to the civil rights movement. She was the author of two books: *Bella! Ms. Abzug Goes to Washington*, 1972; and (with Mim Kelber) *Gender Gap: Bella Abzug's Guide to Political Power for American Women*, 1984.

Born in New York City on July 24, 1920, Bella Savitsky was the daughter of Russian-Jewish immigrants. She attended Bronx public schools and, after graduating from Hunter College, entered Columbia University Law School. In 1944, she married (Maurice) Martin Abzug, a stockbroker and novelist. They had two daughters.

After receiving her law degree and passing the New York bar exam in 1947, Abzug entered private practice, specializing in labor disputes and civil rights

Women's liberation movement leader and Democratic congresswoman from New York Bella Abzug anounces her candidacy to the United States Senate on May 17, 1976. (AP/Wide World Photos)

cases. In the 1950s, she represented clients accused of "subversive activities" by anti-Communist politicians. She lobbied for nuclear disarmament in the 1960s and led protests against United States military involvement in Vietnam in her role as the legislative director for the Women's Strike for Peace (1962–1970).

Abzug became a nationally known figure in 1970 when she was elected to the U.S. Congress—the first Jewish woman to attain this position. She served in the House of Representatives from 1971 until 1976, assuming a leadership role in the antiwar and women's movements. Abzug's campaign against the selective service system and advocacy for national day care centers and ratification of the Equal Rights Amendment (ERA) won her national support. She gave up her congressional seat in 1976 to seek the New York Democratic Party nomination for the U.S. Senate, but narrowly lost the race to Daniel Patrick Moynihan, who eventually won the seat. Abzug went on to run unsuccessfully for mayor of New York City in 1977 and for a congressional seat representing Manhattan's East Side in 1978. Abzug served as co-chair of President Jimmy Carter's National Advisory Committee for Women until 1979, when she was dismissed after criticizing

the president's decision to cut funding for women's programs.

After leaving elective politics, Abzug devoted most of her attention to women's rights. In the early 1980s, she continued to work in support of the Equal Rights Amendment. She served as a special adviser to the Secretary General of the United Nations Conference on Environment and Development and co-founded the Women's Environment and Development Organization (WEDO), which works to give women around the world greater access to political power. She presided over the World Women's Congress for a Healthy Planet in 1991 and addressed the United Nations World Conference on Women in 1995. She died of complications following heart surgery at Columbia-Presbyterian Medical Center in Manhattan on March 31, 1998.

BIBLIOGRAPHY

Abzug, Bella, with Mim Kelber. *Gender Gap: Bella Abzug's Guide to Political Power for American Women.* 1984.
Faber, Doris. *Bella Abzug.* 1991.

Jennifer Mossman

ACLU

See American Civil Liberties Union.

ACMHR

See Alabama Christian Movement for Human Rights.

Affirmative Action

The concept "affirmative action" was first used by President John F. KENNEDY in a 1961 executive order. Kennedy's order provided that federal contractors take affirmative action to prevent racial discrimination in the workplace and to promote information about employment among racial groups, especially blacks, that had been previously excluded from employment.

President Kennedy's executive order was aimed at affirmative action in the workplace. In addition to employment, the CIVIL RIGHTS ACT OF 1964 applied affirmative action's nondiscrimination principle to public accommodations and facilities, federally funded programs, and public education. Through the administration and adjudication of these initiatives, as well as others, the meaning and scope of affirmative action have been refined and enlarged. Originally intended to benefit blacks, affirmative action now provides protection to a broad array of other groups, including Asian Americans, Hispanics, Native Americans, and women.

Affirmative action has been defended, broadly, on two grounds. First, it functions as a remedy for discrimination: either invidious or intentional discrimination, or disparate impact or adverse effect discrimination. The latter results from practices that evince no discriminatory intent but nevertheless have a disparate impact or adverse effect on a protected group. The U.S. SUPREME COURT endorsed the disparate impact rationale for affirmative action in *Griggs v. Duke Power Co.* (1971), the Court's seminal exposition of TITLE VII OF THE CIVIL RIGHTS ACT OF 1964, preventing discrimination in employment.

The second defense of affirmative action is that it is not just a remedy for discrimination but rather, or in addition, a corrective for disadvantage. Under this model, discrimination is more or less irrelevant to affirmative action since the policy is intended as a "no-fault" measure, providing disadvantaged groups the legal and practical means by which they may catch up to those more fortunate, regardless of who is liable for their disadvantage. It is precisely the inability of proving discrimination in individual or class actions (which can be long and costly) that makes affirmative action

such a desirable policy over and above the traditional safeguards of antidiscrimination law.

Proponents of affirmative action claim that the policy has always been about equal opportunity, providing, among other things, redress for past wrongs and their lingering effects, fairness in employment and education, role models for minority and underutilized groups, income to those who for too long were unable to participate on a level playing field with others, particularly in the highest paying and most prestigious jobs, and, perhaps above all, respect.

Critics of affirmative action argue that the policy is no longer concerned with equal opportunity but has become a social technology consumed with achieving equal or proportional group results, granting preferences to legally designated groups in the name of attaining racial balance in the workplace and in education. The effects of the policy have been the promotion of mediocrity, government-sponsored dependency, widespread doubt about the competence of affirmative action beneficiaries, and the division of the country into an archipelago of racial and ethnic enclaves.

Advocates of affirmative action frequently do not contest that the goal of the policy has been achieving of racial and ethnic balance in the workplace and in education. They defend this objective, however, on grounds of "diversity," that the different perspectives and experiences promoted by affirmative action will benefit employers as well as academic programs. Justice Lewis Powell, writing for the U.S. Supreme Court in *Regents of the University of California v. Bakke* (1978), gave credence to the diversity rationale for affirmative action, ruling that race could be one element weighed against other elements in the admission procedures of a medical school, but that a fixed number of places or quotas for minority candidates could not be used (see BAKKE, REGENTS OF THE UNIVERSITY OF CALIFORNIA V.)

Since *Bakke*, the question of how much race could be used in affirmative action programs before constitutional rights were violated has occupied the courts. Critics have assailed the diversity rationale as antithetical to the original vision of civil rights, which is founded, the critics claim, on the principle that race, ethnicity, and sex are irrelevant to hiring decisions and educational admissions, and should not be used as a proxy for how individuals think or behave.

In the late 1980s and 1990s, the Supreme Court has been increasingly sympathetic to the critics' arguments, reining in affirmative action in both state and federal programs. In *City of Richmond v. Croson* (1989), the Supreme Court rejected a small business set-aside for minorities that the city of Richmond, Virginia, had established for city construction contracts. Justice

William Brennan, writing for four justices in *Bakke*, had argued that programs that take account of race but that are aimed at remedying those disadvantages imposed on minorities by previous racial prejudice should be treated as "benign" discrimination, subject to the lesser constitutional standard of intermediate scrutiny. (Intermediate scrutiny allows for programs that serve important governmental objectives and that are substantially related to the achievement of those objectives.) In *Croson*, the Court rejected the logic of benign discrimination, holding that all racial classifications, regardless of the race burdened or benefited, are equally suspect and subject to the rigorous constitutional standard of strict scrutiny. (Strict scrutiny requires of legislation that it serve a compelling governmental interest and be narrowly tailored to meet that interest.) The Court later unified its affirmative action jurisprudence, ruling in *Adarand Constructors, Inc. v. Pena* (1995) that the strict scrutiny standard, applicable to state and local affirmative action in *Croson*, also applied to federal affirmative action programs. *Adarand* overruled an earlier decision of the Court, *Metro Broadcasting, Inc. v. FCC* (1990), which had subjected federal affirmative action programs to the lesser constitutional standard of intermediate scrutiny.

Affirmative action has emerged as one of the most controversial public policies of the late twentieth century. It is not hard to understand why: the policy addresses such fundamental issues in American politics and constitutional law as the meaning of equality, the role of the state and private actors in promoting educational opportunity and job redistribution, and, more generally, the view Americans hold of themselves and of their relationship to others.

The future of affirmative action may be in jeopardy, but the policy still enjoys support among significant sectors of American society. Critics claim that the policy has run its course, and now serves only to entrench a racial and gender spoils system. There is little doubt, however, that affirmative action will survive, if perhaps modified, well into the next millennium, having established an enduring legacy in American civil rights.

BIBLIOGRAPHY

Adarand Constructors, Inc. v. Pena, 115 S.Ct. 2097 (1995).

Belz, Herman. *Equality Transformed: A Quarter-Century of Affirmative Action.* 1992.

Bergmann, Barbara R. *In Defense of Affirmative Action.* 1996.

City of Richmond v. Croson, 488 U.S. 469 (1989).

Eastland, Terry. *Ending Affirmative Action: The Case for Colorblind Justice.* 1997.

Gibson, Dale. "Stereotypes, Statistics and Slippery Slopes: A Reply to Professors Flanagan & Knopff and Other Critics of Human Rights Legislation." In *Minorities and the Canadian State*, edited by Neil Nevitte and Allan Kornberg. 1985.

Glazer, Nathan. *Affirmative Discrimination: Ethnic Inequality and Public Policy.* 1975.

Griggs v. Duke Power Co., 401 U.S. 430 (1971).

Metro Broadcasting, Inc. v. FCC, 497 U.S. 547 (1990).

Orlans, Harold, and June O'Neill, editors. "Affirmative Action Revisited." In *Annals of the American Academy of Political and Social Science.* S23 (September 1992): 50.

Regents of the University of California v. Bakke, 438 U.S. 265 (1978).

Rosenfeld, Michel. *Affirmative Action and Justice.* 1991.

Rossum, Ralph A. *Reverse Discrimination: The Constitutional Debate.* 1980.

Sowell, Thomas. *Civil Rights: Rhetoric or Reality?* 1984.

Anthony A. Peacock

AFL-CIO

The American Federation of Labor (AFL) was organized in 1886 as a federation of autonomous craft unions. These UNIONS organized workers in particular occupations rather than throughout a given workplace or industry. They battled for the eight-hour day, improved wages and working conditions, a degree of autonomy, and the right to organize and strike to improve the conditions and the rewards of work. The AFL unions primarily voiced the aspirations of white, male, and immigrant workers from Europe. During an era of SEGREGATION, most craft unions and the railroad brotherhoods (some of them independent of the AFL) sought to maintain high wages by creating a tight labor market through restricting access to the best jobs to white craftsmen and their sons and relatives. They excluded African Americans and members of other racial minority groups (and many of them excluded women as well) through constitutional provisions banning them from union membership, by keeping them out of apprenticeship training, through union-controlled hiring halls, and by strikes forcing employers not to hire them. All-black AFL locals emerged among railroad porters, longshoremen, laborers, hod carriers, and plasterers, and blacks also belonged to the United Mine Workers (UMW) union and a few other AFL organizations; but most craft unions even in these instances froze African Americans out of higher-paying jobs.

During the early twentieth century, AFL craft unions flourished, but they declined almost to the vanishing point in the early 1930s, when a more inclusive labor movement emerged. Spurred by the devastation of worker living standards wrought by the Great Depression and the failure of existing unions to organize the mass of unorganized industrial workers, John L. Lewis of the UMW (one of the few AFL unions that had consistently organized blacks) and other unionists challenged the AFL leadership at a 1935 convention. The Congress of Industrial Organizations (CIO) soon emerged as a new spearhead for organizing the vast ranks of unrepresented workers, many of them minorities, based on the inclusion of all workers in industry, regardless of race, nationality, gender, or political creed. CIO unions grew episodically during the NEW DEAL and then by leaps and bounds during WORLD WAR II; fourteen million workers, about equally divided between the AFL and the CIO, belonged to unions at war's end.

These developments particularly benefited African Americans, who were overwhelmingly working class, and began to lay the groundwork for labor support for civil rights. Black workers took on increasing numerical and strategic importance in the CIO, as significant numbers of them had long worked in steel, meatpacking, auto, mining, and other industries. They became the first to join and the last to quit CIO organizing drives, and the most committed to the CIO's egalitarian creed. Blacks and left-wing organizers, many of them in the COMMUNIST PARTY and many of them also black, began to exert increasing demands and pressures against the old JIM CROW system in unions and the workplace. Prodded by black leaders such as W. E. B. DU BOIS and Paul ROBESON, the CIO made alliances with the NATIONAL ASSOCIATION FOR THE ADVANCEMENT OF COLORED PEOPLE (NAACP) and other civil rights groups. It also undergirded the New Deal voting coalition that kept President Franklin ROOSEVELT in office and extended union wages and benefits to millions of white and black workers through organization of the workplace. More jobs opened up to blacks when in 1941 the BROTHERHOOD OF SLEEPING CAR PORTERS (an AFL union) president, A. Philip RANDOLPH, threatened a mass march on Washington for equal job rights, causing the federal government to require war manufacturers to hire racial minorities. African-American median income relative to that of whites rose significantly as black workers, and especially a new cohort of black women, gained access to union wages, federally supervised voting in the workplace, and, to a lesser extent, union leadership positions.

In the postwar era, black workers and their allies within the CIO left wing pushed increasingly for equal access to all jobs and union leadership positions. The CIO as a whole also attempted to break the back of conservative control over CONGRESS by organizing the unorganized workers in the South. A major challenge to JIM CROW appeared to be on the horizon, with unionized black workers at its core. This proved to be a false dawn. In most industries, segregated facilities and jobs and separate seniority lines for white and black

persisted, as most white workers as well as employers sought to keep African Americans in hot, dirty, dangerous, unpleasant, and lower-wage occupations. A wave of Red-baiting by employers, the HOUSE UN-AMERICAN ACTIVITIES COMMITTEE, and others, antilabor laws, and violent repression (including a burst of LYNCHING of black servicemen) crushed many postwar organizing efforts, and by 1949 the CIO was in full retreat. It purged most of its left-wing affiliates, largely dispensed with Southern organizing, and became increasingly wedded to the DEMOCRATIC PARTY and American foreign policy. Although the CIO's formal program still demanded equality and civil rights for all, its actions increasingly fell short of black workers' demands.

In 1955, in order to shore up the power of organized labor, the AFL and the CIO merged, bringing together contradictory impulses over the role unions would play in supporting civil rights demands. The AFL unions gained the greater control over the new AFL-CIO, with plumber George Meany as its president. The AFL-CIO at this stage represented nearly 35 percent of American workers, covering much of basic industry as well as the crafts, yet it had not reached out to unorganized and largely minority workers in agriculture and service sectors. Civil rights advocates nonetheless remained hopeful about gaining labor support. Indeed, the AFL-CIO in subsequent years supported the BROWN V. BOARD OF EDUCATION school DESEGREGATION ruling of the SUPREME COURT and the CIVIL RIGHTS ACTS of 1957, 1960, and 1964 as well as the VOTING RIGHTS ACT OF 1965; was a major partner in the LEADERSHIP CONFERENCE ON CIVIL RIGHTS; and in many states supported equal rights laws. Individual unions also contributed significant amounts of funds and people to civil rights struggles, from the MONTGOMERY BUS BOYCOTT in 1955 to the MARCH ON WASHINGTON in 1963. Martin Luther KING, JR., Randolph, Bayard RUSTIN, and other African-American leaders continually sought to expand the "Negro–labor alliance" to sweep segregationists out of elected office and expand EMPLOYMENT, EDUCATION, HOUSING, Social Security, and other equal rights initiatives. As unionism in the 1960s spread to the rapidly growing area of public employment, an increasing proportion of ethnic minority and women workers joined AFL-CIO unions, and their importance to the labor and civil rights struggle overall became obvious during the MEMPHIS SANITATION WORKERS STRIKE in 1968, during which Dr. King lost his life.

To many civil rights advocates, however, the financial and rhetorical support of the AFL-CIO for the civil rights struggle was more than offset by the failure of the federation to discipline national and local unions, industrial as well as craft, that continued to practice segregation and to exclude black workers from the best jobs. The NAACP thoroughly documented union racism, and Randolph continually sought remedies within the AFL-CIO, only to be ignored and then censured (in 1961) for his efforts. Black workers become increasingly disgusted with union failure to implement AFL-CIO rhetoric, and under Title VII of the Civil Rights Act of 1964 (often aided by the NAACP) sued unions and companies alike for maintaining separate seniority lines, preventing blacks from moving into better-paying and more skilled occupations, and upholding segregated facilities. Black workers also formed militant caucuses within industrial unions, particularly the United Auto Workers union, and criticized older white male leaders of the AFL-CIO for being out of touch and relatively unconcerned with the plight of the urban poor, and for failing to organize at the grass roots. During unprecedented movements for change among African Americans and as many industries moved South, union failure to organize the unorganized drastically undercut the power of the civil rights struggle to transform the region and alter racial-economic inequities in the United States.

These failures caught up with the labor movement, as the AFL-CIO went into a period of diminished power during plant closings and business reorganization that swept through American industry from the late 1970s through the 1990s. The massive loss of unionized industries as well as blatant attacks against the right to unionize shattered the power of the both industrial and craft unions. Deindustrialization had a devastating effect on black communities, destroying unionized occupations that had held up incomes among working-class blacks, and especially black men. The focus on individual economic interest and racial scapegoating by the REPUBLICAN PARTY turned many white male workers away from civil rights and the unions, undercutting the political coalition of labor and minorities. African Americans, however, remained organized in higher proportions than whites, and minorities and women remained the strongest supporters for new labor organizing in growing sectors of service and white collar employment. A new leadership in the AFL-CIO during the 1990s began to recognize these realities by including minorities and women in more leadership positions and by attempting to strengthen alliances between minorities, women, and the poor as part of a strategy for organizing the unorganized. Unions now represented only about 11 percent of private sector workers, but more than 30 percent in the public sector. Civil rights leaders such as A. Philip Randolph and Martin Luther King, Jr., had always said that civil rights gains would be hollow without jobs and economic advances for working-class blacks. Whether a new labor and civil rights alliance could halt continuing racial and economic polarization remained uncertain in a globalized economy that allowed capitalists to ship jobs and plants overseas at a moment's notice.

BIBLIOGRAPHY

Foner, Philip S. *Organized Labor and the Black Worker, 1619–1981.* 1982.
Harris, William H. *The Harder We Run: Black Workers Since the Civil War.* 1982.
Honey, Michael K. *Southern Labor and Black Civil Rights: Organizing Memphis Workers.* 1993.
Hill, Herbert. "The AFL-CIO and the Black Worker: Twenty-Five Years after the Merger." *Journal of Intergroup Relations* X (1) (Spring 1982): 1–78.
Zieger, Robert H. *American Workers, American Unions,* 2nd ed. 1994.

Michael Honey

African Blood Brotherhood

The African Blood Brotherhood for African Redemption, also known as the ABB, was organized in 1919 under the guidance of Cyril V. Briggs who was born on the Caribbean island of Nevis in 1888. Briggs later moved to New York City where he was associated first with the Harlem-based *Amsterdam News*, and later with the African-American socialist newspaper, *The Messenger*. In 1919 Briggs became editor of the ABB publication *The Crusader*. The ABB enunciated a program that merged a black nationalist approach to racial self-determination with an internationalist Marxist emphasis on class struggle. In this merger the ABB attempted to operate both as a vanguard leading group for the African-American community, and as the black voice inside the left.

The ABB, which structured itself as a semisecret organization, advocated black armed self-defense against racist attacks. However, with the possible exception of their presence during a 1921 white pogrom against African Americans in Tulsa, Oklahoma (see TULSA RACE RIOT), there is no indication that they were directly involved in such measures.

The organizing of the ABB is related to the 1919 schism in the left which led to splits from the Socialist Party and the creation of U.S. Communist Party (CPUSA) with direct ties to the Third International of Lenin and Trotsky in the new Soviet Union. Briggs was among several black leftists who, dissatisfied with the lack of emphasis on racism and race among the socialists, joined the Communist Party. It was in this same year that the ABB was created by Briggs along with other like-minded black activists including Ben E. Burrell, Grace P. Campbell, W. A. Domingo, Otto E. Huiswoud, William H. Jones, and Richard B. Moore, as an organizationally autonomous group, philosophically affiliated with the Third International's coordination of communist parties worldwide. The ABB's initial organizational autonomy and its strong link with the Third International were crucial elements in the development of its American strategy of merging race and class outlooks. Additionally, 1919 was also the year of "the Red Summer" (referring to blood, not communism) in which at least seventy-five African Americans were killed and many more terrorized in twenty-five "race riots," often involving mass attacks by whites. The ABB's insistence on the salience of race and the need for self-defense drew in part from these and earlier attacks.

The ABB, essentially operating as a black caucus within the early U.S. communist movement, found itself facing left-based resistance to its emphasis on racism and black consciousness, not unlike that which had driven them from the Socialist Party. As a caucus, the ABB basically asserted the communist ideals of anticapitalist liberation and equality, but from a black perspective, emphasizing that "the Negro Question" was also a "national question." The impact of racism meant that black people around the world, said the ABB, had to be viewed as an oppressed people with their own history and culture that was parallel to that of other colonized peoples. From the ABB vantage point, alliances with white workers would require that they discard their beliefs in racial superiority; otherwise such workers would be "only potential allies" (cited in Foner and Shapiro, 1987, 23). For the ABB, working class unity depended on an end to racism within labor and the left, and on white recognition of the distinctive national character of black people. Similarly, class struggle remained a pivotal dimension. It was this class emphasis that propelled the ABB's staunch condemnation of Marcus Garvey's UNIVERSAL NEGRO IMPROVEMENT ASSOCIATION as a "bourgeois" distraction from anticapitalist organizing (see also Marcus GARVEY).

Resistance to the class/race perspective among many white leaders of the CPUSA required that the ABB go over their heads by drawing on its links to Lenin and Trotsky, who were alert to the issues of how to integrate diverse oppressed cultural groups into a framework of Marxist unity. Although the ABB's position on race, black national identity, and class was a largely autonomous development, it dovetailed with the positions of Lenin and Trotsky. ABB members found themselves welcomed by the Third International. Trotsky commissioned Claude McKay, the Harlem writer and ABB member, to write a book entitled *Negroes in America* to help development of more emphasis among communists on black workers in the United States. But, with the removal of Lenin and Trotsky from the stage, and with the rise of Stalin, who evidenced less interest in "the Negro Question," combined with its full organizational merger into the Communist Party in 1925, the ABB lost its autonomous cutting-edge role of attempting to create a race/class intersection within the Communist Party.

Harold Cruse's criticism of the ABB as a "West Indian" operation that was disconnected from American realities because of its leaders' regional origins, helps to illuminate part of the major twentieth-century presence of Caribbean activists in African-American politics of the United States. However, his critique ignores the presence in the ABB of U.S.-born black activists such as Grace Campbell, Edward Doty, Lovett Fort-Whiteman, Haywood Hall, and Otto Hall. More importantly, the ABB accurately tapped into one of the fundamental dilemmas of the left relations with black Americans, which is the persistence of racism among many white workers, along with a class-only perspectives of much of the left (with some notable exceptions such as the Industrial Workers of the World). Precisely because of their understanding of the importance of merging race and class analytically and strategically, the ABB is an important organization that prefigures later developments such as the BLACK PANTHER PARTY and the Detroit Revolutionary Union Movement (DRUM), as well as, in a more muted way, the RAINBOW COALITION. The Panthers and DRUM, as with the ABB, emphasized the continued impact of racism alongside the importance of black self-determination, and struggled to link these dimensions with Marxist/Leninist/Maoist concepts of class struggle and internationalism. Additionally, the Black Panther Party, similar to the ABB, emphasized armed self-defense as one element in its program albeit in actuality rather than only as a programmatic position. The Rainbow Coalition in its early formulation also attempted to link a diverse range of peoples along intersecting class and race/ethnic lines. Research on possible links and parallels among these organizations would be useful. Minimally, we can note that these parallels demonstrate the fundamental persistence of the issue of racism within white working-class organizations, and emphasizes the continued salience of distinctive African-American leftist outlooks in which race is pivotal to unity in any class struggle for equality. In this sense, the "African Blood Brotherhood for African Liberation and Redemption" was not simply ahead of its time, it was also deeply entwined in the racial knot of U.S. society that remains densely tied today.

BIBLIOGRAPHY

Cruse, Harold. *The Crisis of the Negro Intellectual.* 1967.
Foner, Philip S., and James S. Allen, eds. *American Communisms and Black Americans: A Documentary History, 1919–1920.* 1987.
Griffler, Keith. *What Price Alliance? Black Radicals Confront White Labor, 1918–1938.* 1995.
Robinson, Cedric. *Black Movements in America.* 1977.

Afrocentrism

During the 1980s a body of ideas labeled "Afrocentrism" came to be an important part of public discourse in various segments of the African-American community, especially within the discipline of BLACK STUDIES. With the publication of *Afrocentricity: The Theory of Social Change* in 1988, its author, Molefi Kete Asante, became widely recognized as the leading proponent of the Afrocentric perspective, which he described as being indispensable to black studies. After the publication of *Afrocentricity*, the Association for the Study of Classical African Civilization (ASCAC) came into existence as the brainchild of Jacob Carruthers and Maulana Karenga, who believed that the centerpiece of Afrocentric theory was a reconnection of Egypt to Africa, especially in the minds of black people. ASCAC's commitment to historiography was to rewrite Africans into the classical periods. Although there is no single conception of Afrocentricity, the movement was condemned by its critics as "Afrocentrism," which was seen by many as merely an ideological discourse between Afrocentric advocates and their critics.

Opponents of the more extreme tenents of Afrocentrism charged that its advocates lacked scholarly proof of their claims or based such claims on distortions of historical research. They also claimed that many of the arguments of Afrocentrists were implicitly racist and often viciously anti-Semitic. Among the scholars who criticized the movement were Diane Ravitch, Arthur Schlesinger, and Mary Lefkowitz. In her book, *Not Out of Africa: How Afrocentrism Became an Excuse to Teach Myth as History*, published in 1996, Lefkowitz wrote that "the negative purpose" for writing her book was "to show that the Afrocentric myth of ancient history is a myth, and not history." In her attack on the methodology of the Afrocentrists, Lefkowitz proclaimed that "Afrocentrism is not just an alternative interpretation," but that "in effect, Afrocentrists are demanding that ordinary historical methodology be discarded in favor of a system of their own choosing."

Some of the Afrocentric arguments that have come under attack by critics include: Africa and African cultures were the original sources of world civilization; Greek civilization was stolen from Africa; Socrates and Cleopatra were black; peoples of African descent have a unique "humanistic, spiritualistic value system" unmatched by that of any other racial group; European cultural and economic systems are inherently exploitive; and blacks' high melanin content makes them "inherently more creative."

In addition to the external criticisms, Afrocentrists themselves differ in their beliefs. For instance, the collection of supporting scholars around Asante, Carruthers, and Karenga are identified as "Nile Valley" Afrocentrists. These scholars assert the primacy of Egyptian Africa as the creative locus of the major ideas and practices that undergird the foundations of humanity. The Continental Afrocentrists, on the other hand, assert that the entire African continent is the true cultural source of black transatlantic communities. It is a conviction of this group that African social values are more humanistic than those derived from Europe. A third group is the Afrocentric Infusionists, who assert the positive value of infusion or blending Africa-based ideas, concepts, values, and historical data into the curricula. This group seeks close collaboration with public school curriculum specialists. A fourth group is the Social Afrocentrists, who do not see the black experience as so specialized that only blacks may be involved with exploring it.

The intellectual ideas that gave rise to all the various expressions of Afrocentrism may be traced back to a small group of black writers and intellectuals in the nineteenth century who, at various times, stressed the uniqueness and greatness of ancient African cultures; the New Negro Movement, which found powerful expression in the cultural and political activities of the HARLEM RENAISSANCE in the 1920s; and the BLACK POWER movement, a product of the racial challenges and tensions faced by the African-American community during the 1960s. The later movement, which grew out of the struggle for CIVIL RIGHTS, gave rise to black studies as an academic discipline. It has been this discipline that has provided the context for the emergence of Afrocentric ideas.

BIBLIOGRAPHY

Asante, Molefi Kete. *Afrocentricity,* new rev. (3rd) ed. 1988.
Azevedo, Mario, ed. *Africana Studies: A Survey of Africa and the African Diaspora.* 1993.
Franklin, John Hope, and Alfred A. Moss, Jr. *From Slavery to Freedom: A History of African Americans,* 7th ed. 1994.
Karenga, Maulana. *Introduction to Black Studies,* 2nd ed. 1993.

Lefkowitz, Mary. *Not Out of Africa: How Afrocentrism Became an Excuse to Teach Myth as History.* 1996.

Michael H. Washington

Age Discrimination (Ageism)

Certain forms of prejudice and discrimination are so pervasive that they deserve a name of their own. For example, prejudice against people of color is frequently known as "racism"; prejudice against women is commonly referred to as "sexism." In 1969, Robert Butler coined the word "ageism" to refer to prejudice against older people (generally those over age fifty in this context).

Psychologically, Butler's version of ageism can be regarded as an *attitude*, a negative evaluation that serves to orient individuals toward older people as a group. In particular, ageism as an attitude frequently predisposes individuals to *discriminate*; that is, to avoid contact with, victimize, or otherwise do injury to older people on the basis of their age status alone.

Ageism seems to flourish under the social conditions imposed by industrialization. No longer are older people seen as a reservoir of wisdom and practical knowledge; no longer do they possess the power they once maintained over extended family, government, religion, and the ownership of land. Instead, their status deteriorates, and they are asked to disengage from the important roles that they formerly played throughout the life cycle.

Gerontologists agree that many of the employment problems now confronting older workers are due to age discrimination, when workers in their fifties and sixties are denied employment opportunities strictly because of their chronological age. Unfairly stereotyped as incompetent and inadequate, older workers may not get promoted or be retrained even though they are fully qualified to perform a job. When terminated, older workers are much more likely than their younger counterparts to remain unemployed. For example, pollster Louis Harris observed in 1990 that more than 1.1 million Americans over fifty were ready and able to work but remained without a job. Such workers may be in very good health, flexible about their terms of employment, and willing to be retrained. Yet, believing that employers regard them as "too old to hire," they give up looking for work.

Beginning with research conducted in the early 1950s, study after study has indicated that older people tend to be stereotyped as lacking in "versatility." They are typically seen as "resistant to change," "uninterested in technology," "untrainable," "looking to the past," and "slow to comprehend new ideas." Moreover, there has been a fairly widespread perception that older people develop characteristics associated with children. They are regarded as cranky, incompetent, and weak. In 1952, in a classic study of age stereotypes, Tuckman and Lorge found a high level of agreement among graduate students in psychology—sometimes reaching 90 percent—that old people are set in their ways, walk slowly, have poor coordination, have lost most of their teeth, are bossy, and like to doze in a rocking chair. Variations of these findings have been obtained in recent research as well, although perhaps in more subtle form. In 1988, for example, sociologist William Levin found that college students in Boston, San Francisco, and Johnson City, Tennessee tended to characterize older people as less intelligent, competent, healthy, active, creative, attractive, reliable, energetic, flexible, educated, and socially involved than their younger counterparts.

The traditional image of elders may have been joined recently by another set of equally unrealistic, ageist, and even contradictory beliefs; namely, that older Americans are disproportionately powerful in both political and economic terms, that they control much of the nation's wealth, and—far in excess of their numbers in the population—that they occupy positions of authority over younger Americans. Some gerontologists regard this new stereotype as one aspect of a larger image of intergenerational warfare that has been constructed and fostered by policymakers in an effort to divert members of all generations from uniting to demand from the state the fulfillment of basic human needs regardless of age. In this view, the new stereotypes of elders direct the attention of policymakers and the public toward engaging in false conflicts between the generations. However, there is a contrasting viewpoint as well; namely, that ageism reflects a changing reality—that elders really do take more than their share of medical and economic resources, in part because of the growing number of older Americans who depend on Social Security and also because of skyrocketing medical costs due to recent breakthroughs in medical technology, as well as fast-rising costs of basic medical care and prescription drugs.

In more recent formulations, the term "ageism" has been applied not only to discrimination against elders, but to any age group including children. Also more recently, gerontologists have recognized the presence of positive stereotypes of older adults—for example, regarding them as kind, wise, dependable, and happy—which might have led to positive forms of age discrimination such as tax benefits and improved health care and housing options.

Such changes in conceptions of ageism did not develop in a cultural or structural vacuum; indeed, they probably reflect the fact that elders have organized effectively on their own behalf (through such groups as the AMERICAN ASSOCIATION OF RETIRED PERSONS), and that their wealth, status, and power have improved considerably since the early 1980s. Although continuing to survive across generations, negative ageism directed toward the elderly may have declined considerably. At the same time, it could escalate again in the years to come as members of the baby-boom cohort, Americans born between 1946 and 1962, mature into old age and compete with their children's generation for economic resources.

BIBLIOGRAPHY

Atchley, Robert C. *Social Forces and Aging.* 1991.

Butler, Robert N. "Age-ism: Another Form of Bigotry." *Gerontologist* 9 (1969): 243–246.

Bytheway, Bill. *Ageism.* 1995.

Cowgill, Donald O., and Lewelyn Holmes. *Aging and Modernization.* 1972.

Doering, Mildred, Susan R. Rhodes, and Michael Schuster. *The Aging Worker: Research and Recommendations.* 1983.

Estes, Carol L. *The Aging Enterprise.* 1979.

Falk, Ursula A., and Gerhard Falk. *Ageism, the Aged and Aging in America.* 1997.

Harris, Louis, and Associates. *The Myth and Reality of Aging in America.* 1975.

Harris, Louis, and Associates. *Americans Over 55 at Work Program: Research Reports 1 & 2.* 1990.

Levin, Jack. *Sociological Snapshots.* 1996.

Levin, Jack, and William C. Levin. *Ageism: Prejudice and Discrimination Against the Elderly.* 1980.

Levin, Jack, and William C. Levin. *The Functions of Discrimination and Prejudice.* 1982.

Levin, William C. "Age Stereotyping: College Student Evaluations." *Research on Aging* 9 (1988): 35–41.

Palmore, Erdman B. *Ageism: Negative and Positive.* 1991.

Rosen, Bernard, and Thomas H. Jerdee. "The Influence of Age Stereotypes on Managerial Decisions." *Journal of Applied Psychology* 61 (1976): 428–432.

Torres-Gil, Fernando M. *The New Aging: Politics and Change in America.* 1992.

Tuchman, Jacob, and Irving Lorge. "Attitudes Toward Older Workers." *Journal of Gerontology* 36 (1952): 149–153.

Williamson, John B., Diane M. Watts-Roy, and Eric R. Kingson, eds. *The Generational Equity Debate.* 1999.

Jack Levin

Agricultural Workers Organizing Committee

Farm workers have long tried to organize themselves into unions to improve their working conditions. Low wages, long hours, lack of fresh water, and inadequate housing have provoked numerous strikes in the fields. Anyone could start a strike; the challenge has been to organize the forces necessary to win the strikers' objectives.

The United Cannery and Packinghouse Workers (UCAPAWA) organized in the 1930s. The National Farmworkers Union (NFW), led by Ernesto GALARZA, tried to organize farmworkers in the 1940s and 1950s. In 1959, the AFL-CIO tried to organize farmworkers again, with the Agricultural Workers Organizing Committee (AWOC).

AWOC had several weaknesses, including a top-down leadership selected by AFL-CIO leaders, not by farmworkers, and a strategy of working cooperatively with labor contractors. AWOC continued the prior efforts of Ernesto Galarza and the NFW in preventing "braceros" or guest workers, contract workers imported from Mexico, from breaking strikes.

In the spring of 1965, the mostly Filipino farmworkers associated with AWOC conducted a successful three-day strike to raise wages in the grape fields of the Coachella Valley in California. When the harvest moved north to the Delano area, AWOC, led by Filipino leader Larry Itlong, insisted on the same $1.40 per hour wage they had won in Coachella. The Delano area growers refused.

Philip Vera Cruz, a former UFW vice president, described the start of the Great Delano Grape Strike: "On September 8, 1965, at the Filipino Hall at 1457 Glenwood St. in Delano, the Filipino members of AWOC held a mass meeting to discuss and decide whether to go on strike or to accept the reduced wages proposed by the growers. The decision was 'to strike' and it became one of the most significant and famous decisions ever made in the entire history of the farmworkers' struggles in California. It was like an incendiary bomb, exploding out the strike message to the workers in the vineyards, telling them to have sit-ins in the labor camps, and set up picket lines at every grower's ranch. . . . It was this strike that eventually made the UFW, the farmworkers movement, and César Chávez famous worldwide."

AWOC leaders quickly asked César CHÁVEZ's National Farm Workers Association (NFWA) to join the strike. Chávez, whose NFWA was composed mostly of Mexican-American workers, thought a major strike was years away; but he did not believe he could refuse to join workers on strike. The NFWA joined the strike twelve days later.

Agricultural growers had often kept workers from winning strikes by pitting one ethnic group of workers against another. If Mexican laborers went on strike, a Filipino labor contractor might harvest the crop. When Filipino workers threatened strikes, the grower would try to hire Mexican braceros to do the work. However, during the Delano strike, AWOC successfully merged with César Chávez's NFWA, creating what would be known as the UNITED FARM WORKERS, AFL-CIO, a multi-ethnic union with multi-ethnic leadership. The unity of Filipino and Mexican workers, along with the later addition of African-American, Arab, and other farm workers, helped the new union to oppose the grower efforts to set Filipino and Mexican workers against each other.

Labor affiliation proved extremely valuable to the merged union in providing funds and union supporters to assist in winning the grape boycott and later in defending the new UFW from attacks by the larger, crime-ridden Teamsters union.

BIBLIOGRAPHY

Galarza, Ernesto. *Farm Workers and Agri-Business in California, 1947–1960.* 1977.
Scharlin, Craig, and Lillia V. Villanueva. *Philip Vera Cruz: A Personal History of Filipino Immigrants and the Farm-workers Movement.* 1992.

Duane Campbell

Alabama

Alabama, the twenty-second state, was admitted to the Union on December 14, 1819. It later was home to the capital of the Confederacy, and RACE relations have been a major issue throughout the state's history. Some of the civil rights movement's most dramatic challenges to SEGREGATION occurred in Alabama in the 1950s and 1960s.

The Ascent of Jim Crow: 1875–1901

African Americans in Alabama enjoyed full VOTING RIGHTS and equal educational benefits even after RECONSTRUCTION. Alabama's constitutions of 1868 and 1875 guaranteed black suffrage. Conservative Democrats, led by Black Belt cotton planters, protected black suffrage, for legislative representation was based on the eligible voting population, which included freedmen. The 1868 Constitution also mandated equal funding on a per capita basis for black and white students. The legislature established ten normal schools for blacks, as Republicans and Democrats coveted black votes. Tuskegee Institute's inception in 1880 exemplified this political courtship; a grateful Democratic legislator introduced the founding legislation after black Macon County politician Lewis Adams supported his campaign.

As C. Vann Woodward shows in *The Strange Career of Jim Crow* (1955), segregation became legally sanctioned in the late nineteenth century. In Alabama, the dismantling of African Americans' civil rights suited conservative planters, who feared a potential populist alliance of poor whites and blacks. Conservatives used white supremacist appeals to win the votes of poor whites, who disliked the Black Belt's legislative power, based largely on its black population.

The legal assault on black Alabamians' liberties began in 1890. The state legislature permitted counties to levy their own property taxes and allocate funds to the two races' schools with a "just and equitable" standard. Horace Mann Bond showed the predictable results in *Negro Education in Alabama* (1939). Expenditures for teachers' salaries in Wilcox County's white schools were over seven times the expenditures for teachers in black schools by 1907.

The years 1890 through 1905 were a demoralizing time for Alabama's blacks. Forty-eight blacks were lynched in 1891 and 1892; sixteen were lynched in 1901. The Alabama legislature required segregated railroad cars in 1891. A boycott by Montgomery blacks failed to change that city's 1900 ordinance for segregated streetcar seating. In 1902 the Alabama Railroad Commission ordered railroads to maintain segregated train stations.

The culmination of Alabama's JIM CROW legislation came with the state's Constitution of 1901. Through poll taxes and literacy, EMPLOYMENT, and property requirements, the constitution disfranchised all but 3,654 adult black males, 2 percent of the black adult male population, by 1906. This percentage would not change substantially until the 1960s. Sheldon Hackney estimated in *Populism to Progressivism in Alabama* (1969) that 23.6 percent of eligible whites were disfranchised also.

A Period of Vulnerability and Exclusion: 1901–1940

Alabama women remained disfranchised until 1920, when enough states ratified the NINETEENTH AMENDMENT to the U.S. Constitution to make it law. In 1892, the state's first woman suffrage association formed in Decatur. Ellen Hildreth, wife of the Decatur *Advertiser*'s editor, became president of the statewide suffrage association after chapters were formed in Huntsville, Gadsden, and Montgomery. The 1901 Constitutional Convention rejected the organization's appeals, for most delegates feared that black women would gain voting rights. The Alabama Equal Suffrage Association was born in 1912 after prohibition leader Mary Winslow Partridge of Selma and child labor activists Mrs. W. L. Murdoch and Pattie Ruffner Jacobs of Birmingham revived the movement. Repeatedly the legislature rebuffed the suffragists, even rejecting the Nineteenth Amendment.

As Alabama's railroads and steel and textile industries needed black labor, particularly to undermine white labor unions, the state diverted funds from black grammar and high schools to industrial and agricultural schools. A leading black promoter of these types of education was Booker T. WASHINGTON, president of Tuskegee Institute.

Washington and Tuskegee Institute influenced the future civil rights movement. Although Washington urged blacks to demand equal educational funding, at the 1895 Atlanta Exposition he expressed his willingness for blacks to sacrifice political rights for goals of economic advancement. The black professional class that grew around Tuskegee later rejected this "Atlanta Compromise," organizing for political reforms. Tuskegee was also the site of a bizarre exploitation, as the U.S. Public Health Service studied the effects of syphilis on some four hundred poor black men, from 1930 to 1972, without their consent or knowledge.

The notorious ordeal of the SCOTTSBORO boys illustrated Alabama blacks' vulnerability. In 1931, nine black youths were charged with raping two white women on a train going through the northeast Alabama town of Scottsboro. Despite inconsistencies in the women's testimony, the nine defendants were convicted and sentenced to death. The COMMUNIST PARTY-backed INTERNATIONAL LABOR DEFENSE (ILD) intervened, retaining prominent attorneys Walter Pollak and Samuel Leibowitz to appeal the cases. The U.S. SUPREME COURT in 1932 ordered retrials for all defendants because of inadequate counsel, and all were retried and again convicted. The high court reversed Haywood Patterson's and Clarence Norris's second convictions because of unfair exclusion of blacks from county jury rolls. Again new trials ended in convictions, with lifetime prison sentences. In 1937 the state released four of the young men, and four others were paroled in the 1940s. Haywood Patterson escaped prison and fled to Michigan in 1943.

In the early twentieth century, demographic changes occurred in America that would affect the civil rights movement. Agricultural depression compelled thousands of blacks to move to Northern cities for industrial jobs. The remaining black population became increasingly urban. Whereas 10.3 percent of Alabama blacks lived in cities in 1890, by 1930 some 28.4 percent of the black population was urban.

Jim Crow Under Attack: 1940–1965

Urban blacks formed effective civil rights organizations under middle-class leadership. In 1941, for example, Charles GOMILLION, a sociology professor at Tuskegee Institute, helped form the Tuskegee Civic Association (TCA), which started voter registration drives in Macon County in that decade. In 1957, TCA led a devastating boycott against white businesses due to Macon County's resistance to black voter registra-

tion. TCA's lawsuit against a state gerrymander of Tuskegee designed to render black voters powerless resulted in the U.S. Supreme Court's *Gomillion v. Lightfoot* decision (1960), which declared race-based gerrymandering unconstitutional. The growth of black political power hastened the elections of Tuskegee's first black councilman, Institute sociologist Stanley Smith, in 1964, and of its first black mayor, Johnny Ford, in 1972.

Federal courts frequently helped Alabama blacks achieve their civil rights. U.S. District Court Judge Frank JOHNSON, Jr., issued several significant orders from Montgomery. In 1958, he ordered Macon County registrars to submit records to the federal Civil Rights Commission, threatening Governor George WALLACE with jail for encouraging resistance to the order. In *Lee v. Macon* (1963), Johnson ordered the Macon County Board of Education to admit thirteen black students to all-white Tuskegee High School. No Alabama high school had been desegregated since the Supreme Court's BROWN V. BOARD OF EDUCATION decision (1954). As whites deserted Tuskegee High for segregated schools, Johnson prohibited the busing of white students to nearby Notasulga and Shorter high schools and transferred twelve black students there. Finally, in 1967 Johnson expanded *Lee v. Macon* to mandate statewide school DESEGREGATION.

Attorney General and future Governor John Patterson having won an injunction against the NATIONAL ASSOCIATION FOR THE ADVANCEMENT OF COLORED PEOPLE's (NAACP's) activities within Alabama in 1956, other local organizations had to promote change. In Montgomery, Rosa PARKS, a seamstress and NAACP chapter secretary, sparked a protest movement with her arrest for refusing to yield her bus seat to a white passenger. Local NAACP leader E. D. NIXON and ministers such as Rev. Ralph ABERNATHY rushed to Parks's defense, organizing the MONTGOMERY IMPROVEMENT ASSOCIATION (MIA). Dexter Avenue Baptist Church's young pastor, Dr. Martin Luther KING, JR., was elected president of MIA, which organized the successful MONTGOMERY BUS BOYCOTT. The boycott and a U.S. Supreme Court decree ended discriminatory seating practices. With veteran organizer Bayard RUSTIN and other ministers' help, King formed the SOUTHERN CHRISTIAN LEADERSHIP CONFERENCE (SCLC) in 1957, which spearheaded civil rights campaigns throughout the South.

Although King committed the movement to nonviolence, civil rights activists learned that some white Alabamians would violently defend segregation. In 1961, six white and seven black members of the Northern CONGRESS OF RACIAL EQUALITY (CORE) embarked on two buses from Washington, D.C. to New Orleans to challenge segregated interstate travel facilities. Outside Anniston, members of the KU KLUX KLAN set one bus aflame and beat four of the Freedom Riders. A mob assaulted the travelers in Birmingham, as segregationist Commissioner of Public Safety Eugene "Bull" CONNOR offered them no protection. Connor detained ten new Freedom Riders who arrived from Nashville, but upon their release they continued to Montgomery, where they faced violent mobs before departing for Mississippi. The violence convinced Birmingham's white business leaders to dismiss Connor by means of a referendum changing Birmingham's commission form of government to a mayor–council system.

More violence preceded Connor's departure, however. Birmingham's blacks had a strong organization, the ALABAMA CHRISTIAN MOVEMENT FOR HUMAN RIGHTS (ACMHR), led by Reverend Fred SHUTTLESWORTH. Founded in 1956, ACMHR sought black economic advancement and desegregation with boycotts and peaceful demonstrations. In 1956 and 1962, Shuttlesworth's Bethel Baptist Church was bombed. Policemen harassed participants of Birmingham's bus boycott, and Connor closed Birmingham's parks after a federal judge ordered them desegregated.

The local movement climaxed in April and May of 1963, when SCLC joined ACMHR's campaign of demonstrations for desegregated dining and municipal facilities and fair hiring practices. Violating a state court order against marching, King and Abernathy were jailed for eight days, during which time King wrote his famous "Letter from a Birmingham Jail," challenging white moderates to stand for "justice" rather than "order."

In May, Birmingham's black schoolchildren began marching daily and by the hundreds on downtown Birmingham. National television audiences saw Connor's police attack demonstrators with dogs and water cannons. White civic leaders agreed to ACMHR's demands on May 10, but that night rioting ensued after King's brother's home and the A. G. Gaston Hotel were dynamited. On September 15, another blast killed four girls attending Sunday School at the Sixteenth Street Baptist Church; former Ku Klux Klansman Robert Chambliss was convicted of the murders in 1977. Progress continued, however; events in Birmingham motivated CONGRESS to pass the CIVIL RIGHTS ACT OF 1964, and Birmingham's police force was integrated in 1966.

White pressure had forced Autherine Lucy from the University of Alabama in 1956 despite *Tuscaloosa News* editor Buford Boone's Pulitzer Prize–winning defenses of desegregation. In 1963, Governor Wallace again attempted to block court-ordered desegregation of the university; but wishing to avoid the violence that accompanied desegregation of the University of Mississippi in 1962, Wallace only briefly prevented Vivian Malone and James Hood from registering at Foster Auditorium. President John KENNEDY's committal of federalized National Guard troops made this desegregation attempt successful.

King planned to gain public support for federal voting-rights legislation with a grand Selma-to-Mont-

Part of the long line of marchers in the 1965 Selma-to-Montgomery March for Voting Rights. (AP/Wide World Photos)

gomery march in 1965. On March 7, activists from the STUDENT NONVIOLENT COORDINATING COMMITTEE (SNCC) led a march that stretched across the Edmund Pettus Bridge outside Selma, where state troopers and Dallas County sheriff's deputies attacked about eighty demonstrators with tear gas and billy clubs as they knelt to pray. This "Bloody Sunday" violence and severe beatings of three visiting ministers in Selma two days later (which killed Rev. James REEB) led President Lyndon JOHNSON to endorse voting-rights legislation in a nationally televised address the following Friday. On March 25, King and over three thousand participants completed the four-day Selma-to-Montgomery march; but that night, Ku Klux Klansmen murdered Detroit housewife Viola LIUZZO as she drove marchers back to Selma. President Johnson in August signed the VOTING RIGHTS ACT OF 1965, which banned discriminatory tests for voter registration.

Peaceful Accommodation: 1965–Present

The federal action of the 1960s was followed by a period of peaceful adjustment to civil rights gains. By 1966, older blacks viewed cautiously the BLACK POWER doctrine of the militant SNCC members. Reelected as governor in 1970, 1974, and 1982, Wallace appealed to African Americans as a populist after being paralyzed in a 1972 assassination attempt. Symbolizing his desire for forgiveness was his 1976 pardon of Clarence Norris, the last surviving Scottsboro defendant. In 1979, Richard ARRINGTON won election as Birmingham's first black mayor, an office he would hold for two decades. Like Ford in Tuskegee, he maintained close relationships with business leaders and middle-class constituencies, both black and white.

This accommodation continued throughout the 1990s, but room for improvement still existed. A 1996 U.S. Civil Rights Commission study revealed that Alabama's blacks still found pervasive segregation in schools and churches. Until 1999, Alabama was the last state to have an (unenforceable) law banning interracial marriages. Alabama also had the lowest percentage in America of elective offices (8 percent) held by women at the end of the century, although women had broken many educational and employment barriers in the last few decades.

BIBLIOGRAPHY

Ahmed, Nahfiza. "The Neighborhood Workers of Mobile, Alabama: Black Power Politics and Local Civil Rights Activism in the Deep South." *Southern Historian* 20 (1999): 5–24.

Bass, Jack. *Taming the Storm: The Life and Times of Judge Frank M. Johnson and the South's Fight over Civil Rights.* 1993.

Bond, Horace Mann. *Negro Education in Alabama: A Study of Cotton and Steel,* 2nd ed. 1994.

Carter, Dan T. *Scottsboro: A Tragedy of the American South.* 1979.

Clark, E. Culpepper. *The Schoolhouse Door: Segregation's Last Stand at the University of Alabama.* 1993.

Cox, Thomas H. "From Centerpiece to Center Stage: Kelly Ingram Park, Segregation, and Civil Rights in Birmingham, Alabama." *Southern Historian* 18 (1997): 5–28.

Eskew, Glenn T. *But for Birmingham: The Local and National Movements in the Civil Rights Struggle.* 1997.

Fager, Charles E. *Selma, 1965: The March That Changed the South,* 2nd ed. 1985.

Garrow, David J. *Protest at Selma: Martin Luther King, Jr., and the Voting Rights Act of 1965.* 1978.

Garrow, David J. *Bearing the Cross: Martin Luther King, Jr., and the Southern Christian Leadership Conference.* 1988.

Harris, James Tyra. *Alabama Reaction to the Brown Decision, 1954–1956: A Case Study in Early Massive Resistance.* 1978.

Healey, Thomas. *The Two Deaths of George Wallace: The Question of Forgiveness.* 1996.

McMillan, Malcolm Cook. *Constitutional Development in Alabama, 1798–1901: A Study in Politics, the Negro, and Sectionalism.* 1978.

Mueller, Charles Wendell. *A Voice for Justice: The Tuscaloosa News Views the Autherine Lucy Incident.* 1958.

Norrell, Robert J. *Reaping the Whirlwind: The Civil Rights Movement in Tuskegee, Alabama.* 1985.

Permaloff, Anne, and Carl Grafton. *Political Power in Alabama: The More Things Change . . . .* 1995.

Stanton, Mary. *From Selma to Sorrow: The Life and Death of Viola Liuzzo.* 1998.

Toffel, Miriam Abigail, ed. *Women Who Made a Difference in Alabama.* 1995.

Wiggins, Sarah Woolfolk, ed. *From Civil War to Civil Rights: Alabama, 1860–1960.* 1987.

Woodward, C. Vann. *The Strange Career of Jim Crow.* 1955.

Yarbrough, Tinsley E. *Judge Frank Johnson and Human Rights in Alabama.* 1981.

Yelverton, Mildred Griffin. *They Also Served: Twenty-Five Remarkable Alabama Women.* 1993.

Wesley Brian Borucki

Alabama Christian Movement for Human Rights

The Alabama Christian Movement for Human Rights (ACMHR) was founded in Birmingham on June 5, 1956, in response to a court injunction against the NAACP, undermining its local effectiveness. The goals of the new organization, led by Rev. Fred L. SHUTTLESWORTH, included the desegregation of buses, schools, and public facilities. To accomplish these goals, Shuttlesworth and other leaders, by their personal example, encouraged volunteers to violate segregation laws, and then used the arrests to challenge the laws in court.

The years of the ACMHR's greatest activity were 1956–1963. The organization began its activity with a petition drive and suit to pressure the city to hire black policemen. Soon thereafter, Shuttlesworth launched a two-year struggle against bus segregation. In 1957 he briefly attempted to force progress on school integration. On other fronts the ACHMR fought segregation in the parks and cooperated with local college students in a selective buying campaign against discrimination.

From the perspective of the national movement, the ACMHR's greatest contribution was its collaboration with the SOUTHERN CHRISTIAN LEADERSHIP CONFERENCE in the 1963 Birmingham campaign. Most ministers who participated in those demonstrations were ACMHR activists and the organization had provided the training in nonviolence for the children who marched. The ACMHR was what Aldon Morris called a "movement center," organizing local people into supporting or participating in direct action against segregation. As movement centers, the ACMHR and similar groups were the backbone of the early movement, providing the local leadership, infrastructure, and volunteers for the demonstrations.

BIBLIOGRAPHY

Clarke, Jacquelyne Johnson. *These Rights They Seek: A Comparison of the Goals and Techniques of Local Civil Rights Organizations*. 1962.

Eskew, Glenn. "The Alabama Christian Movement for Human Rights and the Birmingham Struggle for Civil Rights, 1956–1963." In *Birmingham, Alabama, 1956–1963*, edited by David Garrow. 1989.

Morris, Aldon D. *Origins of the Civil Rights Movement: Black Communities Organizing for Change*. 1984.

Tracy E. K'Meyer

Alaska

Alaskan social inclusion issues strongly center on the Alaskan Natives' struggle to claim rights to an indigenous land base and participate in mainstream society. The indigenous populations compose four major groups, each with distinct languages and socio-cultural traditions: the Aleut of southwestern Alaska; the Eskimo (Inuit and Yupik) of the western and northern coasts; the Athapascan of the great interior region; and the Tlingit, Haida, and others of the southeast coast. Not until the 1940s did non-Natives actually outnumber Natives in the territory. Correspondingly, socio-cultural change came slowly until after WORLD WAR II. The slowness of Alaskan Natives to assimilate into western society and adopt white middle-class values stimulated persistent white paternalism, negative stereotyping, and economic exploitation in the following decades.

Resolution of severe land claim conflicts by the 1971 ALASKA NATIVE CLAIMS SETTLEMENT ACT (ANCSA) represented a major turning point, with Alaskan Natives receiving substantial lands and monies. The relatively favorable resolution for Alaskan Natives no doubt benefited from the U.S. civil rights movement of the previous two decades that sensitized people to the plight of indigenous and minority peoples. A major intent of ANCSA was to assimilate Alaskan Natives into mainstream American society, transforming them from a communal society to private ownership and free enterprise. A system of regional and village-level profit-making Native corporations was designed to provide better educational and economic opportunity and to guide economic development for increased independence. However, the relatively high incidence of poverty compared to the general population, poor access to quality health care, suppression of religious freedom, and complex subsistence issues persisted. By the 1970s, Natives' demands for increased educational opportunities grew as they sought greater participation in Alaska's rapidly expanding economic and political development. By 1990 over 85,000 Natives resided in Alaska, most of them still living in small rural villages. Despite a steadily increasing Native population, the growth rate remained less than the overall Alaskan population growth rate. Becoming more of a minority, the Native population therefore dropped from around 25 percent of the state population in 1950 to 15 percent in 1990, though Natives were still a majority in several regions.

To address chronic socio-economic problems toward the end of the twentieth century, Alaskan Natives sought to limit the role of the ANCSA corporations, strengthen tribal governments, and resurrect their traditional subsistence economies. The Native villages more aggressively asserted an inherent right to self-rule through tribal governments created to regulate Native affairs, including the establishment of tribal courts, taxation systems, and management of village assets. Although gains were made by the end of the twentieth century in both quality of housing and income in some regions, improvements in day-to-day life and socio-cultural acceptance into mainstream Alaskan society were less evident. Economic discrimination and exploitation still persisted.

Despite recurrent charges of racial discrimination, the Alaskan state government earnestly fought formal recognition of tribal self-government. In 1998 and 1999, Alaskan Natives and sympathizers marched in Anchorage, protesting the state's inability or refusal to address the emotionally charged subsistence issue.

Interior Secretary Bruce Babbitt (back) on a 1997 boat tour of the National Petroleum Preserve on the Alaska Arctic Coast. (AP/Wide World Photos)

Alaska was faced with either instituting a subsistence priority system involving the Natives and other resource users or having the federal government assume management of fish and game throughout the region.

BIBLIOGRAPHY

Chance, Norman A. "Alaska Eskimo Modernization." In *Handbook of North American Indians: Arctic*, Vol. 5, edited by David Damas. 1984.

Goldschmidt, Walter R., et al. *Haa Aani, Our Land: Tlingit and Haida Land Rights and Use.* 1999.

Hosley, Edward H. "Intercultural Relations and Cultural Change in the Alaska Plateau." In *Handbook of North American Indians: Subarctic*, Vol. 6, edited by June Helm. 1981.

Langdon, Steve J. *The Native People of Alaska.* 1993.

Naske, Claus-M. *Alaska: A History of the 49th State.* 1994.

Richard C. Hanes

Alaska Native Claims Settlement Act of 1971

With the status of Alaskan Native land rights yet to be resolved by the mid-twentieth century, many indigenous peoples there continued a traditional subsistence lifestyle relatively unrestrained. However, a collision course between Native Alaskans and U.S. expansionism quickly erupted. Under the 1959 Alaskan Statehood Act, the new state could claim 104 million acres of public lands, much of it ancestral lands still used by Alaskan Natives. In reaction, Native Alaskan political organizations, guided by the Alaska Federation of Natives, grew through the 1960s. Upon the discovery of major oil fields in northern Alaska in 1968, Native claims legally stalled construction of the Alaska Pipeline, critical for transporting oil to the southern Alaskan coast. Industry, the state, and President Richard M. NIXON joined the Alaskan Natives to lobby Congress for a comprehensive resolution. In 1971, Senators Fred Harris (Democrat, Oklahoma) and Ted Kennedy (Democrat, Massachusetts) sponsored a bill in the U.S. Senate, and Congressman Lloyd Meeds (Democrat, Washington) submitted the companion measure in the House of Representatives.

The resulting Alaska Native Claims Settlement Act (ANCSA) passed into law on December 18, 1971. Bargaining from an unusual position of political strength, Alaskan Natives received 44 million acres of land and $962 million in exchange for dropping all claims to the remaining 335 million acres. ANCSA created twelve regional and almost 200 village Native corporations to disperse and invest the funds and guide future Native economic development. The singularly most important legislation to address land ownership and use in Alaska, the Act represented a major turning point by catapulting Native participation into Alaskan socio-political and economic life and reasserting Native Alaskan control over their own affairs.

BIBLIOGRAPHY

Alaska Native Claims Settlement Act Resource Center. http://www.clbw.com/ancsa.htm.

Berger, Thomas R. *Village Journey: The Report of the Alaska Native Review Commission.* 1985.

Mitchell, Donald C. *Sold American: The Story of Alaska Natives and Their Land, 1867–1959.* 1997.

Richard C. Hanes

Albany Movement

Between December 1961 and August 1962, more than 1,000 people, including Martin Luther KING, JR., were arrested during demonstrations to overturn segregation in Albany, Georgia. The Albany movement was the first citywide campaign involving the SOUTHERN CHRISTIAN LEADERSHIP CONFERENCE (SCLC). However, the movement was beset by internal divisions and eventually rebuffed by a highly disciplined police force and an intransigent city government.

Albany was the commercial center of rural southwest Georgia, in which the black community represented about 40 percent of the city's population of 56,000. The movement was launched officially on November 17, 1961, under the leadership of local oesteopath William Anderson. In fact, civil rights activity had begun in earnest in early October 1961 with the arrival of STUDENT NONVIOLENT COORDINATING COMMITTEE (SNCC) fieldworkers Charles Sherrod and Cordell Reagon. On Sunday, December 10, 1961, a further group of eight SNCC students, four black and four white, rode an interstate bus from Atlanta to Albany. Their subsequent arrest outside Albany's bus terminal triggered mass demonstrations leading to almost five hundred arrests.

King himself became involved only after an invitation from Anderson to address a rally on December 15, 1961. Moved by the local fervor, King agreed to lead a march downtown during which both he and Anderson were arrested. At this point SCLC decided to pour resources into the Albany campaign and King vowed to spend Christmas in jail.

However, two days later King was back in Atlanta after local movement leaders, many of whom were wary of outside activists, had agreed to a thirty-day truce with the city government. Privately, King was appalled to discover that the truce did not contain a single written concession toward ending segregation.

King returned to Albany in July 1962 to be sentenced and chose to serve a forty-five-day jail sentence instead of paying a $178 fine. But plans to trigger a renewed mass campaign were stymied after an unwanted anonymous benefactor (who was, in fact, Albany's mayor) paid King's fine. Much to the chagrin of SNCC activists, demonstrations were delayed further during the following week when King felt compelled to obey a temporary federal injunction banning marches.

By the time that King was arrested for a third time on July 27, 1962, local support was dwindling rapidly. Meanwhile, Chief of Police Laurie Pritchett steadfastly refused to be drawn into the type of confrontational response that might have provoked federal intervention. With momentum dissipating, local movement leaders announced another truce in a futile attempt to start negotiations with the city government. Meanwhile King received a suspended sentence and returned to Atlanta having suffered what proved to be his most severe setback in the South.

Reviewing the movement, SCLC staffers acknowledged that their involvement had been poorly planned and that the single goal of citywide integration had been too ambitious. However, the protests demonstrated conclusively that ordinary black Southerners, not just professional activists, were prepared to go to jail for the cause of civil rights. SCLC's experience in Albany also led to a valuable reappraisal of strategy before its subsequent (and far more successful) campaign in Birmingham, Alabama. Locally, SNCC used Albany as the base for a community organizing project throughout southwest Georgia.

BIBLIOGRAPHY

Carson, Clayborne. "SNCC and the Albany Movement." *Journal of Southwest Georgia History* 2 (1984).

Oates, Stephen. "The Albany Movement: A Chapter in the Life of Martin Luther King." *Journal of Southwest Georgia History* 2 (1984).

Ricks, John A., III. " 'De Lawd' Descends and Is Crucified: Martin Luther King, Jr. in Albany, Georgia." *Journal of Southwest Georgia History* 2 (1984).

Stephen Tuck

Albizu Campos, Pedro

(1893–1965), Puerto Rican nationalist leader and lawyer.

Pedro Albizu Campos was born on June 29, 1893, in a "barrio" of the city of Ponce on the south coast of Puerto Rico. Considered Puerto Rico's most celebrated twentieth-century leader in the struggle for self-determination and independence, Albizu was a graduate of the University of Vermont, where he studied chemistry and engineering. He became Puerto Rico's first Harvard graduate when he received a doctorate in law from that university. He struggled gallantly in support of Puerto Rico's inalienable right to independence, but the effort cost him many years of incarceration. Among Puerto Ricans, he is also known as Dr. Pedro Albizu Campos, Don Pedro Albizu Campos, Albizu Campos, simply Albizu, or the respectful "Don Pedro." In Puerto Rico and in Puerto Rican communities in the United States, schools, housing developments, and community agencies are named in his honor. For many, Albizu continues to be an inspiration for the island's quest for self-rule and cultural affirmation.

During WORLD WAR I, Albizu Campos was recruited to serve as an officer in the U.S. Army. He was assigned to an all-black battalion, and this heightened his awareness of the racial conflict that permeated American society. Later, he practiced law in Puerto Rico, primarily defending the interests of small farmers and organized labor against U.S.-owned agricultural interests.

He began his career in politics in 1923 when he joined the Partido Unión de Puerto Rico (the Union Party), which advocated independence for the island. When the Union Party merged with the Partido Republicano and reduced its drive for independence, Albizu resigned and joined the Partido Nacionalista Puertorriqueño (the Puerto Rican Nationalist Party). He simultaneously became the editor of its weekly publication in Ponce, and this provided him with a respected forum to voice his perspectives on various local and international issues.

In 1930, in the halls of the Puerto Rican Athenaeum, Pedro Albizu Campos was elected president of the Nationalist Party after serving as vice president. He had gained the support of party members through his

Pedro Albizu Campos in his San Juan Puerto Rico jail cell, November 3, 1950. (CORBIS/Bettmann)

work in Ponce and his travel throughout Latin America. The election of Albizu gave the party a more aggressive and militant voice. Albizu's leadership also embraced the views of a number of articulate defenders of independence, including noted writer Juan Antonio Corretjer. Under Albizu's leadership, the Nationalist Party considered all strategies in its quest to achieve independence; it accepted strategies that relied on peaceful civil disobedience, the electoral process, and armed struggle, either to defend itself, to aggressively convey a message, or to secure control. The party developed a reputation, however, for its armed confrontation with the authorities on the island and in Washington, D.C. Although Albizu Campos admired the Gandhian approach of civil disobedience, he was highly influenced by the Irish struggle for independence of the 1920s and 1930s. Under Albizu, however, the Nationalist Party initially participated in the island's general elections and peacefully participated in the demonstrations of striking workers.

The party was best known for violent confrontations that resulted in a number of casualties beginning in the 1930s and continuing through the 1950s. The confrontations began with an 1932 assault on the Puerto Rican legislature that led to one death. In October 1935, a Nationalist-led confrontation at the University of Puerto Rico resulted in the death of four party activists and one police officer, with another forty persons wounded. In February 1936, Colonel Frances Riggs, chief of the Puerto Rican Police was assassinated by two Nationalists, Hiram Rosado and Elías Beauchamp. Those two were then slain while in police custody. On Palm Sunday, March 21, 1937, the Puerto Rican police fired upon members of the Nationalist Party, killing twenty-one and wounding more than a hundred fifty. The Nationalists, members of the "Cadets of the Republic," were unarmed. An AMERICAN CIVIL LIBERTIES UNION investigation labeled this event a massacre. In July 1938, an attempt to assassinate colonial Governor Blanton Winship resulted in the death of Colonel Luis Irizarry, who was seated next to the governor. Several Nationalist were arrested and convicted of the crime. Shortly thereafter there was a failed attempt to assassinate Federal Judge Robert Cooper in San Juan. On October 30, 1950, the Nationalists launched an attempted take-over of several Puerto Rican municipalities, and a "Republic of Puerto Rico" was solemnly proclaimed. A suicide commando also attacked the governor's palace. The revolt left twenty-five people dead and more than one thousand under arrest. Albizu Campos, who had been jailed from 1936 to 1943 on charges of sedition, was rearrested and sentenced to fifty-three years in prison on comparable charges. On November 1, 1950, two New York–based Nationalists, Oscar Collazo and Griselio Torresola, attacked the temporary U.S. presidential residence, Blair House, in Washington, D.C. Torresola and a Secret Service agent were killed. Torresola carried a letter from Dr. Pedro Albizu Campos.

On May 25, 1951, U.S. Representative Fred L. Crawford submitted to the Congressional Committee on Interior and Insular Affairs a report on Pedro Albizu Campos and the Nationalist Party. At the time there was in the United States a national anticommunist witch hunt, and the report tried to establish a connection between the Nationalists and the Communist Party of the United States. In reality, Albizu was an avowed Catholic and openly opposed to class struggle in Puerto Rico, as he believed that class divisions would retard the independence effort.

On March 1, 1954, four other Nationalists, also based in New York, launched an assault against members of CONGRESS from the visitors' gallery of the House of Representatives. They were led by Lolita LEBRÓN and included Rafael Cancel Miranda, Irvin Flores Rodríguez, and Andrés Figueroa Cordero. Five member of Congress were wounded. This was the last major Nationalist armed attack against U.S. authorities who held control over Puerto Rico's destiny. At the time, Albizu Campos was very ill, hospitalized but in police custody.

On April 21, 1965, Pedro Albizu Campos died. He was survived by four children and wife Laura Meneses, a native of Peru and also a Harvard graduate. He had spent a total of eighteen years in prison before being pardoned in 1964. By then he was near death. Recent findings strongly suggest that while a prisoner Albizu Campos was subjected to radiation that caused tumors on his legs and his eventual demise. Shortly after his death the University of Havana granted him an honorary doctorate.

For many, Albizu was the conscience of Puerto Rico, a role he accepted as his destiny with a willingness always to accept the consequences as well. Pedro Albizu Campos's greatest contribution was to revive the militant tradition started by Dr. Ramón Emeterio Betances in the 1860s, as both leaders insisted that Puerto Rico be placed within a Caribbean and Latin American context and not retained as a U.S. appendage. Albizu also argued that U.S. control over Puerto Rico was illegitimate because it violated the 1897 Charter of Autonomy. The Charter, an agreement with Spain, included a clause that precluded any change in the island's status without Puerto Rican consent.

For the emerging generation of Puerto Rican activists in the 1960s, the legacy of Albizu Campos would be appropriated and given new meaning. As a symbol of unwavering militant opposition to U.S. colonialism, Albizu could be viewed as a Puerto Rican MALCOLM X.

BIBLIOGRAPHY

Maldonado-Denis, Manuel, ed. *La Conciencia Nacional Puertorriqueña por Pedro Albizu Campos.* 1972.

Ribes-Tovar, Federico. *A Chronological History of Puerto Rico.* 1973.

Rodríguez-Morazzani, Roberto. "Political Cultures of the Puerto Rican Left in the United States." In *The Puerto Rican Movement: Voices from the Diaspora,* edited by Andrés Torres and José Velásquez. 1998.

Tirado-Avilés, Amílcar. "La forja de un líder: Pedro Albizu Campos 1924–1930." *Centro: Journal of the Center for Puerto Rican Studies* IV(1) (1992): 12–23.

Wagenheim, Kal, and Olga Jiménez de Wagenheim. *The Puerto Ricans: A Documentary History.* 1973.

Basilio Serrano

Alcatraz Occupation

The occupation of Alcatraz Island in San Francisco Bay by members of various tribes from November 1969 through June 1971 marked a shift to militant tactics in the NATIVE AMERICAN MOVEMENT, showed a growing generational rift in the movement, and spawned further protests.

A group dominated by Sioux first occupied Alcatraz in 1964, shortly after the United States abandoned its federal prison there. Citing a provision in the 1868 Fort Laramie Treaty allowing Sioux to claim surplus federal property, the activists claimed Alcatraz. They offered the government forty-seven cents per acre for

A group of Sioux Indians invaded and briefly occupied Alcatraz Island on March 9, 1964, in an attempt to assert rights given under an 1868 treaty allowing Native Americans to claim "unoccupied government land." (CORBIS/Bettmann)

the island as a gimmick to call attention to a similar offer the government was making to California Indians for land taken during the Gold Rush of 1849. The occupiers left Alcatraz with little incident, but their protest inspired leaders of the large Bay Area Indian community, created by government relocation programs, to consider converting the former prison into an Indian cultural and community center.

Adam Nordwall (now known as Adam Fortunate Eagle), a Red Lake Chippewa who moved to the Bay Area in 1951 where he become a successful businessman and leader in the Indian community, revived these plans in 1969. He acted when it became known that a Texas businessman planned to develop the island, and after fire destroyed the Bay Area Indian community center. Organizers of the second Alcatraz occupation intended to thwart the island's economic development and call attention to challenges facing the Indian community, as well as win support for converting the island to an Indian community center. Nordwall invited Richard Oakes, a Mohawk and activist in the local Indian college population, to participate briefly, thereby creating a wide-ranging generational alliance in the Indian community. After the occupation failed on its intended date of November 9, 1969, Oakes organized a subsequent occupation by a force of seventy-eight activists, dominated by college-age Indians from various tribes, that began November 20, 1969 and lasted until June 11, 1971.

The NIXON administration feared the public relations repercussions of a violent encounter with Alcatraz protestors if it tried to evict them from the island. Nixon's officials also saw an opportunity to improve the administration's image in the turbulent late 1960s by offering to create a national park dedicated to Indian history and culture. The occupiers refused the proposal, though, wanting to maintain the occupation's value as a political symbol and to obtain not a national park but outright title to the island, which the government would not deliver. The occupation force had shrunk to fifteen by June 11, 1971, when about thirty federal agents landed on Alcatraz and rounded up the remaining protestors, thus ending the occupation.

Although occupiers did not obtain title to Alcatraz, the occupation achieved the short-term goals of preventing the island's commercial development and generating publicity that brought contributions used to found a new Indian center for the Bay Area. The occupation also heightened national awareness of American Indian issues, fostered increased cultural pride in many Indian communities, and energized the Native American Movement, which would see an increase in high-profile protests following Alcatraz.

BIBLIOGRAPHY

Fortunate Eagle, Adam. *Alcatraz! Alcatraz!: The Indian Occupation of 1969–1971.* 1992.

Johnson, Troy R. *The Occupation of Alcatraz Island: Indian Self-Determination and the Rise of Indian Activism.* 1996.

Smith, Paul Chaat, and Robert Allen Warrior. *Like a Hurricane: The Indian Movement from Alcatraz to Wounded Knee.* 1996.

Todd M. Kerstetter

Alexander, Kelly Miller, Sr.

(1915–1985), NAACP leader.

Kelly Alexander, Sr., a Southern black civil rights leader, was elected to the NAACP Board of Directors (1950), vice-chairman of the organization (1976), acting chairman (1983), and chairman (1984). (See NATIONAL ASSOCIATION FOR THE ADVANCEMENT OF COLORED PEOPLE.) His forceful calls for youth representatives on the board, a million-member organization, and AFFIRMATIVE ACTION programs echoed his leadership of the Charlotte (NORTH CAROLINA) NAACP (1940–1948), and his work at the North Carolina NAACP Conference (1948–1984). He pioneered in race reform.

Alexander's parents, owners of a funeral business in JIM CROW Charlotte, raised their four sons with ideals of education, independence, and community service. They named their son Kelly for prominent educator Kelly Miller of Howard University. Older brother Frederick Douglass Alexander (1910–1980) became Charlotte's first black city councilman in 1965, and state senator in 1974. Kelly began a stride toward freedom in 1940, after returning from Tuskegee Institute and mortuary college. He initiated local NAACP ANTI-LYNCHING, equal schooling, fair hiring, and right-to-vote campaigns (see VOTING RIGHTS). At the city's Friendship Missionary Baptist Church in 1943, he co-founded the state's NAACP Conference. He led it courageously, teaming with its branch organizer, field secretary, and attorneys to attack bus, job, and school SEGREGATION. As they mobilized communities, using nonviolent direct action and litigation to breach color lines, Alexander received death threats from the KU KLUX KLAN (KKK). State legislators also attempted to silence the allegedly communist NAACP. Even so, during statewide SIT-INS, the emergence of BLACK POWER, and later protests, Alexander remained outspoken. He abjured armed self-defense and clung to nonviolence (a bomb damaged his home in 1965) while promoting racial integration and justice. North Carolina had one of the NAACP's largest affiliates—122 branches and 35,000 members—when Charlotte's black mayor eulogized Alexander in 1985.

BIBLIOGRAPHY

Bennett, Wylissa R. "The Alexanders: NAACP Family Affair." *Southeast Perspective Magazine* 2 (1996).

Crow, Jeffrey J., Paul D. Escott, and Flora J. Hatley. *A History of African Americans in North Carolina.* 1992.

Douglas, Davison M. *Reading, Writing, and Race: The Desegregation of the Charlotte Schools.* 1995.

Gavins, Raymond. "The NAACP in North Carolina During the Age of Segregation." In *New Directions in Civil Rights Studies,* edited by Armstead L. Robinson and Patricia Sullivan. 1991.

Golden, Harry. *The Right Time: An Autobiography.* 1969.

Waynick, Capus M., John C. Brooks, and Elsie W. Pitts, eds. *North Carolina and the Negro.* 1964.

Raymond Gavins

Alexander, Will Winton

(1884–1956), social activist and administrator.

Born in Morrisville, Missouri, Will Winton Alexander graduated from Scarritt-Morrisville College in 1908 and entered the Methodist ministry. He received a bachelor of divinity degree from Vanderbilt University in 1912 and served for several years as a pastor of churches in Nashville and Murfreesboro, Tennessee. During his ministry, Alexander became increasingly interested in the problems of Southern poverty and racial discrimination. These issues would become the focus of Alexander's social activism.

Alexander left the ministry at the beginning of WORLD WAR I to work for the National War Work Council. In 1919, Alexander helped to found the COMMISSION ON INTERRACIAL COOPERATION (CIC) in an attempt to ease the racial tensions and violence that followed World War I. He served as the CIC's executive director for the next twenty-five years. Alexander also agreed to oversee the organization of Dillard University in New Orleans, and served as its acting president from 1931 to 1935.

Alexander's interest in issues of poverty and farm tenancy led him to write, along with Charles S. Johnson and Edwin Embree, *The Collapse of Cotton Tenancy* in 1935. The authors argued that federal government programs were the only solution to the problem of farm tenancy in the South. Soon after the book's publication, President Franklin D. ROOSEVELT asked Alexander to become assistant administrator of the Resettlement Administration and implement the government's farm programs. When the Resettlement Administration was reorganized and became the Farm Security Administration (FSA) in 1937, Alexander was appointed its administrator.

Alexander served as head of the FSA until 1940, when he left government service to become vice president of the Rosenwald Fund. He had been a trustee of the Rosenwald Fund since 1930, and was its vice president until 1948, when he retired from public service.

BIBLIOGRAPHY

Baldwin, Sidney. *Poverty and Politics: The Rise and Decline of the Farm Security Administration.* 1968.

Dykeman, Wilma, and James Stokely. *Seeds of Southern Change: The Life of Will Alexander.* 1962.

Olson, James S., ed. "Alexander, Will Winton." In *Historical Dictionary of the New Deal.* 1985.

Larissa M. Smith

Ali, Muhammad

(1942–   ), boxer.

Born Cassius Marcellus Clay, Jr., in Louisville, Kentucky, on January 17, 1942, of parents of modest means, Muhammad Ali was perhaps the most famous athlete of the 1960s and 1970s. No black person in American history has ever been quite the public figure that Ali was. His fame has rested on three distinct but related aspects of his public and private lives: first, he was the most gifted heavyweight boxer in history; second, he joined the NATION OF ISLAM; and third, he refused to be drafted into the U.S. Army during the VIETNAM WAR because of his religious beliefs (see CONSCIENTIOUS OBJECTION).

Even as a youngster, Ali was always colorful, gregarious, and fun-loving. He was something of a poor student, with little inclination to study or read. Louisville policeman Joe Martin took a liking to the young man and taught him the fundamentals of boxing, managing his amateur career. Ali dedicated himself to carefully learning the craft of boxing, devising imaginative stylistic adaptations that often violated conventional wisdom in the sport. The amateur phase of his career culminated when he won the gold medal as a light-heavyweight at the 1960 Olympic Games in Rome, where he also recited his own poetry and dazzled audiences with his speed and grace in the ring.

Upon his return from Rome, Ali turned professional, changing his management to a syndicate of prominent white Louisville businessmen. His trainer was Angelo Dundee, who co-owned and operated a gym in Miami. Blossoming into a well-proportioned, six-foot–three-inch, 210-pound frame, Ali seemed almost genetically engineered to be a champion boxer. Despite his dazzling style and highly personable wittiness, Ali was at first not taken very seriously by sportswriters or other boxing insiders as a heavyweight

Heavyweight champion Muhammad Ali answers questions from the press at the Houston federal courthouse where, on March 27, 1967, the court was to review his plea to prevent his induction into the Army. The court refused to block his call-up. To the right of Ali is Martin Luther King, Jr. (AP/Wide World Photos)

contender. When he went up against Sonny Liston, a former convict who was considered too strong and tough, no one thought he had a chance of winning.

Despite being dubbed a seven-to-one underdog by the oddsmakers, Ali handily beat Liston in Miami Beach on February 25, 1964, in seven rounds. What had been happening outside the ring was equally fascinating to most—and unsettling to many. MALCOLM X, who had a ringside seat at the fight with Liston, had been with Ali during much of his training. The fight promoters feared that Ali was associating with members or the black Nation of Islam, an organization little understood at the time and seen by many as a hate group because of its belief in the superiority of blacks and its forthright denunciation of white RACISM. Indeed, the young fighter, who had been attending Muslim meetings for some time, had already joined the Nation. In order to have the fight with Liston proceed, Ali had promised promoters he would not reveal his membership until after the fight. When Ali did so, an-

nouncing also that he was adopting a new Muslim name in place of Cassius Clay, his "slave name," he was immediately denounced by the press and a good portion of the white public. Even significant portions of the black public were skeptical. Ali was no longer a sweet-tempered, bragging kid but something sinister, a threat to boxing, although at this time no athlete on the active boxing scene was living as clean a life as Ali. For the next several months, Ali found himself embroiled in the controversy between Malcolm X—who officially quit the Nation the month following Ali's victory over Liston and formed his own organization— and Elijah MUHAMMAD, head of the Nation of Islam. Ali eventually denounced Malcolm X publicly. It was feared for some time after the assassination of Malcolm X in 1965 that Ali would be a target of retaliation by Malcolm's followers.

After Ali announced his membership in the Nation of Islam, he also became embroiled in conflict with the Selective Service System. He had originally been classified as I-Y (unfit to serve) because he had twice failed the Army's intelligence test. But, faced with a need to escalate the draft, the Army lowered its standards for a passing grade for the test and Ali was now found eligible. Mounting pressure was placed upon the Selective Service to reclassify him under the new standard, which it did. Ali refused to be drafted, however, becoming famous for saying "I ain't got nothing against them Viet Cong" and "Ain't no Viet Cong ever called me nigger." During this time, Ali continued to fight, but he had become perhaps one of the most hated public figures in the United States. Further, despite the fact that his opponents were mostly black, he politicized his fights, making them virtual crusades where he was the knight fighting against the white power structure and his black opponents were merely pawns and dupes for whites. It was this stunning self-dramatization that had a galvanizing effect on his public, especially young Blacks, who were becoming increasingly militant and anti-establishment as a result of what many perceived as the failures of the civil rights movement. In 1967, Ali was convicted of a violation of the Selective Service Act and sentenced to five years in prison—a conviction that was eventually overturned by the Supreme Court, on the grounds that his Islamic beliefs qualified him for conscientious objector status. In the short term following his sentencing, he was stripped of his boxing title, denied a boxing license anywhere in the country, and forced to surrender his passport. He did not fight professionally for nearly four years. While appealing his case, he lectured on college campuses around the country to raise money for his defense. He thus became connected to the ANTI-WAR MOVEMENT and a symbol of the new black militancy of the BLACK POWER era, although his political views were, on the whole, surprisingly conservative. His stance on the war particularly endeared him to Dr. Martin Luther KING, JR., who himself came out against the war in 1967.

Ali returned to boxing in 1970, through a match arranged by black politicians in Georgia. Although he had been officially stripped of his championship title in 1967, the public had never accepted anyone else as champion. But in 1971 Ali actually lost the title to Joe Frazier. He regained the title in Kinshasa, Zaire, in 1974, beating the heavily favored George Foreman. Public opinion, which had started to shift to Ali's favor as more of the American public turned against the Vietnam War, was now fairly solidly behind him when he beat Foreman. Indeed, he was lionized shortly after the Foreman match, starring in a movie based on his life and drawing crowds of thousands whenever he appeared in public.

Unfortunately, Ali, like many boxers, stayed in his profession too long, suffering a savage beating at the hands of Larry Holmes when the now-aging fighter attempted a comeback after retiring. After one final fight, Ali retired for good. He has since been diagnosed as suffering from a Parkinson's Disease–like illness, induced by the punishment he endured at the end of his career as a boxer. Although greatly limited in his ability to speak as a result of his illness, Ali is still a powerful, world-renowned personality.

BIBLIOGRAPHY
Hauser, Thomas. *Muhammad Ali: His Life and Time*. 1991.
Olsen, Jack. *Black Is Best: The Riddle of Cassius Clay*. 1967.
Sheen, Wilfred. *Muhammad Ali*. 1975.

Gerald Early

Alianza Federal de Pueblos Libres

Originally founded by Reies López TIJERINA as the Alianza Federal de Mercedes (Federal Alliance of Land Grants) in 1963, the organization changed its name in 1967 to the Alianza Federal de Pueblos Libres (Federal Alliance of Free Towns). Tijerina formed the organization in an attempt to regain Hispano communal land grants in northern New Mexico, lands granted first by the Spanish crown and then legally recognized by the United States under the terms of the 1848 Treaty of Guadalupe-Hidalgo.

The Alianza first gained national attention in October of 1966 with an attempted occupation of the Echo Amphitheater in New Mexico's Kit Carson National Forest. The next year, the organization received even more publicity when *aliancistas* (Alianza members) occupied the Rio Arriba County courthouse in Tierra Amarilla. The incident resulted in a shootout and the eventual surrender of Tijerina. Tijerina served time in federal prison for his part in the incident.

Before his prison term, Tijerina reached out to Chicano activist César CHÁVEZ and African American civil rights leader Martin Luther KING, JR. In the 1970s and 1980s, Tijerina attempted to bring international attention to the cause by asking the Mexican government to intervene in the land grant issue, which the government refused to do.

Although focused largely on a specific issue, the Alianza's contribution to civil rights in the United States lies in its role in bringing attention to the plight of poor, rural peoples and in encouraging pride in Hispano heritage and history.

BIBLIOGRAPHY
Blawis, Patricia. *Tijerina and the Land Grants: Mexican Americans in Struggle for Their Heritage*. 1971.
Gardner, Richard. *Grito! Reies Tijerina and the New Mexico Land Grant War of 1967*. 1970.
Meier, Matt. "King Tiger: Reies Lopez Tijerina." *Journal of the West* (April 1988).
Nabakov, Peter. *Tijerina and the Courthouse Raid*. 1969.
Tijerina, Reies López. *Mi Lucha por la Tierra*. 1978.

Scott Zeman

All-African People's Revolutionary Party

Stokely CARMICHAEL, famous civil rights activist and a leader of the STUDENT NONVIOLENT COORDINATING COMMITTEE (SNCC) and the BLACK PANTHER PARTY in the 1960s, was an admirer of Kwame Nkrumah. Nkrumah was the first president of the newly independent nation of Ghana and also a proponent of a larger, unified sub-Saharan African state. Unhappy with the Black Panther Party, which he felt was compromised by its frequent willingness to work with white liberals, Carmichael left the United States in 1969 to join Nkrumah, then living in exile in Guinea. In honor of Nkrumah and of Guinea's President Ahmed Sekou Touré, Carmichael changed his name to Kwame Toure.

Toure felt that the best hope for Africans, whether they were in Africa, the United States, or elsewhere, was a liberated and unified Africa. It was to help make this dream a reality that Toure founded the All-African People's Revolutionary Party (A-APRP). The party's goal was to free Africa from outside control through revolution and to unify the continent under a socialist government. Toure believed that only by accomplishing this goal could Africans and people of African descent be free and empowered.

Never very large, the A-APRP owed most of its prominence to founder and leader Toure. Although he continued to make Guinea his home, Toure also traveled widely to gather support for the A-APRP and for the cause of PAN-AFRICANISM. While Toure visited the United States and built some support for his organization there, it never approached the levels of support needed to influence mainstream America. Few African Americans were interested in his message of socialist revolution, and Toure's death in 1998 left the future of the A-APRP in question.

BIBLIOGRAPHY

Mabunda, L. Mpho, ed. *The African American Almanac.* 1997.

Meadows, Eddie S. "Stokely Carmichael." In *Encyclopedia of African-American Culture and History,* edited by Jack Salzman, David Lionel Smith, and Cornel West. 1996.

John F. McCoy

Amendments to the U.S. Constitution

See Thirteenth Amendment; Fourteenth Amendment; Fifteenth Amendment; Nineteenth Amendment.

Amenia Conferences (1916 and 1933)

In 1916, fifty prominent blacks and whites gathered at the Amenia, New York, estate of Joel E. Spingarn, board member of the NATIONAL ASSOCIATION FOR THE ADVANCEMENT OF COLORED PEOPLE (NAACP). The purpose of this initial Amenia Conference was to unite and formulate a collective plan of action regarding blacks' social and political problems.

The purpose and the timing of this conference were deliberate. Booker T. WASHINGTON, the most powerful black leader since the late 1800s, had died only one year earlier, thus creating an opportunity to bring together the major racial uplift camps. Those who were in Washington's camp supported a conservative program that promoted black self-help practices and accommodated southern segregation. Chief among these advocates was Robert Russa MOTON, Washington's successor as the principal of the Tuskegee Institute, the pillar of vocational education for blacks. The competing group was led by W. E. B. DuBois, director of publicity and research for the NAACP, editor of the NAACP's journal CRISIS, and champion of integrationist politics and full civil rights and liberties for blacks.

This conference was designed to unite southern race leaders and the northern-dominated NAACP. Although some of the gathering's unity was cosmetic, there was a general sense that the conference resolutions for further understanding and cooperation between the advocates of the competing philosophies pointed to the end of the Booker T. Washington era and signaled the coming of the NAACP era.

In 1933, the Second Amenia Conference was held at Spingarn's estate. The goals of the second meeting were different from the first. Black Americans had been particularly hard hit by the stock market crash of 1929 and the financial devastation of the Great Depression. President Herbert Hoover's inability to solve the country's financial woes allowed Franklin Delano ROOSEVELT to sweep into office with his promise of what he called a "New Deal." The group of thirty-three men and women that gathered at Amenia in 1933, however, felt there was no guarantee that Roosevelt's NEW DEAL would alleviate the country's plight, much less that of blacks.

On this occasion, then, the NAACP leaders were not searching for a new and united vision regarding racial issues. The NAACP leadership was aware that many blacks were dissatisfied with the organization and its focus on political and civil liberties and its inability to develop a successful plan to eliminate black poverty and unemployment. It was becoming evident that blacks' concern about civil rights was being eclipsed by a desperate search for economic justice and even survival. Indeed, the Second Amenia Conference attendees claimed that new alliances between black and white laborers would be the most effective means of improving the quality of black life. A solitary and racialized focus on civil rights and liberties did not make sense for Depression era America.

Far from advocating a peace between competing uplift philosophies, the Second Amenia conferees made it clear that the NAACP had to get more in touch with Depression era realities. Whereas the First Amenia Conference signaled the solidification of race leadership under the NAACP, the Second Amenia Conference openly challenged this leadership and suggested that a new political program highlighting economic issues was necessary to achieve racial justice.

BIBLIOGRAPHY

NAACP Papers. Library of Congress, Washington, D.C.

Ross, B. Joyce. *J. E. Spingarn and the Rise of the NAACP.* 1972.

Wolters, Raymond. *Negroes and the Great Depression.* 1970.

Young, James O. *Black Writers of the Thirties.* 1973.

Jonathan Scott Holloway

American Association of Retired Persons

Founded in 1958 as a companion organization to a retired teachers service group, the American Association of Retired Persons (AARP) has grown to become the largest nonreligious private organization in the United States. By the end of the century, the AARP also was generally considered the most powerful lobby at the national and state levels, growing into an ardent foe of AGE DISCRIMINATION in American society.

Dr. Ethel Percy Andrus, the first female high school principal in the state of California, began working to create safety nets for the often poverty-stricken and insuranceless retired teachers in her home state after her own retirement. Eventually, Andrus founded the National Retired Teachers Association in 1947, which provided health insurance and other benefits to its members. In response to interest from retirees who were not teachers, Andrus worked to establish the AARP as an independent association. Deeply involved

in the organization at the time of its founding was Leonard Davis, who chartered the Colonial Penn Company to manage AARP insurance packages. Davis's influence over the AARP expanded after Andrus's death in 1967.

Membership in the AARP grew quickly after its founding. In addition to the opportunity to join the insurance program, the organization has published from its inception a generally apolitical magazine, *Modern Maturity*, and enabled members to receive discounts at hotels and restaurants and on pharmaceuticals. Davis eventually departed the AARP, following press reports critical of Colonial Penn's immense profits and subpar insurance plans and federal investigations into the entanglement of the nonprofit AARP and the insurer. The organization survived the crisis

American Association of Retired Persons (AARP) volunteers sorting through mail.
(AP/Wide World Photos)

and continued its growth, enrolling over thirty million Americans over the age of fifty in the 1990s. The AARP's membership is disproportionately white, well-educated, upper-income, and suburban.

Although few AARP members join the association for its political advocacy program, the massive membership is often noted by the organization's lobbyists as they encourage lawmakers to support legislation favored by the AARP. Moreover, in addition to more traditional lobbying resources, the AARP has a unique 150,000-person force of volunteer employees based in congressional districts to activate grassroots pressure on wavering members of CONGRESS.

The association is especially effective in having a substantive impact on the formation of policy in areas such as Social Security, where the AARP is perceived as a source of objective information for members of Congress. On civil rights measures related to the protection of older Americans, the AARP is seen as a more traditional pressure group. The association has won numerous significant legislative victories at the federal level—most notably the Age Discrimination Act of 1975, which protects seniors from discrimination in federal programs, and a 1978 act that repealed mandatory retirement ages for federal workers and, expanding upon a 1967 act that banned discrimination against workers aged forty to sixty-five, protected other workers from mandatory retirement before the age of seventy. In statutes protecting the civil rights of older Americans, employers and program administrators are typically given slightly more flexibility in their application than is the case with civil rights laws protecting racial and ethnic minorities and women. In 1991, for the first time, the AARP publicly opposed the nomination of a SUPREME COURT Justice, with the association's representatives testifying that Clarence Thomas had failed to prosecute violators of federal age discrimination laws while chair of the EQUAL EMPLOYMENT OPPORTUNITY COMMISSION (EEOC).

BIBLIOGRAPHY

Congressional Quarterly, Inc. *Congress and the Nation, Volume II, 1965–1968.* 1969.

"Elderly Grudge Against Thomas," *National Journal.* July 6, 1991:1667.

Morris, Charles R. *The AARP: America's Most Powerful Lobby and the Clash of Generations.* 1996.

Peirce, Neal R., and Peter C. Choharis. "The Elderly as a Political Force—26 Million Strong and Well Organized." *National Journal.* Sept. 11, 1982:1559.

Van Atta, Dale. *Trust Betrayed: Inside the AARP.* 1998.

Jay Barth

American Civil Liberties Union (ACLU)

American civil rights and liberties are not abstract conceptions. They were established, albeit frequently challenged, by constitutional provisions such as the First Amendment and FOURTEENTH AMENDMENT, ordinary statutes, and executive orders. But it was the courage and determination of individuals and groups that have given form and substance to these amendments and to those laws, private claims, and executive orders that have been adopted to fulfill these goals. In the twentieth century, the American Civil Liberties Union has had a significant, if not preeminent role, in this process. The core of the ACLU position on rights and liberties is the broadest and most extensive assertion of freedom of expression.

Jane Addams (1860–1935), social worker and activist, helped found the American Civil Liberties Union in 1920. She was president of the Woman's International League for Peace and Freedom and went on to share the Nobel Peace Prize with Nicholas Murray Butler in 1931. (CORBIS)

The ACLU was created in 1920 by a small group of antiwar and prolabor Progressive era activists. Its board of directors included Harry F. Ward of the Union Theological Seminary, Duncan McDonald, president of the United Mine Workers, Congresswoman Jeannette Rankin, who opposed United States entry into World Wars I and II, Harvard law professor Felix Frankfurter, and Oswald Garrison Villard, editor of *The Nation*, among others. Its early agenda consisted of many legal defenses of working people in an immediate post-World War I era of antilabor activity. From its very beginning in 1920 and for several subsequent decades, Roger Baldwin, an energetic and astute antiwar social reformer and coauthor of an early influential book on juvenile courts and probation, had a definitive leadership role in ACLU.

The agenda for the early years of the ACLU was not limited to labor relations issues. Indeed, the organization had taken on what were then exceedingly unpopular assertions of rights for black people. After a few years, Baldwin and some of his fellow board members felt it necessary to expand the ACLU's civil rights agenda. Consequently, over time many new litigatory commitments were made. These commitments often strained relations with old supporters while not necessarily gaining new ones.

The ACLU has tried to remain committed to the fundamental principle that the defense of civil liberties must be universal. As noted above, this has resulted occasionally in the loss of core supporters and serious public criticism. Some dramatic occasions were the defense of the freedom of speech of Klansmen, the much-debated defense of the Nazi march in Skokie, Illinois, and the defenses of criminal defendants. (See AMERICAN NAZI PARTY; KU KLUX KLAN.) Virtually every historian of the ACLU has concluded that the Union was indeed true to its central purpose—to maintain political and ideological neutrality in its choices of the groups and individuals and causes deemed worthy of the ACLU's intervention. The ACLU's determination to provide universal and unbiased defense of civil liberties has at times been costly in terms of its own supporters and the bitter critics it has encountered. Among the latter, Attorney General Edwin Meese in the 1980s called the ACLU a "criminal's lobby" while conservative critic William A. Donohue attacked the ACLU's reputation for impartiality. Like any organization attempting to defend the rights of frequently unattractive individuals and unpopular causes, the ACLU undoubtedly has made errors in judgment. In balance however, its record of civil rights interventions has been evenhanded and courageous.

BIBLIOGRAPHY

Bean, Barton. "Pressure for Freedom: The American Civil Liberties Union." Dissertation. 1955.
Donahue, William A. *The Politics of the American Civil Liberties Union*. 1985.
Lamson, Peggy. *Roger Baldwin: Founder of the American Civil Liberties Union*. 1976.

John Schmidhauser

American Dilemma, An

Gunnar Myrdal's *An American Dilemma*, published in 1944, has been the most influential social science study of race relations in the United States. Its arguments were prominently employed in official actions that were precursors to the civil rights era, such as *The Report on the President's Committee on Civil Rights* (1948) and the Supreme Court's decision in BROWN v. TOPEKA BOARD OF EDUCATION (1954). During the first half of the 1960s Myrdal's approach carried weight in the formulation of national policy responses to the civil rights movement. While this study was encyclopedic in its accumulation of data and imaginative in its theorizing, its main impact has been ideological and discursive.

At the time of *An American Dilemma's* writing; the national and civic consideration of black-white relationships still operated within the format developed during the decades following the overthrow of RECONSTRUCTION. JIM CROW segregation was intact in the South, as was *de facto* segregation in the North. Governmental modernizing efforts of the Progressives and the New Deal in the first half of the twentieth century had had relatively little impact on racial patterns or policies, and this anomaly did not even generate serious public debate. Myrdal's accomplishment was to formulate black-white relationships in terms compatible with these modernization movements' underlying social engineering and planning assumptions. His formulation promoted egalitarianism and, at the same time, avoided any great social or political conflicts.

In 1938 a major philanthropic foundation brought Gunnar Myrdal to the United States to execute a fresh, but modest, review of the American racial scene. Myrdal was a Swedish economist already noted for both his original contributions to Keynesian welfare-state economics and for his practical work in establishing a new Swedish population policy. Almost from the start he vastly expanded the scope of the project with a workplan to develop a social engineering methodology for making American racial issues manageable, as it were, seeking to craft a Keynesianism for race.

An American Dilemma's major premise was that the nation's core values were organized around an "American Creed" of egalitarianism. No consideration was given to the ambiguous reality that for centuries RACISM was also a major value. The *dilemma* was one for whites in that they deviated from these values in their treatment of blacks. Although the *creed* was cultural and historical, the persistence of discrimination was based only on a model of current behavioral interactions. In a vicious cycle: White prejudices were reinforced by the debased conditions and standards of black people, in turn blacks were debased by the prejudice. Myrdal postulated a counter-mechanism of a virtuous cycle in which improvement in the status of blacks would reinforce the creed, and in turn the strengthened creed would create conditions for the further improvement in the status of blacks. The New Deal's growing welfare-state (see NEW DEAL AND DEPRESSION) provided institutional means to reinforce this cycle.

The descriptive text provided an encyclopedia on black-white relationships. The strongest sections treated economic matters, such as the impact of the New Deal on agrarian tenancy and industrial labor markets. The analysis of black society and its organizational structure depicted a realm unknown to most white readers.

While the Myrdalian theory of race challenged the status quo, issues of power and exploitation played minor roles in it. Nonantagonist resolutions were possible through the skillful alignment of the interests of the various parties and with the modification of behaviors. What almost all Americans considered to be intractable issues of race were reconstructed into an adjustable equilibrium that could respond to effective social policy.

However, in keeping with his theoretical structure Myrdal did not see the black community as a decisive actor in its own behalf, asserting its own interests. Since the dilemma was one that whites confronted, the role of black people was to strengthen whites' egalitarian values. This assimilationist orientation led Myrdal to call "the Negro community a pathological form of an American community."

Upon its publication, *An American Dilemma* had a big impact in scholarly circles, redefining much of the field that came to be known as race relations. Public policy debates used its arguments and frequently cited it as authority for expanding the civil rights of black people. However, by the mid-1960s, as the BLACK POWER movement asserted self-determination, Myrdal's theory, in which whites were almost the only significant actors for change, lost much of its authority. In the next decade political challenges to the welfare state undercut another Myrdalian premise. Neverthe-

less, this book still remains the most cited study of blacks and whites.

BIBLIOGRAPHY

Clayton, Obie, ed. *An American Dilemma Revisited.* 1996.
Ellison, Ralph. "*An American Dilemma*: A Review." In *Shadow and Act.* 1964, pp. 303–317.
Jackson, Walter A. *Gunnar Myrdal and America's Conscience: Social Engineering and Racial Liberalism, 1938–1987.* 1990.
Myrdal, Gunnar. *An American Dilemma*, 2nd ed., 2 vols. 1962 (1st ed., 1944).
Southern, David W. *Gunnar Myrdal and Black-White Relations.* 1987.

Harold M. Baron

American Federation of Labor

See AFL-CIO.

American Friends Service Committee

Founded by Quakers in 1917 to offer conscientious objectors an alternative to military service, the Philadelphia-based American Friends Service Committee (AFSC) quickly developed an interest in racial matters. In the mid-1920s, it established an Interracial Division, which was superseded in the mid-1940s by a Race Relations Division, and in 1950 by a Community Relations Division. Through these divisions, and via a network of formal and informal links with other progressive forces, the AFSC have played an important, but largely unheralded, part in the struggle for racial justice and understanding.

Although membership was never restricted to Quakers, the AFSC's opposition to racial discrimination was rooted in the Quaker belief in the equality of all human beings before God. Also important was the Quaker concept of convincement, whereby the AFSC believed that its own example of good works and racial tolerance would encourage others to see the need to change their racial views and practices. This tactic of moral persuasion was frequently allied to the provision of more direct material assistance to those grappling with the effects of racial oppression. These twin tactics were clearly seen in Washington, D.C., in the early 1950s, when the AFSC helped orchestrate an ultimately successful campaign to desegregate schools and other institutions. While AFSC staffers Irene Osborne and Alma Shurlock worked closely with local activists, their colleague Ralph Rose met with government officials and President Dwight EISENHOWER, emphasizing the moral imperative to end segregation.

During the 1950s and 1960s, the AFSC continued to urge those in power to act against racial discrimination. Yet, the organization also became concerned that this sort of top-down approach to identifying and solving racial problems might be rather paternalistic. It increasingly worked to ferment grassroots social change by encouraging local leaders and institutions to articulate and address their own problems. For example, in the Prince Edward County, Virginia, school crisis of 1959–1964, when authorities closed the public schools rather than desegregate them, the AFSC established an Emergency Placement Project, which arranged for some black students to be schooled in the North, and worked with local organizations to establish a system of Free Schools in the county. Both initiatives provided the sort of experience and training that produced a new generation of more assertive black leaders in the area.

Another key aspect of the AFSC's civil rights work was its Merit Employment Programs, which urged employers to hire qualified minority candidates in nontraditional jobs. In the late 1950s, the AFSC applied this criteria to its own hiring practices by making a black woman, Sarah Herbin, southeastern director of the program—despite the fact that the post was originally earmarked for a white male. Indeed, although the organization was not without its patriarchal tendencies, with men like Henry Cadbury, Lewis Hoskins, Russell Jordan, and Clarence Pickett dominating the executive committee during the 1950s and 1960s, women like Herbin, Barbara Moffett—who served for many years as secretary of the Community Relations Division—Nancy Adams, Helen Baker, Connie Curry, and Jean Fairfax played a vital role in the AFSC's civil rights work.

Arguably the AFSC's most significant contribution to the civil rights struggle was in the realm of ideas. In accordance with its pacifist beliefs, the AFSC actively promoted the use of nonviolent direct action and had links with most of the major theoreticians and exponents of this tactic, including A. J. Muste, Glenn Smiley, and Robert MOSES. William Stuart Nelson, Bayard RUSTIN, and James Lawson were among those who visited India to study Gandhian techniques under the auspices of the AFSC. The AFSC also quickly recognized the potential of Martin Luther KING, JR., as a nonviolent leader. In March 1956, it established an informal committee to channel assistance and advice to King in Montgomery. Three years later, it coordinated and partially sponsored King's own trip to India, and in 1963 it published King's most famous statement on nonviolence, the "Letter From Birmingham Jail." The AFSC continues to promote nonviolent protest as the most effective and ethical means to pursue peace,

human dignity, minority rights, and economic justice in America and throughout the world.

BIBLIOGRAPHY

AFSC. *Race and Conscience in America: A Review Prepared for the American Friends Service Committee.* 1959.
Chafe, William H. *Civilities and Civil Rights: Greensboro, North Carolina and the Black Struggle for Freedom.* 1980.
Curry, Constance. *Silver Rights.* 1995.
Lynn, Susan. *Progressive Women in Conservative Times: Racial Justice, Peace and Feminism, 1945 to the 1960s.* 1992.
Pickett, Clarence. *For More Than Bread: An Autobiographical Account of Twenty-Two Years' Work with the AFSC.* 1953.

Brian Ward

American G.I. Forum

In 1948, a Corpus Christi, TEXAS, funeral home denied a local Hispanic family the right to use its chapel for the wake of their son, Private Felix Longoria, a war hero and Mexican American whose remains were returned to his family three years after his death. In response to this episode and others that demonstrated the obvious neglect and poor treatment of returning Hispanic WORLD WAR II veterans, Dr. Hector Perez Garcia, a decorated Mexican-American war veteran, founded the American G.I. Forum. "Dr. Hector" formed the Forum on March 26, 1948. His earliest goal was to provide good health care for veterans who needed it and were refused because they were "Mexicans." Since that day, the organization has served to herald and protect the inalienable rights of Mexican-American war veterans.

Garcia's frustration with the poor treatment of Mexican-American war veterans surfaced shortly after his own return from World War II, in which he had served as an officer in the Medical Corps. Garcia, whose family had migrated to Texas from Mexico during the Mexican Revolution in 1918, saw many white veterans taking advantage of the services and benefits promised to them by the G.I. Bill. He also witnessed widespread discrimination against Hispanic veterans, who were denied proper health care and equal education and employment opportunities. The many returning Mexican Americans who fought in World War II for the United States saw their expectations of a proper homecoming fade.

The events that unfolded in 1948 in Garcia's community prompted him to take action. More important, these events propelled an even bigger foray, by Garcia and other Texas Mexican Americans, into the general civil rights movement. Spreading quickly throughout the American Southwest, the American G.I. Forum blossomed into a forerunner of the Hispanic civil rights movement as well as a watchdog for improper treatment of other minority groups in the United States and Puerto Rico. Garcia, whose father taught him the importance of a thorough and well-rounded education, was a staunch proponent for the higher education of all Hispanic people. As a result, he and his organization found themselves involved in issues such as the DESEGREGATION of schools, proper voter registration, and other federal legislation protecting the rights of minorities. The American G.I. Forum thus assumed its role as a major player in the civil rights movement in the middle portion of the twentieth century.

Today, the Forum flourishes with over 500 chapters and 6,000 members throughout the United States and Puerto Rico. For his continuous efforts toward the equal treatment of Mexican-American veterans and the overall Hispanic community, Garcia, who died in 1996, has since been linked with other twentieth-century civil rights leaders, including Martin Luther KING, JR., and César CHÁVEZ. The recipient of many outstanding community service awards, the Forum continues to make its presence known and its services available by sponsoring several types of scholarships, promoting youth leadership (see MEXICAN-AMERICAN STUDENT ORGANIZATIONS), and providing information on equal employment opportunities. As a part of the organization's commitment to civil rights, it has developed several national programs throughout its 51 years of service, including the Hispanic Education Foundation (HEF), National Veterans Outreach Program (NVOP), Jobs for Progress (SER), and Women in Community Service (WICS).

BIBLIOGRAPHY

Ramos, Henry A. J. *The American GI Forum: In Pursuit of the Dream, 1948–1983.* 1998.
Sigler, Jay A. *Civil Rights in America: 1500 to the Present.* 1998.

Jamie C. FitzGerald

American Indian Citizenship Act of 1924

One of the more complex issues in relations between American Indians and the federal government has been that of citizenship. Are American Indians citizens of their own tribal nations, the United States, or both? In 1924, the United States government attempted to give a clearer picture of that question. Despite being immune from the draft laws of the United States, more than 8,000 American Indians volunteered to serve during WORLD WAR I. Recognition of their dedicated service, along with strong lobbying efforts put forth by the Alaska Native Brotherhood, motivated the United

States Congress to grant American Indians the rights and privileges of U.S. citizenship. By issuing full citizenship, the government did not take away any rights that American Indians had gained through past treaties or that were expressed in the Constitution. The American Indian Citizenship Act of 1924 permitted American Indians to vote in federal elections, yet some of the individual states passed legislation barring electoral participation in state elections.

Not all American Indians were pleased with the government's actions, and many groups opposed the bill. As one Tuscarora chief, Clinton Rickard, said, "All Indians were automatically made United States citizens whether they wanted to or not. This was a violation of our sovereignty." At the time of the citizenship act's enactment, many policymakers guessed that most of the tribal governments and customs would lose influence and disappear, but that has not occurred. Because the act did not void previous agreements and treaties, American Indians today enjoy a unique DUAL CITIZENSHIP. See also SOVEREIGNTY.

BIBLIOGRAPHY

Champagne, Duane, and Michael A Pare, eds. *Native North American Chronology.* 1995, pp. 104–105.
Sigler, Jay A., ed. *Civil Rights in America.* 1998, pp. 224–225.

Matthew May

American Indian Civil Rights Act of 1968

In the 1960s, many members of Congress and figures in national government championed the cause of American Indians. Senator Robert F. KENNEDY called attention to the plight of many American Indians in New York and around the nation, and it became one of the themes in his candidacy for the presidency in 1968. A congressional committee had spent seven years investigating the history of the denial of civil rights to individual American Indians, by tribal governments, state governments, and the federal government. Hearings were held in Washington, D.C., and around the nation. As a result of these investigations, Senator Sam Ervin of North Carolina introduced and sponsored legislation to reverse this trend in a bill that became known as the American Indian Civil Rights Act.

The legislation was geared toward Native Americans living on reservations and guaranteed them many of the same civil rights and liberties in relation to their tribal governments and authorities that the U.S. Constitution assures to citizens of the United States. The act also limited the rights of tribal authorities to fining criminals up to $1,000 for crimes committed on their reservations or jailing them for six months. Other parts of the legislation directed the secretary of the interior, a Cabinet official, to publish updated versions of treatises on American Indian law for public use.

As with most legislation passed by Congress and directed at a particular group, not all tribes within the American Indian population supported the new law. One of the more vocal groups of opposition to the American Indian Civil Rights Act was the Pueblo tribe, who feared that the U.S. government was once again interfering in the business and operations of a sovereign nation. Many Pueblo officials and leaders feared that the Act would radically change traditional forms of government and culture within the Pueblo nation. In fact, a Pueblo tribe took legal action to test the legitimacy of the Act, and that test made its way to the United States SUPREME COURT.

Much earlier, in 1939, the Santa Clara Pueblo passed an ordinance permitting tribal membership for children of male members who had married outside the tribe, but denied it for children of female members who did the same. Julia Martinez, a full-blooded Pueblo, married a Navajo in 1941 and, accordingly, her daughter was denied membership in the Pueblo tribe, preventing the daughter from participating in elections, from holding secular office, and from retaining inheritance rights. In the 1970s Martinez sued the tribe and cited the American Indian Civil Rights Act for relief. The case reached the Supreme Court and Justice Thurgood MARSHALL wrote the opinion for the Court in the 1978 case SANTA CLARA PUEBLO v. MARTINEZ. Marshall and the Court ruled that federal courts did not have the authority to grant relief based on the language of the legislation, which said that courts might only review tribal ordinances in the context of habeas corpus and that any other scrutiny would be a violation of tribal sovereignty.

BIBLIOGRAPHY

Champagne, Duane, ed. *Chronology of Native North American History*. 1994.
Santa Clara Pueblo v. Martinez, 436 U.S. 49 (1978).

Matthew May

American Indian Movement (AIM)

The American Indian Movement (AIM) was easily the most aggressive Native American political group in a period that saw the rise of several activist organizations. Founded in Minneapolis, Minnesota, AIM began life as a Native American community group organized to protect Native Americans from undue police harassment. The organization grew in importance on a national level and was eventually targeted

for destruction by the FEDERAL BUREAU OF INVESTIGATION.

As organized in 1968 by Dennis BANKS, Clyde BELLECOURT, Eddie Benton-Banai, and George Mitchell, AIM primarily concentrated on problems in the Minneapolis Native American community. Within a year of its founding, however, AIM had become a national organization focused on the revitalization of traditional tribal cultures and spirituality, combating stereotypes and negative images of Native people, protecting Native American civil and human rights, educating Native American children about their own tribal heritages, regaining control over tribal resources and generally advocating Native American tribal self-determination. AIM leaders inevitably became involved in organizing demonstrations and generally spreading the word that Native Americans were not content with their treatment in America.

Although some AIM members, notably John Trudell, had been involved in the takeover of Alcatraz Island in San Francisco Bay in 1969 (see ALCATRAZ OCCUPATION). The organization's first aggressive political

American Indian Movement leader Clyde Bellecourt in 1973. (AP/Wide World Photos)

action to gain widespread national attention was in connection with the 1972 march on Washington, D.C., known as the TRAIL OF BROKEN TREATIES, and the subsequent takeover of the offices of the BUREAU OF INDIAN AFFAIRS (BIA). The demonstrators were to present a document known as the Twenty Points to the NIXON administration outlining Native American demands for the betterment of U.S.–tribal relations. One of the main provisions of the Twenty Points was that federal-tribal relations should be governed by treaties. Federal officials had been notified of the march and the demonstration's organizers had arranged housing for the marchers. The march ended at the BIA building. Accommodations for the marchers failed to materialize and law enforcement officers were called in to remove the protesters from the building. A scuffle ensued and the demonstrators occupied the building. The building was occupied for a week before negotiations—and guarantees of immunity from federal prosecution—finally ended the impasse.

The federal response to the Twenty Points very likely played a part in AIM's next political action, Wounded Knee II (see WOUNDED KNEE OCCUPATION). Basically, the federal government outlined the idea that the AMERICAN INDIAN CITIZENSHIP ACT of 1924 nullified all treaty relationships. U.S. citizenship and treaty rights were, in short, mutually exclusive.

Trouble had been brewing on the Oglala Lakota Pine Ridge Reservation for years. Richard Wilson, the elected tribal president, had formed a paramilitary organization known as the "GOONs" (Guardians of the Oglala Nation) to counter and even terrorize his political rivals on the reservation. The anti-Wilson forces, mostly traditional Oglalas, formed the OGLALA SIOUX CIVIL RIGHTS ORGANIZATION (OSCRO), which, in turn, asked AIM for protection from their own tribal government. The ensuing occupation of the hamlet of Wounded Knee on the Pine Ridge Reservation was an attempt to establish an autonomous Oglala Nation based on the Fort Laramie treaty of 1868. Oglala AIM leader Russell MEANS, along with most of the Lakota protesters, argued that their government under Richard Wilson had been, in actuality, a U.S.-imposed system rather than the lineal descendent of the legal Oglala authority that signed the 1868 treaty. It was, therefore, an illegitimate government. Thus with AIM help, OSCRO formed the Independent Oglala Nation (ION) at Wounded Knee.

The site of the occupation was picked because of its historical significance. It was there in 1890 that the U.S. Army slaughtered nearly three hundred Lakotas. Almost as soon as the occupation began, the protesters were surrounded by GOONs, Bureau of Indian Affairs police, U.S. marshals, and FBI agents armed with the latest military weaponry. Several firefights occurred

during the resulting two-month-long siege and two of the protesters, Frank Clearwater and Buddy Lamont, were killed by federal gunfire. The agreement that ended the siege, which contained a provision that the protesters would not be prosecuted, was soon broken and most of the AIM leadership, including Russell Means, Dennis Banks, John Trudell, Carter Camp, Stan Holder, and Leonard Crow Dog were targeted for arrest by the FBI. Wilson remained in office and won reelection in 1974.

Wilson's reelection did not end the violence. It was widely known on the Pine Ridge Reservation that AIM and the FBI were wary of each other and that violence would be forthcoming. The expected outbreak occurred June 26, 1975 when two FBI special agents, Ronald Williams and Jack Coler, entered the Jumping Bull property near the town of Oglala. An AIM encampment was located on the property. Williams and Coler were supposedly on the trail of a young man who had allegedly stolen a pair of boots. Whatever their reason for coming on the property, they found themselves in a gun battle with AIM members. Both agents and an AIM member, Joe Stuntz Killsright, were killed in the firefight.

The rest of the AIM group escaped and soon became objects of one of the largest manhunts ever in the western United States. Eventually three members of AIM, Dino Butler, Bob Robideau, and Leonard PELTIER, were brought to trial for the murders of Williams and Coler. In the first trial, held in Cedar Rapids, Iowa, Butler and Robideau were found not guilty. Leonard Peltier was extradited from Canada on the basis of false evidence and tried in Fargo, North Dakota, in a far different political climate. The falsification of evidence and perjured testimony led to his conviction April 18, 1977.

Despite the Wounded Knee trials and Peltier's conviction, AIM has nevertheless remained active. The organization has drawn considerable national and international attention to the Peltier case. In 1978, AIM was involved in the "Longest Walk," another national march on Washington, D.C., in the continued attempt to air Native American grievances. Three years later, AIM established Yellow Thunder Camp on federal land in the Black Hills in South Dakota. The establishment of the camp was the first step, according to AIM leaders, in reclaiming this sacred land for the Lakota people. AIM has continued in its political participation, particularly in protesting the false and harmful images of Native Americans in the media, and as sports team mascots, and in calling attention to environmental abuses. In 1998, twenty-five years after Wounded Knee II, a San Carlos Apache group, Call to Action, asked the Arizona chapter of AIM to help in its efforts to institute a new tribal constitution.

BIBLIOGRAPHY

Churchill, Ward, and Jim Vander Wall. *Agents of Repression: The FBI's Secret Wars Against the Black Panther Party and the American Indian Movement.* 1988.

Deloria, Vine, Jr. *Behind the Trail of Broken Treaties.* 1974.

Holm, Tom. "Indian Concepts of Authority and the Crisis in Tribal Government." *Social Science Journal* 19 (July 1982): 59–71.

Matthiessen, Peter. *In the Spirit of Crazy Horse.* 1991.

Ortiz, Roxanne D. *The Great Sioux Nation.* 1977.

Tom Holm

American Indian Religious Freedom Act of 1978

Assimilationist government policies and misunderstandings about Native American religions have historically worked to deny Indians the free exercise of religion guaranteed by the First Amendment. The American Indian Religious Freedom Act of 1978 (AIRFA) was a congressional effort to ensure Indians the same protection enjoyed by other Americans. Sponsored by Senator James Abourezk and Representative Morris Udall, AIRFA was signed by President Jimmy CARTER in August 1978. The Act acknowledged past government violations and committed the government to a policy that would protect and preserve the rights of Native Americans to exercise and express traditional religions. Furthermore, Native Americans should have access to their sacred sites and the use of sacred objects that were necessary for the integrity of their ceremonies.

The most frequent criticism leveled at AIRFA was that the Act was empty legislation. AIRFA directed federal agencies to review their practices and procedures, but did not require substantive policy changes by them. The Act contained neither enforcement mechanisms nor penalties for noncompliance. Other critics argued that AIFRA gave native religions special protections and, therefore, violated the Establishment Clause of the Constitution by permitting American Indians the exclusive use of federal land for religious purposes. Because Indian religions require the performance of certain rituals in certain places, their rights to religious freedom have often collided with the interests of developers.

Court interpretations have been inconsistent in protecting religious liberties, so Native Americans must rely on Congress for protection. The 1993 Native American Free Exercise of Religion Act guaranteed Indians' right to use peyote in religious ceremonies, but other issues remain unresolved.

BIBLIOGRAPHY

Deloria, Vine, and Clifford M. Lytle. *American Indians, American Justice.* 1983.

Vecsey, Christopher, ed. *Handbook of American Indian Religious Freedom.* 1991.

Wilkins, David E. *American Indian Sovereignty and the U.S. Supreme Court.* 1997.

L. Patrick Goines

American Nazi Party (ANP)

After WORLD WAR II, American Nazism was carried on by small groups in the ideological tradition of the German-American Bund of the 1930s. The American Nazi Party was founded in 1959 by "Commander" George Lincoln Rockwell, who had been a commander in the United States Navy. He set up headquarters in Arlington, Virginia, which were often called "Hatemonger Hill." It served as the training and housing facility for the organization that published and distributed *The Rockwell Report* and *The Stormtrooper.* Membership figures suggest that the group consisted of about three dozen core members with another several hundred supporters nationally. Rockwell's philosophy was published in a book entitled *White Power!* (1967), which came to be a popular slogan for neo-Nazis, racialist skinheads, and some Klansmen as these groups began to converge in the 1970s.

Members of the American Nazi Party pose next to their "Hate Bus," which they drove around the country in the spring of 1961. On the far right is party leader George Lincoln Rockwell. (CORBIS/Bettmann)

(See KU KLUX KLAN; WHITE SUPREMACY.) He also published his autobiography, *This Time the World!* (1963). The American Nazi Party was one of many white reactionary groups resisting the civil rights movement. The organization utilized propaganda to sell their ideology, Rockwell spoke on college campuses across the country and ran for governor of Virginia in 1965, and his cadre staged street protests. Rockwell changed the ANP name to the National Socialist White People's Party (NSWPP) in 1965. Matthias (Matt) Koehl, formerly the leader of the Chicago unit, became his deputy commander at the headquarters. In 1967, Rockwell was assassinated in a laundromat parking lot by John Palter, a former member of the party who had been recently expelled.

Koehl, the executor of Rockwell's estate, assumed leadership of the NSWPP. Splinter organizations formed as leaders were dismissed by Koehl in 1970. The name of the organization was changed to the New Order in 1982 and the *NS Bulletin* was the party's only publication by 1984. Two of the more notable figures who left the NSWPP to form other groups were William Pierce, founder of the National Alliance, and Frank Collins, who organized the Chicago-based National Socialist Party of America (NSPA). The latter group came to be known for its plans to hold a rally in 1978 in Skokie, Illinois, which was home to many Jewish Americans. After a highly attention-getting court victory permitted them to hold the Skokie demonstration, they held rallies at Chicago's Federal Building and another one in Marquette Park on Chicago's South Side. Some have said that Marquette Park, where 2,500 demonstrators gathered to confront the neo-Nazis, marked the beginning of the "counter-hate" or "antiracist" movement. Another infamous event involving the NSPA was the 1979 slaying of five Communist Worker's Party members in Greensboro, North Carolina, by the KKK; three of the Klansmen were members of the NSPA. Neo-Nazi groups still constitute one of several main factions in what some have termed the "white power" or "white nationalist" movement.

BIBLIOGRAPHY

Anti-Defamation League. *Hate Groups in America: A Record of Bigotry and Violence.* 1988.

Dobratz, Betty A., and Stephanie L. Shanks-Meile. *White Power, White Pride! The White Separatist Movement in the United States.* 1997.

George, John, and Laird Wilcox. *Nazis, Communists, Klansmen, and Others on the Fringe.* 1992.

Jenkins, Philip. *Hoods and Shirts: The Extreme Right in Pennsylvania, 1925–1950.* 1997.

Rockwell, George Lincoln. *This Time the World!* 1963.
Rockwell, George Lincoln. *White Power!* 1967.

Stephanie Shanks-Meile

Americans for Democratic Action

Americans for Democratic Action (ADA), the leading COLD WAR liberal lobbying and activist organization, has a long history of involvement in civil rights issues. The ADA was founded in January 1947 as a successor group to the wartime Union for Democratic Action. Its organizers, a coalition of labor leaders, political figures, and intellectuals that included James Loeb, David Dubinsky, Reinhold Niebuhr, Walter Reuther, and Joseph Rauh, sought to combine advocacy of an anti-communist foreign policy with strong support for New Deal–style domestic reform.

Although the ADA originally paid little attention to civil rights issues, it became strongly involved with civil rights at the 1948 Democratic National Convention. The ADA lobbied for the incorporation into the party platform of the report of the PRESIDENT'S COMMITTEE ON CIVIL RIGHTS, which prescribed strong federal legislation to ensure racial equality. Hubert Humphrey, a leading ADA member, proposed that the delegates endorse anti-lynching bills (see LYNCHING and ANTI-LYNCHING CAMPAIGN), equal employment opportunity (see EQUAL OPPORTUNITY), black voting rights, and the integration of the armed forces. When the Platform Committee, fearing a Southern walkout, defeated Humphrey's proposal, he brought the question to the entire convention, urging the Democrats to "get out of the shadow of states' rights and walk forthrightly into the sunshine of human rights." The Convention voted to adopt the strong civil rights plank—a victory that signaled the ADA's rise to power.

Over the following years, the ADA continued to work on behalf of black equality, though largely unsuccessfully. Notably, in 1950, as part of a campaign for a permanent FAIR EMPLOYMENT PRACTICES COMMITTEE, the ADA joined with the NATIONAL ASSOCIATION FOR THE ADVANCEMENT OF COLORED PEOPLE and other groups to form the LEADERSHIP CONFERENCE ON CIVIL RIGHTS (LCCR), a civil rights lobbying group and information clearinghouse. However, following the Supreme Court's 1954 BROWN V. BOARD OF EDUCATION school-desegregation decision, the ADA divided between advocates of immediate DESEGREGATION and moderates who distanced themselves from the SUPREME COURT and counseled "gradualism." These differences surfaced at the 1956 Democratic National Convention, where ADA support for civil rights was outmatched by its members' desire for the nomination of Adlai Stevenson, a leading gradualist.

The ADA failed to persuade the convention to endorse the *Brown* decision, especially after Eleanor ROOSEVELT—an ADA icon and a Stevenson supporter—spoke on behalf of moderation.

During the 1960s, the ADA increased its focus on civil rights. ADA leaders drew up the strong civil rights plank that was adopted by the 1960 Democratic National Convention, and the ADA and LCCR lobbied Congress to win support for the CIVIL RIGHTS ACT OF 1964 and VOTING RIGHTS ACT OF 1965. However, the ADA's focus on federal action left it ill-equipped to deal with civil rights groups such as the STUDENT NON-VIOLENT COORDINATING COMMITTEE (SNCC) as these grew more assertive—a conflict encapsulated in the opposition of Rauh and Humphrey to the seating of the SNCC-created MISSISSIPPI FREEDOM DEMOCRATIC PARTY at the 1964 Democratic National Convention. The ADA's civil rights activism gradually declined after 1965, although the organization remains a member of the LCCR.

BIBLIOGRAPHY

Americans for Democratic Action. *Program for Americans, 1966.* 1966.
Brock, Clifton. *Americans for Democratic Action: Its Role in National Politics.* 1985.
Gillon, Steven M. *Politics and Vision: The ADA and American Liberalism.* 1987.

Greg Robinson

Americans with Disabilities Act

Culminating a generation of disability rights activism and legislation, the Americans with Disabilities Act of 1990 (ADA) sought to extend civil rights protections to disabled persons as a "minority . . . subjected to a history of purposeful and unequal treatment." A cross-disability coalition of conservative and liberal advocates drafted and promoted it, drawing a surprisingly broad spectrum of support in Congress and the BUSH administration from leaders with personal experience of disability-based discrimination.

Because "disability" is a highly mutable social role, the ADA established complex rules for determining discrimination and ensuring access. Supporters called them flexible; critics, ambiguous. ADA covers individuals who have "a physical or mental impairment that substantially limits one or more . . . major life activities," have "a record of such an impairment," or are "regarded as having such an impairment." In hiring and promotion, employers may not discriminate against qualified disabled individuals who with or without "reasonable accommodations" can perform the "essential functions" of a job. ADA proscribes selection

A group of handicapped persons demonstrate in support of the Americans with Disabilities Act in Washington, D.C., in 1990. (CORBIS)

measures that tend to screen out disabled applicants by using criteria unrelated to those "essential functions." Employers must provide "reasonable accommodations" unless they can demonstrate that this would impose an "undue hardship" by incurring significant difficulty or expense. State and local governments and public schools must make reasonable modifications to ensure disabled persons have access to their services. Public transit systems must be made accessible when new cars or buses are bought, or new stations are built, or "key" existing stations are altered. Comparable paratransit must be provided to individuals who cannot use fixed-route bus services, unless an undue burden would result. In providing goods and services to the public, facilities such as restaurants, hotels, theaters, doctors' offices, stores, libraries, parks, and private schools may not deny participation to disabled people or offer them participation of unequal or separate benefit. Covered entities must make reasonable modifications in policies and practices and provide auxiliary aids and services to afford access to individuals with disabilities unless the entity can demonstrate that this would fundamentally alter its nature or impose an undue burden on it.

Such entities must remove structural barriers where doing so is readily achievable (i.e., able to be accomplished without much difficulty or expense considering the nature of the action needed, the financial resources of the facility, and its size and type). Otherwise, the services must be offered by alternative methods if those methods are readily achievable. All new construction and alterations must be made accessible to the maximum extent feasible. Companies offering the general public telephone service must provide telephone relay service to individuals who use telecommunication devices for the deaf or similar devices.

Activists have criticized legislative compromises that have permitted: private lawsuits to obtain injunctive relief but not monetary damages, individual complaints to designated federal agencies that enforced it laxly, and exemptions that could extend transportation compliance timetables for twenty to thirty years after 1990. Limited opposition during the legislative phase gave way after passage to substantial resistance from businesses which charged that such legislation imposed excessive regulation and financial burdens on them.

BIBLIOGRAPHY

Johnson, William G., ed. "The Americans with Disabilities Act: Social Contract or Special Privilege?" *The Annals of the American Academy of Political and Social Science* 549 (January) 1997.
West, Jane, ed. *Implementing the Americans with Disabilities Act.* 1996.

Paul K. Longmore

American Woman Suffrage Association

The American Woman Suffrage Association (AWSA) was formed in November 1869 under the leadership of Lucy STONE, a noted suffragist and public speaker. The Boston-based organization was created in response to a rift within the WOMAN SUFFRAGE MOVEMENT over the issue of support for the FIFTEENTH AMENDMENT. The Fifteenth Amendment, ratified in 1870, altogether prohibited the disenfranchisement of African-American men, which had been merely penalized by the FOURTEEENTH AMENDMENT. (The Fourteenth Amendment reformulated states' representation in the House of Representatives so that it was based on the number of male voters; therefore, states refusing to enfranchise African-American men would lose congressional representation.) Elizabeth Cady STANTON and Susan B. ANTHONY objected to the exclusion of women from the Fifteenth Amendment and, in protest, left the American Equal Rights Association, which had succeeded in uniting suffragists and abolitionists just a few years earlier.

Stanton and Anthony formed the National Woman Suffrage Association, which was entirely dedicated to the enfranchisement of women, and sought to modify the Fifteenth Amendment to include a prohibition against denying women the vote. The American Woman Suffrage Association was formed by more conservative activists, who continued to prioritize the ratification of the Fifteenth Amendment over the securing of the vote for women. These women believed that, as a matter of principle, African-American men should be fully enfranchised before women, and furthermore that this was an attainable objective that would improve the prospects for woman suffrage. Accordingly, they actively worked for the ratification of the Fifteenth Amendment. AWSA members were alarmed by the NWSA's proposed social reforms, such as those for more liberal divorce laws, and by the support NWSA received from eccentric activist Victoria Woodhull. Stanton in particular was an ardent supporter of divorce law reform, arguing that the grounds for divorce should include not merely adultery, but drunkenness, cruelty, abandonment, and incompatibility. Lucy Stone, Julia Ward Howe, and others in the AWSA viewed NWSA as anti-African-American and pointed to the support it received from racist George Train. (Train, a Democrat politician, was an overt racist who nonetheless endorsed female suffrage and offered various types of support to Anthony and Stanton; he campaigned for woman suffrage in Kansas in 1867 and financed Anthony's publication, *The Revolution.*)

AWSA membership was limited to participants in traditional suffrage organizations. The AWSA worked on state and local government levels for the enfranchisement of women and, beginning in 1870, launched publication of what became the foremost women's rights periodical of its era, *Woman's Journal,* edited by Lucy Stone and her husband, Henry Blackwell.

In 1890 the AWSA reconciled with the NWSA and the two bodies merged to form the NATIONAL AMERICAN WOMAN SUFFRAGE ASSOCIATION (NAWSA). The merger was achieved in part through the efforts of Alice Stone Blackwell, daughter of Lucy Stone and Henry Blackwell. The organization represented a new degree of militancy that was uncharacteristic of the AWSA, and its formation marked the birth of a cohesive women's movement in the United States.

BIBLIOGRAPHY

Blackwell, Alice Stone. *Lucy Stone: Pioneer of Woman's Rights.* 1971.

Frost-Knappman, Elizabeth, with Sarah Kurian. *The ABC–Clio Companion to Women's Progress in America*. 1994.

Kerr, Andrea Moore. *Lucy Stone: Speaking Out for Equality*. 1992.

Sarah Kurian

Ames, Jessie Daniel

(1883–1972), anti-lynching reformer.

For most of her life, Jessie Daniel Ames was a tireless activist for WOMAN SUFFRAGE and ANTI-LYNCHING campaigns. While she worked with many Progressive-era reform organizations (see PROGRESSIVE PARTY), Ames is best known as the founder of the Association of Southern Women for the Prevention of Lynching (ASWPL). Ames's anti-racist activism grew from her recognition of the contradictions inherent to a women's suffrage struggle that failed to acknowledge the continued disfranchisement of all African Americans (and in the South, often relied upon that exclusion to promote the advancement of white women). Under the organizational umbrella of the COMMISSION ON INTERRACIAL COOPERATION (CIC) in Atlanta, Ames formed the ASWPL in 1930. Like Ida B. WELLS, a prominent, black feminist and anti-lynching activist of the late nineteenth century, Ames (who was white) understood the complex linkages between the denial of black citizenship and that of white women, articulated through lynching. A brutal means of social control in the South, the threat of lynching made possible white oppression of African Americans and the continued coercion of black labor. Similarly, the threat of rape—the most common charge against black, male victims of lynch mobs—justified white women's exclusion from the public world and suggested a need for white men's "protection." Ames recognized that this particular combination left African-American women in a uniquely vulnerable position. They lived with the constant threat of sexual assault by the very same white men who claimed to be protecting Southern womanhood. Yet, because black women were considered wild, uncontrollable seductresses within racist notions of black sexuality similar to those that informed the charges against black men, it was not a crime to rape them. In fact, they were deemed "unrapable" by nature.

A woman of many contradictions, Ames's anti-racist, feminist vision sometimes seemed at odds with her practices and strategies as an activist. The effectiveness of the ASWPL was diminished by her failure to reach out to black reformers or include black women in the organization in any meaningful way.

BIBLIOGRAPHY

Ames, Jessie Daniel. *Whither Leads the Mob?* 1932.

Ames, Jessie Daniel. *Southern Women Look at Lynching*. 1937.

Ames, Jessie Daniel. *The Changing Character of Lynching*. 1942.

Ames, Jessie Daniel. Papers. Southern Historical Collection, University of North Carolina, Chapel Hill.

Association of Southern Women for the Prevention of Lynching Papers. Carter Woodruff Library, Atlanta University, Atlanta.

Hall, Jacqueline Dowd. *Revolt Against Chivalry: Jessie Daniel Ames and the Women's Campaign Against Lynching*. 1979 (with new introduction, 1993).

Hall, Jacqueline Dowd. "Second Thoughts on Jessie Daniel Ames." In *The Challenge of Feminist Biography: Writing the Lives of Modern American Women*, edited by Sarah Alpen. 1992.

Micki McElya

Anthony, Susan Brownell

(1820–1906), woman suffrage movement founder.

Susan Brownell Anthony ranks indisputably as one of the principal figures in the WOMAN SUFFRAGE

Susan Brownell Anthony, reformer and activist in the woman suffrage movement, in an 1875 photograph. (CORBIS/Bettmann)

MOVEMENT in the United States, along with companion activist Elizabeth Cady STANTON. Anthony was born on February 15, 1820, in Adams, Massachusetts. Her father was a Quaker and a cotton manufacturer with progressive ideas on women's education. The eventual failure of her father's cotton mills cost Susan most of her childhood possessions, as well as her inheritance, which was given to her brother to circumvent creditors.

Susan Anthony's concern over women's issues developed in part because of pay discrimination she experienced during her fifteen-year tenure as as teacher in New York, first at a Quaker seminary, then as head of the female wing of the Canajoharie Academy. In 1852 she became involved with the temperance movement, a popular cause among women activists because of the seemingly endemic abusiveness and irresponsibility of alcoholic husbands; Anthony, however, unlike other women in the movement, was alarmed by the bias exhibited by male temperance activists. In the course of her temperance work, Anthony developed a friendship with Amelia Bloomer, popularizer of the so-called "bloomer" costume (featuring a mid-length skirt worn over loose pants). In 1851, Bloomer introduced Anthony to Elizabeth Cady Stanton, an already experienced social activist with whom she immediately struck up a friendship. Stanton encouraged Anthony's involvement in women's issues, particularly woman suffrage, and the two would continue to work together to the end of the century.

Anthony worked to achieve a revision of the New York Married Woman's Property Act of 1848, a law which allowed women to keep property they owned at the time of marriage, but did not allow women to control their own income. The change did not take effect until 1860. Other issues of interest to Anthony included child custody law, women's labor issues, and abolition. Anthony was particularly effective as a founder of activist organizations, notably the National Women's Loyal League, which worked for abolition; the American Equal Rights Association, which worked on behalf of both women and African-American men; and the National Woman Suffrage Association, which took a militant stand in favor of female enfranchisement. As copublisher of *The Revolution*, with Stanton, Anthony created a forum from which she could champion women's rights.

Anthony presented petitions to the U.S. CONGRESS urging that women be enfranchised, and she sought to have the FIFTEENTH AMENDMENT expanded to include women. Anthony campaigned extensively for female suffrage throughout the country, and tested the existing laws in 1872 by casting a ballot in an election—an act which she repeated and for which she was fined one hundred dollars. Anthony's public image evolved, in her lifetime, from one that evoked derision to one that reflected her accomplishments and dedication to reform. She died in Rochester, New York, on March 13, 1906. Although Anthony did not live to see the passage of the NINETEENTH AMENDMENT (1920), the amendment was often referred to as the "Anthony Amendment."

BIBLIOGRAPHY

Anthony, Katharine. *Susan B. Anthony: Her Personal History and Her Era*. 1954.

Barry, Kathleen. *Susan B. Anthony: A Biography of a Singular Feminist*. 1988.

Du Bois, Ellen Carol. *Elizabeth Cady Stanton/Susan B. Anthony: Correspondence, Writing, Speeches*. 1981.

Frost-Knappman, Elizabeth, with Sarah Kurian. *The ABC–Clio Companion to Women's Progress in America*. 1994.

Harper, Ida Husted. *The Life and Work of Susan B. Anthony*. 1898.

Sarah Kurian

Anti-Apartheid Movement

The African-American struggle against apartheid in South Africa stretches as far back as the early 1900s. In 1912, the NATIONAL ASSOCIATION FOR THE ADVANCEMENT OF COLORED PEOPLE (NAACP) helped to create the African National Congress, which opposed violence and fought to end racial discrimination through legal measures. Forty-one years later, the American Committee on Africa formed to coordinate anti-apartheid activities between the United States and South Africa.

In the mid-1960s civil rights activists, students, religious leaders, and organizations such as the NAACP, CONGRESS OF RACIAL EQUALITY, STUDENT NONVIOLENT COORDINATING COMMITTEE, and STUDENTS FOR A DEMOCRATIC SOCIETY gained national recognition for their demand that the United States terminate bank loans to South Africa. In 1984, Randall ROBINSON, head of TRANSAFRICA the African-American lobby for Africa and the Caribbean, led demonstrations lasting over fifty-three weeks in Washington, D.C., to end President Ronald REAGAN's "constructive engagement" policy—which allowed friendly ties between the United States and South Africa although apartheid still existed. However, Reagan argued that the suspension of trade and loans would hurt black South African workers. But in 1986 the U.S. Congress overrode Reagan's veto. The Anti-Apartheid Act of 1986 put a ban on the importation of South African products such as gold; a ban on exports to South Africa of several U.S. products such as computers and nuclear materials; and ended new U.S. loans and investments to that country.

The Anti-Apartheid Act of 1986 and the international liberation movement helped to develop an environment in which support of apartheid became less acceptable in South Africa. This climate led to the release of long-incarcerated Nelson Mandela from prison and to his election as first black president in the spring of 1994.

BIBLIOGRAPHY

Bigelow, Barbara Carlisle, and Issac Rosen. "Randall Robinson." In *Contemporary Black Biography,* edited by Barbara Carlisle Bigelow. 1994.

Nickerson, Albert. "Anti-Apartheid Movement." In *Encyclopedia of African-American Culture and History,* edited by Jack Salzman, David Lionel Smith, and Cornel West. 1996.

Shaunda Partida

Anti-Lynching Campaign

LYNCHING mobs acted simultaneously as prosecutor, judge, jury, and executioner; they did so with no legal authority and with utter disregard for the rights of the accused. Their victims could be anyone alleged to have violated the law or transgressed local customs. Such summary justice fell most heavily on African Americans, as mob violence became a sadistic, public ritual reaffirming racial dominance by whites over any and all blacks. The practice flourished throughout the JIM CROW Southern and border states from the end of RECONSTRUCTION in the late 1870s to the civil rights movement of the 1960s. From 1882 to 1968, there were 4,743 persons lynched in the United States; 3,446 of them African Americans. In the latter instances, less than 1 percent of the mob members were prosecuted and punished. There also existed countless "legal lynchings," whereby a court arbitrarily sentenced a defendant to death or life imprisonment.

From the 1890s into the early 1930s, sixteen border and Southern states had laws against mob violence but without vigorous enforcement. As a beleaguered minority, African Americans lacked the means to contain lynching, although they tried. At the turn of the century, black leaders openly condemned mob action, sought to use their newspapers and organizations against it, and appealed in vain to the White House for federal intervention. One campaigner, Ida B. WELLS, even traveled to Great Britain hoping to rouse an Anglo-American resistance to racist violence.

Effective opposition, however, required an interracial effort at home, and that eventually surfaced with the NATIONAL ASSOCIATION FOR THE ADVANCEMENT OF COLORED PEOPLE (NAACP), the Atlanta-based COMMISSION ON INTERRACIAL COOPERATION (CIC),

public agitation from leftist groups in the 1930s and 1940s, and various influential figures and organizations responding to the campaigns.

Led by James Weldon JOHNSON and Walter WHITE, the NAACP publicized lynching's evils, lobbied for a federal statute (the House passed the measure in 1922, 1937, and 1940, but Senate conservatives prevented enactment each time), and mobilized the liberal, labor, women's, ethnic, and church groups that became the midcentury civil rights coalition. In that sense, the anti-lynching campaigns laid a solid foundation for further civil rights crusades. The CIC represented southern liberals anxious to end mob violence without federal involvement. In 1930 it created the Southern Commission for the Study of Lynching and helped launch the Association of Southern Women for the Prevention of Lynching through which well-placed white women used their influence to induce local officials to halt mob action.

Lynching experienced a steady if erratic decline from the 1890s to the 1960s. Some of the factors that contributed to this decline were the work of its critics, massive black migrations from the South to northern and western urban centers, and the economic and political changes that brought the South into the twentieth-century national mainstream. In addition, the TRUMAN administration's 1948 endorsement of civil rights objectives, and America's Cold War strategies to attract support among Third World nations, helped to diminish the frequency of the practice. Finally, the passage by Congress of civil rights laws from 1957 to 1968 combined to undermine the phenomenon of lynching, without necessarily ending the racism that habitually sustained it.

BIBLIOGRAPHY

Hall, Jacquelyn Dowd. *Revolt Against Chivalry: Jesse Daniel Ames and the Southern Women's Campaign Against Lynching.* 1979.

Raper, Arthur F. *The Tragedy of Lynching.* 1933.

Tolnay, Stewart E., and E. M. Beck. *A Festival of Violence: An Analysis of Southern Lynchings, 1882–1930.* 1995.

White, Walter. *Rope and Faggot: A Biography of Judge Lynch.* 1929.

Zangrando, Robert L. *The NAACP Crusade Against Lynching, 1909–1950.* 1980.

Robert L. Zangrando

Anti-Semitism

The modern concept of civil rights is rooted in the idea that no one should be discriminated against because of voluntary or involuntary membership in a particular group. Individuals who are hemmed in or handicapped in any way because of a group association are, *ipso facto*, denied their rights.

In the Christian world, Jews have been victimized by their faith and have been accused of killing Jesus Christ. For this, they have for centuries been ostracized in various ways. Christian immigrants from Europe brought their Christian beliefs to the New World with them and continued displaying their animosity toward Jews. However, because of the wilderness, the less developed and more classless society, the need for laborers, and the eventual rhetoric of tolerance proclaimed by the U.S. Constitution, anti-Semitism in the United States developed differently from its European origins. In the colonial era, Jews were often circumscribed in their economic and political opportunities. As examples, Peter Stuyvesant, Dutch governor of New Netherland from 1646 to 1664, did not want Jews to settle in his colony when some arrived in 1654; and about 80 years later, the proprietors of Georgia also wished to exclude Jews. Jews who arrived found their employment and political rights denied. Further, they could not become doctors or lawyers in some colonies, or even vote, unless they took an oath swearing that they believed in the divinity of Jesus Christ. Once the American Constitution was adopted in 1789, the federal government did not erect any barriers against Jews, but state governments only gradually began to

give them the vote. Not until 1877, when New Hampshire became the last state to lift the ban, were male Jews able to vote in all of the United States.

Although there have been a number of interpretations of the causes of anti-Semitism, there can be no question but that its basis lay in religious teachings. However, some scholars have focused on the negative image of Jewish businessmen (the "Shylock" image) as unscrupulous, untrustworthy, and immoral in their dealings with gentiles as the prime factor in the development of the animus. Still others have associated the causes of anti-Semitism with political events. A rise in anti-Semitic thought accompanied the development of nationalism in Europe in the nineteenth century. In the United States, Jewish liberalism—especially alleged Jewish affiliation with left-wing "isms" like socialism and communism—has been regarded by some as the cause for hostility toward Jews. What is quite clear, however, is that anti-Semitic thought and anti-Semitic behavior always rise in times of social, economic, and political crises, and frequently become manifest among those individuals or groups who are most frustrated with existing turmoil in their lives. Academic studies have also correlated degrees of anti-Semitism with intensity of religious beliefs; many of the most devout Christians have also been found to be intensely anti-Semitic.

A community member attempts to remove a spray-painted swastika on the gate of a New Jersey Jewish cemetery. (AP/Wide World Photos)

Throughout American history, Jews have often been victimized during societal upheaval. In wartime they have been accused of disloyalty, during economic crises they have been held responsible for the deprivation of others, and among groups particularly disgruntled they have been identified as the perpetrators of misfortune.

Ironically, and despite the inaccurate perceptions of some that Jews do not care about equality for all, American Jews have been in the forefront of civil rights activities. They were active in the formation of the NATIONAL ASSOCIATION FOR THE ADVANCEMENT OF COLORED PEOPLE (NAACP) in 1909 and pioneered in forming community relations and defense organizations such as the Anti-Defamation League, American Jewish Committee, and American Jewish Congress in the twentieth century. Moreover, in terms of finance and participation, Jews were the most active group of white individuals after World War II who worked toward legislation to protect all Americans' civil rights.

BIBLIOGRAPHY

Dinnerstein, Leonard. *Antisemitism in America.* 1984.
Dobkowski, Michael. *The Tarnished Dream.* 1979.
Higham, John. *Strangers in the Land.* 1955.

Leonard Dinnerstein

Anti-War Movements

The earliest recorded anti-war activism in America is probably the refusal to bear arms of the Dutch Mennonites living on Manhattan in the early 1640s. Mennonites, Brethren, and Amish took literally the New Testament injunction "Resist not Evil." Members of these traditional "peace churches" came to be called nonresistants. They refused to pay war taxes, would not pay to be exempted from the militia, and would not perform alternative service. During the Revolutionary War, most anti-war activists came from these peace churches. By the time of the Civil War, anti-war activists practiced CIVIL DISOBEDIENCE, tax refusal, public disturbances, boycotts, and direct actions such as sit-ins. Persons with pacifist ideas not of the peace churches were inducted into the army anyway, held in army prisons, or, in the North, offered their freedom if they would pay a commutation fee. In the South, the Confederate conscription act of 1862 did not provide for an exemption even for members of the traditional "peace churches."

Around 1815, churchmen professing religions not traditionally pacifist founded organizations to promote the cause of peace: the New York Peace Society, Massachusetts Peace Society, American Peace Society, New England Non-Resistance Society, and League of Universal Brotherhood. Rather than Biblical tenets, secular arguments against war began to emerge. For example, in 1814 Noah Worcester wrote "A Solemn Review of the Custom of War," in which he maintained that wars should not be fought to right wrongs because the people killed are not the people most responsible for the wrongful national policy. In the 1830s, members of the American Peace Society criticized U.S. expansionist policy and argued for disarmament. They focused their attention on establishing a world court. In its later years, the lobbying and educational efforts of the APS led directly to the establishment of the Hague Court in 1899, the first permanent tribunal for international arbitration, paving the way for the League of Nations and today's United Nations. The boldest anti-war organization in the nineteenth century was the New England Non-Resistance Society, led by William Lloyd Garrison. Members disavowed allegiance to any government and claimed to be world citizens. After the Civil War, however, secular peace societies never recovered the vitality they had before the war.

With the advent of WORLD WAR I, new organizations appeared; the Women's Peace Party, for example, was founded in 1914. In 1915, its members met with women from other peace groups at a Peace Congress in The Hague. The first organized opposition to the war came in the spring of 1915, with the formation of the Anti-Enlistment League. In two years 3,500 men signed a pledge to refuse enlistment in the war cause. Radical anarchist Emma Goldman and socialist leader Eugene Debs were arrested and fined for their anti-war views. The SOCIALIST PARTY stood virtually alone in its political opposition to World War I. International Workers of the World called for a general strike, in all industries, should the United States enter the fray. But upon U.S. entry into the war, most anti-war activism crumbled quickly. Throughout the 1920s, the Women's Peace Society, the FELLOWSHIP OF RECONCILIATION, the WAR RESISTERS LEAGUE, and a number of smaller ad hoc groups continued to agitate against, and to argue the folly of, World War I. Internationally, a series of steps were taken toward disarmament that culminated in the 1929 Paris Peace Pact, which outlawed war as a solution to international problems. Sixty-two nations signed the pact, including the United States.

As WORLD WAR II approached, anti-war groups such as the American Peace Mobilization opposed U.S. entry into the war against Germany; but when the Germans attacked Russia, most peace groups urged that the United States enter the war against the Nazis. Some organizations, and some members of the news media, however, remained pacifist throughout the war, such as the *Catholic Worker*, with a circulation of over

100,000 in the 1930s, over thirty houses of hospitality, and nine farming communes. Activist priests Daniel and Philip Berrigan and socialist writer Michael Harrington shared in *Catholic Worker* efforts. Members of the *Catholic Worker* remained in the forefront of the peace movement even in the 1960s, working with other nonviolent groups in anti–VIETNAM WAR protests. During World War II, however, the anti-war movement had little effect on public opinion. When the Japanese attacked Pearl Harbor, December 7, 1941, only Jeannette Rankin voted in CONGRESS against the declaration of war. Even the War Resisters League reluctantly acquiesced to the necessity for war, though this organization was quickly revitalized during the Vietnam War, when it grew in size and influence, cosponsoring the first nationwide anti-war demonstration in 1964 as well as the first draft card burning.

Anti-war activities increased after World War II. The Society for Social Responsibility in Science was

Protest against the draft and against the Vietnam War in Washington, D.C., 1967. (CORBIS/Leif Skoogfors)

founded in 1948, and in the 1950s physicist Albert Einstein urged noncooperation in military matters for all scientists. In 1947 the wartime draft was abolished, but the Pentagon pressed for universal conscription. Public opposition was enough to stop the effort. On February 12, 1947, the first draft card burnings took place, at the White House and in New York. Over four hundred men destroyed their draft cards or mailed them to the president during this series of demonstrations. The Pacifica Foundation developed out of the efforts of war resisters, and in 1949 radio station KPFA went on the air, becoming a means of tying together intellectuals, artists, musicians, and political activists. In 1955, twenty-eight persons protested against a nationwide civil defense alert. They were arrested for refusing to take shelter in City Hall Park, in New York.

This kind of civil disobedience, action against compulsory air raid drills, led by such people as the *Catholic Worker*'s Dorothy Day and A. J. Muste, soon produced the core of the Ban the Bomb movement, with the encouragement of *Liberation* magazine, the Committee for Nonviolent Action (CNVA), and the Committee for a Sane Nuclear Policy (SANE). One of the most successful CNVA projects was the attempted sailing of the ketch *Golden Rule* into the nuclear bomb test area in the South Pacific. On numerous occasions pacifists tried to enter the docks where U.S. Navy submarines were being constructed, or to interfere with their launching by swimming out to and boarding them. In 1960, eleven pacifists left San Francisco on a peace walk that would take them across the United States and Europe to Moscow. The walkers reached Red Square in Moscow ten months later, where they conducted a peace vigil and distributed leaflets urging disarmament. Other peace walks took place from major urban centers to Washington, D.C. A. J. Muste (1885–1967), a major figure in the anti-war community, helped establish and edit *Liberation* magazine, was active in the War Resisters League, refused to pay war taxes, and was one of the principal figures in starting the campaign against civil defense drills in New York City. Muste played a leading role during the Vietnam War resistance in the early 1960s, organizing rallies, vigils, and marches to protest expanding U.S. involvement.

The AMERICAN FRIENDS SERVICE COMMITTEE, founded among Quakers in 1917, sponsored workcamps, peace caravans, publications, and other projects during the Vietnam war, demonstrated publicly against American involvement, counseled men about the draft, and joined in direct action projects against the war. The first important anti-war protest of the Vietnam War came in 1964 in New York City. Fifteen hundred people heard A. J. Muste, Norman Thomas, and A. Philip RANDOLPH speak out against the war.

The first national demonstration against the war was a March on Washington organized by STUDENTS FOR A DEMOCRATIC SOCIETY (SDS) in 1965. The same year anti-war teach-ins spread throughout college campuses. In 1967 fifteen hundred young men turned in their draft cards, there was a march on the Pentagon, and youth in the counterculture came to view the whole American society as part of a war culture and simply dropped out of it in the "Summer of Love." In 1969, publication of *The Pentagon Papers* by Daniel Ellsberg enflamed the anti-war movement. Draft card burnings and tax resistance increased dramatically. Peace finally came in 1975. After the Vietnam War many radical pacifists returned to disarmament as the priority issue.

In the post-Vietnam War era, with the end of universal military training, anti-war activism subsided as a movement. Subsequent U.S. military actions, such as the invasions of Granada and Panama in the 1980s, the Persian Gulf War of 1990, and the U.S.-led NATO bombing of Serbia in 1999 provoked little public protest. Anti-war activists, diminished in number, made nuclear disarmament in a post–COLD WAR world their primary goal.

BIBLIOGRAPHY

Chatfield, Charles. *The American Peace Movement: Ideals and Activism.* 1992.
Cooney, Robert, and Helen Michalowski. *The Power of the People: Active Nonviolence in the United States.* 1977.
Cortright, David. *Peace Works: The Citizen's Role in Ending the Cold War.* 1993.
Ellsberg, Daniel. *The Pentagon Papers.* 1972.
Lunardini, Christine A. *The American Peace Movement in the Twentieth Century.* 1994.

Eric Cummins

Arizona

When Arizona was admitted as the 48th state in 1912, its political culture was a unique mixture of Eastern colonialism, Western individualism, Southern Jim Crowism, and Anglo-Irish unionism rooted in an extractive economy of copper mining and cattle ranching. During WORLD WAR I, cotton-farming became the third "C" of Arizona's economy, attracting thousands of migrant workers. Because of its history and geographical location, Arizona's two largest minority groups were American Indians and Mexicans, but the growth of the agricultural sector brought more African Americans into the state as well. Chinese workers built the Southern Pacific Railroad across Arizona in the early 1880s, but Mexican and Anglo-Irish workers united to drive them off the railroads and out of the mines later in that decade.

The result was an economic pyramid organized largely along ethnic lines. Between statehood and WORLD WAR II, Tucson nourished a small but vigorous Mexican middle class of businesspeople and intellectuals. For the most part, however, Mexicans, American Indians, and African Americans labored in "unskilled" or "semiskilled" occupations. They also faced barriers of discrimination that restricted them to separate schools, prohibited them from many public facilities such as restaurants and hotels, prevented them from obtaining well-paying jobs, and restricted them to segregated barrios, slums, or reservations. As prominent African-American mortician and civil rights activist Lincoln Ragsdale said, "Phoenix [Arizona's largest city] was just like Mississippi. People were just as bigoted. They had segregation. They had signs in many places, 'Mexicans and Negroes not welcome.' "

A good example of Arizona's deeply embedded racism was the 1912 state constitution, which upheld a territorial miscegenation law that prohibited "all marriages of persons of Caucasian blood, or their descendants, with negroes, Mongolians or Indians, and their descendants. . . ." In 1931, the state legislature extended the prohibition to "Hindus" and "Malays." The legislature legalized marriage between Indians and Caucasians in 1942 but did not repeal the miscegenation law itself until 1962. For the first fifty years of Arizona statehood, then, not only were interracial marriages forbidden, but people of mixed race with Caucasian blood could not legally marry anyone.

At present there are twenty-one federally recognized American Indian reservations in Arizona. As these peoples—the Diné (Navajos), Hopis, Indeh (Apaches), Yavapais, Walapais, Havasupais, Mojaves, Quechan (Yumas), Cocopas, Maricopas, Tohono O'odham (Papagos), Akimel O'odham (Pimas), and Yoemem (Yaquis)—have struggled to maintain or reclaim their cultural heritage, tribal sovereignty, and at least a portion of their traditional territories, they have confronted numerous challenges from federal, state, and county agencies to limit their self-determination. Although American Indians were granted the right to vote in national elections in 1924, they could not vote in Arizona state or county elections until 1948. Today their struggles revolve around such issues as casino gambling, which the state regulates, and water rights, which involve complex negotiations among federal, state, municipal, and private entities.

Mexicans in Arizona, the largest minority in the state, have experienced perhaps the most ambivalent status. Although legally considered "Caucasian," Mexicans have faced institutionalized discrimination ranging from outright to cloaked forms of segregation. Moreover, Mexican citizens of the United States have often been confused with migrants, both legal and undocumented, from Mexico. During Arizona's constitutional convention prior to statehood, organized labor—generally anti-Mexican at that time—attempted to incorporate Proposition 91 into the constitution. This proposition would have prohibited anyone who could not "speak the English language" from working in "underground or hazardous occupations" and would have limited "alien labor" to no more than 20 percent of the workforce of any "individual, firm corporation, or association." It was defeated, but similar attempts to restrict Mexican labor and keep Mexicans from holding Arizona's best-paying jobs in the mines or on the railroads surfaced again as an initiative in 1914, when voters overwhelmingly approved it. A year later, it was struck down by the U.S. SUPREME COURT for violating the FOURTEENTH AMENDMENT.

Nonetheless, many mining companies continued to pay Mexicans lower wages than Anglo-Irish and European miners for the same jobs. The dual-wage system crumbled after World War II, when Mexican veterans in Clifton-Morenci won a strike against the giant Phelps Dodge copper company in 1946. Mexicans also benefited from a groundbreaking Arizona judicial decision. Even though the "separate but equal" doctrine was not supposed to apply to Mexicans, numerous school districts across Arizona segregated Mexican pupils. In 1953, after declaring that "a half century of intolerance is enough," Judge Fred Struckmeyer ruled that segregated high schools were unconstitutional. Judge Carl Bernstein soon declared that segregated grade schools were unconstitutional as well. These decisions predated BROWN V. BOARD OF EDUCATION by a year.

Those decisions were also victories for Arizona's small African-American population. The Greater Phoenix Council for Civic Unity, an organization of European Americans and African Americans, sponsored the lawsuit that resulted in Struckmeyer's decision after its initiative to desegregate schools was trounced by voters. Local chapters of the NATIONAL ASSOCIATION FOR THE ADVANCEMENT OF COLORED PEOPLE (NAACP) and the NATIONAL URBAN LEAGUE accelerated their attempts to integrate housing and the workplace as well. Their political activism reflected the economic transformation sweeping across Arizona and the rest of the nation triggered by World War II. Prior to the war, Arizona was a predominantly rural state dominated by extractive industries. World War II brought defense plants to the state, and the postwar boom attracted electronics and aeronautics firms with close ties to the Pentagon. Barriers of race—except for Japanese Americans, many of whom had their property confiscated and were imprisoned during the war in internment camps such as Camp Poston on the Colorado River—began to break down as manufacturing and service industries and explosive urbanization rearranged the political ecology of the state.

Barriers of gender weakened as well. During World War II, thousands of Arizona women entered the workplace for the first time, laboring in defense plants and even in the copper mines. Employment dropped after the war, but by 1960 women comprised 32 percent of the workforce, which was also the ratio of their median income (.32) compared to that of men. Between 1969 and 1981, however, the percentage of women professionals rose from 25 percent to 35 percent while the percentage of women administrators climbed from 3 percent to 12 percent. In 1999, women were elected to the top five positions in state government—governor, secretary of state, attorney general, treasurer, and superintendant of public instruction.

Arizona also moved to protect gay and lesbian rights. In 1978, after a young gay man was murdered by several high school students, the Tucson City Council passed one of the first gay hate crimes ordinances in the nation. Even though Arizona is a politically conservative state, a strong libertarian tradition, exemplified by the late U.S. Senator Barry Goldwater, characterizes the thought of many Arizona conservatives. After U.S. Congressman Jim Kolbe announced he was gay, for example, he continued to receive Republican support and won reelection in 1998.

BIBLIOGRAPHY

Hardaway, Roger D. "Unlawful Love: A History of Arizona's Miscegenation Law." *Journal of Arizona History* 27 (1986): 377–390.
Luckingham, Bradford. *Phoenix: The History of a Southwestern Metropolis*, 1989.
Luckingham, Bradford. *Minorities in Phoenix: A Profile of Mexican American, Chinese American, and African American Communities, 1860–1992.* 1994.
Martin, Patricia Preciado. *Songs My Mother Sang to Me: An Oral History of Mexican American Women.* 1992.
Melcher, Mary. "Blacks and Whites Together: Interracial Leadership in the Phoenix Civil Rights Movement." *Journal of Arizona History* 32 (1991): 195–216.
Nishimoto, Richard S. *Inside an American Concentration Camp: Japanese American Resistance at Poston, Arizona,* edited by Lane Ryo Hirabayashi. 1995.
Rothschild, Mary Logan, and Pamela Claire Hronek. *Doing What the Day Brought: An Oral History of Arizona Women.* 1992.
Sheridan, Thomas E. *Los Tucsonenses: The Mexican Community in Tucson, 1854–1941.* 1986.
Sheridan, Thomas E. *Arizona: A History.* 1995.

Thomas E. Sheridan

Arkansas

A state that straddles the Deep South and upper South, Arkansas has struggled to reconcile forces of extremism and moderation in civil rights, particularly in issues of race. The southeastern part of the state is dominated by the delta, where African Americans were brought first as slaves and after the Civil War remained tied to the land as sharecroppers and tenant farmers. Protest efforts in this largely rural region were sporadic and often met with ruthless suppression. In 1919, for example, attempts by African Americans to organize a cotton pickers union resulted in the Elaine Race Riot with the deaths of over 200 men, women, and children at the hands of an armed white mob. Even the biracial effort to organize a SOUTHERN TENANT FARMERS UNION (STFU) in 1934 was stymied through violence, with the union forced to relocate its headquarters to Memphis shortly after its founding. In the northwestern half of Arkansas a landscape of rolling hills meant that cotton farming, and hence slavery, never became established there. As a result few African Americans lived in that part of the state.

Located between the delta and northwest, Arkansas's capital city of Little Rock attempted to cultivate an image of racial moderation after the Civil War, principally in order to attract northern investors. Certainly, the city offered better opportunities for African-American advancement with an influential middle class developing during RECONSTRUCTION, establishing a network of business, political, social, civic, and masonic organizations. In contrast to the delta, urban African-American protests were largely petition- or legal-based, and focused mainly on winning political representation. From the turn of the century to the 1920s, lawyer Scipio Africanus Jones fought to maintain African-American representation in the Republican Party. In 1928, Dr. John Marshall Robinson formed the Arkansas Negro Democratic Association (ANDA) to fight for an African-American voice in the then politically dominant state Democratic party.

The 1930s saw significant changes in the African-American struggle for civil rights. The mechanization and collectivization of agriculture through New Deal programs led to a movement off the land and into the growing towns and villages of the delta that offered greater protection from white intimidation and provided points for potential community mobilization. Federal government entered the lives of African Americans as never before and, although often hindered by discrimination, New Deal programs did at least indicate that help from Washington, D.C., might begin to have some impact on testing southern racial mores. Continued federal assistance for civil rights from the United States Supreme Court in the 1940s, which increasingly began to take a stronger stance against JIM CROW, provided further incentive for increased African-American activism.

Throughout the 1940s African Americans sought to test the boundaries of racial discrimination in Arkansas. In 1940, Pine Bluff lawyer William Harold Flowers organized the Committee on Negro Organizations (CNO) to launch a campaign to increase the number of registered voters in the growing delta settlements. In 1942, teachers in Little Rock, with help from the NATIONAL ASSOCIATION FOR THE ADVANCEMENT OF COLORED PEOPLE (NAACP), filed a successful suit to demand equal pay with whites. The same year Daisy and Lucious Christopher BATES, owners of the Little Rock *State Press* newspaper, demanded and received the appointment of African-American police officers in the city after the shooting of Sergeant Thomas B. Foster by a white city policeman. In 1948 the University of Arkansas Law School at Fayetteville voluntarily admitted Silas Hunt as its first African-American student rather than take the case to the courts. The following year, Edith Mae Irby integrated the University Medical School in Little Rock.

The acid test for how far Arkansas had come in terms of racial progress was the 1954 BROWN V. BOARD OF EDUCATION school desegregation decision. Initial signs appeared encouraging: three school districts with only a small number of African-American students in northwest Arkansas immediately integrated and most state politicians urged calm. However, when the U.S. Supreme Court handed down an ambiguous implementation order for school desegregation in 1955, acceptance of the law began to wane. In order to counteract growing opposition, the Little Rock NAACP launched the 1956 *Aaron v. Cooper* lawsuit to put pressure on the city's School Board to immediately implement plans for desegregation. Although the courts upheld Little Rock's gradualist plan, they affirmed that it must go ahead in September 1957. As the date for integration approached, however, school officials began to panic about the prospects of violence and disruption to their plans by segregationists.

At that point, Governor Orval E. FAUBUS took the matter into his hands. Initially perceived as a moderate, Faubus had made political capital out of the race issue during his election campaign in 1956. In September 1957 he took the radical step of surrounding Central High School with National Guardsmen to prevent desegregation from taking place. After negotiations with the White House, Faubus finally agreed to remove the guard, albeit under protest. Yet when nine African-American students showed up for classes on September 24, 1957, a hostile white mob forced their withdrawal from the school. The next day, President Dwight D. EISENHOWER sent federal troops to escort the nine students safely into classes. The next academic year, after the removal of federal troops, Faubus closed all city's schools rather than integrate them. Only when the business community slowly awakened to the fact that the school crisis was having a detrimental economic impact on the city was the situation

Federal troops escort four African-American students to Little Rock's Central High School on September 26, 1957. The soldiers were called in to carry out President Dwight D. Eisenhower's order to enforce the federal court ruling to integrate the school. (AP/Wide World Photos)

resolved. In May 1959, when segregationist school board members tried to dismiss forty-four teachers for allegedly sympathizing with integration, they were ousted in a recall election. With business candidates in control of the school board, peaceful token integration of the reopened schools took place in September 1959.

After the school crisis, African Americans in Little Rock found it difficult to mobilize effectively for civil rights. The heightened racial tensions in the city together with the demise of the NAACP under a barrage of litigation meant that sit-in and freedom ride protests in the early 1960s were largely unsuccessful. Not until 1963 with the formation of a new community group, the Council on Community Affairs (COCA), together with the help of direct action protests organized by STUDENT NONVIOLENT COORDINATING COMMITTEE (SNCC), did local businessmen agree to negotiate an end to downtown segregation. SNCC's influence in Arkansas grew after 1963 with projects set up at Pine Bluff, Gould, Helena, and Forrest City. Although not given as much media attention or resources as neighboring efforts in Mississippi, SNCC played an important role in stimulating civil rights protests in the Arkansas delta and paved the way for a new surge in African-American voters and an increasingly assertive electorate during the mid- to late 1960s.

The zenith of the civil rights movement in Arkansas came with Republican Winthrop Rockefeller's defeat of segregationist candidate Jim Johnson in the 1966 election for governor. Rockefeller's victory was dependent on 80,000 new African-American votes gained through the efforts of a civil rights coalition including the Arkansas Voters' Project (AVP) funded by the VOTER EDUCATION PROJECT (VEP), SNCC, COCA, NAACP, labor unions, and ex-members of the Women's Emergency Committee (WEC). The latter group had been formed during the school crisis and had played a major role in prompting the business community to end segregationist influence in Little Rock. Further activism from key members of this organization played an important part in the development of the struggle for women's rights in the 1960s and 1970s, indicating the interconnected nature of civil rights struggles within the state.

Although the late 1960s were a high point for civil rights activism in Arkansas, subsequent decades have evidenced an ambiguous legacy. For example, African-American participation in state politics has not expanded beyond initial seats that were won in the 1972 elections. Arkansas still remains the only former Confederate state never to have returned an African American to the U.S. Congress. African-American voter registration is lower now than twenty years ago. In Little Rock, schools have struggled to achieve a meaningful degree of integration despite busing and various rezoning plans. With increasing white flight from the city the term "re-segregation" is now being used. Urban renewal has continued to geographically ensure that the two races live farther apart than ever before. Continuing problems of poverty remain at the heart of many African Americans' inability to compete on equal terms with whites. As in many other parts of the United States, African Americans in Arkansas are still striving to translate the dismantling of the legal apparatus of Jim Crow in the 1940s, 1950s, and 1960s, into practical and continuing day-to-day gains.

BIBLIOGRAPHY

Bartley, Numan V. *The Rise of Massive Resistance: Race and Politics in the South During the 1950s.* 1969.

Bates, Daisy. *The Long Shadow of Little Rock: A Memoir.* 1962.

Blackside, Inc. *Fighting Back (1957–1962),* episode two of the series *Eyes on the Prize, Part 1: America's Civil Rights Years—1954 to 1965.* 1990.

Blossom, Virgil T. *It Has Happened Here.* 1959.

Cortner, Richard C. *A Mob Intent on Death: The NAACP and the Arkansas Riot Cases.* 1988.

Freyer, Tony. *The Little Rock Crisis: A Constitutional Interpretation.* 1984.

Gordon, Fon Louise. *Caste and Class: The Black Experience in Arkansas, 1880–1920.* 1995.

Graves, John William. *Town and Country: Race Relations in an Urban/Rural Context, Arkansas, 1865–1905.* 1990.

Grubbs, Donald H. *Cry From the Cotton: The Southern Tenant Farmers Union and the New Deal.* 1971.

Jacoway, Elizabeth. "Taken By Surprise: Little Rock Business Leaders and Desegregation." In *Southern Businessmen and Desegregation,* edited by Elizabeth Jacoway and David R. Colburn. 1982.

Kirk, John A. *Black Activism in Arkansas, 1940–1970.* Ph.D. thesis, University of Newcastle upon Tyne, UK. 1997.

Murphy, Sara Alderman. *Breaking the Silence: Little Rock's Women's Emergency Committee to Open Our Schools, 1958–1963.* 1997.

Reed, Roy. *Faubus: The Life and Times of an American Prodigal.* 1997.

Report of the Racial and Cultural Diversity Task Force Submitted to the Steering Committee of Future—Little Rock. 1992.

University Task Force on the Little Rock School District. *Plain Talk: The Future of Little Rock's Public Schools* (full text can also be found at the internet site http://www.ualr.edu/~lrsd/). 1997.

John A. Kirk

Armed Forces

Throughout the nation's history, the United States military has grappled with discrimination. In the midst of its birth during the American Revolution, patriot leader General George Washington himself vacillated on whether the colonial Army should admit blacks into its ranks. Ultimately, the Army allowed both freemen and slaves to fight for independence. About five thousand served, fighting in many major battles, including Lexington and Concord, Bunker Hill, Trenton, Brandywine, and Saratoga. When independence

was won, many slaves who had fought for freedom were still denied theirs.

The group with the longest experience of discrimination within the U.S. military, African Americans have continually answered the call to war. Though most states initially prohibited blacks from participating in militias during the Civil War, Union forces gradually began to accept blacks within their ranks. Blacks served in separate regiments and received separate wages. For most of the war, all black soldiers, regardless of rank, received lower wages than those of white privates.

In January 1863, President Abraham Lincoln issued the EMANCIPATION PROCLAMATION, freeing the slaves of the South, many of whom escaped to freedom and joined the Union effort. Though the Union was hesitant to use black regiments in combat, those who did fight distinguished themselves. The Fifty-fourth Regiment of the Massachusetts Volunteer Infantry, for example, led an attack on Fort Wayne, South Carolina, a key Confederate stronghold, and black troops were among the first Union soldiers to enter the fallen Confederate capital of Richmond, Virginia.

About 178,000 African Americans served in the segregated armed forces during the Civil War. During WORLD WAR I (fifty years later), more than 400,000 served. Despite the fighting ability demonstrated by blacks during the Civil War, the U.S. military was still reluctant to let them fight in front lines, and 89 percent of those who participated in the war worked as laborers.

When WORLD WAR II began in Europe in 1939, the U.S. military still maintained segregated forces under a separate-but-equal policy. This changed in 1940, with the passage of the Selective Training and Service Act, which created the country's first peacetime draft and formally established the Selective Service System as an independent federal agency. It also prohibited discrimination on the basis of race in the administration of the draft.

African-American soldiers, however, still predominantly served in segregated regiments and lived and trained in segregated facilities, such as those at the Tuskegee Institute in Alabama. Tuskegee produced the 99th Pursuit Squadron—piloted, manned, and maintained completely by African Americans—a force that prompted the War Department to reconsider the contribution of blacks to the military. By July 1948, President Harry TRUMAN had established the President's Commission on Equal Treatment and Opportunity in the Armed Services. (See PRESIDENT'S COMMITTEE ON CIVIL RIGHTS.) Movement toward equality, however, was slow.

The KOREAN WAR, fought on a much smaller scale than the two world wars, emphasized to U.S. military leaders the inefficiencies and wastefulness of a segregated armed force. By March 1951, the number of new trainees was such that SEGREGATION efforts were overwhelmed, and after the war's end in 1953, the military began to move more decisively to ensure equal treatment.

Racial tension increased across the United States in the 1960s. As the conflict in Vietnam intensified (see VIETNAM WAR), the military relied more heavily on the draft. Despite an increase in racial tension in society at large, African-American soldiers experienced for the first time much the same opportunities as their white counterparts. This is not to say that all was well. In May 1971, a riot occurred at Travis Air Force Base in California, prompting the military to begin instruction on racial cooperation and understanding.

In 1991, the United States led a coalition to expel the invading army of Iraq from the sovereign nation of Kuwait. About 30 percent of the American force in the Middle East was African American. In contrast, women serving in the Middle East at the same time made up 7 percent of the American force.

Although women have always had some involvement in war, it was not until 1948 that they achieved official status in the U.S. military. In that year Congress passed the Women's Armed Services Integration Act, which came in recognition of women's positive efforts during World War II. This act, however, did not give women access to every area of the armed forces. It contained a clause that specifically excluded them from participating in combat. Under the rhetoric of protecting women, the act perpetuated a discriminatory attitude, assuming that women would never want to serve in combat. This cultural stereotype of women as the weaker sex sustained such laws and consequently did not allow women the same access as men to the military.

In the 1970s a movement began to open more possibilities for women in the military. In 1973, when the All-Volunteer Force (AVF) was established, only 1.6 percent of military personnel were women. This small percentage represented women mainly in traditional roles, such as administration or medicine. As programs began to open up, the percentage jumped to 8.5 in 1980. The Air Force flight program opened to female enlistment in 1976. A year later the Coast Guard initiated a mixed-gender program, which proved to be greatly successful. Another significant advancement occurred in 1978, when Army women ceased to be trained in separate programs and were allowed to join their male counterparts. This period of rapid growth was attributed to President Jimmy CARTER, whose efforts were halted when the Army declined to make additional increases in female acceptance. The succeeding period under Ronald REAGAN's

administration was nicknamed a "womanpause" because the Army halted the growth of its acceptance of women at 9 percent, though there was no official law or regulation determining this action.

Since the Women's Armed Services Integration Act of 1948 allowed the individual military branches to create their own policies rather than to follow one standard, women often faced varying degrees of discriminatory treatment. Such treatment led Congress to monitor the Air Force in 1985. This oversight by Congress prompted the Army to reopen most job categories it had previously denied to women, and by 1988 the percentage of active-duty women had increased to about 11 percent.

As more women pursued careers in the military, more became interested in attending military academies. The 1975 Stratton Amendment, signed by President Gerald FORD, granted women permission to attend previously all-male military academies. Women enrolled in West Point and several other institutions and, despite great opposition, many succeeded in graduating at the top of their classes. The main complaint from men was the lowering of physical standards.

The most controversial cases of females in military academies involved the Citadel in South Carolina and the Virginia Military Institute (VMI), the last of the traditionally all-male institutions to admit women. In 1993, Shannon Faulkner won her case for admittance to attend classes at the Citadel. She was greeted with signs that read, "Die Shannon," and stayed at the school for only one week. The Citadel reverted to its prior status as an all-male academy and remained so for three more years. In 1996, the Virginia Military Institute was ordered by the U.S. Supreme Court to admit women or lose its federal funding. VMI complied, and the Citadel followed suit that same year. Though women entered these once all-male bastions of military training, they faced a high level of resentment and aggression from their male counterparts.

Women's achievements in entering the Citadel and VMI are examples of how women have overcome restrictive military regulations. However, such achievements have not necessarily been accompanied by improvements in their treatment by fellow soldiers at a more directly personal level. Female soldiers, in traditionally male careers, have continued to be faced with the difficult matter of sexual harassment. The Tailhook '91 incident is the most infamous, widely publicized case of military sexual harassment. At the annual Tailhook Association Convention, in Las Vegas, Nevada, on September 5–7, 1991, Lt. Paula Coughlin of the Navy was assaulted by a group of naval aviation officers. Her courage to defend her rights as a woman and as a member of the military not only helped to change the way the military views sexual harassment, but caused it to reconsider its rigid policies regarding women in combat. In the aftermath of an extensive investigation, Secretary of Defense Les Alpin directed all branches of the military to open up all but a few combat assignments to women. The only remaining exclusion for women is the ban on direct ground combat, which applies to the Army, the Marines, and some areas of the Air Force.

The vital changes that have occurred in military academies since the 1970s reflect the changes that have occurred throughout the military world in general. The focus is still on physical strength and endurance, but attention is also given to the attainment of leadership and interpersonal skills, as women take on ever-expanding roles in every branch of the military.

While African Americans and women have gained a large measure of acceptance and respect in the military, gay and lesbian soldiers continue to face strong discrimination (see also GAY AND LESBIAN RIGHTS). Until the early 1990s, the military held an intractable stance regarding the sexual orientation of its soldiers. If a gay or lesbian soldier was "found out," he or she would most certainly be discharged—not always honorably.

This position has not so much changed as shifted. In 1993, abandoning an initial attempt to ensure full rights for gays and lesbians in the military, President Bill CLINTON announced a new compromise policy, referred to as "Don't Ask, Don't Tell, Don't Pursue." The armed forces have made an effort to eliminate antigay harassment and have ceased to actively search out gay or lesbian personnel. Such searches in the past were frequently compared to witch hunts, during which the allegation of homosexuality alone often led to discharge for the accused.

Under the "Don't Ask, Don't Tell" policy, the military must maintain a respect for individual privacy in this regard. The policy does not protect the open expression of homosexuality. A soldier may not announce that he is gay, engage in any homosexual act, including simple displays of affection, or marry someone of the same gender without facing discharge from military service.

While the Clinton policy did improve the position of gays in the armed services, they have continued to treat homosexuality as representing a category of persons undeserving of the same rights given to personnel of the female gender or a minority race. And it fell far short of Clinton's initial intent to end the entrenched practice of refusing the service of openly gay or lesbian personnel in the military.

Mere allegations of homosexuality have damaged or ruined the careers of heterosexual soldiers. For instance, airman Sonya Harden's career was ended when her roommate claimed Harden was a lesbian. Harden passed a polygraph test and presented testimony about her heterosexual activities. Her accuser even recanted the claim. Nevertheless, Harden's military career was concluded.

Still, the military persistently maintains its policy on sexual orientation. Despite the evidence shown by countless African-American and female soldiers—that racial or gender difference does not mean deficiency when it comes to military service—despite the increasing acceptance of gays and lesbians in society at large, and despite the increasing efforts of gay rights lobbyists, the military stands rigid—maintaining a bastion of open discrimination into the twenty-first century.

BIBLIOGRAPHY

Astor, Gerald. *The Right to Fight: A History of African Americans in the Military.* 1998.

Katzenstein, Mary Fainsod, and Judith Reppy, eds. *Beyond Zero Tolerance: Discrimination in Military Culture.* 1999.

Salzman, Jack, David Lionel Smith, and Cornel West, eds. *Encyclopedia of African-American Culture and History.* 1996.

Skaine, Rosemarie. *Women at War: Gender Issues of Americans in Combat.* 1999.

Christy Wood

Arrington, Richard, Jr., "Dick"

(1934–   ), mayor, city of Birmingham, Alabama.

Richard Arrington was born in Livingston, ALABAMA on August 19, 1934, and grew up near Birmingham. Upon graduation from high school he attended Miles College, and in 1966 he earned a Ph.D. in zoology from the University of Oklahoma. He returned to teach at Miles where he also served as dean under president Lucius Pitts, an administrator with an interest in social change. Under Pitts, Arrington learned the inner workings of city politics and the dynamics of social reform.

In 1971 Arrington won a seat on the Birmingham City Council. As councilman, he showed a special interest in educational issues, economic development, and police brutality. With his sober temperament and scholarly demeanor, the press gave him increasing attention and respect, focusing on his community activities. Arrington, however, had no political ambition beyond the city council, but fate intervened to change his career.

On June 22, 1979, a white Birmingham policeman shot and killed an eighteen-year-old black woman. Arrington and the black community insisted that Mayor David Vann, Arrington's political ally and friend, fire the officer who killed the young woman. He refused.

With blacks ready to draft him, Arrington decided to enter the 1979 mayoral contest. He used the organization he had founded, the Birmingham–Jefferson County Citizens Coalition, to defeat a strong opponent in a runoff election.

During his twenty years in office, Arrington has repeatedly defeated contenders for his position, but the politician has been unable to garner more than 12 percent of the white vote in a city that has become majority black. The Arrington years have witnessed some notable achievements. With support from the business community, he has diversified the economy in a city where steel is no longer king. He has also encouraged the growth of the University of Alabama at Birmingham, its Medical Center, and technical businesses associated with health care and technology. Historians will likely remember Arrington for his community revitalization projects, strong support of a cultural district, a more professional police force, greater diversification of the city's workforce, and the building of a historic civil rights museum.

BIBLIOGRAPHY

Edds, Margaret. *Free at Last: What Really Happened When Civil Rights Came to Southern Politics.* 1987.
Franklin, Jimmie Lewis. *Back to Birmingham: Richard Arrington, Jr., and His Times.* 1989.
Royster, Beatrice Horn. "Mayor Arrington: His Record and the Economic Future of Birmingham." *Black Business Network* 2 (1983): 2–4.

Jimmie Lewis Franklin

Asian-American Movement

Although Asians in the United States have long been engaged in political action, their efforts never drew public attention until the 1960s. Inspired by the social movements of the time, Asian-American activists joined other groups of color to challenge the country's definition of itself as a democratic pluralist society. Denouncing the historical forces of racism, poverty, war, and exploitation, Asian Americans demanded racial equality and social justice and asserted their cultural and racial distinctiveness. They drew inspiration from diverse intellectual and political sources such as Karl Marx, Mao Tse-tung, Ho Chi Minh, Korean communist leader Kim Il Sung, Latin American guerrilla leader Che Guevara, W. E. B. DuBois, adult educator reformer Paulo Freire, the BLACK PANTHER PARTY, the women's liberation movement, and many other resistance struggles. Critical to the development of the Asian-American movement was the mobilization of black Americans. Beside offering

tactical lessons, the civil rights and BLACK POWER movements had a profound impact on the consciousness of Asian Americans, sensitizing them to racial issues. The anticolonial nationalist movements in Asia—and elsewhere—also stirred racial and cultural pride and provided a context for the emergence of the YELLOW POWER movement.

Although an offshoot of the mass struggles of the 1960s, the Asian-American movement was not only a political movement but one that emphasized race. Like their non-Asian peers at the time, young Asian-American activists participated in New Left activities and organizations such as the FREE SPEECH MOVEMENT, STUDENTS FOR A DEMOCRATIC SOCIETY, and the PROGRESSIVE LABOR PARTY. However, they participated as individuals and had no coalition to draw attention to themselves as a distinct group. Since there was no organizational structure to uphold their own identity, Asian-American activists often felt impotent and alienated. As an example, when the PEACE AND FREEDOM PARTY was formed on the basis of black and white coalitions, Asian-American activists felt excluded because they were neither black nor white.

Outraged by the racism directed against their communities, Asian Americans brought their own perspectives and demands to the social movements of the time. As an example, Asian-American emphasis on race and racism differentiated their antiwar protest from that of whites. For many Asian-American activists, the American war in VIETNAM involved more than the issues of national sovereignty or imperialism; it also raised questions of racism directed against Asian people. Underscoring the racist nature of the war, Asian-American protesters discarded the popular slogans "Give peace a chance" and "Bring the GIs home," and touted their own "Stop killing our Asian brothers and sisters" and "We don't want your racist war." In 1971, the Asian-American contingent refused to join the main antiwar march in Washington, D.C., because the coordinating committee failed to adopt the contingent's antiracist statement for the march.

Although important, this antiracism agenda at times superseded the gender struggles waged by Asian-American women. Because their ethnic and racial identity was critical to their feminism, Asian-American feminists did not distance themselves from the Asian-American movement. They chose instead to work within the Asian-American community to challenge sexism and to introduce gender-related issues into the movement.

With the growth of racial pride among their ranks, young Asian Americans already active in various political movements began to form their own organizations, bringing together members of various Asian groups who considered themselves, and who acted politically together, as Asian Americans. In 1968, activists at the University of California, Berkeley, founded one of the first pan-Asian political organizations: the Asian American Political Alliance (AAPA). Reflecting the various political movements from which its members had come, AAPA took progressive stands against the war in Vietnam and in support of other Third World movements. Shortly after AAPA was formed at Berkeley, sister organizations were established at San Francisco State College, University of California, Los Angeles, and California State University, Long Beach, campuses. Asian-American organizations also mushroomed in other parts of the country. In 1969, through the initiative of west coast students, Asian American organizations began to form on east coast campuses. Similarly, in the midwest, the civil rights, antiwar, and United Farm Workers movements drew together Asian Americans of diverse backgrounds.

One of the most important legacies of the Asian-American movement was the institutionalization of Asian-American studies. Under the slogan of self-determination, Asian Americans and other U.S. Third World students fought for educational space in universities and for an education more relevant and accessible to their communities. These students demanded the right to control their educational agenda, to design their own programs, and to evaluate their instructors. In 1968, after the most prolonged and violent campus struggles in this country's history, Asian-American studies programs were established at San Francisco State College (now San Francisco State University) and at the University of California at Berkeley. In succeeding years, Asian-American courses and programs were established on major campuses throughout the country. In the decade following the San Francisco State strike, the political goals of the strike—for inclusion and equality—reverberated in other Asian-American struggles for social justice. In Los Angeles, San Francisco, Sacramento, Stockton, San Jose, Seattle, New York, and Honolulu, a broad range of Asian-American activists—including high school and college students, tenants, small business people, former prison inmates and addicts, the elderly, and workers—fought for community control over housing, defended education rights, organized union drives, campaigned for jobs and social services, and demanded democratic rights, equality, and justice.

Asian Americans challenged race, class, and gender exploitation not only through political and economic struggles but also through cultural activism. Grounded in the social movements for racial and social justice and in the anticolonial struggles of Third World countries, Asian-American artists/cultural workers founded political-oriented newspapers and journals, formed independent Asian-American media,

painted protest murals on public buildings, and organized basement poetry readings. Through songs, posters, murals, plays, dances, poems, films, and other creative projects, these activist artists performed the important tasks of correcting histories, contesting demeaning stereotypes of Asian-American women and men, demythologizing the United States as the land of opportunity, and creating an Asian-American counterculture that more accurately reflected their history, values, and experiences. Community scholars—through local studies, monographs, documentaries, local studies, historical societies, and ethnic museums—also worked to reclaim Asian-American history. Writing social history from the bottom up, these scholars gave voice to the historically voiceless by actively involving local residents in documenting and interpreting their own history.

Today, Asian-American political activism continues to take many forms and embrace many issues. Some present-day activists engage in direct action and grassroots mobilization; others organize leadership training programs, voter registration drives and redistricting campaigns; still others produced "resistance cultures" through their works in the media and the arts. Together, today's generation of activists fight political disenfranchisement, anti-Asian violence, labor exploitation, police brutality, inequality of housing and education, and cultural misrepresentations. Asian-American struggles for political, economic, and cultural inclusion and equality have significantly advanced American democratic ideals, broadened American culture, and affirmed the principle of equal opportunities for all Americans.

Chronology of Landmark Events

1968   Students go on strike at San Francisco State College to demand the establishment of ethnic studies programs.

1969   Students at the University of California, Berkeley, also go on strike for the establishment of ethnic studies programs.

1970   Asian-American students join nationwide protests against the American invasion of Cambodia and the broadening of the war in Vietnam; the University of California, Los Angeles, establishes the Asian American Studies Center; independent media artists in Los Angeles launch Visual Communications—the nation's first and oldest Asian-American media arts organization.

1979   The Japanese American Citizens League adopts a resolution calling for redress and reparations for the World War II internment of Japanese Americans.

1983   Labor activists in Oakland form Asian Immigrant Women Advocates (AIWA) to organize Chinese, Vietnamese, and Korean immigrant workers.

1985   Labor activists in Boston form the Chinese Progressive Association Workers Center to advocate on behalf of Chinese immigrant women workers.

1989   President George Bush signs into law a reparation program to pay each surviving Japanese-American internee $20,000.

1992   Labor activists in Los Angeles form Korean Immigrant Worker Advocates (KIWA) to work with low-income Korean immigrants in Los Angeles's Koreatown.

BIBLIOGRAPHY

Aguilar-San Juan, Karin. *The State of Asian America: Activism and Resistance in the 1990s.* 1994.

Amerasia Journal 15 (1989): whole issue. This commemorative issue is a salute to the social movements of the 1960s and 1970s and to the legacy of the San Francisco State Strike.

Choy, Curtis. *The Fall of the I Hotel.* This film documents the struggle to save the International Hotel in San Francisco from destruction. The hotel housed mainly elderly Filipino and Chinese bachelors.

Espiritu, Yen Le. *Asian American Panethnicity: Bridging Identities and Institutions.* 1992.

Gee, Emma, ed. *Counterpoint: Perspectives on Asian America.* 1976.

Leong, Russell, ed. *Moving the Image: Independent Asian Pacific American Media Arts.* 1991.

Lowe, Lisa. *Immigrant Acts: On Asian American Cultural Politics.* 1996.

Tachiki, Amy, Eddie Wong, and Franklin Odo, eds. *Roots: An Asian American Reader.* 1971.

Tajima, Renee, and Christine Choy. *Who Killed Vincent Chin?* This film documents the killing of Chinese-American Vincent Chin in Detroit and the subsequent efforts by Asian-Americans to prosecute his killers.

Wei, William. *The Asian American Movement.* 1993.

Yen Le Espiritu

Asociación Nacional México-Americana

Founded in February of 1949 in Phoenix, Arizona, by Mexican-American union leaders, the Asociacion Nacional Mexico-Americana (ANMA) began as a national political organization with the purpose of safeguarding the civil rights of people of Mexican descent. Alfredo Montoya served as president and Isabel González as vice president. At its height, the ANMA probably had fewer than three thousand members and thirty local organizations.

At its first national convention in Los Angeles in 1950, the ANMA adopted a broad-based civil rights platform. By linking ethnicity with a working-class identity, the ANMA viewed Mexican-American civil rights as intimately tied to the rights of other oppressed groups in the United States, especially African Americans.

On the political front, the ANMA opposed the KOREAN WAR, supported workers during the Bayard, New Mexico, strike of 1950–1952, and protested against the BRACERO PROGRAM of importing Mexican workers to the fields of the southwestern United States. When the Immigration and Naturalization Service (INS) launched a massive deportation drive in 1954 known as "Operation Wetback," the ANMA actively opposed the sweep.

In the cultural arena, the ANMA combated stereotyping in the media. In one of its more successful campaigns, it led a boycott against Colgate Palmolive, the sponsor of the Judy Canova radio show, a program that portrayed Mexican Americans as lazy and indolent. The ANMA also spoke out against racial stereotypes in popular songs and films and promoted cultural awareness through its Spanish language paper, *Progreso*, and schools like the Lazaro Cardenas School in Chicago.

Such "radical" activities did not go unnoticed during the McCarthy era. The organization was listed as subversive because of supposed ties to the Communist Party. The ANMA finally succumbed to pressure from the FBI and the INS. After 1954, the ANMA existed in name only.

BIBLIOGRAPHY

García, Mario. *Mexican Americans: Leadership, Ideology, and Identity, 1930–1960.* 1989.

Meier, Matt, and Feliciano Ribera. *Mexican Americans/ American Mexicans: From Conquistadors to Chicanos.* 1992.

Urrutia, Liliana. "An Offspring of Discontent: The Asociación Nacional Mexico-Americana, 1949–1954." *Aztlán*, Spring 1984.

Scott Zeman

Aspira

Aspira is among the oldest of Puerto Rican politico-cultural organizations. Established in New York City as a project of the Puerto Rican Forum in 1961, its purpose is to develop that community through education and youth leadership training. The organization's founders included Dr. Antonia PANTOJA and a cadre of young professionals and grassroots community leaders. They sought to fill a leadership void prevalent in articulating policy and decision making in those public and private spheres that affected the lives of Puerto Rican and other Latino communities.

Aspira is perhaps best known for its role in securing the Aspira Consent Decree (1974), the result of a class action suit against the New York City Board of Education. Led by Aspira and the PUERTO RICAN LEGAL DEFENSE AND EDUCATION FUND, the lawsuit was filed on behalf of a class of children of limited ability at speaking or writing English, their parents, and other Puerto Rican organizations; it centered on language rights in the public schools. A landmark case in bilingual education, the suit rested on evidence that Puerto Rican youth were being denied equal educational opportunities. Few Puerto Rican students were completing high school and fewer still graduated with academic diplomas. The classification of non-English speakers as "slow learners" and the low rates of secondary-level graduates were viewed as discriminatory. Although the New York City Board of Education had instituted a series of measures to provide for the educational needs of Puerto Rican and other students with limited English-speaking abilities, the results were uneven. The students' lack of English-language proficiency and the schools' English-only operational system were identified as major stumbling blocks to academic progress. The Consent Decree established standards for entitlement programs that included bilingual instruction as well as organization, personnel, and other school-related matters. The Board of Education was mandated to implement a bilingual education program for all children who were prevented from participating in the learning process because of English-language limitations.

In accordance with Aspira's original mission, the key to social change was EDUCATION. The organization established student clubs in New York City secondary schools where significant numbers of Puerto Rican and other Latino students were enrolled. The clubs and Aspira's neighborhood chapters counseled and guided youth toward professional, business, academic, and artistic careers and goals. As *aspirantes*, high school students who joined Aspira programs entered into an empowering, nurturing environment. They were tutored in the academic disciplines and enriched in the study of Puerto Rican history and culture. Along with their families, students received counseling regarding higher education. Aspira facilitated tours of college campuses and offered workshops on college requirements, financial aid, and the application process.

Since its origins in a small New York City office staffed by seven individuals, the organization has grown into a national association with offices and extensive programs in Florida, Illinois, New York, New Jersey, Pennsylvania, Puerto Rico, and Washington,

D.C. The guiding principle in the leadership developmental process is expressed in three words: awareness, analysis, and action. School clubs, now federated, make up a national network that encourages cooperation, self-esteem, and community service. Other programs include the Aspira Parents for Education Excellence (APEX); the Teachers, Organizations, and Parents for Students (TOPS); the National Health Careers; the Public Policy Leadership; the Math and Science Academy (MAS); and the Aspira Institute for Policy Research.

BIBLIOGRAPHY

Banks, James A., and Cherry A. Banks, eds. *Handbook of Research on Multicultural Education.* 1994.

Santiago, Isaura Santiago. *A Community's Struggles for Equal Education Opportunity: Aspira vs. the Board of Education.* 1978.

Virginia Sánchez Korrol

Association of Indians in America

The Association of Indians in America (AIA), is the oldest Asian Indian ethnic organization in the United States. Chartered in 1967 in New Jersey, today the AIA has nineteen loosely federated local chapters, each free to undertake on its own social, cultural, or educational programs for immigrants from India and their children. By policy, the AIA now avoids political involvement. The New York metropolitan area, Florida, and Illinois, major centers of Indian immigration, have the largest chapters. Members and officials are largely entrepreneurs or professionals. The organization reflects the interests of this ethnic elite.

From the mid 1970s AIA was involved, through the active efforts of a founding member, in winning Indians separate enumeration on the 1980 U.S. Census, then under revision to reflect civil rights and new immigrant issues. Amidst discussion within the Indian community, the federal commission advising the Census Bureau placed Indians, previously grouped with whites, within a new Asian/Pacific Islander category. The label "Asian Indian" was adopted at the urging of Native Americans on the commission. This new categorization was not universally popular among Indians. However, responses to the 1980 Census showed 387,000 people of Asian Indian descent in the United States, many more than reflected under previous statistical projections.

In a separate effort, AIA had already taken steps by the late 1970s to bring Indians under affirmative action programs. Despite educational and income levels higher than those of other ethnic groups, Indian entrepreneurs and professionals recognized the advantages affirmative action offered in obtaining federal contracts and Small Business Association loans. With the help of another Indian organization this effort was finalized in 1982. Nevertheless many Indian immigrants remain embarrassed by a legal categorization at odds with the community's general economic standing and which links Indians to other disadvantaged racial minorities.

This may be why AIA played no organizational role in protesting the highly publicized 1987 "dotbuster" racial attacks in New Jersey that left a young Indian man dead. Although individual AIA members attended meetings and rallies, it was left to ad hoc groups and a coalition of progressive students to agitate until New Jersey officials prosecuted. This reticence encapsulates the profound ambivalence of many Indian immigrants about civil rights activism and about their own racial—as opposed to class—status within U.S. society.

BIBLIOGRAPHY
"India: A Nation in Our Midst." *New Jersey Home News Tribune* (http://www.thnt.com/India).

Johanna M. Lessinger

Attica Rebellion

On September 9, 1971, inmates at Attica State Prison in New York staged a four-day rebellion. Inmate complaints to Commissioner of the New York State Department of Correctional Services Russell Oswald regarding the prison's unsanitary and inhumane conditions and the brutal treatment of prisoners by correctional officers had gone unheeded. Consequently, inmates began to lose faith in nonviolent forms of protests such as letter writing campaigns. Sparked by rumors of beatings of inmates, the rebellion erupted into a full-scale conflict. The uprising was indictment of a system that many inmates, especially African-American and Puerto Rican, increasingly found intolerable. Young inmates from urban centers affiliated with militant groups such as the BLACK PANTHER PARTY and the Young Lords Party, who followed the philosophies of charismatic young men like George JACKSON (killed at San Quentin Prison in 1971) and Fred Hampton (head of the Chicago Black Panther Party, killed in a police raid in 1969), found their voices during the rebellion. Inmates demanded in

Negotiations continued between inmates' representatives and correctional authorities on September 10, 1971, while other inmates showed their support at the Attica State Correctional Facility. (CORBIS/Bettmann)

their "Immediate Demands" and subsequent "Fifteen Practical Proposals" that they be treated in more humane fashion. The rebellion ended September 13, 1971, as New York State troopers stormed the prison at the request of Commissioner Oswald. The primary goal of state officials was control of the prison. The lives of both hostages and prisoners were a secondary concern. In the end, thirty-nine men, including ten hostages, were killed in the fifteen-minute raid on the prison. In total, forty-three men died in the course of the four-day rebellion.

BIBLIOGRAPHY
New York State Special Commission on Attica. *Attica: The Official Report of the New York State Special Commission on Attica.* 1972.
Wicker, Tom. *A Time to Die: The Attica Prison Revolt*, rev. ed. 1994.

Shirley A. Jackson

B

Baker, Ella J.

(1903–1986), civil rights leader.

Ella Josephine Baker was a founder of the SOUTHERN CHRISTIAN LEADERSHIP CONFERENCE (SCLC) and of the STUDENT NONVIOLENT COORDINATING COMMITTEE, and a civil rights leader and organizer for more than half a century.

Ella Baker was an independent woman—feisty, and outspoken. As one friend put it: "if you don't want to know what Ella Baker thinks, don't ask her." She had her own ideas of how to organize and she pursued them. She worked in a male-dominated arena, but she came to be recognized as a superb organizer despite gender antagonism.

Baker was born in 1903 in Norfolk, Virginia, and at an early age moved to the former plantation on which her grandparents and other relatives had worked as slaves. Her grandparents, Mitchell and Betsy Ross had purchased parcels of the old plantation and she grew up in an extended family of former slaves. Her grandfather, Mitchell Ross, who was the local minister, was a profound early influence. He did not tolerate emotional religious demonstrations. Ella Baker learned from this that one must have content in one's professions of faith, and of ideas.

In the NATIONAL ASSOCIATION FOR THE ADVANCEMENT OF COLORED PEOPLE (NAACP), where she worked for five years, three as a national officer, she consistently fought for the right of local people to define their own issues and pursue them. Baker joined the staff of the NAACP in 1941 and became Director of Branches in 1943. She traveled across the country in this role, but she concentrated in the segregated South, traveling for six months of the year to large cities and rural areas to instill in local people the idea that they could make change.

She resigned from the NAACP in 1946 to take on the responsibility of raising her niece, but her resignation memo made it clear that she was disaffected by the NAACP's bureaucratic way of functioning. She felt that currying favor with the powers that be was not the way. A hard-hitting program, she felt, would, as she put it, force the reigning forces to beat a path to the NAACP's door.

Baker's primary contribution to the civil rights movement was an organizing style which took into account the importance of involving ordinary people in seeking solutions to their problems.

Mainly Baker used a technique of asking questions. She taught as she organized. She also addressed personal problems *before* dealing with the political: a stratagem which cleared the air for dealing with problems at hand.

Baker became a champion of the right of ordinary people to speak out, to define their own problems and devise solutions for them. Urging local people to look at their situations and figure out a plan to make change was the way to create a mass movement, and a grassroots leadership. She was adamantly against the creation of a charismatic leader believing instead in a "group-centered leadership, rather than a leadership-centered group."

Baker continued to espouse these ideas throughout the 1940s, 50s, and 60s. She felt that the MONTGOMERY

Ella J. Baker in her later years emerged into the national spotlight as the godmother or elder spokesperson of civil rights movement. ("Fundi: The Story of Ella Baker," First Run Features)

BUS BOYCOTT of 1955–1956 could lead to a mass organization because she saw that there were innumerable people who had become involved, who had become active and who were potential leaders. She, together with Bayard RUSTIN and Stanley Levison, orchestrated the establishment of the Southern Christian Leadership Conference (SCLC) as a vehicle for the Rev. Dr. Martin Luther KING JR. Together they drafted the working papers for the establishment of the SCLC. Baker became executive director of the SCLC and fought with the ministers consistently to try to make it into a viable mass organization.

Baker left the SCLC to take on a part-time position at the National Student Young Womens Christian Association—part time so that she could devote her major effort to the development of the STUDENT NON-VIOLENT COORDINATING COMMITTEE (SNCC), an outgrowth of the student sit-ins protest against segregated lunch counters. Baker organized a gathering of the student protesters and was instrumental in establishing SNCC as an independent entity unaffiliated with an already established organization.

This turned out to be a major decision for the growth of the 1960s civil rights movement, for the young people of SNCC became the cutting edge of the 1960s movement. Baker said that the protest movement was about "more than a hamburger." Following Baker's precepts the young people of SNCC worked in the rural areas of the South to establish local areas of protest and encourage the development of local leadership.

Baker's next major task was pushing for the seating of the MISSISSIPPI FREEDOM DEMOCRATIC PARTY (MFDP) at the national Democratic Party convention in Atlantic City in 1964, and for the unseating of the state's all-white delegation. She gave the keynote address at the MFDP's state convention in Jackson, Mississippi, at which she declared: "Until the killing of black mothers' sons becomes as important as the killing of white mothers' sons we who believe in freedom cannot rest."

She then went on to head up the MFDP office in Washington, D.C., and then to the Atlantic City headquarters. Baker's job was to convince as many delegations as possible to support the MFDP's challenge to the seating of Mississippi's all-white delegation.

Baker returned to New York after the convention to continue her fight for civil rights and to renew her interest in fighting Northern de facto segregation. She pursued her long-held interest in radical politics: in a 1969 speech declaring "we are going to have to learn to think in *radical* terms." She used the term radical to mean "getting down to and understanding the root cause." She became active in the fight for Puerto Rican independence, for independent political action, and defense of political prisoners. She never gave up the fight.

BIBLIOGRAPHY

Cantarow, Ellen, and Susan Gushee O'Malley. "Ella Baker, Organizing for Civil Rights." In *Moving the Mountain*, 1980, pp. 52–93.

Dittmer, John. *Local People: The Struggle for Civil Rights in Mississippi.* 1994.

Fairclough, Adam. *To Redeem the Soul of America: The Southern Christian Leadership Conference and Martin Luther King, Jr.* 1987.

Forman, James. *The Making of Black Revolutionaries.* 1985.

Garrow, David J. *Bearing the Cross: Martin Luther King, Jr. and the Southern Christian Leadership Conference.* 1986.

Grant, Joanne. *Fundi: The Story of Ella Baker.* Film. First Run Features, 1981.

Grant, Joanne. *Ella Baker: Freedom Bound.* 1998.

Lerner, Gerda. *Black Women in White America.* 1972.

Payne, Charles M. *I've Got the Light of Freedom: The Organizing Tradition and the Mississippi Freedom Struggle.* 1995.

Ransby, Barbara. *Ella J. Baker and the Black Radical Tradition.* Dissertation. 1996.

Youngblood, Susan. *Testing the Current: The Formative Years of Ella J. Baker's Development as an Organizational Leader in the Modern Civil Rights Movement.* Master's thesis. University of Virginia. 1989.

Joanne Grant

Baker, George

See Father Divine.

Bakke, University of California Regents v. (1978)

In the *Bakke* case, the U.S. Supreme Court first struck down an affirmative action program on "reverse discrimination" grounds. In 1968, the regents of the University of California initiated a plan to increase minority representation. Under this scheme, the University of California-Davis Medical School set aside sixteen of its one hundred openings each year for minority students and maintained separate processes for general and "special" minority admissions. In 1973 and 1974, Allan Bakke, a white student, applied to the medical school. Although his evaluation scores were not high enough to be admitted into the general pool of admittees, they were substantially higher than several of the minority students accepted under the special admissions program. The school rejected Bakke's application both years.

Bakke filed suit alleging that the school had excluded him on racial grounds, argued that the special admissions program violated his civil rights under the California and federal constitutions, and asked for an order compelling the school to admit him. In 1978, the U.S. Supreme Court held 5–4 that the California program violated Bakke's rights under the equal protection clause of the FOURTEENTH AMENDMENT and the CIVIL RIGHTS ACT OF 1964. The Court declared that California's admission process had the effect of discriminating against white students, ordered the Davis school to admit Bakke, and struck down the special admissions program. Universities could take race into account as a "plus" factor in making admissions decisions, the Court added, but could not set specific quotas for matriculating minority students.

BIBLIOGRAPHY

O'Neill, Timothy J. *Bakke and the Politics of Equality: Friends and Foes in the Classroom of Litigation.* 1985.
Schwartz, Bernard. *Behind Bakke: Affirmative Action and the Supreme Court.* 1988.

Tim Alan Garrison

Baldwin, James Arthur

(1924–1987), essayist, novelist, and playwright.

James Baldwin used the power of his words to convey the moral significance of the fight for racial equality. He was born in Harlem and grew up there in desperately poor and crowded conditions. Following Richard Wright and other black artists, Baldwin fled the United States for Paris at the age of twenty-four. Although Baldwin spent the remainder of his life as a "commuter" to and from the United States, he knew that he could neither abandon his home nor separate himself from the struggles for racial justice taking place there. He dedicated his forty-year writing career to undermining Americans' dishonesty about the seriousness of racial injustice because he believed that the confinement of African-American citizens to Harlem and other ghettoes revealed the state of American democracy as a whole.

Baldwin's great challenge as a writer was to develop this moral vision without sacrificing the literary value of his work. Among his many novels, the most highly regarded are his earliest: *Go Tell It on the Mountain* (1953), *Giovanni's Room* (1956), and *Another Country* (1962). But it is in his essays, especially in the essays

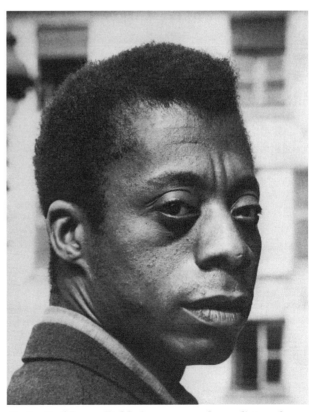

Portrait of James Baldwin, renowned novelist and civil rights activist, shown relatively early in his distinguished career. (CORBIS/Bettmann)

collected in *Notes of a Native Son* (1955) and *Nobody Knows My Name* (1961), that Baldwin best succeeds in joining exquisite prose with relentlessly fierce social critique. Whether reporting on the Southern civil rights movement or relating a personal story from his childhood, Baldwin's essays expose the distance between democratic ideals and American practices. His writings are radical insofar as they penetrate to the core of the prejudices and fears that divide black and white Americans. The most influential of Baldwin's essays, *The Fire Next Time* (1963), remained on best-seller lists for weeks and established Baldwin as a prophetic voice of the civil rights movement.

Baldwin's contribution to the civil rights movement was not only literary. During the early 1960s, he traveled extensively, giving speeches and participating in voter registration drives for the CONGRESS OF RACIAL EQUALITY (CORE) and the STUDENT NONVIOLENT COORDINATING COMMITTEE (SNCC). Baldwin also made public appearances with Martin Luther KING, JR., MALCOLM X, Bayard RUSTIN, Huey NEWTON, and other black leaders. So great was Baldwin's influence that Attorney General ROBERT F. KENNEDY invited him for a private consultation in May 1963.

Profoundly shaken by the killings of Medgar EVERS, Malcolm X, and Martin Luther King, Jr., Baldwin wrote less frequently and less effectively during the later 1960s and 1970s. During this same period his stature as a spokesman waned: Baldwin's willingness to analyze racial identity critically sounded at odds with the views of advocates of BLACK POWER, and his unwillingness to temper his social criticism in the wake of the passage of civil rights legislation was unwelcome to many white Americans.

Baldwin is remembered not only as an advocate of racial justice but also as a symbol of sexual freedom. While he never embraced the gay rights movement, Baldwin was honest about his romantic relationships with other men. He defied the sexual mores of the 1950s and jeopardized his status as a promising "Negro writer" when he published *Giovanni's Room*, a sexually explicit story containing no African-American characters or discussions of race.

When Baldwin died of cancer in 1987, thousands gathered to celebrate his life at a memorial in New York City. Among the literary and political leaders who spoke were Maya Angelou, Amiri BARAKA, and Toni Morrison. Although Baldwin founded no organization and drafted no major civil rights legislation, he left a legacy of words. A resolutely independent thinker, Baldwin dedicated his literary gifts to the work of describing Americans' racial anguish honestly. His six novels, two plays, short stories, poetry, screenplay, children's book, and dozens of essays remain a revolutionary call to conscience for Americans of all races.

BIBLIOGRAPHY

Baldwin, James. *Conversations with James Baldwin*, edited by Fred L. Standley and Louis H. Pratt. 1989.

Baldwin, James. *Collected Essays*, edited by Toni Morrison. 1998.

Baldwin, James. *Early Novels and Stories*, edited by Toni Morrison. 1998.

Bloom, Harold, ed. *James Baldwin.* 1986.

Leeming, David. *James Baldwin: A Biography.* 1994.

Troupe, Quincy, ed. *James Baldwin: The Legacy.* 1989.

Lawrie Balfour

Banks, Dennis James

(1932–   ), Native American civil rights activist.

Dennis Banks (Chippewa) was a foremost activist for Native-American civil rights and TREATY RIGHTS beginning in the late 1960s. Banks found direction for his life while serving a short term in Minnesota's Still-

Dennis Banks, American Indian Movement (AIM) national executive, as he resigns his AIM post at a general meeting of his organization on June 10, 1974. (CORBIS/Bettmann)

water prison, where he realized that Indians of diverse tribal backgrounds could work together—"Indians helping other Indians"—to promote Indian identity and self-expression, and to protect Indian civil and legal rights. Along with other former inmates, Banks founded the AMERICAN INDIAN MOVEMENT (AIM) in Minneapolis/St. Paul, one of the cities to which many reservation Indians had recently come, urged on by a U.S. government policy of "relocation." Banks directed AIM to supply food, HOUSING, jobs, "survival schools," and legal assistance for the many distressed and dislocated native migrants. A foremost AIM activity involved Indian patrols to monitor aggressive police action and diminish police arrests of Native Americans. Expanding AIM's leadership, Banks recruited the demonstrative Russell MEANS (Oglala) from California. AIM inspired younger Indians, and its activism quickly spread to other cities.

Led by Banks and Means, AIM's civil rights demonstrations gained notoriety in the early 1970s. In January 1972 they organized a 200-car caravan from Pine Ridge Reservation in South Dakota to Gordon, Nebraska, to protest the racist murder by drunken whites of a Sioux cowboy. This civil rights protest influenced local officials to proceed with a trial that convicted the murderers. In January 1973, Banks and Means led a civil rights demonstration at Custer, South Dakota, to protest another killing by a white man of a Sioux Indian. This protest led to a riot that spread from Custer to Rapid City. Banks spoke to local and state officials about racism and injustice suffered by Native Americans. However, he was among those arrested for inciting riot and destruction of property at Custer County courthouse. He was convicted in 1975, and became a fugitive from South Dakota until 1984, when he returned to serve fourteen months of a three-year sentence.

In 1972 Dennis Banks joined other Indian leaders in protest against the operations of the U.S. BUREAU OF INDIAN AFFAIRS (BIA), government controls, and treaty rights. They organized the TRAIL OF BROKEN TREATIES, a pan-Indian march to Washington, D.C., to present to federal officials their "Twenty Points" for resolving issues about Indian lands, treaties, tribal SOVEREIGNTY, and Indian rights. Confrontation developed, instead of serious high-level negotiations, and a storm of occupation, damage, and pillage at the Bureau of Indian Affairs lasted five days. Banks attempted to maintain internal security for the Indians and publicize American Indian grievances, but in the end the government rejected the arguments of the "Twenty Points."

AIM's activism then grew militant, most evident on February 1973 at Pine Ridge Reservation, home of the Oglala Sioux, where Indians were bitterly divided over the reservation governance by Tribal Council chief Richard Wilson, a strong supporter of the BIA and federal government controls. AIM leaders Banks and Means were invited by the Oglala Sioux Civil Rights Organization (OSCRO) to challenge Wilson's corrupt rule, as charged by reservation traditionalists (full-bloods), which OSCRO represented. AIM and OSCRO supporters occupied Wounded Knee (see WOUNDED KNEE OCCUPATION), and federal agents laid siege for seventy-one days. With government promises to examine Oglala grievances, the siege ended. But Banks and Means, depicted as "dangerous renegades," were arrested and stood trial that lasted eight months. By October 1974 all counts against the men were dismissed by the judge for improprieties of government evidence and witnesses, and they were acquitted.

Dennis Banks's efforts for Native-American civil rights and the activism of AIM in the early 1970s were really part of a new era in which Native Americans began to achieve their own definition of what their place in American society should be, and to voice the plea for "self-determination" and greater measures of tribal sovereignty.

BIBLIOGRAPHY

Cheatham, Kae. *Dennis Banks: Native American Activist.* 1997.

Josephy, Alvin M., Jr. *Now That the Buffalo's Gone: A Study of Today's American Indians.* 1982.

Lazarus, Edward. *Black Hills, White Justice: The Sioux Nation Versus the United States, 1775 to the Present.* 1991.

Matthiessen, Peter. *In the Spirit of Crazy Horse.* 1991.

Smith, Paul Chatt, and Robert Allen Warrior. *Like a Hurricane: The Indian Movement from Alcatraz to Wounded Knee.* 1996.

Weyler, Rex. *Blood of the Land: The Government and Corporate War Against the American Indian Movement.* 1982.

Frederick Schult

Baraka, Amiri (LeRoi Jones)

(1934–), writer and activist.

Amiri Baraka is a leading African-American writer, intellectual, and political activist who sparked cultural and political organization during the BLACK POWER Movement. Baraka was born Everett Leroy (later LeRoi) Jones in Newark, New Jersey, on October 7, 1934. Baraka attended Newark public schools. Rejecting what he saw as an elitist "middle-class" attitude, Baraka left Howard University and joined the U.S. Air Force in 1954. During his time in the military, Baraka became increasingly interested in literature and began to think of himself as a writer and intellectual.

Playwright, poet, and militant civil rights activist Amiri Baraka is pictured here at the time of his first success, the Off-Broadway production in New York City of his play Dutchman, *June 30, 1964.* (AP/ Wide World Photos)

After his discharge from the Air Force, Baraka moved to New York City. There he quickly established relationships with such important beat, Black Mountain, and New York School writers as Allen Ginsberg, Jack Kerouac, Charles Olson, and Frank O'Hara. In addition to Baraka's writing, his activities as an editor of the journals *Yugen* and *Floating Bear* and as a small press publisher were crucial to the development of a counterculture literature in the late 1950s and early 1960s.

Under the influence of the civil rights movement, the Cuban Revolution, and militant nationalists, such as MALCOLM X, Baraka moved in the direction of political activism during the early 1960s. His poetry and plays, combining the avant-garde style of his "beat" period, the harsh surrealism of the radical Martiniquan poet Aimé Césaire, African-American vernacular speech and popular culture, and often violent assertions of black identity, were models for BLACK ARTS drama and literature.

While Baraka became increasingly involved with militant African-American political organizations in the middle 1960s, it was the assassination of Malcolm X in 1965 that pushed him to his final break with predominantly white artistic circles. Shortly thereafter,

Baraka moved to Harlem, where he was instrumental in creating the Black Arts Repertory Theatre-School, popularizing "Black Arts" as a descriptive term for artistic expression associated with the Black Power Movement. Returning to Newark at the end of 1965, he continued to be a leader in the Black Arts Movement and the political movements of Black Power. An anthology of African-American writing edited by Baraka and Larry Neal, *Black Fire* (1968), was a watershed in the creation of a black cultural nationalist literature.

Baraka also played important roles in many national African-American political events, such as the 1972 Black Political Convention in Gary, Indiana. Drawing on both his national status and his local visibility (the result of his community activism and a savage beating by the Newark police in the 1967 riot, provoked by community resentment toward police brutality and a general sense of political disenfranchisement), Baraka was a leader in the election of Newark's first black mayor, Kenneth Gibson, in 1970. Baraka was heavily influenced by Maulana Karenga (from whom he received the name Amiri Baraka) and Karenga's doctrine of "Kawaida." (Karenga was the leader of the cultural nationalist U.S. organization.) Like Karenga, Baraka advocated a community-based Afrocentric ideology of African-American separatism and self-determination. In the mid-1970s, Baraka moved from cultural nationalism to Marxism-Leninism, a political stance to which he still adheres.

However one evaluates Baraka, he has left an indelible mark on post-World War II American culture. He has written powerfully in many different genres, producing many volumes of poetry, over twenty plays, three jazz operas, a novel, and several nonfiction works, including some of the most influential criticism of African-American music. He not only was a defining figure in the Black Arts movement and a charismatic leader of the Black Power movement, but remains a significant artistic and political voice.

BIBLIOGRAPHY

Baraka, Amiri. *The Autobiography of LeRoi Jones.* 1984.
Harris, William J. *The Poetry and Poetics of Amiri Baraka: The Jazz Aesthetic.* 1985.
Sollors, Werner. *Amiri Baraka/LeRoi Jones: The Quest for a "Populist Modernism."* 1978.

James Smethurst

Barnett, Claude

(1890–1967), journalist.

Claude Barnett, director of the Associated Negro Press (ANP), was born in Florida, but grew up in Illinois. He attended the Tuskegee Institute from 1904 through 1906. After graduation, Barnett moved to Chicago, where he worked in the post office and, in 1913, founded a mail-order photograph business. Four years later, Barnett organized a consortium and founded the Kashmir Chemical Company, a cosmetics firm.

In 1919, with financial aid from the Kashmir company, Barnett founded the Associated Negro Press, a news and clipping service that provided biweekly packets of news releases from various news sources and from its own stringers. Subscribers included individuals and African-American journals. At its height during the 1930s, the ANP provided material to some 200 black newspapers, and was the only national media outlet for stories that were of African-American interest.

Although he was not primarily an activist, Barnett used his influence as director of the ANP to focus popular attention on civil rights issues. For instance, he commissioned detailed daily reports on the trials of the Scottsboro Boys in 1932. In 1930, he met with President Herbert Hoover in an unsuccessful attempt to persuade him to withdraw the nomination of John J. PARKER, a segregationist, to the U.S. Supreme Court. Barnett also published many articles on the problems of Southern black farmers, and in 1930 and 1937 he served as special advisor to the U.S. Department of Agriculture.

The ANP steadily declined in size after 1945, and Barnett was forced to suspend operations in 1964, three years before his death.

BIBLIOGRAPHY

"Barnett, Claude." *Dictionary of American Negro Biography.* 1982.
Hogan, Lawrence Daniel. *A Black News Service: Claude Barnett, the Associated Negro Press, and Afri-American Newspapers, 1919–1945.* 1984.

Greg Robinson

Bates, Daisy Lee

(1914–1999), journalist, NAACP leader, and community activist.

Daisy Bates played a key role in the 1957 Little Rock, Arkansas, School Integration Crisis. As president of the Arkansas NAACP, Bates directly influenced state and community responses to the 1954 BROWN V. BOARD OF EDUCATION decision, helped to instigate the 1956 *Aaron v. Cooper* lawsuit to urge a prompt end to segregation in Little Rock schools, and mentored the nine students who underwent the ordeal of desegregating Central High School in 1957. Daisy, along with her husband Lucious Christopher ("L. C.") Bates,

Daisy Bates is best known for her leadership in the struggle to integrate Central High School in Little Rock, Arkansas, in 1957. (Courtesy Daisy Bates Papers, University of Arkansas Libraries)

bore the brunt of white anger and resentment to school desegregation in Little Rock, with crosses burnt on their lawn, missiles thrown at their home, threatening telephone calls, and harassment from state authorities through numerous lawsuits relating to their NAACP activities. In 1959, the *State Press* newspaper, which the Bateses founded in 1941, and which had played a vital role in early civil rights struggles in Arkansas, was forced to close down because of pressure put on advertisers to withdraw their business. After completing her memoir *The Long Shadow of Little Rock*, from 1962 to 1965 Bates lived in Washington, D.C., working for the Democratic National Committee and the Johnson administration's antipoverty programs. After suffering a stroke in 1965, Bates moved back to Arkansas and from 1968 to 1974 she was active in antipoverty efforts at Mitchellville. In 1984 Bates revived the *State Press*, which she then sold in 1987, while remaining a consultant to the paper.

BIBLIOGRAPHY

Bates, Daisy. *The Long Shadow of Little Rock: A Memoir.* 1962.
Daisy Bates Papers. Special Collections Division, University of Arkansas, Fayetteville.

Daisy Bates Papers. State Historical Society of Wisconsin, Madison.

John A. Kirk

Bell, Derrick A.

(1930–), civil rights activist.

Derrick A. Bell, Jr., is a civil rights activist and trailblazer law professor. He was born on November 6, 1930 in Pittsburgh, Pennsylvania. He learned early about courage and defiance from his mother during the difficult years of the Great Depression. Bell's favorite story about his mother concerns the time when she withheld the rent from her landlord until repairs were made to the back steps of the house.

Bell graduated from Duquesne University in Pittsburgh in 1952 with an A.B. degree in Political Science. He graduated from the University of Pittsburgh Law School. In 1960, he married Jewel Allison Hairston and they became the parents of three sons. After the death his first wife, Bell married Janet Dewart in 1992.

Bell's career has continually been touched by protests and confrontations at various levels. He is a man of commitment and dedication. The legacy of Derrick Bell to the civil rights movement has been his relentless zeal in standing up for justice and equality. He has served as a mentor and role model for African Americans and any other marginalized groups by speaking out or writing about racism, sexism, and tenure practices in academia as well as the larger society. He has been particularly outspoken in both analyzing and battling of legal and constitutional racism.

Derrick Bell is the embodiment of what the civil rights movement represented. He was Harvard Law School's first black tenured professor, at one time Dean of Oregon's Law School, and in 1998 he was teaching at New York University's School of Law. His ardent support of affirmative action—most notably his demand that Harvard's law school hire an African-American woman—has focused attention on the underrepresentation of legal scholars and students of color in American law schools. Finally, he has authored several well-received books about the intersection of legal and race issues.

BIBLIOGRAPHY

Bell, Derrick A. *And We Are Not Saved: The Elusive Quest for Racial Justice.* 1987.

Bell, Derrick A. *Faces at the Bottom of the Well: The Permanence of Racism.* 1992.

Bell, Derrick A. *Confronting Authority: Reflections of an Ardent Protester.* 1994.

Graham, Judith. *Current Biography Yearbook 1993.* 1993.

Dorothy A. Smith-Akubue

Bellecourt, Clyde

(1936–), Chippewa activist.

One of twelve children born to a disabled WORLD WAR I veteran and his wife on the White Earth Reservation, Clyde Bellecourt was first sentenced to the Minnesota Training School for Boys at Redwing in 1949. From there, he graduated to the St. Cloud Reformatory and, after a burglary conviction, to Stillwater State Prison. All told, he spent more than a dozen years in lockup before his thirtieth birthday.

In July 1968, on parole and displaced to Minneapolis, Bellecourt and several other Chippewa ex-convicts founded the AMERICAN INDIAN MOVEMENT (AIM). Patterning itself after the BLACK PANTHER PARTY, the group formed a street patrol to combat police abuse of the local Indian community. It also established an alternative school and several social service programs that continue to function after thirty years.

In 1969, with the eighteen-month "Indians of All Tribes" occupation of Alcatraz Island (see ALCATRAZ OCCUPATION), a wave of Indian activism rolled across the country. AIM became a primary beneficiary as hundreds of new members and a raft of talented leaders poured in. By 1972, the Minneapolis office was coordinating the activities of sixty-seven AIM chapters in the United States and two in Canada.

Bellecourt achieved celebrity as a national AIM officer/spokesperson during this period, as the movement undertook increasingly aggressive actions in its effort to draw attention to Indian rights issues. This culminated in the spring of 1973 with a spectacular seventy-one-day armed confrontation with federal authorities at the hamlet of Wounded Knee, on the Pine Ridge Sioux Reservation in South Dakota (see WOUNDED KNEE OCCUPATION).

In the aftermath of Wounded Knee, AIM suffered severe repression at the hands of the FEDERAL BUREAU OF INVESTIGATION (FBI). More than five hundred felony charges, most of them frivolous, were filed against Bellecourt and other AIM leaders, while a concerted propaganda campaign was directed at discrediting the movement as a whole. Meanwhile, more than sixty AIM members were murdered and another 350 physically assaulted on Pine Ridge alone.

In 1974, Bellecourt himself was seriously wounded during a dispute with AIM's national chairman, Carter Camp, believed to have been provoked by an FBI operative. The incident foreshadowed an internal fragmentation from which AIM never recovered. During the last general membership meeting, held in June 1975, both the national office and the national officer positions were abolished, with local AIM chapters mandated to function autonomously.

Although it was able to sustain the briefly successful INTERNATIONAL INDIAN TREATY COUNCIL during the late 1970s, and to mount sporadic demonstrations, it was clear that AIM was in decline. By 1983, rumors were rife that a dispirited Bellecourt had abandoned politics and returned to his roots, converting what was left of the Minneapolis street patrol into a criminal enterprise. Such speculation was confirmed in 1985, when he was arrested and subsequently confessed to charges of organized drug dealing, mostly among Indian youth.

After a remarkably short stint in Leavenworth, Clyde began what has been called "his most dubious undertaking yet." In 1993, he and an older brother, Vernon, chartered an entity under Minnesota law dubbed "National AIM, Inc." and issued a proclamation that all remaining autonomous chapters had been "expelled" from the movement. More puzzling still, given the background of its chief executive officer, "National AIM" has recorded receipt of several million dollars in federal and corporate funding.

For a time, Clyde Bellecourt made significant contributions to the struggle for native rights. Unfortunately, his overall behavior has been sufficiently questionable as to nullify much of the good he sought to accomplish.

BIBLIOGRAPHY

Means, Russell, with Marvin J. Wolf. *Where White Men Fear to Tread.* 1995.
Smith, Paul Chaat, and Robert Allen Warrior. *Like a Hurricane: The American Indian Movement from Alcatraz to Wounded Knee.* 1996.
Vizenor, Gerald. *Manifest Manners: Postindian Warriors of Survivance.* 1994.
Weyler, Rex. *Blood of the Land: The U.S. Government and Corporate War Against the American Indian Movement,* 2nd ed. 1992.

Ward Churchill

Berry, Mary Frances

(1938–   ), civil rights activist.

As a lawyer, historian, university professor, and chairwoman of the U.S. COMMISSION ON CIVIL RIGHTS, Berry has dedicated her life to winning and protecting criminal and social justice for African Americans and for all women.

Born in Nashville, Tennessee, Berry was educated at Howard University and the University of Michigan, where she received both a Ph.D. and a law degree. She was admitted to the Washington, D.C., bar in 1972.

Her first book, *Black Resistance, White Law: A History of Constitutional Racism in America* (1971), combined her historical and legal training to draw attention to the inequalities of the American criminal justice system and was received with great acclaim. She has taught at universities around the country, including the universities of Maryland, Colorado, and Michigan, as well as Howard University, helping to focus attention on African-American studies. Berry has served on numerous boards and committees, including those of the Organization of American Historians, and was an editor of the *Journal of Negro History* in the late 1970s. She has been a member of the U.S. Commission on Civil Rights since 1980, having served as its chairwoman since 1993. She has also been an advocate for women's rights, writing several books on women's issues from a legal and constitutional standpoint. In her 1999 book, *The Pig Farmer's Daughter and Other Tales of American Justice,* Berry argued that suppressed voices should be heard and explained that inclusion of a culturally broader range of stories in American media and history books would lead to a more trustworthy justice system.

BIBLIOGRAPHY

Berry, Mary Frances. *Military Necessity and Civil Rights Policy: Black Citizenship and the Constitution, 1861–1868.* 1977.
Berry, Mary Frances. *Stability, Security and Continuity: Mr. Justice Burton and Decision-Making in the Supreme Court, 1945–1958.* 1978.
Berry, Mary Frances. *Why ERA Failed: Politics, Women's Rights, and the Amending Process of the Constitution.* 1986.
Berry, Mary Frances. *The Politics of Parenthood: Childcare, Women's Rights and the Myth of the Good Mother.* 1993.
Berry, Mary Frances, and John Blassingame. *Long Memory: Black Experience in America.* 1982.

Noeleen McIlvenna

Betances, Ramon Emeterio

(1827–1898), physician, writer, revolutionary.

Born in Cabo Rojo, Puerto Rico, and educated in Paris, where he earned his medical degree in 1853, Ramon Emeterio Betances returned to his native country in 1854 to practice medicine, gaining recognition during the 1855 cholera epidemic by offering free medical care to the poor. Almost immediately, he became involved in political, abolitionist, and revolutionary activities against the Spanish colonial government.

Fleeing harassment and death threats, Betances lived for thirty-one years in exile, directing from afar resistance efforts such as the Lares Revolt of September

23, 1868, which he planned with Segundo Ruiz Belvis. Betances soon became known to sympathetic Puerto Rican nationalists as "the Father of the Motherland." Though the insurrectionists who raised the Puerto Rican flag in Lares were easily defeated by the Spanish military, Betances was not discouraged. Together with his compatriots Belvis, José Julián Acosta, Francisco Mariano Quiñones, and Julio L. de Vizcarrondo, Betances struggled for years to end slavery in Puerto Rico. Finally, on March 22, 1873, the Spanish National Assembly abolished slavery in Puerto Rico, though the slaves were not actually wholly free until 1876. In 1872 Betances returned to Paris to practice medicine, though his efforts on behalf of Puerto Rican independence continued unabated. From 1895 to 1898 he served as a Cuban diplomatic representative in Paris. During that period, Cuba was itself in the throes of the latest of several successive waves of revolution in an attempt to free itself from Spanish rule and U.S. interference. Puerto Rico remained a Spanish colony until the Spanish-American War broke out in February 1898. The United States invaded and occupied Cuba and Puerto Rico later that year, to the dismay of Betances and his freedom-seeking compatriots.

In addition to extensive writings on medicine, for which Betances was awarded the French Cross of the Legion of Honor, he published many articles in French, Haitian, and Spanish newspapers arguing for independence and for the establishment of some kind of Antillean or Caribbean federation, since he feared that Cuba, Puerto Rico, or other Caribbean lands might not be able to survive alone after independence from Spain. He was also very wary of what a U.S. presence in the region might portend. For him, the terrible significance of the U.S. invasion was that his beloved, yet-to-be-born country had passed from one imperialist government to another. Betances died in Paris on September 16, 1898, shortly after the U.S. occupation of his homeland. The U.S. occupation of Cuba ended by 1909, but Puerto Rico remained a U.S. possession throughout the twentieth century, hovering ambiguously between U.S. statehood and independence.

BIBLIOGRAPHY

Fernandez, Ronald, Serafín Méndez Méndez, and Gail Cueto. *Puerto Rico Past and Present: An Encyclopedia.* 1998.

Hill, Marnesba D., and Harold B. Schleifer. *Puerto Rican Authors: A Biobibliographic Handbook.* 1974.

Kanellos, Nicolás, and Cristelia Pérez. *Chronology of Hispanic-American History.* 1995.

Melodie Monahan

Bethune, Mary McLeod

(1875–1955), educator, political activist, and civil rights advocate.

Destined to become a pioneer in the modern civil rights movement and a champion of democracy and equality for all Americans, Mary McLeod Bethune was born the fifteenth of seventeen children to former slave parents in Mayesville, South Carolina. She attended the Presbyterian Mission School in Mayesville, from 1885 to 1888, and later attended another Presbyterian school, Scotia Seminary, in Concord, North Carolina. She personified the concept of pulling oneself up by one's bootstraps. In 1904 she founded the Daytona Normal and Industrial School for Negro Girls in Daytona Beach, Florida, and in 1935 she established the NATIONAL COUNCIL OF NEGRO WOMEN (NCNW). Today, her school is known as Bethune-Cookman College (B-CC) and is the only historically black institution founded by a black woman. And, NCNW is the largest black women's organization in America and the world, claiming more than four million members. Bethune's legacy also includes leadership in NEW DEAL programs under President Franklin D. ROOSEVELT; she was the first black woman to serve as head of a federal agency, as the director of the Negro Division of the National Youth Administration from 1935 to 1943.

A champion of the masses, Bethune took seriously the meaning of democracy. Acting on principles grounded in the Christian tradition, she championed the cause of civil rights for blacks, women, children, and the poor. The concept of brotherhood—the active love of one another—was at the core of her work as a civil rights advocate. In the days of JIM CROW, Bethune had the courage to write and to speak of her vision of a fair and just America. In the 1930s and 1940s, she was a columnist for both the *Pittsburgh Courier* and the *Chicago Defender*. Also one of the most popular orators of her day, she could relate to people across racial barriers and national boundaries. She wrote and spoke from her heart about democracy, brotherhood, and equality, expressing her own trailblazing spirit while connecting her audience to its history in an effort to ensure a just society. She saw America's racial hatred as a scar that needed healing, which would come only if all Americans worked to achieve it.

In a speech entitled "We the People of the South," Bethune argued that democracy would not just appear and purge the world of evil; instead, people must find the means to do so, and having found it must keep working toward that end. She saw RACISM in the United States as an obstacle but believed that strength of spirit and the power of the will of the people could

Rights activist Mary McLeod Bethune founded the National Council of Negro Women in 1935. She also served as director of the National Youth Administration's Division of Negro Affairs from 1936 to 1943, the highest-ranking black woman in government up to that point. (Archive Photos)

overcome it. Bethune believed that the United States was founded on the principle of justice for all and should guarantee civil rights for all Americans. In 1949 she wrote in a *Chicago Defender* article that civil rights were more than a declaration of law; she postulated that something must come from the inner person when the principles of justice and civil rights were at stake. Building unity among diverse groups of people was crucial to the success of the civil rights movement.

The civil rights movement needed leadership, and Bethune called for persons of great moral stature, who were both informed and militant, brave and astute. In her speeches and writings Bethune recognized that the United States was a world leader, and she clearly understood that other nations looked to the United States as a model; thus American leaders had global obligations. After WORLD WAR II she chastised white American leaders for continuing discrimination against blacks, who, like others, had fought for democracy in Europe. Also she encouraged black leaders

to broaden their understanding of the struggle against oppression. She advised them to see the race problem as an international issue: Blacks in the world were a force to be reckoned with.

A global citizen, Bethune worked tirelessly to make civil rights a by-product of brotherhood, in the United States and abroad. She did not separate her belief in God from her work or her vision. Bethune believed that brotherhood began with a spirit of love, which could lead to removing all barriers to EMPLOYMENT, promotion, HOUSING, transportation, recreation, EDUCATION, and cultural pursuits. In her words, brotherhood called for the "abolition of Jim Crow." In speeches about brotherhood in the United States and abroad, Bethune proclaimed the need for the spirit of love to be demonstrated in the global community. She insisted that parents cannot pass on brotherhood to their children unless they first develop it in themselves. Consequently, the steps to world brotherhood are "to know, to help, to like and finally to love" all people. In taking these steps, people reach out to their children "so that their hearts and their minds will be ready to accept the challenges of world brotherhood and to meet its obligations wherever they appear."

BIBLIOGRAPHY

Flemming, Sheila. *Bethune-Cookman College, 1904–1994: The Answered Prayer to a Dream.* 1995.

McCluskey, Audrey Thomas, and Elaine M. Smith, eds. *Mary McLeod Bethune: Building a Better World.* 1999.

Smith, Elaine M. "Mary McLeod Bethune." In *Black Women in America: An Historical Encyclopedia*, edited by Darlene Clark Hines. 1995.

Smith, Elaine M., ed. "Mary McLeod Bethune Papers: The Bethune-Cookman College Collection, 1922–1955." 1995.

Smith, Elaine M. "Mary McLeod Bethune's Last Will and Testament: A Legacy for Race Vindication." *Journal of Negro History* 86 (1996): 107–122.

Sheila Flemming

Bilbo, Theodore G.

(1877–1947), politician.

Theodore Bilbo served as a U.S. senator (1934–1947) from Mississippi. Twice elected governor, Bilbo advocated progressive reforms and supported New Deal programs. Throughout his political career, he identified with common whites. Yet his liberal record was overshadowed by his racist diatribes, which became more vitriolic with the start of the modern civil rights movement.

As a senator, Bilbo's racist rhetoric received little national scrutiny until 1938 when he called for the removal of African Americans from the United States. Bilbo believed removal would prevent "mongrelization," the greatest evil he could imagine. His plan eventually took shape as the Greater Liberia Bill of 1939, which ironically drew support both from African-American–led organizations interested in African repatriation and from race-baiting whites. The advent of World War II, however, ended discussion of the bill.

Bilbo continued his war against racial equality with attacks on the egalitarian FAIR EMPLOYMENT PRACTICES COMMITTEE (FEPC). As usual, his rhetoric was crude, his ideas reactionary. The shallowness of his thought and the coarseness of his language is captured in his book *Take Your Choice* (1947).

Bilbo's rhetoric turned violent in the wake of the 1944 Supreme Court decision *Smith v. Allwright*, which outlawed white-only primaries. On the eve of the 1946 primary elections, he called for white men to stop blacks from voting. The resulting violence and vote fraud in Mississippi prompted a congressional investigation that blocked Bilbo from returning to the Senate. Before the investigation ended, Bilbo died of complications associated with mouth cancer.

BIBLIOGRAPHY

Bilbo, Theodore G. Papers. University of Southern Mississippi, Hattiesburg, Miss.

Fitzgerald, Michael W. "'We Have Found a Moses': Theodore Bilbo, Black Nationalism, and the Greater Liberia Bill of 1939." *Journal of Southern History* 43 (1997): 293–320.

Morgan, Chester M. *Redneck Liberal: Theodore G. Bilbo and the New Deal.* 1985.

Bradley G. Bond

Birmingham Campaign

The climax of the African-American civil rights struggle occurred in Birmingham, ALABAMA, in 1963. President John F. KENNEDY attributed his decision to propose watershed civil rights legislation to Commissioner Eugene "Bull" CONNOR's use of police dogs and fire hoses against nonviolent activists and school children during the Birmingham Campaign. A joint effort of the ALABAMA CHRISTIAN MOVEMENT FOR HUMAN RIGHTS (ACMHR) and the SOUTHERN CHRISTIAN LEADERSHIP CONFERENCE (SCLC), the demonstrations not only created a crisis in local RACE relations but also forced a resolution to the national race problem.

Drawing on a deep faith in a righteous God, the Reverend Fred L. SHUTTLESWORTH organized the ACMHR to demand black access to the system as consumers and workers. Opposed by the accommodationist traditional Negro leadership class, the ACMHR led the local struggle for INTEGRATION by using direct action tactics that prevented it from attracting a mass base and alienated the black bourgeoisie. The ACMHR protested segregated seating on buses in 1956 and 1958, attempted to desegregate schools in 1957, assisted the Freedom Riders in 1960 (see FREEDOM RIDES), and joined student protests in 1961. In the spring of 1962, SIT-INS by black students provided the momentum that led up to the Birmingham Campaign as the ACMHR promoted a boycott against white merchants. Shuttlesworth appealed to the Reverend Dr. Martin Luther KING, JR., and the SCLC to assist its Birmingham affiliate in the struggle for local race reform. Shuttlesworth hoped King's prestige would attract the black masses and thus force a resolution to the racial conflict. Badly burned by Albany (see ALBANY MOVEMENT), King needed a success to restore his reputation as a national civil rights leader.

In preparation for the campaign, King and the Reverend Wyatt Tee Walker designed a limited strategy of sit-ins and pickets to pressure merchants and local business leaders into forcing the city commission to dismantle segregation. In hindsight, some people have argued that the strategy called for violent confrontations with Commissioner Connor that would fill the jail and thus force the Kennedy administration to intervene on behalf of civil rights. However, filling the jail had failed to alter race relations in Albany, and the Kennedy administration had yet to offer support for the movement.

Sit-ins announced the beginning of the ACMHR–SCLC joint protest on April 3, 1963. Poor planning, open hostility by the traditional "Negro" leadership class, an apathetic black community, and "nonviolent resistance" by Connor and the white power structure appeared to set the Birmingham Campaign on the road to Albany. The limited protest provoked little interest in the national media and led movement organizers to alter strategy in an effort to generate "creative tension." Indeed, the ease with which the campaign changed directions reflected the fluidity of the movement. Increasing its number of targets, the ACMHR–SCLC drained local resources as police arrested its members. Although black spectators gave the appearance of mass support, many African Americans remained apathetic as the traditional Negro leadership class attempted to undermine the protest by accommodating the white power structure. King's decision to go to jail marked a turning point in his life as a leader but did little to increase local support. While behind bars he penned "Letter from a Birmingham Jail," a clear statement of movement ideals. After a month of lackluster demonstrations, a stalemate signaled the defeat of the Birmingham Campaign.

Firefighters turn their hoses full force on demonstrators in Birmingham, Alabama, on July 15, 1963, at the peak of civil rights protest against all forms of discrimination. (AP/Wide World Photos)

Yet on May 2 the movement launched the Children's Crusade, which provided the nonviolent protesters necessary to force the white power structure into negotiations on race reform. At first, Connor arrested the hundreds of school children, but then he turned fire hoses and police dogs on the youngsters. In response black bystanders rioted, presenting an unorganized force for change. The negative images of the Birmingham Campaign carried by the media persuaded the Kennedy administration to react: it sent Assistant Attorney General for Civil Rights Burke Marshall to assist local negotiations. Federal intervention during the Freedom Rides had resulted in a policy of federalism that supported local law and order in segregationist MISSISSIPPI. In Birmingham, Marshall succeeded in fashioning a similar resolution by convincing King to call off the protests without winning any concessions from the local white power structure.

Shuttlesworth bitterly denounced King's betrayal. Originally appearing to be in agreement, the local and national movements had clashed over the approaches to achieving different objectives. The local movement had demanded equal access and job opportunities, and refused to compromise. The national movement had initially promised to support local objectives. Nonetheless, when the opportunity arose to gain federal recognition and thus restore King's reputation, the national movement bowed out of the protest.

National outrage, international pressure, and inner city riots following in the wake of the Birmingham Campaign convinced a reluctant Kennedy administration to propose sweeping legislation that Congress ultimately passed as the CIVIL RIGHTS ACT OF 1964. Consequently the movement achieved its goals of gaining access to public accommodations and equal EMPLOYMENT opportunities, thus reforming national race relations by opening the system to African Americans. Yet this moderate approach to reform had not altered the structure of the system, for integrationists had asked only for inclusion. White resistance exaggerated the significance of the change. In Birmingham, vigilantes contested the token desegregation by bombing the Sixteenth Street Baptist Church, killing four black girls. Only with the implementation of the Civil Rights Act did the city completely desegregate, and only with the VOTING RIGHTS ACT OF 1965 did many African Americans in Birmingham win the right to vote. The appointment of Arthur Shores to the Birmingham council in 1968 and the election of Dr. Richard ARRINGTON as mayor in 1979 represented the strength of the black electorate as a growing black middle class joined whites within the system. Yet other African

Americans remained shut out, having gained little from black political empowerment, equal access as consumers, and equal employment opportunities.

BIBLIOGRAPHY

Eskew, Glenn T. *But for Birmingham: The Local and National Movements in the Civil Rights Struggle.* 1997.

Garrow, David J. *Birmingham, Alabama, 1956–1963: The Black Struggle for Civil Rights.* 1989.

Manis, Andrew M. *A Fire You Can't Put Out: The Civil Rights Life of Birmingham's Reverend Fred Shuttlesworth.* 1999.

Glenn T. Eskew

Birmingham Civil Rights Institute

Three decades after the heroic struggle that pitted nonviolent demonstrators against fire hoses and police dogs, and resulted in the KENNEDY administration's landmark race reform legislation, the Birmingham Civil Rights Institute opened to commemorate the watershed civil rights events that rocked America. An immediate success, the Institute has since become one of ALABAMA's largest visitor attractions. It joints similar facilities in Memphis and Atlanta as memorials to the civil rights movement.

The idea for the Institute originated with David Vann, a white racial liberal who had negotiated with the Reverend Dr. Martin Luther KING, JR., in 1963 and later served Birmingham as mayor. In November 1979, the city council authorized a study to determine the feasibility of the Institute. Resistance from Mayor Rich-ard ARRINGTON initially hindered the effort, but well into his second term the proposal received his backing. In November 1985, the city acquired the block west of Kelly Ingram Park as the site for the Institute. In 1986, the minority architectural firm Bond, Ryder, James and Associates began designing the facility. A local task force, including the mayor's executive secretary Edward S. LaMonte, the University of Alabama at Birmingham's Odessa Woolfolk and Horace Huntley, and archivist Marvin Y. Whiting of the Birmingham Public Library, drafted a mission statement that conceptualized the Institute around three areas: exhibitions, education, and archives.

Collecting information and opinions from movement veterans became a central focus of the Birmingham Civil Rights Institute during its formative stage. The task force consulted the Reverends Fred L. SHUTTLESWORTH, Abraham Woods, and N. H. Smith, Jr., and attorney Arthur Shores. Huntley headed efforts to conduct oral interviews of participants on both sides of the confrontation. The Institute planned to place the collected interviews in the new archives, and the task force consulted these and other materials in determining the content of the exhibits. The task force held the objective of making the Institute a living institution that could document ongoing civil rights struggles throughout the world.

In 1986, Arrington proposed a bond issue to finance the Institute, but the city's majority-black voters voted two to one against the initiative. The mayor and the city council, however, remained firm in their sup-

The headquarters of the Birmingham Civil Rights Institute was designed by J. Max Bond, prominent black architect and scholar. (CORBIS/Raymond Gehman)

port of the project. The city hired Richard Rabinowitz of the American History Workshop to conceptualize the thematic program of the museum and Joseph A. Wetzel and Associates to design the exhibits. Upon defeat of a second bond issue in 1988, the mayor sold surplus city property to raise the $12 million needed to fund the museum and exhibits.

On November 15, 1992, the Birmingham Civil Rights Institute opened with a week-long series of seminars, concerts, and other special events. The museum proved an immediate success with its dramatic representation of segregation and racial conflict. The arched doorways and roofline of the Institute complement the historic black business district and neighboring Sixteenth Street Baptist Church, where four black girls were murdered by a bomb blast in 1963. The architecture also underscores the thematic design of the Institute.

A visitor climbs up into the building's rotunda and enters the exhibit area by crossing a darkened threshold into a theater where a film about black Birmingham is shown. Here the concluding image is of segregated water fountains, which appear as the screen is lifted to reveal life in a JIM CROW environment. After walking through this display, the visitor confronts life-size statues of everyday people, as recorded voices reenact racial incidents. The visitor follows the civil rights struggle as events from Montgomery to Memphis are recounted. Special attention is paid to Birmingham as the visitor views world-famous archival film footage of violent demonstrations that occurred there during the spring of 1963. After climbing up through the exhibit area, the visitor walks out into an open procession of life-cast monochromatic mannequins marching to freedom. Milestones listing African-American advances appear at the head of the processional.

The Institute decided not to incorporate originally proposed abstract notions of reconciliation into its exhibits, although in 1995 it did add an exhibit linking the American civil rights struggle to world concerns over human rights. School children make up many of the visitors, fulfilling the educational objectives of the mission statement, yet problems with developing the archives have prevented the scholarly aspect of the Institute's work from achieving its potential.

BIBLIOGRAPHY

Birmingham Civil Rights Institute Collection, Marvin Yeomans Whiting Papers. Birmingham Public Library, Department of Archives and History, Birmingham, Ala.

Birmingham News, Nov. 17, 1985; July 6, 1986; July 4, 1990; Sept. 6, 1991; Jan. 30, 1992.

Birmingham Post-Herald, Feb. 14 and 23, 1984; Apr. 16, 1986; Oct. 9, 11, 15, 18, and 19, 1991; Nov. 19, 1992.

Glenn T. Eskew

Black, Hugo L.

(1886–1971), U.S. senator and Supreme Court justice.

Hugo Black had a very unusual background for a SUPREME COURT justice. Born in Clay County in the eastern Alabama hill country, he grew up in the heyday of populism and imbibed its belief that government had a role in improving the lives of citizens. Black never attended college, but graduated from the University of Alabama Law School with highest honors in 1906. The class roll noted that he "will use the devil himself with courtesy."

In 1907, Black moved to Birmingham and practiced largely accident and negligence law. He taught Sunday school and joined almost every organization in town; in 1910 and 1911 he served as a part-time police judge. Elected district attorney in 1914, Black eliminated the fee system under which law enforcement personnel were paid on the number of arrests made, and he exposed third-degree confessions in a local jail before resigning in 1917.

Back in private practice after stateside service in WORLD WAR I, Black routinely won over 90 percent of his cases. He lost no more than a few dozen cases out of about 1,500 during his twenty-five-year legal career. Black was a master at cross-examination, and so good at ingratiating himself with jurors that the saying among Birmingham lawyers was, "If you don't watch out, Hugo will get in the jury box with you every time."

In 1923, Black joined the KU KLUX KLAN. He was an officer, the Kladd of his local Klavern, whose duty was to swear in new members; otherwise, he did not partake in Klan activities. Nearly one-half of all white men in the greater Birmingham area were Klan members. This group gave Black a ready-made base of supporters when he ran for the U.S. Senate in 1926. He won the election as the Klan served as his unofficial campaign organization, and in 1932 he was reelected.

Black was the most feared congressional investigator of his day. His investigation into lobbying irregularities by public utilities was instrumental in the passage of the Public Utilities Holding Company Act in 1935, and his inquiry into airline and shipping subsidies led to the Merchant Marine Act of 1936 and ultimately to the establishment of the Civil Aeronautics Board. Black cross-examined witnesses as if he were back in court. "You have me on the hip, Senator," protested one witness. The federal minimum wage law was

Supreme Court Justice Hugo Black emerged over the years as a major champion of civil rights and personal civil liberties. In particular, in 1952 he was a prime mover in persuading the Court to agree to hear the cases that constituted Brown v. Board of Education. (CORBIS/Bettmann)

Black's pet project in the Senate. He introduced it three times before it became law in 1938. No other senator more outspokenly supported Franklin D. ROOSEVELT's plan to "pack" the Supreme Court.

In August 1937, on the heels of the ill-fated Court-packing plan, Roosevelt appointed Black to the Court. "A kick in the face [with] our own foot," one anti–New Deal senator called it. After he was easily confirmed, Black's former Klan membership was revealed to an unsuspecting nation. He admitted it in a low-key radio address while pointing to his humanitarian record, and the uproar soon died.

On the Supreme Court, Justice Black spearheaded a constitutional revolution. He led the redirection of American law toward the protection of the individual. At the same time he sought clear standards in order to limit judicial discretion while giving government room to operate. Black presented his views in clear, simple language that admitted to no doubts. His dissents rang with passion. Language and history are the "crucial factors" in interpreting the Constitution, he wrote.

By 1950, Black had come to think that the "clear and present danger" rule in First Amendment cases, with inherent balancing of disparate interests, did not sufficiently protect freedom of expression. The advent of MCCARTHYISM led him to adopt the view that all speech about public matters is constitutionally protected. This position remains unprecedented in Supreme Court annals. To Black it meant, for example, that all obscenity laws and all libel and slander laws were unconstitutional. "It is my belief," he said in 1960, "that there are 'absolutes' in our Bill of Rights, and that they were put there by men who knew what words meant, and meant their prohibitions to be 'absolute.'"

Black believed that the framers of the FOURTEENTH AMENDMENT intended to make the specific guarantees of the Bill of Rights applicable to the states in the same way that it applies to the federal government. He presented this argument at length in *Adamson v. California* (1947), which he considered his "most important" opinion. The Court followed his lead in many fields, including the right against self-incrimination, coerced confessions and, perhaps most famously, the right to counsel in *Gideon v. Wainwright* (1963). Similarly, the Court's reapportionment decisions built upon Black's dissent in *Colegrove v. Green* (1946). No other justice has been as strong a proponent of jury trial as Black. He saw no textual basis, however, for a constitutional right of privacy, and his record in Fourth Amendment cases might be the most restrictive of that of any justice in history. Noting that "hardships are part of war," he wrote the Court's opinion in *Korematsu v. U.S.* (1944), upholding the internment of all American citizens of Japanese ancestry during WORLD WAR II.

Starting in 1950, Black searched for a case to overturn the "separate but equal" standard. He turned down the opportunity to write the Court's opinion in *Sweatt v. Painter* (1950). After Earl Warren's appointment as chief justice in 1953, wrote Herbert Brownell, attorney general in the EISENHOWER administration, Black "carefully tutored him [Warren] in his views on the Fourteenth Amendment" (as Black tried in differing ways to persuade any new justice). Warren wanted Black to write the Court's opinion in BROWN V. BOARD OF EDUCATION (1954), according to Justice Tom Clark, but Black dissuaded Warren, who wrote it instead.

Black played a key role in the development of the First Amendment's religious guarantees. He wrote the Court's opinions in *Everson v. Board of Education* (1947), the first case that applied the establishment clause to the states, and in *Engel v. Vitale* (1962), which outlawed state-written and mandated prayers in public schools. Commentators called it the "Warren Court," after Chief Justice Warren, but as *Time* magazine noted, it was "more accurately called the 'Black Court,' after its chief philosopher."

The direct-action cases of the 1960s tested Black's philosophy. They involved peaceful Sɪᴛ-Iɴs, which he called sit-downs, and marches. And, as his robust health started to deteriorate, Black's philosophy changed. He believed that Cɪᴠɪʟ Dɪsᴏʙᴇᴅɪᴇɴᴄᴇ could result in anarchy, and he consistently favored the need for preservation of public order over the First Amendment right to assemble. "Marches lead to violence," Black said, insisting that government had the authority to take over an area if necessary. His later opinions lacked their former expansiveness and optimism, and his interpretations were often cramped and confining.

Black's main pursuits off the Court were tennis, which he played regularly and passionately on a court behind his Federal-style home in Alexandria, Virginia, and reading. He read voluminously, largely in history, philosophy, and the classics, marking his books and making his own indexes inside their rear covers. A reporter hearing Black's Senate speeches said that he sounded like "a talking encyclopedia with a southern accent," and his opinions on the Court made history come alive as he related analogous situations and showed continuities in human nature. Black was a man of charm who inspired deep loyalty among friends and associates. Situations, not personalities, animated him. Even though he fought for his views with what he called his "usual tenacity ad nauseam," his fiercest adversaries were among his best friends.

The Supreme Court that rewrote the Constitution in the 1960s was basically Hugo Black writ large, as many of his dissents, more than those of any other justice, became the law of the land. His last opinion came in the Pentagon Papers case in June 1971. The press must be free "to publish news whatever the source, without censorship, injunctions, or prior restraints," Black wrote. " . . . Only a free and unrestrained press can effectively expose deception in government."

Black died on September 25, 1971, universally recognized as one of the handful of great judges in American history and one of the leading figures of the century.

Bɪʙʟɪᴏɢʀᴀᴘʜʏ

Dunne, Gerald T. *Hugo Black and the Judicial Revolution.* 1977.

Frank, John P. "Hugo L. Black: Free Speech and the Declaration of Independence." *University of Illinois Law Forum* 2 (1977): 620.

Newman, Roger K. *Hugo Black: A Biography.* 1994, 1997.

Reich, Charles A. "Mr. Justice Black and the Living Constitution." *Harvard Law Review* 76 (Feb. 1963): 673.

Roger K. Newman

Black Arts Movement

Inspired by the works of Langston Hᴜɢʜᴇs, Zora Neale Hurston, Romare Bearden, Sterling Brown, Claude McKay, Aaron Douglas, Ralph Ellison, James Bᴀʟᴅᴡɪɴ, Richard Wright, and Margaret Walker and fired by the militancy of Robert F. Wɪʟʟɪᴀᴍs and Mᴀʟᴄᴏʟᴍ X, the Black Arts Movement began in 1964 among overlapping circles of writers, artists, and activists. One day after the assassination of Malcolm X, on February 22, 1965, the poet and playwright Amiri Bᴀʀᴀᴋᴀ announced that he would establish the Harlem Black Arts Repertory Theater/School (BARTS). The initial funding for BARTS came from the proceeds of several of Baraka's plays and from benefit jazz concerts featuring such artists as Sun Ra and his Myth-Science Arkestra, Betty Carter, John Coltrane, Jimmy Garrison, Sonny Murray, Grachun Moncur, Virgil Jones, Marion Brown, and Archie Shepp. On May 1, BARTS opened in a four-story Harlem brownstone at 109 West 130th Street. Playing jazz, Sun Ra's group—accompanied by Albert Ayler, Don Ayler, and Milford Graves—led a parade of writers and artists across 125th Street, waving the Black Arts flag, a black-and-gold banner with Afrocentric theater masks of comedy and tragedy. During an eight-week summer program for four hundred students, BARTS set the standard for Bʟᴀᴄᴋ Sᴛᴜᴅɪᴇs: Harold Cruse taught African-American history and culture; Larry Neal, Askia Muhammad Toure, and Max Stanford, political ideology; Sun Ra, Albert Ayler, Milford Graves, Cecil Taylor, and Archie Shepp, music; S. E. Anderson and Sonia Sanchez, reading and writing; Amiri Baraka, A. B. Spellman, Charles Patterson, Lonnie Elders, Adrienne Kennedy, and Douglas Turner Ward, playwriting; Robert Hooks, Lou Gossett, Al Freeman, and Barbara Ann Teer, acting; Minnie Marshall, Sandra Lein, Ella Thompson, Marguerite Delain, and Barbara Alston, dance; Leroy McLucas, filmmaking; and Joe Overstreet, Edward Spriggs, and Vincent Smith, painting, drawing, graphics, and art history.

BARTS marked a turning point in African-American culture, emphasizing black consciousness, self-determination, and cultural revolution against white racism. In solidarity with Bʟᴀᴄᴋ Pᴏᴡᴇʀ, the Harlem BARTS experiment inspired the development of a national Black Arts Movement that made an indelible contribution to the direction of African American culture. As poets like Haki Madhubuti insisted on "the integration of light and dark Black people," the nascent movement delivered a devastating blow to the long-standing prestige of the color caste system in black America. And, challenging the hegemony of white cultural critics and entertainment markets over their work, the young artists declared that their

The creative outpouring of the 1960s and 1970s know as the Black Arts Movement involved just about every genre of art and artist. This undated photo shows playwright Ntozake Shange (right) in a scene from her 1976 play For Colored Girls Who Have Considered Suicide/When the Rainbow Is Enuf. (CORBIS/Bettmann)

audience and critics were to be found in the African-American community. Indeed, Larry Neal declared the centrality of a "Black Aesthetic" in the creation and judgment of African-American works of art.

The Black Arts Movement spread quickly via conventions, festivals, and cultural centers throughout the country. The first national Black Arts conventions were held in Detroit in 1966 and 1967. Black Arts festivals began in Harlem in 1965 and in Newark in 1967, and have continued since 1987 with an annual National Black Arts Festival in Atlanta. The Black Arts Movement inspired the establishment of some eight hundred black theaters and cultural centers in the United States. Writers and artists in dozens of cities assembled to fashion alternative institutions modeled after the Harlem BARTS: Baraka established the Spirit House in Newark; Jayne Cortez, Ed Bullins, Marvin X, and Eldridge CLEAVER, the Black Arts West in San Francisco; Kalaamu ya Salaam, the Free Southern Theater in New Orleans; Dudley Randall, the Concept East Theater and the Broadside Press in Detroit; Barbara Ann Teer and Richard Wesley, the National Black Theater and New Lafayette in New York; Gwendolyn

Brooks and Haki Madhubuti, the Afro-Arts Theater and the Organization of Black American Culture in Chicago. Further, the Black Arts Movement inspired Chicago's giant outdoor mural, the *Wall of Respect,* devoted to the new voices of black liberation, which influenced the creation of murals in communities across the country. A host of new black arts and black studies journals provided vital forums for the development of a new generation of writers and artists: *Umbra, Liberator, Negro Digest/Black World, Freedomways, Black Scholar, Cricket, Journal of Black Poetry, Black Dialogue, Black America,* and *Soulbook.* By 1968 Larry Neal and Amiri Baraka had edited *Black Fire,* a thick volume of poetry, essays, and drama, which drew national attention to the transformation that was under way among African-American artists.

The influences of the Black Arts renaissance are both profound and far-reaching. They are reflected in the painting of Vincent Smith; the photography of Billy Abernathy; the architecture of Earl Coombs; the documentary films of William Greaves and St. Claire Bourne; the drama of Amiri Baraka, Ed Bullins, Charles Fuller, Ntozake Shange, Woody King, Adrienne Kennedy, and Richard Wesley; the novels of Toni Cade Bambara, John A. Williams, Alice Walker, Ishmael Reed, Margaret Walker, William Melvin Kelley, Paule Marshall, Nathan Heard, John O. Killens, Rosa Guy, and Toni Morrison; the acting of Barbara Ann Teer, Yusef Iman, Danny Glover, Lou Gossett, and Al Freeman; the music of Nina Simone, Milford Graves, Marion Brown, Sonny Murray, Abbey Lincoln, and Archie Shepp; and the poetry of Amiri Baraka, Sonia Sanchez, Mari Evans, Haki Madhubuti, Jayne Cortez, Askia Muhammad Toure, Etheridge Knight, Keorapetse Kgositsile, Nikki Giovanni, Gil-Scott Heron, and the Last Poets.

BIBLIOGRAPHY

Neal, Larry. *Visions of a Liberated Future: Black Arts Movement Writings.* 1989.

Woodard, Komozi. *A Nation Within a Nation: Amiri Baraka and Black Power Politics.* 1999.

Komozi Woodard

Black Berets

During the early 1970s the Black Berets became known throughout Bermuda for publicly condemning RACISM, COLONIALISM, and the unequal treatment of blacks in their country's criminal justice system. Inspired by a 1969 Black Power Conference, the Black Berets formed that year under the leadership of John Hilton (Dionne) Bassett. Modeling themselves after the BLACK PANTHERS in the United States, this Bermudan organization supported revolution—leading some to view them as militant "rebels without a cause." The group's actions often resulted in trouble with the law. Throughout their organization's existence, Bassett and his fellow members were jailed for an assortment of political offenses, including flag burning, verbal attacks on the court system, and anti-authoritarian viewpoints expressed in their publication.

With members under suspicion for the murder of Police Commissioner George Duckett, the Black Berets disbanded in 1972 in the aftermath of the crime. While some went on to become community leaders, founding member Bassett eventually fled Bermuda after jumping bail on a stolen firearms possession charge; he lived in peaceful exile for the rest of his life, dying in 1996 of a sudden illness in Syracuse, New York. His funeral was attended by several former group members and supporters. Speaking to the *Bermuda Sun* about the Black Berets nearly twenty-five years after the organization's break up, ex-member Eliyahtsoor Ben Aaharon stated: "Most of our accomplishments [were] intangible. We gave a lot of people

the vision to be self-reliant and hope that they could achieve their dreams."

The goal of the Black Berets was to provide Bermudan youths with a means to uplift themselves through the espousal of progressive political activism. Subsequent organizations inspired in small or large part by the Black Berets include many groups throughout the major urban centers of the United States forming what has been loosely designated as the Youth Peace Movement. These groups generally arise in impoverished areas and serve to provide a bridge for youths to escape the vise of violence, crime, and poverty in favor of a new constructive, nonviolent involvement in their communities.

BIBLIOGRAPHY

Childs, John Brown. "Street Wars and the New Youth Peace Movement." Cited online at: www.2bzmedia.com/childs.htm.

Ebbin, Meredith. "Memorial Service for Black Beret Founder." October 5, 1999 (www.bermudasun.org/issues/mr22/beret.html).

John McCoy

Black Church

The role of the black church in the civil rights movement, 1955 to 1968, is contested by historians. A debate ranges among scholars about its significance beyond the role of high-profile clergy such as Martin Luther KING, JR. Although some scholars, such as Adolph L. Reed, Jr., and Gary Marx, question the centrality of the role of the black church in the movement, others, like Aldon D. Morris and James Melvin Washington, argue for the indispensability of the black church to the movement. Reed critiques the notion of the black church's universal support for civil rights activism and Marx purports an inverse relation between the degree of religious faith and practice and the degree of support for such activism. Morris and Washington in contrast contend that the black church was the essential, central source for mobilization within the movement. The other debates that rage among historians involve the role of women, including black Christian women, in the national civil rights struggle. Local congregations, as well as local community struggles, have profoundly influenced the discussion regarding women and gender.

Black churches participated in the construction of the modern civil rights movement in myriad ways, ranging from the prominent role of the Christian clergy and laity, the use of church facilities for mass meetings, and the employment of religious language to define the issues as well as mobilize people. In addition, black churches played a historic role in the earlier campaigns of the NATIONAL ASSOCIATION FOR THE ADVANCEMENT OF COLORED PEOPLE (NAACP), the 1963 MARCH ON WASHINGTON, the FELLOWSHIP OF RECONCILIATION (FOR), and the CONGRESS OF RACIAL EQUALITY (CORE) through involvement locally in area chapters and nationally through black ecumenical agencies such as the Fraternal Council of Negro Churches.

As early as the 1770s, African-American Christian slaves in MASSACHUSETTS, CONNECTICUT, and NEW HAMPSHIRE petitioned their respective legislatures to abolish slavery. Between the American Revolution and Civil War, black churches joined local and national black leaders in engaging four points of focus in the political struggle for civil rights: the campaign for the free black male vote, antidiscrimination, the abolition of slavery in Northern states, and the abolition of slavery in the Southern states. The black church exercised influence during the RECONSTRUCTION era, often serving as a public forum providing candidates to elected offices on the local, county, state, and federal levels and brokering between political factions in the black community. After the collapse of Reconstruction, black churches continued to be vital in galvanizing support for the diminishing civil rights of African Americans during the rise of SEGREGATION that accompanied the PLESSY V. FERGUSON SUPREME COURT decision, which constituted the "separate but equal" doctrine. For instance, black clergy led and participated in boycotts of segregated streetcars in the early 1900s, in cities such as Atlanta, Montgomery, Jacksonville, New Orleans, Richmond, and Nashville. Religious organizations such as the Women's Convention of the NATIONAL BAPTIST CONVENTION initially attempted to work within the confines of the separate-but-equal doctrine, according to historian Evelyn Brooks Higginbotham; they petitioned for adequate HOUSING and equal care of neighborhoods, equal accommodations, the franchise, equal treatment in the legal system, equal distribution of public education funds, equal treatment of black prisoners, and anti-lynching legislation (see ANTI-LYNCHING CAMPAIGN), but later challenged the doctrine itself.

The black church's involvement in the modern civil rights movement included both a Southern and a Northern campaign. While the Southern campaign received support from the clergy-dominated SOUTHERN CHRISTIAN LEADERSHIP CONFERENCE (SCLC) and the lay-youth-dominated STUDENT NONVIOLENT COORDINATING COMMITTEE (SNCC), much of its activity was led by local leaders and activists, including black clergy and laypeople. SCLC was organized in 1957 as a broad-based agency to coordinate the campaign in the South, and in 1960 SNCC was founded. The Southern campaign attacked de jure, or legalized, segregation. Established civil rights organizations, such as the NAACP, supported by black churches played a pivotal role in both the Southern and Northern campaigns. The Northern campaign, however, centered around de facto segregation. The civil rights struggle in the North consisted of strong local initiatives by grassroots leaders and activists in cities like Chicago, where the Coordinating Council on Community Organizations led the campaign, as well as by groups such as local chapters of organizations like the NAACP.

Within the black church an intense debate ensued concerning the role of the church in the civil rights struggle. However, Martin Luther King, Jr., and others represented a faction spearheading the church's commitment to nonviolent active resistance as integral to the Christian gospel. Minister Joseph H. Jackson, president of the National Baptist Convention from 1953 to 1982, challenged the church's use of CIVIL DISOBEDIENCE as counterproductive, but suggested that the commitment of the church to racial progress was morally based. Minister A. B. McEwen represented various local black clergy across the nation who espoused a doctrine of the innate spirituality of the church, accenting its dissociation from politics and protest. However, after the 1963 March on Washington, a watershed moment occurred within the black church and the civil rights movement wherein the movement gained the moral high ground and wherein the role of the black church in the movement received widespread approval.

According to sociologist Doug McAdam's study, the height of the black church's involvement was the years 1956 to 1959. Afterward the leadership of the movement became more diversified, led by local NAACP officials and students in addition to clergy. However, the role of the black church in the civil rights movement must, by definition, encompass more than the involvement of clergy. As Morris and Washington note, the role of African-American Christian laypeople—as well as the discourse, facilities, networks, and culture of the black church—must be included in any assessment of the black church's participation. The landmark phase of the civil rights movement concludes in 1968 with the rise of the BLACK POWER movement and the embrace of Black Power by the National Committee of Negro Churchmen, which spawned the modern black theology movement and its respective challenges to INTEGRATION and nonviolence.

BIBLIOGRAPHY

Crawford, Vicki L. et al., eds. *Women in the Civil Rights Movement: Trailblazers and Torchbearers, 1941–1965.* 1993.

Morris, Aldon D. *The Origins of the Civil Rights Movement: Black Communities Organizing for Change.* 1984.
Paris, Peter J. *Black Religious Leaders: Conflict in Unity.* 1991.
Reed, Adolph L. *The Jesse Jackson Phenomenon.* 1986.

David D. Daniels III

Black Codes

A series of state laws passed by southern legislatures immediately following the Civil War, black codes restricted the rights of African Americans. South Carolina and Mississippi first instituted black codes in late 1865, although most other former Confederate states soon enacted similar laws.

Ostensibly, the codes identified new rights enjoyed by southern blacks. The codes allowed African-Americans to marry legally, own property, negotiate contracts, testify in court proceedings involving other African Americans, and to be parties in lawsuits. In practice, however, black codes restricted black mobility, maintained white control over the labor force, and regulated race relations. Laborers had to provide evidence of annual employment contracts, and early termination of contracts led to forfeiture of wages. Vagrancy laws subjected the unemployed to fines or other punishment. "Enticement" codes prohibited prospective employers from offering higher wages to laborers already engaged. Restrictions on property ownership and high taxes levied on skilled labor forced most African Americans to remain agricultural or domestic workers. Black codes also banned interracial marriages and criminalized the use of insulting language toward whites. While the codes often failed to specify race as a factor, they were obviously aimed at black southerners.

Enactment of black codes infuriated African Americans, and caused political turmoil in the North by suggesting that southern state legislatures dominated by former Confederates refused to extend civil rights to blacks. Under Congressional or "radical" Recon- struction, new southern legislatures quickly abolished black codes, although the racially discriminatory principles behind the codes soon resurfaced in southern law and practice.

BIBLIOGRAPHY
Cohen, William. "Negro Involuntary Servitude in the South, 1865–1940: A Preliminary Analysis." *Journal of Southern History* XLII (1976): 31–60.
Du Bois, W. E. B. *Black Reconstruction in America, 1860– 1880.* 1935.
Foner, Eric. *Reconstruction: America's Unfinished Revolution, 1863–1877.* 1988.
Franklin, John Hope. *Reconstruction After the War.* 1961.
Litwack, Leon F. *Been in the Storm So Long: The Aftermath of Slavery.* 1979.
Wilson, Theodore B. *The Black Codes of the South.* 1965.

Michelle A. Krowl

Black Colleges and Universities

Most of the earliest African-American educational institutions in the United States were founded and administered by white religious groups or missionary societies who wanted to assist free blacks. The oldest educational establishment for blacks was the Institute for Colored Youth, founded in 1837 by Philadelphia Quakers who wanted to train free blacks to become teachers. The Institute began as a high school but began offering college degrees in the 1930s, and is now

The United Negro College Fund (UNCF) was founded in 1944 to help fund higher education at African- American colleges and universities. The organization is an alliance of forty-one historically black institutions of higher education. (Phyllis Picardi/ Stock South/PNI)

A view of the exterior of the main building at Howard University in Washington, D.C., ca. 1900. (CORBIS)

known as Cheyney University. The first institution in the world to provide higher education in the arts and sciences to blacks, the Ashmun Institute, was also founded in Pennsylvania, in 1854. It was later named Lincoln University, in honor of the slain president. Today there are 103 historically black colleges and universities (sometimes called HBCUs) in the United States, with a combined enrollment of approximately 280,000.

Education, long withheld from African Americans by slave owners who knew of its potential for empowerment, had always been seen by free blacks in both the North and the South as the vehicle for true freedom and economic self-reliance; most African Americans considered an education to be more important than the right to vote. The years following the Civil War, of course, ushered in a new wave of growth for the colleges, but all were funded almost exclusively by private donations and often suffered from a lack of subsidy and attention.

In 1890, the passage of the Second Morrill Act secured the apportionment of public land to be set aside for educational purposes, and Southern states then established a series of new land-grant institutions for free blacks. Some of these schools, however, were undertaken simply to draw funds that could be funneled

to white colleges, and the black schools still tended to languish in comparison.

In their early years, in fact, most of the nation's black colleges and universities were not true institutes of higher education. Due to the incomplete preparation of most Southern public-school graduates, very few were able to offer courses at the college level; most taught at the high school or remedial level. Despite the efforts of many Southern whites to keep funds restricted, several of these institutions—schools such as Fisk, Howard, Morehouse, Spelman, and Atlanta (now Clark Atlanta)—evolved to become highly esteemed institutions in their own right. Most of the nation's great African-American thinkers and many of nation's most prominent civil rights leaders were products of these colleges. However, most HBCUs continued to practice their dual role of providing both college and secondary-level curricula well into the twentieth century. Until the 1954 Supreme Court decision in the BROWN V. BOARD OF EDUCATION case, which effectively ended segregation in public educational institutions, HBCUs were really the only available option for blacks seeking a higher education. By the 1980s, black schools were forced for the first time to actively recruit black students, because historically white colleges now sought their enrollment.

Many black colleges and universities have been increasingly troubled in the latter half of the twentieth century. Since 1976, at least ten have had to close for lack of funding or poor leadership.

Despite a federal rejuvenation program enacted by President Jimmy CARTER in 1980, many schools continue to suffer from insufficient funds. In the late 1990s, students at Ohio's Wilberforce University, founded in 1856 as the nation's first coeducational college for blacks, chose to live in hotel rooms rather than inhabit the dorms, which were condemned as fire hazards. In addition, federal court cases in the 1980s and 1990s called into question the rationale behind maintaining distinctly "black" and "white" schools within the same system—rulings which paradoxically harmed many black colleges by forcing reorganizations, mergers, and closings. While traditions remain strong at HBCUs and most students are fiercely proud of their schools' histories, many black colleges and universities are now faced with challenges that are more profound than ever before: perennially inadequate state and private funding, increasing competition for the brightest students in the higher education market, and the danger of lost identity in the face of rising white enrollment.

BIBLIOGRAPHY

Black American Colleges and Universities. 1994.
Black Colleges and Universities: Charcoals to Diamonds. 1999.
Bowman, J. Wilson. *America's Black & Tribal Colleges.* 1998.
Handbook of Historically Black Colleges and Universities. 1999.
Roebuck, Julian B., and Komanduri S. Murty. *Historically Black Colleges and Universities.* 1993.
Shannon, David T. *Historically Black Colleges: Challenges and Opportunities.* 1982.
Suggs, Ernie. "Fighting to Survive: Historically Black Colleges and Universities Face the 21st Century." *Herald-Sun.* 1997 (http://www.herald-sun.com).
Turkington, Carol A. *Historically Black Colleges and Universities.* 1995.

Craig Collins

Black Convention Movement, Modern

The Modern Black Convention Movement began in 1966 with the Black Arts Convention in Detroit and the National Black Power Conference planning summit in Washington, D.C. Under Amiri BARAKA's influence, elements of the BLACK ARTS MOVEMENT and sections of the BLACK POWER movement merged to fashion the politics of black cultural nationalism and the Modern Black Convention Movement. In the aftermath of hundreds of African-American urban up-

risings, BLACK NATIONALISM developed quickly at the local level. In June 1968, one thousand people drafted a political agenda for municipal elections at the Newark Black Political Convention in New Jersey. By November 1969 hundreds of African-American and Latino leaders joined at the Black and Puerto Rican Political Convention, selecting a slate of candidates for municipal offices in Newark. By June 1970, the Black and Puerto Rican Convention candidates won the Newark elections, breaking a historic executive color bar by installing the first black mayor and the first Puerto Rican deputy mayor in a major northeastern city. In 1972, the Modern Black Convention Movement in Essex County, New Jersey, won a court case, designing a new congressional district and expanding black political representation. Eventually, U.S. Representative Donald Payne, an African American, replaced the veteran Representative Peter Rodino in that congressional seat.

The Modern Black Convention Movement entered the national political arena in 1972 with the National Black Political Convention in Gary, Indiana. Leading up to that Gary Convention to forge independent politics, the movement had generated a series of National Black Power Conferences in Newark in 1967 and in Philadelphia in 1968, culminating in Amiri Baraka's new organization, the Congress of African People in 1970. That Congress of African People sponsored a series of Pan-African political conventions and helped organize the first African Liberation Day in 1972. Meanwhile, the CONGRESSIONAL BLACK CAUCUS formed. All of these political forces laid the groundwork for the maverick Gary Convention in March 1972. In the midst of the 1972 presidential campaigns, the Gary political convention drew 1,800 black elected officials within an assembly of somewhere between eight thousand and twelve thousand African Americans. Similar to the local conventions, the Gary Convention fashioned a National Black Political Agenda to guide black American development in seven major areas: human development, economics, communications and culture, rural development, environmental protection, politics, and international policy.

The Modern Black Convention Movement generated many local organizations, schools, and community institutions, as well as county and state political organs, and at least four national organizations: the Congress of African People, the African Liberation Support Committee, the Black Women's United Front, and the National Black Political Assembly. The Congress of African People joined Black Power politics with PAN-AFRICANISM; the African Liberation Support Committee structured African-American efforts against colonialism on the continent; the Black Women's United Front mobilized communities and fashioned a political agenda joining the struggles against racism, imperialism, and sexism; and the National Black Political Assembly, created by the Gary Convention, charted the road to independent black politics.

Between 1974 and 1976, the Modern Black Convention Movement was locked in ideological and political battles between Black Nationalists and black Marxists on the one hand, and between proponents of independent politics and party politics on the other hand. As the 1976 presidential race approached, the Modern Black Convention Movement split into numerous factions, weakening the thrust of independent black politics.

BIBLIOGRAPHY

Harding, Vincent. *The Other American Revolution.* 1980.
Walters, Ronald W. *Black Presidential Politics in America: A Strategic Approach.* 1988.
Woodard, Komozi. *A Nation Within a Nation.* 1999.

Komozi Woodard

Black–Jewish Relations

Although African Americans and Jewish-Americans have struggled for equal rights since they arrived in this country, until the early twentieth century neither figured prominently in the efforts of the other. Few Jews, for example, were vocal abolitionists. Similarly, African Americans, occupied with pressing questions of freedom and citizenship, rarely involved themselves with issues of religious freedom and tolerance. The end of the nineteenth century brought the two populations into greater contact, with the migration of African Americans and the immigration of large numbers of Eastern European Jews primarily into urban centers, and brought increasing restrictions against both. While discrimination against African Americans was ever the more virulent and widespread, both blacks and Jews were barred from certain neighborhoods, jobs, colleges, and social spaces. Both were targets of hate groups, both faced the threat of violence, and both were at times denied constitutional rights. And both communities organized for their own protection and the assertion of their civil rights.

These organizations ranged from local to national, reformist to radical, separatist to integrationist, grassroots to hierarchical and elite. Some acted in the political sphere, others in the economic or social. Black and Jewish women's groups, fraternal orders, unions, religious bodies, nationalists, socialists, and countless others sought equality and justice for their community. The profusion of efforts brought infighting over membership, strategies, and even goals, but also brought a tremendous energy to the struggle.

In the early twentieth century, when many of these groups formed, individual Jews and African Americans cooperated in these struggles for justice. The NATIONAL ASSOCIATION FOR THE ADVANCEMENT OF COLORED PEOPLE (NAACP), for example, included numerous Jews among its founders. The NATIONAL URBAN LEAGUE (NUL) and the Socialist and Communist Parties were similarly constituted. Of whites involved in progressive and radical politics, a far greater proportion were Jewish than their proportion in the larger population, a fact that remained true throughout the century. Nevertheless, these were individuals, often elites. While black and Jewish newspapers of the day, especially those on the left, featured stories about the plight of the other, by and large the two communities pursued their shared agenda of equality separately.

In fact, most contact between Jews and African Americans occurred not within political organizations but rather in far more strained venues. Jews, less racist than other whites, accepted black neighbors more readily; and neighborhood after neighborhood shifted from Jewish to African American. Jews continued to hold onto their property and businesses, and more often than other whites proved willing to hire African Americans (albeit still in menial positions), or serve black communities as teachers and social workers. As a result, tensions between landlords and tenants, storekeepers and patrons, teachers and students, small employers and their employees, became redefined in the minds of many blacks and Jews as black-Jewish conflicts.

The threat of Nazism brought the beginnings of cooperation between civil rights agencies in the two communities. Urgent to aid European Jews, American Jewish groups asked non-Jewish agencies for help in encouraging the government to act against Nazi aggression. African-American organizations saw in Nazism the opportunity to press for their agenda; equating Nazism with American racism, they hoped, could win adherents to antiracist policies at home. This mutual self-interest led to joint programs against Nazism, which in turn promoted further cooperation after WORLD WAR II. By the 1940s, as leftist organizations, populated by both blacks and Jews, were increasingly forced by growing anticommunist pressures to withdraw from public activism, more centrist black and Jewish organizations like the NAACP, NATIONAL COUNCIL OF NEGRO WOMEN, NATIONAL UNION LEAGUE, American Jewish Committee, Anti-Defamation League, National Council of Jewish Women, and American Jewish Congress, began working together to fight racial and religious discrimination. Joint action on restrictive housing covenants, segregated schools, antidiscriminatory employment legislation, immigration reform, and similar programs brought activist blacks and Jews together in a political partnership which, though still marked by self-interest, reflected a more inclusive conception of it than before.

This political cooperation, which was now more broadly supported by both communities, brought substantial civil rights victories. Nevertheless, longstanding economic tensions continued to threaten relations. The coalition was further weakened in the 1960s as civil rights efforts shifted to the streets. While younger Jews embraced the more confrontational style of organizations like the STUDENT NONVIOLENT CO-ORDINATING COMMITTEE (SNCC), their parents feared they might be moving too fast. By the late 1960s, as these groups shifted toward BLACK POWER and against Democratic Party–style liberalism, conflicts between the two communities became more frequent and more fierce. Having benefitted from liberalism, Jews, mostly white and middle class, counseled patience. Many African Americans, having seen white liberals' failures to deliver on their promises, turned toward more race-conscious positions from separatism to affirmative action.

Meanwhile, a white backlash slowed the civil rights movement. And because Jews enjoyed unprecedented prosperity while racism continued to constrain African-American life chances, personal interactions between the two grew fewer, and some Jews shifted their priorities from civil rights to more internal concerns. Thus, although political cooperation continues on numerous issues such as hate-crimes legislation and enforcement of civil rights laws, and both Jews and blacks remain heavily represented in progressive political efforts, black–Jewish differences have become more visible than black–Jewish collaboration.

BIBLIOGRAPHY

Berman, Paul, ed. *Blacks and Jews: Alliances and Arguments.* 1994.

Diner, Hasia. *In the Almost Promised Land: American Jews and Blacks, 1915–1935.* 1977.

Franklin, V. P., Nancy Grant, and Genna Rae McNeil, eds. *African Americans and Jews in the Twentieth Century: Studies in Convergence and Conflict.* 1998.

Friedman, Murray. *What Went Wrong? The Creation and Collapse of the Black–Jewish Alliance.* 1985.

Kaufman, Jonathan. *Broken Alliances: The Turbulent Times Between Blacks and Jews.* 1988.

Salzman, Jack, ed., with Adina Bach and Gretchen Sorin. *Bridges and Boundaries: African Americans and American Jews.* 1992.

Salzman, Jack, and Cornel West, eds. *Struggles in the Promised Land: Toward a History of Black–Jewish Relations in the United States.* 1997.

Washington, Joseph, ed. *Jews in Black Perspectives: A Dialogue.* 1984.

Cheryl Lynn Greenberg

Black Nationalism

"Black nationalism" refers to a particular kind of NATIONALISM advocated by Africans and peoples of African descent in various parts of the world. Whereas nationalism generally denotes a form of group consciousness and attachment to a "nation," black nationalism is expressed as a desire for unity or solidarity among African peoples on the African continent and in the diaspora. Since the late eighteenth century, Africans have expressed black nationalist sentiments and ideologies in response to their enslavement and oppression at the hands of Europeans. Among the many ideals and objectives associated with black nationalism, the most fundamental have been a belief in religious, economic, and political self-determination, PAN-AFRICANISM, a commitment to race vindication, cultural nationalism, and revolutionary nationalism.

The belief that African people should control their own circumstances and destiny in any society in which they find themselves serves as the cultural basis for self-determinist activities within black communities. The masses of Africans in American society demonstrated their belief in religious self-determination with the founding of black-controlled churches and religious institutions beginning in the 1780s and 1790s. Black nationalist beliefs and attitudes served as a basis for the creation of the African Methodist Episcopal Church (1816), the African Methodist Episcopal Zion Church (1821), and other black-controlled religious denominations.

Closely associated with religious self-determination, and another important element in black nationalism, is a belief in Pan-Africanism. From the early nineteenth century on, black Christians from the United States engaged in missionary activities to spread the gospel to their brothers and sisters in Africa and the Caribbean. At times justifying their activities on the basis of the Biblical passage Psalms 68:28–32 (especially verse 31: "Ethiopia shall soon stretch out her hands unto God"), black Christian missionaries built churches and schools in Africa in an attempt to eradicate what they considered to be "heathenism" and ignorance among the native people. Pan-African sentiments underpinned these missionary activities, performed in the belief that African peoples have a responsibility to assist one another and work together to achieve their advancement and liberation. By the end of the nineteenth century, Africans who had obtained their political freedom in the Americas began to organize PAN-AFRICAN CONGRESSES to mobilize their resources to bring about political liberation for Africans oppressed by European COLONIALISM. Although the various "back-to-Africa" movements in nineteenth-century America, led by Martin DELANY and others, reflected support among the black masses for Pan-Africanism, the various Pan-African congresses were organized by African and African-American elites who viewed themselves as leaders of the African liberation movements.

African-American intellectual elites also engaged in race vindication and used their advanced education and training to challenge the ideas and beliefs in European and American society about the mental and cultural inferiority of African peoples. Black nationalist clergymen, professors, and journalists, including Alexander Crummell, Henry McNeal TURNER, Henry Highland Garnet, Ida Wells-Barnett (see Ida B. WELLS), T. Thomas FORTUNE, W. E. B. DU BOIS, and others, wrote numerous scholarly books, articles, and investigative reports to expose the lies and distortions prevalent in American society about Africans and people of African descent. Race vindication continued to be a major activity of African-American intellectuals throughout the first half of the twentieth century.

In the post–WORLD WAR I period, the black nationalists in the UNIVERSAL NEGRO IMPROVEMENT ASSOCIATION (UNIA) of Marcus GARVEY triumphed over black SOCIALISTS, COMMUNISTS, and integrationists in their competition for support among the black masses. The UNIA advocated economic self-determination, Pan-Africanism, and "Africa for the Africans," as well as black separatism. Whereas earlier black nationalist Christians, such as Henry Highland Garnet and Alexander Crummell, adhered to the idea of Christian brotherhood and were willing to work with sympathetic whites to obtain black advancement, the Garveyites as a matter of principle refused any white support. Marcus Garvey was able to build the largest secular organization among African Americans by preaching black nationalism and practicing black separatism.

With the coming of the Great Depression in the 1930s, many all-black institutions were destroyed (see NEW DEAL AND DEPRESSION), and the black masses came to appreciate the value of being integrated into government and private programs aimed at relieving their economic distress. Appealing to the self-determinist values of the black masses, black leaders at the local and national levels organized boycotts, picketing, and other protests to gain black EMPLOYMENT. When A. Philip RANDOLPH, black labor leader and president of the BROTHERHOOD OF SLEEPING CAR PORTERS, called for an all-black march on Washington in July 1941 to protest employment discrimination by govern-

ment agencies and contractors, his objective was the INTEGRATION of black workers into the national defense industries on the eve of U.S. entry into WORLD WAR II. During the war and in the postwar period, black leaders called for an end to legal SEGREGATION and the integration of African Americans into American society on the basis of EQUALITY, and they utilized self-determinist strategies to obtain these objectives but avoided black nationalist rhetoric.

Self-determinist strategies to obtain integrationist objectives can be seen in the launching of the successful MONTGOMERY BUS BOYCOTT in 1955 to 1956 and the formation of the SOUTHERN CHRISTIAN LEADERSHIP CONFERENCE (SCLC) in 1957. Although sympathetic whites supported the bus boycott and SCLC, these were black-controlled activities and institutions that had broad-based support among the black masses. In the late 1950s and early 1960s, the NATION OF ISLAM's Elijah MUHAMMAD and MALCOLM X advocated black nationalism and separatism and gained some degree of support within the African-American community. However, Martin Luther KING, JR.'s integrationist strategies and campaigns appealed to both black and white Americans. The campaign for civil rights became the most important social reform movement in the United States in the twentieth century.

There was a resurgence in black nationalist ideologies and movements in the late 1960s. Frustration among civil rights activists over the failure of nonviolent protests to bring about the end of black political and economic subordination led to a demand for BLACK POWER. Advocates of Black Power appealed to traditional black nationalist objectives emphasizing religious, economic, and political self-determination. However, unlike earlier nationalists, particularly those in the nineteenth century, many Black Power spokespersons upheld the value and significance of black culture.

Cultural nationalism became an important element in black nationalist thought in the 1960s, with emphasis on the role of artists and intellectuals in the creation of black group consciousness and solidarity. Amiri BARAKA (formerly LeRoi Jones), Nikki Giovanni, Sonia Sanchez, Ed Bullins, Haki Madhubuti (formerly Don L. Lee), and other poets and writers associated with the BLACK ARTS MOVEMENT were committed to producing art and literature for, by, and about black people. In an influential essay first published in 1968 on the relationship between African-American art and Black Power, poet Larry Neal declared that "the Black Arts and Black Power concept both relate broadly to the Afro-American's desire for self-determination and nationhood. Both concepts are nationalistic. . . . The political values inherent in the Black Power concept are now finding concrete expression in the aesthetics of Afro-American dramatists, poets, choreographers, musicians, and novelists." Cultural nationalist Maulana Ron Karenga developed a system of cultural practices and beliefs for African-American families and communities based on East African languages and cultures. Karenga was responsible for the broad acceptance of Kwanzaa as a black alternative or supplement to the Christmas celebration.

In the area of EDUCATION, cultural nationalism served as the ideological basis for the introduction of BLACK STUDIES programs and departments in colleges and universities all over the United States. Black and white students often organized protests and demonstrations to demand that college administrators hire more black faculty members, increase the number of African-American and other minority students, and offer courses on African and African-American history and culture. On many campuses black cultural centers were opened to provide social activities and to organize conferences and public programs on African and African-American history and culture.

Many cultural nationalists supported black capitalism as a means of achieving Black Power, or merely argued that the cultural interests of African peoples should define their political and economic objectives. However, the revolutionary black nationalists Huey P. NEWTON, Bobby SEALE, Eldridge CLEAVER, and the members of the BLACK PANTHER PARTY advocated a "socialist revolution" and aligned themselves with radical white organizations calling for the overthrow of the capitalist system in the United States. In the late 1960s and early 1970s the Panthers demonstrated their willingness to take up arms to defend the black community from attacks by the police, and in their "Ten Point Program" they called for "a United Nations supervised plebescite to be held throughout the Black colony" to determine African Americans' "national destiny." Unfortunately, the Panthers' strategies and objectives were viewed as a threat by the U.S. government, and the group's leaders came under unrelenting attack from the FEDERAL BUREAU OF INVESTIGATION (FBI) and local police forces. By the mid-1970s many of the Panther leaders were incarcerated or in exile, and few of the group's political objectives were realized.

For more mainstream political activists in the late 1960s, black nationalism provided a justification for the movement to create an independent black political party. Many black nationalists argued that political self-determination could not be achieved by working within the DEMOCRATIC or REPUBLICAN parties, and several conferences and meetings were organized to launch a separate black political party. By 1972, however, many black leaders with political aspirations decided that they would support white Democratic candidates and work with the Democrats to gain elective office and to increase black political power.

In the post–civil rights era, most proponents of black nationalism, with the exception of Louis FARRAKHAN and the Nation of Islam, were more willing than their earlier counterparts to work with white liberal, conservative, or progressive groups and organizations to achieve black social, political, and economic advancement. At the same time, however, there have been some recent controversies, particularly in the area of Black Studies. In their original articulation in the late 1960s and early 1970s, the various types of Black Studies programs were considered as manifestations of AFROCENTRISM and they emphasized documenting and interpreting the history and culture of African peoples in North and South America and in Africa. With the rise of the educational emphasis on MULTICULTURALISM and "ethnic diversity" in the 1970s and 1980s, however, some Black Studies programs were integrated into multicultural and ETHNIC STUDIES departments, and large numbers of African-American courses, particularly at predominantly white colleges and universities, were taught by nonblack instructors. In response to these developments, black nationalists inside and outside the academy expressed their renewed preoccupation with Afrocentrism, and argued that only Black Studies courses and programs that adopted an Afrocentric approach were "authentic" and useful for the advancement of the African-American community. Although some Black Studies programs developed strong attachments to the local black community and provided various types of educational services and programs, others did not (or could not), for any number of reasons. Moreover, black scholars and educators outside the Afrocentric camp emphasized their commitment to the training of African-American students and to the production and dissemination of new knowledge and information on both the African and the African-American experience.

The recent controversy over Afrocentrism has revealed many shared interests among black scholars and public intellectuals, and demonstrated more similarities than differences between black nationalist and multicultural approaches to documenting and interpreting the experiences of African peoples in the New World and Africa.

BIBLIOGRAPHY

Asante, Molefi K. *Afrocentricity: The Theory of Social Change.* 1980.

Asante, Molefi K. *The Afrocentric Idea.* 1987.

Bracey, John, et al., eds. *Black Nationalism in America.* 1970.

Franklin, V. P. *Black Self-Determination: A Cultural History of African-American Resistance.* 1992.

Franklin, V. P. *Living Our Stories, Telling Our Truths: Auto-biography and the Making of the African-American Intellectual Tradition.* 1996.

Franklin, V. P., and Bettye Collier-Thomas, eds. "Vindicating the Race: Contributions to African-American Intellectual History." *Journal of Negro History,* Special Issue, 81 (1996): 1–144.

Gates, Henry Louis, and K. Anthony Appiah, eds. *Identities.* 1995.

Gayle, Addison, ed. *The Black Aesthetic.* 1972.

Howe, Stephen. *Afrocentrism: Mythical Pasts and Imagined Homes.* 1998.

Jones, Charles P., ed. *The Black Panther Party Reconsidered.* 1998.

Moses, Wilson J. *The Golden Age of Black Nationalism, 1850–1925.* 1978.

Neal, Larry. "The Black Arts Movement." In *Visions of A Liberated Future: Black Arts Movement Writings,* edited by Larry Neal. 1989.

Seale, Bobby. *Seize the Time: The Story of the Black Panther Party and Huey P. Newton.* 1970.

Stuckey, Sterling. *The Ideological Origins of Black Nationalism.* 1972.

Stuckey, Sterling. *Slave Culture: Nationalist Theory and the Foundations of Black America.* 1987.

Stuckey, Sterling. "Classical Black Nationalist Thought." In *Going Through the Storm: The Influence of African American Art in History.* 1994.

Taylor, Charles, et al. *Multiculturalism: Examining the Politics of Recognition.* 1994.

Van Deburg, William L., ed. *Modern Black Nationalism: From Marcus Garvey to Louis Farrakhan.* 1997.

Wurzel, Jaime S., ed. *Toward Multiculturalism: A Reader in Multicultural Education.* 1988.

V. P. Franklin

A 1969 group portrait of the Black Panther Party leadership. Above right: Eldridge Cleaver. From top to bottom: Bobby Seale, Huey Newton, and Fred Hampton. (AP/Wide World Photos)

Black Panther Party

Inspired by the Southern civil rights movement's victory over JIM CROW segregation, yet responding to the rejection of assimilationist goals and nonviolent tactics by many young urban blacks, the Black Panther Party pioneered revolutionary organizing strategies in the late 1960s and 1970s. Incidents of police brutality had ignited riots in most major U.S. ghettos during the mid-1960s. The Black Panther Party began as one of many efforts by young African Americans to channel their frustration into a political force, heeding MALCOLM X's call to defend their communities "by any means necessary."

Originally called the Black Panther Party for Self Defense, the party was founded by Bobby SEALE and Huey NEWTON on October 15, 1966, in Oakland, California. Newton and Seale began their political collaboration as students at Merritt Community College, where they successfully fought for a BLACK STUDIES curriculum and participated in the Afro-American As-

sociation and the REVOLUTIONARY ACTION MOVEMENT. Having carefully researched California gun laws, they began armed patrols to curb police brutality.

On April 1, 1967, an unarmed black man named Denzil Dowell was killed by police in the neighboring town of Richmond, and his family came to the Black Panther Party for assistance. Organizing armed street rallies and confronting the local sheriff about Dowell's death, the Panthers mobilized massive support. Local Assemblyman Donald Mulford introduced a bill into the state legislature that would make it illegal for the Panthers to carry their arms in public, and the Party took its protest right into the capitol building in Sacramento. Images of the Black Panther Party at the capitol with their black berets, powder-blue shirts, black leather jackets, and guns were broadcast through television and newspapers from New York to London.

The strategy of armed self-defense attracted many to the party, including Eldridge CLEAVER, author of *Soul on Ice* and a writer for *Ramparts* magazine. He was soon followed by STUDENT NONVIOLENT COORDINATING COMMITTEE (SNCC) activist and wife-to-be, Kathleen Neal Cleaver. When Huey Newton was arrested in October 1967 following a confrontation in which police officer John Frey was killed, the Cleavers stepped into leadership positions in the party, traveling coast to coast gathering support for the "Free Huey" campaign.

From the start, the Black Panther Party's ten-point program emphasized social needs. As the Party established a degree of political power, it began to address these needs by providing free direct services, including breakfast for children, sickle cell anemia testing, ambulance services, shoes, escorts for senior citizens, legal aid, and the Youth Institute, which was directed by Erika Huggins and honored by the governor of California for providing the highest level of elementary education in the state. These services allowed the Party to expand and consolidate its political base. About forty chapter offices were opened throughout the United States, and the Party grew to more than 5,000 full-time members.

By the mid-1970s, the Party's emphasis shifted to electoral politics under the leadership of Elaine Brown. For example, in 1977 the Black Panther Party was instrumental in electing Lionel Wilson as the first black mayor of Oakland, breaking the city's one-hundred-year reign of white Republican Party political machine rule.

One characteristic that distinguished the Black Panther Party from most Black Nationalist organizations (see BLACK NATIONALISM) was its class-based analysis and coalition politics. Panthers read Karl Marx, Che Guevara, Franz Fanon, and Mao Tse-tung, identifying themselves as part of an international struggle to overthrow capitalism. They saw their community as a black colony to be liberated from external control in coalition with other liberation struggles. The Panthers built strong practical coalitions with many nonblack organizations such as STUDENTS FOR A DEMOCRATIC SOCIETY (SDS), the PEACE AND FREEDOM PARTY, the Red Guard, and the BROWN BERETS. They were the only major black organization to endorse GAY AND LESBIAN RIGHTS in the early 1970s. Further, they established official diplomatic relations with a number of revolutionary governments internationally, including Algeria, China, Cuba, and Vietnam. At one point, the Vietcong offered to exchange prisoners of war for the release of Huey Newton and Bobby Seale from jail.

The U.S. government saw these activities as a serious threat. FBI Director J. Edgar Hoover ranked the Black Panther Party as the number-one threat to American security, and extensive resources were marshaled to repress the Party's activities (see FEDERAL BUREAU OF INVESTIGATION). The Party was infiltrated, and while police raided its offices, agent provocateurs stirred conflict in chapters from New York to Chicago and Los Angeles. The results were disastrous, resulting in divisions within the party, shoot-outs between Pan-

thers and police, arrests of key leaders including Chief of Staff David Hilliard and the New York 21, and the outright assassination by police of Mark Clark and Deputy Chairman Fred Hampton as they slept.

Ultimately, ideological division and state repression brought about the Black Panther Party's demise. But at a time when the politics of access and the tactics of nonviolent civil disobedience were faltering, the innovative strategies of the Black Panther Party seized the political imaginations of frustrated urban African-American youths. Many gains by moderate black organizations during the period would never have been won if not for the stark alternative the Panthers presented. The Black Panther Party built organized political power where there had been none and transformed the face of urban politics forever.

BIBLIOGRAPHY

Brown, Elaine. *Taste of Power: A Black Woman's Story.* 1992.
Cleaver, Eldridge, and Robert Scheer, ed. *Post-Prison Writings and Speeches.* 1969.
Foner, Philip S., ed. *Black Panthers Speak.* 1970.
Hilliard, David, and Lewis Cole. *This Side of Glory: The Autobiography of David Hilliard and the Story of the Black Panther Party.* 1993.
Jones, Charles E., ed. *Black Panther Party Reconsidered.* 1998.
Newton, Huey P. *To Die for the People.* 1972.
Newton, Huey P. *Revolutionary Suicide.* 1973.
Seale, Bobby. *Seize the Time: The Story of the Black Panther Party and Huey P. Newton.* 1970.

Joshua Bloom

Black Power

Black Power was a collective, action-oriented expression of racial pride, strength, and self-definition that percolated through all strata of Afro-America during the late 1960s and the first half of the 1970s. Interpreted variously both within and outside black communities, the Black Power movement was a logical progression of civil rights era efforts to achieve racial equality. It also was a reaction against the tactics, pace, and certain of the operative assumptions of the earlier movement.

As a political slogan, the term "Black Power" was given a national forum during the summer of 1966 by STUDENT NONVIOLENT COORDINATING COMMITTEE (SNCC) head Stokely CARMICHAEL. Reflecting the frustration felt by civil rights activists whose hopes for a rapid transformation of U.S. racial relationships had proven illusionary, it came to symbolize rejection of black moderate leadership, white liberal allies, and the time-honored integrationist ethic. To Black Power militants, nonviolent approaches to integrationist ends encouraged harmful assimilationist tendencies and seemed productive only of continued dependency. As a result, they sought to effect personal and group empowerment via a variety of initiatives grounded in pluralist and black nationalist ideologies.

Both nationalists and pluralists understood that white power, as manifested in the workings of American economic, political, and intellectual life, constituted a major impediment to black American advancement. They held that in order to surmount this barrier, blacks had to mobilize, close ranks, and build group strength in all areas of community life. With unity achieved, African Americans would form a significant power bloc and be able to exercise true freedom of choice for the first time. Nationalists might then choose to go it alone, either in "liberated" urban enclaves, in a separate nation-state, or simply in the realm of the psyche. Pluralists could hope to parlay their newfound racial solidarity into a representative share of both local and national decision-making power. Thereafter, the myth of the melting pot never again could be used to obscure the role of minority group power in ordering societal affairs.

All manner of Black Power theorists believed that self-definition and psychological liberation were prerequisites for acquiring these more tangible manifestations of power. Noting that a people ashamed of themselves cannot soon hope to be free, they claimed that African Americans had the right to reject organizational structures, values, and methodologies that emanated from sources outside the group experience. Blacks, they said, were a beautiful people with a rich cultural heritage. It was anticipated that a "revolution of the mind" would lead to enhanced group cohesion, alter extant patterns of cultural hegemony, and provide a guiding force for black activism.

Beset by ingrained prejudices, internal dissention, U.S. counterintelligence intrigues, bad press, and the death, exile, or defection of key spokespersons, most Black Power groups were unable to implement their programs in full. Nevertheless, throughout the 1970s and 1980s their deeply felt desire to preserve and honor racial distinctives, to experience individual and group autonomy, could be seen in the determined efforts of other ethnic and gender-based constituencies to define the world in their own terms and thereby begin the quest for empowerment.

BIBLIOGRAPHY

Blackside, Inc. "Power! (1966–1968)." Program 3 of *Eyes on the Prize: America at the Racial Crossroads, 1965–1985.* 1987.

Carmichael, Stokely, and Charles V. Hamilton. *Black Power: The Politics of Liberation in America.* 1967.

Carson, Clayborne. *In Struggle: SNCC and the Black Awakening of the 1960s.* 1981.

McCartney, John T. *Black Power Ideologies: An Essay in African-American Political Thought.* 1992.

Van Deburg, William L. *New Day in Babylon: The Black Power Movement and American Culture, 1965–1975.* 1992.

William L. Van Deburg

Black Studies

The field of Black Studies (sometimes also known as African American Studies and Africana Studies) is the interdisciplinary analysis of the history, experiences, cultures, institutions, and statuses of people of African descent in the Americas, on the continent of Africa, and throughout the African diaspora. Black Studies emerged from the larger African-American civil rights movement for racial equality during the 1960s. Aided by antiwar and New Left activists as well as Latino, Asian, and Native American students, black college students led the academic movement for ethnic "inclusion" and multicultural education (see also ETHNIC STUDIES; MULTICULTURALISM). Their protests resulted in the establishment of the first Black Studies department in the United States at San Francisco State University in 1969. In 1975 the National Council of Black Studies (NCBS) was established as the professional organization for this new field and as an "intellectual extension" of the civil rights movement. Bertha Maxwell Redding (founding NCBS president, often described as the "mother of the Black Studies movement"), Nathan Hare, La Francis Rodgers-Rose, Norman Harris, and Deloris P. Aldridge were key leaders.

Black Studies courses of instruction began off-campus with the civil rights struggle for racial justice in black communities during the 1950s and early 1960s and moved to college campuses during the late 1960s and 1970s. In the midst of multiple protests and campus unrest, members of local student government organizations, as well as national civil rights organizations such as the STUDENT NONVIOLENT COORDINATING COMMITTEE (SNCC), demanded "culturally relevant" education and the academic inclusion of and focus on the lives and experiences of African Americans. Often having been trained in the earlier FREEDOM RIDES, SIT-INS, FREEDOM SCHOOLS, and voter registration marches of the civil rights movement, black students used direct-action tactics, occupied academic buildings, took over student unions, held meetings and committee hearings, organized school walkouts and strikes, and created black cultural centers, houses, and programs. At historically black colleges and universities, such as Howard and Jackson State, as well as at predominantly white universities, such as Columbia (in New York City) and San Francisco State, black students protested the distortion, marginalization, or exclusion of African Americans in Eurocentric college curricula and scholarship. They publicized their "revolutionary" critiques of RACISM and classism in society and charged that the content and process of higher education were racist and produced and reproduced racial inequalities inside the school or academy. Their corrective demands for Afrocentric curricula, black faculty recruitment, financial aid, cultural programs, and liberative education accessible to and empowering of black communities were taken seriously.

Over the past thirty years, Black Studies programs have grown and become institutionalized on campuses throughout the United States. However, during the 1980s and 1990s, conservative national politics and some highly debatable issues posed challenges to and opportunities for the growth of Black Studies. First, opponents have charged that this multidisciplinary area lacks rigor and "intellectual substance" and lowers standards for education and scholarship. Second, Black Studies has been accused of being male-centered and failing to recognize black women's experiences and leadership. Third, critics charge that the area is racially separatist and divisive. In addressing such issues, Black Studies has continued to strengthen its academic research and teaching base, standards for excellence, and social outreach to the black community; forged coalitions with other area studies and mainstream disciplines; obtained competitive funding grants that support and recruit students and faculty; and maintained international linkages among Africana scholars. Moreover, black women's studies scholars, such as Patricia Hill Collins, Deborah King, Bonnie Thornton Dill, and Darlene Clark Hine, have led major transformations of Black Studies, Women's Studies, Ethnic Studies, and mainstream disciplines by developing cutting-edge scholarship, theoretical paradigms, and a new field of race–gender–class intersection studies that analyze the "multiple" and "simultaneous" statuses of black women and other women of color.

BIBLIOGRAPHY

Aldridge, Delores P., ed. "New Perspectives on Black Studies." Special issue of *Phylon: A Review of Race and Culture.* (Spring 1988).

Barnett, Bernice McNair, Rose M. Brewer, and M. Bahati Kuumba, eds. "New Directions in Race, Gender, and Class: African American Perspectives." Special issue of *Race, Gender, and Class* 6, no. 2 (1999).

Belkhir, Jean, and Bernice McNair Barnett, eds. *Race, Gender, and Class in Sociology: Towards an Inclusive Curriculum.* 1997.

Butler, Johnnella E. *Black Studies: Pedagogy and Revolution.* 1981.

Hull, Gloria T., Patricia Bell Scott, and Barbara Smith, eds. *All the Women Are White, All the Blacks Are Men, but Some of Us Are Brave: Black Women's Studies.* 1982.

Karenga, Maulana. *Introduction to Black Studies.* 1993.

Bernice McNair Barnett

Black Towns

Black towns, a post–Civil War phenomenon, were founded by former slaves, such as Isaiah T. Montgomery, or by free blacks, such as Edward P. McCabe, as well as by white abolitionists throughout the industrial Northeast, South, Midwest, and West. They were either small settlements of laborers, recruited by agents and forced to establish their dwellings on the periphery of larger, white enclaves, or settlements created through the careful planning of free blacks and/or abolitionists bent on providing safe havens for runaway slaves. From the mid- to late nineteenth century these all-black enclaves were usually established in proximity to larger, predominantly Anglo-American, towns or cities. Once these black settlements reached the requisite population (generally 1000), officials would apply for incorporation into the county. The town would then be included on county and state maps and a federal post office would be established.

To some extent black towns were a compromise between prevailing patterns of SEGREGATION and a strategic, self-conscious effort to exercise the rights and privileges of free American citizenship, including the right to own property and the right to vote—two basic rights largely denied blacks from the late nineteenth well into the twentieth century. In the South, where African Americans were prevented from voting and legal segregation was a formidable challenge to black dignity and mobility, black towns provided a measure of local autonomy and protection as well as economic opportunity. In Mound Bayou, for example, in the Mississippi Delta, blacks elected their local officials despite the denial of the franchise to most African-American males throughout the state. And some of its citizens attained a measure of economic prosperity. In the twentieth century, Mound Bayou also served as a regional medical training and treatment center for black Mississippians who were refused entry into whites-only hospitals. The Taborian Hospital, established by the Knights and Daughters of Tabor (a black self-help society) in 1942, was strategically located in Mound Bayou to provide hospital services and medical treatment to blacks throughout the Mississippi Delta.

In contrast to the South, where black towns served to offset the effects of legal segregation and public discrimination, Midwestern and Northeastern towns like Brooklyn, Illinois (1874), and Lawnside, New

Jersey (established in 1840 and incorporated in 1926), began as way stations of the Underground Railroad. In these communities black descendents of the original organizers have maintained their viability as all-black towns despite their dependence on industries located outside their boundaries.

Black towns provided opportunities for African Americans to realize ideals advocated by Booker T. WASHINGTON, T. Thomas FORTUNE, and W. E. B. DU BOIS. The longevity of towns like Mound Bayou (Mississippi), Robbins (Illinois), Glenarden (Maryland), and Lawnside (New Jersey), as well as their record of self-determination and economic enterprise, mark the black town as a reminder of the determination of black Americans to realize their ambitions. Though many other towns disappeared or were relegated to insignificance following the CIVIL RIGHTS ACTS OF 1964 and 1965, black towns were the laboratories where African Americans experimented with the intricacies of democratic practice, established institutions, and acquired economic and political skills that prepared them for the challenges of the modern Civil Rights Movement.

BIBLIOGRAPHY

Crockett, Norman L. *The Black Towns.* 1979.

Hamilton, Kenneth M. "The Origins and Early Developments of Langston, Oklahoma." *Journal of Negro History* 62 (July 1977): 270–282.

Meier, August. "Booker T. Washington and the Town of Mound Bayou." *Phylon* 15 (Fourth Quarter, 1954): 396–401.

Rose, Harold M. "The All-Negro Town: Its Evolution and Function." *Geographical Review* 55 (July 1965): 362–381.

Homer Douglass Hill

Bond, Horace Mann

(1904–1972), educator.

Horace Mann Bond, educator and black leader, was born in Nashville, Tennessee, the son of a Methodist minister who named him for public school reformer Horace Mann. Bond attended college at Lincoln University in Pennsylvania, where he graduated in 1923. Over the following years, as he pursued graduate work in education at the University of Chicago, he taught at a variety of African-American colleges. During this time, he published his major work, *The Education of the Negro in the American Social Order* (1934), an exploration of racial discrimination in the schools. In 1939, after earning his Ph.D., Bond became a professor at Dillard University in New Orleans. Six years later, he was named the first African-American president of Lincoln University, his alma mater. He remained at Lincoln until 1957, then accepted an administrative position at Atlanta University, where he remained a noted education scholar and critic of racial bias in intelligence testing.

Bond integrated his professional work with civil rights activism. In 1942 he attended the Durham Conference, an interracial meeting of Southern moderates; there, he helped draft the "DURHAM MANIFESTO" adopted by the Conference, which opposed the principle of segregation. In addition, as a noted scholar of the RECONSTRUCTION era, Bond was recruited in 1953 by the NATIONAL ASSOCIATION FOR THE ADVANCEMENT OF COLORED PEOPLE (NAACP) to write on the politics of public education during Reconstruction for the historical sections of the NAACP's brief in the landmark BROWN v. BOARD OF EDUCATION Supreme Court school desegregation case. Civil rights activist Julian BOND is Horace Mann Bond's son.

BIBLIOGRAPHY

Urban, Wayne J. *Black Scholar: Horace Mann Bond, 1904–1972.* 1992.

Williams, Roger M. *The Bonds: An American Family.* 1971.

Greg Robinson

Bond, Julian

(1940–), civil rights activist.

Julian Bond was a member of the STUDENT NONVIOLENT COORDINATING COMMITTEE (SNCC) and a Georgia legislator, became the first African American to have his name entered in nomination for vice-president by a major party, and was selected as Chairman of the NATIONAL ASSOCIATION FOR THE ADVANCEMENT OF COLORED PEOPLE in 1998.

Bond was born in 1940 to noted educator Horace Mann BOND and Julia Washington. While attending Morehouse College early in 1960, he helped to stage SIT-INS against Atlanta's segregated public facilities. Later that spring he traveled to the founding conference of the STUDENT NONVIOLENT COORDINATING COMMITTEE (SNCC), established as an autonomous civil rights organization with the encouragement of pioneering black activist Ella BAKER. In 1961 Bond married Alice Clopton, with whom he would have two children. The next year he left Morehouse, one semester shy of his degree to become SNCC's communications director, returning to complete his studies in 1971.

Bond was a charismatic and articulate spokesman for SNCC's goal of cultivating indigenous leadership in black communities. His extensive media contacts helped to cast a sporadic spotlight on the physical bru-

Julian Bond, civil rights activist and chairman of the NAACP, is pictured here giving a speech on the Voting Rights Act of 1965 at Harvard University on October 2, 1998. (AP/Wide World Photos)

tality and psychological trauma SNCC workers and local blacks endured as they organized in remote areas, often overshadowed by the choreographed campaigns of more established civil rights groups.

In 1965 Bond won a seat in the Georgia legislature as a Democrat representing black Atlantans, but soon after his victory created a furor when he endorsed a SNCC statement criticizing the Vietnam War. Hostile white legislators, citing "disloyalty," barred him from taking his seat, excluding him again when Bond's constituents promptly reelected him. In 1966, during a third successful campaign, Bond resigned from SNCC; he felt its new leaders had let ideological preoccupation supplant grassroots mobilization, but he refused to criticize the organization publicly. White attempts to crush Bond's nascent political career ironically catapulted him to national prominence as a civil rights *cause célèbre*, a status cemented when a unanimous Supreme Court ended Bond's legislative limbo and restored his seat in the statehouse.

While promoting greater black political participation, Bond joined a group of Georgian Democrats in 1968 to challenge a convention delegation controlled by vitriolic Governor Lester Maddox. Seeking to test the national party's commitment to nondiscrimination pledges made following a rancorous dispute over rival Mississippi delegations in 1964, Bond's delegation won a compromise victory at the Chicago Democratic convention. As violence raged outside, antiwar delegates nominated Bond as vice-president in a thinly veiled parliamentary maneuver to bring their champion Allard Lowenstein to the convention podium. Seven years shy of the constitutional age requirement, Bond withdrew, but his moments as the first black nominee for vice-president for a major party further enhanced his national stature.

After two decades of virtual ostracism in Georgia's House and Senate, Bond entered the Democratic primary for Atlanta's 5th Congressional District in 1986. A favorite of the national press and front-runner in a crowded field, Bond fell victim to lackluster campaigning and media speculation about a substance-abuse problem in a divisive and hard-fought run-off against fellow SNCC veteran John LEWIS. Lewis's narrow upset victory badly damaged the two men's close friendship.

Julian Bond has embodied SNCC's ideology of the "beloved community" in his commitment to see the world in collective terms. As a university professor and political activist in the 1990s he has bridged the worlds of activism and scholarship, insisting on the relevance of past struggles to contemporary students and policymakers alike. Widely respected, he has served as a living symbol of the civil rights movement. Bond's largest audience came as he narrated the sweeping 1987 television documentary series EYES ON THE PRIZE, which chronicled the civil rights era. Early in 1998 the NAACP selected Bond as its chairman to replace the outgoing Myrlie Evers-Williams, long-time activist and widow of slain Mississippi civil rights leader Medgar EVERS.

BIBLIOGRAPHY

Bond, Julian. *A Time to Speak, A Time to Act: The Movement in Politics.* 1972.

Bond, Julian. "Introduction." In *Eyes on the Prize: America's Civil Rights Years, 1954–1965*, by Juan Williams. 1987.

Bond, Julian. "The Politics of Civil Rights History." In *New Directions in Civil Rights Studies*, edited by Armstead L. Robinson and Patricia Sullivan. 1991.

Carson, Clayborne. *In Struggle: SNCC and the Black Awakening of the 1960s.* 1981.

Lewis, John, with Michael D'Orso. *Walking with the Wind: A Memoir of the Movement.* 1998.

Neary, John. *Julian Bond: Black Rebel.* 1971.
Powledge, Fred. *Free at Last? The Civil Rights Movement and the People Who Made It.* 1991.

David C. Carter

Bonnin, Gertrude

(1876–1938), Native American activist.

Gertrude Simmons Bonnin was a noted Native American political activist and author. A granddaughter of Sitting Bull, the Sioux chief, Simmons was born in 1876 at the Yankton Sioux Agency in South Dakota. Although her father was white, she had an entirely Sioux upbringing on a reservation until the age of eight. Simmons graduated in 1895 from a Quaker school for Indians in Indiana, and subsequently entered Earlham College in Richmond, Indiana. She began a teaching career at the Carlisle Indian School in Pennsylvania upon the 1897 completion of her college studies. Under the name "Zitzala-Sa" (her Sioux name, meaning Red Bird), she published essays and short stories in magazines, having benefited from contacts at the school that gave her access to the field of publishing.

Simmons entered the New England Conservatory of Music in Boston in 1899, where she studied the violin and continued her writing, publishing *Old Indian Legends,* her first full-length work, which was a retelling of several Indian stories. Although the atmosphere of the Conservatory was much more to her liking than that of the Carlisle School, she believed she had obligations toward her fellow Sioux and so returned to South Dakota the following year.

In 1902 Simmons married Raymond Talefase Bonnin, an employee of the U.S. Indian Service and a Yankton Sioux. Once the couple moved to a reservation in Utah, Gertrude resumed teaching and worked as a clerk on an Indian reservation. She simultaneously began her Native American activism with membership in the SOCIETY OF AMERICAN INDIANS (SAI), an organization founded in 1911 primarily to encourage the assimilation of Native Americans. Its further objectives included increasing the Native American presence in the Indian Service; the pursuit of Native American land claims and CITIZENSHIP; codification of U.S. laws dealing with Native Americans; and the maintaining of the Indians' cultural heritage. Although there were preexisting advocacy groups for Native Americans, the SAI was the first such organization founded and operated by Native Americans alone.

Gertrude Bonnin moved to the nation's capital after being made secretary of SAI and editor of its publication, *American Indian Magazine.* A gifted orator from her college days, she lectured extensively on Indian rights. She testified before CONGRESS and lobbied on a variety of Indian issues, including living conditions, the depletion of natural resources, and the Indian Citizenship Bill, which was passed in 1924. (See AMERICAN INDIAN CITIZENSHIP ACT OF 1924.) Her travels exposed her to the needs of Native Americans, which she worked aggressively to bring to the attention of government officials in conjunction with other organizations such as the American Indian Defense Association. With the same objective in mind, Gertrude and her husband founded the National Council of American Indians (NCAI), of which she became president after the dissolution of the Society of American Indians in 1926. The NCAI, comprised entirely of Native Americans, attacked the Indian Service. Its campaign bore fruit when the Interior Department commissioned, in 1928, a study of the status of Native Americans as well as the effectiveness of government policies toward them. The scholars involved in the effort produced a report, "The Problem of Indian Administration," also known as the "Miriam Report," after Dr. Lewis Miriam of the Institute for Government Research, who was chief architect of the study.

The Miriam Report represented a milestone in the struggle for Native American rights and fueled the drive for reform by highlighting the poverty, illness, and poor education experienced on reservations. Mrs. Bonnin echoed the findings of the report and stressed the responsibility of the government's BUREAU OF INDIAN AFFAIRS for the situation. As a result of the report, President Herbert Hoover gave leadership roles in the Bureau to members of the Indian Rights Association, an organization that had been allied with Gertrude Bonnin's, and President Franklin D. Roosevelt would endorse the INDIAN REORGANIZATION ACT OF 1934 and the "Indian New Deal"— an offer to make Native Americans more autonomous and give them more freedom to preserve their cultural history.

Shifting attention away from writing and toward music, Mrs. Bonnin composed "Sun Dance," an Indian opera. She continued to work ardently for the amelioration of conditions on reservations as well as the INTEGRATION of Native Americans into mainstream society. Although she was part of the Pan-Indian movement (see PAN-TRIBALISM), she paid special attention to the needs of the Utes and her fellow Sioux. She died in 1938 and is buried in Arlington National Cemetery.

BIBLIOGRAPHY
Gridley, Marion E. *American Indian Women.* 1974.
Mossman, Jennifer, ed. *Reference Library of American Women.* 1999.

Sarah Kurian

Bracero Program (Public Law 78)

Beginning as an international agreement on contract labor between the United States and Mexico in 1942, the Bracero Program provided American farmers and agribusiness with cheap and tractable labor. (*Bracero* derives from *brazo*, the Spanish word for "arm." A *bracero* is one who works with his arms and performs physical labor.) The program persisted until labor and civil rights groups convinced CONGRESS to end it in 1964.

American mobilization for WORLD WAR II required huge increases in agricultural production. But by 1942, the military draft and the lure of better-paying jobs in war industries had diminished the supply of farm labor. The United States and Mexico agreed to allow Mexican nationals to work in American fields as a temporary wartime emergency measure. More than 200,000 *braceros* came north during World War II.

Although intended as a temporary wartime expediency, the power of the farm bloc in Congress—and the need for continued U.S. food exports to Europe—led to the extension of the program through 1947. In 1951, Congress codified the program in statute as Public Law 78 and the program expanded rapidly thereafter, with more than three million *braceros* working American fields between 1950 and 1960.

The Bracero Program guaranteed agribusiness a dependable source of cheap, temporary, and tractable labor. Although the 1951 law required that the program not adversely affect the country's own domestic farm workers, in reality it depressed their wages, made HOUSING scarce, and weakened union-organizing efforts. For the *braceros*, employers often provided inadequate food, housing, and medical care. In 1964, under pressure from labor and civil rights groups, Congress allowed the Bracero Program to expire. Its demise represented a victory for labor, and helped advance American farm workers' struggle for higher wages, benefits, and dignity.

BIBLIOGRAPHY
Craig, Richard B. *The Bracero Program: Interest Groups and Foreign Policy.* 1971.
Galarza, Ernesto. *Merchants of Labor: The Mexican Bracero Story.* 1964.
Gamboa, Erasmo. *Mexican Labor and World War II: Braceros in the Pacific Northwest, 1942–1947.* 1990.

Douglas W. Dodd

Braden, Anne and Carl

(1924–   and 1914–1975), labor and civil rights activists.

Their efforts to dismantle the walls of SEGREGATION landed them in court and on the front pages. The marriage of Anne and Carl Braden was a coming together of social activists. Carl introduced Anne to the LABOR MOVEMENT of the 1940s, and Anne drew Carl to her interest in race relations. Together, the Louisville, Kentucky, couple dedicated themselves to the fight against segregation. The fight took a dramatic turn in March 1954, when a black friend, Andrew Wade IV, approached the Bradens about helping him purchase a home in a newly developed white neighborhood. Although Louisville had a reputation for relatively progressive race relations, HOUSING in the city remained mostly segregated. The segregation was a matter of custom rather than law, and the Bradens readily agreed to help Wade. They bought the house in their name with money supplied by Wade and immediately deeded the residence over to him. When Wade moved to take possession of the house, he was met by an angry mob throwing rocks and burning a cross in the yard. Six weeks later, the house was bombed. When news of the Bradens' role in the transaction was revealed, the couple received numerous death threats. They were accused of conspiring to destroy the house as part of a communist plot to overthrow the state of Kentucky. Indicted for sedition and unable to meet bail, both were imprisoned to await trial. A family friend offered to post bond for Anne, and she was soon released; Carl was tried and convicted of sedition under a law that was more than a hundred years old yet had never been used, and national interest in the case began to grow. The couple used their backgrounds in journalism to help take their story before the public, and donations from a sympathetic audience paid Carl's bond a year after he was first imprisoned. His conviction was reversed on appeal in 1956, and the charges against all of the accused conspirators were dropped.

The Bradens continued to work for social change and incite the anger of government officials. After refusing to testify before the HOUSE UN-AMERICAN ACTIVITIES COMMITTEE, Carl served time in prison from 1961 to 1962. In 1967 Anne and Carl were indicted for sedition once more, this time by Pike County (Kentucky) officials, who accused them of attempting to spread communist theory in order to overthrow the local government. After the SUPREME COURT ruled in another case that state sedition laws were unconstitutional, the case against the Bradens was dismissed.

Throughout their legal battles the Bradens worked as field organizers and codirectors for the SOUTHERN CONFERENCE EDUCATIONAL FUND (SCEF), an organization dedicated to black and white cooperation in the struggle for civil rights. Carl also directed the Training Institute for Propaganda and Organizing. Following his death in 1975, Anne began working with the Southern Organizing Committee for Economic and Social Justice (SOC), continuing her fight for social justice and equality throughout the South.

BIBLIOGRAPHY

Braden, Anne. *The Wall Between.* 1958.
Obituary (for Carl Braden). *New York Times.* February 25, 1975.
Sterne, Emma Gelders. *They Took Their Stand.* 1968.
Thrasher, Sue, and Elliot Wigginton. " 'You Can't Be Neutral': An Interview with Anne Braden." *Southern Exposure* 12 (1984): 79–85.

Rochelle C. Hayes

Bradley, Tom

(1917–1998), Los Angeles mayor.

Tom Bradley was the first African-American mayor of Los Angeles, California, serving an unprecedented five terms in a metropolitan area that was only 15 to 17 percent black. The son of Texas sharecroppers and the grandson of slaves, Bradley also broke color barriers in the Los Angeles Police Department over a twenty-year period, eventually achieving the rank of lieutenant. He earned his law degree from Southwestern University in 1956, and in 1963 was the first black elected to the Los Angeles City Council, where he served three terms. He lost his first bid for mayor in 1969, but won in 1973 and was victorious in the next four elections.

An early hallmark of Bradley's mayoral career was the opening of City Hall and local governance to women and the African-American, Asian, Hispanic, and Jewish communities. He was nationally known for his ability to unify diverse communities without alienating the dominant white population. He ran for governor of California unsuccessfully in 1982 and 1986, and was considered to be on Walter Mondale's shortlist for vice president in 1984. Tom Bradley is best known as a black politician representing a predominately white constituency in a racially divided city. He calmed the fears of white voters by downplaying the issue of race; however, most analyses of his failed gubernatorial bids argue that RACISM played a dominant role in his defeats. A primary criticism of Bradley's political career is that he did not associate himself with black issues or the black community.

In this December 1976 photo, Mayor Tom Bradley of Los Angeles tells newsmen he will not consider a possible nomination to President-elect Jimmy Carter's Cabinet. In 1973 Bradley became Los Angeles's first black mayor and the first African-American mayor of a predominantly white city. He was reelected four times, completing his final term in 1993. (AP/Wide World Photos)

BIBLIOGRAPHY

Bradley, Tom. *Offshore Oil: Costs and Benefits.* 1976.
Bradley, Tom. *There are No Impossible Dreams for Possibility Thinkers.* 1984.
Bradley Administrative Papers, 1963–1993. University of California, Los Angeles, Westwood Campus.
Payne, J. Gregory, and Scott C. Ratzan. *Tom Bradley: The Impossible Dream: A Biography.* 1986.
Pettigrew, Thomas F., and Denise A. Alston. *Tom Bradley's Campaigns for Governor: The Dilemma of Race and Political Strategies.* 1988.
Sonenshein, Raphael. *Politics in Black and White: Race and Power in Los Angeles.* 1993.

Michelle Donaldson Deardorff

Branton, Wiley Austin

(1923–1988), lawyer, political campaigner, and educator.

Wiley Austin Branton remains one of the civil rights movement's unsung heroes. As director of the VOTER EDUCATION PROJECT (VEP) from 1962 to 1965, Branton played a pivotal role in the registration of 600,000 new African-American voters in the South. These votes provided an essential electoral bedrock which, alongside nonviolent protests, heralded the legislative erosion of JIM CROW in the 1960s. Up until his appointment as director of the VEP, Branton had been a civil rights activist in his native state of Arkansas. He was one of the earliest African-American graduates of the University of Arkansas Law School in 1952, and an attorney in the 1956 *Aaron v. Cooper* lawsuit, a precursor of the 1957 Little Rock School Integration Crisis. After leaving the VEP, Branton held numerous high-profile posts, such as Special Assistant to Attorneys General Nicholas Katzenbach and Ramsey Clark (1965–1967), where he worked on the enforcement of the 1965 VOTING RIGHTS ACT; Executive Director of the United Planning Organization (1967–1969), Washington D.C., antipoverty agency; Director of the Social Action Program of the Alliance for Labor Action (1969–1971); and, Dean of the Law School at Howard University (1978–1983). Throughout his career Branton remained active in the legal profession as a partner in Dolphin, Branton, Stafford and Webber (1971–1977), and Sidley and Austin (1983–1988). From 1978 until his death in 1988, he served as Vice-President of the NATIONAL ASSOCIATION FOR THE ADVANCEMENT OF COLORED PEOPLE's (NAACP's) Legal Defense Fund.

BIBLIOGRAPHY

Wiley Branton Papers. Moorland-Spingarn Archives, Howard University, Washington, D.C.

John A. Kirk

Brotherhood of Sleeping Car Porters

Brotherhood of Sleeping Car Porters (BSCP), organized in secret on August 25, 1925, became the first successful African-American labor UNION. The Pullman Company employed black porters from its inception, in 1867, thereby creating an occupation over which African Americans had a monopoly. Because of steady jobs and travel experience the porters were considered the elite of black labor, yet, because they were not unionized, they were also exploited and underpaid. Socialist journalist A. Philip RANDOLPH seized on the porters' grievances, educated them about collective bargaining and the value of trade unionism, and began organizing them. Loyal assistants, such as Milton P. WEBSTER in Chicago, Ashley Totten and Benjamin McLauren in New York, C. L. Dellums in Oakland, and E. J. Bradley in St. Louis, took care of the day-to-day detail and undercover organizing to avoid com-

pany reprisals, while Randolph obtained outside publicity and funding.

Porters' responsibilities included working long hours for little pay, making the railroad cars ready, assisting with luggage, waiting on passengers, converting seats into beds that they then had to make up, polishing shoes with supplies bought with their own money, and remaining on call twenty-four hours a day. Simultaneously, porters were indoctrinated with the idea of company "benevolence." Because many did not understand the difference between a company union and a trade union such as the BSCP, porters' reluctance to join the union (which would also jeopardize their jobs) had to be overcome. Many prominent African Americans opposed the BSCP believing company propaganda that identified Pullman as a great benefactor to the black race. Organized labor was anathema to other African Americans because they believed, with justification, that black workers were discriminated against by white unions. Despite the obstacles, membership shot up, causing Pullman to retaliate with frame-ups, beatings, and firings. Pullman had previously dealt with labor unions, but resisted bargaining with African Americans as equals.

The success of the union ultimately depended on its ability to correct grievances and provide job security; however, when the company remained intransigent the BSCP was forced to call a strike in 1928. Accustomed to taking jobs as strike breakers, African Americans knew other blacks would be eager to take their jobs. In response to rumors that Pullman had nearly 5,000 Filipinos ready to take the places of BSCP members, the head of the American Federation of Labor (AFL) advised Randolph to postpone the strike.

After the aborted strike, membership dropped and the BSCP almost ceased to exist, but the more favorable labor legislation of the Franklin ROOSEVELT administration's NEW DEAL, especially passage of the amended Railway Act of 1934, which outlawed company unions, revived the BSCP. The AFL granted the Brotherhood an international charter in 1935. After twelve years, the Pullman Company finally signed a contract with the BSCP on August 25, 1937, bringing improved working conditions and some two million dollars in income to the porters and their families. When the AFL and the Congress of Industrial Organizations (CIO) merged in 1955, Randolph became a vice-president of the new AFL-CIO, and the BSCP became instrumental in pushing the combined federation to financially back the civil rights movement.

The BSCP provided support for civil rights activity by contributing human resources and some fifty thousand dollars to Randolph's various equality movements as well. Randolph, backed by the Brotherhood, threatened a March on Washington of 100,000 blacks (to take place on July 1, 1941), to demand jobs in defense plants and integration of the armed forces. (see MARCH ON WASHINGTON MOVEMENT.) It resulted in the Roosevelt Administration's issuance of Executive Order #8802, granting a wartime FAIR EMPLOYMENT PRACTICES COMMITTEE in exchange for cancellation of the March. Although weak, FEPC provided job training and economic improvement for many African Americans. In 1948, the porter's union supported, albeit more reluctantly, Randolph's threat of a black boycott of Universal Military Training; the Truman Administration capitulated with integration of the military by Executive Order #9981. The BSCP supported the MONTGOMERY BUS BOYCOTT in 1955, Randolph's Prayer Pilgrimage in 1957, marches in Washington for integrated schools in 1958 and 1959, and the MARCH ON WASHINGTON for Jobs and Freedom in 1963.

After World War II the porters became a diminishing and aging group and in 1978 the BSCP merged with the Brotherhood of Railway and Airline Clerks. The BSCP, however, was always more than an instrumentality of service to the porters. Trained in collective bargaining, porters made demands rather than begging for favors from the white power structure. Hence the BSCP became the vanguard of the early and mid-century civil rights movement.

BIBLIOGRAPHY

Brazeal, Brailsford Reese. *The Brotherhood of Sleeping Car Porters: Its Origin and Development.* 1946.
Brotherhood of Sleeping Car Porters, Chicago Division Papers. Chicago Historical Society, Chicago, Ill.
Brotherhood of Sleeping Car Porters Papers. Library of Congress, Washington, D.C.
Harris, William H. *Keeping the Faith: A. Philip Randolph, Milton P. Webster, and the Brotherhood of Sleeping Car Porters, 1925–37.* 1977.
Pfeffer, Paula F. *A. Philip Randolph, Pioneer of the Civil Rights Movement.* 1990.
Randolph, A. Philip. "One Union's Story." *American Federationist* (November, 1953): 20–23.
Santino, Jack. *Miles of Smiles, Years of Struggle: Stories of Black Pullman Porters.* 1989.
Wilson, Joseph F. *Tearing Down the Color Bar: A Documentary History and Analysis of the Brotherhood of Sleeping Car Porters.* 1989.

Paula F. Pfeffer

Brown, H. Rap

(1943–   ), radical civil rights activist.

Born Hubert Gerald Brown on October 4, 1943, in Baton Rouge, Louisiana, Rap Brown became active in the STUDENT NONVIOLENT COORDINATING COMMIT-

On July 26, 1967, Black Power advocate and national chairman of the Student Nonviolent Coordinating Committee (SNCC) H. Rap Brown is brought before federal authorities for arraignment. He was charged with flight to escape prosecution on Maryland charges of inciting arson. (CORBIS/ Bettmann)

TEE (SNCC) while a Student at Southern University in the early 1960s. He became SNCC Alabama Project Director in 1966 and replaced Stokely CARMICHAEL as National Director in 1967 as SNCC turned sharply away from integrationism and interracialism toward black nationalism and separatism.

An advocate of alliance with the BLACK PANTHER PARTY, of which he was also a leader, armed self-defense of black communities, and community control, Brown epitomized the late 1960s menacing black revolutionary. He coined the phrase "Burn, Baby, Burn," and was quoted widely to the effect that "violence is as American as cherry pie."

As a result, he found himself in and out of jail and, in part because of his militancy, SNCC became a marginalized paper organization. Brown's 1969 book, *Die, Nigger, Die,* and his speeches advocating armed self-defense and draft resistance, made him a press scapegoat for ghetto rioting and a continuing target for police. Marginalized in the aftermath of police destruction of the Black Panther Party and other black radical groups, Brown was convicted in 1973 of involvement in a robbery in New York and sentenced to fifteen years at Attica State Prison, scene of a multiethnic prisoner insurrection two years before (see ATTICA REBELLION).

Converting to traditional Islam in prison, Brown took the name Jamil Abdullah al-Amin, and, following his parole in 1976, settled in Atlanta where he has been a storekeeper and religious community activist, briefly returning to the headlines in 1995 for an alleged gun shooting incident.

Like other New Left radicals of the time, Brown's playing to media stereotypes gave him a few years of negative celebrity. Unfortunately, this came at the expense of serious political analysis and action that might have enabled organizations like SNCC to survive police repression and the post-1960s backlash.

BIBLIOGRAPHY

Brown, H. Rap. *Die, Nigger, Die.* 1969.
Carson, Clayborne. *In Struggle: SNCC and the Black Awakening of the 1960s.* 1981.
Haskins, James. *Profiles in Black Power.* 1972.

Norman Markowitz

Brown, John Robert

(1909–1993), judge.

John R. Brown was a circuit judge of the United States Court of Appeals for the FIFTH CIRCUIT from 1955 until his death in 1992. Brown grew up in the small town of Holdredge, Nebraska, graduating from the University of Nebraska in 1930 and from the University of Michigan Law School in 1932. Following graduation, he decided to move to a more vital, growing part of the country. He chose Houston, Texas, where he became a specialist in maritime law. In 1952, like his later judicial colleagues, Judges Elbert TUTTLE and John Minor WISDOM, Brown was a leader in a pro-EISENHOWER delegation to the Republic National Convention.

President Dwight Eisenhower appointed Brown to the United States Court of Appeals for the Fifth Circuit, and, until 1981, his court dealt with all appeals of lawsuits from federal courts in Texas, Louisiana, Mississippi, Alabama, Georgia, and Florida. (After 1981, Congress created a new Eleventh Circuit, with jurisdiction over Alabama, Georgia, and Florida.) Its location made the Fifth Circuit essential to the effective implementation of the SUPREME COURT's civil rights decisions. Brown, along with Judge John Minor Wisdom of Louisiana, Judge Richard RIVES of Alabama, and Judge Elbert Tuttle of Georgia, became

known as one of "The Four"—four Fifth Circuit judges committed to protecting the rights of African Americans. One of Judge Brown's most important opinions was his 1959 dissent in *Gomillion v. Lightfoot* (see Charles GOMILLION), a case involving a gerrymander that created a twenty-eight-sided district designed to reduce the power of black voters in Tuskegee, Alabama. The Supreme Court agreed with Judge Brown's dissent and reversed the Fifth Circuit's decision, thus helping to launch a more aggressive posture toward discrimination claims in the South.

Judge Brown was chief judge of the Fifth Circuit from 1968 to 1979 and was noted for his administrative skills in dealing with the Fifth Circuit's enormous case load. He was a lively and well-liked man, noted for his use of humor in his judicial opinions. In 1984, Brown took "senior status," which allowed him to hear fewer cases. He continued to hear and decide appeals until shortly before his death in January 1993.

BIBLIOGRAPHY

Bass, Jack. *Unlikely Heroes.* 1981.
Couch, Harvey C. *A History of the Fifth Circuit, 1891–1981.* 1984.
Read, F., and I. McGough. *Let Them Be Judged.* 1978.
Texas Law Review 71 (April 1993): 903–920.

Henry T. Greeley

Brown Berets

The Brown Berets, a militant youth organization associated with the Chicano movement, emerged out of Young Citizens for Community Action (YCCA), a youth group formed by Chicano students working with Father John Luce's Social Action Training Center at the Episcopal Church of the Epiphany, which had become an influential center for youth activism in East Los Angeles.

In late 1967, YCCA opened the Piranya Coffee House to promote community consciousness and as a site for recruiting members. Shortly thereafter, the YCCA adopted a brown beret as a part of its uniform and thus became known as the Brown Berets. During its period of activity from 1967 through 1972, the Brown Berets developed into over twenty chapters and published the newspaper *La Causa*. In May 1969 the Brown Berets opened the East Los Angeles Free Clinic, offering a range of medical services. Emphasizing the right of self-determination and defense against aggression, the Brown Berets were culturally nationalist in orientation, including women as well as men and rejecting cultural assimilation and accommodationist politics. They had a formal code of conduct and ethics and a ten-point program that included housing, cultural events, employment, and education. In practice, they emphasized opposition to police brutality and discrimination in the schools, which led to a police campaign of harassment, infiltration, and disruption.

In general, the Brown Berets participated in some way in all the major events of the Chicano movement during their period of activity, including the East Los Angeles "Blow Outs" in which over 10,000 students walked out of Garfield, Roosevelt, Lincoln, and Belmont High Schools to protest educational discrimination against Chicanos. In late 1969, the Brown Berets formed the Chicano Moratorium Committee, which organized annual marches to protest the disproportionate number of Chicanos dying in the VIETNAM WAR. In 1971, the Brown Berets conducted a March Through Aztlan, marching one thousand miles from Calexico to Sacramento to protest police brutality, racial discrimination, and the Vietnam War. In 1972, they occupied Santa Catalina Island, arguing that the Channel Islands on the coast of southwestern California, not having been specifically named in the Treaty of Guadalupe Hidalgo of 1848, were still sovereign Mexican land. In late 1972, in response to repeated harassment and infiltration by police, the Brown Berets disbanded.

In 1993, the Brown Berets were recommissioned by founder David Sanchez. Since that time the Brown Berets have continued their philosophy of Chicano nationalism, but they have also experienced renewed factionalism and in-fighting. At this writing, the Brown Berets remain active in a number of communities, but are no longer operating under unified leadership. During the same period that the original Brown Beret organization was active in California, an organization called the BLACK BERETS was formed in New Mexico. It followed similar principles.

BIBLIOGRAPHY

Acuña, Rudy. *Occupied America: A History of Chicanos.* 1989.
Brown Beret Information Packet. Ethnic Studies Library, U.C. Berkeley.
Meier, Matt S., and Feliciano Rivera. *Mexican Americans/American Mexicans: From Conquistadores to Chicanos,* rev. ed. 1994.

Ron López

Brownell, Herbert, Jr.

(1904–), U.S. attorney general 1953–1957.

As U.S. Attorney General from January 1953 to September 1957, Herbert Brownell was President Dwight D. EISENHOWER's principal adviser on civil rights. Under him the Justice Department continued the Truman administration's practice of filing *amicus curiae*

briefs in the federal courts in favor of desegregation. In *District of Columbia v. John R. Thompson Co.* (1953), Brownell argued successfully before the Supreme Court that segregation of public restaurants in the nation's capital was unconstitutional. In BROWN V. BOARD OF EDUCATION (1954), Brownell sanctioned a brief on the applicability of the FOURTEENTH AMENDMENT to school desegregation which was stronger than the president preferred and was deemed "outstanding" by new Chief Justice Earl Warren. Post-*Brown*, the Attorney General believed that states should be allowed to move gradually toward school desegregation without federal compulsion, but came to adopt a tougher attitude in response to Southern intransigence. Brownell was the principal legal architect of federal intervention in the Little Rock crisis of 1957. He also drafted the administration's 1957 civil rights bill, but Eisenhower would not support a provision authorizing Justice Department intervention to compel desegregation, which was removed by Congress. The final legislation dealt mainly with black voting rights but lacked effective mechanisms to enforce these. Brownell, whose moderate stance on civil rights appeared progressive compared with the president's, became the focus of segregationist resentment. When he resigned his office to return to private law practice, the Richmond *Times Dispatch* editorialized, "The frightful mess the South, and the country, are in is probably as much his responsibility as that of any living man."

BIBLIOGRAPHY

Anderson, J. W. *Eisenhower, Brownell and the Congress.* 1964.
Burk, Robert F. *The Eisenhower Administration and Black Civil Rights.* 1984.

Iwan Morgan

Brown Power

"Brown Power" is a slogan or declaration of group self-affirmation and articulation of positive group identity, often made as part of a group chant during political and cultural demonstrations, and in Chicano/Latino political material. It is also similar to, or used in conjunction with, other phrases like "Brown Pride," "Brown and Proud," "Chicano Power," and "Chicano Pride."

"Brown Power," adapted from the black nationalist call for BLACK POWER, was first used in the late 1960s, possibly by the BROWN BERETS or by other Chicano nationalist organizations. According to a widely accepted definition, the term "Brown Power" embodied a nationalist, separatist political vision of Chicano community autonomy as well as rejection of cultural assimilation or political accommodation.

Today, the phrases "Brown Power" and "Chicano Power" are still used, although they have come to differ somewhat in their uses and meanings. For some militant Mexican Americans, "Chicano Power" is still the preferred term. On the other hand, the word "Chicano" is not accepted by many older people and newer immigrants, for whom it still carries a pejorative meaning, nor is it accepted by non-Mexican Latinos. "Brown Power" expresses more of a collective affirmation of phenotypical (skin-color) or Latino cultural identity, and hence has a wider, less specific meaning—and thus a broader appeal—than that which originally was articulated in the late 1960s.

BIBLIOGRAPHY

Acuña, Rudy. *Occupied America: A History of Chicanos.* 1989.
Gómez-Quiñones, Juan. *Chicano Politics: Reality and Promise, 1940–1990.* 1990.

Ron López

Brown v. Board of Education

In 1896 the Supreme Court, in PLESSY V. FERGUSON, upheld a Louisiana statute requiring the SEGREGATION of railroad cars as long as the facilities were "separate but equal." That decision provided legal support for more widespread segregation, including segregation in the South's elementary and secondary schools. The Supreme Court's unanimous 1954 decision in *Brown v. Board of Education* struck down that practice.

Brown was the culmination of a sustained litigation campaign conducted by Thurgood MARSHALL and the NATIONAL ASSOCIATION FOR THE ADVANCEMENT OF COLORED PEOPLE (NAACP). Beginning in the mid-1930s, Marshall and his colleagues challenged the exclusion of African Americans from Southern universities. The NAACP's lawyers also attacked the Southern practice of paying African-American teachers less than whites. Together these cases established two propositions that Marshall used to attack segregation directly: separate facilities had to be truly equal, and equality had to be measured with reference to a school's intangible qualities, not only its material endowments.

Brown involved five separate cases from Kansas, Virginia, South Carolina, Delaware, and the District of Columbia. The Supreme Court first heard the cases argued in 1952. The justices were unable to reach a decision and the Court directed the lawyers to reargue the cases, devoting special attention to the original understandings with respect to segregated education.

On May 17, 1954, the Supreme Court rules in Brown v. Board of Education *that segregation in public schools is unconstitutional. The attorneys who argued the case against segregation stand together in front of the U.S. Supreme Court building. From left to right: George E. C. Hayes, Thurgood Marshall, and James Nabrit, Jr.* (CORBIS/Bettmann)

By the time the cases were reargued, Earl WARREN had replaced Fred Vinson as Chief Justice. Warren overcame reluctance from justices Robert Jackson and Stanley Reed and led the Court to its unanimous decision. Warren's brisk opinion found the historical evidence inconclusive, and stated that segregation by law "generates a feeling of inferiority . . . that may affect [students'] hearts and minds in a way unlikely ever to be undone." Warren supported this conclusion with a controversial footnote referring to "modern authority" from social psychologists. The opinion found that "the doctrine of 'separate but equal' has no place" in public education.

The justices knew that DESEGREGATION would be difficult, and they asked the lawyers to argue once again the question of the appropriate remedy. The second *Brown* decision held that the Constitution allowed the states to desegregate their schools "with all deliberate speed." Southerners opposed to desegregation seized upon this phrase to justify tactics of obstruction and delay. Although some border states accomplished significant desegregation quickly, substantial desegregation did not occur in the deep South until the mid-1960s.

Brown was decided at the outset of the modern civil rights movement. Movement leaders stated that *Brown* influenced their activities, if only because it offered a dramatic statement that the nation's highest court believed that the Constitution supported civil rights claims. But the slow pace of desegregation made it easy to criticize *Brown* as ineffective. Responding to Southern recalcitrance, the courts began to insist on more drastic steps such as busing, which made desegregation policy even more controversial. Migration from the South, and from inner cities to suburbs, meant that it was increasingly difficult to accomplish real integration within a single school district, but the Supreme Court held that the Constitution rarely required interdistrict desegregation remedies. By the early 1990s the nation's experiment with judicial efforts to require integration was largely over.

BIBLIOGRAPHY

Kluger, Richard. *Simple Justice.* 1975.
Rosenberg, Gerald. *The Hollow Hope: Can Courts Bring About Social Change?* 1991.
Tushnet, Mark. *Making Civil Rights Law: Thurgood Marshall and the Supreme Court, 1936–1961* (1994).

Mark Tushnet

Bruce, Blanche Kelso

(1841–1898), U.S. Senator.

Blanche K. Bruce, a black RECONSTRUCTION-era political leader in MISSISSIPPI, was elected to the United

Born a Mississippi slave, Blanche K. Bruce was the second African American to be elected to the U.S. Senate and the first to serve an entire six-year term. After Reconstruction he left Mississippi and moved to Washington, D.C., where he became a leader of the city's black elite. (Prints and Photographs Division, Library of Congress)

States Senate in 1874. Born in Farmville, Virginia, in 1841 to a slave woman and a white man—probably her master—Bruce received an education on his master's plantation through a tutor he shared with the master's son. Bruce's master later moved to MISSOURI, taking his slaves with him. During the Civil War, Bruce escaped to KANSAS; in 1864, he moved to Hannibal, Missouri (where slavery had been abolished), and established a school for African Americans.

In 1869, after moving to Bolivar County, Mississippi, Bruce became involved in local politics. In Mississippi, where blacks outnumbered whites, he rose through the ranks of the Republican Party. At one point in his career, Bruce, who had dominated a powerful political machine in Bolivar County, simultaneously held the offices of sheriff, tax collector, and superintendent of education. During his tenure as superintendent he expanded and developed the county's schools, which served over one thousand black and white children. A man of wealth and refinement by the time he was elected to the U.S. Senate in 1874, Bruce became the second black senator elected during Reconstruction. Taking office on March 5, 1875, Bruce frequently spoke out in defense of the rights of African Americans. He opposed all efforts to promote the migration of African Americans to Liberia. As chairman of the investigation into the failed Freedman's Savings and Trust Company, Bruce conducted a highly detailed inquiry into the corrupt handling of approximately $56 million in deposits of former slaves. He served on the Pensions, Manufactures, and Education and Labor Committees, and on the Select Committee on Mississippi River Improvements. In Washington, D.C., Bruce became a member of the city's black elite, and after serving his term in the Senate, Bruce and his wife, Josephine, chose to remain in the nation's capital. There, Bruce held various civil service positions and remained active in politics until his death in 1898.

BIBLIOGRAPHY

Blanche K. Bruce Papers. Howard University.
Gatewood, Willard B. *Aristocrats of Color: The Black Elite, 1880–1920.* 1990.
Harris, William C. "Blanche K. Bruce of Mississippi: Conservative Assimilationist." In *Southern Black Leaders of the Reconstruction Era,* edited by Howard N. Rabinowitz. 1982.
Shapiro, Samuel. "A Black Senator from Mississippi: Blanche K. Bruce (1841–1898)." *Review of Politics* 44 (1982): 85–88.

Alicia E. Rodriquez

Portrait of Ralph J. Bunche, Under Secretary of the United Nations, Nobel Prize laureate, and Member/ Trustee of the Rockefeller Foundation. (Archive Photos)

Bunche, Ralph J.

(1903–1971), Nobel Peace Prize winner, author.

Ralph J. Bunche was the first person of African descent to win a Nobel Peace Prize. Just as he was about to graduate at the top of his class at the University of California at Los Angeles in 1927, Bunche wrote to W. E. B. DU BOIS asking for the older man's help in reaching his goal of service to "my group." By his mid-twenties Bunche was already an accomplished scholar, athlete, and youth leader. Moreover, he was headed to Harvard—Du Bois's alma mater—to study political science, which had been an early interest of the older man. Yet, within a few years their careers would diverge dramatically as Bunche became the ultimate "insider" while Du Bois moved further and further from the mainstream.

Bunche's political views would move from the left to the center over the years as he filled posts of increasing responsibility. Born in Detroit and losing his mother at an early age, Bunche was raised by his maternal grandmother and began to blossom when the family moved to Albuquerque and then Los Angeles in 1918. He followed his racial "firsts" as valedictorian of his high school and college graduating classes with the first doctorate achieved in political science in the United States by an African American. In addition, his dissertation, "French Administration in Togoland and Dahomey," was awarded a prize as the best of the year in the Government Department at Harvard. Taking a position at Howard University in Washington, D.C., there he established the Political Science Department and became the principal black social scientist on the influential Carnegie-Myrdal study on American race relations. He left Howard, at first temporarily, to serve as the only black section head in the Office of Strategic Services during World War II. Bunche then moved to the State Department as the first black desk officer, and then the only black in the U.S. delegation to the meetings that established the United Nations. In these meetings, Bunche sought to promote decolonization through the process of UN Trusteeship of the colonies. His work led the UN to offer him the position of director of the Trusteeship Division which he accepted in 1947.

In 1950, Bunche won the Nobel Peace Prize for his role in the mediation of the Palestinian conflict in the Middle East. He was the first UN official to head peace-keeping operations and played a major role in such crises as Cyprus, Sinai, Yemen, the Congo, and Bahrain. Bunche was the first African American to serve as president of the American Political Science Association and retired as undersecretary-general of the United Nations—the highest ranking black in that body at that time. He also declined a number of other potential firsts, including a position as assistant secretary of state and an offer to teach at Harvard.

After winning the Nobel Peace Prize, Bunche became the best-known black American in the world outside of sports figures such as Jackie Robinson and Joe Louis. At one point he had accumulated more honorary degrees than any living American and a host of schools and streets were named after him. His fame came at the height of the COLD WAR and had an ironic impact on race relations. Defenders of the racial status quo in the United States used Bunche's accomplishments to deny Soviet charges of racial oppression. In other words, prosegregationists viewed Bunche's achievements as evidence that race relations were improving. This despite the fact that Bunche had been a founder of the leftist NATIONAL NEGRO CONGRESS in 1935 and was an ardent supporter of the emerging civil rights movement. In fact, Bunche was a role model for such civil rights leaders as Martin Luther KING, JR., and Andrew Young. Nonetheless, Bunche was denounced as a token by the BLACK POWER movement and largely forgotten by those coming of age in the 1960s. Although he produced a number of influential articles in the 1930s, his only book-length manuscript was *A World View of Race* published in 1936. As his life drew to a close in 1971, Bunche realized that he had been a role model few could follow and endorsed his own version of Black Power. In response to the urban violence of the late 1960s he said: "Racism, white or black, is a sickness, and a society in which it is prevalent is an afflicted society. The black American can attain no major goals in the American society except by his own determined, united, and unrelenting effort. He must believe in himself, he must know and have pride in himself, his background, and his culture. In these respects, Black Power serves a necessary purpose."

BIBLIOGRAPHY

Henry, Charles P., ed. *Ralph Bunche: Selected Speeches and Writings.* 1995.

Mann, Peggy. *Ralph Bunche, U.N. Peacemaker.* 1975.
Rivlin, Benjamin, ed. *Ralph Bunche: The Man and His Times.* 1988.
Urquhart, Brian. *Ralph Bunche: An American Life.* 1993.

Charles P. Henry

Bureau of Indian Affairs

The Bureau of Indian Affairs (BIA), alternatively known as the Office of Indian Affairs, Indian Office, and Indian Department, is the federal agency responsible for administering policies for Indian nations and communities. Its civil rights record is mixed, as it has acted both to protect fundamental liberties and as the agency responsible for implementing land cessions and cultural assimilation. This is partly the result of divergent notions regarding civil rights, since granting Indians the same set of liberties as those of all Americans can be interpreted as undermining important cultural and legal distinctions that mark Indians as something other than just another American "minority."

Formally established in 1824 by Secretary of War John C. Calhoun (an executive decision ratified by Congress in 1832 upon the request of the first Indian commissioner Thomas L. McKenney), the BIA centralized functions previously conducted by officers of the executive branch, and prior to the creation of the U.S. government by the Continental Congress, colonial legislative bodies, and colonial powers themselves. For much of the nineteenth century, the BIA, through its officers in the field—agents and superintendents—was charged with administering U.S. Indian policies that generally operated according to two interrelated aims: separating Indians from their lands and assimilating individuals into the cultural mainstream. This included supervising commercial and diplomatic relations, overseeing the distribution of funds and services as mandated by treaties, and implementing various "civilizing" initiatives. Far more effective at securing lands than in protecting Indian civil rights, policy aims were laid bare during the Indian Removal tragedy of the 1830s and 1840s, which proved that land hunger outweighed promises for full participation in American society, even when Indians agreed to alter their cultural ways.

With the acquisition of vast western lands, the BIA, located within the Interior Department since 1849, accelerated its activities. Under the Peace Policy, implemented in stages from 1869 to 1871, Congress endorsed the practice of consolidating Indians on reservations, but placed BIA agents under the nominal authority of religious (primarily Protestant) denominations and made them subject to oversight by the civilian Board of Indian Commissioners. These initiatives were designed to retard widespread corruption in the Indian service, while the appointment of the first Native American, Ely S. Parker (Seneca), to the post of Indian commissioner, was supposed to enhance the bureau's legitimacy. The successor policy, the General Allotment Act of 1887, aimed to subdivide reservations into individual homesteads, thereby dismantling tribal identities considered so injurious to Indian cultural "progress." For the most part, BIA officials endorsed allotment and implemented it enthusiastically and with little regard for the harm it caused Indians. This practice was coincident with other policy objectives, namely, sending children to off-reservation boarding schools, such as the famous Carlisle Indian Industrial School in Pennsylvania, and prohibitions on religious practices. The BIA, then, proved an effective, and sometimes brutal, tool for implementing policies few Indians desired.

During the twentieth century, policy has shifted between forced assimilation and acceptance of Indian self-determination, and this has rendered the BIA's role more complicated and controversial. While some early twentieth-century activists, notably many Native Americans associated with the assimilationist Society of American Indians, called for outright abolition, others sought to reorient its mission. This second agenda culminated with the INDIAN REORGANIZATION ACT OF 1934, which aimed at restoring the Indian land base, promoting self-government, and recognizing the intrinsic worth of Indian values, life ways, and religious practices—goals which accorded more closely with Indian conceptions of civil rights. But even this did not necessarily translate into a reduced BIA role as officials still directed policy and sometimes came to dominate tribal governments.

Forced assimilation again became policy during the 1950s, as BIA officials were actively involved in selecting tribes "ready" for the withdrawal, or termination, of federally recognized status and hence protections. A policy opposed by most Indians, BIA officials nevertheless played a critical role in its most dramatic failures—"termination" of the Menominee and Klamath tribal governments. But by the 1960s, Indian activists, bolstered by favorable court decisions and a public more sympathetic to Indian rights, had partially reversed policy. The BIA accommodated changing times unevenly. It often reacted negatively to the transfer of authority to other federal agencies or to tribes themselves, and Indian activists came to consider the BIA an agency of oppression. At their best, however, BIA agents supported respect for treaty obligations, fishing rights, and religious freedoms.

This complicated legacy endures. While the Indian Self-Determination and Educational Assistance Act of 1975 allows tribal governments to deliver services formally administered by the BIA, and Indians assert the right to speak for themselves, the federal government continues to dominate many aspects of tribal governance. Tension exists in other areas as well, such as the official sanctioning of "tribal" religions, where general notions of civil rights and tribal prerogatives are in conflict. But most Indians support a continued role for the BIA. The office remains a critical link to official Washington and its mere existence affirms the distinctive nature of tribal sovereignty and, by extension, Indian civil rights.

BIBLIOGRAPHY

Berkhofer, Robert F. *The White Man's Indian: Images of the Indian from Columbus to the Present.* 1978.
Hoxie, Frederick E. *A Final Promise: The Campaign to Assimilate the Indians, 1880–1920.* 1984.
Kvasnicka, Robert M., and Herman J. Viola, eds. *The Commissioners of Indian Affairs, 1824–1977.* 1979.
Philp, Kenneth R., ed. *Indian Self-Rule: First-Hand Accounts of Indian–White Relations from Roosevelt to Reagan.* 1986.
Prucha, Francis Paul. *The Great Father: The United States Government and the American Indians,* 2 vols. 1984.

Brian C. Hosmer

Bureau of Refugees, Freedmen, and Abandoned Lands

Commonly known as the "Freedmen's Bureau," the Bureau of Refugees, Freedmen, and Abandoned Lands was the federal agency that oversaw emancipation in the former slave states after the Civil War. Officially designed to protect the rights of the ex-slaves against intrusion by their former masters, the bureau is seen by some historians as paternalistic. In this view, the Freedmen's Bureau pursued "social control" of the freedpeople, encouraging them to return to work as plantation wage laborers.

The Freedmen's Bureau developed out of wartime private relief efforts directed at the "contrabands" who had fled to Union lines. The bureau emerged at the suggestion of the American Freedmen's Inquiry Commission, an investigative body set up by the War Department. After long debate, CONGRESS established the bureau on March 3, 1865, as a military agency. Intended as a temporary organization to exist for one year after the official end of the rebellion, the bureau had "control of all subjects relating to . . . freedmen from rebel States." In addition, it would undertake white refugee relief and manage confiscated Confederate property. The commissioner of the bureau,

Oliver Otis Howard, was known as the "Christian general" for his philanthropic interests and Congregationalist religious enthusiasm. Howard eventually presided over a network of almost one thousand local military and civilian agents scattered across the South, nearly all of them white.

Initially, Howard and his subordinates hoped to provide the rumored forty acres and a mule to at least some freedpeople from plantations seized by the government during the war. Congress had tentatively authorized some land redistribution, and Howard's office drafted Circular 13, which would have implemented the distribution of land in bureau possession. However, President Andrew Johnson countermanded the proposal, and his policy of widespread pardons for ex-Confederates restored most property to its former owners. Stymied, Howard then felt obliged to evict the freedpeople from the lands given them under the "Sherman grant," which were located on the Sea Islands and coastal areas of South Carolina and Georgia. Thus, by the late summer of 1865, Howard abandoned land redistribution and turned his attention to more attainable goals.

The bureau's remaining areas of activity were broad. It assumed responsibility for aiding the destitute—white and black—and for the care of ill, aged, and insane freedpeople. It also subsidized and sponsored educational efforts directed at the African-American community, developed both by the freedpeople themselves and by the various Northern missionary societies. The founding of Howard University, for example, resulted in large part from the general's efforts. The postwar years witnessed an explosive growth in black education, and the bureau encouraged this development in the face of white Southern opposition. The bureau's agents also assumed the duty of securing minimal legal rights for the freedmen, especially the right to testify in court.

Perhaps the bureau's most enduring, and controversial, aspect was its role in overseeing the emergence of free labor. The bureau fell heir to repressive wartime labor codes, in the Mississippi Valley and elsewhere, designed to stabilize the labor of ex-slaves once behind Union lines. While the agency attempted to protect the freedpeople from impositions by their former masters, the freedpeople also were enjoined to labor diligently. The favored bureau device for adjusting plantation agriculture was the annual labor contract, as approved by the local bureau agent. Tens of thousands of standardized contracts were written and enforced by the bureau in 1865 and 1866. The contracts it approved generally provided for wage labor under circumstances reminiscent of slavery: gang labor, tight supervision, women and children in the workforce, and provisions restricting the physical mobility and deportment of the freedmen.

In practice, bureau agents spent much of their time encouraging diligent labor by the freedmen, quashing rumors of impending land redistribution, and even punishing the freedmen for refractory behavior. In some cases, agents issued and enforced vagrancy codes directed at the freedpeople. Despite encouraging the freedmen to act as disciplined wage laborers, the bureau soon incurred the enmity of the planters. It insisted that corporal punishment be abandoned, and backed this policy up with frequent arrests. It also established a dual legal structure, with local agents acting as judges in those instances where the civilian courts refused to hear blacks' testimony or committed flagrant injustice. Finally, the bureau and the military opposed the efforts of the conservative presidential Reconstruction governments to impose harsh vagrancy laws, through the Black Codes and similar legislation. President Andrew Johnson heeded the complaints of the planters, and in February 1866 vetoed legislation providing for the extension of bureau activities. The Freedmen's Bureau became a focus of the emerging political struggle between Johnson and Congress for the control of Reconstruction. With the increasing power of the Republican Party and especially the Radical faction, the bureau secured powerful political sponsorship. Its functions were extended over Johnson's veto in July 1866. That veto became a major campaign issue in the fall 1866 congressional elections, resulting in Johnson's sweeping repudiation by the Northern electorate. With the enactment of congressional Reconstruction and black suffrage in March 1867, Freedmen's Bureau personnel tended to become involved with the resulting political mobilization. For example, in South Carolina, Assistant Commissioner Robert K. Scott would be elected the state's first Republican governor, and in Alabama several of the initial Republicans were bureau officials. Though they were widely denounced as "carpetbaggers," bureau agents exercised an important role in the politicization of the freedpeople through mass Republican clubs such as the Union League.

The restoration of most of the Southern states under the military Reconstruction acts furnished the immediate cause of the bureau's demise. The agency was always seen as temporary, and with reconstructed Southern governments granting the freedpeople equal legal rights, there no longer appeared to be any need for interference in local legal functions. The expansive powers of the Freedmen's Bureau violated states rights taboos, and the expense of the bureau's programs proved unpopular with the Northern public. The renewal bill of July 1866 provided for the organization's essential termination in two years' time.

Later legislation changed that date to the end of 1868, and after that time only the bureau's education division and efforts to secure bounties owed to black veterans continued. On June 30, 1872, these operations ended, and the Freedmen's Bureau ceased to exist. The timing of the bureau's withdrawal was unfortunate in that it coincided with the emergence of the KU KLUX KLAN across the South.

The Freedmen's Bureau represented the federal government's first substantial foray into direct provision of aid to impoverished citizens. Many of the bureau's aims were laudable, and its accomplishments in promoting black legal rights and education were substantial. Its humanitarian intervention was crucial as well, though the agency's overall record is controversial among historians. In abandoning land redistribution and in promoting the return of ex-slaves to plantation agriculture as hired labor under the contract system, the bureau also assisted in the survival of the plantation economy. In cultural terms, it strongly encouraged Victorian values among the freedpeople, especially male leadership of the family. Thus it can be seen as furthering socially conservative objectives along with more egalitarian ones; but, whatever its limitations, the emancipated population generally viewed the bureau as helpful relative to the Southern power structure.

BIBLIOGRAPHY

Bentley, George R. *A History of the Freedmen's Bureau*. 1955.
Cimbala, Paul A. *Under the Guardianship of the Nation: The Freedmen's Bureau and the Reconstruction of Georgia, 1865–1870*. 1997.
Foner, Eric. *Reconstruction: America's Unfinished Revolution, 1863–1877*. 1988.
McFeely, William S. *Yankee Stepfather: General O. O. Howard and the Freedmen*. 1968.

Michael W. Fitzgerald

Burnham, Louis E.

(1915–1960), civil rights activist, journalist.

Louis E. Burnham was born and raised in Harlem. His Caribbean parents were in the Garvey movement (see UNIVERSAL NEGRO IMPROVEMENT ASSOCIATION). From his early years, Louis was influenced by street-corner speakers such as Marcus GARVEY and A. Phillip RANDOLPH, who used their oratorical skills to organize the community in the struggle for jobs, racial equality, and an end to JIM CROW.

Burnham attended the Townsend Harris High School and City College of New York (CCNY). He developed excellent debating and oratorical skills. In his second year in college, he won the Upsilon Chi Gamma oratorical contest, his subject being "Of What Value Is a National Negro Congress?" It is clear that he had made the commitment to use his public platform skills to organize and fight for justice.

At CCNY he became completely involved in the student progressive movement. He was the president of the Frederick Douglass Society, a black students' organization, and vice president of CCNY's student council. At the same time he was active on the streets of Harlem, joining Adam Clayton POWELL, Jr., in the campaign for jobs on 125th Street and speaking on behalf of the Scottsboro Boys (see SCOTTSBORO CASE) and Angelo Herndon.

After leaving City College, he traveled south, organizing the first chapters of the American Student Union on black campuses. At that time he was also involved in organizing for the Harlem Youth League and the youth chapter of the NATIONAL NEGRO CONGRESS. In 1940 he ran on the American Labor Party ticket for State Assembly.

In 1941 Louis Burnham moved to Birmingham with his new wife Dorothy Burnham to take a position as executive secretary of the SOUTHERN NEGRO YOUTH CONGRESS (SNYC). He traveled throughout the South, speaking on college campuses, in the churches, at trade union meetings, and to rural youths. He played a key role in that period, organizing youths and adults throughout the South to join the struggle for civil rights, jobs, and education. During this period he helped to organize the Southern Association of Sharecroppers, Tenant Farmers, and Wage Laborers. With the other leaders of the SNYC, he organized the highly successful Southern Youth Legislature at the South Carolina Conference of the SNYC, in 1946, which brought together hundreds of Southern youths and participants like Paul ROBESON, Modjeska SIMKINS, and W.E.B. DU BOIS.

In 1948 Louis Burnham was organizing for the Birmingham conference of the SNYC. The SNYC immediately met with resistance from Birmingham Mayor Eugene "Bull" CONNOR and the Birmingham police force when they were informed that the conference meetings would not be segregated. Louis and the ministers of the churches were detained and threatened by Bull Connor, and a few of the churches withdrew their support. The Rev. Herbert Oliver offered his church, the Alliance Gospel Tabernacle, for the meeting, but both he and Senator Glen Taylor, the 1948 vice presidential candidate for the PROGRESSIVE PARTY, were arrested when Taylor (who was white) attempted to enter the church through the door designated for "colored."

Later in 1948, Burnham campaigned with Glen Taylor and Henry WALLACE in support of the Progressive Party and its program. In 1951 the newspaper

FREEDOM was born, with Louis Burnham as its editor. The paper provided a voice for Paul Robeson and many other black progressives who were hounded and persecuted during the McCarthy period (see MCCARTHYISM). Regular contributors included Paul Robeson, Lorraine HANSBERRY, George Murphy, Alice Childress, Vicki Garvin, W. E. B. Du Bois, and many others. The paper covered news of freedom struggles around the world. As editor Burnham was able to get correspondents from the Caribbean and from Africa to report on the struggles against COLONIALISM. Education, tenants' organizations, trade union battles, and black culture were all part of the mix in *Freedom.* Paul Robeson's regular column, "Here's My Story," reflected the political and cultural life of this great leader, who was persecuted and deprived of a livelihood because of his dedication to freedom.

Louis Burnham worked as a journalist for the *National Guardian* from 1957 to 1960. In this setting he was able to bring to an integrated audience the news of the struggle for human rights being waged in the African-American community and throughout the world. He covered news about school INTEGRATION, the HOUSE UN-AMERICAN ACTIVITIES COMMITTEE's witch hunt against those fighting Jim Crow practices and on behalf of VOTING RIGHTS and labor struggles (see LABOR MOVEMENT).

Meanwhile he continued speaking to audiences all over the country—teaching, preaching, and campaigning for justice, equality, and liberty. On February 12, 1960, during Negro History Week Celebrations, Burnham collapsed on the platform while speaking about the history and future of the civil rights movement. The *National Guardian* wrote "The life and work of Louis Burnham was linked to the great upsurges taking place toward human equality in the world today and tribute is paid to his effectiveness in the activities and movements to which he devoted his life."

BIBLIOGRAPHY

Burnham, Louis. *Behind the Lynching of Emmet Louis Till.* 1955.
Burnham, Louis, and Norval Welsh, eds. *A Star to Steer By as Told by Hugh Mulzac: Captain of the Booker T. Washington.* 1963.
Dittmer, John. *Local People: The Struggle for Civil Rights in Mississippi.* 1994.
Obituary. *National Guardian,* May 9, 1960.

Donny Barnett

Bush, George Herbert Walker

(1924–   ), U.S. president, 1989–1993.

George Bush, the forty-first president of the United States, was raised in a wealthy New England family. He completed his formal education at Yale and made his fortune as an oilman in West Texas. His civil rights record is a study in contrasts and inconsistencies. His private life is one without the taint of bigotry. In his last year at Yale, he organized the campus fund-raising drive for the United Negro College Fund. While a young businessman in the South, his liberal civil rights attitudes were a liability.

Bush became increasingly active in politics in the 1960s as a Goldwater Republican. In 1964 he was unsuccessful when he ran against Ralph Yarborough for a Texas senate seat. He attacked Yarborough for his liberal stand on civil rights, particularly his vote for the CIVIL RIGHTS ACT OF 1964. While Bush expressed racial sympathy for the social and political injustices suffered by African Americans, he argued that interference by the federal government would be ineffective and a threat to the civil rights of all citizens. He emphasized the use of moral persuasion as the best method for gaining civil equality. During his 1966 campaign for a seat in the House of Representatives, Bush received press coverage when he sponsored an African-American girls' softball team that won an integrated tournament. He won with the help of 35 percent of the Hispanic and African-American voters.

In 1966, as a discussion in Congress on a bill to end discrimination in housing progressed, Bush remained opposed to federal action. Yet despite the political consequences back in Houston, he voted for the Civil Rights Act of 1968 which was intended to guarantee open housing. After the assassination of Dr. Martin Luther KING, JR., Bush visited the Rev. Ralph ABERNATHY's Resurrection City in Washington, D.C.

Ronald Reagan picked Bush as his running mate for the 1980 presidential campaign. Vice President Bush was instrumental in directing funds and other federal assistance to the Atlanta Police Department to help capture the murderer of twenty-eight African-American children and to deal with the aftermath of those crimes. In the 1988 presidential campaign, Bush was accused of racial politics when he attacked Governor Michael Dukakis for a Massachusetts prison program that released Willie Horton, an African American who had committed heinous crimes during his furlough.

Shortly after this election, President Bush appeared with African-American leaders and condemned bigotry, but civil rights initiatives from his administration were few and not of great significance. The president's 1991 appointment of Clarence Thomas to the Supreme Court was controversial. Thomas was an African American who was critical of affirmative action programs. Sexual harassment charges against Thomas further weakened the effect of this appointment. In 1990 the president vigorously campaigned for Senator

Jesse Helms of North Carolina. The Helms campaign had attempted to intimidate African-American voters. In 1990 Congress passed a civil rights bill with the aim of assisting women and minorities in proving workplace discrimination. Bush vetoed the bill, insisting that it supported racial quotas. However, in 1991 he signed a similar bill.

BIBLIOGRAPHY

Bush, Barbara. *Barbara Bush: A Memoir.* 1994.
Duffy, Michael, and Dan Goodgame. *Marching in Place: The Status Quo Presidency of George Bush.* 1992.
Germond, Jack W., and Jules Witcover. *Whose Broad Stripes and Bright Stars? The Trivial Pursuit of the Presidency.* 1988.
Parmet, Herbert S. *George Bush: The Life of a Lone Star Yankee.* 1997.
Woodward, Bob. *The Commanders.* 1991.

Frank R. Martinie

Busing

This controversial SCHOOL DESEGREGATION method arose from the U.S. SUPREME COURT's frustration over resistance to its unanimous 1954 BROWN V. BOARD OF EDUCATION decision. The Court's declaration in *Brown II* (1955), that school districts should desegregate with "all deliberate speed," became an excuse for districts' slow implementation.

In the 1960s the Supreme Court moved more aggressively against dual school systems. In *Green v. New Kent County School Board* (1968), the Court voided a Virginia county's "freedom of choice" plan, which produced little desegregation due to whites' pressure on black families not to enroll children in white schools and blacks' reluctance to go where they were obviously not wanted. The Court further allowed district courts to supervise desegregation plans.

Following Earl WARREN's retirement and Warren Burger's appointment as Chief Justice, the Court expressed its impatience most dramatically in *Alexander v. Holmes County Board of Education* (1969). In this decision thirty-three Mississippi districts were ordered to desegregate "at once."

Busing soon followed these precedents that expanded federal courts' power. Black families sued the Charlotte–Mecklenburg County (North Carolina) School Board over the closing of black schools. Seeing that two-thirds of Charlotte's 21,000 black students attended schools that were more than 99 percent black, Federal District Judge James McMillan approved educational specialist John Finger's plan to bus black and white students between clustered inner-city and outlying schools. After the FOURTH CIRCUIT Court of Appeals rejected busing of elementary school students,

the plaintiffs, represented by North Carolina native and NAACP-affiliated attorney Julius LeVonne Chambers, appealed to the Supreme Court. The conservative Burger and liberal justices William Brennan and Thurgood MARSHALL rallied unanimously behind a compromise opinion in *Swann v. Charlotte-Mecklenburg Board of Education* (1971), which endorsed McMillan's order without elementary-school busing and fixed enrollment ratios.

Busing was difficult enough in geographically large Southern districts with histories of *de jure* SEGREGATION. Federal courts unleashed greater controversy by implementing busing outside the South to rectify *de facto* segregation. In 1973, the Supreme Court first legitimated busing outside Dixie in *Keyes v. Denver School District No. 1*, finding Denver schools had racially gerrymandered feeder patterns. Families (that included a total of over 4,000 children) wealthy enough to do so moved to suburbs in order to avoid busing.

In Boston, Federal Judge W. Arthur Garrity's 1974 busing decree sparked hostile reaction, particularly from South Boston's Irish and East Boston's Italian communities. Led by housewife Pixie Palladino and School Committeewoman Louise Hicks and supported by President Richard NIXON, anti-busing protesters staged 1960s-style marches for neighborhood schools. Boston's School Committee, having long fought Massachusetts's Racial Imbalance Act (1965)—which mandated busing—canceled plans to balance enrollment at a new elementary school. The subsequent lawsuit of area blacks prompted Garrity's order. Violent racial incidents plagued affected high schools such as South Boston and Hyde Park High Schools.

Detroit's busing case ensued when the Michigan legislature, fearful of white protest, repealed a desegregation provision within legislation approving decentralization of Detroit's School Board. The NAACP sued the Board and state defendants, including Governor William Milliken. Finding Detroit schools segregated in 1972, Federal District Judge Stephen Roth accepted a white Detroit parents organization's metropolitan busing proposal. The state school board formulated a busing plan encompassing fifty-three districts. On the state's and suburbs' appeal, the Supreme Court in its five-to-four MILLIKEN V. BRADLEY (1974) decision rejected interdistrict busing, declaring that plaintiffs must prove intentional discrimination by the state and suburbs.

In *Milliken II* (1977) the Court ordered Michigan to compensate Detroit schools for past segregation. District Judge Robert DiMascio in 1978 approved a moderate intradistrict desegregation plan that transported 9 percent of Detroit's students. Success of school desegregation in Detroit, where the African-

Buses with African-American students head for South Boston High School in October 1974. The buses have a police escort in preparation for any outbreak of violence. (Archive Photos)

American population grew from 4 percent in 1920 to 63 percent in 1980, was limited. Court supervision ended in 1989 with little improvement in the Detroit schools' standardized test results.

As the five-to-four Milliken ruling symbolized, busing, like affirmative action, divided the former liberal consensus on civil rights. Writing in *Public Interest*, for example, Daniel Patrick Moynihan declared, "Desegregation is one thing, busing another," and Nathan Glazer condemned an "imperial judiciary" that dictated painstaking requirements.

Today pro-busing analysts, such as Gary Orfield and his colleagues, criticize the Supreme Court's retrenchment on desegregation in the 1980s and 1990s by justices more sympathetic to neighborhood schools. The decisions *Riddick v. School Board of the City of Norfolk, Virginia* (1986), *Board of Education of Oklahoma v. Dowell* (1991), and *Freeman v. Pitts* (1992) freed school districts from federal courts' supervision once they were judged unitary (as opposed to a dual system, with separate black and white schools), allowing districts to return to neighborhood schools. The *Missouri v. Jenkins* decision (1995) allowed time limits on *Milliken II* equalization measures even if positive results were not documented.

BIBLIOGRAPHY

Cooper, Phillip J. *Hard Judicial Choices: Federal District Court Judges and State and Local Officials.* 1988.
Formisano, Ronald P. *Boston Against Busing: Race, Class, and Ethnicity in the 1960s and 1970s.* 1991.
Glazer, Nathan. "Towards an Imperial Judiciary?" *Public Interest* 41 (Fall 1975): 104–123.
Kalodner, Howard I., and James J. Fishman, eds. *Limits of Justice: The Courts' Role in School Desegregation.* 1978.
Moynihan, Daniel Patrick. "The Schism in Black America." *Public Interest* 27 (Spring 1972): 3–24.
Orfield, Gary, Susan E. Eaton, and the Harvard Project on School Desegregation. *Dismantling Desegregation: The Quiet Reversal of* Brown v. Board of Education. 1996.
Schwartz, Bernard. *Swann's Way: The School Busing Case and the Supreme Court.* 1986.

Wes Borucki

Byrd, Harry Flood

(1887–1966), politician, segregationist.

As governor of VIRGINIA (1926–1930), United States Senator (1933–1965), and longtime leader of the state DEMOCRATIC PARTY, Harry Byrd dominated the politics of the Old Dominion for over forty years. A self-made newspaperman and apple orchardist, Byrd was a successful governor who, unlike many Southern politicians of his day, rarely made use of race in political campaigns and was responsible for the 1928 passage of Virginia's anti-lynching law.

However, the economic and demographic revolutions unleashed by WORLD WAR II threatened Byrd's control of Virginia politics. Frustrated by continuing federal interference in state affairs and encouraged by the opponents of racial desegregation in the state, Byrd moved to shore up his political authority by adopting a policy of "massive resistance" to the 1954 BROWN V. BOARD OF EDUCATION decision. After a period of "deliberate" waiting, he and his lieutenants compelled the state legislature to pass legislation in 1956 that would prevent school integration. Two years later, facing court orders to integrate, Governor Lindsay Almond shut down three school systems rather than admit black students. Much to Byrd's dismay, fed-eral and state courts in January 1959 overturned Virginia's school-closing laws, forcing the reopening of these schools on an integrated basis. It was the most significant defeat of his career.

As a respected senior senator, Byrd also was instrumental in forging regional opposition to the *Brown* decision. Coining the term "massive resistance," he vigorously supported the SOUTHERN MANIFESTO of Senator Strom THURMOND and joined other Southern senators in unsuccessfully filibustering every civil rights bill proposed between 1957 and 1965.

BIBLIOGRAPHY

Ely, James. *The Crisis of Conservative Virginia: The Byrd Organization and the Politics of Massive Resistance.* 1976.
Heinemann, Ronald L. *Harry Byrd of Virginia.* 1996.
Wilkinson, J. Harvie, III. *Harry Byrd and the Changing Face of Virginia Politics, 1945–1966.* 1968.

Ronald L. Heinemann

C

California

The Native American people of California, with the spread of the white population throughout the early 1800s, endured as much suffering as any Native American population in America. Constantly pushed west by a series of treaties (see TRAIL OF BROKEN TREATIES), their lands were completely swallowed up in the 1840s, when the U.S. boundary reached the Pacific. In 1850, the year California became a state, a new set of treaties was negotiated between the federal government and Western natives, in which all Native American lands were ceded and all hostilities renounced by the natives, in exchange for provisions, cattle, and tracts of land—about 8 percent of California's entire land area—to be set aside on reservations.

Settlers were outraged at what they saw as an over-generous offer, however, and the state's U.S. senators lobbied so hard against these measures that the Senate refused to ratify them. Instead, a more modest system was adopted, in which the natives occupied lands that also served as U.S. military installations. Amid angry rhetoric and exaggerated fears about an Indian backlash, the next two decades saw a series of brutal massacres that were mostly carried out by whites against Native Americans. Throughout the 1850s, for example, the state government spent more than $1 million in payment to local volunteers for the suppression of "Indian hostilities." By the 1860s, the Native American population of California, stricken mostly by disease and starvation, had been reduced to less than a third of its original number, to far fewer than 100,000. By the turn of the twentieth century, it had shrunk to fewer than 16,000.

At about the time that Native Americans were being subdued by the new state government, the legislature was also responding on another front to a rising "nativist" feeling among white Californians (see NATIVISM). The Treaty of Guadalupe Hidalgo, which in 1848 ended the Mexican-American War, had transferred the rich territory of Alta California (Upper California) to the United States and provided the explicit provision that all Mexicans who wanted to remain in the territory would automatically become U.S. citizens at the end of one year's residence. Within a year, however, the discovery of gold in the Sierra Nevada caused an eruption of conflicting land claims. Most of the Mexicans who did not lose their claims were defeated by the state legislature's 1850 "foreign miners' license tax" and its indiscriminate application to all Mexicans, regardless of their duration of residence. The exorbitant tax drove about two-thirds of the 15,000 Mexican miners out of California to their homeland.

The Gold Rush of 1849 also brought a substantial population of ethnic immigrants to California—a little more than 2,000 African Americans (most of them free, but including some slaves) and, after civil war broke out in China, about 25,000 Chinese fortune seekers, who came to constitute 10 percent of the state's population, by far the largest foreign minority in California. There were many obstacles to equality for both groups: by state law, African Americans and Native Americans in California were not allowed to vote or to testify against white people in court, and a state judge, in the 1854 *People v. Hall* case, pronounced that the Chinese immigrants were legally Indians because they had both probably descended from the same Asiatic ancestors. To fight these provisions, which threatened the livelihood and property rights of all ethnic residents and immigrants, African Americans in San Francisco formed the state's first civil rights organization in 1852, the Franchise League, which in 1863 won the right of African Americans to testify in court. However, black men in California were not allowed to vote until the FIFTEENTH AMENDMENT to the U.S. Constitution was ratified in 1869.

Chinese immigrants became almost the only group burdened with the foreign miners' license tax, which accounted for nearly one-quarter of the state's revenue until the tax was repealed as unconstitutional in 1870. Another legal weapon against the Chinese was a 1790 law, which stated that only "free white persons" could become naturalized citizens of the state. This law—flagrantly unconstitutional and undemocratic—became the basis for many forms of discrimination against Chinese immigrants for nearly a hundred years, until it was finally struck down by federal immigration statutes in 1952 (see CITIZENSHIP; IMMIGRATION AND IMMIGRANTS).

When the transcontinental railroad was undertaken in 1862, it was the industrious Chinese who were called on by many foremen to lay track through the dangerous and bitterly cold passages of the Sierra Nevada. They were paid well but otherwise poorly provided for—the weather was so harsh that many had to dig into the ground at night to keep from freezing to death. In the cities, the diligence of many Chinese laborers had made them owners of some enterprises, a fact that poor whites perceived as a threat. In the 1860s, anti-Chinese sentiment swelled, culminating in an 1871 race riot in Los Angeles's Chinatown, during which eighteen or nineteen Chinese were murdered. By 1902, California officials had persuaded the federal government and President Theodore Roosevelt to pass a federal bill prohibiting the immigration of Chinese people into the United States.

The flood of immigration to the United States throughout the early 1900s was strongly felt in California. While limits on Chinese immigration were in place, Japanese flocked to California, relatively undisturbed until the 1905 formation in San Francisco of the Asiatic Exclusion League. Laws were enacted to prevent these immigrants from land ownership and to exclude their children from public schools. By 1910, however, there were more than 40,000 Japanese immigrants in California, many of them working on farms in the Central Valley, and in 1920, when the Japanese population reached about 72,000, an Anti-Alien Measure was enacted to keep even first-generation Japanese immigrants from owning land. The influx of foreign immigrants was accompanied by the migration, especially to Los Angeles, of tens of thousands of African Americans from other parts of the country. By 1940, nearly 125,000 African Americans lived in California, most of them working in low-paying service-sector jobs.

Despite its former status as a Mexican territory, California contained only about 50,000 people of Mexican ancestry by 1910. Revolution in Mexico, however, accompanied by WORLD WAR I, set into motion a long process of mass immigration across California's southern border. By 1945, among Mexican cities only Mexico City had a larger Mexican population than Los Angeles, and Latinos in the latter half of the twentieth century grew to constitute by far the largest ethnic minority in California.

The women's movement of the late nineteenth century was strongly represented in California by activists such as Charlotte Perkins Gilman and Laura De Force Gorman, who successfully lobbied for the admission of women lawyers to the state bar and won an equal-rights provision for women in the state constitution. Although the state was among the first to grant women the right to vote (see WOMAN SUFFRAGE MOVEMENT), it took many years for California women to succeed in obtaining elective office. As late as 1975, California ranked forty-eighth among states in the percentage of state elective offices held by women.

WORLD WAR II and its aftermath created dramatic circumstances among the state's ethnic populations. The war served as justification for perhaps the most blatantly racist abuse in the history of the federal government—the removal of all Japanese Americans to concentration camps throughout the war years (see JAPANESE AMERICAN INTERNMENT CASES). Public sentiment, so strongly anti-immigrant before the war, was turned by this injustice to one of sympathy; one by one, California's discriminatory laws began to fall— the CHINESE EXCLUSION ACT was repealed in 1943 and, in 1952, the Supreme Court struck down the state's alien land law. It was not until 1988, however, that Congress authorized financial compensation to each of the surviving Japanese-American citizens and resident aliens interned during the war (see also JAPANESE AMERICAN REDRESS AND REPARATIONS MOVEMENT).

Jobs in defense-related industries created during WORLD WAR II attracted nearly a quarter of a million African-American workers to California, most of whom were concentrated in cities on the San Francisco Bay, where new shipyards were producing thousands of merchant ships. These newcomers, however, faced discrimination in both housing and employment; "restrictive covenants," clauses in real estate contracts forbidding future sales to nonwhites, were still legal, but were struck down by the U.S. Supreme Court in 1948. Beginning in 1959, the state legislature began to pass measures that would enforce fair housing and employment measures. But the state had a long way to go before it would accommodate the large number of African Americans who had migrated to its cities.

Californians of Mexican descent became more urbanized and integrated during and after World War II, but they too suffered much discrimination. During the 1960s, many younger Mexican Americans began a crusade in search of ethnic identity. Many Mexican Americans began to call themselves *La Raza* ("the people") or Chicanos. The term *Chicanos*, though a shortened form of *Mexicanos*, grew to embrace all Americans of Spanish-speaking origin, a population caught in a debilitating cycle of underemployment and poor education. Though Latinos outnumbered African Americans in the state by more than two to one, they had great difficulty in gaining political power.

By the 1960s, the political power of African Americans in California was considerable. The event that did most to galvanize the African-American political will was the voters' approval of Proposition 14, a measure that effectively repealed the state's fair-housing laws and made California HOUSING more segregated than in almost any other state. This discrimination, along with an episode of police brutality, sparked a riotous rebellion in the Los Angeles neighborhood of Watts in 1965 (see WATTS RIOT). While some African Americans responded to the riot with a call for increased INTEGRATION, others, led by the militant Oakland-based BLACK PANTHER PARTY, responded that integration was futile and that self-reliance would be the key to African-American success. Though the party eventually declined in importance, African-American political power increased steadily over the next few decades.

The growth of Latino political power was also accelerated in the 1960s, but it did not spring from the cities. The migrant workers of California's agricultural Central Valley, most of them Mexican Americans or immigrants, banded together to protest the long history of their mistreatment at the hands of growers. The UNITED FARM WORKERS' union, led by César CHÁVEZ, proclaimed a statewide boycott of stores that sold grapes picked by strikebreakers. The strike lasted five years, until the growers gave in and granted union pickers an unprecedented minimum wage. Throughout the 1960s and 1970s, Chávez and his union became a rallying point for Latino students and political reformers, though a large percentage of California's Mexican Americans remained unskilled, low-income laborers. In the 1980s, a widespread effort was made to organize and strengthen Latino political power.

The decade of the 1990s revealed some disturbing facts about race relations in California. Although African-American political representation increased in the 1970s and 1980s, it was clear to most observers that discrimination and other social problems were still rampant. Soaring unemployment, accompanied by drug abuse, crime, and gang violence, plagued urban ghettoes such as south central Los Angeles. A 1992 acquittal of four police officers accused of beating black motorist Rodney King sparked another bloody riot in the area. For the first time, African Americans, frustrated by the poor quality of their lives, began leaving the state in considerable numbers—many returning to the Southern states from which their ancestors had migrated a few generations earlier.

Meanwhile, the rise of Latino political power was most clearly illustrated by the election of the state assembly's first Latino Speaker in 1996. California Asians and Latinos, now constituting a considerable political alliance, had become the driving force behind an effort to change a 1965 immigration law that had favored Europeans with relatives in the United States. The effort led to a backlash, however, that was illustrated by two key ballot measures adopted by voters during the 1996 elections: Proposition 187, which limited the provision of government services to illegal immigrants (most of them Mexican) and Proposition 209, designed to end preferential treatment or discrimination based on race, sex, color, or ethnicity. Dubbed the CALIFORNIA CIVIL RIGHTS INITIATIVE by its supporters—among them a few prominent African-American leaders—Proposition 209 ended years of AFFIRMATIVE ACTION programs that had lent support to traditionally disadvantaged people seeking education and employment. After its approval by voters in 1997, however, the measure was subject to successful legal challenges by the AMERICAN CIVIL LIBERTIES UNION and other civil rights advocates.

BIBLIOGRAPHY

Camarillo, Albert. *Chicanos in California: A History of Mexican Americans in California.* 1990.

DeWitt, Howard A. *Readings in California Civilization.* 1989.

Hoexter, Corinne K. *From Canton to California: The Epic of Chinese Immigration.* 1976.

Mitchell, Don. *The Lie of the Land: Migrant Workers and the California Landscape.* 1996.

Phillips, George H. *The Enduring Struggle: Indians in California History.* 1996.

Pitt, Leonard. *California Controversies.* 1968.

Rawls, James J., ed. *New Directions in California History: A Book of Readings.* 1988.

Rawls, James J., and Walton Bean. *California: An Interpretive History.* 1993.

Rice, Richard B., William A. Bullough, and Richard J. Orsi. *The Elusive Eden: A New History of California.* 1996.

Rolle, Andrew. *California: A History.* 1998.

Wheeler, B. Gordon. *Black California: The History of African-Americans in the Golden State.* 1992.

Craig Collins

California Agricultural Strikes of the 1930s

Depression conditions in the 1930s, with their corresponding decline in consumer demand and high unemployment rates, put severe downward pressures on agricultural wages.

Labor patterns in California had from Spanish times relied on large land holdings and indentured (later casual) workers. In addition, agricultural work tended to be ethnically based—Indian laborers worked for Spanish landholders. Later Hispanic, Asian, and black workers came to predominate, although in the 1930s, many white Anglos, such as the "Okies" who fled the Dust Bowl, were forced to take up agricultural work. The Joad family in John Steinbeck's *The Grapes of Wrath* typified these laborers.

There had been earlier attempts at organizing migrant labor, especially under the INDUSTRIAL WORKERS OF THE WORLD (IWW), resulting in such infamous events as the 1913 Wheatland hop-field riot in the Sacramento Valley. It was with the approach of the Great Depression, however, that the situation became critical. In 1927 Mexican harvest workers formed the Confederacion de Uniones Obreras Mexicanas that struck the cantaloupe fields in 1928. Employers used the threat of deportation to break the strike.

In 1929 the Trade Union Unity League (TUUL) of the Communist Party began organizing Mexican harvesters. The state responded with prosecutions under the California Criminal Syndicalism Act of 1919, but by 1932 the TUUL had created the Cannery and Agricultural Workers Industrial Union (CAWIU). With farm wages at less than one-half the 1929 levels, 1933 saw a California crop pickers revolt with strikes expanding to involve 48,000 laborers. Serious incidents of anti-union vigilantism proliferated as did the arrest of organizers, but in scattered instances strikes succeeded.

In the autumn of 1933 a cotton pickers strike erupted in the San Joaquin Valley and soon spread. On October 10 ranchers fired on strikers at Pixley, wounding eleven and killing two. Governor James Rolfe and the ROOSEVELT administration established an arbitration board of prominent Californians, with a settlement ultimately imposed through the dual threat of state relief cut-offs for strikers and an end to government-guaranteed loans to farmers.

In subsequent agricultural strikes, many California counties adopted anti-picketing ordinances in order to weaken union efforts. Anti-communist campaigns in the press and by state governmental agencies also greeted attempts by the CAWIU to support other unions' strikes, such as the 1934 West Coast longshoreman's strike. In 1935 fourteen union leaders were tried in Sacramento under the state's Criminal Syndicalism statute and raids were conducted against the offices of various communist organizations. Six defendants were acquitted, while eight were found guilty. Subsequent attempts in the legislature to repeal the Criminal Syndicalism law failed.

In March 1935, the Communist Party ordered the abolition of the CAWIU as part of its "popular front" strategy in appealing to traditional labor unions and liberal organizations, and some CAWIU organizers ended up working for the CIO's United Cannery, Agricultural, Packing and Allied Workers of America (UCAPAWA).

Throughout the 1930s and 1940s an organization known as the United Farmers (UF) attacked unionization efforts and strikes with propaganda tools, political lobbying, and vigilante violence. In 1941 the U.S. Supreme Court in *Edwards v. California* reversed several anti-union convictions under the Indigent Act, asserting the principle of the free movement of persons across state borders.

The agricultural strikes in California in the 1930s marked an important chapter in labor history, but also a vital chapter in the struggle for the civil rights of labor organizers, ethnic minorities, the poor, and advocates of unpopular political causes.

BIBLIOGRAPHY

Daniel, Cletus E. *A History of California Farmworkers, 1870–1941.* 1981.

Loftis, Anne. *Witnesses to the Struggle: Imagining the 1930s California Labor Movement.* 1998.

Starr, Kevin. *Endangered Dreams: The Great Depression in California.* 1996.

Patrick M. O'Neil

California Civil Rights Initiative

The California Civil Rights Initiative, popularly known as Proposition 209, called for outlawing RACE, sex, ethnicity, or national origin as a reason for discriminating against or granting preferential treatment to any person or group. The precursor to Proposition 209 was a tumultuous University of California Board of Regents meeting on July 20, 1995. Fourteen regents voted to abolish "preferential treatment" on the basis of race or gender in connection with University of California admissions, EMPLOYMENT, and contracts. Students, faculty, staff, and administrators were shocked that the regents had not closely consulted with them or the chancellors (all nine of whom had opposed the regents' decision). Regent Ward Connerly later became chair of the "Yes on 209" Committee to end AFFIRMATIVE ACTION in the state of CALIFORNIA. But the 1996 campaign generated much confusion among voters. In fact, supporters of affirmative action went to court to argue that a civil rights initiative should clearly be in *support* of civil rights. It was not only dishonest to use terms that misrepresented the anti–affirmative action thrust of the proposition, they stated, but the proposition itself was flawed in its assertion that it would shield white women and people of color from discrimination.

Nevertheless, the "money strings" behind the "Yes on 209" political action group were superabundant. The office of the California Secretary of State reports that the group raised $5,239,287, and of this amount approximately $3 million came from the wealthy pockets of contributors who donated at least $10,000 each. By contrast, the largest grass-roots campaign to defeat Proposition 209 raised only $2,185,086, with single donors of $10,000 or more accounting for only $1.5 million. The role of money in this campaign cannot be underestimated: the large financial contributions by Proposition 209 supporters translated into a major media advertising campaign and their ability to pay for five television commercials to every one aired by anti–Proposition 209 forces. On election day in November 1996 the progressive efforts of groups across the state representing the cultural, racial, social, and economic diversity of California, were defeated. The words "affirmative action" were not featured on the ballot, and many believe that a misunderstanding of the initiative accounted for the election results of 54 percent in favor and 46 percent opposed (a *Los Angeles Times* poll indicated that when the term "affirmative action" was used, a higher proportion of people opposed the initiative).

Entitlement and denial of privileges—as opposed to slavery, JIM CROW, RACISM, and SEXISM—have become the buzzwords in this new anti-affirmative discourse that has since engulfed the nation. What has become apparent from this contested debate is the significance of discursive power. As Stuart Hall puts it, it's "not a question of what is true but what is made to be true." Since the 1996 ban on state-based affirmative action programs, a Jim Crow relapse in higher education has become evident at the University of California. For example, at the Berkeley campus there was a 52 percent drop of black and Hispanic students in the fall 1998 class. Clearly, a significant crisis that began with the regents' vote has made it ever more challenging to balance diversity within a multiracial state.

BIBLIOGRAPHY

Coleman, Trevor. "Affirmative Action Wars." *Emerge* 9 (March 1998).

Stall, Bill. "Prop 209's Fate May Hinge on Two Words." *Los Angeles Times*, October 31, 1996.

Hall, Stuart. "Subjects in History: Making Diasporic Identities." In *The House That Race Built*, edited by Wahneema Lubiano. 1998.

Healy, Patrick. "Berkeley Struggles to Stay Diverse in Post-Affirmative-Action Era." *Chronicle of Higher Education* 29 (May 1998).

Taylor, Ula. "Proposition 209 and the Affirmative Action Debate on the University of California Campuses." *Feminist Studies* (Spring 1999).

Wallace, Amy, and Dave Lesher. "UC Regents, in Historic Vote, Wiped Out Affirmative Action Diversity." *Los Angeles Times* (July 1995).

Ula Y. Taylor

Campos, Pedro Albizu

See Albizu Campos, Pedro.

Carmichael, Stokely (Kwame Toure)

(1941–1998), civil rights leader, chairman of the Student Non-Violent Coordinating Committee, and black activist.

Stokely Carmichael, who later adopted the name Kwame Toure, was born in Port-of-Spain, Trinidad, in 1941. In 1960, Carmichael attended historically black Howard University rather than the numerous white colleges and universities that offered him scholarships. During his college years, he joined the CONGRESS OF RACIAL EQUALITY (CORE), an interracial organization, founded in 1942, that formulated and implemented a policy of "direct action" civil rights protest. Inside CORE, Carmichael was involved in efforts to end racial segregation and participated in lunch counter sit-ins, protests at public facilities, "freedom rides" to desegregate interstate bus transportation, and voter education campaigns throughout the South.

After graduating from college in 1964, Carmichael focused his attention on black voter registration in southern rural areas, such as Lowndes County, Mississippi. (See LOWNDES COUNTY BLACK PANTHER PARTY.) Here, Carmichael did his most significant work as a civil rights leader in the STUDENT NONVIOLENT COORDINATING COMMITTEE (SNCC). The group

Stokely Carmichael hands out anti-war leaflets outside an Atlanta, Georgia, induction center in 1967. (AP/ Wide World Photos)

was organized by black college students in the South in 1960 following a series of successful sit-ins to end racial segregation in restaurants and at lunch counters throughout the region. Sparked in part by this kind of militant politics, the Lowndes County Freedom Organization (LCFO) was formed in 1964 in Mississippi. Carmichael played a key role in the evolution of this group. The LCFO, which was a political group independent of and separate from both the Democratic and Republican parties, chose the panther as its emblem and was the forerunner of the national revolutionary organization the BLACK PANTHER PARTY (BPP).

Personifying the increasing militancy and radicalization of many protest groups in the United States, Carmichael was elected the head of SNCC in 1966 and coined the rallying slogan "BLACK POWER!" during the march of James MEREDITH through northern Mississippi. Carmichael implemented a militant black nationalist stance within SNCC, formed a close alliance with the BPP, and promoted PAN-AFRICANISM, an ideology of cooperation and community of all people of African descent throughout the world. On June 29, 1967, Carmichael was "drafted" into the Black Panther

Party and given the rank of Field Marshall. From 1966 to 1968, Carmichael was a key leader in Black Power coalitions, which radicalized the civil rights movement agenda by their revolutionary call for the redistribution of wealth and power in the United States and their advocacy of armed self-defense. However, responding to the backslash against civil rights militancy and the FEDERAL BUREAU OF INVESTIGATION (FBI's) Counterintelligence Program (COINTELPRO) to neutralize radicals, Stokely Carmichael left the United States for Guinea in 1973, but continued to fight for Pan-Africanism until his death. By choosing to live in Guinea and holding steadfastly to a vision of "revolutionary" Pan-Africanism, his influence among African Americans dwindled in the early 1970s. Carmichael has written *Stokely Speaks: Black Power Back to Pan-Africanism* (1971) and *Black Power: The Politics of Liberation in America* (1967, with Charles V. Hamilton).

BIBLIOGRAPHY

Carmichael, Stokely, and Charles V. Hamilton. *Black Power: The Politics of Liberation in America.* 1967.
Morris, Aldon. *Origins of the Civil Rights Movement.* 1984.
Payne, Charles M. *I've Got the Light of Freedom: The Organizing Tradition and the Mississippi Freedom Struggle.* 1995.
Van Deburg, William L. *New Day in Babylon: The Black Power Movement and American Culture, 1965–1975.* 1992.
Zinn, Howard. *SNCC: The New Abolitionist.* 1965.

Donny C. Barnett

Carr, Johnnie Rebecca Daniels

(1911–   ), civil rights leader.

Johnnie Rebecca Daniels was the youngest of seven children born to Anna and John Daniels in Montgomery, Alabama. As a southern black girl from a rural working-class family, Johnnie Carr's early life was one of toil. At the Montgomery Industrial School, she was trained in the low-level service jobs available to most black women at that time. She married Jack Jordan in 1927 and had two daughters. After a long separation and then divorce in 1943, she met and married Arlam Carr, an insurance salesman, in 1944. During the 1950s, Carr was an insurance agent, official in her local church, community organizer, and secretary of the local chapter of the NATIONAL ASSOCIATION FOR THE ADVANCEMENT OF COLORED PEOPLE (NAACP).

In December 1955, when Mrs. Carr's former classmate and good friend Rosa PARKS, a seamstress and local NAACP secretary, was arrested and charged with violating laws requiring racial SEGREGATION in city bus transportation, Carr showed her passion for justice and her "aggressive" civil rights activism. Unlike many black women domestics, Carr was agent for a black insurance company and was not as vulnerable to job retaliation as they were; she took a leading role in the MONTGOMERY IMPROVEMENT ASSOCIATION (MIA), an organization founded to organize the MONTGOMERY BUS BOYCOTT. As chair of the MIA's Job Committee, Carr collected and distributed funds to blacks who were blacklisted or fired from jobs in retaliation for their participation in the boycott that protested Parks's arrest. In 1967, Mrs. Carr was elected president of MIA. Still president in the late 1990s, she has been the longest-sitting occupant of the position, which was first held by Martin Luther KING, JR.

BIBLIOGRAPHY

Barnett, Bernice McNair. "Invisible Southern Black Women Leaders of the Civil Rights Movement: The Triple Constraints of Gender, Race, and Class." *Gender & Society* 7 (2) (1993): 162–182.

Barnett, Bernice McNair. "Sisters in Struggle: Invisible Black Women Leaders of the Civil Rights Movement, 1940–1975." Forthcoming.

King, Martin. *Stride Towards Freedom.* 1955.

Morris, Aldon. *Origins of the Civil Rights Movement.* 1984.

Papers of Johnnie Carr. Martin Luther King, Jr. Center for Nonviolent Social Change, Atlanta, Ga.

Bernice McNair Barnett

President Jimmy Carter. (Library of Congress)

Carter, James Earl, Jr. (Jimmy)

(1924–   ), U.S. president, 1977–1981.

Jimmy Carter was Democratic president of the United States, 1977–1981. As Georgia governor (1971–1975), he symbolized the New South in accepting that the civil rights revolution was fundamental to the modernization of his state and region. As president Carter sought to strengthen the national foundations of this revolution. His administration expanded black appointments to federal office (12 percent of its appointees were African American, compared with 4 percent under Ronald REAGAN), enhanced enforcement of minority hiring by federal contractors, and promoted "set-aside" programs reserving fixed percentages of government contracts to black firms, notably through the Omnibus Minority Business Act of 1978. Despite his reservations about inflexible quotas, Carter bowed to black pressure and sanctioned a Justice Department brief favoring racial classifications for affirmative action in *Regents of the University of California v. Bakke.* Though the 1978 Supreme Court judgment in this case disappointed civil rights advocates, the administration continued to proffer briefs in favor of race-conscious remediation and helped to win two major

judgments endorsing quotas—*Kaiser Aluminum and Chemical Corp. v. Weber* (1979) and *Fullilove v. Klutznick* (1980). Carter's sympathy for civil rights also influenced his human rights foreign policy and desire for better U.S. relations with black Africa. However, Carter's concern about inflation made him resistant to black demands for economic redistribution, a major concern of the civil rights agenda in the recession-hit 1970s. Nothing better exemplified this than his failure to fight against amendments that undermined the job-creation provisions of the Humphrey-Hawkins Full Employment Act of 1978.

BIBLIOGRAPHY

Abernathy, M. Glenn. "The Carter Administration and Domestic Civil Rights." In *The Carter Years: The President and Policy Making,* edited by M. Glenn Abernathy, Dilys Hill, and Phil Williams. 1984.

Carter, Jimmy. *Keeping Faith: Memoirs of a President.* 1982.

Dumbrell, John. *The Carter Presidency: A Re-evaluation.* 1993.

Kaufman, Burton I. *The Presidency of James Earl Carter, Jr.* 1993.

Iwan Morgan

Carter, Robert L.

(1917–), civil rights advocate, judge.

Robert L. Carter was born in Florida and raised in New Jersey. After graduating from Lincoln University (Pennsylvania) in 1937 and Howard University Law School in 1940, Carter received a master's degree in law from Columbia University. After serving in the Army Air Corps during World War II, Carter joined the legal staff of the NAACP Legal Defense and Education Fund in 1945. Inexperienced in trial work, Carter quickly became Thurgood Marshall's chief assistant, responsible for the office's day-to-day administration.

Often restive about what he perceived as Marshall's cautious pace challenging discrimination, Carter helped devise the litigation strategy for the School Desegregation cases (see Brown v. Board of Education). In the face of some skepticism, Carter insisted on including testimony from social psychologist Kenneth Clark on the damage segregation inflicted on the self-image of African-American schoolchildren. The Supreme Court's opinion in *Brown* mentioned this evidence in a footnote that became controversial among the decision's critics, who thought it inappropriate for a constitutional decision to rest on that sort of empirical evidence, and among its supporters, who thought that resting the decision on such evidence gave it a less firm footing.

When the Internal Revenue Service, prodded by southern senators, insisted that the NAACP and its Legal Defense Fund separate, Carter became general counsel to the NAACP in 1956. He coordinated the NAACP's defense against attacks by southern attorneys-general, who attempted to close down the NAACP by charging it with subversive activities and by seeking the names of NAACP members. Although Carter persuaded the Supreme Court to rule in the NAACP's favor in almost every case, the southern attacks did interfere with the organization's ability to operate in the South until the early 1960s.

Carter argued twenty-six cases in the Supreme Court, winning twenty-five of them. Believing that he deserved to be named Marshall's successor, Carter was extremely upset when Marshall himself persuaded the Legal Defense Fund board to name Jack Greenberg to the position Marshall vacated on his appointment to the federal bench in 1961. Relations between the NAACP and the Legal Defense Fund deteriorated through the 1960s.

Carter resigned as the NAACP's general counsel in 1968 after the NAACP's board, without notifying him, fired a white staff lawyer who had published an article in the *New York Times* criticizing the Supreme Court as "Nine Men in Black Who Think White." He became a partner in a New York law firm.

In 1972, on the recommendation of Republican Senator Jacob Javits, President Richard Nixon named Carter, a Democrat, to the federal trial bench in New York, where he served until he took senior status in 1988. Among his most notable rulings was a 1980 decision finding that the New York City police department had discriminated against African Americans and Hispanics, and requiring that 50 percent of all new hires be African American or Hispanic.

BIBLIOGRAPHY

Greenberg, Jack. *Crusaders in the Courts.* 1994.
NAACP Papers. Library of Congress, Manuscript Division, Washington, D.C.
Tushnet, Mark. *Making Civil Rights Law: Thurgood Marshall and the Supreme Court, 1936–1961.* 1994.

Mark Tushnet

CASA

See Center for Autonomous Social Action.

Castro et al. v. People of California

For years following World War II, concerns over the quality of education among the expanding Mexican-American population of East Los Angeles were raised to city school authorities, but with few results. Overcrowding in inferior facilities, blatantly racist behavior by teaching staffs that included few Hispanics, the cultural insensitivity of the curricula, high dropout rates, and poor access to higher education were among the many grievances. Encouraged by gains of African Americans in raising the public consciousness about civil rights issues, the activist Chicano Movement emerged in 1967, influencing frustrated students in East Los Angeles schools. By early 1968 protest plans among students began to take shape.

Sudden cancellation of a school play at one of the predominantly Chicano high schools in early March triggered student action. For a week and a half, over ten thousand students, predominantly in five Chicano high schools but at other schools as well, boycotted class. Known as the East Los Angeles School Blowouts, students and sympathizers participated in walkouts, marches, Sit-Ins, and speeches. School officials summoned city police to prevent vandalism and violence. Though little violence initially occurred, aggressive police actions resulted in near riots, leading to injuries and a broad-based reaction from the community.

Weeks later, high school teacher Sal Castro and twelve others—dubbed by the press the "L.A. 13"—

were arrested and charged with conspiracy to break the peace by planning the protests. Castro was suspended from his teaching position but was later reinstated after students and other members of the East Los Angeles community demonstrated on his behalf. Tensions in the community remained elevated until the mid-1970s when a California appellate court threw out the case, *Castro et al. v. People of California*, based on violations of the thirteen defendants' constitutional rights.

No other event served so well to unite the Mexican-American community of East Los Angeles. The founding of the Educational Issues Coordinating Committee (EICC) to unify community activities was a direct result of the walkouts. Eventually, the EICC was replaced by the Mexican-American Education Commission, a formal part of the Los Angeles School Board.

BIBLIOGRAPHY

Bernal, Delores Delgado. "Grassroots Leadership Reconceptualized: Chicana Oral Histories and the 1968 East Los Angeles School Blowouts." *Frontiers* 19 (1998): 113–115.

Chávez, John R. *Eastside Landmark: A History of the East Los Angeles Community Union, 1968–1993.* 1998.

Marin, Marguerite V. *Social Protest in an Urban Barrio: A Study of the Chicano Movement, 1966–1974.* 1991.

Richard C. Hanes

Catt, Carrie Chapman

(1859–1947), suffragist and peace activist.

Carrie Chapman Catt first became interested in women's rights when she discovered at age 13 that her mother could not vote. Raised on a farm in Iowa, she attended Iowa State Agricultural College, paying her way by dishwashing and teaching summer school. After serving briefly as superintendent of schools in Mason City, Iowa, Catt began writing a weekly newspaper column on women's issues. She became involved with the woman's suffrage campaign in Iowa in the late 1880s, and was soon traveling the country giving speeches and organizing local suffrage campaigns. An excellent organizer and pragmatic politician, Catt twice served as the president of the NATIONAL AMERICAN WOMAN SUFFRAGE ASSOCIATION (NAWSA), from 1900 to 1904 and from 1915 to 1920. As president of NAWSA, Catt focused exclusively on the issue of suffrage and on securing passage of a federal amendment granting women the right to vote. Catt sought to distance NAWSA from radical causes and militant tactics. Despite her personal pacifism, she led the organization to support the war effort during WORLD WAR I. The successful passage of the NINETEENTH AMEND-

Woman suffragist leader Carrie Chapman Catt marches in a suffragette parade in New York City, ca. 1912. (CORBIS/Bettmann)

MENT in 1920 was largely the result of Catt's organizational skills. Catt was also an internationalist who believed women around the world had much in common. In 1902, she helped found the International Woman Suffrage Alliance. With a victory for suffrage ensured, Catt helped found the LEAGUE OF WOMEN VOTERS, a nonpartisan group designed to educate women to use their new political power. Catt spent the last twenty years of her life working for world peace. She formed the Committee on the Cause and Cure of War in 1925, advocated disarmament and American entry into the World Court, and lobbied for the Kellogg-Briand Pact to outlaw war.

BIBLIOGRAPHY

Fowler, Robert Booth. *Carrie Catt: Feminist Politician.* 1986.

Van Voris, Jacqueline. *Carrie Chapman Catt: A Public Life.* 1987.

Renee Romano

Censorship

Censorship is as old as human history. In ancient Greece, Spartan rulers prohibited certain forms of poetry, music, and dancing, and Plato tried to expurgate Homer. Roman censors checked on the morals of the people. The earliest censorship imposed by the Christian church was the Apostolic Constitutions of the Church Fathers. They forbade Christians to read "any books of the Gentiles, since the Scriptures should suffice for the believer." Starting in 1476, the English king required that anyone wishing to print anything had to secure a license from a royal official, who could at will censor any passages. This system of prior restraint ended in 1694, but any Englishmen who criticized the government could still be prosecuted. Under the law of treason, until 1720 a person could be executed merely for trying to publish a book that questioned the king's authority.

The struggle against censorship in America began in 1734, when the John Peter Zenger case established the precedent that criticism that is true is not libelous. (Zenger had criticized the royal governor of the colony of New York.) This ran contrary to Sir William Blackstone's observation in his *Commentaries on the Law of England in 1765* that "the liberty of the press . . . consists in laying no *previous* restraint upon publications; and not in freedom from censure for criminal matter when published." Whether a root purpose of the First Amendment was to change the restrictive English common law has been a matter of heated debate. Some scholars have claimed that all the framers wanted was to adopt Blackstone's standard. Others with at least as strong historical ammunition have asserted that the First Amendment, as Justice Hugo L. BLACK stated, was "a bold effort . . . to establish a country with no legal restrictions upon the subjects people could investigate, discuss, and deny." It was this "central meaning of the First Amendment"—that damaging and even false criticism of government and its officials must be tolerated, and that the "mere label" of a libel suit could not defeat that freedom—that lay at the heart of Justice William J. Brennan, Jr.'s, opinion for the SUPREME COURT in *New York Times v. Sullivan* (1964), a decision that paved the way for the press to cover the civil rights movement in the South without fear.

Obscenity

In the nineteenth and continuing into the early twentieth centuries, state courts routinely denied free-speech claims concerning obscenity, the most frequently litigated freedom-of-expression category. The first federal obscenity law was not passed until 1842 as part of the customs law, and only four states passed obscenity laws before the Civil War.

The appearance of erotic literature in the mid nineteenth century combined with the development of the camera to increase public concern about obscenity.

A blindfolded man looking at artwork is an illustration of censorship. (Robert Maass/CORBIS)

CONGRESS responded in 1873 by passing the Comstock Act, which outlawed the mailing of obscene materials. It was named after its prime proponent, Anthony Comstock of New York, who later, as a special agent of the U.S. post office, allegedly said in court during the trial of a woman who had mailed photographs he considered immoral, "Your Honor, this woman gave birth to a naked child."

American judges long gave the broadest possible interpretation to the Comstock Act. The courts adopted the standard of an 1868 English case and let a work remain banned if its "tendency" within even isolated passages might "deprave and corrupt those whose minds are open to such immoral influences." Customs officials regularly seized books coming into the country from Europe that they deemed dangerous to the nation's morals. One of these books was James Joyce's novel *Ulysses.* In 1934 a federal judge ruled that the book could enter the country, ruling that a book must be taken "as a whole."

In 1925 the Supreme Court declared for the first time that the speech and press clauses of the First Amendment, which had previously applied only to the federal government, also applied to the states. Then, in *Near v. Minnesota* (1931), one of the landmark First Amendment decisions in American history, the Court ruled that, with only very limited exceptions, the government could not restrain the press. "The fact that the liberty of the press may be abused by miscreant purveyors of scandal [Near published an anti-Semitic newspaper] does not make any the less necessary the immunity of the press from previous restraint in dealing with official misconduct," Chief Justice Charles Evans Hughes wrote. "Subsequent punishment for such abuses is the appropriate remedy, consistent with constitutional privilege." The only exceptions the Court noted were publishing military secrets in time of war, the use of obscenity, and incitement to riot or forcible overthrow of the government.

The last exemption was based on the "clear and present danger" rule Justice Oliver Wendell Holmes enunciated in *Schenck v. United States* (1919): "whether the words used . . . create a clear and present danger that they will bring about the substantive evils that Congress has a right to prevent." Schenck arose in the context of subversive speech and in 1969 the Court expanded its protection, announcing in *Brandenburg v. Ohio* that a person could be punished only if he advocated the use of force or violation of the law immediately and with words "likely to incite or produce such action." The Court ruled in *New York Times Company v. United States* (1971) that not even the prosecution of the *New York Times* and the *Washington Post* in 1971 for releasing the Pentagon Papers, a classified govchernment study of some of the decisions leading to extensive American involvement in the VIETNAM WAR, met the "heavy burden" of justifying the use of prior restraint.

Motion Pictures

The *Near* case notwithstanding, motion-picture licensing boards across the country previewed films to determine their suitability to be shown to adults as well as children. Over fifty state and local censorship boards were active during the first half of the twentieth century. In addition, local license commissioners sometimes determined a movie's appropriateness. New York City enacted the first board in 1912; Maryland enacted the last state board, which went out of business in 1981; and Dallas's, the last surviving local board, closed a few years later.

The standards the groups used were necessarily vague, ranging from "immoral" or tending to "corrupt morals" and "other than moral, educational, amusing or harmless." In 1954, New York state's censorship board for a short time banned an Academy Award–winning True-Life Adventure documentary film from Walt Disney, *The Vanishing Prairie*, which showed a buffalo giving birth (in apparent violation of New York statutory law, which did not limit bans of depictions of this activity to humans) and was therefore "indecent." In the South the criterion "prejudicial to the best interests of the people of said City" was often used to keep off the screen films with a racial context, such as *Pinky* in the early 1950s. (See also FILM.)

The Supreme Court in 1952 ruled that New York state could not deny a license to a movie (Joseph Burstyn's *The Miracle*) that the state licensing board had found to be "sacrilegious." While this kept New York's licensing scheme intact, the Court gradually found other standards unconstitutional. The justices also insisted over the next decade on procedures that ensured the prompt determination by a court as to whether a particular film was unfit to be shown.

The movie industry's Production Code from 1930 into the mid-1960s served as a form of self-censorship and as a private type of prior restraint. It was established to prevent the threat of government censorship and private boycott. By requiring that the content of movies produced by the major studios be approved before they could be shown in theaters controlled by the industry, it limited what was shown on the screen. Similarly, the current ratings system was established in 1968 to forestall censorship, and, despite many complaints such as its failure to provide reasons for ratings, it has done just that.

Books

Books have been suppressed on moral or ideological grounds. Publishers in the early twentieth century submitted manuscripts to the New York Society for the Suppression of Vice, a private group acting with the city's imprimatur, which could arrest anyone it believed had violated the law by publishing "offensive" material. Detroit's censorship board prevented more than one hundred books from being sold in the city from 1950 to 1952. During the twentieth century, literary suppression tended to increase during periods of political conservatism. Accusations of censorship reported to the American Library Association on the day after Ronald REAGAN's victory in the 1980 election tripled.

Changes in Society

In 1957 the Supreme Court considered obscenity at length for the first time. Justice Brennan wrote that "all ideas" were constitutionally protected unless they were "utterly without redeeming social importance," and that obscenity lacked constitutional protection. The Court struggled to define obscenity as events were overtaking the subject. *Playboy* magazine was founded in 1953; rock and roll became part of American culture. In 1966 the Court tightened the obscenity test to include, additionally, questions of whether the material is "prurient" (likely to excite lustful thoughts) and whether it is "patently offensive" to "contemporary community standards." Obscenity became the only remaining permissible ground for denying a movie a license; and, as Justice Brennan once said, during the 1960s a book could be proscribed only if the Supreme Court disapproved it—which rarely happened.

In 1973 the Court altered its obscenity test to include considerations of whether the material is prurient to an average person in a particular community, whether it describes sexual conduct in a patently offensive way, and whether if taken as a whole it "lacks serious literary, artistic, political, or scientific value." This standard allowed that definitions of "obscenity" might vary considerably in different communities. But the justices were swimming against strong currents. By then, only the most overt obscenity was prosecuted; such material was widely accepted across much of American society and, given a surging crime rate, prosecutors had other things to do than prosecute obscenity cases.

Technology, moreover, was changing the face of censorship. Cable television became widespread. More important was the advent of the Internet (see INTERNET, CENSORSHIP AND THE). In 1995 Congress passed the Communications Decency Act, which made it criminal to send "indecent" material on-line unless the sender tried to prevent the material from being distributed to anyone under eighteen.

The Supreme Court, in *Reno v. American Civil Liberties Union* (1997), overturned the law, noting that "the interest in encouraging freedom of expression in a democratic society outweighs any theoretical but unproved benefit of censorship." (During trial in this case, a government witness, a special agent, entered "XXX" into a search engine on one of the computers in the courtroom. Super Bowl 30 was one of the 120 sites that came up on the screen.) The Court granted the Internet the highest form of First Amendment protection and did so in the quickest time it has ever granted that protection to any media. Convergence of the media will present those who favor censorship in a democracy with their greatest challenge.

BIBLIOGRAPHY

Boyer, Paul. *Purity in Print.* 1982.
Burns, James MacGregor, and Stewart Burns. *A People's Charter.* 1991.
De Grazia, Edward, and Roger K. Newman. *Banned Films: Movies, Censors and the First Amendment.* 1982.

Emerson, Thomas I. *The System of Freedom of Expression.* 1970.
Wagman, Robert. *The First Amendment Book.* 1991.

Roger K. Newman

Center for Autonomous Social Action

The Center for Autonomous Social Action, more commonly known as Centro de Acción Social Autónomo or CASA, grew out of conflict in the 1960s over U.S. deportation policies of Mexicanos. Founded in 1968 in Los Angeles by Bert CORONA, longtime Chicano political activist and labor organizer, the organization fought for the rights of undocumented immigrant Chicano workers, considered illegal aliens by U.S. authorities. CASA established a number of centers around southern California and elsewhere in the nation to provide legal and social services to Chicano immigrants seeking to regularize their status, to combat their economic exploitation, and to influence U.S. immigration policies (see IMMIGRATION AND IMMIGRANTS). Using the slogan "Raza Si, Migra No!" (No Deportation!), CASA sought to mobilize mass worker resistance. The organization also became associated with Chicano interests in fighting U.S. imperialism in Latin America, particularly the Puerto Rican struggle for independence (see PUERTO RICAN LIBERATION). CASA succeeded in making immigration a focal point of political activism; however, the goal of uniting Mexican-American and Mexican workers, as well as generating support for undocumented workers, was never realized. The Mexican-American community was divided over the issue of undocumented workers because of concerns over job competition, which for many outweighed distress over civil rights and oppressive U.S. policies.

Radical youthful elements soon gained influence in the organization and attempted to transform it into a political party (see MEXICAN-AMERICAN STUDENT ORGANIZATIONS). CASA became one of two Mexican-American Marxist organizations to grow out of the 1960s CHICANO MOVEMENT. Unable to build a strong base, the primarily Chicano anti-deportation organization turned political party gradually lost financial support, ultimately disappearing by 1978.

BIBLIOGRAPHY

Garcia, Mario T. *Memories of Chicano History: The Life and Narrative of Bert Corona.* 1994.
Hammerback, John C., Richard J. Jensen, and Jose A. Gutierrez. *A War of Words: Chicano Protest in the 1960s and 1970s.* 1985.

Muñoz, Carlos, Jr. *Youth, Identity, Power: The Chicano Movement.* 1989.

Richard C. Hanes

Centro de Acción Social Autónomo

See Center for Autonomous Social Action.

Chaney, James; Goodman, Andrew; and Schwerner, Michael

Civil rights workers.

The murder of James Chaney (1943–1964), Andrew Goodman (1943–1964), and Michael Schwerner (1939–1964) during the 1964 FREEDOM SUMMER focused the nation's attention on MISSISSIPPI's violence and lawlessness.

Organized by a coalition of civil rights groups working in Mississippi, Freedom Summer brought volunteers to work on voter registration, teach in freedom schools, and organize the MISSISSIPPI FREEDOM DEMOCRATIC PARTY (MFDP). Struggling against massive resistance and pervasive violence, organizers hoped that white volunteers would bring the nation's laws and attention into Mississippi and force the federal government to protect those attempting to register to vote and exercise their rights as citizens.

In 1963, Michael Schwerner, a white Jewish social worker from New York City joined the CONGRESS OF RACIAL EQUALITY (CORE) and, with his wife Rita Schwerner, opened a community center in Meridian, Mississippi. There they met James Chaney, an African-American Meridian native, who worked closely with the Schwerners. At the June 1964, Oxford, Ohio, training program for summer volunteers, Chaney and Schwerner met Andrew Goodman, a white Jewish college student who agreed to work with them in the Meridian movement.

The three men returned to Mississippi and on June 21 investigated the burning of planned freedom school host, Mt. Zion Methodist Church in Neshoba County. On their way home, Deputy Sheriff Cecil Price arrested, jailed, and held them without a telephone call until 10:30 P.M. while he conspired with members of the KU KLUX KLAN. After Price released them, the Klan members, who had nicknamed Schwerner "Goatee" and targeted him for elimination, forced the three men to stop their car. Chaney, Goodman and Schwerner were taken to a deserted road where they were shot, killed, and then buried in an earthen dam under construction.

The COUNCIL OF FEDERATED ORGANIZATIONS (COFO) office began searching for the men as soon

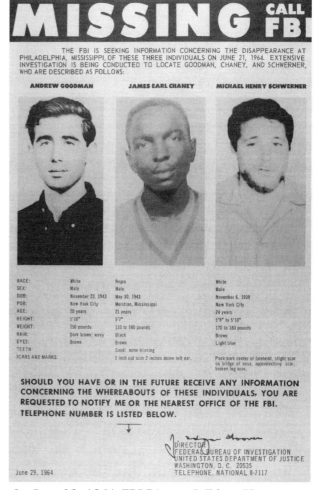

On June 29, 1964, FBI Director J. Edgar Hoover announced that the search for the three civil rights activists working in Mississippi would be expanded to five states. Posters like the one shown here were distributed throughout Mississippi, Alabama, Tennessee, Arkansas, and Louisiana. (CORBIS/Bettmann)

as they failed to return, but the FBI and Justice Department were reluctant to get involved. The case received considerable news coverage and the publicity forced President Lyndon JOHNSON to order a massive FBI search and investigation. On August 4 an informant's tip led the FBI to the bodies of the missing men. In October 1967, after years of delay, seven men, including Cecil Price, were convicted and sentenced to three to ten years in jail for depriving Chaney, Goodman, and Schwerner of their civil rights. The jury acquitted or failed to reach a verdict on the remaining defendants. None were tried on state murder charges.

Unfortunately, the deaths of these three men confirmed the analysis of Mississippi activists that, due to racism, the public and the federal government were more likely to insist on rights for, and safeguard the lives of, whites. The murder of several other African Americans that summer went unnoticed, while bodies of African-American men recovered during the search were ignored. Thus, the movement's success in focusing the nation's attention on the violent resistance to voting and civil rights in Mississippi was accompanied by growing disillusionment among activists confronted by the inescapable reality that black lives were valued less than white lives and by the national Democratic party's rejection of the MFDP, organized to provide a voice to those excluded from the political process by such violence.

BIBLIOGRAPHY

Belfrage, Sally. *Freedom Summer*. 1965.

Cagin, Seth, and Philip Dray. *We Are Not Afraid: The Story of Goodman, Schwerner, and Chaney in the Civil Rights Campaign for Mississippi*. 1988.

Dittmer, John. *Local People: The Struggle for Civil Rights in Mississippi*. 1995.

Mars, Florence. *Witness at Philadelphia*. 1976.

Emilye Crosby

Charles, Robert

(1865/6–1900), migrant worker.

Robert Charles was born shortly after the end of the Civil War, probably in Copiah County, Mississippi, where he grew up. His parents were former slaves who became sharecroppers after the end of the war. As a youth, Robert Charles was intelligent, though a bit reserved, and a hard worker. He worked for the LNO&T Railroad in Vicksburg until a dispute with a white co-worker (a signalman) led to a gunfight. He went into hiding and adopted the alias "Curtis Robertson" out of fear of being lynched (see LYNCHING). In 1890, he moved to New Orleans, Louisiana, and joined the International Migration Society, whose goal was to "transport American Negroes back to Africa."

For the next ten years Charles remained in New Orleans. For much of the latter part of the nineteenth century, New Orleans had been a near-exemplar city in the area of interracial relations. Following the 1896 Supreme Court decision in PLESSY V. FERGUSON, however, the sizable black community in New Orleans began to experience frequent harassment from the New Orleans police as well as a new city policy of segregation. By the summer of 1900, racial tensions had reached a critical point, exacerbated by an acute job shortage.

On the evening of July 23, 1900, Robert Charles, at this point unemployed, was accosted by New Orleans police, one of whom threatened him with a billy club. At first, Charles ran; then, as the officers opened fire on him, he pulled out his own gun and, bleeding from a wound, shot two of his pursuers. Charles then went into hiding, and the police commenced a house-to-house search. On July 25, white citizens now began an angry spree of harassment against blacks throughout New Orleans, killing three and beating over fifty others, as well as looting black-owned houses and businesses and setting fire to the city's best black school building. On July 27 Charles was cornered in a house where he had taken refuge. As the police, encouraged by a white mob, shot their way in, Charles shot back, killing four police and wounding three more before he himself was shot dead. White newspapers afterward referred to him as "worthless" and as a "bloodthirsty champion of African supremacy," though in truth he was neither. Ten blacks were arrested for complicity in Charles's concealment but were later released. On the testimony of white witnesses, six whites were arrested for murder, but they too were released.

BIBLIOGRAPHY

Hair, William Ivy. *Carnival of Fury*. 1976.

Shaunda Partida

Chávez, César Estrada

(1927–1993), labor leader and civil rights activist.

César Chávez was born near Yuma, Arizona, where his family owned a grocery store and some farmland. During the Great Depression, his family was forced off the land when it fell behind on mortgage payments. Like thousands of other rural families in the Southwest, the Chávez family moved to California, where family members worked as temporary farm laborers. It was during this period that César Chávez experienced many of the hardships faced by migrant farm workers: corrupt labor contractors, extremely low wages, and poor living and working conditions. It was also during this time that he got his first glimpse of union organizing when his father, Librado Chávez, became active in several union activities, including a successful effort to organize workers at a dried-fruit packing plant in San Jose.

After serving two years in the Navy during World War II, César Chávez married Helen Fabela in 1948 and moved to Delano, California, a town near San Jose. While working as a migrant laborer in grape and cotton farms, he met Fred Ross, an organizer for Saul Alinsky's COMMUNITY SERVICE ORGANIZATION (CSO). Chávez joined the CSO in 1952 in its campaign to register and mobilize Mexican Americans; and within six years, he became national director of the organiza-

On June 4, 1986, United Farm Workers leader César Chávez puts up posters in New York City advocating a boycott to protest the use of toxic pesticides in the growing of grapes. (CORBIS/Bettmann)

tion. However, the CSO refused to take up the cause of organizing migrant farm workers; so he resigned from the organization in 1962 and created a new union for farm workers, the National Farm Workers Association (NFWA). By 1965, Chávez had organized over 1,700 families in the Delano area. When a largely Filipino union, the AGRICULTURAL WORKERS ORGANIZING COMMITTEE (AWOC), struck against growers over low wages, Chávez and the NFWA decided to join the struggle.

In March 1966, César Chávez led the NFWA on a three hundred–mile march from Delano to the state capitol building in Sacramento. The march, which was inspired by the 1964 Freedom March from Selma to Montgomery, Alabama, drew national attention to the plight of farm workers. Even before the protestors reached Sacramento, one of the major table-wine producers formally recognized the NFWA and agreed to refrain from hiring farm workers through labor contractors. For the next two years, the union signed contracts with a few other vineyards in central California.

It also bolstered its strength by affiliating with the AFL-CIO to form the UNITED FARM WORKERS (UFW). Despite these early gains, UFW contracts with growers covered fewer than six thousand workers. The largest table-grape growers in California still refused to negotiate with the group, and they circumvented the union's boycott by shipping grapes under different labels.

Faced with increasing resistance from the state's major grape growers, Chávez called for a nationwide boycott of California table grapes beginning in January 1968. The boycott drew support from labor unions, Chicano associations, civil rights activists, and college students. The UFW set up boycott organizations in over forty major cities, and mayors of several cities endorsed the campaign against California table grapes. The leadership of César Chávez proved crucial, not only in envisioning and implementing a nationwide boycott but also in preventing the movement from taking a violent turn. When some farm workers threatened to use violent tactics against growers in early 1968, he initiated a hunger fast to affirm the principles of nonviolence advocated by Mohandas GANDHI and Dr. Martin Luther KING, JR. The fast was the first of several that Chávez would undertake on behalf of farm workers.

The 1968 grape boycott was a tremendous success for César Chávez and the UFW. Public opinion polls found that over 17 million Americans had stopped eating grapes because of the boycott. Faced with significant losses in revenue, many growers acceded to the demands of the UFW, including higher wages, health insurance, formal grievance procedures, and safe working and living conditions.

Despite its notable victories, the UFW soon faced challenges from the Teamsters Union, which began to sign contracts on terms that were more favorable to growers than to farm workers. It also faced legislative challenges from growers, who sponsored a ballot proposition in 1972 that would outlaw farm worker boycotts and would limit union elections to nonseasonal employees. Chávez and the UFW were able to overcome both challenges by the mid-1970s. The Teamsters decided to refrain from contesting the union's elections in 1977, and the UFW was able to defeat the ballot initiative by informing and mobilizing voters. The UFW also made legislative gains in 1974 with the support of Governor Jerry Brown, a pro-union Democrat. The California legislature passed the Agricultural Labor Relations Act, a landmark bill that established collective bargaining and secret-ballot union elections for all farm workers. Thus, with favorable legislation and a lack of competition from the Teamsters Union, the UFW reached the peak of its strength during the late 1970s.

Beginning in the early 1980s, however, the union lost many of its contracts with growers, and Chávez found less and less public support for consumer boycotts. At the same time, many activists within the UFW resigned from the organization. Some complained that Chávez exerted too much personal control over day-to-day decisions, whereas others felt that Chávez was relying too heavily on hunger strikes and boycotts and not devoting enough resources to organizing farm workers.

As internal problems weakened the UFW, the 1982 election of a Republican governor proved disastrous to the organization. Soon after taking office, Governor George Deukmejian cut the budget for the Agricultural Labor Relations Board, appointed members to the board who were favorable to growers, and failed to act on farm worker grievances. During this period, contracts with the UFW declined substantially, and union membership fell precipitously from sixty thousand in 1982 to below twelve thousand by 1987. Even as Chávez undertook a hunger strike in 1988, the union continued to decline in significance. By the time of his death in 1993, the UFW had lost most of its membership and had relinquished most of the gains in wages that it had made during the previous decades.

Despite the decline of the UFW, César Chávez is still noted for his accomplishments in organizing farm workers and in drawing national attention to farm worker grievances. President Bill CLINTON recognized his achievements in 1994 by posthumously awarding him the Medal of Freedom, the nation's highest civilian honor. Even today, Chávez remains a source of inspiration for Latino activists, union organizers, community leaders, and civil rights activists.

BIBLIOGRAPHY

Dunne, John Gregory. *Delano: The Story of the California Grape Strike.* 1966.

Ferris, Susan, and Ricardo Sadoval. *The Fight in the Fields: César Chávez and the Farmworkers' Movement.* 1997.

Griswold del Castillo, Richard, and Richard A. Garcia. *César Chávez: A Triumph of Spirit.* 1995.

Hammerback, John C., and Richard J. Jensen. *The Rhetorical Career of César Chávez.* 1998.

Jenkins, J. Craig. *The Politics of Insurgency: The Farm Worker Movement in the 1960s.* 1985.

Kushner, Sam. *The Long Road to Delano.* 1975.

Levy, Jacques. *César Chávez: Autobiography of La Causa.* 1975.

Matthiessen, Peter. *Sal Si Puedes: César Chávez and the New American Revolution.* 1969.

Mooney, Patrick H., and Theo Majka. *Farmers' and Farm Workers' Movements.* 1995.

Taylor, Ronald. *Chávez and the Farm Workers.* 1975.

Yinger, Winthrop. *César Chávez: The Rhetoric of Nonviolence.* 1975.

S. Karthick Ramakrishnan

Chicago Campaign of 1966

See Chicago Freedom Movement.

Chicago Freedom Movement

By 1965 the civil rights movement had secured enormous victories in the South. The passage of the CIVIL RIGHTS ACTS OF 1964 dismantled the remaining vestiges of JIM CROW segregation and the VOTING RIGHTS ACT OF 1965 prevented the systematic exclusion of black southerners from the political process. As the lives of black southerners improved, outside the South little had changed. In urban areas across the country black Americans were trapped in slum ghettos, forced to attend overcrowded, understaffed schools, and disproportionately stuck in the lowest-paid jobs. *De facto* segregation in HOUSING and EDUCATION, along with dire ghetto conditions, precipitated a series of urban riots that swept the country in the summer of 1965.

In response to the cries from blacks trapped in northern ghettos, in the summer of 1965 Dr. Martin Luther KING, JR.'s organization, the SOUTHERN CHRISTIAN LEADERSHIP CONFERENCE (SCLC), announced its plans to conduct a northern tour. The SCLC wanted to extend the movement's victories to the urban North and to test the extent to which nonviolent direct action would work outside the South. After touring a series of cities, the SCLC selected Chicago as the site for its first northern drive. A group of Chicago activists known as the Coordinating Council of Community Organizations (CCCO) joined forces with the SCLC to launch the Chicago Freedom Movement.

The SCLC encountered a number of obstacles in Chicago. First, *de facto* had replaced *de jure* segregation. Hence, the launching of a civil rights movement in Chicago meant confronting barriers far more elusive than the segregated lunch counters of the South. Second, Chicago was much larger than most southern cities. In 1965 Chicago was home to close to one million blacks, many of whom were poor and residing in the city's two enormous slum ghettos. Third, machine politics had replaced political disfranchisement. In 1965 Chicago was the political dominion of Richard J. Daley, the nation's most powerful mayor. Daley's political machine in many ways contributed to and benefited from the proliferation of slum housing in the city. Fourth, many influential black leaders who were affiliated with the city's political system denounced the SCLC's presence in Chicago. Despite these constraints, in the summer of 1966 the SCLC–CCCO coalition conducted a series of open housing demonstrations in Chicago's all-white neighborhoods and dramatized for an entire nation Chicago's segregated housing conditions. The demonstrations powerfully illustrated the underrecognized similarities between the North and the South. During one march an onlooker threw a fist-size rock that struck Dr. King in the head. On another occasion angry whites overturned and burned the cars of movement activists.

While the open housing demonstrations revealed the depths of northern RACISM, unlike the southern campaigns the Chicago Freedom Movement did not generate a distinct victory. Dr. King and his staff had hoped that a successful Chicago campaign would generate national housing legislation and provide a model for nonviolent direct action that could be used to attack racial inequality nationwide. But the SCLC underestimated the difficulty involved in organizing a civil rights movement in Chicago. Logistical difficulties, a powerful political machine, class differentiation within Chicago's black community—and unsupportive black leaders—prevented the Chicago Freedom Movement from securing the clear-cut northern victory that movement activists sought.

BIBLIOGRAPHY

Anderson, Alan B., and George W. Pickering. *Confronting the Color Line: The Broken Promise of the Civil Rights Movement in Chicago.* 1986.

Carson, Clayborne, David J. Garrow, Gerald Gill, Vincent Harding, and Darlene Clark Hine, eds. *The Eyes on the Prize: Civil Rights Reader.* 1991.

Fairclough, Adam. *To Redeem the Soul of America: The Southern Christian Leadership Conference and Martin Luther King, Jr.* 1987.

Garrow, David J. *Bearing the Cross.* 1986.

Garrow, David J., ed. *Chicago 1966.* 1989.

Hampton, Henry, and Steve Fayer. *Voices of Freedom: An Oral History of the Civil Rights Movement from the 1950s through the 1980s.* 1990.

Ralph, James R. *Northern Protest.* 1993.

Young, Andrew. *An Easy Burden: The Civil Rights Movement and the Transformation of America.* 1996.

Waite, Lori. "Overcoming Obstacles and Challenges to Social Movement Mobilization: The Case of the Chicago Freedom Movement." Ph.D. dissertation, Northwestern University. 1998.

Lori G. Waite

Chicano Movement

During the 1960s, the Chicano Movement, or *El Movimiento*, emerged as a culmination of various currents of grass-roots movements. In time it would call for and champion community activism, educational reforms, political action, literary and artistic cultural expressions, and labor-organizing movements to combat the RACISM, educational discrimination, SEGREGATION, and poverty faced by Mexican Americans. Developing a new political identity and calling themselves Chicanos, followers of *El Movimiento* criticized and turned away from the integrationist strategies of previous Mexican-American civil rights organizations. Encouraged by the independence movements abroad and the civil rights movement in the United States, and increasingly by the black liberation movement, Chicanos espoused cultural nationalism as a means of community empowerment. Through the new ethos of Chicanismo and the declaration that the Southwest was in reality the ancestral land of the Aztecs, Chicanos reclaimed their rights and presence in that region, which they named Aztlán. Previous Mexican-American civil rights movements had been heavily influenced by local and regional concerns, but during the 1960s efforts to bridge these regional divisions resulted in an increased national movement.

The American public was first made aware of this national movement through the Delano Grape Boycott of 1965. By the 1960s, most Chicanos were urbanites; however, the farm workers' labor-organizing efforts turned their leader, César CHÁVEZ, into a national leader. Through the boycott, Mexican Americans easily identified with the economic oppression of the farm workers. Inspired by the boycott, Mexican Americans throughout the United States increasingly protested their subordinate social and economic conditions. Appropriated as a Chicano leader, Chávez never fully endorsed the emerging Chicano nationalism; nevertheless, the boycott forecast the potential advancement of a unified community effort. The boycott solidified the growing desire, by regional leaders, to form national rather than strictly local and regional organizations to advance the civil rights of all Mexican Americans.

One of the most important regional organizers who aided the cause of cultural nationalism was Rodolfo "Corky" GONZÁLES. A former Golden Gloves boxer-turned-businessman, Gonzáles joined the "Viva Kennedy" campaign that marked, for the first time, the entry of middle-class Mexican Americans into national politics. Under President Lyndon JOHNSON's administration, Gonzáles was named director of the WAR ON POVERTY program in Denver, Colorado. Frustrated by the lack of political rewards for and political integration of Mexican-American Democratic support, Gonzáles broke away from liberal, mainstream politics and in 1965 founded the CRUSADE FOR JUSTICE, a broad-based civil rights organization that at first preached

A Chicana protester in a crowd of demonstrators during a march to the Capitol building in Sacramento, California, on August 7, 1971, to denounce discrimination against Americans of Mexican descent. (CORBIS)/Bettmann)

dents at the university level. Renaming itself EL MOVIMIENTO ESTUDIANTIL CHICANO DE AZTLÁN (M.E.Ch.A.), the organization's goal was twofold: student activism in local communities, and on college campuses, advocating increased attention and educational resources to meet the specific cultural needs of Mexican-American students and their communities. *El Plan* also demanded the development of Chicano Studies departments on college campuses. M.E.Ch.A. chapters championed and supported the 1968–1971 Los Angeles high school walk-outs that called attention to the inadequate funding, poor educational materials, and the 50 percent dropout rate in the five predominately Mexican-American East Los Angeles high schools.

Another major outcome of the 1969 NCYLC conference was a call for the creation of an independent local, regional, and national political party. That same year, José Angel GUTIÉRREZ and Mario Compeán, both influential leaders of the Texas-based Mexican American Youth Organization (MAYO), helped form LA RAZA UNIDA PARTY (RUP) that targeted the Crystal City, Texas, school board elections (see CRYSTAL CITY ELECTORAL REVOLT). Through high school walk-outs and successful grass-roots community organizing efforts, Gutiérrez effectively elected RUP's candidates to the school board and the city council. By 1972, the call for a national La Raza Unida Party brought together the preeminent regional Chicano leaders González, Gutiérrez, Compeán, and Reies López TIJERINA, leader of the New Mexico Tierra Amarilla land grant movement. An itinerant Protestant minister, López Tijerina joined the land grant movement that charged the current landowners and the federal government with deception and fraud. The land grant movement sought to regain the communal land grant rights initially granted Mexican Americans by the Spanish crown or Mexican government. López Tijerina not only reinvigorated the movement but garnered national attention when he attempted, but failed, to make a citizen's arrest of the district attorney of Rio Arriba County on June 5, 1967; the attempt ended in violence and a federal manhunt. Acquitted of the charges, López Tijerina emerged as a recognizable Chicano leader.

As with other civil rights movements, the VIETNAM WAR fostered Chicano militancy. On August 29, 1970, the BROWN BERETS, a militant Chicano organization styling itself after the BLACK PANTHER PARTY, called for a national Chicano Moratorium to protest not only the VIETNAM WAR but also oppression by police. The Moratorium became one of the country's largest antiwar protests in Los Angeles with nearly twenty thousand people in attendance. Overreacting to a minor incident, the police attacked the peaceful demonstra-

nonviolence and Chicano nationalism. In time this organization developed an alternative school and defense committees, and in March 1969 hosted the National Chicano Youth Liberation Conference (NCYLC). Gonzáles helped to draft a document entitled *"El Plan Espiritual de Aztlán,"* which became the Chicano Movement's manifesto, declaring that nationalism was the organizational glue to bind religious, political, class, and economic factions within the Mexican-American community. The ultimate goal of Chicano nationalism was self-determination and control over the Chicano barrios' educational, economic, political, and judicial institutions.

Two months later, in Santa Barbara, California, the Chicano Coordinating Council of Higher Education, a statewide educational network, implemented the cultural/nationalist ideology of *El Plan*, which described the development of a national student organization dedicated to creating a master plan that would include curriculum reform, the establishment of needed auxiliary social and educational services, and increased admission and retention of Chicano stu-

tors. In the ensuing violence a Chicano reporter, Reuben Salazar, was killed.

The Chicano Movement declined by the early 1970s. External pressures, especially the effective law enforcement infiltration of Chicano militant groups, undermined the radicalism of *El Movimiento.* Internally, several factors contributed to its decline. Personal rivalries based on regionalism led to the demise of RUP and Chicana feminists challenged the paternalism of cultural nationalism and its male leaders. By the late 1970s, regionalism again divided Chicano communities.

BIBLIOGRAPHY

Acuña, Rodolfo. *Occupied America: A History of Chicanos,* 3rd ed. 1988.

Garcia, Ignacio M. *United We Win: The Rise and Fall of La Raza Unida Party.* 1989.

Garcia, Ignacio M. *Chicanismo: The Forging of a Militant Ethos Among Mexican Americans.* 1997.

Muñoz, Carlos, Jr. *Youth, Identity, Power: The Chicano Movement.* 1989.

Navarro, Armando. *The Crystal Experiment: A Chicano Struggle for Community Control.* 1998.

Vigil, Ernesto B. *The Crusade for Justice: Chicano Militancy and the Government's War on Dissent.* 1999.

Maria Raquel Casas

Chicano Student Movement of Aztlán

See Movimiento Estudiantil Chicano de Aztlán.

Children's Defense Fund

The Children's Defense Fund (CDF) is a Washington, D.C.-based advocacy organization led by former civil rights attorney Marian Wright EDELMAN. It advocates for programs and policies that assist children, primarily those who are poor, minority, or disabled. The faith-based moral imperative of its advocacy is reminiscent of elements of the 1950s and early 1960s civil rights movement.

Founded in 1968 as the Washington Research Project (WRP), it initially acted as a public interest law firm monitoring the enforcement of federal civil rights and antipoverty legislation. As such, WRP acted as legal counsel to the 1968 POOR PEOPLE'S CAMPAIGN and as the campaign's liaison to the federal government. It also provided assistance to the civil rights movement–based Child Development Group of Mississippi in shielding its HEAD START and funding of the project from attack by Mississippi Senator John Stennis.

As support for programs to assist poor African Americans and others waned in the early 1970s, WRP focused more strongly on children, with the premise that programs assisting them would also benefit the wider community and appeal to a broader political base. Moreover, Edelman increasingly came to believe that early intervention for children acted as a cost-effective investment in them and their communities. Since 1973, when WRP became the Children's Defense Fund, the organization has successfully advocated for juvenile offenders and disabled students at the federal and state levels, and for the expansion of Head Start, subsidized childcare, and Medicaid. Among its losses, however, are campaigns for a national health insurance program and against the dismantling of Aid to Families with Dependent Children.

BIBLIOGRAPHY

Greenberg, Polly. *The Devil Has Slippery Shoes: A Biased Biography of the Child Development Group of Mississippi.* 1969.

"Interview with Marian Wright Edelman." In "The Rights of Children." *Harvard Educational Review,* Reprint series, 9 (1974).

Steiner, Gilbert Yale. *The Children's Cause.* 1976.

Young, Andrew. *An Easy Burden: The Civil Rights Movement and the Transformation of America.* 1996

Charles F. Casey-Leininger

Children's Rights Movement

The Children's Rights Movement (also called the Children's Advocacy Movement) emerged most notably in the middle 1970s in the United States, although the history of child advocacy in this country could certainly be traced back to periods well over a hundred years prior. Comprised of a relatively small number of concerned citizens, parents' groups, youth organizations, and professional advocates in law, education, health care, government, psychology, and corrections, the children's rights movement, in its most recent incarnation, never gained the sort of national attention or political coherence of other civil rights and liberation movements of the era. It was never a "mass action" or broad-based movement. Important for children's advocacy at the time was the general "culture of rights" that had grown up in the United States over the preceding two decades. Amidst well-known national debates on the rights of racial or ethnic minorities and women, the plight of children was articulated within the conventions of the prevailing reformist or revolutionary rhetoric. What were the demands of the movement? Around which issues did the loosely coordinated organizations and advocates rally? Let us briefly summarize the major components of children's oppression in the United States as they were formulated by advocates of the time.

In their landmark anthology, *The Children's Rights Movement: Overcoming the Oppression of Young People*, Beatrice and Ronald Gross (1977) stated, "A good case can be made for the fact that young people are the most oppressed of all minorities. They are discriminated against on the basis of age in everything from movie admissions to sex. They are traditionally the subjects of ridicule, humiliation, and mental torture by adults. Their civil rights are routinely violated in homes, schools, and other institutions. They often cannot own money or property. They lack the right to trial by jury before being sentenced to jail." Children, it was argued, are politically disenfranchised, economically disadvantaged, legally unprotected, and vulnerable to the abuses and exploitation of adult society. As a critical response to such observations, children's rights advocates enacted a number of counter-measures, from reformist to revolutionary in scope.

Advocates called for an end to neglect and abuse (mental, physical, and sexual) in the public institutions which determined so much of young people's life chances—schools, juvenile detention units, counsel-

A young girl works in the spinning room at the Globe cotton mill in Augusta, Georgia, in January 1909. (CORBIS)

ing centers, hospitals, and courts. Similarly, social workers, teachers, religious leaders, and community groups were called upon to encourage reform in the parenting and child-rearing strategies (which were often authoritarian, violent, and paternalistic) utilized by so many families. National campaigns, usually coordinated at the local level, were launched to stem the tide of violence against children, while efforts to increase the funding of vital social services for children—especially poor children were pursued (i.e., schools, health care, housing, etc.). Perhaps the most noted national organization to emerge from the movement was the CHILDREN'S DEFENSE FUND (CDF), founded by Marian Wright EDELMAN in 1973. Edelman, a veteran of the civil rights movement and the WAR ON POVERTY, saw the fight for children's rights as an extension of the concerns of the sixties, the most salient way to broaden the base for political change.

For all its national prominence, however, the CDF must be situated within the more fundamental divisions inherent to the Children's Rights Movement itself. On the one hand, along with Edelman and the CDF, there were advocates who supported a "caretaker" approach to children's rights. Generally, these groups argued that children, while not able to take care of and make critical decisions for themselves, should be provided with capable and informed caretakers. On the other hand, "child liberationists" argued that children should be afforded most, if not all, of the rights granted to adults in the United States. The guiding principle of the latter approach was, of course, self-determination, a direct counter to the perceived paternalism of the caretaker program. These divisions made for much heated debate, only some of which was productive to the movement as a whole. To date, the CDF and other children's advocacy groups continue to battle for the programs and initiatives they catalyzed nearly twenty-five years ago. As such, their battles are as much with each other as with the general public or various state agencies.

Timeline

1930   The first national Children's Charter is drafted at the White House Conference on Children's Rights.

1959   United Nations General Assembly adopts the Declaration of the Rights of the Child.

1965   Project Head Start is created to combat juvenile poverty and educational failure in elementary schools nationwide.

1966   Presidential adviser James Coleman publishes his report *Equality of Educational Opportunity*, a major source of information for children's advocates in the following years.

1967 The U.S. Supreme Court case *In Re Gault* grants children some of the constitutional rights afforded adults charged with crimes. It is the first Supreme Court decision to recognize children as human beings before the Constitution.

1967 The National Commission on Resources for Youth is founded, expressly to promote opportunities for responsible participation of youth in society.

1969 The U.S. Supreme Court holds that high school students cannot be expelled for expressing their political beliefs under the First Amendment. The students involved had worn black armbands in protest of the U.S. war in Southeast Asia.

1972 Youth Liberation of Ann Arbor publishes what is, perhaps, the first manifesto of youth organizations in the Children's Rights Movement, entitled *We Do Not Recognize Their Right to Control Us.*

1973 The Children's Defense Fund is founded by Marian Wright Edelman.

1973–76 The United States issued a number of international directives to extend its newly emerging national "commitment" to children. This occurred after numerous studies indicating the dire conditions of children worldwide (high rates of poverty and infant death, low literacy rates and lack of educational opportunities, low per capita incomes, poor health care systems, polluted water, famine, and overcrowding). More recently, however, U.S. foreign aid, and domestic spending for child-oriented programs have dwindled.

1974 *U.S. News & World Report* publishes the first extensive national coverage of the Children's Liberation Movement in an article entitled, "Nationwide Drive for Children's Rights."

1979 The International Year of the Child established by UNICEF and the United Nations General Assembly. It proclaimed four major purposes:
  1. To heighten awareness of people, communities, and governments about the importance of the child—as a child and as the adult of tomorrow.
  2. To deepen understanding of what a child requires to enable him or her to develop his or her full potential.
  3. To increase sympathy for unmet needs, and awareness of the possibilities of action to improve conditions.
  4. To bring about a commitment to children on the national and international level

deep and persistent enough to produce necessary changes.

1980 The Children Defense Fund–sponsored Child Welfare Act is passed by Congress.

1987 The Children's Initiative, a composite measure consisting of nine federal programs, is enacted.

BIBLIOGRAPHY

Adams, Paul, et al. *Towards the Liberation of the Child.* 1972.
Archard, David. *Children: Rights and Childhood.* 1993.
Berger, Nan. *The Rights of Children and Young People.* 1967.
Gross, Beatrice, and Ronald Gross, eds. *The Children's Rights Movement: Overcoming the Oppression of Young People.* 1977.
Jenks, Chris, *Childhood.* 1996.
Nazario, Thomas A., ed. *In Defense of Children: Understanding the Rights, Needs, and Interests of the Child.* 1988.
Wringe, C. A. *Children's Rights: A Philosophical Study.* 1981.

Jared Sexton

Chinese American Citizens Alliance

In 1895 in San Francisco, Chun Dick founded the Native Sons of the Golden State (NSGS), an organization of native-born male Chinese Americans that modeled itself after the patriotic Native Sons of the Golden West. Reorganized by Walter U. Lum and others in 1904, the NSGS members strove to fully enjoy and defend their American citizenship, cultivate their minds through the exchange of knowledge, effect a higher character among themselves and observe the principles of brotherly love and mutual help. In 1912 the Grand Lodge, the organization's national headquarters, opened at 1044 Stockton Street in San Francisco. Other communities—San Francisco, Los Angeles, and Oakland—formed local chapters. Eventually lodges were established nationwide. In 1915 the organization adopted a new name—the Chinese American Citizens Alliance—which was formalized in 1928. From 1924 to 1988 the CACA published *The Chinese Times*, a Chinese-language daily newspaper advocating its interests.

Being a member of the CACA established a person as a Chinese-American community leader and many members were encouraged to participate in local, state, and national politics, community welfare programs, and educational programs. In 1976 membership was extended to women.

The CACA has been instrumental in changing many unfair laws, especially those related to immigration and discrimination, raising the Chinese-American community's political consciousness, fostering a most positive image of Chinese people in the United States, and improving the quality of life for Chinese Americans. Through the years the CACA joined with other organizations in supporting legal actions aimed at equality and justice.

BIBLIOGRAPHY

Chung, Sue Fawn. "Fighting for Their American Rights: A History of the Chinese American Citizens Alliance." In *Claiming America: Constructing Chinese American Identities During the Exclusion Era*, edited by K. Scott Wong and Sucheng Chan. 1998.

Hong, Y. C. *A Brief History of the Chinese American Citizens Alliance*. 1955.

Sue Fawn Chung

Chinese Consolidated Benevolent Association

Commonly known as the Chinese Six Companies, the Chinese Consolidated Benevolent Association (CCBA) is an umbrella organization with representatives from the *huiguan*. The *huiguan* are mutual-aid associations composed of migrants from the same district. In the nineteenth century, they provided social activities, temporary lodging, employment assistance, and burial services. Each district association also settled quarrels and debts among its members.

Officers from the existing district associations came together in 1862 to form the CCBA. This federation had an executive council made up of association presidents and a board of directors determined by proportional representation. Its original function was to arbitrate disputes between migrants from different associations, but the CCBA began handling affairs that affected the interest and welfare of the Chinese immigrant community as a whole. Although not democratic, the CCBA served as the representative of the Chinese immigrants to the rest of America. Public officials consulted the CCBA whenever they sought the opinion of the Chinese community. Before the Chinese Consulate was established in the late 1870s, the CCBA also was spokesman for the Chinese government in its relations with overseas Chinese.

Chinese immigrant elites in New York, Honolulu, Portland, and Seattle created similar coordinating organizations, but San Francisco, the city with the largest Chinese community in America, had the most prominent of these federations. San Francisco's CCBA founded a Chinese-language school to teach children Chinese language, history, and philosophy and established community medical services for sick and indigent immigrants. It hired guards to protect Chinatown stores and properties, reflecting the organization's domination by merchants.

When an organization to defend the rights of all Chinese immigrants became necessary in the 1880s, the CCBA became active in combating anti-Chinese sentiment. It used protests, appeals, and memorials to city, state, and federal governments to raise awareness of the mistreatment of Chinese immigrants. It protested the persecution of Chinese miners and later challenged a 1900 quarantine of Chinatown. In 1905, the CCBA sponsored a speaking tour for Ng Poon Chew, a Christian pastor and the founder of the newspaper *Chung Sai Yat Po*, who informed audiences about anti-Chinese activities and unjust immigration laws. In addition to moral suasion, the CCBA expressed its resentment toward immigration policy by participating in the 1905 Chinese boycott of American goods.

Through membership dues and exit permits, the CCBA collected a legal war chest to hire European-American lawyers to represent the Chinese community. Among the numerous cases was the CCBA's attempt to overturn the Geary Act (1892), a law authorizing immediate deportation if a Chinese immigrant could not produce registration documents or a white witness to verify the immigrant's residency since 1880. Hoping to launch a test case to declare the act unconstitutional, the CCBA ordered Chinese immigrants to refuse to register. The unfavorable ruling in *Fong Yue Tiang* v. *United States* (1892) was a blow to the CCBA's prestige and led to an internal power struggle.

The CCBA was also heavily involved in Chinese politics. By the middle of the twentieth century, the CCBA had a close association with the *Kuomintang* or Nationalist Party of China. Because its leaders held high positions in the party hierarchy, the CCBA bolstered the party's influence in Chinese immigrant communities.

BIBLIOGRAPHY

Chan, Sucheng. *Asian Americans: An Interpretive History*. 1991.

Hoy, William. *The Chinese Six Companies*. 1942.

Lai, Him Mark. "Historical Development of the Chinese Consolidated Benevolent Association/*Huiguan* System." In *Chinese America: History and Perspectives, 1987*. 1987.

Ma, L. Eve Armentrout. "Chinatown Organizations and the Anti-Chinese Movement, 1882–1914." In *Entry Denied: Exclusion and the Chinese Community in America, 1882–1943*, edited by Sucheng Chan. 1991.

Nee, Victor G., and Brett de Barry Nee. *Longtime Californ': A Documentary Study of an American Chinatown*. 1974.

S. H. Tang

Chinese Equal Rights League

The Chinese Equal Rights League, established on September 1, 1892, was the first civil rights organization formed by persons of Asian ancestry in the United States. Its origins lay in a meeting held on July 30, 1884 in New York City, when fifty naturalized U.S. citizens of Chinese ancestry met to discuss the possibility of forming an organization to "obtain representation and recognition in American politics." The meeting was reported in the *New York Times* in an article entitled "The Chinamen Organizing." Obtaining political representation was a difficult goal to reach because the then-existing naturalization laws, a clause in the 1868 Burlingame Treaty between China and the United States, and the 1882 CHINESE EXCLUSION ACT all denied Chinese immigrants the right of naturalization. However, because at that time applications for naturalization were handled by the local courts, a small number of Chinese had managed to acquire naturalized citizenship before the federal courts unequivocably denied them such a right. Unable to become citizens, and hence unable to vote, the vast majority of Chinese immigrants were barred from political participation.

The passage of the Geary Act in 1892 not only extended Chinese exclusion for another ten years, but set up draconian measures to find, apprehend, and deport any Chinese caught without the registration card he or she was required to carry. This act gave concerned Chinese Americans the impetus to establish the Chinese Equal Rights League. Its 150 founding members elected Lee Sam Ping, a Philadelphia merchant, as president, and Wong Chin Foo, a newspaper editor and popular public speaker, as secretary. The league held a rally three weeks later and passed a resolution to oppose the implementation of the Geary Act. The league also issued a pamphlet appealing to the American people for equal treatment. "America is our home through long residence," the pamphlet declared. "Character and fitness should be the requirements of all who are desirous of becoming citizens of the American Republic."

Five years later, the league campaigned to urge Congress to rescind all the Chinese Exclusion Laws and to grant Chinese the franchise, but to no avail. In 1898, in an attempt to prove its members' patriotism, the league proposed to form a militia company to fight in the war against Spain. Though such a group never came into being, some eighty Chinese did enlist in the U.S. Navy and fought in the Battle of Manila Bay. In retrospect, though the league did not succeed in any of its efforts, it certainly deserves a place in the history of the struggle for civil rights.

BIBLIOGRAPHY

Zhang, Qingsong. "The Origins of the Chinese Americanization Movement: Wong Chin Foo and the Chinese Equal Rights League." In *Claiming America: Constructing Chinese American Identities During the Exclusion Era,* edited by K. Scott Wong and Sucheng Chan. 1998.

Sucheng Chan

Chinese Exclusion Acts

The 1882 Chinese Exclusion Act was Congress's response to the anti-Chinese movement in California which had overwhelming support in the American West. Opposition came from some employers of Chinese labor, merchants in the China trade, and Christian denominations interested in converting Chinese. U.S. Senator George F. Hoar, a Massachusetts Republican, was one of the few Americans to oppose Chinese exclusion on principle. The 1868 Burlingame Treaty with China, which recognized the mutual right of Chinese and Americans to immigrate, was an impediment to exclusion, but China agreed, in 1880, that the United States could "regulate, limit or suspend" the immigration of Chinese laborers. In 1882 Congress suspended the immigration of Chinese laborers for twenty years, but President Chester A. Arthur vetoed the bill while indicating that he would accept a "shorter experiment." Congress then quickly passed, and Arthur signed, an act suspending the immigration of Chinese laborers for ten years.

Although titled the Chinese Exclusion Act, the 1882 statute exempted teachers, students, merchants and their families, and "travellers for pleasure." The law was extended for ten years in 1892 and made "permanent" with similar exemptions in 1902. Until 1888 Chinese laborers already in the United States could obtain a certificate entitling them to return, but the so-called Scott Act of 1888 canceled all outstanding certificates. Many Chinese laborers with such certificates were barred from returning.

The provisions of the exclusion laws that allowed the entry of some Chinese—mostly merchants and their families—were hotly contested. It was eventually stipulated that laundry proprietors were not merchants and an 1893 law specified that the status of anyone who sought entrance as a merchant had to be attested to "by the testimony of two credible witnesses other than Chinese." One unintended consequence of the exclusion acts was an expansion of constitutional protections for resident aliens. Chinese litigants brought a large number of cases testing the exclusion acts and other anti-Chinese legislation; in YICK WO v. HOPKINS (1886) the U.S. SUPREME COURT established that the FOURTEENTH AMENDMENT applied to all persons within its jurisdiction. The IMMIGRATION ACT OF 1924, which barred the immigration of "aliens ineligible to citizenship," all but ended Chinese immigration for twenty years.

In 1979 a monument was unveiled at Angel Island Immigration Station to honor Chinese immigrants almost a hundred years after the passage of the Chinese Exclusion Acts. (Photo by Connie Young Yu)

In 1943 Congress, at the urging of President Franklin D. ROOSEVELT, repealed the fifteen statutes that effected Chinese exclusion, gave Chinese persons a tiny annual quota of 105, and made them, alone of all Asians, eligible for naturalization. The public campaign for repeal, the discussion in Congress, and the statements of President Roosevelt all stressed, not the rights of Chinese Americans, but the lifting of "an unfortunate barrier between allies."

The Chinese Exclusion Act and its subsequent repeal have a larger significance than is readily apparent. It can now be seen that the original act was a hinge on which American immigration policy turned: once Chinese had been excluded it was easier to enact other restrictions. Similarly its repeal signaled the beginning of a less racially exclusive immigration and naturalization policy: within nine years all ethnic/racial bars to immigration and naturalization had been removed.

BIBLIOGRAPHY

Daniels, Roger. *Asian America: Chinese and Japanese in the United States Since 1850.* 1988.
McClain, Charles J., Jr. *In Search of Equality: the Chinese Struggle against Discrimination in Nineteenth-Century America.* 1994.
Riggs, Fred. *Pressures on Congress: A Study of the Repeal of Chinese Exclusion.* 1950.
Salyer, Lucy. *Laws Harsh as Tigers: Chinese Immigrants and the Shaping of Modern Immigration Law.* 1995.

Sandmeyer, Elmer C. *The Anti-Chinese Movement in California,* rev. ed. 1991.

Roger Daniels

Chinese for Affirmative Action

A Chinese-American civil rights organization, Chinese for Affirmative Action was founded in San Francisco in 1969 by five Chinese-American political activists: Alice Barkley, Lambert Choy, Lillian Sing, L. Ling-chi Wang, and Germaine Wong. Its initial goal was to promote equal employment opportunities for Chinese Americans. Two other objectives were soon added: to encourage Chinese Americans to participate in political and civic affairs and to ensure that Asian Americans receive their fair share of public resources and services.

Since its founding, Chinese for Affirmative Action has accomplished a great deal. Through negotiation and political action, the organization has helped to increase job opportunities for Asian Americans in the construction industry; in civil service, at the municipal, county, state, and federal levels; in the mass media; in financial institutions, especially banks, insurance companies, and stock brokerages; and in higher levels of the service sector. Not only have more Asian Americans been hired in the mass media, but various broadcast stations have also responded to requests for more sensitive reporting and more ethnically inclusive programming.

Although the organization has focused its activities in the greater San Francisco Bay area, its impact has been felt in wider circles. Several of its members and officers have mounted efforts for educational reform, including filing a successful lawsuit (see LAU V. NICHOLS) that mandated bilingual programs in the public schools and ensuring that the University of California, Berkeley, not impose discriminatory quotas on Asian-American students.

BIBLIOGRAPHY

Der, Henry. "Affirmative Action Policy: Asian Pacific Islanders and the 'Glass Ceiling'—New Era of Civil Rights Activism?" In *The State of Asian Pacific America—a Public Policy Report: Policy Issues to the Year 2020*, edited by LEAP Asian Pacific American Public Policy Institute and UCLA Asian American Studies Center. 1993.

Der, Henry, Colleen Lye, and Howard Ting. *Broken Ladder: Asian Americans in City Government Reports*. 1986, 1989, and 1992.

Sucheng Chan

Congresswoman Shirley Chisholm giving a forceful speech during her 1972 campaign for the Democratic Party nomination for president. In 1969 Mrs. Chisholm had become the first African-American woman to serve in the U.S. Congress. (AP/World Wide Photos)

Chisholm, Shirley Anita

(1924–   ), first black woman elected to the U.S. Congress, activist.

Shirley Chisholm has had a long career as a political activist and advocate for racial, economic, and gender equality. The daughter of working-class West Indian immigrants, Chisholm (*née* Shirley St. Hill) was born in Brooklyn, but was sent to live with her maternal grandmother in Barbados when she was three years old. Growing up on a farm in Barbados, Chisholm was educated in British-influenced island schools; she credits her confidence, self-esteem, and discipline to the years she spent there. When she was ten years old, Chisholm returned to Brooklyn. Raised in an interracial neighborhood by parents who stressed the importance of education and religion, Chisholm learned racial pride from her father, a labor organizer and follower of Marcus GARVEY.

In 1942, Chisholm entered Brooklyn College, graduating cum laude with a major in sociology. Deciding on a career in teaching, she worked at a child care center while earning a master's degree in early childhood education from Columbia University. After seven years, Chisholm became the director of a large child care center. By 1959, she had become a consultant to the New York City Division of Day Care, responsible for supervising ten day care centers and promoting the development of others. She married twice,

to Conrad Chisholm in 1949 and to Arthur Hardwick, Jr., in 1979. She never had any children of her own.

While Chisholm's professional career began in teaching, she quickly became involved in politics. Starting from a position as a volunteer in various community service organizations, Chisholm began working with the seventeenth assembly district Democratic club in the early 1950s. While the political club was dominated by whites, the seventeenth district was increasingly comprised of blacks and Puerto Ricans. Chisholm spent several years involved in grassroots political organizing where she learned the valuable lesson that political organizations are designed to keep power in the hands of the powerful. She soon joined an alternative political organization that sought to oust the white political machine. In 1964, Chisholm was elected to the New York State Assembly as a Democrat, a position she held for four years. In 1968, she beat Republican candidate James Farmer, the former head of the CONGRESS OF RACIAL EQUALITY, to win election to the U.S. CONGRESS as the representative from the twelfth congressional district.

Throughout her seven terms as a Congresswoman, Chisholm repeatedly proved her political independence from both the Democratic party and from political tradition. Running on the slogan, "unbought and unbossed," Chisholm strove to serve the needs of her constituents through her skill in pragmatic politics. She protested her original Congressional Committee assignment (to the Agricultural Committee) as "irrelevant" and demanded to be reassigned; she fought to extend the minimum wage to domestic workers, to limit spending on defense and increase spending on social services, and to improve education and child care facilities. In 1972, Chisholm made a serious bid for the Democratic nomination for the presidency, running, she claimed, because someone had to be the first to challenge the notion that only white men could be president. Seen as politically unpredictable, Chisholm often earned the wrath of other black politicians, who felt she was too independent.

As much a feminist as an advocate of civil rights, Chisholm claims that being a woman was more of a disadvantage in her political career than being black. Throughout her career, Chisholm has urged women to refuse to accept gender stereotypes and to become more actively involved in politics. In 1971, along with feminists like Betty FRIEDAN and Bella ABZUG, Chisholm helped found the National Women's Political Caucus. She has also served as honorary president of the National Abortion Rights Action League, contending that poor women must have access to safe abortions.

After retiring from Congress in 1982, Chisholm spent several years teaching politics and women's studies at Mount Holyoke College in Massachusetts. Chisholm has stayed involved in politics through her extensive lecturing, by cofounding the National Political Congress of Black Women in 1984, and by participating in Jesse JACKSON's presidential campaigns in 1984 and 1988. In 1993 she was nominated by President Bill Clinton to serve as Ambassador to Jamaica, although she had to turn down the position because of problems with her eyesight. Although she has retired to Florida, Chisholm remains an active political voice. In recent years she has warned of an erosion of the gains of the civil rights era and of the dangers of cutting social spending. Current politicians, Chisholm claims, are suffering from "compassion fatigue," a condition that never plagued the congresswoman from New York.

BIBLIOGRAPHY

Chisholm, Shirley. *Unbought and Unbossed.* 1970.
Chisholm, Shirley. *The Good Fight.* 1973.
Mueller, Michael. "Shirley Chisholm." In *Contemporary Black Biography,* Vol. 2, edited by Barbara Carlisle Bigelow. 1992.
Scheader, Catherine. *Shirley Chisholm: Teacher and Congresswoman.* 1990.

Renee Romano

Cinema

See Film.

Citizenship

Since the nation's founding, citizenship in the United States has been organized within the complex and contradictory frameworks of equality and exclusivity. Citizenship denotes a particular relationship between the state, which includes federal, state, and local government apparatuses, and the governed. The Declaration of Independence originally defined this relationship as one based fundamentally upon consent, arguing that governments derive "their just powers from the consent of the governed." As the primary vehicle for conferring this legitimacy, the right to vote is one of the most significant components of the relationship between the American state and its people. Not only does it form this concrete link, but the franchise also defines the citizenry generally as the community of voters. Thus, although citizenship includes many other connections to government, such as access to social services and the protection of law, the franchise has come to stand as the most powerful symbol of civil rights in the United States, forming the focal point for a variety of struggles for full citizenship.

The notion of equality among citizens is a foundational principle of American civil rights as well as a central myth of the national culture. Equal citizenship means that, ideally, all members of the American public hold the same rights and responsibilities, and are afforded uniform protections by law to exercise them. Yet, this "equality" has been severely constrained by the fact that not all people within the nation have been recognized as members of the American community, or as citizens, at various times. Native Americans, African Americans, women, immigrants, the poor, the sexually nonconforming, the disabled, and prisoners are among the many who have been denied, and often continue to be denied, full inclusion in the citizenry. Historically, these very exclusions have served to define the boundaries of American citizenship, by designating who did *not* belong to the national community.

Beginning with the obvious contradictions of a new nation founded on "equality" and "freedom" yet dependent upon the enslavement of black people, African-American freedom struggles have persistently exposed the exclusivity inherent in these nationalist ideologies. Black civil rights activism has played a unique role in the history of American citizenship, providing a strategic model for other excluded populations and setting a number of legal precedents for wider inclusion. Moreover, black-nationalist critiques of this liberal rights model of INTEGRATION have informed a variety of identity-based political movements in post-1968 America.

A group is gathered to take the oath of citizenship on Ellis Island, with the Statue of Liberty barely visible in the background, ca. 1990. (AP/Wide World Photos)

Citizenship is most literally regulated through law in the United States. A series of Supreme Court cases and constitutional amendments form one significant narrative in the history of African-American civil rights struggles. In the context of national debates over slavery, the *Dred Scott* decision of 1857 (see Dred Scott v. Sandford) declared that all enslaved people and their descendants could not be citizens of the United States. This decision also established a distinction between federal and state laws that would continue to plague African Americans' quest for full inclusion in the American citizenry until the 1960s. In his majority opinion, Justice Roger B. Taney argued that black people were inherently incapable of citizenship as an "inferior class of beings," and were never intended to be members of the American public defined by the Constitution. He claimed that because state laws dictating the chattel-slave status of black people existed prior to federal law, the exclusion had been clear in the minds of the Framers and held precedence. Thus, Taney drew a separation between national and state citizenship, defining the latter as the primary arena of civil rights. The maintenance of this distinction in subsequent decisions, such as the *Slaughterhouse Cases* (1873), would make legal apartheid in the Southern states possible throughout the first half of the twentieth century.

Although enslaved people had been freeing themselves since the beginning of the Civil War, the Emancipation Proclamation officially ended slavery in 1865. With the North's victory, the Thirteenth Amendment mandated emancipation constitutionally in December of that year. Within months, however, eight Southern states had established contradictory laws, known as Black Codes, that limited black freedoms and continued disfranchisement. With the onset of Radical Reconstruction, the Fourteenth and Fifteenth Amendments to the Constitution were passed to enforce the full citizenship of freed men. To the great dismay of women's suffrage activists, the enfranchisement mandated by the Fifteenth Amendment continued to exclude all women of any race. It would be nearly fifty years before the Nineteenth Amendment granted the vote to women.

The revolutionary promise of Radical Reconstruction came to an abrupt end with the Compromise of 1877, which marked the federal government's retreat from its protection of African-American citizenship. Although a conservative Supreme Court had been limiting the intent of the Fourteenth Amendment in deference to "States' Rights" since its passage, the last part of the nineteenth century witnessed a series of devastating decisions that legalized Southern Segregation. In the *Civil Rights Cases of 1883*, the Court ruled that as long as state laws did not explicitly segregate public accommodations by race, the federal government held no mandate to enforce equal access. With its decision in Plessy v. Ferguson (1896), the

Court went a step further, finding that the racial segregation of Southern railroads was legal within the infamous logic of "separate but equal."

It was not until the 1950s that African Americans began to successfully dismantle segregation and their forced exclusion from the citizenry. With its decision in BROWN V. BOARD OF EDUCATION(1954), the Supreme Court, under the leadership of Chief Justice Earl WARREN, returned to the Fourteenth Amendment's equal protection clause to find the segregation of public schools illegal. This marked a turning point for the civil rights movement as the case set a precedent for subsequent DESEGREGATION campaigns, culminating in the CIVIL RIGHTS ACT OF 1964, outlawing public segregation and racial discrimination in the workplace and in schools, and the VOTING RIGHTS ACT OF 1965.

As these disjunctures between federal law, state law, and local, everyday practice illustrate, the legal system is only one arena in which citizenship is defined, limited, and expressed. Conflicting notions of equality and exclusivity, grounded in collective racial, gender, CLASS, and sexual identities saturate the national culture. In this respect, both African Americans and others have yet to achieve full inclusion in the national community, as they continue to struggle alongside many other populations for the recognition of their equal citizenship.

BIBLIOGRAPHY

Franklin, John Hope. *From Slavery to Freedom: A History of African Americans*, 7th ed. 1994.

Gordon, Linda. *Pitied But Not Entitled: Single Mothers and the History of Welfare, 1890–1935.* 1994.

Karst, Kenneth L. *Belonging to America: Equal Citizenship and the Constitution.* 1989.

Lowe, Lisa. *Immigrant Acts: On Asian-American Cultural Politics.* 1996.

Ruiz, Vicki L., and Ellen Carol DuBois, eds. *Unequal Sisters: A Multicultural Reader in U.S. Women's History,* 2nd ed. 1994.

Warner, Michael, ed. *Fear of a Queer Planet: Queer Politics and Social Theory.* 1993.

Micki McElya

Citizenship Schools

Political education or reeducation is an essential task in any social movement. Broadly construed, it includes both consciousness-raising and civics. The Citizenship Schools (CS) provided a major model for the civil rights movement's efforts to mobilize and train African-American citizens in the South. Begun under the auspices of the HIGHLANDER FOLK SCHOOL in 1957, the CS used adult literacy training as the core of a rural leadership development program. Supported by

grants from the Marshall Field Foundation, the program and key African-American staff member Mrs. Septima CLARK moved to the SOUTHERN CHRISTIAN LEADERSHIP CONFERENCE (SCLC) when the Folk School closed in 1961. With Andrew YOUNG as director, it became SCLC's principal grass-roots program working across the South. From its new base in Knoxville, Tennessee, the renamed Highlander Educational Center also provided training in voter education for other civil rights organizations, notably the STUDENT NONVIOLENT COORDINATING COMMITTEE (SNCC) and the CONGRESS OF RACIAL EQUALITY (CORE). The first CS teacher, Bernice ROBINSON, passed on her experience to SNCC and CORE field workers in MISSISSIPPI, southwest GEORGIA, and other trouble spots. The underlying Highlander philosophy of empowerment through active participation was thus spread significantly by the Citizenship Schools.

Highlander developed the schools at the invitation of Mr. Esau Jenkins of Johns Island, near Charleston, SOUTH CAROLINA. The stress on literacy reflected the primacy of the literacy test as an obstacle to black voter registration in the Deep South. A longstanding member of the NATIONAL ASSOCIATION FOR THE ADVANCEMENT OF COLORED PEOPLE (NAACP) and a schoolteacher, Mrs. Clark knew formal techniques of literacy teaching, and her younger cousin, Robinson (a beautician), was able to listen to the adult students and devise a scheme relevant to them. Beginning in 1957, classes met two nights a week for a two-or three-month period during the slack winter farm period (commonly December to February). The formal goal of the CS was voter registration, but central to its success were the personal ties that developed between teacher and students and the immediate personal benefits students enjoyed from the skills they acquired.

The Citizenship Education Program at SCLC was primarily a teacher-training scheme. Using Marshall Field Foundation money, local people—usually activists, such as Fannie Lou HAMER—attended the Dorchester Center outside Savannah (Tennessee) to train as CS teachers. On their return, they set up classes of (usually) twelve adults and received a small monthly payment to cover expenses. Mrs Clark and her colleagues, notably Dorothy COTTON and Annell Ponder, would visit the schools to check on progress, and the teachers would return to Dorchester for refresher courses. As the schools spread across the South, their curricula changed to suit the needs of different places and to address pupils' concerns. Many students were women and so issues of planned parenthood and child care were addressed. Former CS teachers launched HEAD START programs and CS supervisors attended courses on how to submit Community Action Plans and other proposals funded under the WAR ON POV-

ERTY. Attempts to extend the Citizen Education Program to Northern communities using a Ford Foundation grant in 1967 failed, and after the VOTING RIGHTS ACT OF 1965 eliminated literacy tests, many literacy programs lapsed back into overly formal schemes geared narrowly toward employment rather than empowerment.

BIBLIOGRAPHY

Glen, John. *Highlander: No Ordinary School.* 1996.
Ling, Peter. "Local Leadership in the Early Civil Rights Movement: The South Carolina Citizenship Education Program of the Highlander Folk School." *Journal of American Studies* 29 (1995): 399–422.
Tjerandsen, Carl. *Education for Citizenship: A Foundation's Experience.* 1980.

Peter J. Ling

Civil Disobedience

Civil disobedience, disobeying the law for reasons of conscience, has a long tradition in America. As early as 1638, Ann Hutchinson's insistence upon the priority of personal conscience brought her into conflict with and eventual banishment by Puritan authorities in Massachusetts, where early Quakers, too, were hanged for the "heresy" of their belief in the "Inner Light" of personal conscience. In the following years, Quakers, Mennonites, Brethren, and Amish refused to pay war taxes, would not pay to be exempted from the militia, and would not perform alternative service. In the period prior to and following the Revolutionary War, Friends (Quakers) carried out an extensive campaign for the abolition of slavery. In 1780, they started the first anti-slavery society. As secular arguments against violence began to emerge in the early nineteenth century, members of the American Peace Society criticized U.S. expansionist policy, argued for disarmament, and focused their attention on establishing a world court. One of the boldest organizations in the nineteenth century was the New England Non-Resistance Society, led by William Lloyd Garrison, who disavowed allegiance to any government and claimed to be a world citizen. Mohandas GANDHI of India was influenced by the work and thought of Garrison, and Henry David Thoreau's celebrated essay "Civil Disobedience" owes much to the Christian anarchism articulated by Garrison. This essay urges individuals to act according to the dictates of conscience even though this entails resistance to the state.

During slavery, both abolitionists and slaves fighting RACISM used the technique of the boycott. Slaves themselves resisted through work slowdowns and running away, in addition to a limited number of armed

insurrections. A black boycott of segregated Boston schools lasted eleven years, resulting in the first major city initiation of INTEGRATION in public schools in 1855. Many of the pacifist-abolitionists of this period were also active in the early women's movement, such as the eminent abolitionist Sojourner Truth. Frederick DOUGLASS urged Elizabeth Cady STANTON to call for women's suffrage as early as 1848.

In WORLD WAR I, thirty-five hundred men signed a pledge to refuse enlistment in the war cause, and there were four thousand conscientious objectors, some of whom served harsh sentences in military prisons. Anarchist Emma Goldman was arrested for speaking out against the war, fined $10,000, sentenced to ten years in prison, and later deported. At the same time, Eugene Debs, leader of the Socialist Party proclaimed, "I have no country to fight for; my country is the earth and I am a citizen of the world." He was arrested and sentenced to ten years in prison. The American Union Against Militarism (AUAM), precursor to the AMERICAN CIVIL LIBERTIES UNION, emerged at this time to protect the civilly disobedient. In the WOMAN SUFFRAGE MOVEMENT in 1917 at a silent vigil at the White House, probably the first demonstration ever held at the president's mansion, Alice PAUL and over two hundred women from twenty-six states were arrested for "obstructing sidewalk traffic"; ninety-seven were imprisoned. During the early 1930s reports began coming from India of Gandhi's use of nonviolent tactics and civil disobedience on a massive scale to win independence for his nation from Great Britain. In WORLD WAR II, about six thousand men refused to cooperate at all with the draft and served prison sentences. Others volunteered for special projects, such as working as attendants in mental hospitals, or offering their bodies as human guinea pigs in medical experiments.

After the war, fear that the next war would be a nuclear war and that such a war would have neither victors nor survivors turned many people to nuclear pacifism. Physicist Albert Einstein urged scientists not to cooperate in military matters. In 1947 the wartime draft was abolished, and public opposition stopped the Pentagon's effort to impose universal conscription. On February 12, 1947, the first draft card burnings took place, at the White House and in New York. Subsequently, over four hundred men destroyed their draft cards or mailed them to the president. The 1950s began an era of civil disobedience against compulsory civil defense drills, when people were arrested for refusing to take shelter in the Ban the Bomb movement. Peace activists also sailed boats into nuclear bomb test areas in the South Pacific. Radical activist A. J. Muste (1885–1967) was one of the first to popularize the sit-down strike. He was arrested repeatedly for his work

Protesters are hosed by police on a Birmingham, Alabama, street corner during the spring 1963 civil rights campaign. (AP/Wide World Photos)

on behalf of labor, civil liberties, and peace. Muste influenced Martin Luther KING, JR., and such groups as the STUDENT NONVIOLENT COORDINATING COMMITTEE (SNCC) and the SOUTHERN CHRISTIAN LEADERSHIP CONFERENCE (SCLC) in their adoption of nonviolence as a tactic. Muste took a leading role during the VIETNAM WAR in the early sixties, organizing events to protest expanding U.S. involvement.

By 1948 the CONGRESS OF RACIAL EQUALITY (CORE) had begun sponsoring SIT-INS at segregated restaurants. CORE cosponsored with the FELLOWSHIP OF RECONCILIATION (FOR) the first FREEDOM RIDES, on Greyhound and Trailways buses through the upper South to desegregate interstate buslines. In 1955, Rosa PARKS refused to obey segregated seating on city buses in Montgomery, Alabama, and an ensuing boycott of city buses continued for several months. Prompted by actions such as these, CONGRESS passed the CIVIL RIGHTS ACT OF 1957. Dr. Martin Luther King, Jr., had been a student of the civil disobedience of Gandhi since his days at Crozer Theological Seminary. In 1957 he founded SCLC and engaged in numerous protests. In 1960, lunchcounter sit-ins started at Greensboro, North Carolina, quickly spread to more than fifty cities and led directly to the integration of public facilities in the South.

The ANTI-WAR MOVEMENT of the 1960s began a time of resumed draft card burnings, war resistance, and noncooperation. In 1967, fifteen hundred young men turned in their draft cards. People regularly sheltered AWOL soldiers and deserters and provided for their safety much as abolitionists had established an Underground Railroad for runaway slaves during the Civil War. There were an estimated eighty thousand to one hundred thousand military deserters and draft evaders during the Vietnam War. In the 1980s and 1990s the Right to Life movement adopted sit-in and civil disobedience tactics in its effort to blockade abortion clinics.

BIBLIOGRAPHY

Cooney, Robert, and Helen Michalowski. *The Power of the People: Active Nonviolence in the United States.* 1977.

Downton, James, Jr., and Paul Wehr. *The Persistent Activist: How Peace Commitment Develops and Survives.* 1997.

Herngren, Per. *Path of Resistance: The Practice of Civil Disobedience.* 1993.

Levi, Margaret. *Consent, Dissent, and Patriotism.* 1997.

Weber, David R., ed. *Civil Disobedience in America: A Documentary History.* 1978.

Eric Cummins

Civil Liberties

"Civil liberties" is a political term long associated with Western political traditions and sometimes mistakenly used interchangeably with "civil rights." Concepts connoted by these two terms, while sharing some mutual qualities, are not synonymous, as can be noted in a study of their origins and meanings. They do, however, represent an important development in the Western political experience regarding (1) the relationship between citizen and state; (2) individual rights and government authority; (3) how civil government and society should be organized; and (4) the role and purpose of civil government in a democratic society.

Many scholars maintain that the origin of the civil liberties concept dates back to the days of ancient Greece when the citizens of democratic Athens were able to enjoy political independence and exercise individual liberties free of governmental restrictions and interference. Among the liberties the citizens enjoyed were freedom of speech and assembly. Civil liberties in ancient Athens were inherent to citizenship. A review of ancient Western history reveals that civil liberties preceded the development of civil rights.

Although the original idea of civil liberties may have had certain foundations in antiquity, the civil liberties concept of the modern age dates from the seventeenth century in Europe, which witnessed the emergence of LIBERALISM, capitalism, and visions of liberal democracy. It was during this period that civil liberties as envisioned by America's founders came to be coherently defined and developed. Classic liberal thinkers such as John Locke argued that all democratic regimes should be based on popular consent and a commitment to civil liberties. The liberalism espoused by Locke in the seventeenth century represented a newly emerging middle-class philosophy that promoted the rights of the individual and firmly opposed the authoritarian social order that had undergirded European medieval society. The absolute power claimed by the monarchy as a consequence of rule by divine right, as well as the rigid caste and mercantile system that served to support the feudal social order, eventually would be challenged successfully by liberalism. The philosophy of liberalism called for a new vision for organizing civil government and society. At its core was an emphasis upon civil liberties, individual rights, and the goal of limiting governmental authority. One of the features that eventually came to define liberalism was the tendency to suspect governmental power and fear tyrannical rule.

Given the experiences and realities of a feudal system in which a minority (monarchy, aristocracy, and nobility) exercised rights and authority and the majority (serfs and peasants) were without rights and political influence, liberal thinkers argued that a new social order needed to be established. They maintained that government was established by consent and based on a contract with individuals to protect their natural or individual rights and to restrain government authority. Civil liberties, they proclaimed, would be the basis for a society in which freedom could be maximized and individuals would have the opportunity to realize their full potential. This perspective strongly influenced the form of government that would be established in the emerging Western democracies of the eighteenth century.

In the American political context, this new liberal vision emphasizing civil liberties was articulated by the nation's framers in the Declaration of Independence and given concrete form in the Bill of Rights. Sharing Locke's negative view of the state, they sought to restrain governmental authority and to ensure protection of the individual's life, liberty, and property from arbitrary political usurpation. The Bill of Rights identifies the freedoms that are to be protected from governmental interference: RELIGION, speech, assembly, petition, and due process for persons accused of a crime. Within the context of American political experience, the civil liberties enunciated in the Bill of Rights are to be restricted only if the government can provide compelling argument and evidence that these liberties are being abused or that national security or public welfare requires such abridgment. The framers originally intended for the provisions of the Bill of Rights to apply only to the federal government. But since 1925 the U.S. SUPREME COURT has moved to "incorporate" the Bill's provisions, eventually applying almost all of them to state governments (see *Gitlow v. New York*).

Conceptualizing and deploying civil liberties to protect the individual against arbitrary power was a major contribution of classic liberal thinkers to the progress of democratic theory and practice. Not until the nineteenth century was the premise, now almost universally accepted, advanced that another tyranny, one referred to by John Stuart Mill as "social tyranny," might ravage the freedom of individuals or groups even in the context of political democracy. In his 1859 work *On Liberty*, Mill pointed out that civil society may itself impose a tyranny as insidious as that of traditional political tyranny. Thus, Mill argued, individuals and groups require protection from civil society and from civil government. Social tyranny typically is imposed by an oppressive majority upon a vulnerable or defenseless minority through social customs, practices, and law. Slavery and racial discrimination are two forms of social tyranny that have been evident in U.S. history.

Liberal thinkers came to understand that in order to ensure equality and provide all individuals with the opportunity to realize their full potential, both civil rights and civil liberties needed to be incorporated into America's constitutional system. Coming to embrace a positive view of the state, modern liberal thinkers and activists made the case that government should take the initiative to ensure that the dignity and rights of all people are respected. Civil rights are secured through positive acts by the government to guarantee the protection of individuals against discrimination or arbitrary treatment by other individuals, groups, or governments themselves. Like civil liberties, they are sometimes made part of the Constitution; but more commonly, civil rights are codified in the form of legislation and statutes. They entered the American constitutional system when it became apparent in the nineteenth and twentieth centuries that the civil liberties provisions of the Bill of Rights failed to protect minorities against discrimination by private actors and by state and local governments.

After the Civil War, the federal government devoted itself for a time to the goal of ending the twin tyrannies of slavery and racial oppression. The RADICAL REPUBLICANS of the RECONSTRUCTION Congress took positive actions to ensure the civil rights of African Americans by initiating constitutional amendments and enacting major legislation. New amendments adopted were the THIRTEENTH AMENDMENT, which abolished slavery and involuntary servitude; the FOURTEENTH AMENDMENT, which granted citizenship and civil rights protection and declared that no state shall "deny to any person within its jurisdiction the equal protection of the laws"; and the FIFTEENTH AMENDMENT, which prohibited the denial of VOTING RIGHTS on "account of race, color, or previous condition of servitude."

Congress also passed important civil rights statutes (the CIVIL RIGHTS ACTS OF 1866, 1870, and 1871) to affirm and implement the protections and policy commitments that had been established in the aforementioned amendments. In a far-reaching effort to end racial SEGREGATION in public accommodations (e.g., transportation, restaurants, hotels, and theaters), Congress passed the CIVIL RIGHTS ACT OF 1875.

The Reconstruction Congress made impressive progress in its effort to resolve America's race problem, but unfortunately the progress was short-lived. In 1883, for example, the U.S. Supreme Court declared the Civil Rights Act of 1875 unconstitutional. The Court ruled that the Congress had been in error in assuming that the equal protection clause of the Fourteenth Amendment gave it the power to pass legislation outlawing segregation. In rescinding the law, the Court took the position that the Fourteenth Amend-

ment was applicable only to state-imposed segregation, not discrimination practiced by private citizens.

Although the 1883 decision was a setback for efforts to advance civil rights for African Americans, the Court rendered an even more crushing decision in 1896 with its ruling in PLESSY V. FERGUSON. There were two principal reasons why the *Plessy* decision had dire consequences for civil rights. First, the decision placed segregation outside the reach of the Fourteenth Amendment by invoking the infamous "separate but equal" doctrine. Second, it legitimized racial apartheid in almost every aspect of American life, including public accommodations, EMPLOYMENT, voting, and EDUCATION. Despite these setbacks, African Americans in the twentieth century would mount a mass movement to pressure policymakers to end racial segregation in America.

Civil rights organizations such as the NATIONAL ASSOCIATION FOR THE ADVANCEMENT OF COLORED PEOPLE (NAACP) and its Legal Defense Fund, the CONGRESS OF RACIAL EQUALITY (CORE), the SOUTHERN CHRISTIAN LEADERSHIP CONFERENCE (SCLC), and the STUDENT NONVIOLENT COORDINATING COMMITTEE (SNCC), among others, became the driving forces in the war on segregation. Because of their mass actions, policymakers throughout the federal government, since the 1940s, have formulated and implemented policy that supports civil rights for all Americans.

President Franklin D. ROOSEVELT, in response to A. Phillip RANDOLPH's threatened "March on Washington" in 1941, issued Executive Order 8802 prohibiting racial discrimination in defense-related industries and government. Seven years later, President Harry S. TRUMAN, in response to civil rights protests, issued Executive Order 9981, which ended segregation in the U.S. military.

The NAACP Legal Defense Fund began in the late 1930s a series of desegregation court battles that culminated in the unanimous landmark 1954 Supreme Court BROWN V. BOARD OF EDUCATION decision overturning the "separate but equal" precedent of *Plessy*. The *Brown* decision, many observers contend, is the Court's most significant ruling in support of civil rights.

Responding to mass protests and direct action movements of the 1950s and 1960s, Congress passed a series of statutes that sought to secure civil rights for African Americans and other disenfranchised minorities in the areas of public accommodations, employment, housing, and voting. The civil rights legislation enacted by Congress included the CIVIL RIGHTS ACTS OF 1957, 1960, 1964, and 1968, and the VOTING RIGHTS ACT OF 1965. Among these statutes, the Civil Rights Act of 1964 is generally regarded as the most consequential in promoting equality, with provisions protecting individuals against racial discrimination in public accommodations and employment on the basis of "race, color, religion, sex, or national origin."

Thus, civil rights can be distinguished from civil liberties in that the latter are extrapolated from the Bill of Rights and promote individual freedoms by placing restraints on governmental authority, whereas the former support political and social equality as the government takes positive actions to protect individuals from discrimination by other individuals and groups.

BIBLIOGRAPHY
Locke, John. *Second Treatise on Government.* 1690.
Mill, John Stuart. *On Liberty.* 1859.
Woodward, C. Vann. *The Strange Career of Jim Crow,* 3rd ed. 1974.

Booker Ingram

Civil Liberties Act of 1988

The Civil Liberties Act of 1988 was an unprecedented piece of legislation that granted a presidential apology and monetary redress payments to Japanese Americans and Aleutians who were wrongfully treated by the United States government during WORLD WAR II. The legislation also established a community education fund for Japanese Americans and a community restoration fund for the Aleuts.

During World War II, over 110,000 Americans and legal U.S. residents of Japanese ancestry were forcibly evacuated from the West Coast and incarcerated for up to five years in American concentration camps (see JAPANESE-AMERICAN INTERNMENT CASES). These camps were located in remote interior areas of the continental United States. Similarly, Aleuts from the Alaskan Aleutian Islands were involuntarily incarcerated in deplorable housing facilities: former mining and cannery operations in Alaska. Affected individuals lost property, employment, and educational opportunities. Additionally, detrimental psychological and social damage resulted from this violation of civil liberties. In 1948 the Japanese-American Evacuation Claims Act of 1948 provided monetary reimbursement for lost physical property. A significant prohibitive requirement, however, was the necessity for proof of the value of the lost property (e.g., receipts). Only an estimated ten cents on every dollar lost was recovered by Japanese Americans through this legislation.

From the 1950s through the 1970s, several favorable SUPREME COURT rulings and an increased presence of Japanese Americans in Congress set the stage for the JAPANESE AMERICAN REDRESS AND REPARATIONS MOVEMENT. In 1981 President Ronald REAGAN and the Congress appointed a nine-member federal commission, the Commission on Wartime Relocation and Internment of Civilians, to study the experiences

of Japanese Americans and Aleuts during World War II and to make recommendations. The commission held hearings in nine cities and heard testimony from over 750 individuals. In 1983 the commission released its unanimous findings: that the exclusion and incarceration were the result of "wartime hysteria, RACISM, and a failure of political leadership." The commission also recommended a presidential apology and individual monetary redress payments to each affected Japanese American, individual monetary payments to each affected Aleut, and the establishment of a community fund for each respective community.

Legislation was introduced in both the 98th and 99th Congresses. The bills died in their assigned subcommittees both times. In the 100th Congress, changes favorable to the passage of the legislation occurred: most notably, the Democrats' return to the Senate majority and changes in key House chairs. The bill was entitled the Civil Liberties Act and on the House side the bill was numbered H.R. 442 in reference to the highly decorated Japanese-American army unit in World War II (the Senate eventually also adopted this same number). The House passed H.R. 442 on September 17, 1987, by a margin of 243–141. The Senate passed its version on April 10, 1988, by a vote of 69–27. After a conference-committee version was passed, President Reagan signed the bill on August 10, 1988.

The Act provided an apology and individual redress payments of twenty thousand dollars to each affected Japanese American. Additionally, a community public education fund was established. The Act also provided individual redress payments of twelve thousand dollars to each affected Aleut, along with the establishment of a community restoration fund. Subsequent legislation passed in 1989 granted redress payments entitlement status. As a result the vast majority of the payments were made by 1993. The redress required by the Civil Liberties Act was completed in 1998. At its completion over 82,000 individuals received a presidential apology and monetary redress payments.

BIBLIOGRAPHY
Horii, William. *Repairing America: An Account of the Movement for Japanese American Redress.* 1988.
Maki, Mitchell, Harry H. L. Kitano, and S. Megan Bechtold. *The Impossible Dream: How Japanese Americans Obtained Redress.* 1999.

Mitchell Maki

Civil Rights Act of 1866

As the first piece of federal civil rights legislation to be enacted into law, the Civil Rights Act of 1866 represents a milestone in both civil rights and constitutional history. The THIRTEENTH AMENDMENT abolished slavery in 1865, but the actual meaning of EMANCIPATION remained vague during the immediate post–Civil War era. Spurred by the conservative RECONSTRUCTION policies of President Andrew Johnson, who tolerated the proliferation of discriminatory state laws known as BLACK CODES, Republican congressional leaders turned to the idea of a federal civil rights law that would define and protect the rights of black citizens and facilitate an orderly reconstruction of the ex-Confederate South. The ensuing struggle over the Civil Rights Act of 1866 widened the rift between the executive and legislative branches of the federal government, pushing the contending forces toward a political and constitutional crisis that culminated in President Johnson's impeachment in 1868. In the process, congressional leaders expanded and clarified the implications of emancipation, effectively negating the DRED SCOTT V. SANDFORD decision of 1857, which had expressly denied black Americans the fundamental rights of national citizenship.

The primary author of the Civil Rights Act of 1866 was Senator Lyman Trumbull, a moderate Republican from Illinois who chaired the powerful Senate Judiciary Committee. During the early months of the Johnson administration, Trumbull emerged as a vocal supporter of the president's Reconstruction policies and displayed little interest in "radical" ideas such as black male suffrage. Nevertheless, by late 1865 he had become a strong advocate of federal legislation that would protect black civil rights and deter interracial violence in the postwar South. In early January 1866, he introduced two important bills: one that extended the life and broadened the authority of the Freedmen's Bureau and a second that promised to protect the civil rights of all American citizens, regardless of race or color. Using expansive language, Trumbull's civil rights bill enumerated the "fundamental rights belonging to every man as a free man" and asserted that no state or local law could abrogate or restrict these rights. The guaranteed rights of national citizenship included the right "to make and enforce contracts, to sue, to inherit, purchase, lease, sell, hold, and convey real and personal property," as well as full access to "all laws and proceedings" designed to protect "the security of person and property." The bill also authorized federal prosecution of anyone, including state and local officials, who attempted to prevent a citizen from exercising these rights.

Trumbull's bill represented the first statutory attempt to define the rights of American citizenship. Although it made no mention of the thorny issue of black political rights, the bill's national scope—technically its provisions were not limited to any race or region—and its obvious potential to transform federal–state relations ensured a spirited congressional debate. Some RADICAL REPUBLICANS expressed dissatisfaction with the bill's failure to include suffrage as a fundamental civil right, others wanted to strengthen the measure's provisions for land acquisition and homesteading among Southern freedmen, and still others were dismayed that the bill's enforcement clauses did not provide for continuous federal scrutiny of discriminatory action at the state and local levels. Under Trumbull's plan, the federal courts, not the military, would shoulder the heavy responsibility of enforcing civil rights. Repeated attempts to strengthen the bill failed, and the Radicals had little choice but to accept what many considered to be half a loaf when the bill came to a final vote in March. Like the Freedmen's Bureau bill, which had passed in February, the civil rights bill received near unanimous support from Republicans in both houses. Also like the Freedmen's Bureau bill, it was promptly vetoed by President Johnson, who issued a stinging rejection of both the details and the underlying philosophy of the congressional Republicans' proposed civil rights legislation. According to Johnson, the Republicans' civil rights bill marked "another step, or rather stride, toward centralization and the concentration of all legislative powers in the National Government." The defiant and dismissive tone of Johnson's veto message, which combined an extreme STATES' RIGHTS philosophy with undisguised RACISM, shocked Republican leaders, who on April 9 overrode the veto. For the first time in American history, CONGRESS had overridden a presidential veto involving a major piece of legislation.

The rancorous aftermath of the veto controversy, combined with lingering confusion about whether state or federal courts had the primary responsibility for adjudicating civil rights matters, made enforcement of the Civil Rights Act of 1866 extremely difficult. Moreover, during the congressional deliberations on the Trumbull bills, some Republican leaders became convinced that the Thirteenth Amendment provided an inadequate constitutional foundation for civil rights legislation. Thus, they began to prepare a new constitutional amendment that offered a clear codification of the fundamental rights of citizenship. Ratified in 1868, the FOURTEENTH AMENDMENT theoretically strengthened the equal protection and due process implications of the 1866 Civil Rights Act, just as it later encouraged Republican leaders to enact the Civil Rights Acts of 1870, 1871, and 1875. This continuing legislative effort stoked the fires of partisan conflict, raised the hopes of African Americans and other civil rights advocates, and produced a new language of civil justice. Nevertheless, by the end of the Reconstruction era it was clear that civil rights legislation had exerted little influence on the realities of everyday life among African Americans. The Supreme Court's CIVIL RIGHTS DECISIONS OF 1883 effectively gutted all four civil rights acts, confirming white America's waning interest in civic equality. Nearly a century would pass before another generation resurrected the legislative promises of 1866, instituting a Second Reconstruction that frequently invoked the language, spirit, and legalisms of the first effort to extend basic civil rights to all Americans.

BIBLIOGRAPHY

Foner, Eric. *Reconstruction: America's Unfinished Revolution, 1863–1877.* 1988.
Hyman, Harold M. *A More Perfect Union: The Impact of the Civil War and Reconstruction on the Constitution.* 1973.
Hyman, Harold M., and William M. Wiecek. *Equal Justice Under Law: Constitutional Development, 1835–1875.* 1982.
Kaczorowski, Robert J. *The Politics of Federal Judicial Interpretation: The Federal Courts, the Department of Justice, and Civil Rights, 1866–1876.* 1985.
Nieman, Donald G. *Promises to Keep: African-Americans and the Constitutional Order, 1776 to the Present.* 1991.

Raymond Arsenault

Civil Rights Act of 1875

The Civil Rights Act of 1875 was the fourth and final piece of civil rights legislation approved during the RECONSTRUCTION era. Introduced by Senator Charles SUMNER of Massachusetts in May 1870, the bill that ultimately became the Civil Rights Act of 1875 was designed to counter white Southerners' resistance to the FOURTEENTH AMENDMENT. In its original form, the Sumner Bill prohibited racial discrimination in public accommodations, conveyances, and schools, mandating equal access to hotels, theaters, churches, railroad cars, steamboats, schools, and cemeteries licensed by state or federal authorities. However, before the bill was enacted into law in February 1875, Republican disunity and bitter Democratic opposition led to the removal of the school and cemetery sections. Weakened by the Democrats' strong showing in the 1874 congressional elections, the Republican leaders of the lame-duck Forty-third Congress were convinced that the Reconstruction effort had become a political liability. After Democrats in the House of Representatives successfully blocked the bill with parliamentary maneuvers, Speaker of the House James G. Blaine of Maine and Representative James Garfield of Ohio—both moderate Republicans who recognized that only a handful of die-hard Radicals considered the DESEGREGATION of schools and cemeteries to be essential—fashioned a compromise facilitating the passage of a truncated version of Sumner's proposal. President Ulysses S. Grant, who had provided the Sumner Bill with only lukewarm support, favored the Blaine–Garfield compromise and immediately signed the watered-down civil rights act into law. In preceding months, the Grant administration's Reconstruction policies had provoked widespread criticism—especially in Louisiana, where General Philip Sheridan had meted out harsh discipline to five unreconstructed Democratic legislators; so Grant was pleased to steer a middle course between radical enthusiasm and conservative reaction.

Even in its diluted form, the Civil Rights Act of 1875 carried the potential to expand the federal government's commitment to civic equality. As historian Eric Foner has written, the Act "represented an unprecedented exercise of national authority, and breached traditional federal principles more fully than any previous Reconstruction legislation." Going well beyond the CIVIL RIGHTS ACT OF 1866 and those of 1870 and 1871 (which collectively focused on the basic rights of citizenship, property-holding, and voting), the new law empowered the federal government to effect a broad reconstruction of Southern life; indeed, scrupulous enforcement of the Civil Rights Act of 1875 would have revolutionized race relations across the nation. Unfortunately for African Americans, it soon became apparent that Republican leaders in Washington were reluctant to enforce such a far-reaching measure. Beginning in the final year of Grant's presidency and continuing through the subsequent administrations of Presidents Rutherford B. Hays, James Garfield, and Chester A. Arthur, federal officials offered little encouragement to black plaintiffs bringing suit under the new law. Nevertheless, by the early 1880s the public accommodations section of the act had spawned more than a hundred test cases involving alleged racial discrimination. As these cases made their way through various courts, few observers were sanguine about the plaintiffs' prospects; indeed, nearly everyone, including most radical Republicans, had already concluded that the act was a paper tiger, a symbolic relic of a fading reform impulse.

To the dismay of civil rights advocates, this judgment became official in 1883, when, by a vote of eight to one, the U.S. SUPREME COURT declared the Civil Rights Act of 1875 unconstitutional. Only Justice John Marshall Harlan dissented from the Court's assertion that the Fourteenth Amendment's prohibition of racial discrimination did not extend to the activities of private individuals. Speaking for the Court, Justice Joseph P. Bradley, a New Jersey Republican, insisted that only discrimination enforced by state action was unlawful: "It would be running the slavery argument into the ground to make it apply to every act of discrimination which a person may see fit to make as to the guests he will entertain, or as to the people he will admit into his coach or cab, or admit to his concert or theatre, or deal with in other matters . . . " (*Civil Rights Cases*, 109 U.S. 3). Black leaders decried the decision as a betrayal of the promises inherent in the Fourteenth Amendment, but few whites mourned the passing of the Civil Rights Act of 1875. Democratic Party leaders, especially in the South, hailed the Court's action as a return to democratic principles, and few Republicans were willing to defend a law that had been struck down by a Republican-dominated Court; all eight of the justices who declared the act unconstitutional had been appointed by Republican presidents. The demise of the Civil Rights Act of 1875 accelerated the retreat from Reconstruction, leaving generations of African Americans bereft of civil rights and vulnerable to the ravages of racial discrimination. Nearly a century would pass before the basic principles of the 1875 act would find new life in the CIVIL RIGHTS ACT OF 1964.

BIBLIOGRAPHY

Foner, Eric. *Reconstruction: America's Unfinished Revolution, 1863–1877.* 1988.

Franklin, John Hope. "The Enforcement of the Civil Rights Act of 1875." In *Race and History: Selected Essays, 1938–1988.* 1989.

McPherson, James. "Abolitionists and the Civil Rights Act of 1875." *Journal of American History* 52 (1965): 493–510.

Wyatt-Brown, Bertram. "The Civil Rights Act of 1875." *Western Political Quarterly* 18 (1965): 763–775.

Raymond Arsenault

Civil Rights Act of 1957

71 Stat. 634

The Civil Rights Act of 1957 was the first civil rights law enacted since RECONSTRUCTION and marks the start of the modern civil rights legislative era, the so-called Second Reconstruction. The 1957 act marked a slow start for such legislation, more symbolic than substantive, and in its final form it was regarded as a triumph for southern opponents of federal civil rights legislation. Its enactment occurred against a backdrop of the DEMOCRATIC PARTY and the REPUBLICAN PARTY vying for support in the South. President Dwight EISENHOWER carried Texas, Virginia, Florida, and Louisiana in the 1956 election. Republicans feared close association with civil rights causes would endanger their hard-won gains in the South; and traditional southerners could argue against Northern Democrats making their party too strong a champion of civil rights, lest Republican gains in the South increase further.

With fear of civil rights issues in both parties, President Eisenhower nevertheless called for enactment of a civil rights bill. As described in Eisenhower's 1957 State of the Union Message, the House bill that became the Civil Rights Act of 1957 contained four main provisions: it established a Commission to investigate civil rights violations and to make recommendations; it created a Civil Rights Division within the Department of Justice; it permitted the federal government to seek injunctive relief to protect civil rights; and it contained provisions allowing for federal enforcement of the right to vote.

The House passed the bill with all of its major provisions intact. Major support came from labor and civil rights groups. In the Senate, the powerful influence of southern senators all but gutted the measure. southern senators, including Sam Ervin, Majority Leader Lyndon JOHNSON, and Richard RUSSELL, successfully opposed the provision authorizing the Attorney General to seek federal injunctive relief against civil rights violators. They argued that allowing federal court initiatives would result in "government by injunction" throughout the South. The provision had to be assessed against the background of the SUPREME COURT's 1954 decision outlawing school DESEGREGATION, which was still undergoing massive resistance in the South. Southern opponents viewed the provision as a mandate for the federal government to sue to foster school desegregation. Senator John F. KENNEDY spoke in favor of the provision. But the federal government would have to wait for legislative blessing of broad government-backed civil rights suits.

Senator Johnson helped oversee the compromise that led to enactment of the bill. With President Eisenhower's assent, Johnson persuaded northern senators from both parties to join southern senators in rejecting the provision authorizing broad federal action. As a southern senator with presidential ambition, Johnson could appear loyal to his southern roots but also claim a pivotal role in national civil rights legislation.

Even federal authority to protect the right to vote, as opposed to civil rights generally, was watered down. Rather than allow for traditional contempt sanctions for violation of court orders, Senate opponents insisted on a right to jury trial. Senator Joseph O'Mahoney (Dem., Wyoming) added an amendment assuring the right to jury trial in criminal contempt proceedings. Southern senators believed that white juries in the South would be less threatening to the status quo than federal judges. Johnson supported the insertion of the jury trial right. With that amendment, the bill passed the Senate. The House accepted the Senate's deletion of federal authority to enforce nonvoting civil rights, but balked at insertion of the jury trial provision. Ultimately, the Senate view dominated because those cited for voting rights violations were assured a jury trial de novo in cases involving substantial contempt penalties.

Though civil rights legislation had been passed, southern senators believed they had achieved a major victory. Senator Russell stated that limiting this first modern civil rights law was the "sweetest victory" in his twenty-five years as a senator. The bill passed only because Southern senators were so content with it that it was not worth the bother of filibustering.

In historical perspective, southern senatorial joy may have been premature. The bill that passed was weak, but the Civil Rights Commission it created would investigate and report on civil rights matters. Information gathered would contribute momentum for further federal civil rights legislation, including the CIVIL RIGHTS ACT OF 1960; and the bill did establish a modern federal legislative presence in the area of civil rights. That presence would grow in the Civil Rights Act of 1960, the CIVIL RIGHTS ACT OF 1964, and the VOTING RIGHTS ACT OF 1965.

BIBLIOGRAPHY

Brauer, Carl M. *John F. Kennedy and the Second Reconstruction.* 1977.
"Civil Rights, 1957." Hearings before the Subcommittee on Constitutional Rights of the Committee on the Judiciary, U.S. Senate, 85th Cong., 1st Sess. 1957.
Woodward, C. Vann. *The Strange Career of Jim Crow,* 3rd ed. 1974.

Theodore Eisenberg

Civil Rights Act of 1960

74 Stat. 86

With little accomplished by the CIVIL RIGHTS ACT OF 1957, pressure continued in CONGRESS for additional civil rights legislation. Performance under the 1957 act only highlighted the need for further laws. The key substantive provision, which authorized the federal government to seek injunctions to protect voting rights, had been utilized in only one case; yet it was clear that race-based voting rights violations were widespread. The Civil Rights Commission created by the Civil Rights Act of 1957 documented massive denials of black voting rights in the South.

The EISENHOWER administration again proposed legislation, but it tailored the legislation to reflect its experience with the 1957 act. The proposal did not include a measure authorizing federal protection of all civil rights; such a provision had been gutted by the Senate in 1957. The Civil Rights Act of 1960 sought to protect the franchise.

The administration proposed creation of a system of voting referees. Referee-based protection of voting

rights could be invoked only via federal court action brought under the Civil Rights Act of 1957. The referees authorized to register black voters would be appointed by the federal courts. The Civil Rights Commission favored a plan under which voting registrars, appointed from Washington, would be authorized to register voters without the need for any judicial action.

Debate over the bill began in the Senate after it was introduced by Senate Minority Leader Everett Dirksen of Illinois; but a filibuster precluded Senate action, and major consideration of the bill commenced in the House. There the administration's voting referee plan prevailed over the Commission's voting registrar plan.

The bill that emerged from the House had four main provisions: The act required state election officers to retain voter registration and qualification records in federal elections. Patterns or practices of abridgment of voting rights on account of race could be addressed by federal courts by declaring individuals qualified to vote. Federal courts also could appoint federal voting referees to take evidence and report to the court on the treatment of black voters. In a departure from the voting rights theme, the 1960 act imposed criminal penalties for obstruction of court orders, a provision designed to limit resistance to the SUPREME COURT's school DESEGREGATION decisions. The act made it a federal offense to cross state borders to avoid prosecution for destroying buildings or other property.

Senate action quickly followed House passage of the bill. Despite the earlier filibuster, Southern senators now regarded the bill as sufficiently tame not to warrant serious opposition. Within fifteen days of House passage, the Senate had passed a bill. After the House agreed to minor Senate amendments, the Civil Rights Act of 1960 was signed into law by President Dwight Eisenhower on May 6, 1960. Thurgood Marshall described it as "not worth the paper it's written on," whereas Lyndon JOHNSON termed it "one of Congress' finest hours."

BIBLIOGRAPHY

Brauer, Carl M. *John F. Kennedy and the Second Reconstruction.* 1977.
Landsberg, Brian K. *Enforcing Civil Rights: Race Discrimination and the Department of Justice.* 1997.
Woodward, C. Vann. *The Strange Career of Jim Crow,* 3rd ed. 1974.

Theodore Eisenberg

Civil Rights Act of 1964

78 Stat. 241

The Civil Rights Act of 1964 was the first major civil rights legislation since RECONSTRUCTION. It followed the largely ineffectual CIVIL RIGHTS ACT OF 1957 and CIVIL RIGHTS ACT OF 1960, and it could be enacted only because it had substantial presidential support. John F. KENNEDY proposed the measure in response to frustration with southern resistance to court DESEGREGATION orders and violent treatment of civil rights protesters. Lyndon JOHNSON's support of the act following Kennedy's assassination signified his rejection of southern regionalism on civil rights matters. The act was the first substantial civil rights law passed by CONGRESS since Reconstruction. The Senate invoked cloture to overcome southern resistance, marking the first major legislative defeat for southern senators on civil rights matters.

The act's eleven titles are of varying importance. Titles I and VIII reinforce earlier voting rights provisions and limit the use of literacy tests to measure voter qualifications. Titles III and IV authorize the Attorney General to bring court proceedings to challenge segregated public facilities and schools. Title V amends provisions governing the Civil Rights Commission created by the 1957 act. In a procedural measure designed to protect federal court jurisdiction over civil rights matters, Title IX authorizes appeal of orders remanding to state courts civil rights cases that have been removed to federal court. It also authorizes the Attorney General to intervene in equal protection cases. Title X establishes a Community Relations Service to assist communities in resolving discrimination disputes. Title XI deals with miscellaneous matters. The most important provisions are: Title II, which prohibits discrimination in public accommodations; Title VI, forbidding discrimination in federally assisted programs; and Title VII, forbidding employment discrimination.

Title II's ban on discrimination in public accommodations and Title VII's ban on employment discrimination are limited to entities affecting interstate commerce. Congress thus sought to avoid a nineteenth-century SUPREME COURT holding that Congress lacks power under the FOURTEENTH AMENDMENT to the Constitution to outlaw private discrimination. Congress's power to regulate insterstate commerce is not limited to public entities. The Supreme Court sustained the constitutionality of the act shortly after its enactment.

With the 1964 act's constitutionality established, it began to play a role in ensuring civil rights. Title II's ban on discrimination in public accommodations established black's entitlement to equal treatment in the highly visible areas of transportation and sleeping accommodations. It achieved swift compliance with little litigation.

Equalizing employment opportunity was not so simple. TITLE VII OF THE 1964 CIVIL RIGHTS ACT generates many cases in the agency charged with its administration, the EQUAL EMPLOYMENT OPPORTUNITY COMMISSION (EEOC), and is the basis for thousands of federal court cases each year. The proof necessary to establish a Title VII violation has occupied both Congress and the Supreme Court. Two leading cases, *McDonnell Douglas Corp. v. Green* (1973) and *Griggs v. Duke Power Co.* (1971), authorize two different methods of proving discrimination. Under either method, a plaintiff must first exhaust the necessary remedies with the EEOC or a state antidiscrimination agency. The *McDonnell Douglas* decision requires a plaintiff to show that he or she applied and was rejected for a job for which he or she was qualified, and that the employer continued to try to fill the position; the employer then must justify its actions. Under *Griggs*, proof by a plaintiff that employment selection criteria have a disproportionate adverse impact on minorities requires the employer to justify the criteria. In the CIVIL RIGHTS ACT OF 1991, Congress expressly endorsed the disparate impact branch of the Supreme Court's Title VII jurisprudence; but Congress left unclear exactly when disparate impact is sufficient to establish a violation of Title VII, and courts remain largely on their own in this area.

The question of sex discrimination has a peculiar relation to the 1964 act. Opponents of the act introduced its ban on sex discrimination in the hope that

President Lyndon Johnson shakes hands with civil rights leader Martin Luther King, Jr., and is about to sign the Civil Rights Act on July 2, 1964. (CORBIS/ Bettmann)

expanding the act's scope would weaken its chances for passage; but the bill passed with the additional ban, which revolutionized the legal status of female workers. In some ways, the ban on sex discrimination is the most far-reaching of Title VII's provisions. The modern doctrines prohibiting sexual harassment in the workplace were developed in cases decided under Title VII as sex discrimination cases. The Supreme Court held Title VII applicable to sex harassment cases in *Meritor Savings Bank v. Vinson* (1986), and the Court interpreted Title VII to preclude sexually hostile workplaces in *Harris v. Forklift Systems, Inc.* (1993). Title VII's ban on sex discrimination reaches beyond traditional refusals to hire or obvious pay disparities. In *General Electric Co. v. Gilbert* (1976), the Supreme Court held that excluding pregnancy from a health plan does not constitute discrimination on the basis of sex; Congress responded by amending Title VII to overturn the result. In *Los Angeles Department of Water and Power v. Manhart* (1978), the Court held that Title VII forbids a requirement that females, who live longer than males and therefore can expect to receive greater total retirement benefits from a pension plan, contribute more to a pension than males.

Amendments to Title VII by the Civil Rights Act of 1991 gave it more potent remedies. For the first time, Title VII plaintiffs were allowed to seek compensatory and punitive damages, as well as the traditional forms of equitable relief available under the original 1964 act. In addition, the 1991 amendments authorize jury trials. Since 1991, there has been a massive shift toward jury trials and away from bench trials in employment discrimination cases.

In the case of sex, religion, or national origin discrimination, Title VII provides a defense to a discrimination claim if these characteristics constitute a bona fide occupational qualification. The Supreme Court found in *Dothard v. Rawlinson* (197) that a bona fide occupational qualification justifies requiring male prison guards for at least some classes of male prisoners. But in *International Union v. Johnson Controls, Inc.* (1991), the Court held that an employer's gender-based fetal protection policy violated Title VII; an employer could not exclude females from jobs in which exposure to lead might endanger fetuses.

Title VII's modern expansiveness owes much to the Burger Court, which is generally regarded as conservative in civil rights cases. Chief Justice Warren E. Burger's opinion for the Court in *Griggs v. Duke Power Co.* invented the doctrine of disparate impact and thereby removed the requirement that discriminatory intent be an element of Title VII cases. This holding is significant for Title VII cases because it puts pressure on large employers to have racially and sexually balanced workforces lest a disparate impact case be brought against them. Disparate impact theory has been incorporated in other areas, including discrimination in housing under the Civil Rights Act of 1968.

In litigated cases under Title VII itself, disparate impact theory has not fared especially well. In *New York City Transit Authority v. Beazer* (1979), the Court refused to invalidate an employment selection standard (exclusion of drug users) with disparate impact on minorities. In *International Brotherhood of Teamsters v. United States* (1977), the Court refused to extend *Griggs* to invalidate seniority systems that predate Title VII. And in *Wards Cove Packing Co. v. Atonio* (1989), the Court was viewed as quite hostile to disparate impact claims. *Wards Cove Packing Co.* helped foster the 1991 act's express endorsement of disparate impact theory.

Outside the employment arena, Title VI of the 1964 act has played a major role. Title VI is the principal antidiscrimination measure for programs receiving federal funds that are not affected by other antidiscrimination measures. In the case of public institutions, however, much overlap exists between Title VI's prohibitions and those contained in the Fourteenth Amendment. The Supreme Court has not clearly defined the relation between the two. In *Regents of the University of California v. Bakke* (1978), a majority of justices suggested that Title VI and the Constitution are coterminous, but did not purport to overturn the Court's earlier holding in *Lau v. Nichols* (1974), widely read as extending Title VI to cases of discrimination not banned by the Constitution.

Title VI continues to shape the role of antidiscrimination principles in educational institutions that receive substantial federal aid. Several subsequent antidiscrimination laws, such as Title IX of the Education Amendments of 1972, the Age Discrimination Act of 1975, and the Rehabilitation Act of 1973, are modeled after Title VI. Athletic programs, often segregated by sex, have been a fertile area of activity. Title IX of the 1972 amendments has played a major role in the increasing number and size of female sports programs through all levels of schooling.

The Civil Rights Act of 1964 has also played a substantial role in litigation about some controversial forms of affirmative action. In *United Steelworkers of America v. Weber* (1979), the Burger Court concluded that Title VII permitted at least some private affirmative action employment programs. In the aforementioned *Regents of the University of California v. Bakke* (1978), Title VI provided the setting for the Court's first important pronouncement on affirmative action programs. Affirmative action programs have had an uncertain legal status for the many years since the *Bakke* decision.

The Civil Right of Act of 1964's contributions to equality defy precise measurement. The act helped change the public life of Southern communities through its public accommodations provisions. It also helped foster an environment in which almost no one in America publicly advocates race or sex discrimination in employment. It contributed to a major shift in attitudes and practices in the workplace and in personal relations outside the workplace. Some strong patterns of racial and sexual employment discrimination remain, but the less overt forms of discrimination may be beyond the power of formal legislation to remedy.

BIBLIOGRAPHY

Bloch, Farrell. *Antidiscrimination Law and Minority Employment: Recruitment Practices and Regulatory Constraints.* 1994.

Donohue, John J., III, and Peter Siegelman. "The Changing Nature of Employment Discrimination Litigation." *Stanford Law Review* 43 (1991): 983–1033.

Epstein, Richard A. 1992. *Forbidden Grounds: The Case Against Employment Discrimination Laws.* 1992.

MacKinnon, Catherine A. *Sexual Harassment of Working Women.* 1979.

Schlei, Barbara L., and Paul Grossman. *Employment Discrimination Law,* 2nd ed. 1983.

Theodore Eisenberg

Civil Rights Act of 1968

See Fair Housing Act.

Civil Rights Act of 1991

105 Stat. 1071

Public Law 102-166, known as the Civil Rights Act of 1991, is federal legislation enacted to amend the CIVIL RIGHTS ACT OF 1964. CONGRESS enacted the legislation to improve the protection afforded under federal civil rights laws in cases of intentional employment discrimination and workplace harassment based on race, color, disability, religion, sex, or national origin. The act also confirms statutory authority and provides guidelines for adjudicating suits involving the disparate impact on employees of neutral employment policies and practices. The act addresses these issues by providing additional remedies for discrimination; codifying the concepts "business necessity" and "job related" enunciated by the SUPREME COURT in the 1971 *Griggs v. Duke Power Co.* decision and other cases; and modifying several 1989 and 1991 Supreme Court decisions. The act also provides protection for U.S. citizens employed abroad and employees of the House of Representatives (but not the Senate) and legislative agencies within its scope and encourages the use of alternative means of dispute resolution other than litigation.

The Civil Rights Act of 1991 made significant changes to the remedial provisions of TITLE VII OF THE 1964 CIVIL RIGHTS ACT. The most significant change from the 1964 act was a shift in the type of relief available in Title VII cases. Under the 1964 act, an aggrieved employee could obtain only equitable relief, which required an employer to cease discriminatory practices, but no monetary damages. Under the 1991 act, successful employees could also obtain monetary relief, including punitive damages and attorney and expert fees. The availability of such damage awards means that Title VII cases can now be tried before a jury, pursuant to the Seventh Amendment, which requires jury trials in most cases where damages are awarded. Most commentators have focused on the amendment's shortcomings in the area of disparate impact claims and Congress's failure to clarify the extent to which the legislation is to apply retroactively.

There was much public controversy and legislative debate during the amendment process. In 1990, President George BUSH vetoed the Civil Rights Act of 1990, introduced to recapture most of the rights lost by employees in 1989 Supreme Court decisions and to push for more aggressive initiatives against employment discrimination. Commentators called the 1990 act a dramatic and far-reaching retort to the Supreme Court. The president characterized the 1990 legislation as a bill that would force employers to establish hiring quotas to ward off litigation. After the veto, the civil rights community attempted to negotiate compromise language with major corporate business coalitions. On Capitol Hill, Republicans and Democrats seeking veto-proof legislation that would avoid the label "quota bill" offered several compromise amendments.

Given the controversy surrounding this legislation, the 1991 act was accompanied by very little legislative history. Like the Civil Rights Act of 1964, the 1991 act was a quickly adopted compromise ending extended legislative debate over prior rejected proposals. The speed of the vote was in part influenced by the testimony of Anita Hill in the Clarence Thomas confirmation hearings and the popularity of white supremacist David Duke as a gubernatorial candidate in Louisiana. There were no committee hearings, no reports, and only abbreviated floor debate on the final provisions of the act. Professor Ronald Rotunda characterizes the legislative history as "manufactured," consisting of snippets and vague statements made in empty congressional chambers. The American Law Institute has identified three main sources of legislative history for the act: First, the prior failed attempts at passing the Civil Rights Act of 1990 produced vigorous floor debate. Second, various members of Congress making arguments on the Senate floor in favor of and opposing the bill submitted memoranda into the record. Third, Senator John Danforth submitted a three-paragraph Interpretive Memorandum addressing the definition of the terms "business necessity" and "job related" in section 105 of the act, which dealt with the burden of proof in disparate impact cases.

Professor Rotunda has concluded that when the Civil Rights Act of 1991 had been passed and signed by President Bush, "each side declared victory."

BIBLIOGRAPHY

Cathcart, David A., et al. *The Civil Rights Act of 1991.* 1993.

Clegg, Roger, et al. *The Civil Rights Act of 1991—A Symposium.* 1994.

Gueron, Nicole. "An Idea Whose Time Has Come: A Comparative Procedural History of the Civil Rights Act of 1960, 1964, and 1991." *Yale Law Journal* 104 (1995): 1201.

Pub. L. No. 102-166, 105 Stat. 1071 (1991).

Rotunda, Ronald D. "The Civil Rights Act of 1991: A Brief Introductory Analysis of the Congressional Response to Judicial Interpretation." *Notre Dame Law Review* 68 (1993): 923.

Wendy Brown Scott

Civil Rights and Civil Liberties

See Civil Liberties.

Civil Rights Cases of 1883

See Civil Rights Decision of 1883.

Civil Rights Congress

The Civil Rights Congress (CRC) emerged in 1946 through the consolidation of the INTERNATIONAL LABOR DEFENSE, the NATIONAL NEGRO CONGRESS, and the National Federation of Constitutional Liberties. Sensing a change in the U.S. political climate and the coming of a "red scare," the three parent organizations decided to try to protect themselves by merging. Still, CRC quickly came under assault as a leading "Communist front."

Headed for most of its existence by the fiery African-American attorney William L. Patterson, CRC specialized in cases of racial and political repression. It had chapters from coast to coast, and its more prominent members included writers such as Jessica Mitford and Dashiell Hammett and the singer-activist Paul ROBESON; at its peak it had approximately ten thousand members.

CRC rose to the defense in 1946 of Willie McGee, an African American charged falsely with the rape of a white woman in rural MISSISSIPPI. This case was similar in many ways to the case of the "Scottsboro Nine," black youths in ALABAMA who were similarly charged with interracial rape. As was done in the Scottsboro case, CRC fought this case to the highest courts in the land, in addition to making it a global question: there were demonstrations at U.S. embassies all over the world. Despite the protests, McGee was executed.

Such crusades were an essential part of the process that led to the decline of legalized racial segregation: JIM CROW. How could the United States purport to be a paragon of human rights virtue during the COLD WAR struggle with the Soviet Union when African Americans particularly were treated as third-class citizens? Jim Crow had to cease.

This was a major theme played on by CRC during its existence. Thus, CRC promoted the case of the Martinsville Seven, black youths in VIRGINIA charged with interracial rape. Rosa Lee Ingram, a black female tenant farmer in GEORGIA who was arrested after repelling an assault by a white male land baron, also was defended avidly by CRC. CRC spoke up vigorously on behalf of the growing numbers of blacks who were imprisoned for a variety of reasons.

However, the most controversial cases involving CRC concerned the defense of COMMUNIST PARTY USA members. After the top leadership of the party was arrested and convicted in 1949 for conspiring to teach Marxism–Leninism, which was said to call for the overthrow of the U.S. government, CRC became the leading organization defending these pariahs. As prosecutions of Communist leaders unfolded nationally, CRC—though it was made up of both Communists and non-Communists—was viewed widely as little more than a "Communist front."

The "black" and "red" aspects of CRC's agenda were epitomized by Patterson, in that he also happened to be a leading member of the Communist Party and had led the crusade in the 1930s to save the Scottsboro defendants. In 1951 he presented a petition to the United Nations charging the U.S. government with countenancing genocide against African Americans. Published as a book, *We Charge Genocide!*, this petition sold in the thousands in the United States and abroad. When Patterson went to Europe to publicize this document, his passport was taken from him by the federal government upon his return. Paul Robeson, who worked closely with Patterson on this effort, also had his passport taken away.

As the "red scare" grew in intensity, CRC came under increasing pressure. Soon it seemed that its major function was to defend itself, as it was dragged into court repeatedly by state and federal authorities.

Finally, in 1956, as a new civil rights movement was being inaugurated in Montgomery, Alabama, by Rosa PARKS and Dr. Martin Luther KING, JR., CRC went out of business. However, the legacy it left inspired the BLACK PANTHER PARTY and other militant organizations that arose in the 1960s and thereafter.

BIBLIOGRAPHY
Horne, Gerald. *Communist Front? The Civil Rights Congress, 1946–1956.* 1987.
Patterson, William. *The Man Who Cried Genocide: An Autobiography.* 1971.

Gerald Horne

Civil Rights Decision of 1883

The CIVIL RIGHTS ACT OF 1875 was passed by the United States CONGRESS and signed into law the following year. The law, which was preceded by two other congressional bills regarding civil rights, was passed to combat the refusal of many white-owned establishments (such as hotels and railroads) to make their facilities and services equally available to African Americans. The law prohibited discrimination on the basis of race in public establishments and guaranteed "full and equal enjoyment" in such places. Those in violation of the law were subject to prosecution. Although this law was intended to allow African Americans enjoyment of fundamental liberties and rights under the Constitution as United States citizens, it was continually violated following its enactment. Subsequently, many owners who refused service unlawfully were sued, and some of the convictions were appealed to the U.S. SUPREME COURT. In reviewing these cases, the justices of the Court decided that the patterns of fact were quite similar and decided to consolidate them on the basis of addressing one issue: the constitutionality of the Civil Rights Act of 1875. The Court declared the act unconstitutional and, therefore, overturned all the convictions in the consolidated cases.

Justice Joseph Bradley wrote the opinion on behalf of the Court, which voted 8–1 to strike down the Civil Rights Act of 1875. The Court's reasoning was based on its interpretation of the THIRTEENTH AMENDMENT and FOURTEENTH AMENDMENT to the United States Constitution, which were passed to abolish slavery and to establish citizenship for anyone born in the United States, respectively. Bradley wrote that neither of these amendments granted Congress the power to protect African Americans—or anyone else, for that matter—against the decisions and actions of private individuals, even if those private individuals owned hotels, railroad carriers, or other services used by the public. The Court decided that the Thirteenth Amendment em-

powered Congress to act on "the subject of slavery and its incidents" and that "the denial of equal accommodations . . . imposes no badge of slavery or involuntary servitude upon the party." As for the Fourteenth Amendment, it did not apply to the prohibition of racial segregation since it was the actions of private individuals—and not the state—that resulted in the denial of services outlined in the consolidated cases.

The lone dissenter on the Court was Justice John Marshall Harlan, who disagreed with the reasoning of his colleagues, calling it "too narrow and artificial." Harlan argued that discrimination against African Americans solely on the basis of race in state-licensed facilities did bring both the Thirteenth and Fourteenth Amendments into play and that Congress had the authority to prohibit such discrimination. Harlan added that the Constitution's Commerce Clause handed Congress the authority to legislate in cases involving railroads. Harlan also warned that, although it had the power to declare legislation unconstitutional, the Court should not do so unless the legislation clearly violated the Constitution. The Civil Rights Act of 1875, Harlan believed, was not one of those cases.

The decision in the combined civil rights cases of 1883 hampered the ability of the federal government to prevent racial discrimination and provide for equal justice under the law for African Americans. Many Southern states took the opportunity to continue and even codify discriminatory practices, which were embodied in the JIM CROW laws.

BIBLIOGRAPHY
Civil Rights Cases. 109 U.S. 3 (1883).
West's Encyclopedia of American Law, Vol. 3, pp. 4–6. 1998.

Matthew May

Civil Rights History 1: Up to 1865

The origins of two great civil rights struggles in United States history lay in the period before 1865. African Americans, although nearly all enslaved by the end of the seventeenth century, gradually gained their freedom in the North and witnessed the triumph of emancipation throughout the nation. At the same time, women took the first steps toward full participation in the American polity by organizing and advocating the right of suffrage. Thus by the end of the Civil War, America's civil rights movements had begun.

Eighteenth-century political theory played a pivotal role in African-Americans' struggle to secure freedom. When the American Revolution began, slavery existed all along the Atlantic seaboard, although the southern colonies depended most heavily upon slave labor. The revolutionary generation's commitment to natural rights philosophy and their belief that slavery contradicted American attempts to achieve their liberty from Britain prompted northern states to begin abolishing slavery, either by statute, constitutional mandate, or judicial decree. The declining economic viability of slavery in the North also contributed to abolitionism there. By 1830, only about two percent of the total black population of the North remained in bondage. The rhetoric of liberty and political equality prompted even southern slaveholders during the late eighteenth century to express antislavery sentiments, as many upper South elites confessed their moral doubts about slavery and enacted laws that loosened restrictions on private manumission. Not a single southern or border state, however, abolished slavery. The United States Constitution reflected the revolutionary generation's divided feelings about the "peculiar institution." While the framers agreed that CONGRESS could end the importation of African slaves by statute after twenty years (1808), they simultaneously sanctioned slavery by deciding that slaves counted as three-fifths of a person for purposes of representation and by providing for the return of fugitive slaves.

Religious egalitarian ideals also inspired much of the antislavery movement. During the late eighteenth century northern Quaker antislavery societies, for example, which emphasized the equality of all people before God, exerted considerable influence in the passage of Pennsylvania's law abolishing servitude. By the early nineteenth century, young New England Protestants, influenced by the wave of religious revivals of the day, took the lead in advocating immediate and unconditional emancipation. Evangelicals such as Theodore Dwight Weld and those influenced by them such as William Lloyd Garrison viewed slavery as a sin—a violation of Biblical teaching that "God is no respecter of persons" and Christ's command to love one's neighbor as oneself. These abolitionists' harsh, uncompromising critique of southern slaveholders shocked northerners and southerners alike. Though they often eschewed political parties, evangelical abolitionists formed antislavery societies, preached sermons describing the horrors of bondage, and published newspapers, tracts, and other antislavery literature.

By the middle of the 1840s, the national debate over slavery intensified, as political and religious antislavery ideals became increasingly a part of public discourse. In 1845 Frederick DOUGLASS, a former slave, published his *Narrative*, one of the most powerful documents of the antislavery movement. In this and other writings, Douglass attacked slavery, racism, and the hypocrisy of American political and religious beliefs. Meanwhile, the introduction of the Wilmot Proviso of 1846, which would have banned the existence of slav-

The front page of The North Star, *the newspaper founded by Frederick Douglass in 1847.*

ery in new territories gained in the Mexican-American War, combined with controversy over the rendition of fugitive slaves, resulted in a strict fugitive slave law that put the national government squarely on the side of slaveholders. In response, Harriet Beecher Stowe wrote *Uncle Tom's Cabin,* one of the most widely read books of the century. Stowe evoked the moral outrage of the northern public through her sympathetic portrayal of slaves and the hardships they endured at the hands of masters and slave traders. Motivated in part by Stowe's work, many northern states passed personal liberty laws, in defiance of national policy, to protect runaways from reenslavement. Such state legislative enactments demonstrated the growing crisis over the issue of African-American rights.

While the nation debated the future of slavery, the civil rights of free blacks in the South and the North deteriorated. During the mid-1830s, in the aftermath of Nat Turner's slave revolt and the emergence of the northern antislavery movement, free blacks who had enjoyed the right of suffrage in North Carolina and Tennessee lost that right in those states, and in no southern state did free blacks enjoy the rights of citizenship after this time. Although free blacks in the

North possessed a greater degree of liberty than their southern counterparts, the guarantees of full civil and political rights eluded them. Between 1850 and 1857, Illinois, Indiana, Iowa, and Oregon all prohibited the migration of blacks within their borders, and white voters in these states gave these measures their overwhelming approval. Moreover, the northern states that allowed black suffrage by 1860—Maine, Massachusetts, New Hampshire, Rhode Island, and Vermont—contained only six percent of the North's total black population. Still, these grim realities motivated African Americans in the North to work for change. During the 1850s, blacks in several northern states formed organizations to repeal restrictions on the black population, assist runaways, secure voting rights, and end discrimination in public facilities.

American women, who had less ground to make up than slaves, made considerably less progress in their struggle for rights. Under English common law, a married woman's legal existence disappeared under that of her husband. This condition, known as "coverture," meant that a married woman could not own separate property, enter into contracts, sue or be sued. Frontier conditions and economic realities in colonial America led courts and legislatures to ameliorate some of these harsh restrictions. Women in the colonies often served as attorneys in the absence of their husbands, received land claims from colonial governments, and at times sued and entered contractual agreements in their own names. A few colonial courts even embraced the right of married women to own and control property independently of their husbands. In addition, women possessed a small degree of formal political power, and some, especially large landholders, voted in local elections. On the eve of the American Revolution only three states disfranchised women who otherwise met property and residency requirements.

Revolutionary ideology both impeded and advanced women's rights. Republican ideals promoted the notion of "separate spheres" for men and women, and the few rights women had exercised during the seventeenth and eighteenth centuries largely disappeared. New state constitutions brought an end to women's suffrage. Courts became less inclined to enforce a widow's traditional legal claim to one-third of her husband's estate, while married women lost the ability to contract, to sue or be sued, and to buy and sell property. Confined to the domestic sphere, women were to serve as "republican mothers," who would instill civic virtue in their offspring. Although the ideology of republican motherhood all but eliminated women's legal rights and political participation, educational opportunities for middle and upper class white women dramatically expanded during this period. Proponents of female education argued that learning produced the ideal republican mother, better suited to nurture and train the next generation. Female academies and colleges thus sprang up all over the country during the first half of the nineteenth century.

If education aided the cause of women's rights, social reform provided opportunities for women to enter the public realm. Beginning in the 1830s, women formed temperance societies, benevolent societies, and abolitionist groups. In doing so, they extended their role as moral guardians from the home into public life. Female antislavery societies first appeared in New England in 1832. Such participation in politics sparked controversy at the same time that it encouraged activism. Sarah Grimké, a noted abolitionist, responded to critics of women's public agitation on the slavery question by publishing *Letters on the Condition of Women and the Equality of the Sexes*, which questioned nearly all the Scriptural arguments on which male domination had relied. By the end of the 1830s, the "woman question" had become a major source of division within the antislavery movement.

Nowhere was this debate over women's place more apparent than at a world antislavery convention in London in 1840. Forced to sit behind a curtain apart from the male delegates, Elizabeth Cady STANTON and Lucretia Mott determined to organize a women's rights movement in America. Meeting with about one hundred others in 1848 in Seneca Falls, New York, Stanton and Mott issued a "Declaration of Sentiments" that proclaimed that "all men and women are created equal." The document, modeled after the Declaration of Independence, catalogued women's legal, social, and cultural subordination. The Seneca Falls Convention also passed a series of resolutions claiming women's right to speak in public, a single moral standard for the sexes, and the right of suffrage. Despite eloquent support from Frederick Douglass, the suffrage resolution was the only resolution that did not pass unanimously. Inspired by the success of the convention, subsequent meetings in Ohio and Massachusetts in 1850 gave further momentum to the movement.

Market capitalism, more than feminism, produced the only major change in women's legal status before 1865. In a number of states, the risks and rewards of the speculative economy spurred legislators to enact married women's property acts, which protected wives from the financial indiscretions of their husbands. In 1839 Mississippi passed the first of these measures to free the estates of wives from the clutches of their husbands' creditors. New York's 1848 legislation resulted more directly from feminists' lobbying. The New York law, unlike Mississippi's, did not allow men to protect their property simply by transferring it to their wives;

the measure insulated only the wife's separate property. By 1850 seventeen states granted some legal capacity to women to own or manage their own property.

The Civil War, the result of years of debate over slavery and its extension, advanced the cause of black freedom but did little to alter the status of women. The wartime Republican-dominated Congress abolished slavery in the nation's capital, outlawed the institution in the territories, and repealed the Fugitive Slave Act of 1850. President Abraham Lincoln's EMANCIPATION PROCLAMATION of 1863, although it only freed those slaves in the Confederacy who were not under the control of the Union Army (those, in other words, whom Lincoln had no real power to emancipate), helped bring about the gradual end of slavery by 1865. Word of the Proclamation encouraged many slaves to desert southern plantations and join the Union Army, and their successful military service helped sway Northern opinion in favor of total abolition. After the Union triumphed in the Civil War, the THIRTEENTH AMENDMENT, ratified on December 6, 1865, abolished slavery. Although women assumed new roles as nurses, business managers, and even spies during the war, no great legal advances were forthcoming.

Throughout much of the antebellum era, antislavery and women's rights had been closely connected. As abolitionist Abby Kelly remarked, women had "good cause to be grateful to the slave," for in "striving to strike his irons off, we found most surely that we were manacled ourselves." Yet, women abolitionists often felt the need to choose one reform over the other, and, believing that abolition was the great reform of the age, at times sacrificed women's rights for the cause of antislavery. Eighteenth-century political theory, religious sentiment, and market economics all helped create and sustain these early civil rights advances. But African Americans and women would have a long time to wait before attaining full equality under the law. The most significant achievements in civil rights in the United States would occur during the twentieth century.

BIBLIOGRAPHY

Hall, Kermit L. *The Magic Mirror: Law in American History.* 1989.

Litwack, Leon. *North of Slavery: The Negro in the Free States, 1790–1860.* 1961.

Maltz, Earl M. *Civil Rights, the Constitution, and Congress, 1863–1869.* 1990.

Melder, Keith E. *Beginnings of Sisterhood: The American Woman's Rights Movement, 1800–1850.* 1977.

Stanton, Elizabeth Cady, Susan B. Anthony, and Matilda Joslyn Gage. *History of Woman Suffrage,* Vol. 1. 1881.

Timothy S. Huebner

Civil Rights History 2: 1865–1918

The period of 1865 to 1918 runs from the end of the Civil War until the end of WORLD WAR I. During the first ten years of this period, the Constitution was substantially amended and CONGRESS enacted many federal civil rights laws. However, the courts proved hostile to most of these laws and to the expansion of federal power, striking down the laws and reading the constitutional amendments narrowly. By 1900, African Americans, Chinese, Japanese, Indians, and women in the United States had few civil rights. Violence by the white majority against African Americans increased as LYNCHING became a tool of terror. Despite these setbacks, African Americans began to seek ways to combat RACISM and enter the mainstream of society. In addition, women continued to fight for the right to vote (see WOMAN SUFFRAGE MOVEMENT). By 1918, legal and political changes were in the wind.

The end of the Civil War meant both the end of slavery and the beginning of a new era in race relations. Congress, led by the RADICAL REPUBLICANS, enacted and passed on to the states the Thirteenth, Fourteenth, and Fifteenth Amendments for ratification. The THIRTEENTH AMENDMENT, ratified in 1865, abolished slavery. The FOURTEENTH AMENDMENT, ratified in 1868, gave CITIZENSHIP to the newly freed slaves and made the protections of due process and equal protection binding against the states. The FIFTEENTH AMENDMENT, ratified in 1871, prohibited the denial of the right to vote based on race. Congress used these amendments as authority to enact the first federal civil rights laws of the new era. These laws sought to protect the newly freed slaves from the vigilantism of the KU KLUX KLAN (see also KU KLUX KLAN ACT) and the oppression of southern state governments that had enacted BLACK CODES, which restricted the civil rights of black people. The reluctance of the southern states to change their behavior led to federal military occupation and the beginning of RECONSTRUCTION.

Through 1876, federal troops ensured that African Americans could enjoy their full civil rights in the South. Blacks were elected to state and local government and to Congress. This hopeful period went into steep decline, however, following the presidential election of 1876, when Southern Democrats conceded a tight election to the Republican Rutherford B. Hayes in exchange for withdrawal of federal troops from the South. Southern states quickly changed political conditions, disenfranchising blacks and setting about to create a racially segregated society that justified its existence through the concept of "separate but equal" (see SEGREGATION). In 1896 the U.S. SUPREME COURT endorsed this concept in PLESSY v. FERGUSON, allowing states to mandate racial segregation in public accommodations, transportation, and public education.

Indians, women, and Chinese fared no better between 1865 and 1918. The U.S. government and the westward wave of settlers forced Indians onto reservations. With the battle of WOUNDED KNEE in 1890, the armed conflict between Indians and U.S. troops ended. Indians became a subject people. Susan B. ANTHONY and Elizabeth Cady STANTON organized the Women's Suffrage Association in 1869, seeking a constitutional amendment giving women the right to vote. Although they were met with ridicule by the male power structure, they and other suffrage leaders campaigned across the country throughout this period. Chinese immigration was limited in 1880, when Congress enacted the first CHINESE EXCLUSION ACT. These exclusionary policies were extended for another ten years in 1892. In 1908 the United States and Japan signed a treaty that restricted Japanese immigrants.

Several civil rights leaders emerged in the late 1800s and early 1900s. Booker T. WASHINGTON, a leading black educator and founder of the Tuskegee Institute, became a national leader on race relations in 1895 when he spoke at the Atlanta Exposition. Washington argued that blacks should seek economic security through vocational education and not seek social integration or political power. Mary Church TERRELL helped found the NATIONAL ASSOCIATION OF COLORED WOMEN in 1896, which sought to end discrimination and foster social reform. Ida Bell Wells-Barnett (see Ida B. WELLS), a journalist, began a crusade in the 1890s against the LYNCHING of African-American men in the South. W. E. B. DU BOIS, an African American intellectual, founded the NIAGARA MOVEMENT in 1905 with the goal of ending segregation and discrimination. Four years later Du Bois helped found the NATIONAL ASSOCIATION FOR THE ADVANCEMENT OF COLORED PEOPLE (NAACP). In 1911 the NATIONAL URBAN LEAGUE was organized to help African Americans secure equal employment. Professor Kelly Miller was a founding member. Finally, Marcus GARVEY founded the UNIVERSAL NEGRO IMPROVEMENT ASSOCIATION in 1914, which sought economic power and the creation of a powerful black community.

Although the courts in the early 1900s were generally hostile to civil rights litigation, there were some exceptions. In 1911, the Supreme Court ruled in *Bailey v. Alabama* that southern law criminalizing breach of tenant farmer contracts amounted to unlawful servitude banned by the Thirteenth Amendment. In 1915, the Supreme Court, in *Guinn v. United States*, declared an Oklahoma grandfather clause, allowing whites to avoid restrictive voting tests, void under the Fifteenth Amendment.

W. E. B. Du Bois, historian, sociologist, editor.

BIBLIOGRAPHY

Hall, Kermit L. *The Magic Mirror: Law in American History.* 1989.

Kluger, Richard. *Simple Justice: The History of* Brown v. Board of Education *and Black America's Struggle for Equality.* 1976.

Palmer, Kris E., ed. *Constitutional Amendments: 1789 to the Present.* 1999.

Sigler, Jay A. *Civil Rights in America: 1500 to the Present.* 1998.

Williamson, Joel. *The Crucible of Race: Black–White Relations in the American South Since Emancipation.* 1984.

Frederick K. Grittner

Civil Rights History 3: 1919–1945

WORLD WAR I and the Great Migration of African Americans to northern urban centers altered the political and social landscape of black America. Spurred by wartime industrial opportunities in the North, nearly 1.5 million black southerners moved to northern cities from 1914 through the 1920s. Although racial discrimination and segregation restricted black opportunities in the North, blacks enjoyed free access to the ballot. As their numbers increased, the black vote in the urban North gradually became a factor of national consequence.

At the same time, the participation of African Americans in World War I—the war that promised "to make the world safe for democracy"—stirred the aspirations of a new generation determined to "make democracy safe for the Negro." Returning veterans formed organizations such as the League for Democracy, which advocated political activism and self-defense and joined in establishing new branches of the NATIONAL ASSOCIATION FOR THE ADVANCEMENT OF COLORED PEOPLE (NAACP) throughout the South. Others, like Charles Hamilton HOUSTON, enrolled in law school, determined to fight racial injustice through the courts.

Rising expectations were met by a wave of anti-black violence (see RACIAL DISTURBANCES AGAINST BLACKS). LYNCHINGS increased in the South, and there were more than twenty-five race riots throughout the country during the summer of 1919. In many instances, blacks fought back. But in the era of the "Red Scare" (see McCARTHYISM), a time of heightening public fears about "bolshevism" and labor unrest, state repression, supported by federal surveillance, effectively quashed the political initiatives spawned by the war. It is notable that in the midst of what was basically a reactionary period, the WOMAN SUFFRAGE MOVEMENT finally succeeded in its long battle. In 1920, the ratification of the NINETEENTH AMENDMENT secured the vote for women.

In the face of such repression, Marcus GARVEY's appeal to black racial pride and independent economic development attracted a large following. Garvey established his UNIVERSAL NEGRO IMPROVEMENT ASSOCIATION in Harlem in 1918. By the early 1920s, the UNIA had branches around the country and represented the largest mass black organization in the United States. Even though the movement faded rapidly after Garvey's imprisonment on mail fraud charges and eventual deportation in 1926, Garveyism had a major impact on the development of BLACK NATIONALISM.

The AFRICAN BLOOD BROTHERHOOD (ABB), a secret black nationalist organization founded in New York in 1918, embraced a more radical political agenda than the Garvey movement. The ABB called for armed self-defense against lynching, full equal rights for blacks, and an end to SEGREGATION laws. Having drawn inspiration from the Bolshevik Revolution and the labor protests of the postwar era, the leadership of the ABB merged into the COMMUNIST PARTY USA (CPUSA) in the early 1920s. By the end of the decade, the CPUSA's increasing attention to issues of racial and economic justice through organizations like the League for the Struggle for Negro Rights enhanced its appeal among segments of the black community. In 1931, the INTERNATIONAL LABOR DEFENSE (ILD), the legal arm of the CPUSA, came to the defense of nine young black men who had been falsely accused of raping two white women in Alabama. The ILD's role in the SCOTTSBORO CASE combined litigation and mass protests and marked a major departure in the struggle for civil rights.

The Great Depression and the New Deal

African Americans lived on the margins of the nation's economic life and were among the first to experience the devastating impact of the Depression. As more traditional organizations like the NAACP and the NATIONAL URBAN LEAGUE groped for a way to respond to the crisis, Communist Party groups organized Unemployment Councils in the cities to fight for relief and were major catalysts in organizing sharecroppers and tenant farmers in the South. Whereas many established leaders, like the NAACP's Walter Francis WHITE, scorned the Communist Party, others, like Charles Houston, argued that the Left's uncompromising resistance to prejudice "made it impossible for any aspirant to Negro leadership to advocate less than full economic, political, and social equality."

Meanwhile, WASHINGTON, D.C. became a primary arena for activists seeking to ensure fair application of NEW DEAL programs while also lobbying for the broad democratic reforms promised by the Roosevelt administration. In 1933, Robert WEAVER and John P. Davis designated themselves as the Negro Industrial League, set up an office on Capitol Hill, and defeated the racial wage differential proposed under the National Recovery Act. Their success led to the establishment of the Joint Committee on Economic Recovery, a coalition of civil rights groups that lobbied for full inclusion of African Americans in government-sponsored programs while publicizing incidents and patterns of racial discrimination.

The National Labor Relations Act in 1935, which secured the right of labor to organize, was a major civil rights gain for white and black workers. A year later, the Congress of Industrial Organizations (CIO), a national federation of industrial unions (see AFL-CIO), was established. The national CIO's policy of no discrimination recognized the centrality of black workers in leading industries and also expanded the possibilities for interracial unionism (see also UNIONS). In response, many younger black leaders elevated economic justice and working-class solidarity to a major focus of black civil rights activism. The NATIONAL NEGRO CONGRESS (NNC) and the SOUTHERN NEGRO YOUTH CONGRESS, which were organized in the late 1930s, actively supported the organization of black workers and lobbied the AFL and CIO to support a strong civil rights platform.

Some New Deal programs, such as the Works Progress Administration (WPA), broadened opportunities for young African Americans. Future civil rights leaders, among them Pauli MURRAY and Ella BAKER, had formative experiences in community organizing and workers' education while participating in WPA-sponsored projects. At the same time, federally sponsored writing, art, and theater projects supported many black artists and also contributed to the documentation and preservation of black history. Government-sponsored interviews with former slaves created a rich documentary source for future historians.

During the 1930s, the NAACP established a permanent presence in Washington, D.C. Executive Secretary Walter White established a close working relationship with First Lady Eleanor ROOSEVELT and became a leading figure in the liberal-labor coalition that developed around the New Deal. The glue in this

A. Philip Randolph (1889–1979), labor and civil rights leader, founder, in 1925, of the Brotherhood of Sleeping Car Porters, president of the National Negro Congress (1937–1940). He organized the 1941 March on Washington Movement, which led to executive orders banning the exclusion of blacks from employment in defense plants and outlawing segregation in the armed services. (AP/Wide World Photos)

coalition was, in large part, the black vote, which had become a pivotal factor in key northern industrial states. In 1936, the majority of black voters joined with labor and urban ethnic voters in providing FDR with his landslide victory, eclipsing the singular dominance of white southerners in the DEMOCRATIC PARTY. For the next three decades, the Democratic Party would be the major site of the struggle to define a national policy on civil rights.

Even as northern black voters emerged as a critical factor in national politics, nearly 80 percent of African Americans lived in the South, where they were, for the most part, disenfranchised. During the 1930s, NAACP legal director Charles Hamilton Houston and his assistant, Thurgood MARSHALL, concentrated much of the NAACP's organizing efforts in the South. Starting in 1934, Houston and Marshall began a systematic legal campaign to challenge racial discrimination in public education, a challenge that would culminate in the BROWN V. BOARD OF EDUCATION decision twenty years later. Working with a small network of black lawyers around the South, Houston and Marshall worked to develop community participation and support, explaining the mechanics of the legal fight and linking it to broader community concerns. Indeed, they viewed the legal campaign as part of a larger effort geared to cultivating local leadership, building NAACP membership, and ensuring that the NAACP was a vehicle for political organizing and local activism.

Federal relief and job programs and the democratic rhetoric of the New Deal, along with the efforts of the NAACP, the growth of industrial unionism, and pockets of student and Communist Party activism, sparked a revival of political interest and activism among southern blacks. During the 1930s, black southerners increased their efforts to vote in the "all-white" Democratic Party primaries, underscoring a growing identification with the national Democratic Party of President Franklin D. ROOSEVELT (as opposed to the state Democratic parties, which barred them from participating). Southern blacks protested discrimination in the local administration of New Deal–sponsored programs. In 1934 in Arkansas, black and white sharecroppers organized the SOUTHERN TENANT FARMERS UNION to demand federal enforcement of the guarantees proved by the New Deal's Agricultural Adjustment Administration.

In the 1938 Democratic primaries, Franklin Roosevelt, frustrated by growing southern opposition in CONGRESS to New Deal reforms, targeted two leading Southern senators and a congressman for defeat. The failure of Roosevelt's "purge" effort underscored the fact that most of the New Deal's staunchest supporters in the South could not or did not vote. Black and white New Deal supporters met in Birmingham that November and founded the SOUTHERN CONFERENCE FOR HUMAN WELFARE (SCHW). In its effort to expand political democracy in the South, the SCHW also mounted a challenge to racial segregation. The SCHW spearheaded the effort for federal anti–poll tax legislation and supported voter registration and education efforts among blacks and whites throughout the region.

By the end of the 1930s, Southern Democrats had joined with Republicans in blocking further New Deal legislation and led the way in slashing relief spending and dismantling major New Deal programs. Conservative charges that Communists were involved in the New Deal and the LABOR MOVEMENT found a powerful forum with the establishment of the HOUSE COMMITTEE ON UN-AMERICAN ACTIVITIES. Although mobilization for World War II supported the conservative resurgence in Washington, few could anticipate the still vaster changes that would be unleashed by the war. As the SCHW's field secretary Osceola McKaine observed in the spring of 1941, "We are living in the midst of perhaps the greatest revolution within human experience. Nothing, no nation, will be as it was before when the peace comes."

World War II

The demographic, economic, and political contingencies of war made RACE and civil rights issues of national consequence. The war advanced the transformation of black culture and consciousness generated by the northward migration of the preceding two decades. Nearly one million blacks served in the ARMED FORCES. The massive MIGRATION of black southerners to centers of war production in the North in response to WORLD WAR II marked the largest internal migration in American history.

The *Pittsburgh Courier* popularized the DOUBLE V CAMPAIGN, which committed African Americans to fight on two fronts: against fascism abroad and for racial equality at home. President Roosevelt tried to ignore black demands, being careful not to do anything that might stir up the opposition of powerful southerners in Congress. But when A. Philip RANDOLPH threatened to lead 10,000 blacks in a 1943 March on Washington (see MARCH ON WASHINGTON MOVEMENT), the president finally issued an executive order banning discrimination in defense industries and federal agencies. The order established the FAIR EMPLOYMENT PRACTICES COMMITTEE to monitor compliance. It was the first federal agency dedicated to protecting civil rights since RECONSTRUCTION.

During the war, African Americans pressed forward with the struggle for civil rights and made significant gains in several areas. At the same time, there was growing racial violence in both the South and the

Black mezzo-soprano Marian Anderson sings into an NBC radio microphone during her famous 1939 concert at the Lincoln Memorial. (Culver Pictures/PNI)

North, along with the dismantling of major New Deal programs. The war against fascism intensified the flagrant disparities between the promise and the practice of democracy. Indeed, one of the most shameful incidents of government-sponsored racial discrimination occurred during the war and involved Japanese-Americans. In 1942, the federal government ordered the relocation of more than 100,000 Americans of Japanese descent from their homes on the West Coast to internment camps (see JAPANESE AMERICAN INTERNMENT CASES), where they were forced to stay for the duration of the war. Fear and racial prejudice drove the policy, which was implemented by California Governor Earl WARREN.

Racial tensions heightened during the war. There were thirteen reported lynchings in 1940–1941; the victims included Elbert Williams, founder of an NAACP branch in Brownsville, Tennessee. Roughly 80 percent of the nearly one million African Americans who served in the segregated armed forces were trained in the South, where they were subject to local segregation ordinances. There were numerous incidents of black soldiers being shot by armed bus drivers and local police. Often, blacks fought back. Racial tensions erupted into riots near military bases and in urban areas that experienced rapid growth during the war. The worst riot occurred in Detroit in 1943. It claimed the lives of twenty-five blacks and nine whites.

NAACP field secretary Madison Jones reported that the war had "caused the Negro to change almost instantly from a fundamentally defensive attitude to one of offense." Indeed, black civil rights efforts accelerated in the face of growing white resistance. One of the most significant measures of the acceleration of civil rights activism during the war is the dramatic increase in NAACP membership throughout the country. The rate of increase in the South was three times greater than in the rest of the country. Groups like the SNYC and the SCHW, along with progressive CIO unions, also fueled the expansion of civil rights activity.

After the Supreme Court outlawed the all-white primary in 1944, black voter participation in the South increased more than three times (see VOTING RIGHTS). In 1944, when South Carolina refused to abide by the Court's ruling, African Americans organized the Progressive Democratic Party (PDP) and sent a delegation to the 1944 Democratic National convention to challenge the seating of the Regular Democrats. The question before the national Democratic Party was whether it would tolerate a state organization that barred black voters. The Credentials Committee turned the PDP away on a technicality; it would be twenty years before a similar challenge was mounted from Mississippi (see MISSISSIPPI FREEDOM DEMOCRATIC PARTY).

During the war, Vice President Henry WALLACE set a new standard for national leadership on the issue of civil rights. Wallace visited Detroit in the aftermath of the 1943 race riot. Addressing a crowd of more than 20,000, Wallace proclaimed that "education for tolerance" was critical to securing the social gains of the previous decade. In a speech seconding the nomination of FDR at the 1944 convention, Wallace told delegates that the Democratic Party must be a liberal party; its future depended on it. Republicans, after all, had the best conservative brains and the wealthiest corporate supporters. Liberalism, he explained, was an affirmative philosophy, committed to "both political and economic democracy regardless of race, color or religion." Wallace's bold defiance of Southern Democrats probably cost him a place on the presidential ticket in 1944, but his challenge to the Democratic Party could not be ignored indefinitely. Indeed, after the Republican sweep in the 1946 midterm elections, Democrats made an aggressive appeal to black Northern voters and finally adopted a strong civil rights platform at the 1948 convention.

By the end of World War II, a loose coalition of civil rights, labor, and progressive groups like the CIO Political Action Committee, the SCHW, and the HIGHLANDER FOLK SCHOOL had cohered around a broad movement to expand political and economic democracy. This coalition was undermined, however, by the conservative reaction that accompanied the COLD WAR and by heightening white racism and resistance to any racial change in the South. Nevertheless, the foundation for a sustained civil rights movement remained anchored in the cumulative gains of the NAACP legal campaigns and its extensive network of branches in the South and throughout the nation.

BIBLIOGRAPHY

Grant, Joanne. *Ella Baker: Freedom Bound.* 1998.
Kelley, Robin D. G. *Hammer and Hoe: Alabama Communists During the Great Depression.* 1990.
Kirby, John B. *Black Americans in the Roosevelt Era: Liberalism and Race.* 1980.
McNeil, Genna Rae. *Groundwork: Charles Hamilton Houston and the Struggle for Civil Rights.* 1985.
Murray, Pauli. *The Autobiography of a Black Activist, Feminist, Lawyer, Priest, and Poet.* 1989.
Naison, Mark. *Communists in Harlem During the Depression.* 1985.
Rosengarten, Theodore. *All God's Dangers: The Life of Nate Shaw.* 1989.
Savage, Barbara. *Broadcasting Freedom: Radio, War and the Politics of Civil Rights.* 1999.
Sullivan, Patricia. *Days of Hope: Race and Democracy in the New Deal Era.* 1996.
Weiss, Nancy J. *Farewell to the Party of Lincoln: Black Politics in the Age of FDR.* 1983.

Patricia Sullivan

Civil Rights History 4: 1946–1965

From 1946 to 1965, the civil rights struggle in the United States was waged primarily by African Americans and was concentrated in the rural areas, small towns, and cities of the southern states where racial SEGREGATION and paternalistic race relations prevailed. The goals of liberty, justice, and social, political, and educational rights were eventually realized at the national level with heightened political liberalism and a war on RACISM as well as at the international level with liberation struggles for democracy and freedom around the world. Although white majority women, Native Americans, Asian Americans, Latinos, gays, and lesbians struggled during these years, it was not until the mid-1960s that their activism really crystallized on a large scale. Irrespective of the existing racial, ethnic, gender, class, and sexual-orientation identities, divisions, and contradictions, the prevailing tone of this entire period was one of reformism—a belief in the efficacy of improving rather than overthrowing society—as well as one of hope and optimism that the legislative, judicial, and executive branches could be used to change unjust laws, make new laws, and enforce civil rights guaranteed to all American citizens by the U.S. Constitution.

For several reasons, the twenty years between the end of WORLD WAR II in 1945 and the Selma, Alabama, VOTING RIGHTS marches in 1965 (see also ALABAMA) marked the most significant phase of modern U.S. reformist collective actions, which happened to be led by African Americans. First, this period of struggle produced fundamental changes in the social and political conditions of black people. Second, it dismantled the system of de jure (by law) racial segregation in the South, which legally required the social and physical separation of blacks and whites in public as well as in private establishments. Third, although less successfully, it challenged the hypocrisy and rigidity of the system of de facto (by custom) racial segregation in the regions of the West, Midwest, and North, which subtly separated blacks and whites via residential patterns and customs rather than by the overt JIM CROW laws of the South. Fourth, the struggles of this period had far-reaching political impact as they abolished discriminatory voting laws, high poll taxes, and literacy tests that made it virtually impossible for African Americans and Mexican Americans to exercise their constitutionally guaranteed right to vote as citizens. These developments change the face of both southern and national politics by challenging the dominance and power of the elite classes and driving a wedge between the traditional solidarity of agrarian landowners and urban merchants.

Finally, this period marked the most successful phase of civil rights struggles of African Americans, whose efforts paved the way for subsequent multiple protests by other groups. The various African-American strategies—court litigations, marches, demonstrations, SIT-INS, pray-ins, FREEDOM RIDES, voter education drives, organizational tactics, and a directly confrontational style—served as forerunners of and models for the struggles of Latinos/as, Chicanos/as, Asian Americans, Native Americans, students, women, gays, lesbians, welfare recipients, farm workers, the handicapped, and other groups.

Legislative Acts and Court Litigations, 1946–1954

The years following World War II produced favorable conditions for improving life for many Americans. The war created a boom in jobs for women, African Americans, and other racial and ethnic minorities in large cities, to which masses of southern blacks migrated, especially in the North and West. During this period, over 150,000 African Americans migrated to cities, but there they often encountered racial discrimination, violence, riots, and lynch mobs (see LYNCHING). In response, black leaders and organizations developed networks inside the black community and visible support coalitions outside the black community, such as organized labor, philanthropic organizations, white clergy, and liberal politicians. African Americans, who had fought in two world wars and had tasted the fruits of urban life and middle-class status, were disillusioned by their continued second-class citizenship. Some questioned the incongruity in American values and practices at home when they and their families and friends had fought for democracy and freedom overseas. Americans of all races and ethnicities witnessed the war deaths of thousands of their young people and began to challenge racial injustice, violence, lynching, segregated education, and labor exploitation. Black Americans, however, systematically called into question southern Jim Crow laws, which mandated the physical and social separation of blacks and whites in public places such as restaurants, courthouses, hotels, theaters, schools, transportation facilities, hospitals, prisons, jails, and cemeteries.

During these early postwar years, the fight against such overt discrimination was waged primarily through the courts by the NATIONAL ASSOCIATION FOR THE ADVANCEMENT OF COLORED PEOPLE (NAACP), founded in 1909. The SUPREME COURT responded to the NAACP's war on racism in a series of favorable decisions, including the 1946 ruling against segregation in interstate commerce and the landmark 1954 BROWN V. BOARD OF EDUCATION ruling against racial segregation in public schooling. Thurgood MARSHALL, chief lawyer for the NAACP LEGAL DEFENSE AND EDUCATIONAL FUND (LDEF), with the assistance of NAACP attorney Constance Baker MOTLEY, successfully argued the 1954 case. A year later, de jure racial segregation was tackled directly via an economic boycott (see MONTGOMERY BUS BOYCOTT).

Although the main thrust of their activism was not apparent until the late 1960s some other disadvantaged groups did become somewhat active for the first time during the post–World War II era. Mexican Americans founded the COMMUNITY SERVICE ORGANIZATION (CSO) in 1947 in Los Angeles and the AMERICAN G.I. FORUM (AGIF) in 1948 in Three Rivers, Texas, in order to organize a number of successful voter registration drives as well as to protest a funeral home's refusal to bury a Mexican-American soldier killed while fighting for democracy on foreign soil in World War II. It was not surprising, therefore, that the Supreme Court's 1954 decision in *Hernandez* v. *Texas* found that Latinos/as were being discriminated against in the United States and not treated as equal to whites in terms of rights. The AGIF, the Mexican American Political Association (MAPA), and the Political Association of Spanish-Speaking Organizations (PASSO) were all direct predecessors to the CHICANO MOVEMENT organizations that emerged in the 1960s to challenge the assimilationist politics of previous generations.

The tide also seemed to turn slowly for Asian Americans, particularly for Japanese Americans who had been removed from their homes and property and relocated in camps during the war. In 1946, the last of the Asian-American internment camps were closed and, by 1948, the Japanese American Evacuation Claims Act, signed by President Harry S. TRUMAN, authorized some compensation for the financial losses incurred by Japanese Americans during the internment. (The U.S. government eventually compensated the Japanese Americans for property loss at the rate of about 10 cents per dollar.) In 1952 the McCARRAN-WALTER IMMIGRATION ACT was passed, ending the exclusion of Asian immigrants, who had been prohibited from entering the United States with the passage of the IMMIGRATION ACT OF 1924. Asian Americans were granted naturalization rights during this period.

The gains for Native-American Indians were mixed, however. In 1946, the INDIAN CLAIMS COMMISSION was established to hear cases related to possible compensations due Indians for loss of their land and property through broken treaties (see TREATY RIGHTS). The NATIONAL CONGRESS OF AMERICAN INDIANS (NCAI), which had been organized in 1944, mobilized to support this cause as well as voting rights guarantees. Eventually, in 1948, Native Americans were granted the right to vote in New Mexico and Arizona; but, six years later, congressional acts of 1954 terminated the relationship between the federal government and several Indian tribes, including the Klamath tribe in Oregon, the Menominee of Wisconsin (see MENOMINEE DRUMS), and the California Indians. Termination resulted in many tribes' losing their federally recognized status, annuities, and the services needed on poverty-stricken Indian reservations to which they had been forcibly relocated and moved. Termination also forced many Indians off the reservations and into urban areas where problems of second-class status continued to plague them.

Economic Boycotts and School Desegregation, 1955–1959

The 1955 Montgomery bus boycott marked what debatably has been considered by some to be the beginning of the modern civil rights movement, although others have argued that the 1960s student movement was the beginning. In December 1955, a boycott of the city buses in Montgomery, ALABAMA, was organized when seamstress Rosa PARKS, a highly

respected church member and local NAACP officer, was arrested and jailed for refusing to give up her seat on a racially segregated bus. The Women's Political Council (WPC), a middle-class black women's organization headed by college professor JoAnn Gibson Robinson, and the Club From Nowhere (CFN), a working-class organization headed by domestic and cook Georgia Gilmore, worked cooperatively with the MONTGOMERY IMPROVEMENT ASSOCIATION (MIA), a clergy-led middle-class organization headed by the Rev. Martin Luther KING, JR., to organize, coordinate, and sustain the boycott. Ralph David ABERNATHY, Johnnie CARR, Mary Francis Burkes, Inez Ricks, as well as service workers, teachers, domestics, and many others, faced whites' retaliations, but the year-long boycott succeeded in eliminating racial segregation on the city's buses.

Racial segregation in high schools and colleges was also challenged during this period. In 1956, Autherine LUCY FOSTER waged an unsuccessful effort to desegregate the University of Alabama, but James MEREDITH forced the University of Mississippi to open its doors four years later. The most notable victory of this period, however, occurred in 1957, when the Arkansas NAACP leader and local teacher Daisy BATES successfully led nine black students (the LITTLE ROCK NINE) in the desegregation of Central High in Little Rock, ARKANSAS. In spite of the fact that Governor Orval FAUBUS closed all the public schools in the state for the following 1958 academic year rather than succumb to President Dwight D. EISENHOWER's enforcement of the Supreme Court's order, this victory gave impetus to cumulative increases in civil rights activism elsewhere. In Alabama, for example, the SOUTHERN CHRISTIAN LEADERSHIP CONFERENCE (SCLC) was founded by black ministers; they chose Rev. Martin Luther King, Jr., as SCLC's first president. Using the social gospel—Christianity's New Testament Bible teachings of Jesus Christ—and Mahatma Gandhi's tactics of nonviolent CIVIL DISOBEDIENCE, King would become the most significant black leader of modern history. King and other SCLC leaders trained activists in the use of civil disobedience and led mass demonstrations in various cities of the South until the stage was set for a newer and younger organization of daring shock troops to emerge.

Sit-ins, Freedom Rides, and Voting Marches, 1960–1965

On February 1, 1960, four black students sat down at a racially segregated lunch counter at Woolworth's department store in Greensboro, NORTH CAROLINA, and refused to leave when they were denied service. This launched the sit-in movement that spread throughout the South and led to the founding of the STUDENT NONVIOLENT COORDINATING COMMITTEE (SNCC), an organization led by black college students, including Diane Bevel NASH, Julian BOND, Stokely CARMICHAEL, and Marion Barry. With Ella BAKER as their mentor, SNCC developed a participatory-democratic leadership and organizational style.

The ALBANY MOVEMENT for voting rights guarantees and desegregation of public facilities had mixed results in southern GEORGIA in 1961–1962. SNCC activists Charles Sherrod, Shirley Sherrod, Cordell Reagon, and Bernice Reagon joined local Albany attorney C. B. King, schoolteacher McCree Harris, and others who had already been organizing before SCLC and Martin Luther King, Jr., swept into town and brought national media attention to the area. The CONGRESS OF RACIAL EQUALITY (CORE), an interracial organization founded in 1942, joined with SNCC workers in May 1961 and thereafter to organize and lead FREEDOM RIDES that tested interstate transportation laws against racial segregation. Riders were threatened, beaten, jailed, and even killed by white opposition groups; but Diane Bevel Nash and other college students nevertheless put their bodies on the line, stayed in jail, and refused bail. In 1963, SCLC and other organizations waged a successful economic boycott of segregated stores in Birmingham, Alabama. That summer, over 200,000 protesters participated in the MARCH ON WASHINGTON, where King articulated his hopes and dreams for racial justice. Following the bombings, brutality, and deaths of activists in freedom rides, FREEDOM SUMMER, and FREEDOM SCHOOLS organized by Robert P. MOSES and Charles Cobb, the CIVIL RIGHTS ACT of 1964 was passed.

After almost two decades of struggle, however, many African Americans throughout most of the South were still not able to vote; therefore, major voting rights marches were conducted in Selma, Alabama, in 1965. The violence against children and women, as well as the murders of black and white activists, gave impetus to the passage of the VOTING RIGHTS ACT of 1965, which guaranteed citizenship rights to African Americans and which later extended these rights to Latinos/as. This Act was given practical meaning by the teachings of Septima Poinsette CLARK, Andrew YOUNG, Dorothy COTTON, and others, who traveled throughout the South to train community leaders and teach literacy, as well as encourage citizenship for voting participation in adult schools. By the end of 1965, the legal bastions of southern segregation had been all but destroyed.

The Chicano struggle in the American West and Southwest gained momentum following the successes of African Americans. A migrant farm workers' grape strike led by César CHÁVEZ and Dolores HUERTA of the UNITED FARM WORKERS (UFW) succeeded in Delano, California, a town in the San Joaquin Valley. In the Midwest, Rodolfo "Corky" GONZALEZ formed the CRUSADE FOR JUSTICE (CJ), which came to epitomize the Chicano movement that emerged in the 1960s. When the U.S. Congress passed an immigration act limiting the number of Mexican immigrants to the

Massive crowds participated in the March on Washington, D.C., in 1963, demanding "an end to bias now." (Magnum Photos, Inc.)

United States to 20,000 annually, the issue of racially biased immigration laws was taken up by the CJ and later by LA RAZA UNIDA PARTY, a Chicano political organization led by José Angel GUTIERREZ in Crystal City, Texas, in 1970 (see also CRYSTAL CITY ELECTORAL REVOLT).

Under the leadership of Joseph Garry, a Coeur d'Alene leader from Oregon and World War II veteran, the NATIONAL CONGRESS OF AMERICAN INDIANS, which had been active on behalf of Native American causes since the 1940s, led a successful campaign in the early 1960s to convince the administration of President John F. KENNEDY to overturn the termination period for recognition and aid for Native American tribal groups. This reversed a 1950s trend whereby the federal government had been terminating its recognition of and consequent aid to various Native American tribal groups, without their consent. (See also SOVEREIGNTY.)

The IMMIGRATION ACT OF 1965 discontinued the ban on Asian immigration and facilitated not only the the subsequent doubling and tripling of Asian Americans in the country but also had an impact on the differences in goals, patterns, interactions, and identities of American-born and foreign-born Asian-American activists of the post-1965 era.

In conclusion, the year 1965 was one that marked not only many gains in civil rights for African Americans and other groups but was also a turning point in the tone and tactics of modern civil rights struggles. Essentially, this reformist period's belief in and call for a "beloved community" and nonviolent civil disobedience would give way to a surge of militancy by multiple protest groups in the United States. The post-1965 period would witness different calls for revolution (a complete restructuring and overthrowing of the existing society) and a militant, separatist approach with much broader goals and a willingness to use violence as a means of self-defense. Within the context of increased political conservatism, urban riots, poverty, and multiple protests by African Americans as well as New Left students, and anti-war and other groups, the goals for civil rights broadened beyond *rights* to economic and political *power*—and beyond the United States to oppressed people throughout the globe. Thus, this period's ending marked a beginning of a new phase of civil rights struggles the following year, as SNCC and CORE expelled whites from top leadership positions and Stokeley Carmichael called for BLACK POWER. The BLACK PANTHER PARTY (BPP)—organized by HUEY NEWTON and BOBBY SEALE in Oakland, California, in 1966 and advocating armed self-defense as well as political power, racial pride, and community and school control for blacks—mirrored or foreshadowed the radicalism of

the white student/New Left's Weather Underground, the women's Redstockings, the Chicano BROWN BERET and Crusade for Justice, the Gay Liberation Front, and other organizations of the post-1965 era. Coalitions of African Americans, Native Americans, Latinos, Asian Americans, women, students, gays, lesbians, welfare recipients, and others would build upon gains and setbacks of the 1946–1965 reformist period, take "the revolution" to different geographical, philosophical, and tactical levels, and make their battleground the urban areas of the Northeast, West, and Midwest as well as college campuses throughout the United States.

BIBLIOGRAPHY

Adam, Barry. *The Rise of the Gay and Lesbian Movement.* 1988.

Ancheta, Angelo N. *Race, Rights, and the Asian American Experience.* 1998.

Barnett, Bernice McNair. "A Structural Analysis of the Leadership and the Roles of Martin Luther King, Jr., in the Civil Rights Movement, 1955–1968." Ph.D. dissertation, 1989.

Barnett, Bernice McNair. "Invisible Southern Black Women Leaders of the Civil Rights Movement and the Triple Constraints of Gender, Race, and Class." *Gender & Society* 7, no. 2 (1989): 162–182.

Barnett, Bernice McNair. "Black Women's Collectivist Movement Organizations: Their Struggles During the Doldrums." In *Feminist Organizations: Harvest of the New Women's Movement*, edited by Myra Marx Ferree and Patricia Y. Martin. 1995.

Branch, Taylor. *Parting the Waters.* 1989.

Deloria, Vine, Jr. *Custer Died for Your Sins.* 1967.

Gray, Fred. Interview with Bernice McNair Barnett. February 1987.

Gitlin, Todd. *The Sixties: Years of Hope, Days of Rage.* 1988.

Higginbotham, A. Leon. Interview with Bernice McNair Barnett. October 1993.

Hing, Bill Ong. *Making and Remaking Asian Americans Through Immigration Policy, 1850–1990.* 1993.

Johnson, Troy, Joane Nagel, and Duane Champagne, eds. *American Indian Activism: Alcatraz to the Longest Walk.* 1997.

King, C. B. Interview with Bernice McNair Barnett. March 1987.

McAdam, Doug. *Political Process and the Development of Black Insurgency.* 1982.

Morris, Aldon. *Origins of the Civil Rights Movement.* 1984.

Munoz, Carlos. *Youth, Identity, and Power: The Chicano Movement.* 1989.

Payne, Charles. *I've Got the Light of Freedom.* 1995.

Vivian, C. T. Interview with Bernice McNair Barnett. February 1987.

Williams, Juan. *Eyes on the Prize: America's Civil Rights Years.* 1989.

Wong, Paul. "The Emergence of the Asian American

Movement." *Bridge* 2, no. 1 (1972): 35–36.

Bernice McNair Barnett

Civil Rights History 5: 1966 to the Present

The traditional narrative describing the civil rights movement ends in 1965. Passage of the VOTING RIGHTS ACT OF 1965 was the culmination of the efforts of African Americans to overthrow segregation and obtain the franchise. Having held together throughout the early 1960s, the coalition that produced these momentous accomplishments soon fell apart. The NATIONAL ASSOCIATION FOR THE ADVANCEMENT OF COLORED PEOPLE (NAACP) and the NATIONAL URBAN LEAGUE retained their commitment to working within the system to achieve additional reforms through lobbying and litigation, while the STUDENT NONVIOLENT COORDINATING COMMITTEE (SNCC) and the CONGRESS OF RACIAL EQUALITY (CORE) turned to more radical goals and tactics. Occupying middle ground, the SOUTHERN CHRISTIAN LEADERSHIP CONFERENCE (SCLC) continued to embrace nonviolence and integration, but increasingly pursued a civil rights agenda that emphasized economic as well as political equality.

The depiction of the civil rights movement as abruptly ending in 1965 is misleading. First of all, groups such as the NAACP, Urban League, and SCLC soon gained another important legislative victory. The FAIR HOUSING ACT (CIVIL RIGHTS ACT OF 1968) established fair housing requirements throughout the nation and protected civil rights workers. Second, although civil rights advocates did not receive as much national support as in the 1960s, they did manage to expand existing civil rights legislation to prohibit sexual discrimination in education (Title IX of the Educational Amendments Act, 1972), and to extend coverage of the Voting Rights Act in 1970, 1975, and 1982. (See VOTING RIGHTS AMENDMENT OF 1970; VOTING RIGHTS AMENDMENT OF 1975.) Finally, at the local level, southern blacks used their newly acquired right to vote to elect African Americans to office who helped their communities to achieve a greater measure of political democracy and economic opportunity than existed under the system of white supremacy. Besides electoral politics, the black freedom struggle stimulated a new flourishing of African-American art, music, literature, and history.

Nevertheless, these gains took place in an altered political environment. The national civil rights coalition unraveled in the mid-1960s. Led by SNCC and CORE, militants promoted the doctrine of BLACK POWER. They espoused black autonomy and pride, rejected integration, and urged self-defense against violence. Drawn from his own experiences as a SNCC organizer in the South and influenced by the separatist preaching of MALCOLM X, in 1966, Stokely CARMICHAEL publicized Black Power during a march in Mississippi to protest the shooting of James MEREDITH. The first black to graduate from the University of Mississippi, Meredith had returned to the state to encourage black voter registration. With Meredith wounded, his cause was taken up by Carmichael, Martin Luther KING, JR., and Floyd McKISSICK of CORE. The NAACP and the Urban League denounced Black Power. King, although he disliked the antiwhite connotations of the slogan, chose to show black solidarity against white violence and repression in Mississippi. For the remaining years of the 1960s, SNCC and CORE condemned the VIETNAM WAR, expelled whites from their ranks, and defended the urban insurrections that exploded in American cities during the latter half of the sixties. Along with other black militant groups such as the BLACK PANTHER PARTY, originating in Oakland, California, they ran up against the FEDERAL BUREAU OF INVESTIGATION (FBI) and local police which used their power to destabilize these organizations.

Meanwhile, Dr. King became increasingly critical of American capitalism, militarism, and materialism. In 1966, he carried nonviolent demonstrations to Chicago in support of open housing, and encountered fierce resistance from whites without scoring a major victory. By 1968, he had become an outspoken critic of the war in Vietnam and had broken with the Johnson Administration. In April 1968, King was preparing a massive march on Washington on behalf of poor people of all races when he was assassinated in Memphis while supporting a strike of sanitation workers. SCLC survived King's death but failed to exert the influence it had when he was alive.

Since 1968, civil rights advocates have supported AFFIRMATIVE ACTION to achieve equality. Sanctioned by the SUPREME COURT, affirmative action furnished opportunities to open up jobs and admissions to educational institutions to qualified blacks as long as rigid quotas were not imposed. During the 1970s and 1980s, advocates for affirmative action walked a fine line in distinguishing permissible recruitment goals from invalid quotas. Although the Supreme Court limited affirmative action in *University of California Regents v. Bakke* (1978), it did not rule out the use of race as a criteria for consideration. Building on congressional legislation against sex discrimination, affirmative action programs also incorporated women, white as well as black, and other underrepresented minory groups, including Latinos, Native Americans, and in some instances Asian Americans.

Along with affirmative action, BUSING became a controversial issue. The Supreme Court in *Swann v. Charlotte-Mecklenburg* (1971) approved busing to integrate southern school systems with a history of official racial discrimination. This ruling was also applied to northern locations such as Boston. Northern whites joined their southern counterparts in defending neighborhood schools and received support from President Richard NIXON. In many locales, busing became a moot issue as whites fled towns and cities (and others who stayed behind set up private academies), thereby leaving public schools attended mainly by blacks and other racial minorities. Many of these communities of color, especially blacks, have also withdrawn support for busing, concentrating instead on securing increased funding to improve local schools.

While busing and affirmative action came under attack as "reverse discrimination" in the 1970s and 1980s, African Americans in particular have successfully pursued electoral politics to revive the principles of the civil rights movement. Along with progressive whites troubled by the conservative Republican policies of Ronald REAGAN, they rallied around the campaigns of Jesse JACKSON for the Democratic presidential nomination. The former assistant to Martin Luther King competed in Democratic primaries in 1984 and 1988. Although failing in his bid, he hammered together a multiracial "Rainbow Coalition," including disaffected black and white Democrats, and managed to finish second in 1988. His campaigns stimulated increased black voter registration and bolstered support for such policies as divestment of funds from the apartheid regime in South Africa.

The decade before the end of the millennium witnessed a serious civil rights retreat. The Supreme Court severely hampered affirmative action and states such as California prohibited its use. The Court also limited the possibility of creating majority-black electoral districts, which increase the chances of African Americans winning a greater share of public offices. Furthermore, although middle-class blacks have prospered since the mid-1960s, a growing number of black women and children have found themselves mired in poverty. Under these circumstances, the twenty-first century awaits another civil rights movement to complete the unfinished business of the preceding one.

BIBLIOGRAPHY

Blackside, Inc. *Eyes on the Prize II: America at the Racial Crossroads, 1965–1985.* Videorecording, eight episodes. 1989.
Califano, Joseph. *Governing America: An Insider's Report from the White House and Cabinet.* 1981.
Carson, Clayborne. *In Struggle: SNCC and the Black Awakening of the 1960s.* 1981.
Fairclough, Adam. *To Redeem the Soul of America: The Southern Christian Leadership Conference and Martin Luther King, Jr.* 1987.
Formisano, Ronald, P. *Boston Against Busing: Race, Class, and Ethnicity in the 1960s and 1970s.* 1991.
Frady, Marshall. *Jesse: The Life and Pilgrimage of Jesse Jackson.* 1996.
Garrow, David J. *Bearing the Cross: Martin Luther King, Jr., and the Southern Christian Leadership Conference.* 1986.
Graham, Hugh Davis. *The Civil Rights Era: Origins and Development of National Policy.* 1990.
Lawson, Steven F. *In Pursuit of Power: Southern Blacks and Electoral Politics, 1965–1982.* 1985.
Lawson, Steven F. *Running for Freedom: Civil Rights and Black Politics in America Since 1941,* 2nd ed. 1997.
Lukas, J. Anthony. *Common Ground: A Turbulent Decade in the Lives of Three American Families.* 1985.
Meier, August, and Elliott Rudwick. *CORE: A Study in the Civil Rights Movement, 1942–1968.* 1973.
Sindler, Alan P. *Bakke, DeFunis, and Minority Admissions: The Quest for Equal Opportunity.* 1978.
Sitkoff, Harvard. *The Struggle for Black Equality, 1954–1992.* 1993.
Van Deburg, William, L. *New Day in Babylon: The Black Power Movement and American Culture, 1965–1975.* 1992.
Weisbrot, Robert. *Freedom Bound: A History of America's Civil Rights Movement.* 1990.

Steven F. Lawson

Civil Rights Law

The civil rights of Americans have been secured by the enactment of constitutional amendments and laws as well as by the rendering of judicial decisions. Following the Civil War and again in the 1960s, CONGRESS enacted a group of federal civil rights statutes that used the power of the federal government to prevent the abridgement of civil rights by government and private individuals. In contrast to the post–Civil War statutes, which only addressed racial discrimination, modern civil rights legislation also prohibits discrimination based on religion, national origin, gender, age, and disability. In addition, state and local governments have enacted laws that prohibit discrimination.

Civil rights law, because of its great potential for changing society, has always generated controversy. From the 1870s until the 1950s, federal courts limited the use of federal civil rights laws and embraced the status quo that permitted racial segregation and discrimination. From the 1954 BROWN V. BOARD OF EDUCATION decision until the early 1990s, the pendulum swung the other way, with the courts broadly interpreting civil rights law. By the late 1990s, however, a more conservative judiciary had begun to limit the scope of these laws.

Immediately following the Civil War and then again in the 1960s, Congress enacted a group of civil rights statutes that used the power of the federal government to outlaw gross violations of civil rights. Here, President Lyndon Johnson signs the Fair Housing Act, April 11, 1968. (AP/Wide World Photos)

Federal Civil Rights Laws

In the aftermath of the Civil War, RADICAL REPUBLICANS in the Congress were determined to protect the civil rights of African Americans. They enacted the THIRTEENTH, FOURTEENTH, and FIFTEENTH AMENDMENTS partially out of concern that future congresses could easily revoke statutory solutions. The Thirteenth Amendment abolished slavery and gave Congress the power to eradicate all vestiges of involuntary servitude. The Fourteenth Amendment proved to be the most profound and far-reaching of all federal RECONSTRUCTION legislation. In its three main clauses, the amendment guaranteed citizens protection from the actions of state and local officials, based on of equal protection, due process, and the concept of privileges and immunities. The Fifteenth Amendment declared that federal and state government could not deny or abridge the right to vote because of race, color, or previous condition of servitude.

Radical Republicans used these constitutional amendments as the basis for many pieces of civil rights legislation. The CIVIL RIGHTS ACTS of 1866, 1870, and 1871 are usually called the Reconstruction Civil Rights Acts, referring to the period following the Civil War. The provisions of these acts are both civil and criminal in nature, and several of these statutes have assumed great importance in modern civil rights litigation. The most important of these statutes, 42 U.S.C.A. § 1983, provides that any person who under color of law subjects another individual to the deprivation of any federal right shall be liable to the injured party in an action at law or in equity. A similar provision in the federal criminal code imposes penal sanctions against persons who willfully engage in such conduct.

The federal government ceased to enforce these and other Reconstruction statutes in the southern states after federal military occupation ended in 1876. African Americans lost their right to vote and were excluded from juries as the white power structure reasserted control of the political and legal systems in the South. In addition, the U.S. SUPREME COURT struck down civil rights laws, including a broad statute that barred racial discrimination in public transportation and accommodations, in large part because the Court perceived a dangerous tilt in the federal-state power relationship. By the end of the nineteenth century the Supreme Court had made clear that it favored giving the states more power than the federal government in regulating the actions of their citizens. The 1896 decision in PLESSY V. FERGUSON, which endorsed the concept of "separate but equal," legitimized state-mandated racial segregation.

In the early part of the twentieth century, the NATIONAL ASSOCIATION FOR THE ADVANCEMENT OF COLORED PEOPLE (NAACP) began to use the federal courts to successfully challenge various types of voting discrimination. By the 1940s it had initiated litigation against segregated public education that led to the landmark case of *Brown v. Board of Education*, which overturned the "separate but equal" doctrine.

The modern civil rights movement that began in the 1950s was met by public and private resistance in the South. Congress responded by enacting a series of laws designed to end discrimination based on race, ethnicity, gender, and age: The Equal Pay Act of 1963, the CIVIL RIGHTS ACT OF 1964, the VOTING RIGHTS ACT OF 1965, the Age Discrimination in Employment Act of 1967, and the FAIR HOUSING ACT OF 1968. The Equal Pay Act mandates that men and women be paid equally when performing the same work. The Civil Rights Act of 1964 prohibits segregation or discrimination in places of public accommodation, such as hotels, restaurants, and public transportation and outlaws employment discrimination. In addition, the law established the EQUAL EMPLOYMENT OPPORTUNITY COMMISSION, which enforces these provisions of the statute. The Voting Rights Act prohibits voting discrimination, while the Age Discrimination Act prohibits employment discrimination based on age. The Fair Housing Act prohibits discrimination in the rental and sale of housing. The Supreme Court found these acts constitutional, which signaled federal dominance over matters previously thought to be within the scope of state and local governments. A generation later, Congress extended protection to persons with disabilities when it passed the AMERICANS WITH DISABILITIES ACT OF 1990 (ADA). The ADA is a broad statute that prohibits disability discrimination in employment, housing, and public accommodations and mandates that public and private facilities be made accessible to disabled persons.

Civil Rights Law in the Courts

Court decisions have been an essential part of the development of civil rights law. Beginning with the Slaughterhouse Cases in 1871, the Supreme Court limited the scope of the Fourteenth Amendment, fearing federal usurpation of powers properly held by the states. The reluctance of the federal courts to use the Equal Protection Clause of the Fourteenth Amendment did not give way until the 1940s, when the Supreme Court announced the "suspect classification" concept that still guides civil rights law. A suspect classification is presumptively impermissible discrimination that curtails the civil rights of a single group, such as members of a racial minority. The Supreme Court has held that certain kinds of government discrimination are inherently suspect and must be subjected to strict judicial scrutiny. Under "strict scrutiny" the government has the burden of proving that the challenged policy is constitutional. The government must show that its policy is necessary to achieve a compelling state interest. If this is proved, the state must then demonstrate that the legislation is narrowly tailored to achieve the intended result. Although strict scrutiny is not a precise test, it is far more stringent than the traditional rational basis test, which only requires the government to offer a reasonable ground for the legislation.

Race is the clearest example of a suspect classification. In LOVING V. VIRGINIA (1967) the Supreme Court scrutinized a Virginia statute that prohibited interracial marriages. The Court noted that race was the basis for the classification and that therefore it was suspect. The Court struck down the law because Virginia failed to prove a compelling state interest in preventing interracial marriages. Legislation discriminating based on religion or ethnicity, as well as those statutes that affect fundamental rights also are inherently suspect.

Age and gender, however, have not been recognized as suspect classifications. Though the Supreme Court has refused to make gender a suspect classification, it has developed the intermediate or heightened scrutiny test. As articulated in *Craig v. Boren* (1976), "classifications by gender must serve important governmental objectives and must be substantially related to the achievement of those objectives." Thus, intermediate scrutiny lies between strict scrutiny and rational basis.

Though gender is not a suspect classification, the courts have been sensitive to acts of gender discrimination. The Supreme Court, in *United States v. Virginia* (1996), issued a landmark case on gender-based discrimination when it ruled that the Virginia Military Institute (VMI), a publicly funded military college, had to give up its all-male enrollment policy and admit women. The Court rejected Virginia's contention that single-sex education yields important enough educational benefits that justified the exclusion of women from VMI. The generalizations offered concerning the differences between men and women that justified the exclusion of women lacked merit because they were too broad and stereotypical.

Most civil rights actions involve one plaintiff, one defendant, one injury, and an established legal theory that shapes and restricts the litigation. Other cases, however, involve more wide-ranging attacks on the way units of government conduct their business. This type of lawsuit is usually brought as a class action on behalf of a large group of plaintiffs. This type of civil rights action has been labeled "structural reform" litigation. Structural reform litigation seeks to vindicate constitutional rights and values by forcing government to change the way it treats people. The remedy sought is systemic in nature: an injunction that requires affirmative steps to prevent constitutional violations from occurring. The plaintiffs seek to prevent recurrence of past wrongs and to reduce the future threat to their constitutional rights. School desegregation cases are examples of structural reform, as the plaintiffs do not seek money damages but affirmative steps to correct unlawful segregation.

This form of litigation moved beyond school desegregation in the 1970s. Federal courts became involved in administering state prison systems, ordering the construction of public housing in cities, and deinstitutionalizing persons with mental illness and developmental disabilities. The Supreme Court, however, has restricted the ability of federal courts to supervise municipal police departments. Congress enacted the Prison Litigation Reform Act of 1995 to limit the ability of federal courts to issue injunctions mandating prison reform.

During the 1980s and 1990s a backlash developed against civil rights decisions of previous decades. A prominent example is the use of AFFIRMATIVE ACTION in employment to remedy past illegal discrimination outlawed by the Civil Rights Act of 1964. Affirmative action is a concerted effort by an employer to rectify past discrimination against specific classes of individuals by giving temporary preferential treatment to the hiring and promoting of individuals from these classes until such time as true EQUAL OPPORTUNITY is achieved. Affirmative action has been controversial because many individuals believe that giving preferential treatment to members of a protected class is "reverse discrimination." In *Regents of the University of California v. Bakke* (1978) and *U.S. Steelworkers Union v. Weber* (1979), the Supreme Court upheld affirmative action in the context of racial discrimination and allowed its use to correct gender discrimination in *Johnson v. Transportation Agency, Santa Clara County* (1987). However, by the late 1980s the Supreme Court began to issue decisions that limited affirmative action to individuals who could prove they were the victims of past discrimination. A decade later affirmative action remained under attack, as states began to enact laws and constitutional amendments that forbid the use of race in college admissions decisions.

The 1990s also saw federal courts ending their oversight of school districts that had previously maintained racially segregated schools. In cities such as Boston, federal judges had taken over control of the city schools to ensure that integration occurred. The Supreme Court acknowledged that the era of federal oversight that started in *Brown v. Board of Education* was drawing to a close. In *Board of Education of Oklahoma City Public Schools v. Dowell* (1991), the Court rejected a stringent standard, which would have limited the ability of school districts to seek an end to court-im-posed desegregation plans, in favor of a standard that envisions an end to such plans. The decision signified a turning point in civil rights litigation, shifting the debate on desegregation from when an order should be issued to when it should be dissolved. One year later the Court, in *Freeman v. Pitts* (1992), held that district courts may relinquish supervision and control in incremental stages, before full compliance has been achieved in every facet of school operations.

State and Local Civil Rights Law

State and local governments have passed civil rights laws that prohibit discrimination in employment, housing, and public accommodations. Unlike the federal government, a number of states and cities have extended legal protection against discrimination to gays and lesbians. Such actions have proved controversial in some localities. A Colorado constitutional amendment that sought to prevent local governments from enacting civil rights ordinances protecting gay and lesbians was overturned by the Supreme Court in *Romer v. Evans* (1996). However, the following year the Court let stand a Cincinnati, Ohio charter amendment that removed gays, lesbians, and bisexuals from coverage by an anti-discrimination ordinance. The federal court of appeals found the amendment constitutional because it was rationally related to the city's valid interest in conserving public costs that accrued from investigating and adjudicating sexual orientation discrimination complaints.

BIBLIOGRAPHY

Curtis, Michael Kent. *No State Shall Abridge: The Fourteenth Amendment and the Bill of Rights.* 1986.
Graham, Hugh Davis. *The Civil Rights Era: Origins and Development of National Policy.* 1990.
Hall, Kermit L. *The Magic Mirror: Law in American History.* 1989.
Kluger, Richard. *Simple Justice: The History of* Brown v. Board of Education *and Black America's Struggle for Equality.* 1976.
Williamson, Joel. *The Crucible of Race: Black–White Relations in the American South Since Emancipation.* 1984.

Frederick K. Grittner

Civil Rights Memorial

In 1988 Morris Dees, president of the SOUTHERN POVERTY LAW CENTER (SPLC), spoke at a national meeting of the NATIONAL ASSOCIATION FOR THE ADVANCEMENT OF COLORED PEOPLE (NAACP). In his speech he mentioned many people who were killed while working to secure civil rights for African Americans, and

The centerpiece of the memorial is the circular black granite table, on whose surface are inscribed the names of forty men, women, and children who lost their lives in the civil rights movement between 1954 and 1968. (Willima Johnson/Stock, Boston/PNI)

he was surprised when some of the younger people who were present did not recognize their names. This experience led him to conclude that a monument to the civil rights movement and those who died for it should be built. The directors of the SPLC agreed, and the organization commissioned architect Maya Lin to design a civil rights memorial.

Lin, who had designed the Vietnam War Memorial in Washington, D.C., sought to design a memorial that would inspire those who viewed it to reflect on the civil rights movement and the price exacted for its successes. Using monies raised from a property sale, SPLC paid for the construction of the memorial at the site of the entrance to its Washington Street headquarters in Montgomery, Alabama. The centerpiece of the memorial is a circular black granite table. On the top surface of the table are inscribed the names of the forty men, women, and children who lost their lives in

the movement between the BROWN V. BOARD OF EDUCATION decision in 1954 and the assassination of Martin Luther KING, JR., in 1968. A black granite wall stands behind the table. On it are inscribed words from the Book of Amos, which King often used when referring to the civil rights movement: " . . . until justice rolls down like water and righteousness like a mighty stream." A thin curtain of water runs over the table and wall.

On November 5, 1989, six thousand people gathered to witness the dedication of the memorial. Family members of many of the people whose names are inscribed on the monument were present. Thousands of visitors from around the world have visited the memorial in the years since its dedication.

BIBLIOGRAPHY

Cantor, George. *Historic Landmarks of Black America.* 1991.
"Maya Lin." In *American Decades CD-ROM*, edited by Jim Edwards. 1998.

John F. McCoy

Civil Rights Restoration Acts

See Civil Rights Act of 1991.

Claims Commission Act

See Indian Claims Commission Act.

Clark, Kenneth and Mamie

(1914–   and 1917–1983), psychologists and advocates for children.

Kenneth and Mamie Clark both earned their doctorates in psychology at Columbia University, the first African Americans to be admitted to that program. In the late 1930s and 1940s, the Clarks conducted a series of tests on children, placing identical dolls—one white and one brown—side by side and asking the children to choose the doll they liked best and the doll that looked "bad." They presented their findings, of serious self-esteem problems among African-American children who lived or attended schools in segregated settings, in a number of papers. These tests were then repeated in the early 1950s as part of the legal challenge to SEGREGATION in southern schools by the NATIONAL ASSOCIATION FOR THE ADVANCEMENT OF COLORED PEOPLE (NAACP). Kenneth Clark organized support for, and largely wrote, the social science brief that became the basis for the SUPREME COURT's 1954 DESEGREGATION decision, BROWN V. BOARD OF EDUCATION. This document, based, in part, upon the

Clarks' work, was cited by the Supreme Court in its famous "footnote 11." It was the first time that social science evidence had become the basis for a Supreme Court decision of such magnitude.

Mamie and Kenneth Clark founded the Northside Center for Child Development in 1946, and Mamie Clark directed it until her retirement in 1979. Northside, the first mental health center for children to be run by African-American professionals, provided the most up-to-date ethnically and racially integrated psychological and counseling services for children in Harlem and northern Manhattan. In addition to its mental health mission, the Center was deeply involved in the critical historical events of the post–WORLD WAR II era: the struggle for integration of Northern public education; Harlem's and New York's Wars on Poverty; the Model Cities and urban renewal efforts of the late 1960s; crises in Jewish and African-American relations; decentralization and community control; community action; and community mental health.

In 1942, Kenneth Clark became the first full-time African-American instructor hired by the City College of New York, and he began a career as a social psychologist that spanned six decades. The author of numerous books and hundreds of articles, Clark analyzed the failure of the American educational system and American society in general to provide equal access for African-American children and a healthy environment in which to grow and prosper. Among his most important works were *Prejudice and Your Child* (1955), one of the first booklength analyses of the effects of segregation and discrimination on child development; *Dark Ghetto* (1965), which not only described the despair and hopelessness that had led to Harlem's high rates of drug abuse, delinquency, teenage pregnancy, and truancy, but found the cause of what he termed this "pathology of the ghetto" in the destruction wrought by powerlessness, by the society's RACISM, and by economic and social dislocation; and *Pathos of Power* (1974), an analysis of the nature of power relationships in major cities and the United States as a whole. From 1967 through 1975 he was president of the Metropolitan Applied Research Center (MARC), a group of social scientists and other professionals that researched and published many books and articles analyzing the effect of segregation on urban social, economic, and educational systems, and developed strategies for overcoming powerlessness, discrimination, and inequality.

Although a lifelong supporter of INTEGRATION, Kenneth Clark was committed first to the education of all children, and, most particularly, African-American and Hispanic children who were denied equal opportunity in the nation's schools. Though he refused to abandon the long-range goal of integration, in the

mid-1960s he supported community control of de facto segregated schools as "primarily a desperate attempt [by African-American parents] to protect their children in the schools they are required to attend." As a member of the Board of Regents of the State of New York from 1966 to 1986, he continued to press for quality education for all children regardless of race.

BIBLIOGRAPHY

Chesler, Marc, Joseph Sanders, and Debra S. Kalmuss. *Social Science in Court: Mobilizing Experts in the School Desegregation Cases.* 1988.

Keppel, Ben. *The Work of Democracy: Ralph Bunche, Kenneth B. Clark, Lorraine Hansberry, and the Cultural Politics of Race.* 1995.

Markowitz, Gerald, and David Rosner. *Children, Race and Power: Kenneth and Mamie Clark's Northside Center.* 1996.

Gerald Markowitz

Clark, Septima Poinsette

(1898–1987), educator and civil rights activist.

Born in Charleston, SOUTH CAROLINA, to Peter and Victoria Poinsette, Septima Clark was the quintessential activist-educator, combining a career of teaching, leadership training, political organizing, and educational activism in the South. Clark founded "CITIZENSHIP SCHOOLS" in which she pioneered the teaching of adult literacy and implementation of collectivist and culturally relevant learning techniques.

Clark attended Avery Institute in Charleston, graduating in 1916, after which she began teaching on John's Island and other economically depressed islands surrounding Charleston. She returned to teach at Avery Institute from 1919 to 1921. From 1921 to 1929, Clark lived and taught in North Carolina and Ohio. In 1929 she returned to South Carolina. While teaching in public schools during the day and in backroom adult citizenship schools at night, Clark earned a B.A. from Benedict College in 1942 and an M.A. from Hampton Institute in 1945. In 1956, after four decades in the classroom, Clark was fired from her position as a school teacher and denied the pension she was due from the state of South Carolina, because she refused to give up her membership in the NATIONAL ASSOCIATION FOR THE ADVANCEMENT OF COLORED PEOPLE (NAACP).

After her firing, labor activist Myles HORTON recruited Clark to develop an educational and leadership training program for the HIGHLANDER FOLK SCHOOL, an interracial organization Horton founded in 1932 in Tennessee. Later, civil rights leader Martin Luther KING, JR., and the SOUTHERN CHRISTIAN

Educator and civil rights leader Septima Clark in 1974. (AP/Wide World Photos)

BIBLIOGRAPHY

Barnett, Bernice McNair. "Septima Poinsette Clark, Participatory Democracy, and the Struggle for Black Education." *Voices* (Spring 1996): 3–4.

Barnett, Bernice McNair. *Sisters in Struggle: Invisible Black Women Leaders of the Civil Rights Movement, 1940–1975.* Forthcoming.

Clark, Septima Poinsette. *Ready from Within.* 1986.

McFadden, Grace Jordan. *The Oral Recollections of Septima P. Clark.* 1980.

Papers of Septima P. Clark. College of Charleston, Robert Scott Small Library, Charleston, S.C.

Bernice McNair Barnett

Class

The industrial and political revolutions of the eighteenth century led to major transformations in western societies. Social rankings within agrarian feudal societies were restructured into classes based largely on monetary wealth. The relation of the individual, or class of individuals, to the industrial work process determined social status. U.S. society became composed of an upper class, a middle class, a working class, and later an underclass.

The upper class, comprised of commercial and industrial capitalists, controls most of the nation's wealth and wields considerable influence on U.S. political decisions and economic policy. By the 1990s, the wealthiest top ten percent of Americans controlled almost seventy percent of the nation's wealth. Inherited wealth aided by tax-free investments and superior educational and economic opportunities serve to perpetuate the upper class and class system inequalities.

Those dependent on wages from jobs designed to sustain the capital of the upper class are the middle and working classes. Technical and professional workers, businessmen, and farmers constitute the middle class, which merges into the upper and lower classes toward both ends of the income spectrum. Property ownership and indebtedness to financial institutions owned by the upper class are key characteristics. Members of the working class hold low-skilled, low-paying manual labor jobs and skilled or semi-skilled jobs earning somewhat larger incomes. Typical working class traits are lack of property, dependence on wages, and inability to accumulate wealth. Living standards are relatively low, they are largely excluded from societal decision-making, and access to higher education is restricted. Changes in the American economy late in the twentieth century from traditional manufacturing industries to a post-industrial information and service economy created a chronically unemployed segment of society known as the underclass, isolated from mainstream society and living in decaying inner cities.

LEADERSHIP CONFERENCE (SCLC) based in Atlanta, Georgia, took over the citizenship schools that she founded and appointed Clark as co-director of teacher education.

Although she endured hardships, job retaliation, and physical violence, Mrs. Clark persevered in her efforts to make political transformation possible in the South. Emphasizing nonhierarchical community-based leadership, participatory democracy, and respect for all races and classes, Septima Clark left an enduring legacy, helping to give meaning to the 1965 VOTING RIGHTS ACT as she made it possible for thousands of illiterate black southerners to learn to read and write, pass literacy tests for voting, and empower themselves for full citizenship in American society.

The Persistence of Class Discrimination

The American class system has persisted since the nation's birth. The notion of social equality was so restricted in the late eighteenth century that neither the term nor even the concept of equality appeared in the Constitution or Bill of Rights. For example, originally only white adult males with property enjoyed voting rights, not blacks, women, or the poor. Not until 1868, following the Civil War, was the concept of equality written into constitutional law with the FOURTEENTH AMENDMENT's equal protection clause.

The growth of U.S. cities and reinforcement of social class stratification in the nineteenth century was integrally linked with expanding industrialization. Industrialization and the resulting process of urbanization led to formation of the classic city pattern by the 1930s. Commercial centers containing financial districts located in downtown areas were encircled by slums and enclaves of working-class neighborhoods often distinguished by ethnic or minority predominance, industrial and manufacturing pockets, and the white middle-class residential neighborhoods growing toward the ever-expanding city boundaries. The city became a geographical and socioeconomic mosaic with a striking correlation between RACE, CLASS, and residence.

Prior to 1940, almost ninety percent of blacks lived in poverty, relegated to low-paying farm and domestic housekeeping employment. Few could be considered middle class. Beginning with WORLD WAR II, income for blacks rose significantly as blue-collar industrial work expanded. Although income increased four times higher than in 1939, it was still only half of corresponding white income and almost forty percent were still living in poverty. Just as urban areas were experiencing a new wave of southern blacks migrating in search of employment during the post-war economic boom, white taxpayers along with jobs and capital began moving in mass to the suburbs leaving the cramped ghettos and polluting industries behind. Having lost desperately needed tax revenue, the inner cities became characterized by poorly equipped schools, low income housing, crime, and homelessness. The exodus left cities with declining property values and lost political and social importance.

In effect, the postwar social system continued to offer special privileges to particular socioeconomic classes largely based on racial affiliation, and gender to a lesser degree. The white middle-class suburbanites valued racial, religious, and social class homogeneity. However, prohibitions on racial and gender discrimination posed by the Equal Pay Act of 1963 and the CIVIL RIGHTS ACT OF 1964 partially addressed socioeconomic inequalities. Class action lawsuits addressing discrimination based on race and gender became more common. African Americans and other minorities of color, however, still found access restricted to positions of power, many job markets, quality housing, and higher education.

In an effort to combat economic inequality, civil rights leaders including Dr. Martin Luther KING, JR., organized a POOR PEOPLE'S CAMPAIGN in 1967. The strategy was to conduct extensive CIVIL DISOBEDIENCE in Washington, D.C. over an extended period of time. King sought legislation ensuring full employment, creating a guaranteed income, and promoting low-income housing. However, his assassination shortly before inception of the campaign, poor coordination, weak support, and aggressive police tactics caused the campaign to fall short of its goal.

Post-Industrial Barriers

A robust national economy in the late 1960s and early 1970s coupled with affirmative-action policies did stimulate change. African Americans entered white-collar jobs and skilled, well-paid blue-collar employment in substantial numbers creating a newly expanded black middle class. Some even joined the upper class. Inroads into the political arenas occurred as well with approximately forty blacks in Congress by the 1990s. Two distinct classes of blacks evolved. One included black professionals moving away from the ghettos to mainstream economic markets and the suburbs, and the other, an impoverished underclass, grew as industrial jobs declined. Though African Americans constituted only twelve percent of the population in 1990, a third of the underclass was black. The breakdown of family structure became epidemic with most black families headed by females in 1991. The number of black children raised in poverty escalated dramatically. In 1990, forty-five percent of black children lived in poverty compared to sixteen percent of white children. The cycle of poverty became increasingly apparent, trapping the lower and underclass members. Faced with high crime, poor living conditions including housing, limited educational opportunity, lack of adult role models, and poor health, many held little hope of breaking from the cycle.

Though having little overt recognition, a generally condoned institutionalized system of class inequality persisted in the United States in the late twentieth century. RACISM remained a key factor. It became increasingly evident through the economically robust 1990s that technological developments improved the life of some, but not others. Economic globalization, corporate downsizing, prominent anti-unionism, laissez-faire government policies, and escalating education costs served to concentrate wealth even more and provide better services only for the few. Emergence of the information age added knowledge as yet another socially stratifying factor. Despite rising concern with diversity and multiculturalism, race remained a principal determinant of socioeconomic class affecting employment and educational opportunities to gain knowledge, as well as access to health services and equal justice.

BIBLIOGRAPHY

Andersen, Margaret L., and Patricia H. Collins, eds. *Race, Class, and Gender: An Anthology.*1992.
Andrain, Charles F. *Public Health Policies and Social Inequality.* 1998.
Fine, Michelle, et al., eds. *Off White: Readings on Race, Power, and Society.* 1997.
Jaynes, Gerald, and Robin M. Williams. *A Common Destiny: Blacks and American Society.* 1989.
Kalra, Paul. *The American Class System: Divide and Rule.* 1995.
Marshall, Gordon. *Repositioning Class: Social Inequality in Industrialized Society.* 1997.
Simon, Thomas W. *Democracy and Social Injustice: Law, Politics, and Philosophy.* 1995.
Stehr, Nico. "The Future of Social Inequality." *Society* 36 (1999): 54–59.
Vanneman, Reeve, and Lynn Weber Cannon. *The American Perception of Class.* 1987.
Wilkinson, Doris Y. "Gender and Social Inequality: The Prevailing Significance of Race." *Daedalus* 124 (1995): 167–178.

Richard C. Hanes

Clay, Cassius

See Ali, Muhammad.

Cleage, Albert B., Jr.

(1911–   ), clergyman and civil rights activist.

Albert B. Cleage, Jr., a clergyman and minister of the Shrine of the Black Madonna in Detroit, Michigan, is the author of some of the earliest works on black theology. The son of a prominent Detroit physician, Cleage received his education at Wayne State University and at Oberlin School of Theology, where he affiliated with the United Church of Christ. In the 1940s, Cleage began his ministry at Congregational churches in Kentucky and Massachusetts and at the interracial Fellowship Church in San Francisco. When called to the pastorate of Detroit's Central Congregational Church in 1951, Cleage expanded his political involvement in civic issues, earning a reputation as a radical community activist who articulated a Christian brand of black nationalism, similar to Elijah MUHAMMAD's NATION OF ISLAM as preached by MALCOLM X.

In 1966, increasingly disenchanted with the mainline civil rights movement, Cleage unveiled a fifteen-foot painting of the Black Madonna, which signaled the transformation of his church into the Shrine of the Black Madonna and the launching of the Black Christian Nationalist Movement. In *The Black Messiah*, a 1968 collection of his sermons, Cleage contends that Jesus Christ was black, and gives historical evidence in support of his claim. In 1970, Cleage changed his name to Jaramogi Abebe Agyeman, and two years later published his second book, *Black Christian Nationalism: New Directions for the Black Church.* In 1978, the Shrine of the Black Madonna reorganized as a denomination called the Pan African Orthodox Christian Church.

BIBLIOGRAPHY

Chapman, Mark L. *Christianity on Trial: African-American Religious Thought Before and After Black Power.* 1996.
Cleage, Albert B., Jr. *The Black Messiah.* 1968.
Cleage, Albert B., Jr. *Black Christian Nationalism: New Directions for the Black Church.* 1972.
Temme, John M. "The Black Messiah and Albert B. Cleage, Jr.: A Retrospective at 25 Years." *Trinity Seminary Review* 17 (Spring 1995): 23–31.
Ward, Hiley H. *Prophet of the Black Nation.* 1969.

Cynthia Taylor

Cleaver, Eldridge

(1935–1998), writer and political activist.

Eldridge Cleaver was born on August 31, 1935 in Wabaseka, Arkansas. His family moved to Phoenix and ultimately the Watts section of Los Angeles. In his youth, Cleaver was often arrested. He wrote *Soul on Ice* while serving a two-to-fourteen-year term at Soledad Prison, where he had become a Black Muslim and read Karl Marx, among others. He developed a contradictory mix of revolutionary fervor and a self-professed "enthusiasm" for raping women.

Later a senior editor for *Ramparts* magazine, ex-convict Eldridge Cleaver encountered the newly created BLACK PANTHER PARTY in February 1967, and was recruited to membership by the party's cofounder Huey NEWTON. Cleaver's rise to national prominence resulted from the 1968 publication of his manifesto, *Soul on Ice*. His writing skills were harnessed by the party through his appointments as both minister of information and editor of the *Black Panther* newspaper, which began circulation in April 1967.

Cleaver unsuccessfully ran for president of the United States for the PEACE AND FREEDOM PARTY in 1968. In April of the same year, he was shot and beaten

Writer, political activist, and one-time presidential candidate Eldridge Cleaver, in exile in 1969 when this picture was taken. His right hand is raised, giving a peace sign. (AP/Wide World Photos)

by police along with fellow Panther Bobby Hutton, who was killed. Subsequently, Cleaver was sent back to prison on a parole violation. Released on bond two months later, Cleaver vowed he would never return to prison. By September, he had gone into hiding, as his parole was again overturned.

In November 1968, Cleaver and his wife Kathleen, also a Panther leader, were forced into exile. They moved to Cuba and ultimately Algeria, where the international chapter of the Black Panther Party was formed. The Cleavers encouraged the party to join an international front against U.S. imperialism.

Although the party initially emphasized its right to bear arms, it ultimately developed a comprehensive strategy to serve, build, and empower African-American neighborhoods nationwide. Cleaver placed a heavier emphasis on violence and cooperation with white radicals than Newton, contributing to an ideological split from Newton. The FEDERAL BUREAU OF INVESTIGATION's (FBI's) COINTELPRO also facilitated the split, as agent provocateurs monitored the dissention in the party leadership and passed false notes between Newton and Cleaver. In February 1971, Cleaver called for Newton to stand trial to judge his commitment to revolution. Cleaver and the New York

Panthers called for the expulsion of both Newton and David Hilliard. Newton expelled the exiled Cleaver from the party as a result.

After returning to the United States in 1975, Cleaver had a religious "conversion," discussed in his 1978 book, *Soul on Fire*, which altered his revolutionary political beliefs. He was sent back to prison for a parole violation and released in 1980. In 1986, he unsuccessfully ran for the Republican nomination for the U.S. Senate in California.

Cleaver joined evangelist Billy Graham in religious crusades and became a regular spokesperson for some California-based organizations, urging young people to turn to God. He joined Panther cofounder Bobby SEALE on a speaking tour. Seale indicated that despite Cleaver's Republicanism, he remained somewhat critical of Republican policies, having tossed a copy of Newt Gingrich's "Contract with America" across the stage during one speaking engagement. Cleaver died on May 2, 1998.

BIBLIOGRAPHY
Cleaver, Eldridge. *Soul on Ice.* 1968.
Cleaver, Eldridge. *Post-Prison Writings and Speeches.* 1969.
Rout, Kathleen. *Eldridge Cleaver.* 1991.

David J. Maurrasse

Clinton, William Jefferson "Bill"

(1946–), U.S. president, 1993–2001.

Forty-second president of the United States of America, Bill Clinton's most tangible claim to civil rights links has been through the African-American community. In his campaigns for governorship of ARKANSAS he carefully cultivated support among blacks and won one of his most loyal voting bases there. As an acknowledgment of this, Clinton promoted black political allies to prominent state posts during his terms of office (1978–1980, 1982–1992). This loyal African-American base of support was repeated nationally in Clinton's presidential campaigns, as were his rewards of political positions in appointments to the White House cabinet. Civil rights luminaries such as Vernon JORDAN and Jesse JACKSON have been among Clinton's closest confidants while in office. He has also been viewed as a strong supporter of women's rights.

In other areas Clinton's civil rights record is much less assured. While first running for president, he famously upheld Arkansas' use of the death penalty by failing to issue a stay of execution for a convicted prisoner. One of his earliest failures as president was his backdown over allowing gays to serve openly in the U.S. military. A succession of alleged affairs and the Monica Lewinsky scandal surely brought into question

Clinton's attitudes toward women at a personal level. Arguably, Clinton's continued drift toward the center and the right while in office has undercut much of the potential for progress in civil rights. For someone who took presidential office with such high expectations for change, Clinton's civil rights record must ultimately be seen as one of missed opportunities and unfulfilled promise.

BIBLIOGRAPHY

Allen, Charles, and Jonathon Portis. *The Comeback Kid: The Life and Career of Bill Clinton.* 1992.

Landau, Elaine. *Bill Clinton and His Presidency.* 1997.

Maraniss, David. *First in His Class: The Biography of Bill Clinton.* 1995.

John A. Kirk

Cloud, Henry Roe

(1886–1950), educator, minister, government official.

Henry Roe Cloud believed in and worked for the assimilation of Native Americans into American society on the basis of greater freedom and opportunity. He was born on December 28, 1886, to Winnebago parents in Nebraska and named Wonah'i layhunka. Educators at the Genoa, Nebraska, government boarding school anglicized his name to "Henry Clarence Cloud." He also attended the Santee Normal Training School, a mission school on the Santee Indian Reservation, where he learned printing and blacksmithing skills and converted to Christianity. In 1902 he began studies at a college preparatory school founded by D. L. Moody in Northfield, Massachusetts. He graduated from the Mount Hermon School in 1906 and entered Yale University that fall. He earned a B.A. degree from Yale in 1910, studied at Oberlin for a year, obtained a Bachelor of Divinity degree in 1913 from Auburn Theological Seminary in New York state, and was ordained as a Presbyterian minister in 1913. While at Yale University, Dr. and Mrs. Walter C. Roe adopted Henry Cloud, and he adopted their name as his middle name. In 1914 Cloud earned an M.A. degree from Yale, and in 1932 he received a Doctor of Divinity degree from Emporia College in Kansas.

Henry Roe Cloud served as vice president of education on the board of the SOCIETY OF AMERICAN INDIANS (SAI), a pan-Indian reform group established in 1911 (see PAN-TRIBALISM). In 1914 at an SAI conference in Madison, Wisconsin, Henry Cloud met Elizabeth Bender, a Minnesota Ojibwa who had attended Hampton Institute and was active in SAI. On June 12, 1916, they married. During their marriage they had five children. Cloud was a founder of the Roe Indian Institute in Wichita, Kansas, and served as its superintendent until 1930. In 1920 the school's name was changed to the American Indian Institute. The institute emphasized academic learning and leadership development rather than vocational education, which was more commonly emphasized in other Indian schools. At the American Indian Institute, Cloud came to feel that Indian youths needed a Christian influence in their lives. Another of his major goals there was to prepare Indian men for college.

In 1923, Cloud was appointed to the "Committee of 100," a group under the direction of Secretary of Interior Hubert Work, organized to investigate and analyze the government's Indian policies. Cloud served as a staff member, researcher, and coauthor of the 1928 *Meriam Report*, conducted by the Institute for Government Research and presented to the Secretary of Interior. In published form, Lewis M. Meriam's *The Problem of Indian Administration* (1928) revealed the depth of Indian poverty and deprivation on reservations. The study identified the source of the problems in the government's allotment policy and called for reform of the administration of Indian affairs and changes in federal Indian policy. The report was useful during the New Deal reforms of the 1930s (see NEW DEAL AND DEPRESSION).

From 1931 to 1933, Cloud served in the Office of Indian Affairs, and as a special field representative, he conducted investigations at Indian agencies. In 1933, Commissioner of Indian Affairs John Collier appointed him as superintendent of the Haskell Indian School in Lawrence, Kansas. Cloud served at Haskell until 1936, when he became assistant supervisor of Indian education in the Office of Indian Affairs. In the meantime, he traveled throughout North Dakota and South Dakota to generate support for the Wheeler-Howard INDIAN REORGANIZATION ACT (1934). He spent much time helping Indians organize under this new policy, which provided for greater Indian self-government and cultural self-determination. For his accomplishments, the Indian Council Fire gave Cloud the Indian Achievement Award in 1935.

During the 1940s Cloud served as Superintendent of the Umatilla Indian Agency in Pendleton, Oregon, and at the Portland regional office of the U.S. BUREAU OF INDIAN AFFAIRS. There he helped organize the records of the Grande Ronde and Siletz Indian Agencies in preparation for the Indian Claims Commission settlement. Throughout his life Cloud worked for the betterment of Indian people and judged that his Christian version of leadership education and assimilation effectively helped to develop the first college-educated group of Indian leaders. He died of a heart attack on February 9, 1950, and is buried in Beaverton, Oregon.

BIBLIOGRAPHY

Cloud, Henry Roe. "From Wigwam to Pulpit." *Southern Workman* (July 1915): 400–406.

Crum, Steven J. "Henry Roe Cloud, A Winnebago Indian Reformer: His Quest for American Indian Higher Education." *Kansas History* 2, no. 3 (Autumn 1988): 171–184.

Granger, Loretta May. "Indian Education at Haskell Institute, 1884–1937." Masters thesis, University of Nebraska. 1937.

Meriam, Lewis M., et al. *The Problem of Indian Administration.* 1928.

Yale University. *Obituary Record, 1949–1950.* 1951.

Rodger C. Henderson

Cobb, Ned

(1885–1973), Sharecroppers' Union member.

Ned Cobb was a black tenant farmer in ALABAMA who joined the Sharecroppers' Union in the 1930s to fight the system of debt peonage. Cobb's abilities as a storyteller preserved a history in the oral tradition, and his stories are told under a pseudonym in Theodore Rosengarten's *All God's Dangers: The Life of Nate Shaw.*

The son of a former slave, Cobb raised nine children on a farm in the JIM CROW era. The system of furnishing, whereby a white storeowner or planter extended credit at exploitative rates of interest to a sharecropper in return for payment in kind after the harvest, kept many black farmers under the economic and social control of the white creditors. This corruption was supported by force when necessary.

In 1931, the price of cotton had fallen sharply, and increasing numbers of seizures of farm livestock and equipment were occurring. In order to make a stand against this system, Cobb joined the secret, Communist-organized, Sharecroppers' Union in 1932. Armed with a .32 Smith and Wesson, Cobb faced off deputy sheriffs who were attempting to foreclose on one of his neighbors. He was shot, brought to trial, and served twelve years in prison for his actions. Despite offers of parole, Cobb refused to tell white authorities anything about the organization. He saw the stand against the deputies as his defining moment and later regarded the union, a part of the struggle for black autonomy, as a connection between the end of slavery and the civil rights movement of the 1960s.

BIBLIOGRAPHY

Daniel, Pete. *The Shadow of Slavery: Peonage in the South, 1901–1969.* 1972.

Rosengarten, Theodore. *All God's Dangers: The Life of Nate Shaw.* 1974.

Noeleen McIlvenna

Cohen, Felix S.

(1907–1953), legal/ethical philosopher, activist, attorney, and teacher.

Born in New York City, the son of Russian Jewish immigrant philosopher Morris Cohen, Felix Cohen was a prodigy. Taking his Ph.D. in philosophy from Harvard University at age twenty-two, he then studied law at Columbia University, was admitted to the New York bar in 1932, and published his influential *Ethical Systems and Legal Ideals* a year later.

In 1933, Cohen became assistant solicitor general of the Interior Department's BUREAU OF INDIAN AFFAIRS under newly appointed Indian Commissioner John Collier. His first task involved drafting the 1934 INDIAN REORGANIZATION ACT, a cornerstone of the "Indian New Deal," reversing a half-century of federal assimilation policy and replacing it with one facilitating native self-governance.

Cohen was next asked to conduct a comprehensive study of Indian rights under U.S. law. The result, first published in 1941, was the *Handbook on Federal Indian Law*, a monumental compilation and analysis of treaties, statutes, and regulations still considered by many to be the definitive work of its kind.

Cohen resigned his position in 1948, when it became clear that post–ROOSEVELT era Indian policy would evolve in a manner antithetical to his own beliefs. He went into private practice, defending native clients against federal paternalism, authored an influencial series of essays on Indian law, and began to experiment with combining legal and direct action strategies.

The force and effectiveness of Cohen's approach led to his being denounced as a "Communist" by Indian Commissioner Dillon S. Myer, investigated by the FEDERAL BUREAU OF INVESTIGATION (FBI), and adopted as a tribal member by the Blackfeet, who gave him the name "Double Runner." His untimely death prevented his achievements from ever reaching full flower. Nonetheless, in only two decades he managed to lay the foundation upon which Indian rights were pursued throughout the remainder of the twentieth century.

BIBLIOGRAPHY

Cohen, Lucy Kramer, ed. *The Legal Conscience: Selected Papers of Felix S. Cohen.* 1960.

Drinnon, Richard. *Keeper of Concentration Camps: Dillon S. Myer and American Racism.* 1987.

Kelly, Lawrence C. *Assault on Assimilation: John Collier and the Origins of American Indian Policy Reform.* 1983.

Taylor, Graham D. *The New Deal and American Indian Tribalism.* 1980.

Ward Churchill

Cold War

The Cold War, a decades-long conflict between the United States and the former Soviet Union, had a paradoxical and contradictory impact on the struggle for civil rights in the United States.

In the immediate post–WORLD WAR II period, opposition to a policy of hostility toward Moscow was spearheaded by such leading African-Americans as W. E. B. DU BOIS and Paul ROBESON. They felt that the wartime unity between Moscow and Washington should be continued after 1945. They were appreciative of Moscow's support for those struggling against colonial powers in Africa—the allies of the United States in London, Paris, Brussels, and Lisbon. They thought that the increased military spending that the Cold War would bring inevitably would hamper the effort of the government to address pressing concerns of the working class generally and African Americans specifically, particularly in such areas as education and health. However, the firing of Du Bois in 1948 from his high-level post in the organization he had helped to found, the NATIONAL ASSOCIATION FOR THE ADVANCEMENT OF COLORED PEOPLE (NAACP), signaled that the Cold War would not continue to be a pressing

concern of most of those who played leading roles in the civil rights movement.

On the one hand, the isolation and marginalization of figures such as Du Bois and Robeson constrained the ideological options available to black America, making it more difficult to generate opposition to U.S. wars in Korea and Vietnam. Du Bois himself was placed on trial in 1951 because of his advocacy of opposition to nuclear weapons; after a massive international campaign he was acquitted, though the NAACP nationally did not stand by his side. As these left-wing individuals were isolated, a radical critique of U.S. society focused on maldistribution of wealth was similarly sidelined. This disparity led directly to a major failing of the civil rights movement: minorities gained the right to eat at a lunch counter but discovered they did not have sufficient funds to pay the bill.

On the other hand, as the United States strained to portray the Soviet Union as a major violator of human rights, it found it necessary to get its own house in order. U.S. politicians found that their message would carry more weight—particularly in Africa, Asia, and Latin America—if people of color in their own country were accorded simple civil rights, including the right to vote. JIM CROW had to go, in no small measure

Senator Joseph McCarthy of Wisconsin pointing at a map during a 1954 hearing of his Permanent Subcommittee on Investigations, a product of the Cold War. A dejected Joseph N. Welch sits nearby, hand on head. (UPI/CORBIS/Bettmann)

because of international pressure and the desire of the United States to improve its global image.

These contradictory trends came to a head during the VIETNAM WAR. After Dr. Martin Luther KING, Jr. made an impassioned anti-war speech at Riverside Church in New York City in April 1967, he was widely denounced because of the perception that he had strayed beyond his field of expertise and had jeopardized the support of the JOHNSON administration, CONGRESS, and other powerful elites for further civil rights reform. Dr. King and his supporters felt that the "butter" needed by his constituency could not be obtained as long as tax dollars were being spent disproportionately on the "guns" of Vietnam; moreover, as a philosopher of nonviolence, Dr. King felt he could hardly support a U.S. war against a developing nation.

A longer-term effect of the Cold War was its circumscribing of acceptable ideological discourse, as opposition to the war, support for unions, and other measures supported by large numbers of African Americans were often derided as "Communist-inspired." Thus, there were supporters of civil rights who were reluctant to back the African National Congress led by South Africa's Nelson Mandela because of its alliance with the South African Communist Party. By the time the Berlin Wall crumbled in 1989 and the Soviet Union dissolved in 1991, the discourse of civil rights had strayed a long way from that expressed when Du Bois was a leader of the NAACP and Robeson was hailed widely among African Americans as a tribune.

BIBLIOGRAPHY

Horne, Gerald. *Black and Red: W. E. B. DuBois and the Afro-American Response to the Cold War, 1944–1963*. 1986.

Stewart, Jeffrey, ed. *Paul Robeson: Artist and Citizen*. 1998.

Gerald Horne

Colonialism

In general, scholars agree that colonialism involves the organized domination by one nation of an external or different geographical unit, nation, culture, race, or people. According to V. Y. Mudimbe in *The Invention of Africa* (1988), the terms " 'colonialism' and 'colonization' basically mean organization, arrangement," and "derive from the Latin 'colere,' meaning to cultivate or to design." Hence, colonization involved the designing of colonized nations as economic and political subordinates of the colonizer, often referred to as the "mother country."

European colonization of other races in the late nineteenth and twentieth centuries had its beginnings in the fifteenth century, when commercial interests in Europe, led by Portugal and Spain, sponsored voyages of exploration in search of precious metals and new routes to the spice markets in India and the Far East. In 1488, Bartholomeu Dias rounded the southernmost tip of Africa. His discoveries led to further Portuguese exploration of India. In 1492, while searching for a westward route to Asia, Christopher Columbus landed on an island in the Caribbean and claimed it for Spain. His voyage opened up the "New World" to further exploration and colonization by European nations, including Portugal, the Netherlands, France, and England. These nations would also claim colonies in the East Indies and Africa.

Whereas the early voyages of exploration were spurred primarily by European quests for precious stones and spices, Africa's late nineteenth-century and early twentieth-century colonization, especially, was shaped by several factors. These factors include the emergence of internal rivalry among European nations, the desire to spread Christianity, the need for raw materials for European industries, and investment opportunities for surplus capital. Some scholars, however, describe late nineteenth- and early twentieth-century colonization of Africa as a continuation of European expansionism into other parts of the world. Some critics have condemned colonization as a racist enterprise, for the colonizers often defined themselves as racially superior to the colonized and morally responsible for "civilizing" the "inferior races."

In Africa, the Europeans found themselves contesting for territories, especially around the mouth of the Congo. The Berlin Conference was organized in 1884–1885 to settle political and trade disputes, but it went on to establish formal guidelines for trade and European occupation of Africa. At the end of the conference, the European nations began a frenzied scramble for Africa, leading eventually to the continent's arbitrary partitioning. By 1914, much of Africa, except Ethiopia, was under European colonial rule.

In response to oppressive colonial policies, many colonized people began to demand autonomy. In India, the Indian National Congress (the National Congress) emerged in the 1880s; and in England, the Pan-African movement founded by Caribbean and American blacks in London in 1900 became an advocate of civil rights and autonomy for blacks. Despite these movements, colonized nations would not gain independence until after World War II or even later.

At the end of World War II, many former colonies began to agitate for independence. Several factors encouraged this resurgence of nationalist sentiments: notably, Europe was no longer a strong economic, military, and political power overseas. Nationalism in the colonies was often championed by indigenous people, who were either educated in Europe or fought in the world wars, and who upon their return home began to demand independence. Also, in their home countries, many Europeans could no longer morally justify colonization as a Christian enterprise. In 1947, India, Great Britain's largest overseas colony, became independent, followed by Ghana in 1957 and Nigeria in 1960. Other British colonies gradually gained independence during the 1960s and 1970s.

Unlike the British, the French, who were reluctant to grant total independence to their colonies, argued for partial independence with French aid, or for total independence without aid. Only Guinea chose independence without aid, in 1958. The French, however, were challenged in Indochina and North Africa, especially Algeria. But by the end of the 1970s, most of the African nations had become independent, as had the countries of French Indochina.

Although the term "colonialism" is often used to describe the domination of another country by an external power, in the late 1960s and early 1970s some radical African-American civil rights activists and scholars compared the colonization of Africans to the oppression of blacks in the United States. Consequently, these critics described the status of African-Americans, especially in ghetto communities, as "internal colonialism." The activists drew on Franz Fanon's critique of colonialism and PAN-AFRICANISM's vision of a united black liberation struggle. These radical activists called for revolution to overthrow a capitalist system that they perceived as colonizing. Such scholars as Kenneth CLARK, in *Dark Ghetto* (1965), and Harold Cruse, in *Rebellion or Revolution?* (1968), described race relations in America as "domestic colonialism." Stokely CARMICHAEL and Charles Hamilton, in their work *Black Power* (1967), extended Clark's paradigm and argued that like African and "Third World" nations, African-American communities were economic, social, and political colonies of the U.S. government. This internal colonization, they claimed, was maintained either directly or by "indirect rule," through "local blacks who are responsive to the white leaders, the downtown, white machine, not to the black populace." Carmichael and Hamilton, however, acknowledged that unlike the case of "classic colonialism," where the colony is the source of cheap raw materials, black communities in America, as colonies, exported "human labor." Nonetheless, they insisted that black Americans, like colonized subjects in Africa and the Third World, experience not only economic and political marginalization but also psychological anguish and cultural alienation from their own people, as well social degradation and dehumanization by the colonizer (pp. 30–31).

In summary, the various attempts to define colonialism, either in its "classic" usage or in the more radical interpretation of formerly colonized people, civil rights activists, and scholars, underscore the domination of one group, race, or culture by another; but many critics of colonialism also see colonization as an expression of racism. They state that racial superiority was used to justify colonization, which created power inequity between the colonizers, who perceived themselves as "superior," and the colonized, who were defined as "inferior."

BIBLIOGRAPHY

Blauner, Robert. "Internal Colonialism and Ghetto Revolt." In *The Black Revolt*, edited by James A. Geschwender. 1971.

Carmichael, Stokely, and Charles V. Hamilton. *Black Power: The Politics of Liberation in America.* 1967.

Cruse, Harold. *Rebellion or Revolution?* 1968.

Freund, Bill. *The Making of Contemporary Africa: The Development of African Society Since 1800.* 1984.

Martin, Phyllis M., and Patrick O'Meara, eds. *Africa.* 2nd ed. 1995.

Mazrui, Ali, and Toby K. Levine, eds. *The Africans: A Reader.* 1986.

Mudimbe, Valentine Y. *The Invention of Africa.* 1988.

Maureen N. Eke

Colonization Movements

Nineteenth-century colonization plans sought to relocate African Americans from the United States to a place (often Africa) where they might develop a separate black state. Usually associated with periods of great frustration with the state of race relations, this form of black nationalism was often posited as an alternative to struggling for civil rights within the nation. It almost always embodied a rejection of America, and sometimes melded with millennial hopes for the "redemption" of Africa. While colonization schemes were often considered fantastic and unworkable, they were typically offered as alternatives to equally untenable hopes for meaningful freedom and political inclusion within the nation.

Early black colonizers include Paul Cuffe (1759–1817), a Massachusetts merchant who transported several dozen blacks to Sierra Leone, and the fugitive slaves who established settlements in Canada in the 1830s. Setbacks in the antislavery struggle in the 1850s led to a wave of colonization schemes by Henry Highland Garnet, James Theodore Holly, Alexander Crummell, and Martin Robison DELANY. While the possibility of inclusion promised by the Civil War dampened colonizationism, Radical Reconstruction's failure (complete by 1877) witnessed its reemergence in the form of the 1878 migration of the "EXODUS-TERS," several thousand disillusioned black sharecroppers who fled the repressive regime of Southern white Redemptionists to Kansas. During the JIM CROW era (1890s) some radicals championed colonization, notably Henry McNeil TURNER, an African Methodist Episcopal bishop. The Great Migration of Southern blacks to the North, which began in the 1890s, embodied the spirit of colonizationism in that it represented the struggle for black autonomy and escape from a repressive racial system.

BIBLIOGRAPHY

Miller, Floyd J. *The Search for a Black Nationality: Black Emigration and Colonization, 1787–1863.* 1975.

Redkey, Edwin S. *Black Exodus: Black Nationalist and Back-to-Africa Movements, 1890–1910.* 1969.

Patrick Rael

Colorado

The history of civil rights in Colorado can be characterized by struggles arising from Anglo-European settlement in an area already occupied by Native American and Mexican populations. Antidiscrimination laws have been present in Colorado since the 1890s, and the 1949 state constitutional amendment granted citizens equal rights protection under the law. However, the struggle for equality under the law has been a process of local enforcement and of legal definition.

After being granted citizenship in 1923, Native Americans in Colorado used the courts to regain their rights to their cultural practices. Colorado's central location between the southwestern and plains tribes has made the state a logical headquarters for the NATIVE AMERICAN RIGHTS FUND and other agencies, which actively pursue Native American rights in the state and across the country. Native Americans in Colorado have become a noted voice in politics through such leaders as Denver lawyer Vine DELORIA and U.S. Senator Ben Nighthorse Campbell. Colorado law has generally viewed Native Americans as one autonomous group, but there are more than a dozen tribes in Colorado that continue to assert their individual and legal identities as American citizens.

Members of Colorado's Latino population have also faced problems in maintaining their cultural integrity and rights as citizens against the dominant Anglo-European culture. Additionally, Latinos have faced continual internal conflicts between early Mexican-American families and the later influx of migrant workers from Mexico. Even though actively involved in the formation of the state constitution as members of the legislature in the 1870s, Colorado Latinos have found themselves perennial victims of discriminatory labor, housing; and educational practices. In the 1960s

and 1970s, political activists, such as Rodolfo "Corky" Gonzales who founded the Crusade for Justice, attempted to radically reassert Latino autonomy. This struggle between cultural autonomy and political balance continues to typify Latino civil rights issues in Colorado.

Although African Americans have fared better than Latino residents in Colorado overall, discrimination against both minorities has been prevalent in every area of daily life. Colorado African Americans secured antidiscrimination statutes in 1885, 1895 and 1917, which, unfortunately, paid little more than lip service to equal rights. Significant changes did not occur, however, until the late 1960s and the 1970s, in housing, employment, and school desegregation.

Women gained suffrage in Colorado in 1893, as it became the first state (as opposed to territory) to enfranchise women. By the 1960s, the effects of the national women's rights movement were being felt in Colorado. Although the Equal Rights Amendment was never ratified nationally, Colorado incorporated the amendment into its constitution in 1972. This era brought such women as Pat Schroeder and Mary Estill Buchanan into state and national politics, where they continued to be advocates for women's rights.

During the 1990s, Colorado was at the center of the most significant gay-rights case in the United States. The passage of Amendment 2 would have canceled gay-rights ordinances and barred the enactment of any other gay-rights laws or policies by state or local governments. Although it was approved by voters, the Colorado Supreme Court invalidated the amendment on the grounds it denied homosexuals an equal voice in government, and in May 1996, the U.S. SUPREME COURT declared Amendment 2 unconstitutional.

BIBLIOGRAPHY

Abbott, Carl, et al. *Colorado: A History of the Centennial State,* 3rd ed. 1994.

Aguirre, Adalbert, Jr., and David Baker. "The Execution of Mexican American Prisoners in the Southwest." *Social Justice* 16, 4 (1989): 150–161.

Atkins, James A. *Human Relations in Colorado, 1858–1959.* Denver, CO: Office of Instructional Services, 1961.

Bardwell, George E. *Segregation: A Social Account.* Denver, CO: Colorado Civil Rights Commission, 1971.

Chaer, Robert. *Civil Rights in Denver, Then and Now: An Interview with Helen Peterson. Agency Director. 1948–1953 and 1962–1970.* Denver, CO: Agency for Human Rights and Community Relations, 1997.

Deutsch, Sarah. *No Separate Refuge: Culture, Class and Gender on an Anglo-Hispanic Frontier in the American Southwest, 1880–1940.* 1987.

Eastman, Max. "Class War in Colorado." In *Civil Strife in America: A Historical Approach to the Study of Riots in America,* by Norman S. Cohen. 1972.

Friesen, Daniel E. D. *Colorado Labor and Employment Law.* 1998.

Gearhart, Dona G. "Coal Mining Women in the West: The Realities of Difference in an Extreme Environment." *Journal of the West* 37, 1 (1998): 60–68.

Hughes, J. Donald. *American Indians in Colorado.* 1977.

Lyons, Oren, et al. *Exiled in the Land of the Free: Democracy, Indian Nations, and the U.S. Constitution.* 1991.

Marin, Christine. *A Spokesman of the Mexican American Movement: Rodolfo "Corky" Gonzales and the Fight for Chicano Liberation, 1966–1972.* R and E Research Associates, 1977.

Monnett, John H., and Michael McCarthy. *Colorado Profiles: Men and Women Who Shaped the Centennial State.* 1989.

Norman, Mary Ann. "Civil Rights in Colorado: An Examination and Analysis of Five Cases." *Journal of the West* 25, 4 (1986): 38–43.

Reese, Joan. "Two Enemies to Fight: Blacks Battle for Equality in Two World Wars." *Colorado Heritage* no. 1 (1990): 2–17.

UMAS, compilation of newspaper articles by members of United Mexican American Students of the University of Colorado at Boulder. 1970.

White, Richard. *"It's Your Misfortune and None of My Own": A New History of the American West.* 1991.

Pamela Cowen
Sue Marasco

Comité, El

El Comité was formed in 1970 on the West Side of Manhattan, in New York City, under the leadership of Fedérico Lorca, as a response to a housing crisis created by the city's Urban Renewal/Model Cities Program. The program called for the demolition of low-income housing to make room for middle- to upper-income housing units, in an area predominantly populated by Latinos, mostly Puerto Ricans. El Comité, comprised mostly of working people, Vietnam veterans, and ex–gang members, was formed as part of a squatters' movement organized as a political response to the city government. The organization soon expanded, spreading to other areas in New York and Boston. In 1975, El Comité held a constitutional assembly leading to the official organization of El Comité-Movimiento de Izquierda Nacional Puertorriqueño (Puerto Rican National Left Movement).

Although its broader goal was the formation of a multinational Communist party that would lead the United States into socialism, El Comité–MINP's primary activities focused on issues relevant to Puerto Ricans living in the United States, such as housing, education, and employment. They supported independence for Puerto Rico, as did many of the other leftist organizations at the time. However, they argued that Puerto Ricans on the mainland were not part of the Puerto Rican nation but instead constituted a national minority within the U.S. working class. The organization was also actively supportive of international issues. For instance, it supported Cuba through demonstrations and rallies at the United Nations; and it educated people on the links between working-class struggles in the United States and those in Cuba, Nicaragua, and Angola.

One of the organization's greatest accomplishments was a conference held in 1971 around the campaign to free five Puerto Rican Nationalist prisoners. El Frente Unido Pro Presos Politicos Puertorriqueños, a coalition of organizations interested in the freedom of the Puerto Rican prisoners, was formed at the conference. The organization also published a local community paper, *Unidad Latina*, which soon increased its circulation to become a citywide paper. *Unidad Latina* was used by the group's members as an instructional tool, informing the community of both local and international struggles. Members of the organization also helped build the Latin Women's Collective, a group of women who were critical of the feminist movement, perceiving it as an antimale movement that did not address issues relevant to women of color.

The organization's decline began with the decision by key members in the organization to pursue their revolutionary interests in Puerto Rico. In 1978 Fedérico Lorca, the original leader of the organization, went to Puerto Rico to join the independence and leftist movements on the island, leaving a great gap in the leadership of the organization. The group's expansion also led to diversification of its membership, which resulted in a division between those who wanted to continue with grassroots organizing activities and those who believed the priority should be to educate the masses in Marxist–Leninist ideology. These differences resulted in irreparable splits in the organization. In 1981, El Comité–MINP was dissolved.

BIBLIOGRAPHY

Martell, Esperanza. "'In the Belly of the Beast': Beyond Survival." In *The Puerto Rican Movement: Voices from the Diaspora,* edited by Andrés Torres and José E. Velazquez. 1998.

Velazquez, José E. "Another West Side Story: An Interview with Members of El Comité–MINP." In *The Puerto Rican Movement: Voices from the Diaspora,* edited by Andrés Torres and José E. Velazquez. 1998.

Elizabeth Garcia

Commission on Civil Rights

See U.S. Commission on Civil Rights.

Commission on Interracial Cooperation

The Commission on Interracial Cooperation (CIC), formed in Atlanta, GEORGIA, in 1919 in the aftermath of racial strife, sought to restore harmony between blacks and whites, with the understanding that white Southerners might gradually accept equality as long as SEGREGATION was maintained. CIC members believed that segregation could exist without black people being discriminated against, not realizing that segregation itself was a form of discrimination. The premise was that blacks could hope to improve their status in Southern society if they adhered to the rules of JIM CROW and did not interfere with the well-guarded folkways of "separate but equal." If CIC could decrease violence and lessen tension between the races, it would deem its work successful.

CIC's highest mark, therefore, came when it sponsored internationally acclaimed black singer Roland Hayes in concert in Atlanta in 1925. Instead of blacks being confined solely to the poorer balcony seats of the city auditorium, they were allowed seats from the top to bottom of an entire side, as long as whites had the other side. This vertical segregation arrangement represented for W. Will ALEXANDER, CIC's executive director, a symbol that segregation had been dealt a small blow. It was as far as CIC was willing to go. Little relief for blacks came even as liberal white Southerners invited black participation in an organization that moved toward the concept of equality.

CIC maintained its low-profile approach to racial equality through 1944, Alexander having served as its executive director for its twenty-five-year history. In 1944 many CIC members joined in founding the SOUTHERN REGIONAL COUNCIL, another organization that worked to create equality among the races in the United States.

BIBLIOGRAPHY

Kelley, Robin D. G. *Hammer and Hoe: Alabama Communists During the Great Depression.* 1990.
Killian, Lewis M. *White Southerners.* 1985.
Reed, Linda. *Simple Decency and Common Sense: The Southern Conference Movement, 1938–1963.* 1991.

Linda Reed

Communism

See Communist Party USA.

Communist Party USA

Detractors of civil rights organizations frequently turned to red-baiting as a means of discrediting the movement. Although accusations of communist influence were highly exaggerated, they were not entirely unfounded. American communists have a long history of support for African Americans' civil rights, and in some respects they might be regarded as pioneers in the struggle against RACISM.

Unlike most other interracial Marxist-oriented organizations, the Communist Party USA (CPUSA) made "Negro rights" one of its top priorities. After 1928, the CPUSA adopted a position that appears at odds with the goal of "racial integration" as we know it, however. Compelled in part by the Communist International as well as by some of the black comrades within its ranks, the Party argued that the black majority in the "black belt counties" of the South had a right to self-determination, including the right to secede from the United States if they so desired. The point was not to promote separatism but to insist on black people's right to choose. Consequently, the policy resulted not in a separatist movement but in active

A Communist Party demonstration in 1930, during the early months of the Great Depression. (Library of Congress)

support for black civil rights—including the formation of groups such as the League of Struggle for Negro Rights (1930), led by none other than poet Langston HUGHES. Through the INTERNATIONAL LABOR DEFENSE (ILD), the Communist Party played a crucial role in defending black rights in the streets and the courtroom. Of course, the ILD took up a wide range of cases involving "class war prisoners," its most famous case in the 1930s being the defense of nine young black men known to the world as the SCOTTSBORO BOYS—falsely accused of raping two white women in ALABAMA.

In 1935, in accordance with the Commitment's Seventh World Congress, the CPUSA called for a Popular Front against fascism, de-emphasized its Marxist ideology, and eventually supported President Roosevelt's New Deal coalition. Communists not only joined mainstream black civil rights organizations in greater numbers, but they became the primary force behind black coalition efforts like the NATIONAL NEGRO CONGRESS (1935–1946). Black communists also initiated a number of campaigns, including a boycott of the film *Gone With the Wind* and a movement to "End JIM CROW in Sports," collecting some 10,000 signatures demanding the integration of African Americans in major league baseball. In the South, communists worked with Southern liberals to found the SOUTHERN CONFERENCE FOR HUMAN WELFARE (1938) and related organizations that were committed to economic justice and equality. Young black communists, in particular, formed the SOUTHERN NEGRO YOUTH CONGRESS (SNYC). Founded in 1937, SNYC attracted a number of energetic activists, many of whom were young, middle-class intellectuals who came of age in the South during the New Deal era. From the time of its founding to its demise in 1948, SNYC's program emphasized the right to vote, job security, the right of black workers to organize, general improvement in the health, EDUCATION, and welfare of African-American citizens, and militant opposition to police brutality and SEGREGATION in public spaces. Although SNYC was never large, its agenda proved far more radical than any of the existing civil rights organizations at the time.

When communists shifted to a pro-war position after Germany invaded Russia in 1941, African-American leadership, for the most part, adopted an uncompromising stance vis-à-vis the war effort, insisting on a "double victory" against RACISM at home and fascism abroad. While the Communist Party essentially opposed the DOUBLE V CAMPAIGN—arguing that too much black militancy could undermine the war effort—rank-and-file communists and liberals close to the Party continued to fight on the civil rights front throughout the war, demanding, among other things, the full integration of the armed forces and the im-

plementation of the FAIR EMPLOYMENT PRACTICES COMMITTEE. In spite of these measures, the Party's opposition to the "Double V" slogan left many African Americans feeling that it had abandoned them for the sake of the war.

After the war, the Party continued to defend black rights in the courts and streets through the CIVIL RIGHTS CONGRESS (CRC), a left-wing legal defense organization created in 1946. Led by communist William L. Patterson, CRC gained notoriety for its militant defense of African Americans falsely accused of crimes, communists accused of "un-American" activities, and for its historic petition to the United Nations charging the U.S. government with genocide against African Americans. However, McCarthyite repression (see McCARTHYISM) and the Party's leftward turn weakened the CPUSA considerably. By 1956, it had become a shadow of its former self, never to achieve the status it once enjoyed in the 1930s and 1940s.

Nevertheless, during the following decade—the heyday of the civil rights movement—black communists and ex-communists such as Jack O'Dell, Mae Mallory, Abner Berry, Hosea Hudson, to name but a few, participated in organizations such as the SOUTHERN CHRISTIAN LEADERSHIP CONFERENCE (SCLC) the NATIONAL ASSOCIATION FOR THE ADVANCEMENT OF COLORED PEOPLE (NAACP), and the STUDENT NONVIOLENT COORDINATING COMMITTEE (SNCC). More significantly, by the early to mid-1960s young activists in SNCC and the CONGRESS OF RACIAL EQUALITY (CORE) began to seriously question the viability of the civil rights movement and consider more radical roads to black freedom. Drawn to the revolutions in China and Cuba, as well as to the Marxist-led movements in Africa and Latin America, activists such as James FORMAN and Stokeley CARMICHAEL set out to develop an independent communist or socialist position for the purposes of building a black radical movement.

BIBLIOGRAPHY

Allen, James S., and Philip Foner, eds. *American Communism and Black Americans: A Documentary History, 1919–1929.* 1987.

Foner, Philip S., and Herbert Shapiro. *American Communism and Black Americans: A Documentary History, 1930–1934.* 1991.

Haywood, Harry. *Black Bolshevik: Autobiography of an Afro-American Communist.* 1978.

Horne, Gerald. *Communist Front? The Civil Rights Congress, 1946–1956.* 1988.

Isserman, Maurice. *If I Had a Hammer: The Death of the Old Left and the Birth of the New Left.* 1987.

Kelley, Robin D. G. *Hammer and Hoe: Alabama Communists During the Great Depression.* 1990.

Naison, Mark D. *Communists in Harlem During the Depression.* 1983.

Solomon, Mark. *The Cry Was Unity: African Americans and the Communist Party.* 1998.

Sullivan, Patricia L. *Days of Hope: Race and Democracy in the New Deal Era.* 1996.

Robin D. G. Kelley

Community Service Organization

The Community Service Organization (CSO), originally called the Community Political Organization, evolved from a Mexican-American steelworkers' UNION and Ed Roybal's unsuccessful run for Los Angeles City Council in 1947. With its ideological roots in the Civic Unity Leagues organized by Ignacio "Nacho" Lopez, the CSO organized community forums and registered voters. Although Roybal, a decorated combat veteran and a public health educator lost in his first attempt, he was successful in 1948, becoming the first Mexican American to be elected a Los Angeles city councilman since 1881.

Once Roybal took office, the CSO was organized as a public service and advocacy organization with the assistance of Fred Ross, a disciple of Saul Alinsky's Industrial Areas Foundation (IAF). The CSO focused on the problems of poor Chicanos and the community generally, organizing for access to health services and full citizenship and fighting discrimination in housing, schools, and public facilities, as well as police brutality and abuses by city officials.

In the early 1950s, the CSO grew quickly, branching out to cities and towns throughout California, even establishing chapters in Arizona. In 1952, the young César CHÁVEZ helped to form the first CSO chapter in San Jose's Sal Si Puedes barrio. Chávez was soon organizing CSO chapters throughout California's Central Valley. He, Dolores HUERTA, and others around the state gained important organizing experience and helped to build a statewide organization.

By the mid 1950s, however, Chávez, Huerta, and others left the CSO in favor of joining or founding more militant or labor-oriented organizations. Chavez and Huerta both rejected aspects of the CIO's relatively conventional forms of organizing—for voter registration and naturalization, protesting police brutality, and demanding civil rights—in favor of organizing agricultural workers, which ultimately led to the birth of the UNITED FARM WORKERS union.

After 1958, the CSO lost IAF funding, leading to a drop in Chicano voter registration. Nonetheless, the CSO continued to be active in California Chicano communities and statewide politics, securing voter registration funding from and contributing cadre to Viva Kennedy clubs in the 1960 presidential election and other electoral efforts.

In the late 1960s, the CSO cooperated with the AMERICAN CIVIL LIBERTIES UNION in the investigation of police abuses in Los Angeles. By 1967, the CSO had become a part of the "old guard" of Mexican-American politics in California, especially Los Angeles. Members of newer organizations, especially youth activists, increasingly criticized the CSO for taking what was seen as a reformist, accommodationist, and mainstream approach. Despite this criticism, the CSO was a critical precursor to the CHICANO MOVEMENT in Los Angeles and other parts of California. In the 1970s the CSO regained some of its numbers and again became active in the Los Angeles community.

BIBLIOGRAPHY

Acuña, Rodolfo. *Occupied America: A History of Chicanos,* 3rd ed. 1987.

Matthiessen, Peter. *Sal Si Puedes: Cesar Chavez and the New American Revolution.* 1969.

Rosales, Francisco A. *Chicano! The History of the Mexican American Civil Rights Movement,* 2nd ed. 1997.

Ron Lopez

Congreso del Pueblo de Habla Espanola

See Congress of Spanish-Speaking People.

Congress

The role of Congress in civil rights policy has developed through five historical periods. First, from the ratification of the Constitution in 1789 to the outbreak of the Civil War in 1861, the states rather than Congress defined most civil rights. Although the Revolution expanded American rights and liberties far beyond European norms, the states were not bound by the Bill of Rights, and state laws generally restricted the exercise of rights in voting, political office-holding, education, professional employment, contracts, and judicial participation to propertied white males. Congress, concentrating on national expansion, dealt with Indian policy and slavery.

The second period began with the Civil War. Secession removed conservative southern representatives from Congress and empowered northern radical Republicans, who passed constitutional amendments banning slavery (the THIRTEENTH AMENDMENT, ratified in 1865); guaranteeing equal individual rights (FOURTEENTH AMENDMENT, 1868); and guaranteeing male voting rights irrespective of race (FIFTEENTH AMENDMENT, 1870). Congress during RECONSTRUCTION (1865–1877) also passed laws to protect the freedpeople from violence, to enforce their political rights, and to guarantee certain economic rights (property ownership, contract). These policies were designed to build a stable economic and political order in the agricultural South.

The third period of congressional civil rights policy was the longest, running from the end of Reconstruction (1877) to American involvement in WORLD WAR II in 1941. It featured a return of civil rights policymaking to the state and local level, especially in the South, where conservative state governments controlled by white Democrats built a caste system of racial segregation. African Americans endured unequal public education, economic discrimination, political powerlessness, and systematic humiliation.

In Congress, efforts by liberal reformers to protect black southerners from the worst abuses—for example, bills during the 1930s to make racial lynching a federal crime—were blocked by white southerners in Congress. To defeat civil rights legislation they used the seniority system, which produced powerful Southern committee chairmen because the South's one-party system returned incumbent Democrats to Congress; the House Rules Committee, where Southern representatives, often with conservative Republican allies, bottled up bills that threatened segregation in the South; and the Senate "filibuster," where final votes were prevented by unlimited debate rules that required supermajorities (usually two-thirds) to close debate and permit a floor vote. As a consequence Congress, which sent the woman suffrage amendment (NINETEENTH AMENDMENT) to be ratified by the states in 1920, passed no civil rights laws challenging racial oppression in America between 1875 and 1957.

The fourth period of civil rights policymaking in Congress, reaching from 1945 to 1968, launched the modern era of expanding national regulation. The war against fascism during 1941–1945 brought the American economy out of the Great Depression and strengthened the forces of civil rights reform. Racial segregation clashed with the United Nations Charter and damaged American prestige in Cold War competition against the Soviet bloc. The SUPREME COURT's school desegregation decision of 1954 and the black civil rights movement in the South increased pressure on the White House and Congress to ban racial discrimination. A campaign of nonviolent civil disobedience to protest segregation, led by the Rev. Dr. Martin Luther KING, JR., and televised worldwide in dramatic demonstrations throughout the South, mobilized national opinion against Southern segregationists and gave the elected branches in Washington a mandate for action.

Congress, following ineffective voting rights statutes in 1957 and 1960, responded to reform proposals by Presidents John KENNEDY and Lyndon JOHNSON by passing four landmark bills: the CIVIL RIGHTS ACT OF 1964, the VOTING RIGHTS ACT OF 1965, the IMMIGRATION AND NATIONALITY ACT OF 1965, and the FAIR HOUSING ACT of 1968. To protect women's rights, Congress in 1963 required equal pay for equal work and in 1964 added sex discrimination to the jurisdiction of the newly created EQUAL EMPLOYMENT OPPORTUNITY COMMISSION. The breakthrough laws of the 1960s were both radical and traditional. They were radical because they extended centralized regulation from Washington to areas previously controlled by state and local authorities or the private marketplace—schools, colleges and universities, business firms, labor unions, owners of hotels and restaurants and places of amusement, voting registrars, realtors, and landlords. They were traditional because they applied American liberalism's classic formula of equal individual rights. The Constitution, in this vision, was color-blind—and sex-blind as well.

The fifth period of congressional civil rights policy coincides with the era of divided partisan government following Richard NIXON's presidential victory in 1968. With few exceptions, the Democrats controlled Congress and the Republicans controlled the presidency and nominations to the federal courts. These roles were reversed in the 1990s, when Democrat Bill CLINTON in a three-way contest (1992) won the presidency with a plurality, then in the next election (1994) the Republicans captured control of both houses of Congress. Despite this reversal, the partisan dynamics of split government continued. Split-party control encouraged party warfare between the president and Congress, especially as a conservative reaction by American voters against the racial rioting and radical protest of the late 1960s sent increasingly conservative Republican presidents and successor vice-presidents to the White House—Richard Nixon and Gerald FORD during 1969–1977, Ronald REAGAN and George BUSH during 1981–1993. Democrats, controlling Congress (and, during Jimmy CARTER's single term in 1977–1981, the White House as well), sought to protect and expand social welfare programs while Republican presidents, most notably Reagan, sought to cut taxes and curb social expenditures.

The political result of this arrangement, somewhat surprisingly, favored expanding civil rights regulation from Washington. Republican presidents campaigned against tax-and-spend "big government" Democrats, and appointed conservative judges to the federal courts. However, needing to compromise with Congress and fearing an anti–civil rights label, Republican presidents after the 1960s signed a series of laws expanding rights-based protections to newly mobilized constituencies. These statutes expanded coverage to include women in educational institutions in 1972, the physically and mentally handicapped in 1973, non-native speakers of English in 1974, and the elderly in 1975.

Some of the congressional actions extended equal-treatment policy to new areas—for example, passage of the EQUAL RIGHTS AMENDMENT in 1972, and subsequent legislation barring sex discrimination in insurance and lending. Most, however, expanded protection in vaguely worded statutes that left the details of regulation to enforcement agencies in Washington—the EQUAL EMPLOYMENT OPPORTUNITY COMMISSION (EEOC) for employers, the Labor Department for government contractors, and the Office of Civil Rights for schools, colleges and medical institutions. Federal courts and bureaucracies, not Congress, shaped specific policies in an expanding regime of rights regulation that grew controversial as enforcement officials shifted emphasis from nondiscrimination to affirmative action.

Despite conservative trends in the American electorate, civil rights regulation expanded during the 1970s and 1980s. The civil rights coalition, effectively coordinated by the LEADERSHIP CONFERENCE ON CIVIL RIGHTS, drew powerful support from more than 160 member organizations representing African Americans, Hispanics, feminists, and the handicapped as well as unions and religious bodies.

The immigration reforms of 1965 strengthened the coalition to a degree unanticipated. After 1965 more than twenty-five million immigrants came to America. Three-fourths of them came from Latin America and Asia and hence were eligible as minorities for affirmative-action programs in employment and government contracts.

Congress in 1977 established a numerical set-aside in government contracting for minority business firms, the first racial classification made by Congress since the Civil War era. In the 1980s President Reagan, despite his opposition to minority preferences, signed laws requiring voting districts with minority majorities and establishing minority business set-asides in defense and transportation appropriations. Similarly, President Bush in 1990 signed the AMERICANS WITH DISABILITIES ACT, extending disability protection to 43 million Americans, and also the Civil Rights Act of 1991, which approved certain race-conscious remedies and for the first time brought sexual harassment under federal jurisdiction.

By the 1990s polls showed wide support for nondiscrimination measures to protect minorities, women, and the disabled, including affirmative-action "outreach" provisions involving special recruitment, train-

ing, and education. But the spread of affirmative-action preferences for minorities drew growing opposition in the 1980s and 1990s. Resentment by white and, increasingly, Asian men and women against preference policies for blacks and Latinos was intensified by the pressures of global economic competition and immigrant participation in affirmative-action programs. In 1989, a conservative Supreme Court majority began sharply narrowing the range of race-conscious remedies under affirmative action. In the 1990s, populist resentment surged in California, where voters in 1994 passed Proposition 187 denying tax-funded social, medical, and education benefits to illegal immigrants. In 1996 they passed Proposition 209, barring minority and gender preferences in state government. Yet Congress, even under Republican control, remained reluctant to engage the volatile race issue, and President Clinton defended affirmative action.

Congress in the last third of the twentieth century outlawed discrimination against minorities, women, and the disabled in education, employment, and housing. These reforms helped destroy segregation in the South, helped triple the size of the black middle class, and dramatically diversified the workplace, the marketplace, school and campus, and government. But Americans enter the twenty-first century deeply divided by the concept and practice of group versus individual rights and equal treatment versus equal results.

BIBLIOGRAPHY

Berger, Morroe. *Equality by Statute: The Revolution in Civil Rights.* 1967.

Berkowitz, Edward D. *Disabled Politics: America's Program for the Handicapped.* 1989.

Congressional Quarterly. *Congress and the Nation,* Volumes I (1945–1968) through VIII (1989–1992).

De Hart, Jane Sherron. "Equality Challenged: Equal Rights and Sexual Difference." In *Civil Rights in the United States,* edited by Hugh Davis Graham. 1994.

Foner, Eric. *Reconstruction.* 1988.

Fuchs, Lawrence H. "The Changing Meaning of Civil Rights, 1964–1994." In *Civil Rights and Social Wrongs: Black-White Relations Since World War II,* edited by John Higham. 1997.

Graham, Hugh Davis. *The Civil Rights Era: Origins and Development of National Policy, 1960–1972.* 1990.

Graham, Hugh Davis. "Legislatures and Civil Rights." In *Encyclopedia of the American Legislative System,* edited by Joel H. Silbey. 1994.

Graham, Hugh Davis. "Since 1964: The Paradox of American Civil Rights Regulation." In *Taking Stock: Policy and Governance in the Twentieth Century,* edited by Morton Keller and H. Shep Melnick. 1998.

Harrison, Cynthia. *On Account of Sex: The Politics of Women's Issues, 1945–1968.* 1988.

Higham, John. "The Three Reconstructions." *New York Review of Books* 44 (Nov. 6, 1997): 52–56.

Lawson, Steven F. *Running for Freedom: Civil Rights and Black Politics in America Since 1941.* 1991.

Sitkoff, Harvard. *A New Deal for Blacks: The Emergence of Civil Rights as a National Issue.* 1978.

Skerry, Peter. *The Ambivalent Minority: Mexican Americans and the Voting Rights Act.* 1993.

Thernstrom, Abigail. *Whose Votes Count? Affirmative Action and Minority Rights.* 1987.

Whalen, Charles and Barbara. *A Legislative History of the 1964 Civil Rights Act.* 1986.

Hugh Davis Graham

Congressional Black Caucus

The Democratic Select Committee (DSC) was established in 1969 following the election of three new African Americans, all Democrats, to the United States House of Representatives. These freshmen joined with six established African-American members of Congress to form the Democratic Select Committee. While African-American members had served in Congress between 1870 and 1901, only four held seats in the House in the years between 1901 and 1955. After the 1968 elections, enough African Americans were elected to make a formal organization viable. The caucus was founded in order to influence or promote legislation that was particularly significant to African-American citizens and to promote legislative activity

for human rights for all people in the United States and around the world. In 1971, at its first annual dinner in Washington, D.C., the group became known as the Congressional Black Caucus (CBC), under the chairmanship of Charles Diggs (D-Mich.).

The CBC's voice was immediately heard on a national scale. After requesting a meeting with President Richard NIXON, which was repeatedly delayed by the president, the group boycotted Nixon's 1970 State of the Union address. The meeting finally occurred in March 1971, and the CBC outlined no fewer than sixty-one points of action, which included community and urban development, and educational, judicial, and civil rights initiatives for Nixon's consideration. Since then, the CBC has been consulted routinely by various administrations on matters of importance to the caucus and has championed causes such as the administering of sanctions against the South African government for its apartheid policies (see ANTI-APARTHEID MOVEMENT). The CBC has also voiced its opposition to the disproportionate number of African Americans who fought in Operation Desert Storm, and on many other issues.

The election of more African Americans will certainly increase the power and influence of the CBC, and its success has inspired other minority groups in Congress, such as women and Hispanic Americans, to form caucuses of their own. On the other hand, 1990 saw the election of a conservative black Republican to Congress, Gary Franks of Connecticut. Franks has re-

Charles Rangel with other members of the Congressional Black Caucus outside the Capitol in 1980. (AP/Wide World Photos)

fused to participate in the CBC and has even openly attacked it for its liberal Democratic bias.

BIBLIOGRAPHY

Clay, William L. *Just Permanent Interests: Black Americans in Congress, 1870–1991*. 1992.
"Congressional Black Caucus." In *Special Interest Group Profiles for Students*, edited by Kelle S. Sisung. 1999.

Matthew May

Congress of Industrial Organizations

See AFL-CIO.

Congress of Racial Equality (CORE)

The Congress of Racial Equality (CORE) was one of the leading civil rights organizations in the protracted and sometimes fierce struggle for black equality. Founded in Chicago in the spring of 1942 by an interracial group of young, middle-class intellectuals, CORE quickly became an important organizational actor in the modern civil rights movement. Most of CORE's founders were pacifist graduate students at the University of Chicago whose affiliation with a pacifist organization, the FELLOWSHIP OF RECONCILIATION (FOR), strongly influenced the philosophy and style of CORE. The original founders of CORE believed strongly in interracialism, were committed to the tactic of nonviolent direct action, and wanted to use this tactic to achieve racial equality in the United States.

CORE's purpose was to use interracial groups, trained in the technique of nonviolent direct action, to attack American racism. CORE's founders were heavily influenced by the work of the Indian leader Mahatma GANDHI and were interested in ways of adapting Gandhian tactics and principles to the American scene. In the early 1940s interracial groups of CORE activists were among the first to use nonviolent direct action tactics such as sit-ins, picketing, and boycotts, to attack de facto segregation in Chicago and other northern cities.

CORE's first foray into the South occurred in 1947 with the "Journey of Reconciliation," a two-week bus trip designed to test Southern compliance with a then-recent U.S. SUPREME COURT ruling against racially segregated seating on interstate buses. The 1947 trip was the catalyst for CORE's biggest achievement in the modern civil rights movement—the 1961 FREEDOM RIDE. Precipitated by another Supreme Court decision that extended the prohibition against segregated seating on interstate buses to terminal facilities, the Free-

Floyd B. McKissick, civil rights activist, in 1965, shortly after he was named to succeed James Farmer as the national director of CORE. (AP/Wide World Photos)

dom Ride catapulted CORE and its newly appointed National Director, James FARMER, into nationwide prominence. Unlike the 1947 Journey of Reconciliation, which was limited to the upper South, the 1961 Freedom Ride penetrated deep South states. Several riders were savagely beaten and hospitalized during the ride when racist white mobs attacked and burned their bus. The group was battered so badly that CORE leaders considered prematurely terminating the trip, until black student leaders from the newly organized STUDENT NONVIOLENT COORDINATING COMMITTEE (SNCC) took over the ride.

The successful 1961 Freedom Ride carved out a central niche for CORE in the modern civil rights movement and broadened its membership base. But by the late 1960s, after the passage of key civil rights legislation eradicated legal segregation, CORE, like other civil rights groups, grappled for new programs. The advent of BLACK POWER precipitated a new militancy within CORE and the larger civil rights movement. Militant factions emerged within CORE who were not as committed to the principals of nonviolence and interracialism as the original pacifist founders had been.

Although CORE's membership has declined since its heyday in the 1960s, its contributions to the black struggle for equality are numerous. In addition to staging some of the first sit-ins and boycotts, the innovative 1961 Freedom Ride will ensure CORE's place in civil rights history.

BIBLIOGRAPHY

Bell, Inge P. *CORE and the Strategy of Nonviolence.* 1968.
Haines, Herbert. *Black Radicals and the Civil Rights Mainstream, 1954, 1970.* 1988.
Meier, August, and Elliott Rudwick. *CORE A Study in the Civil Rights Movement 1942–1968.* 1973.
Morris, Aldon D. *The Origin of the Civil Rights Movement.* 1984.

Lori G. Waite

Congress of Spanish-Speaking People

In the latter years of the Great Depression, an important new pan-Hispanic organization launched a broad civil rights agenda to attack discrimination directed against Mexican Americans, Mexican immigrants, Puerto Ricans, and Cubans in the United States. The idea for the organization belonged to Congress of Industrial Organizations (CIO) union activist Luisa MORENO, a Guatemalan immigrant who entered the United States in the late 1920s. The Congress of Spanish-Speaking People (herein referred to as Congress) was founded in 1939 in Los Angeles, the first national advocacy organization to articulate a political and social reform platform that attempted to address issues adversely affecting Mexicans in the Southwest and Midwest, Puerto Ricans in the Northeast, and Cubans in Florida. Though the Congress was short-lived, it was significant, not only because it was the first group to unite Spanish-speaking organizations throughout the nation around a civil rights agenda, but because it set a precedent for other organizations during the 1940s and beyond.

During a decade when most Americans struggled to survive economically, Spanish-speaking groups, chronically poor populations, were particularly hard hit by job losses and wage cuts in industries that had paid some of the lowest wages to workers anywhere in the United States. In addition, because they were viewed as un-American and as aliens who took jobs away from citizens, Mexicans and Puerto Ricans in particular suffered a double jeopardy during the Depression as segregated racial minorities at the bottom of the socioeconomic ladder. Indeed, the problems of Mexicans during the 1930s were made all the worse by

the U.S. Department of Labor and the Immigration Service's decision to deport to Mexico hundreds of thousands of Mexican immigrants and their American-born children as a way of lessening the economic crisis. These conditions during the 1930s—a decade of deep despair for Mexicans and other Spanish-speaking people—prompted local leaders and organizations to ban together into a national organization to fight the mounting discrimination and injustices faced daily by Hispanic peoples.

The Congress was a broad-based confederation of local and regional organizations among Hispanics (delegates from over a hundred different groups representing 874,000 members convened at the first meeting) that was supported by a variety of progressive labor unions such as the CIO, the International Longshoremen's and Warehousemen's Union, the International Union of Mine, Mill, and Smelter Workers, and left-oriented groups such as the Hollywood Anti-Nazi League and the Women's Committee of the American League for Peace and Democracy. Because of Luisa Moreno's contacts in the labor movement, the influence of organized labor was particularly evident. So, too, was the monetary support from liberals and socialists from the Hollywood motion picture industry, a connection attributable to the Congress's first elected National Secretary, Josefina Fierro, whose spouse was screen writer John Bright, one of the so-called "Hollywood Ten."

Though based in Los Angeles with an elected leadership and a committee structure organized around key issues, the Congress was composed of dozens of local chapters located in cities and towns across the country where Hispanics were regionally concentrated. The political agenda of the Congress revolved around five action platforms: (1) defense of the civil rights of Spanish-speaking people by fighting racial and class discrimination; (2) mobilize political action to contest public polices that adversely affected Hispanics; (3) encourage and support the unionization of Hispanic workers through existing labor unions; (4) protect and advocate for the rights of the foreign born; and (5) condemn fascism at home and abroad. To implement this agenda, the Congress established committees on discrimination and civil rights, on education and health, and on labor unity, while others dealt with housing issues, the status of immigrants and foreign affairs such as the Good Neighbor Policy between the United States and Latin American nations.

Between 1939 and the end of World War II, the Congress and its leaders confronted discrimination against Hispanics in employment and in policy brutality cases. It also advocated effectively against policies that negatively affected Spanish-speaking people, especially those that denied government relief and defense industry jobs to Mexican Americans. But before the Congress had an opportunity to fully press forward its political agenda, the war years left it vulnerable as many young leaders were drafted into the military and other leaders—including Moreno and Fierro—were red-baited and consequently later faced criminal charges as suspected communists. Indeed, from 1944 through 1951, the Congress was identified as a communist-front organization by state and federal committees reporting on un-American activities. Several of the organization's leaders were routinely harassed by the FBI and some were forced into exile in Mexico. Though a small corps of Congress leaders continued to carry out the civil rights agenda of the organization as best they could during the war years, the organization did not recover in the postwar era from the loss of leadership and continued red-baiting by authorities.

The Congress of Spanish-Speaking People was one of the few organizations in the twentieth century that successfully organized different Hispanic communities in the United States. Short-lived and a casualty of World War II and the anticommunist hysteria of the emerging cold war era, the organization nonetheless laid a foundation for a community-based, antidiscrimination agenda that was carried on by many former Congress members and other organizations during the 1950s and 1960s.

BIBLIOGRAPHY

Camarillo, Albert. *Chicanos in California: A History of Mexican Americans.* 1984.

Camarillo, Albert. "Mexicans and Europeans in American Cities: Some Comparative Perspectives, 1990–1940." In *From 'Melting Pot' to Multiculturalism: The Evolution of Ethnic Relations in the United States, and Canada*, edited by Valeria Gennaro Lerda. 1990.

García, Mario T. *Mexican Americans: Leadership, Ideology, and Identity, 1930–1960.* 1989.

Gutiérrez, David G. *Walls and Mirrors: Mexican Americans, Mexican Immigrants, and the Politics of Ethnicity.* 1995.

Ruiz, Vicki L. *Out of the Shadows: Mexican Women in the Twentieth Century.* 1998.

Sánchez, George J. *Becoming Mexican American: Ethnicity, Culture and Identity in Chicano Los Angeles, 1900–1945.* 1993.

Albert Camarillo

Connecticut

It was during the British colonial period that African-American slaves were first imported to the area that is now the state of Connecticut. The state's economy had little place for slaves, however, and even before the state passed a gradual emancipation law in 1784, the slave population was exceedingly small. By 1800, slavery was all but gone from the state, but RACISM and discrimination against African Americans remained. They did not have the vote, few jobs were open to them, and access to education was also very poor.

Kept apart from white society, Connecticut's African-American population developed their own culture. Although not numerous in the state, free African-Americans were concentrated in major cities like New Haven and Hartford, where they could find work in low-paying, menial positions. In these cities African Americans built their own churches, clubs, and civic organizations. As these communities grew, some members made headway against biases and ill-treatment— winning the right to have their children attend public schools, for example. Local leaders also emerged during this period, most notably Amos Berman, a New Haven minister, who was a leader of the state's abolitionist movement.

Although the Civil War and the constitutional amendments that followed greatly expanded the legal rights of African Americans across the nation, they did little to change the day-to-day situation in Connecticut. African Americans remained second-class citizens in the state, although they were spared the repression of the JIM CROW system. While they could and did vote after the passage of the FIFTEENTH AMENDMENT in 1870, their numbers were too few to exert much influence on government. One noteworthy exception to this was the decision by the state government to end all school SEGREGATION in 1868.

The race relations status quo began to shift in the early twentieth century. Tens of thousands of African Americans moved to Connecticut during the two World Wars and the decades that followed as part of the general MIGRATION of African Americans to the North. By 1950, the state's African-American population was over 50,000, and by 1960 it had expanded to 107,000. This dramatic increase in the state's African-American population was mainly concentrated in the cities. In part encouraged by the civil rights movement in the South, local NAACP chapters and other organizations formed across Connecticut in the 1950s and 1960s to protest the continuing mistreatment of African Americans by white society. African Americans began to win elections, at first to positions in the state government, but eventually followed by the mayoralties of New Haven and Hartford as well as a seat in Congress. While most of this progress was won peacefully, the transition to a more color-blind society was marred by riots in Connecticut's cities in 1967, 1968, and 1969.

From the time that Connecticut was colonized, Connecticut's Native American population was relatively sparse, consisting of the Narragansatts, the Pequots, the Quinnipiacs, and several very small groups known as the River Tribes. It is generally estimated that the total population of all these tribes was no more than 7,000 people when the first white settlers arrived. In 1633 and 1634, massive epidemics of the plague and smallpox wiped out substantial portions of the Native American population in Connecticut, including more than 75 percent of the coastal Quinnipiacs (who had also been ravaged by the warlike Pequots and occasional aggressive forays into the region by the Mohawks and other New York tribes). By 1850, the Quinnipiacs were virtually extinct. Much of Connecticut's Native American population in subsequent years migrated to Quinnipiac territory from neighboring areas. In recent years there has been some resurgence in Connecticut's Native American population, though little of the original indigent population is thought to remain. Because of their sparse numbers, organized rights movements among Connecticut Native Americans have not formed a major part of Connecticut civil rights history, though the historical record is replete with interesting anecdotal events.

Griswold v. Connecticut is probably the most famous law suit pertaining to civil rights to involve the state of Connecticut. In this case Estelle Griswold and other members of the Connecticut branch of the Planned Parenthood League were accused of providing information on birth control, in violation of state law. Although they had been providing this information to married couples, they were convicted in the state's courts and each fined $100. Appeals brought the case before the U.S. Supreme Court in 1965. In its decision, the Supreme Court overturned the conviction of Griswold because it found that Connecticut's birth-control law violated the privacy of married couples and was therefore invalid. While acknowledging that the Constitution did not explicitly provide for this right to privacy, the Court felt that the right could be inferred from the language of the First, Third, Fourth, Fifth and Fourteenth Amendments. This landmark decision firmly established the concept of a constitutional right to privacy, and paved the way for later rulings on privacy rights, most notably *Roe v. Wade* (1973).

BIBLIOGRAPHY

Bradshar, Harold. *The Indians of Connecticut.* Reprint. 1996.
Encyclopedia of African-American Culture and History, edited by Jack Salzman, David Lionel Smith, and Cornel West. 1996.
Fraser, Bruce. *The Land of Steady Habits: A Brief History of Connecticut.* 1988.
Pierson, William D. *Black Yankees: The Development of an Afro-American Subculture in Eighteenth-Century New England.* 1942.

John F. McCoy

Connor, Theophilus Eugene "Bull"

(1897–1973), segregationist, public official.

As Birmingham's Commissioner of Public Safety (1937–1953, 1957–1963), Connor became infamous nationwide with his oppressive treatment of civil-rights demonstrators in 1963, inadvertently helping the drive toward the CIVIL RIGHTS ACT OF 1964.

Born in Selma, Alabama, Theophilus Eugene Connor was first employed as a railroad telegrapher like his father. In 1922 he became radio announcer for the Birmingham Barons baseball team. His style of "shooting the bull" earned him his nickname.

Connor won election to the Alabama legislature in 1934, where he sponsored civil-service reform. Elected Birmingham's Commissioner of Public Safety in 1937, he promoted his progressive image by fighting racketeering.

Reactionary on racial issues, Connor pledged to enforce segregation ordinances when the SOUTHERN CONFERENCE FOR HUMAN WELFARE met in Birmingham in 1938. Leading Alabama's Dixiecrat secession from the 1948 Democratic Convention, Connor left office in 1953 after a sex scandal involving his secretary. Reelected in 1957, Connor failed to investigate bombings of black-owned homes in integrating neighborhoods. He did not protect Freedom Riders in 1961. Connor ordered firemen and policemen to attack young demonstrators in April and May 1963, with dogs and high-pressure water hoses, garnering national television coverage. The Rev. Dr. Martin Luther KING, JR., and Rev. Fred SHUTTLESWORTH led these protests for integration of public accommodations and fair employment opportunities, to which local businessmen agreed.

Implementation of a city referendum for a mayor-council government ended Connor's term that May. He later was president of Alabama's Public Service Commission (1964–1972).

BIBLIOGRAPHY

Cox, Thomas H. "From Centerpiece to Centerstage: Kelly Ingram Park, Segregation, and Civil Rights in Birmingham, Alabama." *Southern Historian* 18 (1997): 5–28.
Eskew, Glenn T. *But for Birmingham: The Local and National Movements in the Civil Rights Struggle.* 1997.
Nunnelley, William A. *Bull Connor.* 1991.

Wes Borucki

Conscientious Objection

Conscientious objection first became an issue in 1658 in Maryland when Richard Keene refused to be trained as a soldier. For this act he was "fined and abused by the sheriff." During the American Revolution some towns provided for exemptions from military service on grounds of conscience. No such exemptions existed in the Federal Militia Act of 1862, or otherwise during the Civil War until 1864. Consequently, pacifists paid for their religious beliefs by spending time in military jails. In 1864 religious exemptions were granted liberally, and most objectors accepted noncombatant assignments. The issue did not become a matter of debate again till WORLD WAR I, when CONGRESS limited exemptions to members of traditional and "well-recognized" pacifist religions—Quakers, Mennonites, and Amish, for example. In 1917 the law was liberalized to recognize nonreligious opposition to war although no absolute exemption from military service was legally possible. Conscientious objectors (CO's) had no option but to serve as noncombatants in the military.

In World War I, out of 24 million registrants, approximately 65,000 filed claims for CO status. Twenty-one thousand of these were drafted and sent to military camps, where they were subjected to verbal and physical abuse. About 80 percent abandoned their CO stand and became soldiers. Approximately fourteen hundred draftees refused military service altogether. Some were segregated and kept in army camps, where they were brutally mistreated. Other "absolutists" were court-martialed and sentenced to death or long years in prison for treason. The death sentences were eventually commuted, but seventeen CO's died in prison. Most were released from prison soon after war's end.

The Selective Service and Training Act of 1940 slightly liberalized exemptions. Those opposed to war on religious grounds would in the future be put to work on projects of "national importance under civilian direction." Still, no exemption was made for "absolutists" or nonreligious objectors. During WORLD WAR II, CO's were once again a tiny proportion of the draft-age population, about two-tenths of 1 percent. Approximately seventy-three thousand men claimed to be CO's. About twelve thousand did alternative service in camps, six thousand absolutists went to prison, twenty-five thousand served as noncombatants, and the remainder failed to get CO status. Absolutists were now tried in civilian courts, not court-martialed for treason. Imprisoned CO's were held in federal rather than military prisons, with a maximum sentence of five years. In 1951, during the KOREAN WAR, the Universal Military Training and Service Act was passed, whereby CO's were permitted to perform specified civilian tasks as alternative service. The number of CO's jumped markedly, to 1.64 percent.

During the VIETNAM WAR, dramatically increased inductions were accompanied by raids on local draft boards to destroy draft records. Draft protests met with severe penalties, but, over time, sympathetic juries in some locales tolerated such practices. The U.S. invasion of Cambodia in 1970 and the deaths of student war protestors at Kent State and Florida State universities provoked massive nationwide antidraft activities. More than twenty-five thousand draft cards were returned to draft boards following the deaths of the students. Conscientious objection also increased during this period, to 5.6 percent in 1968 and 14.2 percent in 1970. This change partially reflects a liberalization of exemption. The SUPREME COURT in *Seeger v. United States* (1965), upheld in *Welsh v. United States* (1970), found that conscientious objection no longer required a belief in a supreme being. Still, objection had to be to all wars, not a particular war. This condition was affirmed by the Supreme Court in *Gillette v. United States* (1971). Those objectors refused CO status under the new conditions were subject to five years in prison and a $10,000 fine. As the war progressed, few draft boards exacted such harsh penalties. Of the 3,275 Selective Service violators sent to prison in the Vietnam era, many could have easily avoided any penalty but chose instead to bear witness against the war by submitting themselves to punishment.

BIBLIOGRAPHY

Brock, Peter. *Twentieth Century Pacifism*. 1970.
Cooney, Robert, and Helen Michalowski. *The Power of the People: Active Nonviolence in the United States*. 1977.
Levi, Margaret. *Consent, Dissent, and Patriotism*. 1997.
Lunardini, Christine A. *The American Peace Movement in the Twentieth Century*. 1994.

Eric Cummins

Conservatism

Like most important political concepts, conservatism, American-style, has changed over the course of its history and contains self-contradictory elements. Though modern conservatism is often said to originate in the opposition to the French Revolution, American conservatives, or Americans who became conservatives in the early Republic, by no means wished to repudiate the American Revolution of 1776. Indeed, throughout the nineteenth and into the twentieth century, some Northern conservatives were sympathetic to the antislavery cause and then later, as was the case with Senator Henry Cabot Lodge of Massachusetts, sought to defend the civil and political rights of the freedpeople.

Civil rights themselves were destined to be a major issue in American history because of the contradiction between the universalist claims of the Declaration of Independence ("unalienable rights") and the fact of chattel slavery, which denied slaves not only civil rights but freedom itself. Civil rights issues have not been exclusively linked with the status of African Americans. The exclusion of white women from equal political and legal recognition was addressed, at least rhetorically, in the Seneca Falls Convention of 1848 when the Declaration of Independence was rewritten to include them.

Conservatism by definition implies a certain bias against change, particularly rapid and imposed change. This means that conservatives were (and are) rarely in the forefront of efforts to extend civil rights to excluded groups within the American society and polity. Historically, conservative reluctance to extend civil rights derives from a presumption that existing arrangements—existing social and political elites, settled practices and ways of life—will be disrupted by appeals to abstract principles or values which, for instance, African Americans or women have often voiced in opposition to their exclusion. That said, there is nothing in most variants of American conservatism dictating that civil rights, as such, be withheld from the excluded. Only those brands of conservatism, often southern in origin, that have made fixed racial differences central to their vision, have locked themselves into an exclusionary ideology.

What follows, first, is a kind of typology of American conservatism to indicate both how the various types of American conservatism differ but also what they all share. Second, there will be a brief examination of post-1960s conservatism and its relation to civil rights issues in a post–civil rights era.

Four Traditions of Conservatism

Historically, the first form of American conservatism, properly so-called, was the antimodern model. Originating as the most radical, antebellum Southern response to abolitionism, this antimodernist conservatism was articulated most clearly by Virginia's George Fitzhugh. According to Fitzhugh, the modern world, especially the French Revolution and free-market, free-trade capitalism, was founded on mistaken ideas of human equality and freedom. Rather, the ideal social and political order is one in which individuals and groups are arranged hierarchically with an elite having the social, legal, and political responsibility of looking after the less capable. Fitzhugh took an idealized version of plantation society as his model of what his neofeudal society might look like. Needless to say, there was no room in this conservative tradition for slaves and or even for a good number of whites to enjoy equal rights.

Never popular in pure form (it frightened poor and middling whites), Fitzhugh's paternalistic conservatism was to turn up in this century in the writings of the Vanderbilt Agrarians, especially in Allen Tate's

work and in the writings of Richard Weaver after World War II. Overall, this antimodernist conservatism has always been more a cultural ideal than a political or social blueprint.

A second type of conservatism organized around the idea of states' rights was also southern in origin, though not necessarily conservative in implication and never confined solely to that region. The states' rights variety of conservatism insisted that the individual states should retain control over their basic institutions, including the requirements for and entailments of citizenship, education, and voting.

The historical narrative undergirding constitutional conservatism claimed the Union was originally a compact of sovereign states, any one of which could leave if it so chose. Besides, and prior to, secession, states had the power/right not to enforce federal laws which they felt to be unconstitutional. Thus, states could allow slavery if they so chose, and then, after the THIRTEENTH, FOURTEENTH, and FIFTEENTH AMENDMENTS were passed, could segregate the races, establish (restrictive) voting requirements, and segregate educational institutions as long as certain minimal constitutional standards were met. Indeed, the constitutional arguments against full civil rights for African Americans advanced by the South in the 1950s and 1960s sounded remarkably like those advocated by defenders of slavery between 1830 and 1865.

A third, more generic, form of conservatism places a premium on preserving existing moral, social, and political forms. In practice, this has usually meant a commitment to the triumph of majority (white or male) views on civil rights for minorities and to traditional (usually Christian and earlier classical) assumptions about human nature in general and gender, racial and cultural differences in particular. Here the dictum coined by sociologist William Graham Sumner and cited with considerable frequency from the late nineteenth century on into the 1960s captures this position: "Stateways Can Not Change Folkways," which is sometimes paraphrased as "you can't legislate morality."

But if change is necessary, equalization of the status of a particular group—African Americans or women or some other minority—should always be a gradual process, arising out of a "natural" adjustment on the part of the dominant society and of the supplicant minorities. It certainly should never be imposed by the federal government. The constitutional and political implication of this localistic conservatism is that a major reinterpretation of the Fourteenth Amendment, such as was announced in the BROWN v. BOARD OF EDUCATION decision of 1954 when the "separate but equal" principle was overturned, should not have been left to the Supreme Court. Rather, such a shift should have taken the form of a constitutional amendment or perhaps federal legislation formulated by the Congress.

The fourth model of American conservatism is anything but hostile to modernity; nor is it necessarily localistic or too solicitous of existing social and cultural realities. Originating in nineteenth-century liberalism, free-market conservatism fully accepts the modern capitalist system and makes its smooth functioning central to all other individual or collective goods. The dominant ideology of the Reagan era, it contends that equality and freedom for all people are best served by allowing market mechanisms to determine wages and prices and qualifications for positions in the private and public sector. The best remedy for racial discrimination is a free market which will pick out the most talented or most efficient, irrespective of race, gender, religion or ethnicity. At its most pragmatic, this position accepts the need for legislation guaranteeing equal rights but shies away from active intervention by governmental authorities in the social and economic sphere.

Clearly, these four traditions of conservatism present anything but a single focus or emphasis (though they do frequently overlap). They divide over issues of modernity (for or against individualism, equality, and freedom); the source of normative values and direction (traditional culture, constitutional or social localism, market mechanisms); and the relative importance of biological vs. environmental explanations of human behavior. But what unites all these forms of conservatism is a clear hostility to an interventionist state in the form of "social engineering."

Since the 1960s

Since the 1960s American conservatism as embodied in the Republican Party and as articulated by conservative intellectuals has been dominated by the fourth tradition of conservatism, the "free-market" model. It has basically accepted the legislative achievements of the civil rights movement as embodied in the CIVIL RIGHTS ACT OF 1964 and the VOTING RIGHTS ACT OF 1965 and, in some cases more grudgingly, the BROWN V. BOARD OF EDUCATION decision of 1954. Since 1964, however, the Republican Party has adopted a "Southern strategy," according to which it can gain political power without the support of African Americans by appealing to the white South and other formerly Democratic white voters on issues sometimes related obliquely to race and sometimes not.

Overall, there are several implications worth noting. First, American constitutional thinking no longer differentiates, as it once did, between civil rights and political rights: to be a citizen is to enjoy equal political rights. But though conservatives have moved toward the center on matters having to do with the legal and political rights of African Americans, women, and other minorities, they have firmly opposed, or sought to limit: preferential treatment of minorities as general compensation for past injustices or as a way of achieving diversity; busing or other forms of "social engineering" to achieve racial balance in schools; and the continued aggrandizing of power to the federal government. At the new turn of the century, it is a measure of a new, rather conservative national consensus on civil rights that many social and economic liberals and one-time supporters of the civil rights movement, not least among them certain African-American intellectuals, have come to share with conservatives a firm belief that civil rights remain attached to the individual rather than inhering in a group identity and that "equality of opportunity," not "equality of results," is what civil rights are supposed to protect.

BIBLIOGRAPHY

Allitt, Patrick. *Catholic Intellectuals and Conservative Politics in America, 1950–1985.* 1993.

Genovese, Eugene D. *The World the Slaveholders Made.* 1969.

Friedman, Milton. *Capitalism and Freedom.* 1962.

Herrnstein, Richard J., and Charles Murray. *The Bell Curve: Intelligence and Class Structure in American Life.* 1996.

Kilpatrick, James J. *The Southern Case for School Segregation.* 1962.

Loury, Glenn C. *One by One from the Inside Out.* 1995.

Nash, George. *The Conservative Intellectual Movement in America since 1945.* 1976.

Oakeshott, Michael. *Rationalism in Politics.* 1991.

Phillips, Kevin P. *The Emerging Republican Majority.* 1969.

Sowell, Thomas. *Civil Rights: Rhetoric and Reality.* 1984.

Thernstrom, Stephen, and Abigail Thernstrom. *American in Black and White: One Nation Indivisible, Race in Modern America.* 1997.

Twelve Southerners. *I'll Take My Stand.* 1931.

Voegelin, Eric. *The New Science of Politics.* 1952.

Weaver, Richard. *The Southern Tradition at Bay: A History of Postbellum Thought.* 1968.

Wills, Gary. *Nixon Agonistes.* 1970.

Wish, Harvey, ed. *Ante-bellum: Writings of G. Fitzhugh and H. R. Helper on Slavery.* 1960.

Richard H. King

Constitution, Amendments to

See Thirteenth Amendment; Fourteenth Amendment; Fifteenth Amendment; Nineteenth Amendment.

Constitutionalism

In liberal democracies like America, the term "constitutionalism" refers to the principles of legitimate government: that government must be limited, dependent upon the consent of the governed, and maintained by the rule of law. Prior to the American and French revolutions, constitutionalism generally referred to those historical laws, institutions, and conventions that defined a people and its government. Government was constitutional if it acted within the limits established by the informal constraints of long-accepted legal practices and traditions. Such an informal constitutionalism was the hallmark of the most distinguished political regimes of Greek and Roman antiquity, as well as of such modern political regimes as Great Britain, whose "unwritten" constitution has been described as the product of no particular generation or governing document but of political experience dating back centuries.

Since the late eighteenth century, constitutionalism has generally referred to a formal or written document that establishes a government by defining its structure, authorizing and allocating its specific powers, and providing a means for constitutional amendment. Modern constitutionalism arose upon the defects of pre-modern constitutionalism, in particular, the failure of pre-modern constitutionalism to specifically define the limits of governmental power. America's revolutionary colonists, who had accepted the principles of the British constitution, discovered that that same constitution provided little relief against the machinations of the British Parliament. The remedy to this predicament was simple enough: Establish limitations to legislative, executive, and judicial power in a "fixed" constitution.

The relationship of civil rights to American constitutionalism is best viewed in light of what was originally understood to be the relationship between liberalism and democracy or, more specifically, the relationship between the natural or inalienable rights of individuals, on the one hand, and the right of democratic majorities to rule as they see fit, on the other.

The Preamble to the Constitution makes clear that the document was ordained and established by "the People of the United States." However, the Constitution was not merely the product of "popular sovereignty" or the "will of the people"; it originated in pre-constitutional or pre-political rights that limited the powers of government and that were intended to guide the popular will. It was the specific object of the Constitution to provide a form of government that would protect and promote these rights.

Although there has been dispute over the precise source of the Constitution's authority, the most succinct formulation of its animating principles is found in the Declaration of Independence. The Declaration referred to those truths that were held to be "self-evident": that all men are "created equal" and that they are endowed with the "inalienable rights" to life, liberty, and the pursuit of happiness. According to the Declaration, government is charged with the task of securing these rights through the exercise of just powers derived from the consent of the governed. Insofar as government fails to provide for these ends, the people are entitled to alter or abolish it.

Whether the Constitution, over its history, has adequately provided for the ends of government has been the subject of much commentary. This is particularly so in the case of civil rights. In the nineteenth century, the denial of the civil and political liberties of black Americans led to passage of the RECONSTRUCTION Amendments; the THIRTEENTH, FOURTEENTH, and FIFTEENTH AMENDMENTS to the Constitution. In the twentieth century, the NINETEENTH AMENDMENT protected the right to vote against denials or abridgments by reason of sex.

Defining the exact meaning of the Reconstruction Amendments, and giving them effect, has occupied the attention of the American judiciary and federal and state governments since the Civil War. Over the last fifty years, the struggle to define the meaning of equality in American constitutionalism has arisen most emphatically in disputes over the meaning of equal protection under law and the scope of coverage provided by legislation that has codified the guarantees of the Reconstruction Amendments—the most prominent examples of this being the CIVIL RIGHTS ACT OF 1964 and the VOTING RIGHTS ACT OF 1965. Public policies, such as AFFIRMATIVE ACTION, have also fueled disputes over the meaning of equality in the American constitutional order.

Although constitutionalism in the United States may be defined by the balance between liberalism and democracy, the liberal democratic equation has been shaped as much by disputes over rights not involving issues of equality as by conflicts involving these issues. Litigation over the meaning of the religion clauses—involving the relationship between church and state—as well as the free speech and free press clauses of the First Amendment, the search and seizure protections of the Fourth Amendment, the right against self-incrimination provided by the Fifth Amendment, and the non-enumerated privacy rights held to be protected by the Fourteenth Amendment have all generated controversy, as have disputes involving the definition of other constitutional rights.

Closely related to the problem of how to define civil rights and their relation to democratic government has been the issue of judicial review, the right of courts to determine the constitutionality of laws. The judicial activism of the Court of Chief Justice Earl WARREN from 1953 to 1969, as well as later courts, has pitted advocates of a broad construction of civil rights against those who believed that such a construction would enervate the legislative and executive branches of government, as well as federal–state relations. The broad policy functions that the judiciary has assumed in the last half of the twentieth century have raised the question of how these have affected other institutional arrangements in the American constitutional system that are intended to protect individual liberties: the separation of powers, federalism, and electoral representation, for instance. How institutional structure in the United States might best provide for civil rights while respecting republican principles has become an increasingly salient issue.

While critics of expansive civil rights maintain that government has undermined America's civic character, as well as responsibility under law, by granting too many rights to too many groups, advocates of a broad construction of civil rights have viewed this as a salutary development, providing more avenues of redress for those who have suffered discrimination and disadvantage. Regardless of who is correct, American constitutionalism in the United States continues to be defined by the manner in which it provides for those liberties that have guided the American experiment and that America's forms of government were intended to serve.

BIBLIOGRAPHY

Diamond, Martin. "The Declaration and the Constitution: Liberty, Democracy, and the Founders." In *As Far as Republican Principles Will Admit*, edited by William A. Schambra. 1992.

Dicey, A. V. *Introduction to the Study of the Constitution*. 1915.

Farrand, Max, ed. *The Records of the Federal Convention of 1787*, 3 vols. 1911.

Hamilton, Alexander, James Madison, and John Jay. *The Federalist Papers*. 1961 ed.

Hayek, Friedrich A. *The Constitution of Liberty*. 1960.

Hickok, Eugene W., ed. *The Bill of Rights: Original Meaning and Current Understanding*. 1991.

Pritchett, C. Herman. *The American Constitutional System*. 1963.

Rossum, Ralph A., and G. Alan Tarr. *American Constitutional Law*, 2 vols. 1999.

Schochet, Gordon J. "Introduction: Constitutionalism, Liberalism, and the Study of Politics." In *Constitutionalism*. Roland J. Pennock and John W. Chapman, eds. 1979.

Story, Joseph. *Commentaries on the Constitution of the United States*, 3 vols. 1833.

Anthony A. Peacock

Convict Labor

In the earliest American prisons, work was given prisoners only as a favor. Later, forced labor was seen as a form of rehabilitation and atonement. Convicts worked in prison-owned industries or were leased to private companies. Since U.S. courts have never held that prisoners have a constitutional right to be paid wages for their work, most states and lessees provided merely a token wage. The convict lease system thus provided industrialists in some parts of the United States with the steady, cheap labor necessary for modernization at high profit. Statutes limiting the use of convict labor as unfair competition became a priority of the rising union movement, and by the mid-twentieth century prison labor was largely confined to public works projects, some by chain gang, and prison industries. The issue of the competition of convict with free labor continues to be controversial. Today, the use of prison labor for private profit is again widespread, especially with the advent of work-release programs and the trend toward private prisons. This poses serious threats to prisoner rights.

The U.S. Supreme Court acknowledges no constitutional right of a prisoner to a job, although he or she cannot refuse if asked to work. Courts have upheld solitary confinement as a legal punishment for refusing to work. Because the THIRTEENTH AMENDMENT defines imprisonment as just cause for involuntary servitude, most courts do not consider inmates "employees" and their labor does not belong to themselves but to the state. Consequently, demands by prisoners to be paid the prevailing minimum wage have failed.

Increasingly, states are subcontracting the construction and operation of prisons to private, for-profit companies, some of which are now traded on the New York Stock Exchange. Today financial and political interests are joining to create criminal justice policy. One result is that the prison population has skyrocketed, fed by a widening criminalization of behaviors. An unlimited supply of new prisoners seems to be the raw material needed to guarantee long-term growth of the prison industry.

BIBLIOGRAPHY

Christie, Nils. *Crime Control as Industry*. 1993.

Lichtenstein, Alex. *Twice the Work of Free Labor: The Political Economy of Convict Labor in the New South*. 1996.

Mushlin, Michael, editor. *Rights of Prisoners*. 1993–1998 (updated annually).

Roberts, Ira P., editor. *Prisoners and the Law*. 1993.

Rothman, David J. *The Discovery of the Asylum: Social Order and Disorder in the New Republic*. 1971.

Eric Cummins

CORE

See Congress of Racial Equality.

Corona, Bert

(1918–), labor activist.

A long-time community organizer and labor activist, Corona's life captures much of the history of Mexican protest politics in California in this century. Born in El Paso, Texas, to immigrant parents who left Mexico during the Revolution, Corona grew up in a household sympathetic to Pancho Villa and the ideals of popular struggle and social justice. After moving to California in 1936 to attend college, Corona launched his career as a professional organizer. For more than six decades, Corona participated in unionization drives, civil rights crusades, and political campaigns in an effort to improve conditions for workers and ethnic Mexicans alike.

Bert Corona, Mexican-American rights activist, teaching a class. (AP/Wide World Photos)

A consistent concern for Corona was the rights of laborers, both documented and undocumented. Working at a drug company to support his studies, Corona in 1937 helped unionize the drug industry in Southern California. As a member of the Congress of Industrial Organizations (CIO), Corona later participated in the successful effort to unionize the region's waste-materials industry. During the 1950s, Corona supported strikes among imported Mexican contract workers, or *braceros*. Unlike many Mexican-American activist contemporaries, Corona sought to organize the *braceros* instead of viewing them strictly as competition for domestic workers.

Corona was also a founding member of many key Mexican-American civil rights organizations. While a student, Corona joined the first college group devoted to improving educational opportunity for Mexican Americans, a group that became known as the Mexican American Movement. In 1938, Corona, along with other CIO members, joined the short-lived Congreso Nacional de Pueblo de Habla Española (the National Spanish-Speaking Congress), a Los Angeles-based group that aspired to create a national pan-Latino civil rights alliance. After World War II, Corona played a central role in the northern California efforts of the Community Service Organization as well as the more left-leaning ASOCIACIÓN NACIONAL MÉXICO-AMERICANA. As a member of these grassroots groups and others, Corona worked to end segregation, protest against police abuse, protect undocumented immigrants, and register voters.

Years of struggle convinced Corona of the need to enhance Mexican-American political clout. In 1960, Corona was among the founders of the Mexican American Political Association (MAPA), formed to ensure the election of ethnic candidates in California. In recognition of MAPA's influence, Corona was asked in 1964 to cochair the Viva (Lyndon) Johnson! effort nationally. In 1968, he headed the Viva (Robert) Kennedy! endeavor.

A socialist since the 1930s, Corona was disappointed with the limits of domestic reform during the Johnson administration. Despite some generational tensions, Corona became active in the youth-dominated Chicano movement of the late 1960s and early 1970s. Corona joined Chicano mass protest against the VIETNAM War and strongly supported the LA RAZA UNIDA PARTY, the movement's third-party effort. In conjunction with younger activists, Corona renewed his efforts to defend the undocumented through the founding of an immigrant rights group called El Centro de Acción Social Autónoma (Center for Autonomous Social Action), or CASA. Corona continued to fight against anti-immigrant legislation into the 1990s.

BIBLIOGRAPHY

Campbell, Duane. "Bert Corona: Labor Radical." *Socialist Review* 19 (1989): 41–55.

Corona Papers. Green Library, Stanford University, Stanford, Calif.

García, Mario T. *Memories of Chicano History: The Life and Narrative of Bert Corona.* 1994.

Lorena Oropeza

Cortez Lira, Gregorio

(1875–1916), border hero.

Gregorio Cortez was a very precise man and an expert horseman. The first quality made him a fugitive. The second almost allowed him to elude capture during one of the largest manhunts in U.S. history. On June 12th, 1901, Sheriff T. T. (Brack) Morris arrived at Cortez's Texas farm looking for a horse thief. He asked his deputy, Boone Choate, to inquire of Cortez if he had traded a horse (*caballo*). Cortez replied no, he had traded a mare (*yegua*). Choate, unable to understand, told the sheriff that Cortez said no. From there the misunderstanding escalated. Within minutes Morris critically wounded Cortez's brother, Romaldo. In turn, the sheriff was mortally wounded by Cortez.

Cortez was later surrounded by a posse, led by Morris's friend, Sheriff Robert M. Glover. In the ensuing gunfight, Cortez killed Glover. Soon he was the object of a massive manhunt. In his desperate flight to the border, Cortez covered several hundred miles. Finally, after riding and walking many days, an exhausted Cortez was captured only miles from the border.

Gregorio Cortez was tried several times between 1902 and 1905 on a variety of charges. During these trials he spoke eloquently on his own behalf. His ordeal united Mexicans and Mexican Americans from all backgrounds, who closely identified with Cortez's defense of his rights. Although acquitted of Morris's murder, he was found guilty of murdering Glover. In 1905, he was sentenced to life in prison. In 1913, Governor O.B. Colquitt granted Cortez a conditional pardon.

After his release, Cortez went to Mexico and fought in the Mexican Revolution. Wounded in battle, he returned to South Texas to convalesce. There, during a wedding celebration, Cortez became ill. He died in Anson, Texas, in 1916.

BIBLIOGRAPHY

The Ballad of Gregorio Cortez. Videocassette. 1988.

"Gregorio Cortez"—Tragedia. Parts 1 and 2. Pedro Rocha y Lupe Martinez. Vocalion 8351. 1929.

Paredes, Américo. *With His Pistol in His Hand: A Border Ballad and Its Hero.* 1958. Recording.

Peña, Manuel. "Folksong and Social Change: Two Corridos as Interpretive Sources." *Aztlán* 13 (1982): 13–42.

Sonnichsen, Philip. "More about the Corrido 'Gregorio Cortez.'" (http://www.sp.utexas.edu/jm/gcortez3.html)

Juan R. García

Cortina, Juan Nepomuceno

(1824–1894), Mexican revolutionary and Texas folk hero.

Cortina was born in Camargo, Tamaulipas, the son of Trinidad Cortina and Maria Estefana Goseascochea on May 16, 1824. At age twenty-two as a corporal in the Defensores de la Patria, a company of the Guardia Nacional de Tamaulipas, Cortina served as a scout in the Tamaulipas Brigade during the battles of Palo Alto and Resaca de la Palma. At the beginning of the "unhappy war" in 1846, he married a first cousin, Maria Dolores Tijerina. After her death he wed Rafaela Cortez, a widow several years his senior. Two children, Felicita and Faustina, were born of the second union.

In the years after the war, Cortina established a small ranch at San José, near his mother's large Rancho del Carmen, six miles upriver from Brownsville. At the same time, Cortina came to possess a burning hatred of a clique of judges and unscrupulous Brownsville attorneys, whom he accused of expropriating land from many Mexican Texans who were unfamiliar with the American judicial system. Although largely illiterate, Cortina became a charismatic leader to many of the Mexicans who lived along both banks of the Rio Grande.

The incident that ignited what came to be called the Cortina War occurred on July 13, 1859, when Cortina witnessed the Brownsville City Marshal, Robert Shears, brutally arrest a Mexican Texan who had been employed at Rancho del Carmen. In the impending confrontation, Cortina shot the marshal and rode out of town with the prisoner. On September 28, 1859, Cortina rode into Brownsville again, this time at the head of some seventy-five men and seized control of the town. Five men, including the city jailer, died during the raid, as Cortina and his men raced through the streets shouting "Death to the Americans" and "Viva Mexico." When several of the town's leading citizens appealed to Mexican authorities in Matamorso, the influential José Maria Carbajal crossed the river to negotiate with Cortina. Cortina agreed to evacuate the town and retreated to the family Rancho del Carmen, where, on September 30, 1859, he issued a proclamation asserting the rights of Mexican Texans and demanding the punishment of anyone violating these rights. Cortina issued a second proclamation on November 23 asking Governor Sam Houston to defend the legal interests of Mexican residents in Texas.

In December 1859, Cortina, at the head of several hundred revolutionaries, successfully defeated the Texas Rangers before being defeated himself by the Rangers and United States Army at Rio Grande City on December 27, 1859.

During the French intervention in Mexico, Cortina rose to become a powerful *caudillo*, a general in the liberal army of Benito Juarez, and twice governor of Tamaulipas. During the early 1870s, Cortina was accused by American authorities of masterminding the theft of thousands of cattle in South Texas. In the collateral violence of the "Skinning War," some of Cortina's men raided as far north as Corpus Christi. In retaliation for such raids, Texas Rangers invaded Mexico, burned, plundered, and indiscriminately hanged Mexicans. In May 1875, American diplomatic pressure resulted in Mexican President Sebastian Lerdo de Teja ordering Cortina's arrest and confinement at the prison of Santiago Tlatelolco in Mexico City. Two months later Cortina pronounced in favor of Gen. Porfirio Diaz and fled Mexico City. Back on the border, Cortina was again arrested, this time by orders of Diaz, and again imprisoned in Mexico City, where he died of pneumonia at Azapotzalco on the outskirts of the city on October 30, 1894. He was buried with military honors in the Panteon de Dolores.

BIBLIOGRAPHY

Douglas, James Ridley, "Juan Cortina; El Caudillo de la Frontera." M.A. thesis, University of Texas at Austin, 1987.

Goldfinch, Charles W., and Jose T. Canales. *Juan N. Cortina: Two Interpretations.* 1974.

Thompson, Jerry. *Juan Cortina and the Texas-Mexico Frontier, 1859–1877.* 1994.

Jerry Thompson

Cotton, Dorothy Lee

(1931–   ), educator.

As an officer in the minister-led SOUTHERN CHRISTIAN LEADERSHIP CONFERENCE (SCLC), Dorothy Cotton has been one of the driving forces behind civil rights campaigns and programs to educate illiterate black adults throughout the racially segregated South, where literacy tests were used to deny them their political right to vote.

Cotton was born in 1931 to working-class parents Claude and Sarah Forman in North Carolina. When she was three years old, her mother died; she was raised primarily by her father. While doing domestic work to finance her education, Cotton earned a B.A.

degree in English and library science in 1958 at Virginia State College and an M.A. in speech therapy in 1960 at Boston University. She returned to the South, also in 1960, at which point Wyatt T. Walker, an SCLC officer, gave her a job with the Conference in Atlanta, Georgia. Later, in 1963, the SCLC's president, Martin Luther KING, JR., asked Cotton to join Septima CLARK and Andrew YOUNG as co-directors of the Citizenship Education Program, which aimed to increase adult literacy for voter education, registration, and political empowerment. Cotton, Clark, and Young traveled throughout the South to recruit blacks into the program. Many who could mark only an X for their signature, were introduced to texts of the U.S. Constitution, Bill of Rights, and FOURTEENTH AMENDMENT. With Septima Clark as the exemplar, Cotton and others taught multitudes of African Americans how to read, write, and understand their rights as citizens.

In 1972, Cotton left the SCLC to become director of Child Development and HEAD START in Alabama. From 1975 to 1978, she worked for human services agencies. From 1982 to 1991, she was Dean of Students at Cornell University. Since 1991, Dorothy Cotton has given lectures on civil rights empowerment.

BIBLIOGRAPHY

Barnett, Bernice McNair. "Invisible Southern Black Women Leaders of the Civil Rights Movement and the Triple Constraints of Gender, Race, and Class." *Gender & Society* 7, 2 (1993):162:182.

Barnett, Bernice McNair. "Sisters in Struggle: Invisible Black Women Leaders of the Civil Rights Movement, 1940–1975." Forthcoming.

Branch, Taylor. *Parting the Waters: America's Civil Rights Years.* 1986.

Clark, Septima Poinsette. *Ready from Within.* 1986.

Cotton, Dorothy. Interview with author, February 1987.

Bernice McNair Barnett

Council of Federated Organizations (COFO)

In February of 1962, Bob Moses of the STUDENT NON-VIOLENT COORDINATING COMMITTEE (SNCC), Tom Gaither of the CONGRESS OF RACIAL EQUALITY (CORE), and Aaron HENRY and Medgar EVERS of the NATIONAL ASSOCIATION FOR THE ADVANCEMENT OF COLORED PEOPLE (NAACP) met in Jackson to form the Council of Federated Organizations (COFO), a Mississippi civil rights confederation incorporating all national, state, and local protest groups operating in the state. Historically, COFO has been viewed primarily as an umbrella agency set up to facilitate the transfer of funds from outside agencies (such as the VOTER EDU-

CATION PROJECT) to groups working within the state. Moses has challenged that characterization, pointing out that black Mississippians "wanted to have the feeling that all of their organizations were working together," and thus they developed strong ties to COFO. "The Negro people in Mississippi," observed CORE's Dave Dennis, "needed some organization which could belong to them (as opposed to their belonging to it) which could serve as a unifying force among the isolated Negro communities."

Aaron Henry was COFO's president, but most influential in the operation were Moses as program director and Dennis as assistant director. COFO staff retained their organizational affiliations. With the largest number of field workers in the state, SNCC became the dominant partner. The state conference of the NAACP was part of COFO, but the national organization, traditionally opposed to such alliances, was not.

Although it sponsored projects in local communities across the state, COFO is best known for the 1963 Freedom Vote, a mock election designed to prove that black Mississippians were denied the right to vote; and for the 1964 FREEDOM SUMMER, in which upwards of a thousand volunteers, most of them northern white college students, came to Mississippi to work with local people on a variety of projects. COFO also gave birth to the MISSISSIPPI FREEDOM DEMOCRATIC PARTY (MFDP), which challenged the seating of the all-white racist state delegation in 1964 at the national party convention in Atlantic City.

Atlantic City was a turning point in the civil rights movement, for the failure of the MFDP challenge convinced many COFO activists to reject alliance with white liberals and to pursue nationalist programs instead. COFO survived into 1965, but the interorganizational tensions that had been kept in check surfaced when the national office of the NAACP persuaded the state conference to withdraw from the COFO coalition. SNCC also believed that COFO had outlived its usefulness, and in March of 1965 recommended that COFO be abolished, with its resources shifted to the MFDP.

Although perhaps inevitable, the decision to abolish COFO was shortsighted, for it had been the one civil rights group representing the interests of virtually all black Mississippians. Moreover, with COFO's demise, SNCC and CORE became less active in the state. COFO was unique in the civil rights movement, for Mississippi was the only southern state where civil rights organizations, competing for publicity and money, agreed to cooperate, realizing that they were facing a common enemy and could not afford the luxury of destructive interorganizational warfare.

BIBLIOGRAPHY

Dittmer, John. *Local People: The Struggle for Civil Rights in Mississippi.* 1994.

Payne, Charles. *I've Got the Light of Freedom: The Organizing Tradition and the Mississippi Freedom Struggle.* 1995.

John Dittmer

Court of Appeals for the Fifth Circuit

See Fifth Circuit.

Court of Appeals for the Fourth Circuit

See Fourth Circuit.

Courts

The American judicial system is unique, perhaps above all, because of the broad policymaking role it assigns to courts. This role originates, among other things, in three features of the American legal system: (1) judicial independence from the legislative and executive branches of government; (2) the power of judicial review, the prerogative federal and state courts enjoy to determine the constitutionality of laws; and (3) the American common-law tradition, adopted with modifications from England.

A principal feature of the American constitutional order is the separation of powers, the separating of the legislative, executive, and judicial branches of government. As Alexander Hamilton argued in "Federalist No. 78," an independent judiciary, holding office during good behavior, is necessary for the impartial and consistent administration of laws, as well as for the maintenance of a limited government or a limited constitution.

Although the power of judicial review is not explicitly provided for in the federal Constitution, it was conferred upon federal courts in *Marbury v. Madison* (1803), where the U.S. SUPREME COURT, following Hamilton's argument in "Federalist No. 78," held that the constitutional review of legislation was necessary if constitutional supremacy was to be maintained, and that this power could only reside in the judiciary, not the legislative or the executive branches of the federal government. As a result of conferring the power of judicial review upon federal and state courts, the real controversy over the courts' powers has involved methods of interpretation, of how, specifically, the Constitution should be read.

The common-law tradition, utilized throughout the United States with the exception of Louisiana, grants significant law-making powers to federal and state courts by allowing courts to make law as well as interpret it. The doctrines of the common law are not written down in any statute or ordinance but depend upon authoritative legal principles, drawn from social customs and practices, established through the consideration of legal disputes.

As a result of the broad policymaking powers American courts enjoy, they have become arenas for the resolution of important political and legal conflicts, including civil rights issues. Although resolution of these conflicts has often involved straightforward questions of constitutional or statutory interpretation, civil rights litigation has been complicated by the federal court structure, the division of the judicial system into federal and state courts. Jurisdictional controversies have erupted over whether federal or state courts may address specific issues, and whether courts in one jurisdiction may impose orders on governments in other jurisdictions. Although state courts are the workhorses of the federal judicial system, handling many more cases per year than the federal courts, the most significant decisions bearing on civil rights have originated in the federal courts, particularly the Supreme Court, which, because of its authority, has become the focus of public policy disputes.

Throughout its history, the Supreme Court has used its broad powers of review both to enhance and to restrict civil rights. In DRED SCOTT V. SANDFORD (1857), for instance, the Court proclaimed that blacks could not be, or become, citizens. In PLESSY V. FERGUSON (1896), it sustained racial SEGREGATION. In BROWN V. BOARD OF EDUCATION (1954), by contrast, the Court rejected the *Plessy* holding as it applied to state educational facilities.

The aforementioned cases illustrate not only the power of the judiciary to decide questions of civil rights, but the potential the courts possess to shape the meaning and the scope of civil rights outside the sphere of judicial conflict. This latter issue became particularly salient in the last half of the twentieth century, as the Court heightened its scrutiny of civil and political liberties. Scholars have argued that American politics has been transformed by decisions such as *Brown* and *Roe v. Wade*, the 1973 decision granting a constitutional right to abortion. *Brown* has been credited with having created a revolution in civil rights by raising awareness of the plight of black Americans nationwide, precipitating a movement that would culminate in the CIVIL RIGHTS ACT OF 1964 and the VOTING RIGHTS ACT OF 1965. Similarly, *Roe* has been credited with having crystallized the struggle of women to achieve equality in American law, forging a national women's coalition, and creating the conditions for the popular acceptance of legally accessible abortions.

Critics of this interpretation claim that *Brown* and *Roe* did not so much create a transformation in civil rights and women's politics as reflect political and social movements that were already pushing American politics in the direction these decisions went. In addition, *Roe*, according to many of its critics, did not further women's rights or unify American women. Quite the contrary—by constitutionalizing one side in a contentious political dispute, it alienated a majority of the national electorate and divided Americans, particularly women, into a disparate array of ideological and hostile camps. Supreme Court critics have also argued that although *Brown* and the civil rights and voting rights legislation of the 1960s were salutary developments in American law, the Court subsequently transformed the very meaning of civil rights from a concept concerned with equal individual opportunity to a mandate for equal group results.

Although there remains ambiguity about whether or not the Supreme Court's broad construction of civil rights in the latter half of the twentieth century significantly redefined the civil rights agenda, its effect on civil rights strategy appears less ambiguous. Following *Brown* and *Roe*, civil rights and women's groups devoted increased resources to pursuing political strategies through legal channels. In turn, many of the legal advocacy groups that were created or augmented in response to the Court's expanded civil rights jurisprudence had a significant effect on legislative reform of civil rights law in the 1970s, 1980s, and 1990s.

If the specific influence American courts have had on civil rights remains an equivocal legacy, the conviction that courts should intervene to preserve constitutional and civil rights in the face of intemperate or capricious majorities, hostile to such rights, is still broadly accepted. Whether courts should, and to what extent they can, intervene in public affairs on behalf of civil rights beyond minimal guarantees of such rights remains a controversial issue that continues to occupy civil rights scholars and observers.

BIBLIOGRAPHY

Bickel, Alexander M. *The Least Dangerous Branch: The Supreme Court at the Bar of Politics.* 1962.

Bork, Robert H. *The Tempting of America: The Political Seduction of the Law.* 1990.

Calvi, James V., and Susan Coleman. *American Law and Legal Systems.* 1997.

Ely, John Hart. *Democracy and Distrust: A Theory of Judicial Review.* 1980.

Hamilton, Alexander, James Madison, and John Jay. "Federalist Nos. 78–83." In *The Federalist Papers.* 1961.

Horowitz, Donald L. *The Courts and Social Policy.* 1977.

Rosenberg, Gerald N. *The Hollow Hope: Can Courts Bring About Social Change?* 1991.

Rossum, Ralph A., and G. Alan Tarr. *American Constitutional Law.* 1999.

Sowell, Thomas. *Civil Rights: Rhetoric or Reality?* 1984.

Tarr, G. Alan. *Judicial Process and Judicial Policy-Making.* 1999.

Wilson, James Q. "Chapter 10: The Judiciary." In *American Government.* 1997.

Anthony A. Peacock

CPUSA

See Communist Party USA.

Crisis, The

The Crisis is the magazine of the NATIONAL ASSOCIATION FOR THE ADVANCEMENT OF COLORED PEOPLE (NAACP). The publication was founded in 1910 by W. E. B. Du Bois, who served as its editor until 1934. Du Bois made the statement that the periodical emerged during "a critical time in the history of the advancement of men." Therefore, at the suggestion of William English Walling, a founder of the NAACP, the original title was *The Crisis: A Record of the Darker Races.*

Although Du Bois stated that the mission of *The Crisis* was "to set forth those facts and arguments which show the danger of race prejudice, particularly as manifested today toward colored people," the magazine reflected Du Bois's philosophy concerning the existence of an African-American intelligensia. Under Du Bois's editorship its content resembled a literary and scholarly journal more than a magazine of general audience interest. In addition to editorial commentary on various civil rights issues confronting African Americans, *The Crisis* published literary works and feature stories on Pan-African affairs. Contributors included Langston HUGHES, George Bernard Shaw, Mahatma GANDHI, and James Weldon JOHNSON.

Du Bois was succeeded as editor by Roy WILKINS, who held the post for fifteen years—until 1949. Wilkins's editorship spanned the Great Depression and WORLD WAR II. *The Crisis* turned its attention to JIM CROW policies, lynchings, and discrimination in the U.S. armed forces. (*See* ANTI-LYNCHING CAMPAIGN; LYNCHING; NEW DEAL AND DEPRESSION.) Another editorial addition under Wilkins was a series, "First Ladies of Colored America," which highlighted successful and accomplished black women in various professional endeavors. The magazine also included pictorial essays on beauty queens at historically black colleges and universities.

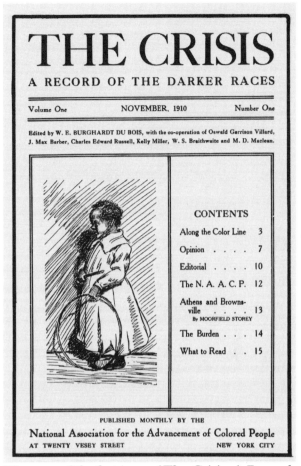

The cover of the first issue of The Crisis, A Record of the Darker Races, *the NAACP newspaper edited by W. E. B. Du Bois that was first published in November 1910.*

Wilkins was succeeded by James W. Ivy, who was editor during the great civil rights era (1950–1966). It was during this period that the magazine added its voice to the consensus of black newspapers and other periodicals supporting the legal challenges to discrimination in education, housing, employment, public accommodations, and voter registration.

Under the seven-year editorship of Henry Lee Moon (1967–1974), *The Crisis* added color photography and continued to address both domestic and international issues of particular interest to African Americans in the post-civil rights era. In 1994 the magazine's subtitle became "The Most Progressive Voice of Black America," but with the birth of *The New Crisis* magazine in 1998, its subtitle was changed to "The Magazine of Opportunities and Ideas." The latter change was accompanied by the rise of Roger Wilkins to the chairmanship of the magazine's editorial board. Wilkins, a Pulitzer Prize-winning journalist and widely recognized radio commentator, is the nephew of Roy

Wilkins. Although *The Crisis* began as a monthly publication, *The New Crisis* is a bimonthly periodical (dated February/March, April/May, July, September, October/November, and December/January) featuring contemporary design and major corporate advertising in the late 1990s. The content still reflects the agenda established by Du Bois in its coverage of affairs relevant to Africans and all world populations that have resulted from the African diaspora. *The Crisis* has always stressed the linkages between African Americans and the peoples of Africa and the Caribbean.

BIBLIOGRAPHY
The Crisis, Vols. 1–103.
Lewis, David L. *W. E. B. Du Bois: Biography of a Race, 1868–1919.* 1993.
Walden, Daniel, ed. *W. E. B. Du Bois: The Crisis Writings.* 1972.

Clint C. Wilson II

Critical Race Feminism

The term "Critical Race Feminism" (CRF) identifies a body of legal scholarship that focuses on the legal rights of women of color. In the words of Professor Mari Matsuda, these women experience "multiple consciousness" based upon simultaneously confronting both RACISM and SEXISM. Traditional legal analysis has ignored their plight, subsuming them under generic discussions regarding "people" or the "reasonable man." Legal scholarship on race or ethnicity may assume or imply that the situation of women of color is identical to that of men of color. Feminist writing may presume that white women's experiences represent all women or may relegate other women to the footnotes or the margins of the analysis.

According to Professor Kimberle Crenshaw, the law must "demarginalize" the legal status of women of color. CRF writings attempt to do just that in their coverage of such diverse areas as EDUCATION, EMPLOYMENT, HOUSING, health, welfare reform, and criminal, international, and comparative law. Specifically, issues of AFFIRMATIVE ACTION, sexual harassment, mothering, domestic violence, stereotyping, customary practices such as female genital surgeries, and the relationship of CRF to traditional feminist legal theory have been addressed.

CRF is linked with several other progressive trends within legal scholarship, most notably Critical Legal Studies, Critical Race Theory, and feminist jurisprudence. Very recently, Latino Critical Studies, Asian Critical Studies, Critical White Studies, and Queer Legal Theory have intersected with CRF thought as well. CRF also draws inspiration from black feminist or "womanist" thought in literature and the social sciences.

Like Critical Legal Studies, CRF attacks preexisting legal schools of thought that regard the law as neutral and objective. CRF "deconstructs" or exposes how various legal systems have served to perpetuate unjust race, class, and gender hierarchies that keep women of color on the bottom of society.

CRF writers may incorporate the controversial narrative or storytelling technique first made popular by Critical Race Theory founders Derrick Bell and Richard Delgado. Opponents of Critical Race Theory such as Professors Daniel Farber, Suzanna Sherry, and Judge Richard Posner have found this technique to be highly subjective, nonlegal, and overly emotional.

CRF authors are interested not only in abstract legal theories but also in practical solutions to the problems facing women of color. Remedies may involve the law as a necessary but not sufficient component and may encompass disciplines such as sociology, history, anthropology, political science, and economics. Redress can include: individual lawsuits; class action litigation; law reform; implementation of new federal, state, or local programs; coalition building; protests and boycotts; counseling; and working with nongovernmental organizations and grassroots activists.

Among the more than fifty law professors who have written articles or books that could be characterized as CRF scholarship are professors Sumi Cho, Kathleen Cleaver, Kimberle Williams Crenshaw, Lani Guinier, Angela Harris, Berta Hernandez, Anita Hill, Mari Matsuda, Dorothy Roberts, Celina Romany, Judy Scales Trent, Patricia Williams, and Adrien Wing.

BIBLIOGRAPHY
Crenshaw, Kimberle Williams. "Demarginalizing the Intersection of Race and Sex: A Black Feminist Critique of Antidiscrimination Doctrine, Feminist Theory, and Antiracist Politics." *University of Chicago Legal Forum* (1989): 139–167.
Harris, Angela P. "Race and Essentialism in Feminist Legal Theory." *Stanford Law Review* 42 (1991): 581–616.
Matsuda, Mari. "When the First Quail Calls: Multiple Consciousness as Jurisprudential Method." *Women's Rights Law Reporter* 14 (1992): 297–303.
Wing, Adrien Katherine, ed. *Critical Race Feminism: A Reader.* 1997.
Wing, Adrien Katherine, ed. *Global Critical Race Feminism: An International Reader.* 2000.

Adrien Katherine Wing

Critical Race Theory

Critical Race Theory (CRT) is a term that describes the scholarly production of a group of more-or-less leftist legal theorists who place "race consciousness" at the center of their analyses. CRT writings have a dual character, representing simultaneously a "left[ist] intervention into race discourse and a race intervention into left discourse." Thus, CRT challenges both liberal theories of the law that subsume RACE under the category of CLASS and "racialist" notions that regard the law as a mere reflection of the social subordination of race. CRT scholarship argues that traditional approaches to "race" and civil rights fail to account for the complex ways in which law is both a reflection of and a cause of accepted concept of "race," "racial" supremacy, and inequity. Drawing upon methods of literary critical deconstruction akin to those of the Critical Legal Studies (CLS) movement that developed in the late 1970s, CRT demonstrates that notions of "color-blindness"—underpinning predominant legal approaches to race—rely on inherently hypocritical conceptions of race and RACISM.

CRT's critical stance coalesced in the 1980s, at the beginning of what some CRT thinkers identify as the "post–civil rights era"—the beginning of the courts' dismantling of earlier civil rights victories. Together CRT and CLS argued that law, far from being "reasonable" and apolitical, supports power arrangements that are advantageous to its creators, but CRT distinguished itself from its predecessor CLS over the issue of whether "race matters." Controversial hiring and curricular decisions at the Harvard Law School in 1980 also precipitated the group's formation when students of color protested the replacement of civil rights litigator Derrick A. BELL, Jr. and his course on race and law. In opposing Harvard's "color-blind" approach, students organized the "Alternative Course," following Bell's curriculum and gathering minority legal scholars from around the country.

CRT authors often advocate ideas that mainstream and conservative pundits find distasteful or unconventional, such as Lani Guinier's proposal for "cumulative voting" to protect minority interests and Richard Delgado's "oppositional storytelling" for introducing as courtroom testimony narratives of the legally marginalized. Analysts hostile to CRT have charged that CRT writings promote "undemocratic" practices like "jury nullification" and "gerrymandering."

The range of CRT writing suggests that radical alternative approaches to legal and political mechanics are necessary to confront the enshrined idea that racism is simply the conscious act of a racist individual rather than a systemic jurisprudential attitude and structure. In addressing issues such as AFFIRMATIVE ACTION, education and curricular reform, voting, penal and welfare reform, IMMIGRATION, economic opportunity, environmental racism, and criminal and constitutional law, CRT recognizes that "race" is not biological but that there are material consequences to being categorized according to race in the United States. Thus, CRT challenges not only mainstream and conservative attitudes but also those of the liberal civil rights traditions, which proclaim the "self-evident" equality (equal rights and protection) of each individual, by exposing the mechanisms of thought that make such a racially blind meritocratic faith untenable.

Writers whose work falls within the CRT compass include Derrick Bell, Anthony E. Cook, Kimberlé Crenshaw, Richard Delgado, Neil Gotanda, Lani Guinier, Mari Matsuda, Gary Peller, Kendall Thomas, and Patricia Williams.

BIBLIOGRAPHY

Crenshaw, Kimberlé, Neil Gotanda, Gary Peller, and Kendall Thomas, eds. *Critical Race Theory: The Key Writings That Formed the Movement.* 1995.
Delgado, Richard, and Jean Stefancic, eds. *Critical Race Theory: The Cutting Edge.* 1999.
Johnson, Alex M., Jr., ed. *Readings in Race and Law: A Guide to Critical Race Theory.* 1998.
Matsuda, Mari J., Charles R. Lawrence III, Richard Delgado, and Kimberlé Crenshaw, eds. *Words That Wound: Critical Race Theory: Assaultive Speech and the First Amendment.* 1993.

Joseph R. Slaughter

Crusade for Justice

Of all the Chicano civil rights organizations of the 1960s and 1970s, none had a greater impact on the intellectual thought of civil rights activists than did the Crusade for Justice. Founded in Denver, Colorado in 1967, it produced two of the most important documents of the CHICANO MOVEMENT and was one of the first organizations to attempt to bring Mexican-American activists together to discuss the problems in the barrios of the United States.

The Crusade for Justice, or Crusada por la Justicia as it was originally called, was the brainchild of Rodolfo "Corky" GONZALES. A WAR ON POVERTY warrior in the early 1960s, he became disillusioned with federal assistance programs because of their bias in favor of African Americans, as well as their failure to promote concrete solutions to poverty, school dropout rates, and violence in the barrio.

The Crusade departed from the traditional civil rights organizations with its holistic approach to Chicano empowerment. It sought to organize families rather than individuals, it endeavored to make Chicanos proud of who they were, and it promoted a tenacious self-help approach to problems. It set up a K–12 bilingual school; developed dance, choir, and theater groups; established an organization to promote political discussions among barrio residents; and started a community newspaper. The Crusade also refused to accept outside funding, choosing instead to make the organization dependent on the support of the Mexican-American community.

In its early years, the organization published two important documents. The first was an epic poem by its founder, titled "Yo Soy Joaquín/I Am Joaquín." This poem sought to dramatize the historical struggle of Mexican Americans to find justice. It became a catalyst for the development of Mexican-American literature, theater, and political rhetoric. The second document came out of the first Chicano Youth Liberation conference of 1967. "El Plan de Aztlán," or the Plan of Aztlán, laid out a plan of action for activists in pursuit of justice for Mexican Americans. No other document would be so widely quoted or be so powerful an indictment by Chicanos of American prejudices as was the Plan of Aztlán.

The Crusade for Justice also served as one of the prime promoters of the Raza Unida Party, of links to progressive movements in Latin America, and of coalition with African Americans and Native-American activists. By the late 1970s, the organization began to fade because of internal conflicts and radicalization; however, its founder and its documents would be remembered as major players in the quest for Mexican-American civil rights.

BIBLIOGRAPHY

Acuña, Rodolfo. *Occupied America.* 1972.
Castro, Tony. *Chicano Power: The Emergence of Mexican America.* 1974.
Documents of the Chicano Struggle. 1971.
García, Ignacio M. *United We Win: The Rise and Fall of La Raza Unida Party.* 1989.
García, Ignacio M. *Chicanismo: The Forging of a Militant Ethos Among Mexican Americans.* 1997.
Gómez-Quiñones, Juan. *Chicano Politics: Reality and Promise, 1940–1990.* 1990.
Gonzales, Rodolfo. "Yo Soy Joaquín." *El Gallo* (1967).
Larralde, Carlos. *Mexican American Movements and Leaders.* 1976.
Marín, Christine. *A Spokesman of the Mexican American Movement: Rodolfo "Corky" Gonzales and the Fight for Chicano Liberation, 1966–1972.* 1977.
Muñoz, Carlos, Jr. *Youth, Identity, Power: The Chicano Movement.* 1989.

Ignacio M. García

Crystal City Electoral Revolt

In 1970, the words "Chicano Power!" were put into practice in this small south Texas town when a total of five candidates of Mexican-descent running for office under the banner of La Raza Unida Party took control of the city's school board and city council. Once in office, La Raza Unida adherents revamped the school curriculum and redirected city spending to address Mexican-American concerns. The electoral success inspired Chicano movement activists all over the Southwest to pursue third-party politics.

A similar victory in Crystal City six years before had gone flat. The self-proclaimed Spinach Capital of the World, the town lay within the heart of Texas's Winter Garden area. The dominant agricultural industry, however, masked long-standing economic, educational, and political inequality. In 1970, Mexican Americans were roughly 80 percent of the Crystal City population of 10,000, but most either followed the migrant trail or worked locally in the fields that were owned by the town's Anglo-American elite. Farmwork commonly interrupted schooling: according to one estimate, in 1960, Mexican Americans aged 25 years or older in the town averaged 2.3 years of education. Political power, moreover, was concentrated in the hands of the minority. The exception was the period between 1963 and 1965, when an all Mexican-American slate captured the city council with the support of the teamsters, who were interested in expanding union strength locally, and a statewide group called the Political Association of Spanish-Speaking Organizations. Lacking experience and grassroots support, however, the Mexican Americans lost their reelection bid and Crystal City reverted to Anglo control.

A volunteer during that 1963 campaign was a young man named José Angel Gutiérrez, a native of Crystal City. Later, while pursuing his studies in San Antonio, Gutiérrez met a group of students who in 1967 formed the MEXICAN AMERICAN YOUTH ORGANIZATION (MAYO). Despite the innocuous name, MAYO members quickly became known in south Texas for their confrontational manner as they supported high school boycotts and protested police abuse. In 1969, the organization launched an ethnic empowerment effort in south Texas with recently acquired federal development funds.

Gutiérrez returned to Crystal City with his wife, Luz, and child. The family's arrival coincided with simmering discontent at the local high school. The Gutiérrezes began to cultivate support for a student boycott by organizing a group called Ciudadanos Unidos (United Citizens). The school protest proved a great success, and Ciudadanos Unidos became the backbone of Crystal City's La Raza Unida Party.

A direct translation of the party's name has "United Race," but the name referred to a united Mexican American population. It had been used in conjunction with a series of ethnic mobilization conferences in

Texas. After April 1970, however, La Raza Unida represented the Chicano alternative party.

In Crystal City, Raza Unida school board members, including José Angel Gutiérrez, initiated a curriculum that focused upon the Mexican-American experience, backed the bilingual announcing of football games, and banned army recruiters at the high school. Federal assistance to the district nearly doubled the first year Raza Unida candidates were in office. Meanwhile, Raza Unida Party city council made certain that the town hired law enforcement officers sympathetic to the Mexican-American population.

Victories for the party extended beyond Crystal City. Also in April 1970, every La Raza Unida Party candidate running in nearby Carrizo Springs and Cotulla emerged triumphant for a total of six electoral wins, including the Cotulla mayorship. Attempts to win offices at the county level that November, however, were stymied by Democrats who launched a series of technical challenges.

La Raza Unida faced constant opposition from the Democratic Party, which was accustomed to Mexican-American voter support. In contrast, the Republican Party apparently courted some La Raza Unida Party members with offers of money. Nevertheless, La Raza Unida steered an independent course. In 1971, the party in Texas developed a statewide platform and decided to back a candidate for governor the following year. By 1972, activists in Colorado, California, and New Mexico had run as Raza Unida candidates for state and local offices. Yet outside of south Texas and its majority Mexican-American population, La Raza Unida, despite repeated attempts, never came close to winning.

Even in Crystal City, problems arose. Although triumphant at the polls, the party split into rival camps. La Raza Unida, moreover, was never able to create an alternate economic base for the town's impoverished farmworkers. Still, the town's revolution via the ballot box symbolized for movement activists, as well as many Democrats and Republicans, the potential electoral clout of Chicanos.

BIBLIOGRAPHY

García, Ignacio M. *United We Win: The Rise and Fall of La Raza Unida Party.* 1989.

Gutiérrez, José Angel. "La Raza and Revolution: The Empirical Conditions for Revolution in Four South Texas Counties." Master's thesis, Saint Mary's University, San Antonio, Texas. 1968.

"Fighting for Political Power," episode four of the documentary *Chicano! History of the Mexican American Civil Rights Movement.* Series Producer, Hector Galan. Distributed by National Latino Communication Center Educational Media. 1996.

Navarro, Armando. *Mexican American Youth Organization: Avant-Garde of the Chicano Movement in Texas.* 1995.

Shockley, John Staples. *Chicano Revolt in a Texas Town.* 1974.

La Verdad newspaper (Crystal City, Texas).

Lorena Oropeza

D

Daughters of Bilitis

The Daughters of Bilitis (DOB) is the first known lesbian civil rights organization in the United States. It was founded in San Francisco in September 1955 by eight women who came together to organize a social space for lesbians outside of bars. The original eight members differed in their perception of the group's function, however, and two of the original members, Del MARTIN and Phyllis LYON, steered the group toward a civil rights agenda. Martin and Lyon worked alongside ONE, Inc., a Los Angeles–based "homophile" (homosexual rights) organization and San Francisco's MATTACHINE SOCIETY, another homophile organization, and in the fall of 1956 the Daughters of Bilitis initiated public meetings focused on lesbian issues. By the end of that year, DOB's function had shifted to a political organization invested in using the public sphere to fight for lesbian civil rights (see GAY AND LESBIAN RIGHTS). In November of 1956 the Daughters of Bilitis had begun publishing a monthly newsletter, *The Ladder*, which was distributed continuously and nationally until 1972. Except for the short-lived and limited publication of Lisa Ben's *Vice Versa* (1947–1948), DOB's *Ladder* was the first widely distributed lesbian periodical. *The Ladder* quickly became the organization's mouthpiece and, literally, its ladder to public visibility and social mobility. On the inside cover of each edition ran the organization's statement of purpose, which listed "education of the variant" as its primary concern. (Following the lead of scientist Alfred Kinsey, homophile activists saw homosexuality—female or male—as a *variation* on the scale of human sexuality rather than a *deviation* from a norm.)

DOB worked to help lesbians adjust to society—a society often hostile toward homosexuals—by sponsoring educational seminars on lesbian history, promoting the production of lesbian arts and literature, and distributing information that challenged the myths of homosexuals' pathology and criminality. DOB also worked to educate the public about lesbianism and break the wall of silence and negative images that rendered lesbians either invisible or stereotyped. Through information campaigns, DOB asserted a more complex image of "the lesbian." It sponsored surveys of San Francisco's lesbian population, encouraged its members to cooperate with scientists in their research, and asserted a new presence in legal and political affairs. While the Daughters of Bilitis fought to articulate its own voice, it also encouraged professionals to advocate for lesbians. The members worked innovatively to reach pastors, politicians, doctors, scientists, and lawyers. In 1956, for example, DOB mailed a copy of its second issue of *The Ladder* to all the female lawyers listed in the San Francisco telephone book, and while most of the recipients angrily asked to be removed from DOB's mailing list, one woman, Juliet Lowenthal, became a friend of DOB through the mailing. She would figure prominently in the organization a few years later when she and her husband, at the behest of the Daughters of Bilitis, prepared an amicus curiae brief in *Vallerga v. Azar*, an important California appeals case that worked to secure the right to public assembly for homosexuals.

Between 1955 and 1970, the Daughters of Bilitis, which took its name from an obscure French poem about woman–woman love ("Songs of Bilitis" by Pierre Louys), grew into a national lesbian rights organization. Chapters emerged in New York, Boston, Philadelphia, Los Angeles, Providence, San Diego, Chicago, New Orleans, Dallas, and Cleveland. The San Francisco chapter of DOB established an infrastructure that allowed the organization to grow beyond its initial goals; it allowed a feminist voice to emerge in lesbian and gay politics; and it provided a space for lesbian activists to converge. It also provided a venue for dialogue among lesbian generations, across male and female homophile organizations, and between gay and straight feminists. The Daughters of Bilitis protected its vision of education and information, and it saw the increased visibility of lesbians translate directly into enhanced social services and civil rights.

BIBLIOGRAPHY

Faderman, Lillian. *Odd Girls and Twilight Lovers: A History of Lesbian Life in Twentieth-Century America.* 1992.
Martin, Del, and Phyllis Lyon. *Lesbian/Woman.* Rev. ed. 1991.

Nan Alamilla Boyd

Davis, Angela

(1944–   ), civil rights activist, educator, and author.

Born the daughter of middle-class educators in Birmingham, Alabama, Angela Yvonne Davis grew up in the midst of the violent and oppressive system of JIM CROW SEGREGATION and witnessed the development of the burgeoning civil rights movement in her community. As a young woman, Davis had a broad education at home and abroad, which allowed her to develop a radical critique of the interactions of RACE, CLASS, and gender in American society.

While pursuing a graduate degree in California, Davis became involved in the BLACK POWER movement and organized on behalf of the STUDENT NONVIOLENT COORDINATING COMMITTEE (SNCC) and the BLACK PANTHER PARTY. In 1968, Davis joined the black cell of the COMMUNIST PARTY in the Los Angeles area. Because she was a communist, Davis was targeted by state officials, who sought to remove her from her teaching position at UCLA. Subsequently, Davis was forced to turn her attentions to defending her political rights in the face of state repression accompanied by threats, police harassment, and FEDERAL BUREAU OF INVESTIGATION (FBI) scrutiny. The attempt to oust Davis made national headlines.

Angela Davis, activist, professor, and Communist Party vice presidential candidate in 1980 and 1984, at a 1986 press conference. (CORBIS)

Davis used the media attention to focus the national spotlight on her political interests, namely, the campaign to free the Soledad Brothers: George Jackson, John Clutchette, and Fleeta Drumgo, prisoners who had organized for revolutionary change in Soledad Prison. When a prison guard was killed, the Soledad Brothers were convicted and sentenced to die for the murder despite a lack of evidence tying them to the crime.

During the battle to free the Soledad Brothers, Jonathan Jackson, George Jackson's seventeen year-old brother, attempted the violent takeover of a California courtroom, in August 1970; and gunfire from San Quentin guards killed Jonathan Jackson and Judge James Haley. Davis was not involved in this event; but Jackson had used a weapon registered in Davis's name during the takeover, so the FBI placed Davis on its most-wanted list for the murder of a federal judge. After two months as a fugitive, Davis was captured and charged with the crime.

While incarcerated before her trial, Davis experienced the brutal system she had worked fervently to expose; but she was bolstered by remarkable amounts of support from the American public. A wide coalition of people that crossed racial and political lines fought to free Angela Davis. During the late 1960s and early 1970s Davis became a unique figure, a black woman who was a lightning rod for issues of race, class, and gender.

On June 4, 1971, Angela Davis was acquitted of charges of kidnapping, murder, and conspiracy. Although the mass movement organized to free her had been successful, Davis was devastated by the August 1971 death of George Jackson, who was killed under mysterious circumstances in Soledad Prison. After her acquittal, Davis resumed her struggle on behalf of prisoners.

Davis has continued to speak and work for the rights of others. As both a professor of the history of consciousness at the University of California, Santa Cruz, and an activist, Davis educates and organizes on behalf of African Americans, women of color, and prisoners. Davis has demonstrated a lifetime commitment to protesting oppression of all forms.

BIBLIOGRAPHY

Davis, Angela Y., ed. *If They Come in the Morning: Voices of Resistance.* 1971.

Davis, Angela Y. *The Black Woman's Role in the Community of Slaves.* 1971.

Davis, Angela Y. *Angela Davis: An Autobiography.* 1974.

Davis, Angela Y. *Women, Race and Class.* 1981.

Davis, Angela Y. *Women, Culture and Politics.* 1989.

Davis, Angela Y. *Blues Legacies and Black Feminism: Gertrude "Ma" Rainey, Bessie Smith, and Billie Holiday.* 1998

Blair L. Murphy

Davis, Benjamin Jefferson, Jr.

(1903–1964), lawyer, journalist.

Benjamin Davis, Jr., received an LL.B. degree from Harvard University in 1929. He began his law practice in Atlanta, where he gained international fame as the principal attorney for the young communist Angelo Herndon, who had been charged with violating an 1861 Georgia law against slave insurrections. Herndon was arrested in 1932 after leading a protest demonstration of black and white workers and indicted for attempting to incite an insurrection. The prosecution claimed that Herndon's mere possession of communist literature was, if he were convicted, punishable by death. Davis's defense rested on the grounds that the insurrection statute was unconstitutional and that Herndon's First Amendment rights had been denied. Herndon was convicted and sentenced to eighteen years in prison. In 1935 Davis abandoned his law practice, joined the Communist Party, moved to New York

City, and became a leading spokesman of the party as editor of the *Harlem Liberator* and, in 1936, as staff writer for the *Daily Worker*, the official news organ of the American Communist Party. Davis also had joined forces with William L. Patterson, the International Labor Defense, and the Communist Party in a five-year struggle to have the Herndon decision overturned. In 1937 the U.S. Supreme Court invalidated the Georgia statute. In New York City, Davis was elected to the City Council in 1943 and, in 1945, ran and won on the Communist Party ticket. In 1949 he lost a bid for a third term and was expelled from the City Council in November 1949 after being indicted, along with other Communist Party members, in July 1948 for violating the 1940 Smith Act. Davis was convicted and spent three years and four months in prison. In 1962 he was indicted for violation of the 1950 McCARRAN ACT. Davis died before the 1962 indictment trial began.

BIBLIOGRAPHY

Cruse, Harold. *The Crisis of the Negro Intellectual.* 1967.

Horne, Gerald. *Black Liberation/Red Scare: Ben Davis and the Communist Party.* 1994.

Martin, Charles H. *The Angelo Herndon Case and Southern Justice.* 1976.

Phillip McGuire

Davis, Benjamin O., Sr.

(1880–1970), first African-American general.

Benjamin O. Davis, Sr., joined the U.S. Army in 1898. In 1940 he became the first African American promoted to the rank of brigadier general. During World War II, Davis was assigned to the Office of the Inspector General. As a member of the Office, he grappled with the problem of segregation and racial discrimination suffered by black soldiers. Davis's investigations of black complaints, however, revealed optimism and high morale among black soldiers when in fact their morale was low throughout the war. In fact, Davis almost succeeded in blocking various recommendations submitted to the War Department by William H. HASTIE (the first black Civilian Aide to Secretary of War Henry L. Stimson, 1940–1942) which aimed to eliminate or modify the racial policies of the Army. Some evidence indicated that the War Department's appointment of Davis to the Inspector General's Office was made because the department knew Davis would not seriously challenge the Army's basic policy of segregation. While a few historians view Davis as having a major impact on race relations and used quiet diplomacy to effect policy changes that eventually led to the dismantling of segregation and racial discrimination

Benjamin O. Davis, Sr., the first African-American general in the U.S. Army, during World War II. (U.S. Army)

in the Army, he was an appeasing accommodationist in the tradition of Booker T. WASHINGTON who accepted segregation and racial discrimination of black soldiers. In reality, Davis was an adjuster of racial ills and black soldier complaints rather than a leading voice for racial justice and social change within the Army. He retired in 1948.

BIBLIOGRAPHY

Dalfiume, Richard M. *Desegregation of the U.S. Armed Forces: Fighting on Two Fronts, 1939–1953.* 1969.
Fletcher, Marvin E. *America's First Black General: Benjamin O. Davis, Sr. 1880–1970.* 1989.
McGuire, Phillip. *He, Too, Spoke for Democracy: Judge Hastie, World War II, and the Black Soldier.* 1988.

Phillip McGuire

Dawes Severalty Act

The General Allotment Act of 1887, commonly called the Dawes Severalty Act, was the culmination of a long-standing effort to assimilate American Indians into mainstream society. Fundamental to this Americanization process was the breaking up of communally held tribal lands and assigning Indians individual tracts of land to which they would have exclusive ownership. It was believed that allotting land in severalty this way would awaken wants in the Indians, thereby creating ambition and a desire for property. As Indians were transformed from tribal members into self-supporting yeoman farmers, the government could reduce its relationship with and expenditures to Native Americans.

Though allotment plans began as early as 1633, a comprehensive effort emerged only after the Civil War. In the 1870s, groups of reformers known as the "Friends of the Indian" called for the dissolution of the reservations. They argued that segregating Indians on reservations created "ethnic slums" and prevented Indians from learning the skills necessary to compete in American society. A land-hungry public that wanted to divest Indians of their lands also supported breaking up the reservations.

Working closely with Indian reform groups, Massachusetts Senator Henry Dawes became the principal supporter of allotment in CONGRESS. Its most prominent opponent, Colorado Senator Henry Teller, argued that the diversity among Indian tribes would make a universal allotment bill unworkable. Such sweeping legislation could not take into account variant geography or Indian traditions. Though President Grover Cleveland noted that allotment in severalty was just another means of separating Indians from their land, he signed the Dawes Act on February 8, 1887.

Initially exempting the Five Civilized Tribes, among others, the Dawes Act authorized the allotment of one hundred sixty acres to the head of each Indian family, eighty acres to each single person over age eighteen and each orphan under eighteen, and forty acres to other single persons under eighteen. Allottees became U.S. citizens, but the government held their lands in trust for twenty-five years. After the trust period, Indians would receive the land in fee simple. The government would select allotments for individuals who did not choose their own. Once Indians received their allotments, the Secretary of the Interior could negotiate with the tribe to purchase remaining reservation lands. Millions of acres of Indian lands were now considered surplus and opened to white settlement.

Congress gradually made numerous changes to the Dawes Act and loosened restrictions. Allotments became equalized at eighty acres for all Indians, and Indians were permitted to lease their lands. The 1906 Burke Act empowered the Secretary of the Interior to grant fee simple patents of allotments to Indians deemed competent to handle their affairs even before the twenty-five-year trusteeship ended.

By 1934, when the INDIAN REORGANIZATION ACT ended the allotment program, hope had given way to failure. Fraudulent practices by whites and the sale of surplus lands had reduced the Indian land base from 138 million to 48 million acres. Of the lands the Indians retained, approximately one-half were desert or semiarid. Almost one-half century of allotment left nearly 100,000 Indians landless and many others impoverished.

BIBLIOGRAPHY

Carlson, Leonard A. *Indians, Bureaucrats, and Land: The Dawes Act and the Decline of Indian Farming.* 1981.
Gibson, Arrell Morgan. *The American Indian: Prehistory to the Present.* 1980.
Prucha, Francis Paul. *The Great Father: The United States Government and the American Indians.* 1984.
Sturtevant, William C., ed. *Handbook of North American Indians*, Vol. 4. *History of Indian–White Relations.* 1988.
Washburn, Wilcomb E. *Red Man's Land/White Man's Law* 1995.

L. Patrick Goines

Deacons for Defense and Justice

White resistance to the civil rights movement in Louisiana was especially characterized by vigilante violence. By 1964, civil rights workers from the STUDENT NONVIOLENT COORDINATING COMMITTEE (SNCC) and the CONGRESS OF RACIAL EQUALITY (CORE) came under severe attacks. In Jonesboro, Louisiana, black people armed themselves to protect their communities and civil rights workers. KU KLUX KLAN activities became so rampant that in July 1964 a dozen black men organized an armed group called the Deacons for Defense and Justice. These men were over the age of twenty-one; most were in their thirties and forties. Some had military experience from World War II and the Korean War. All were disciplined in self-defense tactics and maneuvers. Their emergence in Jonesboro became a major deterrent to Klan violence.

However, it was in Bogalusa, Louisiana, that the Deacons made their name as the "military" arm of the Bogalusa Civic and Voters League, the local organization that organized and led the civil rights movement in Washington parish. The Deacons of Bogalusa were more militant than their Jonesboro brothers, because Bogalusa was more notorious than Jonesboro for organized violence against black people, police officers who were sympathetic to the Klan, and a mayor who demonstrated very little, if any, control over the police.

On February 1, 1965, the Bogalusa chapter of the Deacons for Defense and Justice was established to provide an armed and ready deployment in black communities and to monitor the police and the Klan. The Bogalusa Deacons quickly became a major force; patrolling black communities, warning the police against random intervention against black people, and exchanging gunfire.

The Bogalusa Deacons were led by one Charles Sims, a fast-talking, streetwise insurance salesman, who was well known for his wit and marksmanship. Sims was generally regarded as a "dedicated man, who would take a back seat to no man." To Sims the Deacons "were not just a militant organization that believed in weapons, but were formed to protect our people." Whites in Bogalusa knew and understood Sims's effectiveness in the black community.

The *Bogalusa Daily News* was bitterly opposed to the Deacons and Sims. Five months after the Bogalusa Deacons were established, the *Daily News* editorialized that "Charles Sims is always in the middle of racial strife. He describes himself as an insurance agent, but his main occupation these days is [as] war leader of a militant group of Negro men always willing to fight for their belief in the civil rights movement."

By the end of 1965, the Bogalusa Deacons had gained legendary status, because Klan violence had virtually ceased. In large measure, the Deacons effectively used deceptive tactics against the Klan and police. Inflating their numbers and weapons, the Deacons deterred the Klan in its violent activities.

At its zenith the Bogalusa Deacons had approximately two dozen members and no more than hunting rifles and pistols for weapons, but they were well organized in their effort to protect black neighborhoods. Not only did the Deacons defend the black communities against white terrorism, but they also guarded against Uncle Tomism within the black communities.

The Bogalusa Deacons had a real impact in helping to remove the fear that white violence had created in the hearts and minds of black people. They were not a symbolic organization, but rather, they were strategic to the Bogalusa Civic and Voters League's goal of ending de jure and de facto segregation. There were also chapters in Homer and Tallulah, Louisiana.

Additional chapters of the Deacons were formed in 1965 in Alabama, Mississippi, Florida, South Carolina, and North Carolina, and in April 1966 a chapter was formed outside of the South, in Chicago, Illinois. The Deacons went into sharp decline by 1968, but their legacy was lasting. Their militancy made them a model of emulation for California's Bay Area BLACK PANTHER PARTY and other revolutionary nationalist organizations of the late 1960s.

BIBLIOGRAPHY

Feinberg, Leslie. "Deacons for Defense and Justice." *Workers World* (June 20, 1996). Reprint available from Workers World News Service, http://www.workers.org.

Peterson, Franklyn. "The Deacons: They Fight for Survival." *Sepia* (May 1967): 10–14.

Rickey Hill

Dees, Morris Seligman, Jr.

(1936–   ), lawyer, civil rights activist.

The son of an Alabama tenant farmer and cotton gin operator near Mount Meigs, Alabama, Dees grew up among sharecroppers victimized by racism and poverty; his early goal was financial success rather than justice. In high school, he raised farm animals and earned college money. At the University of Alabama, where he earned his law degree in 1960, he bought property and established a mail order book business. While practicing law in Montgomery, he built one of the South's largest publishing companies. In 1969, he sold the business and committed himself to fighting for Alabama's downtrodden minorities.

In 1971, with partner Joseph J. Levin, Jr., he established the Southern Poverty Law Center (SPLC) to counter discrimination against the poor by legal action and education. In the 1990s, the SPLC expanded existing education and legal protection programs, but emphasized exposing hate groups and militias. Winning civil damages proved to be an innovative tool for bankrupting hate groups.

Dees used his direct mail experience as finance chairman for liberal political campaigns—those of George McGovern in 1972, Jimmy Carter in 1976, and Edward Kennedy in 1980. His publications include *A Season for Justice* (1991), *Hate on Trial* (1993), and *Gathering Storm: America's Militia Threat* (1996). He has earned awards from groups as diverse as the Alabama Future Farmers of America, the JAYCEES, civil rights groups, the National Education Association, and the University of Alabama.

BIBLIOGRAPHY

Dees, Morris. *A Season for Justice.* 1991.
Southern Poverty Law Center at http://www.splcenter. org/centerinfo/morris.html (12/31/98).

J. Herschel Barnhill

Morris Seligman Dees, Jr., attorney, advocate for the poor, and co-founder of the Southern Poverty Law Center. (Archive Photos, Inc.)

Delany, Martin Robison

(1812–1885), author and intellectual.

Martin Delany was born free in Charles Town, Virginia (now Charleston, West Virginia) to a free seamstress and a plantation slave. Delany's life is distinguished by his wide range of abilities and interests. In the early 1840s, Delany studied medicine and edited one of the first African-American newspapers, the *Mystery*. From 1847 to 1849, he coedited the *North Star* with Frederick Douglass. In 1850–1851, Delany attended Harvard Medical School; he was asked to leave after white students protested his presence. Delany's pioneering work on the predicament of black Americans appeared in 1852: *The Condition, Elevation, Emigration, and Destiny of the Colored People of the United States, Politically Considered.* Delany's 1854 address, *The Political Destiny of the Colored Race,* argued for the wisdom and necessity of African-American emigration. Delany explored the Niger Valley in 1859, seeking land for his emigrationist plan in West Africa. In this busy period, he published his novel, *Blake* (1859–1862) and the *Official Report of the Niger Valley Exploration Party* (1861).

During the Civil War, Delany recruited African Americans for the Union army, and in 1865 he was

Major Martin Delany, M.D., author and Freemason, was the first African American to become a commissioned officer in the United States Colored Troops during the Civil War. (Archive Photos)

BIBLIOGRAPHY

Griffith, Cyril E. *The African Dream: Martin R. Delany and the Emergence of Pan-African Thought.* 1975.

Levine, Robert S. *Martin Delany, Frederick Douglass, and the Politics of Representative Identity.* 1997.

Painter, Nell Irwin. "Martin R. Delany: Elitism and Black Nationalism." In *Black Leaders of the Nineteenth Century,* edited by Leon Litwack and August Meier. 1988.

Rollin, Frank (pseudonym for Frances A. Rollin). *Life and Public Services of Martin R. Delany.* 1883.

Sterling, Dorothy. *The Making of an Afro-American: Martin Robison Delany, 1812–1885.* 1971.

Ullman, Victor. *Martin R. Delany: The Beginnings of Back Nationalism.* 1971.

Gregg D. Crane

Delaware

The history of civil rights in Delaware has been largely shaped by developments prior to the Civil War. Slavery was introduced to Delaware in 1639 and reached its zenith during the late colonial period when 20 to 25 percent of the colony's population was enslaved. A strong manumission movement began during the American Revolution and by 1810 approximately three-fourths of the state's African Americans were free.

Although on the eve of the Civil War only 8 percent of its blacks remained enslaved, Delaware continued to resist the abolition of slavery until the THIRTEENTH AMENDMENT forced it and KENTUCKY—the last two surviving slave states—to abandon the institution in December 1865.

During the antebellum years, Delaware led all other states in the percentage of its population made up of free blacks. By 1840 the figure reached 22 percent, which was far higher than that found in any other state. White paranoia about the large percentage of free blacks was fortified by the news of Nat TURNER's Rebellion in Virginia in 1831. Driven by racial fears, Delaware's General Assembly passed a series of BLACK CODES that denied the right of free African Americans to vote, to attend public schools, or to serve on juries. For free blacks, testifying before courts, owning guns, leaving the state, and assembling in groups were seriously restricted "privileges." After 1849, refusing the offer of employment from whites could lead to being sold into servitude for one year. An out-of-state observer noted that Delaware's antebellum free blacks enjoyed only "a mongrel liberty, a mere mock freedom." Indeed, in few other states in the South were free African Americans as oppressed as in Delaware.

In the decades following the Civil War, Delaware's Democratic Party won election after election by committing itself to the state's antebellum tradition of

commissioned a major. After the war, Delany worked for the Freedmen's Bureau in South Carolina. Disenchanted with RECONSTRUCTION, Delany subsequently championed Southern home rule and even became a supporter of Wade Hampton, an ex-Confederate running for governor of South Carolina. Delany's interest in emigration reemerged in the late 1870s. In 1879, he published *Principia of Ethnology: The Origin of Races and Color.*

Certain themes appear throughout Delany's varied career and writings: the social and political necessity of gleaning black leadership from a well-spoken, cultured, and intellectual elite; the economic ideal of creating African-American prosperity through skill, energy, and ingenuity; and the nationalist goal of creating a homeland for a transnational or pan-African coalition of people of color whose rights are guaranteed and protected by their own political power, not the supposed benevolence of a white majority.

denying civil rights to blacks. It was only in 1901, when the Democrats were no longer in power, that Delaware finally got around to ratifying the Thirteenth, FOURTEENTH, and FIFTEENTH AMENDMENTS.

When most of the former slave states demonstrated a blatant disregard for the civil rights of African Americans at the end of the Civil War, the federal government used its army to temporarily "reconstruct" their governments and their racial policies. Because of its loyalty to the Union during the Civil War, however, the federal government did not force "RECONSTRUCTION" on Delaware.

In 1875 the Delaware General Assembly finally established public schools for blacks, but until 1922 insisted that they be funded primarily by taxes placed only on the state's African-American population. The resulting segregated black schools were so underfunded that they were deplorable. From 1922 to 1926 Pierre S. du Pont improved the situation by personally spending between five and six million dollars to build eighty-six schools for blacks. Despite this and other advances of the 1920s, schools for blacks continued to be the impoverished stepchildren of the state's public school system.

In 1950, black attorney Louis L. Redding convinced the Delaware Court of Chancery to order the integration of the University of Delaware. Two years later Redding successfully challenged public school segregation in Delaware in two cases that were also argued before the Delaware Court of Chancery. The state appealed the rulings to the U.S. Supreme Court, which combined them with three other cases as BROWN V. BOARD OF EDUCATION. Despite the *Brown* ruling in 1954, which declared public school segregation unconstitutional, it was not until 1967 that Delaware's last segregated school was closed. In northern Delaware, de facto school segregation continued until 1978, when federal court-ordered busing brought white students into Wilmington and black students to suburban schools.

Theaters and restaurants were also racially segregated in Delaware until the early 1960s. Race-restricted housing sales and rent contracts were not outlawed by state law until 1969.

During most of the late nineteenth century, poll taxes and physical intimidation kept potential African-American voters at home. Although participation by black voters increased in the early twentieth century, in rural and small town Delaware they were nevertheless politically powerless.

In Wilmington, African Americans were a little more successful in exercising political power. In 1901 they elected Thomas Postles as the first in a continuous line of black city councilmen. It was not until 1948, however, that the first African American was elected

to Delaware's General Assembly. By 1992, Wilmington's African Americans represented a majority of the city's population and elected James Sills as the city's first black mayor, and then reelected him four years later.

Delaware's women also sustained a long struggle to gain their civil rights. Until well after the Civil War, Delaware College (the University of Delaware), the state's only postsecondary institution, refused to admit female students. Although finally admitting women in 1872, the college excluded female students after 1885. In 1914 an affiliated women's college was opened in Newark, just south of the Delaware College campus; but it was not until 1945 that the Women's College was closed and the University of Delaware's classrooms were gender integrated. By contrast, Delaware State College (Delaware State University), the state's historically black college, admitted women with its first students in 1892.

As elsewhere in early America, property rights were denied to married women of Delaware. In 1865 and in subsequent years, the Delaware General Assembly enacted a series of laws that granted some property rights to married women.

For women, gaining the right to vote was a much more difficult struggle. The Delaware Constitution of 1792 specifically banned women from voting. Beginning in 1869, Mary Ann Sorden of Greenwood led the voices demanding the franchise for Delaware's women. Subsequently, however, a petition to the state constitutional convention of 1897 and numerous requests to the state legislature were unsuccessful. The establishment of a suffragist office (the Congressional Union) in Wilmington in 1913, under the directorship of Mabel Vernon, and a suffragist parade through the city the following year increased statewide support for women's suffrage.

By late March of 1920, ratification by only one more state legislature was needed to make the NINETEENTH AMENDMENT the law of the land, and Delaware seemed on the verge of providing that final vote. From March to early June the eyes of the nation focused on tiny Delaware as supporters and opponents of women's suffrage poured into Dover, putting pressure on the General Assembly and creating a circus atmosphere. However, as it had done for the Thirteenth, Fourteenth, and Fifteenth Amendments, Delaware's General Assembly refused to ratify the Nineteenth Amendment. It took Tennessee's ratification of the Nineteenth Amendment a few months later to give Delaware's women the right to vote.

Legal protection for the civil rights of Delaware's gay and lesbian community has been very recent and is incomplete. Although sexual orientation was added to the state's hate crimes list in 1997, there are no state laws protecting the gay and lesbian community against discrimination in housing, employment, credit, and public accommodations. Delaware does not recognize same-sex marriages performed within the state, and in 1996 the General Assembly passed a law prohibiting the recognition of same-sex marriages performed in other states.

BIBLIOGRAPHY

Hiller, Amy M. "The Disfranchisement of Delaware Negroes in the Late Nineteenth Century." *Delaware History*, 13, 2 (1968): 124–170.

Hoffecker, Carol E. *Beneath Thy Guiding Hand: A History of Women at the University of Delaware*, 1994.

Hoffecker, Carol E. "Delaware's Women Suffrage Campaign." *Delaware History* 20 (1982–1983): 149–167.

Hoffecker, Carol E. "The Politics of Exclusion: Blacks in Late Nineteenth-Century Wilmington, Delaware." *Delaware History* 16 (1974): 60–89.

Kee, Ed. "The Brown Decision and Milford, Delaware, 1954–1965." *Delaware History* 27, 4 (1997–1998): 205–243.

Livesay, Harold C. "Delaware Negroes, 1865–1915." *Delaware History* 13, 2 (1968): 87–123.

Williams, William H. *Slavery and Freedom in Delaware, 1639–1865*. 1996.

Wolters, Raymond. *The Burden of Brown: Thirty Years of School Desegregation*. 1984.

Woolard, Annette. *A Family of Firsts: The Reddings of Delaware*. Ph.D. dissertation, University of Delaware. 1963.

Woolard, Annette. "Parker v. University of Delaware: The Desegregation of Higher Education in Delaware." *Delaware History*, 22 (196): 111–126.

Williams H. Williams

Deloria, Vine, Jr.

(1933–), Native American activist, author.

Vine Deloria, Jr., earned recognition as a literary/political activist among Native Americans in the civil rights movement of the 1960s. First among his similarly distinguished forbears was François Des Laurias, son of a French trader and a tribal mother, who accepted federal designation as a band chief for mixed-bloods on the Yankton Sioux Reservation. Philip J. Deloria succeeded his father as chief in 1877, then relinquished the office and gained credentials as an Episcopal priest to assume responsibility for the Episcopal mission system on the Standing Rock Reservation. At the new location, Philip enrolled himself and his family, which included Vine Deloria, Sr. (also an Episcopal priest), and Ella Cara Deloria (an anthropologist). Vine Deloria, Jr., became a fourth-generation activist when he chose careers in law and academia.

Custer Died for Your Sins (1969), *We Talk, You Listen* (1970), and *God Is Red* (1973) plus a dozen other substantial titles educated a generation of students and

Vine Deloria, Jr., Native American literary figure and political activist, served as executive director for the National Congress of American Indians. (The Library of Congress)

scholars about the struggles of Native-American peoples, their histories, cultures, and societies. The name of Vine Deloria also appeared in the Indian Council Fire annual selection of extraordinary tribal leaders. He served as executive director of the NATIONAL CONGRESS OF AMERICAN INDIANS, worked for the National Office for Rights of the Indigent, and became a member on the Board of Inquiry on Hunger and Malnutrition in the United States.

Clearly, the younger Vine Deloria emerged as a leader among influential civil rights advocates. He also earned recognition from academic peers while he educated a generation of young scholars at the universities of Arizona and Colorado.

BIBLIOGRAPHY

Biolsi, Thomas, and Larry J. Zimmerman, eds. *Indian and Anthropologists: Vine Deloria, Jr., and the Critique of Anthropology.* 1997.

Herbert T. Hoover

Deming, Barbara

(1917–1984), political activist, writer.

Born and raised a child of privilege, Barbara Deming became one of the United States' most well-known radical activists and writers for peace, justice, and equality. Her life and interests spanned the major movements of this century: she marched and worked for disarmament and then for civil rights; she protested the war in VIETNAM; she struggled finally for WOMEN'S RIGHTS and for GAY AND LESBIAN RIGHTS.

Barbara Deming was the second of four children, the only girl, born into a family that was influenced by her mother's association with an artistic group of friends based in Greenwich Village, New York City, and by her father's association with Republican politics. All four children were educated at the Quaker Friends School of Fifteenth Street Meeting, in New York. During Deming's teens, the family owned a home across the Hudson River from New York, where friends included many writers, poets, and artists. At Bennington College in Vermont, Deming majored in literature and drama. She received her B.A. degree in 1938 and an M.A. in drama from Case Western Reserve University in Cleveland, Ohio, in 1940.

In 1959 Barbara Deming and her partner Mary Meigs traveled to India, where Barbara became interested in the work of Mohandas GANDHI on nonviolence. An encounter with Fidel Castro during the newly established Cuban Revolution in 1960 moved her focus to peace and justice. Within months of returning to the United States she had become involved

Barbara Deming, activist and writer for peace. (Archive Photos)

with the Committee for Nonviolent Action and was writing articles for *The Nation* and other movement journals.

In her earliest writing Deming rejected the notion that there was more than one movement, stressing that the deeper issue was whether or not one was going to be willing to respect one's fellow man. In 1962, when advisors for the Nashville, Tennessee, to Washington, D.C., Walk for Peace told the peace walkers not to walk as an integrated group and to talk only about peace, Deming could not agree. By the end of that walk, Deming succeeded in convincing other walkers that they should be integrated—which they soon were. Later that year, Deming corresponded with Martin Luther KING, JR., urging him to join the struggle for racial equality to the struggle for peace worldwide. He replied to her, as he had to others who inquired similarly, that the best help for peace would be to register the nearly five million disfranchised Negro voters. Deming could not disagree with King's analysis and began to urge, instead, that the Peace Movement join the Civil Rights Movement by integrating all of their marches.

Barbara Deming's book *Prison Notes* is an account of the 1963–64 *Montreal to Guantánamo* walk. While participating in the walk, she and thirty-five others were arrested in Albany, Georgia, for demanding that they be allowed to walk as an integrated group. In jail for twenty-seven days, the peace walkers fasted while others negotiated for their release without agreeing that they would walk as segregated groups. When they were released, they resumed their walk in the place where they had been arrested, and after some tense telephone calls, were allowed to proceed out of town. Their commitment to nonviolence, the strategies they employed in bringing attention to their cause, and their tenacity in achieving their goal had a lasting effect on the ALBANY MOVEMENT and other civil rights groups in the South.

BIBLIOGRAPHY

Deming, Barbara. *Prison Notes.* 1966. Reprinted as *Prisons That Could Not Hold.* 1995.
Deming, Barbara. *Revolution and Equilibrium.* 1971.
Deming, Barbara. *We Are All Part of One Another: A Barbara Deming Reader.* 1984.
McDaniel, Judith. "Introduction: The Women She Loved." In *I Change, I Change: The Poetry of Barbara Deming.* 1996.

Barbara Deming's papers are primarily housed at the Schlesinger Women's History Library at Radcliffe College in Cambridge, Mass. A few early papers are at Boston University's Mugar Library. The papers are open to scholars and historians.

Judith McDaniel

Democracy

Modern democracy, as white people in Europe and America understood it, originated in the United States sometime between the late eighteenth and early nineteenth centuries, when British and colonial American precedents coalesced in new definitions of citizenship and ideals of popular self-government. Some scholars who find the essence of democracy in challenges to authority believe it began in the 1770s with the American Revolution. Others who emphasize the importance of a legal structure date the start of democracy in 1791 with the adoption of the first ten amendments to the United States Constitution—the Bill of Rights. Whatever their judgment on those years, however, almost all scholars agree that the assertiveness, the organization, and the sheer number of white men entering public life during the first quarter of the nineteenth century transformed American politics.

At the core of nineteenth-century democracy lay the assumption that upon reaching adulthood white men would direct their own working lives individually and would govern themselves collectively as equal members of the sovereign people. Women, dependent by custom and law, did not qualify for this fraternal democracy, and slavery, denying all claims to self-determination, stood as its very opposite. Although more and more white men came to hate slavery before the Civil War, few of them accepted blacks as potential members of the sovereign people. Only a handful of free black men in New England had the right to vote.

Civil War, and the South's RECONSTRUCTION following it, dramatically altered these relationships. The THIRTEENTH AMENDMENT (1865), ending slavery, expressed the triumph of self-directed work; the FOURTEENTH AMENDMENT (1868), laying broad ground rules for citizenship, specified men's right to vote; and the FIFTEENTH AMENDMENT (1870), addressing racial discrimination, reaffirmed black men's right to vote. Though violence and prejudice often overrode the law, these changes established national standards of inclusion that benefited especially those black men who left the South. At the same time, constitutional voting rights just for men formalized women's inferior status. Stung by this humiliation, former abolitionists such as Elizabeth Cady STANTON and Susan B. ANTHONY who had once argued from principles of universal equality now asserted the superiority of white women over black men in their campaign for women's suffrage.

That became a routine argument as the longstanding white bias in American democracy expanded and hardened during the first quarter of the twentieth century. States across the South disfranchised blacks and severely limited their rights under the law, a trend the federal government did nothing to resist. In fact, its colonial rule over the Philippine Islands created an additional category of inferior subjects, and both state and federal laws denied citizenship to Asian immigrants.

These efforts to exclude people of color went hand in hand with changes that generally restricted access to the governing process. As new administrative agencies removed government further from ordinary citizens and new rules complicated the act of voting, turnouts fell from 80 percent of those eligible in the presidential election of 1896 to less than 50 percent in 1924. Partial recoveries around 1940 and again around 1960 did not alter the long-term trend. Voter turnout in 1996 approximated that of 1924, and off-year congressional elections attracted substantially lower numbers. Throughout the twentieth century the old sources of citizen authority eroded. Fewer and fewer adults directed their own work; more and more functions of government fell beyond their control.

If strengthening a distant federal government made more citizens apathetic, it also qualified more of them to participate. White women profited first. A rush of support coming out of WORLD WAR I enacted the NINETEENTH AMENDMENT, or the Woman's Suffrage amendment (1920). Many women of color, however, did not share in those benefits until restrictions on Asian-American citizenship were lifted after WORLD WAR II and, at the climax of a long struggle, the VOTING RIGHTS ACT (1965) brought southern African-Americans into the electorate.

As turnouts dropped, individual rights increasingly replaced electoral politics at the heart of twentieth-century American democracy. By the 1920s it was already common to describe citizens as a crowd of individuals who voted to protect their rights as consumers. By World War II, other popular yardsticks were measuring individual rights against the prospects of a secure old age, the freedoms that President Franklin D. ROOSEVELT was promoting, and the Bill of Rights, which the United States SUPREME COURT was now enforcing against state and local as well as federal violations. In the second half of the twentieth century an explosion of rights raised the standards of fairness in the workplace, protection for unpopular speech, justice at the hands of the law, and malpractice by professionals. By 1990 the disabled won their own federal bill of rights, and many state courts were developing one for children. At the end of the century, the most popular American test of democracy in another country was its record on human rights.

Giving the individual center stage in American democracy left a number of important issues unresolved. Some of these sought boundaries for individual rights. Which aspects of human reproduction belonged with private rights and which with public policy? Did democratic individualism include a right to die? Were special provisions to compensate previously disadvantaged groups compatible with democratic individualism? At the end of the century, a growing body of critics who complained of an excessive individualism advocated greater attention to collective rights, community traditions, and public controls.

Another set of issues returned to the first principle of American democracy, popular self-government, with concerns about the relation between money and power. Did the expense of campaigning turn elected officials into representatives of wealth rather than of their constituents? Did the dependence of mass media on advertising undermine independent criticism and shrink differences of opinion? Limiting the role of money in politics faced two major obstacles: resistance from the beneficiaries of the existing system, and in-

difference from those who thought the worst of all public officials. Evidence that a majority of adults considered the government not only hostile to their welfare but also impervious to reform pointed to the most serious problem facing American democracy on the eve of a new century.

BIBLIOGRAPHY

Boorstin, Daniel J. *The Americans: The Democratic Experience.* 1973.

DuBois, Ellen Carol. *Feminism and Suffrage: The Emergence of an Independent Women's Movement in America, 1848–1869.* 1978.

Kettner, Joseph H. *The Development of American Citizenship, 1608–1870.* 1978.

Kousser, J. Morgan. *The Shaping of Southern Politics: Suffrage Restriction and the Establishment of the One-Party South, 1880–1910.* 1974.

McGerr, Michael E. *The Decline of Popular Politics: The American North, 1865–1928.* 1986.

Sandel, Michael J. *Democracy's Discontent: America in Search of a Public Philosophy.* 1996.

Silbey, Joel H. *The American Political Nation, 1838–1893.* 1991.

Sitkoff, Harvard. *The Struggle for Black Equality, 1954–1992.* Rev. ed. 1993.

Sunstein, Cass R. *Democracy and the Problem of Free Speech.* 1993.

Wiebe, Robert H. *Self-Rule: A Cultural History of American Democracy.* 1995.

Wood, Gordon S. *The Radicalism of the American Revolution.* 1991.

Robert H. Wiebe

Democratic Party

In the first decade of the American Republic, the Federalists dominated politics. They believed in an active central government that would pursue policies enhancing commerce and industry, with the larger aim to make America an important and powerful nation. The Democratic Party, its roots among the anti-Federalists of the Founding Era, formed in opposition.

The Democrats' first president was Thomas Jefferson, elected in 1800. He envisioned a country of self-reliant small farmers and tradesmen who would govern themselves at the state and local level. Essentially, the Democrats were founded as a party dedicated to reining-in a potentially too-powerful central government so that ordinary people would have control over their own lives in their communities. Democrats believed in the principle of state and local control of nearly all public affairs—this has been frequently referred to as STATES' RIGHTS in the political lexicon. This philosophy reflected well the then-federation nature of the American political system, which allowed states nearly total discretion in most public matters. The Democrats tended to be most popular in rural and farm-oriented areas of the country, particular the agrarian Southern states.

A crucial turning point in the history of the party occurred after the Civil War in the 1860s. Republican President Abraham Lincoln successfully reunited the Union, but in the aftermath of the war and Lincoln's assassination, "RADICAL REPUBLICANS" put in place in the South an occupying force during the so-called RECONSTRUCTION period (1865–1877). These congressional Republicans instituted governance by Northern Republicans, carpetbaggers, and some of the newly freed slaves with the twin aims of punishing the South and guaranteeing the rights of the freedmen. This did not sit well with the Southern Democratic elite, who finally, in 1877, cut a deal to end the occupation and rapidly worked toward reinstating something resembling the status quo ante in race relations. The Republicans eventually lost interest in working to secure the rights of African Americans in the South in the 1890s, and the Southern Democrats put in place a one-party rule based on a rigid system of SEGREGATION of the races and second-class citizenship for blacks. Most important, the Democrats in the South ruthlessly denied blacks VOTING RIGHTS. In the rest of the country Democrats abided by the principle of States' Rights and ignored the plight of freedmen and women and those African Americans born into freedom following the Civil War.

As late as the 1920s, the Democratic Party was so inimical to the interests of African Americans that members of the KU KLUX KLAN had effective veto power when it came to nominating candidates for the presidency. Changes were in the offing, however. Some of the state Democratic Parties had far more progressive positions regarding the poor and those outside the mainstream than did the Southern Democrats. One of the more progressive Democrats, Franklin Delano ROOSEVELT of New York, was elected president in 1932 in the midst of the Great Depression. His proactive stance in response to economic distress included redistributive economic policies that worked to the advantage of the poor around the country, including millions of African Americans. For the first time, in the 1936 presidential election, large numbers of black voters began pulling the Democratic lever because of their support for Roosevelt—this despite the fact that Roosevelt did little to secure voting rights and other basic civil rights for African Americans. But his popular economic policies were wildly successful politically, bringing together an unlikely coalition that included racial minorities, white Southerners, union members, Catholics, and Jews. This wide-ranging

Democratic umbrella was called the "New Deal" (see NEW DEAL AND DEPRESSION).

As long as the Democrats did not attack segregation and the denial of basic rights for African Americans in the South, this improbable combination of supporters held together—which it did, for the most part, into the 1960s. But there were significant ruptures long before that. In 1948 President Harry TRUMAN supported a strong civil rights plank at the party's convention. This precipitated the walkout of ardent Southern segregationists, led by then-Democrat J. Strom THURMOND of SOUTH CAROLINA. In favor of Thurmond's "DIXIECRATS," ALABAMA didn't even place Truman's name on the ballot in the fall election that year, and some Deep South states for the first time left the Democratic column in presidential politics. These states came back to the fold in the 1950s, and 1960 nominee John KENNEDY made a point of choosing a Southerner as his running mate, Senate Majority Leader Lyndon JOHNSON of TEXAS, with the aim of holding together the New Deal coalition.

But the times were changing. Blacks had supported Kennedy over his Republican opponent Richard NIXON by about two to one in the election, and were crucial to his winning some states. The president's soaring rhetoric, committing the nation to "pay any price" for freedom, attracted African Americans. (Ironically, Kennedy's words were probably meant more as a rallying cry for the COLD WAR than as a call for racial justice.) Although Kennedy proved initially hesitant to move on civil rights, for fear of alienating powerful Southern Democrats in CONGRESS, civil rights leaders, did have some access to him. Eventually, as Southern reaction against blacks' civil rights protests of the era became increasingly violent, Kennedy made a nationally telecast speech in favor of civil rights in June 1963. The party seemed poised to seize the moment. But it was the Southern Democrat Johnson, upon ascending to the presidency after Kennedy's assassination in November 1963, who followed through by providing the necessary leadership to pass the monumental CIVIL RIGHTS ACT OF 1964. Johnson knew what would be the political consequences of his accomplishments, but this did not deter him. The party would lose the South for a generation. This longtime bulwark of the Democratic coalition—the eleven states of the old Confederacy—would shortly become a sure bet in the Republican column.

The Democratic Party had come a long way from the days of Klan influence and States' Rights to a position favoring federal intervention, in order first to relieve suffering and provide jobs during the Great Depression in the 1930s, and subsequently to secure the basic civil rights and voting rights of African Americans in the 1960s. In the key symbolic event signaling the end of the party's once rigid commitment to States' Rights, the 1964 Democratic Convention forced the all-white MISSISSIPPI state party to compromise by including blacks as future delegates. In presidential politics it took the party a full generation to recover from the loss of the support of the South to the Republicans. Even so, no Democratic presidential candidate since 1964 has garnered a majority of the popular vote nationwide, and what had at one time been the Democrats' strongest region remains its weakest, even with Southern Democrats Bill CLINTON and Al Gore at the top of the ticket in 1992 and 1996.

For more than a generation now, the Democratic Party has retained the overwhelming support of the African-American community—to the tune of about 90 percent in most elections—in large measure because its leadership has continued vigorously to support some efforts by the federal government to enforce existing and new civil rights laws. Democratic African-American politicians have risen to previously unreachable positions of political power in the last thirty years, particularly in the nation's largest cities, in the president's Cabinet, and in the Congress.

BIBLIOGRAPHY

Black, Earl, and Merle Black. *Politics and Society in the South.* 1987.
Sorauf, Frank J., and Paul Allan Beck. *Party Politics in America.* 1992.
Sundquist, James L. *Dynamics of the Party System.* 1983.
Tindall, George Brown. *Disruption of the Solid South.* 1972.

John Haskell

Depression

See New Deal and Depression.

DePriest, Oscar

(1871–1951), politician.

Oscar DePriest, the first Northern black member of CONGRESS, was born in Alabama. His father, a teamster, took the family to Kansas in 1878, during the EXODUSTERS movement. In 1889, DePriest moved to Chicago, where he worked as a housepainter and decorator. He later built a considerable fortune as a real estate investor and agent in the city's black ghetto.

In 1915, with the support of the local Republican machine, DePriest was elected to the Chicago City Council, becoming the city's first African-American alderman. In 1928, following the death of the incumbent, DePriest easily won the race for Congress from Illinois's 3rd Congressional District. His victory, which made him the first black in Congress in the twentieth century, demonstrated the increasing political power of urban blacks.

DePriest's six years in Congress were uneven. He supported black efforts to gain access to public accommodations in Washington and in 1933 introduced a measure banning discrimination in the new Civilian Conservation Corps. He also received national visibility when First Lady Lou Henry Hoover initially refused to invite his wife to tea at the White House with other congressional wives. However, as a Republican, DePriest opposed NEW DEAL federal programs for the poor, and he did not sponsor any civil rights legislation except for a weak antilynching bill he introduced in 1934 in an attempt to woo election-year voters. After being defeated for reelection in 1934, DePriest returned to his real estate business, and served on the Chicago City Council from 1943 to 1947. Chicago's Oscar DePriest Elementary School was named to memorialize him.

BIBLIOGRAPHY

Nordin, Dennis. *The New Deal's Black Congressman.* 1997.
"Oscar DePriest." *Dictionary of American Negro Biography.* 1982.

Greg Robinson

Desegration

In its most technical sense, *desegregation* is the elimination of legally mandated distinctions based on race (or, in some versions, the elimination of such distinctions when they contribute to maintaining a system of racial hierarchy). *Brown v. Board of Education* (1954) held school segregation unconstitutional. (See BROWN V. TOPEKA BOARD OF EDUCATION.) Desegregation might have meant simply ending the assignment of students to schools based on their race. Student assignments to the nearest school to their homes would be desegregation in that sense. Anticipating substantial resistance to that sort of desegregation, the Court in *Brown II* (1955) said that desegregation should occur "with all deliberate speed." Resistance to desegregation did occur, and only a few schools in the deep South had both white and African-American students in them by 1964. Prodded by the U.S. Department of Health, Education, and Welfare, and threatened with the denial of federal financial assistance, school systems in the Deep South accelerated the pace of desegregation after 1964. The SUPREME COURT became impatient with systems that continued to resist desegregation, and in *Green v. New Kent County School Board* (1968) held that school systems had to adopt desegregation plans that "promise realistically to work *now*."

Busing was a key element of the desegregation of schools and was supported by federal courts. (Bettmann Archive/Newsphotos)

The Court's impatience led to a subtle shift in its understanding of desegregation. To know whether desegregation plans were working, the Court came to ask not whether assignment by race had been eliminated, but whether the systems had a substantial degree of integration, so that, for example, there were few schools in a district that were identifiable as white or African-American schools.

In the immediate aftermath of *Brown*, one prominent North Carolina federal judge wrote that *Brown* required only desegregation, not integration. By the late 1960s, however, the Court was in fact requiring substantial integration. Accomplishing that in large districts, where there was frequently a significant amount of residential segregation, often required the schools to transport children rather long distances. In the 1970s the courts began to decide cases involving segregation in Northern school districts, and invoked the same sorts of remedies that had been used in the South. The combination of these new Northern cases with the widespread use of busing remedies generated substantial political opposition, supported by the NIXON administration. The Supreme Court began to relax its requirements after new justices arrived starting in 1969. By the 1990s the Court had held that school districts could eliminate some judicial supervision when they had complied only in part with prior desegregation orders, and that they could eliminate all such supervision if they showed that racially identifiable schools did not result from school board decisions but from residential segregation not supported by law.

The desegregation process was somewhat easier in other areas of legally mandated racial discrimination.

Some whites responded with violence to demonstrations aimed at ensuring compliance with the law in interstate transportation facilities such as bus depots, and at demonstrations aimed at changing the law in places of public accommodation. But, after these outbursts of violence, desegregation proceeded relatively smoothly, in part because business owners themselves generally had little to gain from resistance.

BIBLIOGRAPHY

Armor, David J. *Forced Justice: School Desegregation and the Law.* 1995.

Barnes, Catherine A. *Journey from Jim Crow: The Desegregation of Southern Transit.* 1983.

Kluger, Richard. *Simple Justice.* 1976.

Wilkinson, J. Harvie. *From Brown to Bakke: The Supreme Court and School Integration, 1954–1978.* 1979.

Mark Tushnet

Detroit Museum of African American History

See Museum of African American History.

Disability Rights

"Disability rights" refers to the broad-based movement to support creation and enforcement of public policies that protect and advance the rights and the opportunities of people with a disability. The disability rights movement is relatively new within the overall civil rights movements in the United States. It followed and drew lessons from the earlier civil right movements of African Americans and women. The disability rights movement reflects the recognition that many features of contemporary society—physical and social—have worked, sometimes unintendedly, to restrict the rights and the opportunities of people who experience physical or mental impairment. Physical obstacles include buildings and other facilities that people with disabilities cannot access or use in order to pursue the economic, political, and social opportunities that most other Americans take for granted. Other barriers are not physical yet often have a very damaging impact on the lives of people with disabilities. The social stigma and common misconceptions about the needs, capabilities, and potential contributions of disabled individuals, coupled with unease in associating with them, have worked persistently to deny opportunity to these Americans and to isolate them.

A comprehensive survey of disabled individuals conducted in the mid-1980s documented the extensiveness of disability in American society and profiled the status and the perceptions of persons with physical and mental handicaps. The study found that 44 percent of those surveyed had some form of physical disability; 13 percent suffered sensory impairment (e.g., blindness, deafness), 6 percent reported mental disability, 5 percent had respiratory ailments, and 16 percent suffered from other disabling diseases (e.g., heart and blood diseases). The study also found that compared to nondisabled persons, handicapped individuals received much less education, were far more likely to be unemployed, and earned less income when employed. Over half of those surveyed reported that their disabilities prevented them from achieving their full potential in life and 56 percent said that their handicaps prevented them from moving about in the community, attending cultural and sports events, and socializing with friends outside of the home.

Early efforts to assist people with disabilities, dating back to the nineteenth century, centered on raising funds and support to provide services and facilities for specific disabled populations, such as schools for deaf or blind persons. Throughout the twentieth century, groups representing the interests of people with specific types of disabilities proliferated, including such well-known entities as the March of Dimes, Easter Seals, and the United Cerebral Palsy Association. These organizations proved effective in serving the unique needs of specific groups of disabled persons and bringing their situation to the attention of the nondisabled population.

Efforts to aid people with disabilities moved into the policymaking area early in the twentieth century, focusing first on services, then on income assistance, and finally upon disability rights. Vocational rehabilitation policy, enacted by the U.S. CONGRESS immediately following WORLD WAR I, provided support and assistance to help injured persons (including those hurt in the war) to overcome their injury and return to work. Later, in the 1950s, another policy innovation occurred in the form of income support provided through the Social Security system to aid individuals with permanent injury that prevented their participation in the workforce. Beginning in the late 1960s, public policies regarding people with disabilities shifted to ensuring their rights and eliminating discrimination in their lives.

In the first initiative, the Architectural Barriers Act of 1968, Congress required that all new federal buildings be accessible to persons with disabilities and that accessibility features be added to existing buildings when renovations were undertaken. In 1973, as part of the reauthorization of the REHABILITATION ACT, Congress enacted several provisions intended to advance the rights of people with disabilities. The most prominent provision, Section 504, was short in length but powerful in ultimate impact. It prohibited all recipients of federal financial assistance, including all state and local governments, from discriminating on the basis of handicap. The provision stimulated many changes in governmental services, including removal of barriers to government buildings, creation of handicapped parking spaces, and purchase and operation of lift-equipped buses capable of serving patrons using wheelchairs. These laws were enacted through the efforts of a small set of policymakers who recognized the discrimination experienced by people with disabilities and the need for their legal protection.

In 1975, recognizing that children with disabilities had been inadequately served by public schools across the nation, Congress enacted the Education for All Handicapped Children Act. This law required that schools create and implement individual education plans designed to serve the specific educational needs of each disabled child. Passage of this law was due in large measure to the persistent efforts of groups of parents with disabled children who fought vigorously to expand educational opportunities for their children.

The disability rights movement culminated in the passage of the AMERICANS WITH DISABILITIES ACT OF 1990 (ADA). Groups representing individuals with specific disabilities, ranging across the full spectrum of physical and mental handicaps, coalesced to support passage of the ADA, which clarified the legal protections provided to people with disabilities through earlier federal laws, including the responsibilities of public-sector entities to remove physical and programmatic barriers to government services and facilities. The ADA also, for the first time, extended legal protections into the private sector, requiring that all but the smallest firms serving the public—including hotels, retail stores, restaurants, and movie theaters—make accommodations to meet the needs of people with disabilities.

As with other civil rights policies, disability rights policies have involved controversy and debate. From the late 1960s through passage of the ADA, the political debates were centered largely in policymaking arenas such as Congress, where legislators, groups representing people with disabilities, and parties regulated by federal laws offered differing perspectives about the appropriate scope of disability rights. With passage of the ADA, political controversies have shifted away from the law-making arena to the courts, where the parties seek judicial interpretations of the precise meaning of ADA provisions as they are applied in specific cases. Preliminary evidence from studies on implementation of the ADA during its first decade show that the act is creating changes in the public and the private sectors. Given the magnitude of public and private organizations regulated by the ADA, however, it will take more time for policymakers to understand the full impact of the ADA and its effectiveness in eliminating discrimination against people with disabilities.

BIBLIOGRAPHY

Berkowitz, Edward D. *Disabled Policy: America's Programs for the Handicapped.* 1987.

International Center for the Disabled and the National Council on the Handicapped. *Bringing Disabled Americans into the Mainstream.* 1986.

Percy, Stephen L. *Disability, Civil Rights, and Public Policy: The Politics of Implementation.* 1989.

Stephen Percy

District of Columbia

Because the U.S. Congress has maintained oversight of the national capital throughout its nearly two-hundred-year history, civil rights issues in Washington, D.C., have been intimately connected with national trends. A country that accommodated slavery under its new constitution also sanctioned slavery in territory seeded for the new capital by the Southern states of VIRGINIA and MARYLAND. As the abolition movement strengthened, it focused on the District of Columbia and, nearly one hundred years later, when a national civil rights movement built momentum in Southern states, it ultimately targeted Washington too. Despite significant civil rights victories, however, social justice remains an unfulfilled goal, not just for the city's African-American majority, but for gays, lesbians, and Latinos. (See also HOME RULE FOR WASHINGTON, D.C.)

The early presence of slavery in Washington drew the attention of abolitionists who saw in Congress's power of exclusive jurisdiction over District affairs the power to terminate the institution of slavery there. Following an 1836 report that called interference with slavery "unwise, impolitic, and dangerous to the union," Congress adopted a gag rule that required that petitions calling for emancipation in the District be automatically tabled without debate. Other efforts to advance the rights of the growing free black population in Washington failed until the succession of the Southern states left a sympathetic Republican majority in control of Congress. Under prompting by RADICAL REPUBLICANS, Congress ended discrimination on street railways in 1862, abolished slavery that same year, altered the civil code for Washington to eliminate all reference to race, and, in 1867, granted the franchise to black men at a time when that right was denied in many Northern states. Senator Charles SUMNER, a leader in those efforts, rejected a WOMAN SUFFRAGE amendment offered at the same time because, he said, it would complicate the effort to enfranchise black men.

In 1871, in a backlash against the growing political powers of African Americans in Washington, Congress shifted the District's form of government from an entirely elected mayor–council form to a territorial government, in which the governor and the upper body of the legislature were appointed by the president. Abolitionist and District resident Frederick DOUGLASS was among those who described the change as a setback to African-Americans' civil rights. But even as Congress limited the District's elections, it remained attentive to black constituents by enacting strong civil liberties legislation that required restaurants and other establishments to serve customers regardless of color. In 1874, Congress ended the experiment in territorial government, substituting a fully appointed commission to govern District affairs. Although an integrated public transportation system remained as a legacy of Radical Republicans, schools remained fully segregated and, following the SUPREME COURT's decision declaring the CIVIL RIGHTS ACT OF 1875 unconstitutional, most civil suits contesting limits to accessing public accommodations in Washington were dismissed. When Congress codified District laws in 1901, it simply omitted the portion containing civil rights regulations. Following his inauguration as president in 1913, Woodrow Wilson took segregation still a step further by barring African-American civil servants from sharing dining facilities and restrooms with whites as they had done previously.

The hardening of the color line in Washington prompted a strong reaction from the city's growing black professional and managerial classes. Four years after the NATIONAL ASSOCIATION FOR THE ADVANCEMENT FOR COLORED PEOPLE (NAACP) was founded in New York City, Washington established its own chapter, and it quickly grew to be the largest in the country. Protests against federal discrimination did not immediately succeed, but several efforts to segregate streetcars were defeated as local civil rights leaders rallied to oppose congressional legislation introduced to make Washington conform to practices in the Deep South.

Washington's civil rights movement gained momentum in 1933 when a group of young men formed what they called the New Negro Alliance to pressure businesses operating in predominantly black areas to hire African Americans. They secured at least part of their objective when the Supreme Court in 1938 affirmed the Alliance's right to picket stores that failed to hire African Americans. Still, Washington remained a largely segregated city through WORLD WAR II. Such a situation was increasingly embarrassing to a federal government that was soon waging a cold war, as African diplomats were repeatedly denied access to public facilities in the city. Sharply critical reports from the PRESIDENT'S COMMISSION ON CIVIL RIGHTS in 1947, and the National Committee on Segregation in the National Capital—a voluntary organization composed of ninety prominent civil leaders—helped prod federal authorities into integrating recreational facilities.

In 1949 both black and white civil rights activists tested the exclusion of African Americans from public accommodations by sitting in at a downtown Washington restaurant. They subsequently claimed in court that civil rights legislation passed in the 1870s was still in effect, even after its omission from the published city code. The Supreme Court upheld the activists' position in 1953. The high court ruled favorably again in the case *Bolling v. Sharpe*, challenging Washington's segregated schools as part of the May 17, 1954, BROWN V. BOARD OF EDUCATION decision. Although Washington school superintendent Carl Hansen claimed to want to make integration work, his decision to group all students according to ability in separate learning tracks prompted further dissent. In 1966 Julius Hobson, president of the Washington chapter of the CONGRESS OF RACIAL EQUALITY, filed suit, charging that the system discriminated against poor black students. Judge Shelly Wright's decision a year later accepted Hobson's argument and instituted compensatory funding and BUSING measures to balance resources among schools, as well as terminating the track system.

Subsequent civil rights efforts were directed primarily at restoring home rule for Washington, D.C. With the city achieving a black majority in the mid-1950s, activists declared congressional opposition to granting the District self-governance a civil rights issue. In the mid-1960s, Marion Barry, who had served as first chair of the STUDENT NONVIOLENT COORDINATING COMMITTEE in the South before moving to Washington in the early 1960s, organized a "Free D.C." campaign based around boycotts of local merchants who failed to support home rule. The U.S. Senate repeatedly backed home rule legislation (see HOME RULE FOR WASHINGTON, D.C.), but House District committee chairman John McMillan of South Carolina prevented any bills from reaching a final vote on the floor until he was finally beaten in the Democratic primary in 1972 as part of a concerted registration campaign by civil rights leaders. In 1974 Congress finally enacted legislation granting the city the right to elect its own mayor and city council.

The visibility of a civil rights movement in Washington has had its effect on other groups, including gay federal employees who found their jobs at risk at a time when government officials were saying that homosexuality constituted a threat to national security. Starting in 1950, following Senator Joseph McCarthy's first claims of Communist subversion, gays were routinely dismissed from their positions in government. (See MCCARTHYISM.) One who fought back was Franklin KAMENY, an astronomer with the Army Map Service, who in 1957 challenged his dismissal on grounds that discrimination based on sexual identity was comparable to discrimination based on race or religion. When the Supreme Court dismissed his case in 1961, he adopted—along with other leaders including Jack Nichols and Barbara Gittings—the methods of the civil rights movement to transform the MATTACHINE SOCIETY of Washington—which had been formed as a largely self-help organization—into an active opponent of sexual discrimination. Modeling itself after the NAACP, the Mattachine Society brought additional court cases, circulated flyers, and, in 1965, picketed the U.S. Civil Service Commission, which continued to dismiss homosexuals from government even if they had not been charged with breaking any law.

Several court victories boosted Mattachine Society efforts, but by the 1970s it was considered too elite an organization to sustain more overtly political goals. After Kameny made gay rights a public issue as a candidate for the new position of nonvoting delegate to the U.S. Congress in 1971, the campaign for gay rights became largely the work of the GAY ACTIVISTS ALLIANCE (GAA), created in New York in 1969. In 1973 D.C. GAA succeeded in securing passage of the D.C. Human Rights Law, one of the first efforts nationally to ban discrimination against gays and lesbians. The same year, the Civil Service Commission dropped the contested terminology "immoral conduct" from the list of disqualifications for federal employment, thus bringing to an end overt discrimination on the basis of sexual orientation. Franklin Kameny received both an apology from the Commission and appointment to the District's first Human Rights Commission.

Even as gay and lesbian activists became increasingly visible in Washington, so too did a growing Latino population. In order both to forge a common identity between different nationalities and to secure and protect their rights, Hispanics initiated an annual festival in 1970. In 1991 that relatively apolitical activity shifted, in the aftermath of three days of rioting that followed the shooting of a Latino man by an African-American policewoman. Forming the D.C. Latino Civil Rights Task Force, the Hispanics elected a young Salvadoran, Pedro Aviles, to be their spokesperson and prepared an extensive report of grievances. Modeling their own efforts on the civil rights struggle of African Americans, Task Force members submitted their findings both to the mayor and the U.S. Civil Rights Commission. Their criticisms ranged from particular omissions of services, such as Spanish-speaking counselors to deal with alcohol and drug abuse, to the broader concern that these recently arrived immigrants were not proportionately represented in the city or the metropolitan area workforce. Leadership of the Task Force has changed hands several times, but the organization continues to seek access to local political power and assurances of adequate services.

BIBLIOGRAPHY

Cadaval, Olivia. "'Tirarlo a la Calle/Taking It to the Streets': The Latino Festival and the Making of Community." In *Washington History* 4 (1992–93).

Gillette, Howard, Jr. *Between Justice and Beauty: Race, Planning, and the Failure of Urban Policy in Washington, D.C.* 1995.

Johnson, David K. "'Homosexual Citizens': Washington's Gay Community Confronts the Civil Service." In *Washington History* 6 (1994–1995).

Melder, Keith, compiler. *City of Magnificent Intentions: A History of the District of Columbia.* Rev. ed., 1997.

Wolters, Raymond. *The Burden of Brown: Thirty Years of School Desegregation.* 1984.

Howard Gillette, Jr.

Divine, Father

See Father Divine.

Dixiecrats

In early 1948, after President Harry TRUMAN presented a proposed civil rights program to CONGRESS, a group of Southern Democrats organized against the growing racial liberalism of the national DEMOCRATIC PARTY. When a committee of the Southern Governor's Conference failed to secure concessions on civil rights from Democratic National Committee officials, Mississippi Governor Fielding Wright called together a regional conclave, which met in Jackson, Mississippi on May 10, 1948. There, 1,500 delegates vowed to work for recognition of STATES' RIGHTS at the upcoming Democratic National Convention, and if they could not block Truman's nomination for the presidency, to break off from the party and meet again to discuss further action. South Carolina Governor Strom THURMOND, the meeting's keynote speaker, stated that "all the laws of Washington and all the bayonets of the army cannot force the Negro into our homes, our schools, our churches, and our places of recreation."

On May 15, 1948, at the Democratic National Convention in Philadelphia, Truman was nominated for the presidency, defeating Southern candidate Richard RUSSELL of Georgia, and the convention narrowly approved a strong civil rights plank in the party platform.

After the vote, the Mississippi delegation and half of the Alabama delegation rose and left the convention hall. Two days later, six thousand states' rights supporters, including five state governors and both of Mississippi's U.S. senators, met in Birmingham, Alabama, to form the States' Rights Democrats (soon dubbed "Dixiecrats" by North Carolina journalist Bill Weisner). Although party organizers were motivated by opposition to labor unions and the welfare state as well as civil rights, their chief interest was the preservation of the racial status quo. Former Alabama Governor Frank Dixon, the meeting's keynote speaker, denounced Truman's effort to reduce the South "to the status of a mongrel, inferior race." The convention voted to select its own presidential candidates, hoping to prevent either Truman or REPUBLICAN PARTY candidate Thomas E. Dewey from gaining an electoral college majority. The election would then be thrown into the House of Representatives, where Southern votes could be used to bargain for concessions on civil rights. The convention chose Thurmond as its candidate for president and Wright for vice president.

Thurmond and Wright campaigned throughout the Southern states. Although Thurmond officially disclaimed white supremacy, he called for the "defense" of states' rights and SEGREGATION from the federal government's "Gestapo" tactics. Many Southern voters opposed the Dixiecrats as extremists, and although many Southern elected officials sympathized with the rebels, most refused to risk their prominent positions in the regular Democratic Party. However, Dixiecrats seized control of election machinery in Louisiana, Mississippi, and South Carolina so that Thurmond appeared on the ballot in the standard Democratic column, and in Alabama, where Truman did not even appear on the ballot. In the November election, Thurmond polled 1.2 million votes, winning the four states where he appeared as the Democratic candidate. However, Truman captured the rest of the South, and won the presidency.

The States Rights' Democratic Party dissolved soon thereafter, and its members returned to the Democratic Party. Still, the Dixiecrat revolt foreshadowed later sectional realignments over civil rights.

BIBLIOGRAPHY

Cohodas, Nadine. *Strom Thurmond and the Politics of Southern Change.* 1993.

Donaldson, Garry. *Truman Defeats Dewey.* 1999.

Egerton, John. *Speak Now Against the Day: The Generation Before the Civil Rights Movement in the South.* 1994.

Lubell, Samuel. *The Future of American Politics.* 1952.

Greg Robinson

Doar, John Michael

(1921–   ), assistant attorney general.

John Doar served as a U.S. assistant attorney general during the Kennedy and Johnson administrations. Doar was born in Wisconsin in 1921 and was educated at Princeton University and the law school of the University of California, Berkeley. Before joining the U.S. Department of Justice in 1960 as a first assistant in the Civil Rights Division, Doar was in private practice in Wisconsin. A Republican, he joined the Justice Department believing that he could help his party make headway in the American South by enforcing federal voting laws and breaking the Democratic Party's hold in the Southern states.

After witnessing the violence and intimidation that Southern conservative whites used to keep eligible black voters away from the polls, Doar became committed to working toward the goals and principles of the civil rights movement and in 1964 was named head of the Justice Department's Civil Rights Division. Doar traveled extensively in the South to assist in Justice Department investigations and participated in a number of significant events and court cases. These included James MEREDITH's attempts to register at the University of Mississippi in 1962. Doar was at Meredith's side each time he tried to register. Similarly, Doar was a participant in efforts to integrate the University of Alabama in 1963. Doar was assigned to prosecute the 1964 murders of civil rights workers James CHANEY, Andrew GOODMAN, and Michael SCHWERNER. Murder is a state crime; Doar had to prosecute using civil rights law and argued successfully that the civil rights of the deceased had been purposefully violated. Doar left the Justice Department in 1967; in 1973 he served as chief counsel for the House Judiciary Committee's investigation of the Watergate affair. In 1974, after Richard Nixon resigned from office, Doar returned to private practice in Washington, D.C.

BIBLIOGRAPHY

Branch, Taylor. *Parting the Waters: America in the King Years, 1953–63.* 1988.

Brauer, Carl. *John F. Kennedy and the Second Reconstruction.* 1977.

Papers of Burke Marshall, Assistant Attorney General for Civil Rights. John F. Kennedy Library.

Alicia E. Rodriquez

John Michael Doar (right) entering the Montgomery, Alabama, federal courthouse. Doar was U.S. Assistant Attorney General for Civil Rights during the Kennedy and Johnson administrations. (AP/Wide World Photos)

Dobbs, John Wesley

(1882–1961), black civic and fraternal leader.

John Wesley Dobbs epitomizes a generation of black leaders who battled for political reform in the segregated South. A Georgia native, Dobbs worked as a railway mail clerk, but was better known as the unofficial mayor of Atlanta's prosperous Auburn Avenue neighborhood.

As Grand Master of the Prince Hall Masons in Georgia from 1932 until his death, Dobbs saved the fraternity from financial ruin during the Depression. Unlike many of their counterparts, the Masons continued to offer insurance benefits and other social services in lodges across the state.

In 1936, Dobbs founded the Atlanta Civic and Political League. Its goal was to register black voters and thus realize the numerical strength of African Americans in the city, and it became a model for a succession of similar organizations. Bypassing Atlanta's poll tax laws, the League grew in numbers and influence, forcing white politicians to recognize the interests of this black voting bloc. In the 1940s, the city agreed to Dobbs's demands for the hiring of black police officers and improvements in segregated leisure facilities.

On the platform, Dobbs presented a strongly moralistic brand of politics and emphasized black pride. He was an active campaigner for the Republicans, briefly switching allegiance to the Democrats during the New Deal.

Despite his advancing years, Dobbs figured in the early civil rights movement. A close friend to the King family, he took part in the Desegregation of Atlanta's downtown stores in 1960. He was also a director of the Southern Conference Educational Fund. In 1973 Dobbs's grandson, Maynard Jackson, Jr., became the first black mayor of Atlanta.

Bibliography

Pomerantz, Gary. *Where Peachtree Meets Sweet Auburn: The Saga of Two Families and the Making of Atlanta.* 1996.

Andrew M. Kaye

Dodge Revolutionary Union Movement

In the 1930s and 1940s, Detroit was perhaps the most important industrial center where both class consciousness and race consciousness intersected, for both black and white workers and for the trade union and political groupings that sought to lead them. Also, Detroit saw the period's most important race riot (1943) and the successful use of antiblack Racism to defeat a labor-backed mayoral candidate in 1945. The effort to unite white and black workers—especially to win the support of black workers, who combined the most militant class consciousness with a defensive race consciousness—was an ongoing challenge for the powerful left wing of the United Automobile Workers (UAW) union in the city.

Even with former Socialist Party member Walter Reuther's victory over the powerful Communist-led left faction of the UAW in the late 1940s and the purge of both white and African-American left labor activists such as Coleman Young (active in the Negro National Labor Council in the early 1950s and later the mayor of Detroit in the post-1960s era), the city, its labor movement, and its growing African-American community retained many traditional radicals. Later the area was home to many New Left radicals, often centered at the nearby University of Michigan at Ann Arbor.

In the aftermath of the Detroit ghetto riot of July 1967—which black and white radicals called the Great Rebellion—black radical activists and members of the Student Nonviolent Coordinating Committee (SNCC), the Michigan Freedom Now Party, and other groups launched an alternative newspaper, the *Inner City Voice* (*ICV*), which defined itself as both the voice of the community and the voice of the revolution. Although it provided both agitation and analysis on a wide variety of domestic, anti–Vietnam War, and Third World liberation issues, *ICV* consistently called for class-based revolutionary action against the auto companies, the UAW bureaucracy, and the larger "white power structure" of the city and the nation.

Faced with attacks by the American Legion, conservative vigilante groups, the UAW, and politicians who accused them of fomenting new riots, the *ICV* group, whose core consisted of about thirty black activists, sought to transform themselves into a revolutionary vanguard through the study of revolutionary ideas and political action. At the same time, they sought to make the paper into an organizing center, a journal of revolutionary ideas and specific information to inspire revolutionary action.

On May 2, 1968, in the aftermath of the assassination of Martin Luther King, Jr., and ghetto riots across the United States, members of the *ICV* group became the leading force behind the Dodge Revolutionary Union Movement (DRUM), which launched a wildcat strike of four thousand mostly African-American workers at Dodge Main. Among DRUM's most important leaders was General Gordon Baker, a worker at Dodge Main and an *ICV* group member, who had traveled to Cuba in 1964, in opposition to the U.S. government ban, and had been involved in a variety of revolutionary groups. "General" was his first name, as a witness later explained to a bemused member of the Senate Internal Security Committee, not a military rank.

Dodge Main, the central assembly plant for Chrysler, had become the most important employer of young black workers, as General Motors and Ford moved factories out of the city. At this facility, 100 percent of the superintendents, 95 percent of the foremen, 90 percent of the skilled workers, and 90 percent of the skilled apprentices were white. Although DRUM had sought to unite black and white workers (and some whites had participated in the wildcat strike, which dealt with speedup and other working conditions), Dodge's attempt to focus on and punish blacks served to strengthen DRUM's position among the black workers. Trying to connect class and race consciousness in antiracist politics, DRUM increasingly sought to mobilize both the community and the workers against Chrysler and the UAW leadership.

Although the DRUM activists were subsequently defeated in a UAW local election at Dodge Main by methods widely regarded as corrupt, the insurgency spread, as radical workers formed DRUM-influenced Revolutionary Union Movements (RUMs) at United Parcel Service (UPS) and among hospital workers and *Detroit News* workers.

DRUM also extended its influence to the most important city university, Wayne State, which had both major connections to the establishment trade union movement and a significant African-American student component at a time when New Left radicals at the University of Michigan and other Big Ten universities were beginning to lead campaigns to increase the access of African Americans and other minorities to public universities. *ICV* editor John Watson was elected as the first African-American editor of *South End*, the Wayne State University newspaper, and steered the paper and the student movement into support for DRUM, and its various RUM spinoffs, along with solidarity with Third World liberation struggles.

At the beginning of the NIXON administration, in an atmosphere of growing repression of labor unions and racist appeals to conservative white workers ("hard hats") and a middle-class "silent majority," DRUM leaders, including Baker, Mike Hamlin, and John Watson, created a more ambitious organization, the League of Revolutionary Black Workers (LRBW), in Detroit in June 1969. The League sought, through building activist groups at various factories and other enterprises, to construct a radical labor movement and transform it into a revolutionary political force.

The League reflected the media consciousness of the period by working with New York–based radical filmmakers to produce *Finally Got the News* (1970), a powerful and influential documentary that told the story of DRUM and the League from the assemblyline and in interviews with leaders such as Baker, Ron March, and Chuck Wooten. The film gave it important credibility in New Left radical and radical labor circles, encouraging attempts to develop RUMs among black workers in California, New York, and elsewhere.

Documentaries such as *Finally Got the News*, *Working*, and Barbara Kopple's later Oscar-winning work *Harlan County*, influenced a variety of late-1970s Hollywood films. *Norma Rae* and *Blue Collar*, particularly, brought both trade union themes and portrayals of life on the assemblyline to Hollywood films for the first time since the early cold war years.

Compared by some to the Industrial Workers of the World (IWW) in its ability to gain publicity and its commitment to a revolutionary transformation of society, the League, as DRUM's successor, campaigned against police brutality locally, established bookstores and a book club, and, through the influence of James FOREMAN, a former SNCC leader, associated itself with the Black Economic Development Conference (BEDC), which campaigned for $500,000,000 in reparations from churches to fund black economic development. Monies derived from the BEDC were to help the League gain a paid staff and fund its activities.

In the early 1970s, the League was torn apart by complicated factional rivalries, as some members split to form a nationally oriented Black Workers Congress; some leaders of DRUM and the RUMs modeled after

it returned to the UAW fold; and some, most significantly General Baker, joined the Communist Labor Party (CLP). These rivalries—even though personality conflicts and power struggles were a major component of them—can be viewed both as an example of the factionalism that has undermined radical and revolutionary movements everywhere, and as a failure to resolve the contradictions between class-conscious politics and the needs and aspirations of racially oppressed workers through a goal-directed program.

Thus, a combination of increased corporate and government repression, along with the policy and personal rivalries, destroyed DRUM, the RUMs, and the League, stifling the political infrastructure of DRUM-inspired organizations by the middle 1970s. However, individuals involved with the movement that DRUM and the other organizations sought to lead emerged as important political and trade union figures in post-1960s Detroit.

When Coleman Young, himself a victim of the postwar union purges in Detroit and McCarthyite attacks through the 1950s, became the first African-American mayor of Detroit in 1973 (a position he would hold for nearly two decades), he appointed DRUM and League activists to his administration. Ken Cockrel, an African-American attorney who had emerged as a major League spokesman, was elected to Detroit's Common Council, in the mid-1970s, where he became a leader and, before his sudden death in 1989 at age fifty one, the most likely candidate to replace Young as mayor. Justin Ravitz, Cockrel's white law partner and a prominent League lawyer, was elected to Detroit's criminal court for a ten-year term in 1972, on a platform committed to reforming the police and judicial system. Known as Detroit's and the country's only "Marxist judge" (a designation he accepted proudly), Ravitz permitted the judicial airing of a wide variety of civil rights and civil liberties issues.

Unlike many of the groups that called for BLACK POWER or tried to create "alternative" schools, workplaces, and lifestyles in the tradition of both separatist nationalists and the old anarchists and utopian socialists, DRUM and the League of Revolutionary Black Workers sought to combine theory and practice to coordinate the struggles for working-class liberation through revolutionary Socialism and African-American liberation from racist oppression. In Detroit, DRUM and the League sustained a radical tradition that, even after a third of a century of reaction to the social movements of the 1960s, remains a potent force in the political, trade union, and cultural life of the city's working people.

Finally, in the renewal of a culture of protest, as expressed in contemporary campaigns in defense of Abu Mumia Jamal, in demonstrations, protests, and strikes among trade unionists at the beginning of a new century, and in support for the building of a labor party, DRUM's legacy continues to be expressed.

BIBLIOGRAPHY

Allen, Ernest. "Dying from the Inside: The Decline of the League of Revolutionary Black Workers." In *They Should Have Served that Cup of Coffee*, edited by Dick Cluster. 1979.

Georgakas, Dan, and Marvin Sukin. *Detroit: I Do Mind Dying*, 2nd ed. 1998.

Geschwender, James. *Class, Race, and Worker Insurgency: The League of Revolution Black Workers*. 1977.

Dan Georgakas, whose *Detroit: I Do Mind Dying* is both the major work on DRUM and a classic of 1960s labor protest, has presented League of Revolutionary Black Workers materials to the Walter P. Reuther Library at Wayne State University, Detroit, Michigan.

Norman Markowitz

Dombrowski, James Anderson

(1897–1983), administrator and civil rights activist.

A skillful civil rights organizer, James Dombrowski championed workers' and African Americans' economic and civil rights for over five decades. Born in Tampa, Florida, Dombrowski served in World War I as an army airplane mechanic. He graduated from Atlanta's Emory University in 1923. As a graduate student at Union Theological Seminary, Dombrowski joined Southern textile workers' protests. His dissertation, "The Early Days of Christian Socialism in America," completed at Columbia University in 1933, demonstrated his socialist views.

The HIGHLANDER FOLK SCHOOL of Monteagle, Tennessee, hired Dombrowski that same year. There, he facilitated civil rights conferences and labor organizing efforts. Later, as the SOUTHERN CONFERENCE FOR HUMAN WELFARE's (SCHW's) executive director (1942–1946), Dombrowski promoted state affiliates from Nashville and edited SCHW's magazine, *The Southern Patriot*. Local newspapers' portrayal of her husband as a Communist made Ellen Krida Dombrowski reclusive, but undaunted, James organized events like the 1948 SOUTHERN NEGRO YOUTH CONGRESS in Birmingham, Alabama, which violated local SEGREGATION ordinances.

In 1946 Dombrowski became director of SCHW's non-political arm, the SOUTHERN CONFERENCE EDUCATION FUND (SCEF). He later organized rallies for the U.S. Supreme Court's BROWN V. BOARD OF EDUCATION decision and participated in Birmingham's civil rights demonstrations. In 1963 Louisiana authorities charged Dombrowski with subversion: confiscating files from SCEF's New Orleans office. Dombrowski sued state officials for wrongful arrest. In *Dombrowski v. Pfister* (1965), the Supreme Court ruled for Dombrowski, declaring that the requirement of plaintiffs to exhaust state court actions before seeking federal redress had a "chilling effect" on constitutionally protected activities. Dombrowski thus left a legal legacy before he retired in 1966.

BIBLIOGRAPHY

Adams, Frank T. *James A. Dombrowski: An American Heretic, 1897–1983*. 1992.

Egerton, John. *Speak Now Against the Day: The Generation Before the Civil Rights Movement in the South*. 1994.

Glen, John M. *Highlander: No Ordinary School*. 1996.

Wesley Brian Borucki

"Don't Buy Where You Can't Work" Campaigns

Other than the American civil rights movement, few twentieth-century political movements have galvanized black communities into action like the "Don't Buy Where You Can't Work" campaigns. Initiated during the Depression era in mostly northern cities, these campaigns sought to boycott white stores in black communities that refused to hire black employees. The "Don't Buy" movement used mass protest and direct action tactics such as economic boycotts and picketing as potent political weapons. The reticence of traditional civil rights groups such as the NATIONAL ASSOCIATION FOR THE ADVANCEMENT OF COLORED PEOPLE (NAACP) and the Urban League to use direct action tactics created frustration in many black communities. Thus the "Don't Buy" campaigns represented the emergence of a new form of militant black activism which yielded faster results and, in some instances, united diverse segments in black communities.

African Americans living in segregated communities resented the presence of white-owned stores in their midst that refused to employ blacks or employed them only in menial positions. Moreover, without laws barring racial discrimination in private industry, such practices continued unabated. Hence, the "Don't Buy" pickets and boycotts became viable weapons that forced white-owned stores in black communities to hire blacks in skilled and white-collar positions. As these campaigns gained in popularity during the Depression, they spread to more than thirty cities across the country, becoming one of the first black direct action movements of that era.

The earliest "Don't Buy" boycott appeared in Chicago in the late twenties. Its target was a small chain

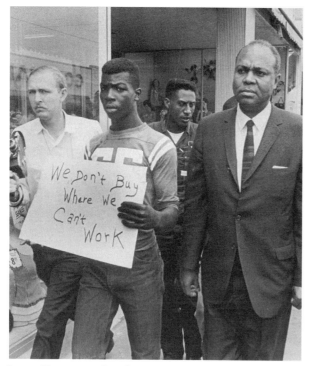

James Farmer and a demonstrator in a 1965 boycott campaign in Bogalusa, Louisiana. (AP/Wide World Photos)

of grocery stores in Chicago's black ghetto that refused to employ African Americans. Referred to as "Spend Your Money Where You Can Work," this first campaign sparked a larger boycott against Woolworth stores located in Chicago's "Black Belt" that also resisted hiring black employees. An aggressive black newspaper, the *Chicago Whip*, published fiery editorials endorsing the campaign. News of Chicago's success sparked similar campaigns across the country, particularly in New York between 1932 and 1941. Influenced by Chicago's example, blacks in Brooklyn and Harlem initiated "Don't Buy" campaigns against various white stores. The charismatic black minister Adam Clayton POWELL, Jr., whose aggressive leadership helped place numerous blacks in Harlem in hundreds of white-collar jobs, enhanced the success of the New York campaigns.

The Depression era "Don't Buy" campaigns sought to improve employment opportunities for black Americans at a time when few weapons existed for blacks to use against racial discrimination. These campaigns clearly paved the way for future collective movements, such as A. Philip RANDOLPH's 1941 March On Washington Movement, and ultimately the modern civil rights movement. The victories of later black protests could not have been won without the foundation laid by these earlier efforts. Thus, the "Don't Buy" cam-

paigns are an important link in the historical chain of black activism and a crucial episode in the prehistory of the modern civil rights movement.

BIBLIOGRAPHY

Drake, St. Clair, and Horace Cayton. *Black Metropolis, A Study of Negro Life in a Northern City.* 1993.

Greenberg, Cheryl Lynn. *"Or Does It Explode?" Black Harlem in the Great Depression.* 1991.

Meier, August, and Elliott Rudwick. "The Origins of Non-violent Direct Action in Afro-American Protest: A Note on Historical Discontinuities." In *Along the Color Line, Explorations in the Black Experience.* Meier, August, and Elliott Rudwick, eds. 1976.

Lori G. Waite

Double-Duty-Dollar Campaign

Black economic ideologies not only fueled the age of Booker T. WASHINGTON (1880–1915) but also inspired strategies used in the later years of JIM CROW. The double-duty-dollar strategy, advocating "spend your money where you can work," sought to consolidate black spending and create jobs.

Gordon Blaine HANCOCK, clergyman, journalist, and economics professor at Virginia Union University in Richmond, coined the term "double-duty dollar" in 1925. For almost four decades, he advocated it to numerous black and interracial audiences, as well as in his Associated Negro Press syndicated column, which appeared in 114 newspapers. Hancock was disturbed because blacks had suffered disproportionately severe unemployment during the Great Depression (see NEW DEAL AND DEPRESSION), received an unequal share of government relief, and were customarily excluded from labor UNIONS. As a remedy, he argued that blacks should mobilize their purchasing power and should patronize black-owned enterprises, thereby assuring themselves some income and employment while leveraging their fair hiring demands of white employers. Race and class survival, above all, hinged on wage earners, entrepreneurs, and professionals sharing the fabled "black dollar." Hancock urged that those who possess this black dollar not return it immediately to the white merchant, but should permit others in the community to use it. In 1930, for food and clothing alone, African Americans expended an estimated $4.5 billion.

Hancock's call to rein in these dollars resonated, inspiring self-help and the freedom struggle. His cause embraced race pride and solidarity, as did such consumer causes as "race first," "buy black," and "jobs for Negroes." Like them, it shaped the advertisements of black banks, life insurance companies, and retail and service firms, especially in urban areas. It drew strong support from organizations, including the Richmond Urban League; the Baptist General Association of Virginia; Phi Beta Sigma fraternity, with its annual "bigger and better Negro business" drives; the National Association of Teachers in Colored Schools; and the Colored Merchants' Association, through cooperative buying and group advertising. Meanwhile, the double-duty-dollar appeal was echoed by *The* CRISIS editor W. E. B. DU BOIS in his 1934 plan to develop a segregated economy. Although it forced Du Bois out of the NATIONAL ASSOCIATION FOR THE ADVANCEMENT OF COLORED PEOPLE (NAACP), that proposal sharpened the debate on economics and SEGREGATION. Howard University economist Abram L. Harris (1899–1963) viewed the buy-black doctrine as racial protection for businessmen who wanted to control and exploit the market that the masses made possible. Harris demanded a class-based, multiracial approach to liberation. Double-duty-dollar advocates, nevertheless, aspired to hold the race's purse strings. In 1935 in the South's seventeen largest cities, an aggregate of 890,000 blacks spent $308 million (a sum comparable to U.S. export trade with Argentina, Brazil, and Chile). Nine of these cities had black business communities of national importance. Atlanta, Georgia; Houston, Texas; Memphis, Tennessee; New Orleans, Louisiana; and Richmond and Newport News, Virginia, saw double-duty-dollar campaigns that culminated in "don't buy where you can't work" picket lines and boycotts. Self-help, indeed, did much to generate and guide nonviolent direct action. From 1929 to 1941, major "don't buy" protests swept thirty-six cities, eleven of them in the South. These struggles linked blacks' dollar consciousness to the evolving civil rights movement in the North and South.

BIBLIOGRAPHY

"The Double-Duty Dollar: An Address by Gordon B. Hancock on Education Day, Tidewater Fair, Durham, North Carolina, October 20, 1933." In *Rare Virginia Pamphlets*. Alderman Library, University of Virginia, Charlottesville, VA.

Gavins, Raymond. *The Perils and Prospects of Southern Black Leadership: Gordon Blaine Hancock, 1884–1970*. 1993.

Harris, Abram L. *The Negro as Capitalist: A Study of Banking and Business among American Negroes*. 1936.

Jaynes, Gerald David, and Robin M. Williams, Jr., eds. *A Common Destiny: Blacks and American Society*. 1989.

Johnson, Charles S. *The Negro in American Civilization: A Study of Negro Life and Race Relations in the Light of Social Research*. 1930.

Meier, August. *Negro Thought in America 1880–1915: Racial Ideologies in the Age of Booker T. Washington*. 1966.

Meier, August, and Elliott Rudwick. *Along the Color Line: Explorations in the Black Experience*. 1976.

Myrdal, Gunnar. *An American Dilemma: The Negro Problem and Modern Democracy*. 1944.

Pierce, Joseph A. *Negro Business and Business Education: Their Present and Prospective Development*. 1947.

Walker, Juliet E. K. *The History of Black Business in America: Capitalism, Race, Entreneurship*. 1998.

Raymond Gavins

Double V Campaign

The African-American struggle for full citizenship took heightened form during the WORLD WAR II years. The slogan "Double V"—"victory abroad over Nazism and victory at home over racism and inequality"—enabled African-American leaders to build coalitions and garner public support for an ongoing civil rights campaign. Double V was, however, more than a slogan; it was an ideology that invoked the necessity of a vigilant fight for democracy. Organizations and individuals across the political and programmatic spectrum found common ground under the ideological umbrella of the Double V.

The slogan "Double V" was coined officially by Robert Vann's *Pittsburgh Courier* in 1942, but the campaign for Double V emerged, in part, from the "rising wind" of black internationalism in the late 1930s. As early as Benito Mussolini's invasion of Ethiopia in 1935 and Adolf Hitler's snubbing of black athletes at the 1936 Olympic games, African-American leaders connected the African-American struggle for justice at home to the battle against fascism overseas. By 1941, while the United States contemplated entry into the Second World War, African-American leaders crafted a language and program in support of U.S. involvement in the war that linked the advancement of democracy abroad to justice for African Americans at home.

A. Philip RANDOLPH's 1941 proposed March on Washington symbolized the possibilities of the Double V campaign. The threat of 100,000 united African Americans marching on Washington to demand equal rights moved President FRANKLIN D. ROOSEVELT to issue Executive Order 8802 banning discrimination in defense industries. The proposed March on Washington sent a powerful message that victory for democracy in the world required the full extension of democracy to African Americans.

BIBLIOGRAPHY

Thomas, Joyce. "The 'Double V' was for Victory: Black Soldiers, the Black Protest, and World War II." Ph.D. dissertation. 1993.

Winkler, Allan W. *Home Front USA: America During World War II*. 1986.

Peter Lau

Douglass, Frederick

(1818–1895), abolitionist, orator, journalist.

Born Frederick Augustus Washington Bailey in Talbot County, Maryland, the son of a slave woman and, likely, her white master, Douglass became the most important African-American leader of the nineteenth century. Upon his escape from slavery at age twenty, he adopted a new surname from Sir Walter Scott's *The Lady of the Lake*. Douglass immortalized his formative years in the first of three autobiographies, *Narrative of the Life of Frederick Douglass* (1845). This work and two subsequent revisions mark Douglass's signal contribution to American letters. As antislavery propaganda and as personal revelation, they are the finest examples of the slave narrative tradition.

As abolitionist, orator, and editor, Douglass achieved international fame as a radical critic of slavery, RACISM, and hypocrisy. His currency was language rather than elective office or law. He preached his own brand of American idealism, but his lifelong insistence on the citizenship birthrights of blacks makes him one of the true founders of the civil rights crusade. Douglass welcomed the Civil War in 1861 and interpreted

disunion, total war, and EMANCIPATION as a second American Revolution.

In RECONSTRUCTION, Douglass allied himself with the radical Republican vision of an activist federal government and racial equality. Although his leadership in his later years became emblematic, Douglass remained an activist for the maligned revolution represented by the THIRTEENTH, FOURTEENTH, and FIFTEENTH AMENDMENTS. In the 1890s he joined with Ida B. WELLS to attack LYNCHING and demand protection of the civil and political liberties of blacks. The civil rights revolution in America needed an ideological indictment of slavery and racism upon which to grow. No one provided a deeper mine of such moral language than Douglass, who in 1852 declared the Declaration of Independence the "ringbolt" of the "nation's destiny," and then condemned his Fourth of July audience for their "inhuman mockery" in inviting him, the voice of the slaves, to celebrate the day.

BIBLIOGRAPHY

Andrews, William L., ed. *Critical Essays on Frederick Douglass.* 1991.

Blassingame, John W., and Jack McKivigan, eds. *The Frederick Douglass Papers,* 4 vols. 1979–1992.

Blight, David W. *Frederick Douglass' Civil War: Keeping Faith in Jubilee.* 1989.

Martin, Waldo E. *The Mind of Frederick Douglass.* 1984.

McFeely, William S. *Frederick Douglass.* 1991.

Preston, Dickson J. *Young Frederick Douglass: The Maryland Years.* 1980.

Sundquist, Eric J., ed. *Frederick Douglass: New Literary and Historical Essays.* 1990.

David W. Blight

Abolitionist, journalist, orator, and social reformer Frederick Douglass. (The Library of Congress)

Draft Riots

In many cultures, collective crowd action has traditionally been accepted as a legitimate means of resisting perceived injustice. Paradoxically, rioters have often viewed their unruly, violent actions as consistent with the maintenance of social order. The New York City Draft Riots of 1863, inspired by outrage among some citizens over the passage of the first military conscription act in American history, demonstrated this long-standing trend, and resulted in the deadliest rioting in U.S. history.

Many poor immigrants particularly resented the draft because it allowed wealthy citizens to avoid Civil War service by paying a commutation fee of three hundred dollars or by hiring a substitute. Although violent protests occurred in cities and towns throughout the North, New York City, with its tradition of deadly mob violence, was the site of the worst such events. Democratic politicians and editors strongly encouraged the city's large immigrant population to resist serving in an armed struggle to free African Americans. Immigrant workers generally despised blacks, from racism generally and, specifically, the economic competition blacks represented. With much of the city's population thus fiercely committed to resistance, the draft went anything but smoothly.

On July 13, 1863, the city erupted. Working-class crowds burned the building where the draft had begun, and embarked on a five-day orgy of destruction and murder. The mostly Irish Catholic mobs targeted police, troops, the wealthy, Republicans, anyone who voiced opposition to their actions, and especially African Americans. Victims were beaten, stabbed, shot, hanged, burned, and drowned. Rioters looted and burned homes and buildings, including the Colored Orphan Asylum. On July 16, federal troops began arriving in the city and violently reclaimed control. Determined not to back down in the face of opposition, the administration went ahead with the draft after first bringing in sufficient reinforcements to discourage further resistance.

Recent scholars have been able to confirm only slightly over one hundred riot-related fatalities although the evidence is fragmentary. Relatively few rioters stood trial for their crimes, and none served long prison sentences. Although the draft continued, few of the rioters would ultimately serve in the military. In a conciliatory move, the city council raised sufficient funds to pay commutation fees for those too poor to afford them.

BIBLIOGRAPHY

Bernstein, Iver. *The New York City Draft Riots: Their Significance for American Society and Politics in the Age of the Civil War.* 1990.
Cook, Adrian. *The Armies of the Streets: The New York City Draft Riots of 1863.* 1974.
McPherson, James M. *Battle Cry of Freedom: The Civil War Era.* 1988.

Michael Thomas Smith

Dred Scott v. Sandford (1857)

In 1846 Dred Scott commenced a lawsuit against Harriet Emerson, the widow of his former owner, Dr. John Emerson. Scott claimed he was free because Dr. Emerson had taken him to Fort Snelling in the Wisconsin Territory (present-day Minnesota) where Congress had prohibited slavery under the Missouri Compromise of 1820. Scott also claimed to be free because Dr. Emerson had taken him to the free state of Illinois.

In 1850 a Missouri court freed him on the theory that he had become free while living in Illinois and at

In the Dred Scott v. Sandford *decision of 1857, the Supreme Court ruled that free blacks were not citizens of the United States and that Congress lacked the power to prohibit slavery in the western territories.* (Library of Congress)

Fort Snelling, and once free, he was always free. This decision was consistent with a long line of Missouri cases, dating from 1824. The Missouri cases rested on the English case *Somerset v. Stewart* (1772), where Lord Mansfield of the Court of Kings Bench had ruled that any slave brought to England was entitled to his freedom. Almost all northern states accepted this proposition, as did some southern states, including Louisiana, Kentucky, Missouri, and very briefly Mississippi.

In 1852 the Missouri Supreme Court overturned Scott's victory, declaring that because of northern hostility to slavery, Missouri would no longer respect the law of the free states, which ended bondage for slaves taken into their jurisdiction. Declaring that the North had been overcome by a "dark and fell spirit . . . whose inevitable consequence must be the overthrow and destruction of our government," the Missouri court rejected its history of freeing slaves who had lived in free states.

In 1854 Scott renewed his quest for liberty in the federal courts, suing his new owner, John F. A. Sanford (his name is misspelled as Sandford in the official report of the case), who was the brother-in-law of his late master, Dr. Emerson. Scott sued under the clause in Article III of the U.S. Constitution which allows a citizen of one state to sue a citizen of another state in a federal court. Scott argued that he was a "citizen of Missouri" and thus could sue Sanford, a "citizen of New York," in federal court. In defending his claim to Scott, Sanford argued that Scott could not sue in a federal court because "Dred Scott, is not a citizen of the State of Missouri, as alleged in his declaration, because he is a negro of African descent; his ancestors were of pure African blood, and were brought into this country and sold as negro slaves." In essence, Sanford argued that blacks, because of their race, could never be citizens of the United States.

United States District Judge Robert W. Wells rejected this argument, concluding that *if* Dred Scott was free, then he could sue in federal court as a citizen of Missouri. However, after hearing all the evidence, Wells rejected Scott's claim to freedom, basing his charge to the jury on the earlier Missouri decision that Scott was still a slave. Judge Wells did not consider whether the Missouri court had incorrectly applied the Missouri Compromise of 1820, which was a federal law.

Scott then took his case to the United States Supreme Court. There, in a 7-2 decision, the Court ruled that the Missouri Compromise, under which Scott claimed to be free, was unconstitutional because it deprived southerners of their property in slaves without due process of law or just compensation, in violation of the Fifth Amendment. In reaching this conclusion, Chief Justice Roger B. Taney determined that slavery had special constitutional protection because of the special needs of that property and its owners. This decision shocked northerners, who had long seen the Missouri Compromise as a central piece of legislation for organizing the settlement of the West and for accommodating differing sectional interests.

In a bitterly proslavery opinion Chief Justice Taney also denied that blacks could ever be citizens of the United States. Taney wrote:

> The question is simply this: Can a negro, whose ancestors were imported into this country, and sold as slaves, become a member of the political community formed and brought into existence by the Constitution of the United States, and as such become entitled to all the rights, and privileges, and immunities, guaranteed by that instrument to the citizen? One of which rights is the privilege of suing in a court of the United States in the cases specified in the Constitution.

For Taney, the answer to these questions was an emphatic "no." Ignoring the fact that free black men in most of the northern states, as well as North Carolina, could vote at the time of the ratification of the Constitution, Taney declared that African Americans:

> are not included, and were not intended to be included, under the word "citizens" in the Constitution, and can

therefore claim none of the rights and privileges which the instrument provides and secures to citizens of the United States. On the contrary, they were at that time [1787–1788] considered as a subordinate and inferior class of beings who had been subjugated by the dominant race, and, whether emancipated or not, yet remained subject to their authority, and had no rights or privileges but such as those who held the power and Government might choose to grant them.

According to Taney blacks were "so far inferior, that they had no rights which the white man was bound to respect."

Taney's opinion outraged many northerners, especially members of the new Republican Party. Abraham Lincoln attacked the decision throughout his debates with Stephen A. Douglas in 1858 and again during the presidential campaign of 1860. The decision forced Republicans to take a firm stand in favor of black citizenship and fundamental rights for blacks. Some Republicans went further, arguing for black equality and suffrage.

Although the *Dred Scott* decision denied civil rights to blacks, the Lincoln administration and the Civil War Congress ignored it. During the War Congress banned slavery in all the western territories, despite Taney's assertation that such an act was unconstitutional. In 1866 Congress sent the FOURTEENTH AMENDMENT to the states, which declared that all persons born in the nation were citizens of the United States and of the state in which they lived. The ratification of this amendment, in 1868, made the civil rights aspects of *Dred Scott* a dead letter. The decision nevertheless remains a potent symbol of the denial of civil rights, and the constitutionalization of racism, under the Constitution of 1787.

BIBLIOGRAPHY

Angle, Paul. *Created Equal? The Complete Lincoln-Douglas Debates of 1858.* 1958.

Fehrenbacher, Don E. *The Dred Scott Case: Its Significance in American Law and Politics.* 1978.

Finkelman, Paul. *Dred Scott v. Sandford: A Brief History With Documents.* 1997.

Paul Finkelman

DRUM

See Dodge Revolutionary Union Movement.

Dual Citizenship

Representative Homer Snyder of New York developed the Indian Citizenship Bill. On June 2, 1924, the

United States Congress passed the AMERICAN INDIAN CITIZENSHIP ACT (42 US Statute 253). This legislation granted all noncitizen Indians the rights of citizenship and authorized the Secretary of Interior to give to all Indians born within the territorial boundaries of the United States certificates of citizenship. The 1924 Indian Citizenship Act did not impair, limit, or remove any civil, political, or property rights Indians held by treaty arrangement or by the U.S. Constitution. The law allowed Indians to vote in federal elections. By the time Congress passed the 1924 legislation probably two-thirds of Indian people were already citizens. Some had served in World War I, others had taken allotments of land according to the 1887 DAWES SEVERALTY ACT, and some Indian women had married white men. The law extended CITIZENSHIP to approximately 125,000 noncitizen reservation Indians in 1924. Inclusion of specific provisions that U.S. citizenship would not limit other Indian rights was important. The U.S. Supreme Court had decided that Indians with U.S. citizenship could not benefit from federal Indian programs (*In re Heff*, 1905) but then had reversed that ruling in 1916 (*U.S. v. Nice*). In general, Indians live under a dual system of citizenship as citizens of the United States and of a tribe. By the Citizenship Act of 1924, Indians' trust relationships with the United States were not affected. Nevertheless, a major purpose was to merge Indians into the general citizenry and assimilate them into American society.

Through many varied stages, Indians became citizens of the United States. In 1881, the Women's National Indian Association sought citizenship for Indians by petitioning the Congress for this basic right. In 1884 the Supreme Court decided that a tribal member could not voluntarily withdraw from a tribe and become a U.S. citizen. In effect, the FOURTEENTH AMENDMENT excluded Indians from citizenship (*Elk v. Wilkins*, 1884). In the General Allotment Act of 1887, Henry Dawes wrote in provisions that granted citizenship to Indians taking individual allotments of land and leaving the tribe and living a "civilized life." After receiving their allotments, Indians became U.S. citizens and became subject to a state's criminal and civil law. In 1888 Congress enacted legislation that granted citizenship to Indian women who married white men. The World War I era brought additional changes.

In 1919 Representative Homer Snyder prepared the Indian Veterans Citizenship Bill. On November 6, 1919, Congress enacted legislation extending citizenship to World War I Indian veterans (41 US Statute 350). Over 12,000 Indians, most of whom were volunteers, had served in the U.S. military service during World War I. Full citizenship "with all the privileges pertaining" to it was given to Indian veterans who received honorable discharges.

Many Indians never liked the idea of becoming United States citizens. Among the Iroquois, including the Onondagas, Mohawks, and others, there was resistance to citizenship. They emphasized tribal sovereignty and Indian nationhood. One Mohawk said of the 1924 Citizenship Act, "The law of 1924 cannot . . . apply to Indians, since they are independent nations. Congress may as well pass a law making Mexicans citizens." The Onondaga also opposed the Indian Citizenship Act (1924) among other federal enactments. Leon Shenandoah has said, "We are a separate nation and intend to govern our affairs without outside interference." In reality, powers are shared and exercised by the federal government, tribal authorities, and, to some extent, by state governments.

In the past, states placed severe limitations on Indians' voting rights. Some states required that in order to vote one had to be a citizen. This rule kept all reservation Indians from voting before the 1924 Indian Citizenship Act. States also disfranchised nonreservation Indians who could not establish that they had ended their tribal relationship. Four states passed laws that required voters to be "civilized." Other kept from the polls all "Indians not taxed." Three states required that voters be citizens, residents, and taxpayers. Indians were disqualified from voting in some states because they were wards of the federal government. Because Indians lived on reservations, some states said they were not citizens of a state. Literacy tests, poll taxes, and other methods were used to keep Indians from voting.

Even though Indians became U.S. citizens in 1924 and could vote in federal elections, many states kept them from voting in state and local elections until the 1950s and 1960s. For example, the federal government forced New Mexico to grant its Indian people the right to vote in state and local elections. Indians are not only citizens of the United States but of the states where they live. As such they have the same civil rights as all other citizens. It took some struggle to establish the facts expressed in the Fourteenth Amendment, which states that all persons "born or naturalized in the United States . . . are citizens of the United States and of the state wherein they reside." Indians are guaranteed "equal protection of the laws" as are all citizens. But states have denied Indian citizens the right to hold public office, vote, attend public schools and serve as jurors. States have justified these denials on the special rights Indians benefit from by federal treaties. Also, states claimed such inequities were justifiable because Indians do not pay certain taxes. Therefore, "Indians should not have all the benefits of state citizenship because they do not share all of the burdens." Others have argued that "it should be sufficient for American Indians to have tribal membership and United States citizenship without having to be an official resident of a particular state."

The Indians' right to vote is protected by the federal government. The right to vote is the fundamental civil right in a democratic society. It is the basic right of citizenship. The FIFTEENTH AMENDMENT (1870) guarantees that a citizen shall not be denied the right to vote because of race. The Twenty-Fourth Amendment protects citizens against imposition of a poll tax. The August 6, 1975, additions to the 1965 VOTING RIGHTS ACT protect the voting rights of non-English speaking citizens by permitting voting in more than one language. Indians are specifically protected by this law. Civil rights laws also defend and protect Indian citizenship.

On April 11, 1968, Congress passed the Civil Rights Act (87 US Statute 77), a law that guarantees Indians on reservations the same civil rights and liberties in relation to tribal authorities that the Constitution guarantees to all persons in relation to federal and state governments. (See AMERICAN INDIAN CIVIL RIGHTS ACT OF 1968.) In effect the 1968 law extended the rights of the BILL OF RIGHTS (1791) and Fourteenth Amendment (1868) to tribal members on reservations in relation to their tribal government. The law protected the individual's rights against tribal government actions. Some Indians feared the 1968 act would alter the traditional forms of government on reservations and encroach upon tribal sovereignty. The federal government, in protecting an individual's rights, might restrict tribal authority to make decisions for the whole Indian nation. The 1968 law also limited the tribes' rights to fines for crimes committed on reservations to $1,000 or six months in jail. Title IV of the act repealed PL 280 (1953) that gave some states authority to extend criminal and civil jurisdiction to reservations. Now, states had to obtain tribal consent before they could extend the state's jurisdiction over Indian reservations.

In describing Indian citizenship Wilma Mankiller has observed of Indians, "We are more of a republic than a reservation and exist in a complex set of laws in relationship to the U.S. government." Of this complex relationship of federal to tribal law she says, "We view it as a dual citizenship." All Indians born in the United States, or outside the country to American citizen Indian parents, are U.S. citizens. They have all the rights and responsibilities of citizenship. They are as well citizens of the state wherein they reside. US citizenship was generally conferred on Indians in 1924 but before that date some treaties, allotment acts and other measures extended citizenship to individual Indians. Moreover, Indians have citizenship as tribal members. American citizenship does not limit the relationship between the federal government and Indian tribes.

BIBLIOGRAPHY

Calloway, Colin G. First Peoples: A Documentary Survey of American Indian History. 1999.

Castile, George Pierre and Robert L. Bee, eds. State and Reservation: New Perspectives on Federal Indian Policy. 1992.

Cohen, Felix S. Felix S. Cohen's Handbook of Federal Indian Law. Edited by Rennard Strickland. 1982.

Lee, R. Alton. "Indian Citizenship and the Fourteenth Amendment." South Dakota History, 4 (1974).

Murdock, Donald B. "The Case for Native American Tribal Citizenship." Indian Historian 8 (1975): 2–5.

Pevar, Stephen L. The Rights of Indians and Tribes. 1992.

Smith, Michael T. "The History of Indian Citizenship." Great Plains Journal 10 (1970): 25–30.

Stein, Gary C. "The Indian Citizenship Act of 1924." New Mexico Historical Review 47 (1972): 257–273.

Wolfley, Jeanette. "Jim Crow, Indian Style: The Disenfranchisement of Native Americans." American Indian Law Review 16 (1991): 167–202.

Ziontz, Alvin J. "After Martinez: Indian Civil Rights Under Tribal Government." University of California, Davis, Law Review 12 (1979): 1–35.

Rodger C. Henderson

Du Bois, William Edward Burghardt

(1868–1963), historian, sociologist, intellectual.

W. E. B. Du Bois was born in Great Barrington, Massachusetts, and raised in its ethnically diverse and seemingly tolerant New England environment. Years later, when Du Bois wrote his masterpiece, The Souls of Black Folk (1903), he revealed that despite the diversity of Great Barrington and the relative racial tolerance of the North, he still suffered racial slights in his childhood. These slights spurred him to leave the North and attend Fisk University in Nashville, Tennessee, in part to discover what it was like to live in a virtually all-black environment. His revelations about black life in the South and the intense racial discrimination that characterized it pushed Du Bois to devote his life to securing full civil rights for African Americans.

Du Bois's civil rights strategy was markedly different from those of many other early fighters for justice. Somewhat paradoxically his approach was decidedly elitist and placed its faith in the hands of what he termed the "Talented Tenth." His desire to work through channels like the American Negro Academy—an intellectual society dedicated to "civilizing the race," which he helped establish and eventually lead—was fueled by his educational experiences after Fisk, when he enrolled at Harvard University with advanced standing and completed a second B.A. in 1890. From 1890 to 1895, Du Bois pursued doctoral studies

W. E. B. Du Bois, ca. 1945. (Archive Photos)

at both the University of Berlin and Harvard. When he received his Harvard Ph.D. in 1895, he was the first black to do so from that school.

Over the next several years, Du Bois was affiliated with Wilberforce University, the University of Pennsylvania, and Atlanta University. While working as a researcher at Penn, Du Bois produced *Philadelphia Negro*, a thorough survey of black Philadelphia, the methodology of which helped establish the field of urban sociology. At Atlanta, Du Bois edited fourteen social-science surveys of black America. These works alone would have justified his centrality to American sociology, history, and African-American Studies.

Du Bois, however, was not content to pursue civil rights gains merely by scholarly projects that made plain how American social injustice followed a racial line. Instead, Du Bois took a lead role in early nationalist and politically militant organizations (see BLACK NATIONALISM). In 1900, he served as secretary of the First Pan-African Conference in London (see PAN-AFRICAN CONGRESSES) and in 1905 he founded the NIAGARA MOVEMENT. The (all-black) Niagara Movement was made up of middle-class reformers who opposed the accommodationist politics of Booker T. WASHINGTON. During the short existence of the Niagara Movement (1905–1909), its members issued a series of manifestos that decried the social and politi-

cal repression of blacks. "In the past year the work of the Negro hater has flourished in the land," the first manifesto declared. "Stripped of verbose subterfuge and in its naked nastiness, the new American creed says: fear to let black men even try to rise lest they become the equals of whites."

The call for civil rights reforms that came from the Niagara Movement was in stark contrast to Washington's conservative race politics. Washington, the head of Tuskegee Institute and the most prominent advocate of industrial EDUCATION for blacks, supported the separation of the races in "all things social." His position made him a popular figure in white America and he quickly became the most powerful black in the United States. Du Bois railed against Washington, claiming that his politics only worsened race relations and perpetuated blacks' second-class citizenship; he challenged Washington's politics on the grounds that it asked blacks to give up three things: "political power," "insistence on civil rights," and the "higher education of Negro youth."

Even though Du Bois disagreed with Washington, he could not approach the latter's influence. In 1909, however, the balance of power slowly began to shift when Du Bois joined with several white progressives to found the NATIONAL ASSOCIATION FOR THE ADVANCEMENT OF COLORED PEOPLE (NAACP). Du Bois, the sole black among the original officers of the Association, served as the director of publicity and research and also edited *The* CRISIS, the journal of the NAACP. Du Bois's power and influence came through his editorial control of that journal. The NAACP was officially a nonpartisan organization, but Du Bois never hesitated to make his personal positions known. During World War I he came under heavy criticism for calling on black America to support Woodrow Wilson's efforts to save Europe. Du Bois believed that if blacks demonstrated their patriotism abroad they would be rewarded at home; a few years later, Du Bois realized that his hope was misplaced. He publicly decried the lynching of returning soldiers, the disfranchisment of blacks, and the broken promises of American democracy. He warned the country, "We return. We return from fighting. We return fighting. Make way for Democracy! We saved it in France, and by the Great Jehovah, we will save it in the United States of America, or know the reason why."

Du Bois's vocal and independent politics were soon increasingly unwelcome in the NAACP. As subscriptions to *The Crisis* plummeted during the Great Depression, pressure mounted within the NAACP to rein him in. At the same time, Du Bois was developing a new race-based Marxist analysis of society that distanced him from the NAACP's middle-class legalist approach to civil rights and justice. In 1934, Du Bois resigned from the organization, making clear that his new economic philosophy, which called for black economic cooperatives, had no home in the NAACP. Du Bois's class analysis was further articulated when he published *Black Reconstruction* the following year; even though an emphasis on the economic and material aspects of black reconstruction is accepted today, he was roundly criticized for these views in 1935.

Du Bois settled back into academic life with a new appointment at Atlanta University, only to return to the NAACP in 1944 as the director of special research. His second stint with the organization was significantly shorter than the first. Still the outspoken political independent, Du Bois was dismissed from the NAACP in 1948. In that year, he endorsed the presidential candidacy of PROGRESSIVE PARTY candidate Henry WALLACE. During this period he renewed his involvement in PAN-AFRICANISM and repeatedly called for the self-government and independence of colonial Africa. Immediately after being dismissed by the NAACP, Du Bois began serving as cochair of the Council of African Affairs and became involved in the international peace movement. In 1950, he ran unsuccessfully for the United States Senate as the candidate for the Progressive Party in New York. The following year he was indicted for failing to register as an agent of a foreign government. This indictment came because of his chairmanship of the Peace Information Center, a Stockholm-based antinuclear weapons group. At the time of his arrest Du Bois denied the charges, declaring that he was not an agent for any government but an agent for peace. Even though he was acquitted of the charges, he was labeled a communist sympathizer and was denied a passport for the next seven years.

In 1959 he went to Moscow to receive the Lenin Peace Prize. Three years after winning back the right to travel abroad, Du Bois bitterly concluded that African Americans would never win justice and full civil rights in the United States. In 1961, he declared his allegiance to the Communist Party, renounced his United States citizenship, and accepted President Kwame Nkrumah's invitation to move to Ghana. Two years later, on the eve of the historic March on Washington for Jobs and Freedom, Du Bois died in Ghana. Even though he was a declared communist and a citizen of another country, he was remembered by the leaders on that momentous day as one of the fathers of civil rights in America.

BIBLIOGRAPHY

Aptheker, Herbert, ed. *The Correspondence of W. E. B. Du Bois,* Vol. 1. *Selections 1877–1934.* 1973.
Aptheker, Herbert, ed. *The Correspondence of W. E. B. Du Bois,* Vol. 2. *Selections 1934–1944.* 1976.
Aptheker, Herbert, ed. *The Correspondence of W. E. B. Du Bois,* Vol. 3. *Selections 1944–1963.* 1978.
Lewis, David Levering. *W. E. B. Du Bois: Biography of a Race, 1868–1919.* 1993.
Lewis, David Levering, ed. *W. E. B. Du Bois: A Reader.* 1995.
Logan, Rayford, and Michael Winston. *Dictionary of American Negro Biography.* 1982.

Jonathan Scott Holloway

Durham Manifesto

Known as the "capital" of the Southern black middle class because of its many successful African-American businesses, Durham, North Carolina, was the logical place for regional leaders to convene as the Southern Conference on Race Relations, on October 20, 1942, to address problems of increasing racial tension, Gordon Blaine HANCOCK, a black sociologist and moderate, directed the conference; Luther Porter JACKSON and P. B. Young, owner and editor of the *Norfolk Journal and Guide,* took leading roles. Among the fifty-two participants were Charles Spurgeon Johnson of Fisk University, Benjamin MAYS of Morehouse College, and Rufus Clement of Atlanta University, former members of the COMMISSION ON INTERRACIAL COOPERATION (CIC).

On December 15, 1942, the conference issued the Durham Manifesto, a position paper that stated the delegates' fundamental opposition to racial inequality. The statement, addressing "current problems of racial discrimination and neglect," made a plea for equal pay and opportunities in industry, the abolition of poll taxes and all-white primaries (see VOTING RIGHTS), the protection of civil rights, and a federal ANTI-LYNCHING law. It also urged white moderates to actively support blacks in combating racial discrimination. However, it was carefully written to avoid a direct demand for DESEGREGATION of schools and other public accommodations, issues that were then felt to be too inflammatory.

White moderates responded with a conference of their own, and in June 1943, the two groups met in Richmond, Virginia, where it was decided that the Commission on Interracial Cooperation would replaced by a new organization, the SOUTHERN REGIONAL COUNCIL. Many felt the Durham Manifesto too aggressive, but the common platform drafted by the two groups also avoided directly addressing the issue of SEGREGATION. While the Durham Manifesto emphasized racial equality and not desegregation, it marked a major step in defining the antisegregationist position of Southern black moderates.

BIBLIOGRAPHY

Gavins, Raymond. *The Perils and Prospects of Southern Black Leadership: Gordon Blaine Hancock, 1884–1970.* 1977.

Logan, Rayford Whittingham, ed. *What The Negro Wants.* 1944.

Maxwell, Louise P. "Durham Manifesto." In *Encyclopedia of African-American Culture and History,* edited by Jack Salzman, David Lionel Smith, and Cornel West. 1996.

Melodie Monahan

Durr, Virginia Foster

(1903–1999), Southern liberal activist.

Virginia Foster was born to white Southern privilege in Birmingham, Alabama, just as the legal structures of racial SEGREGATION were being secured; but her experiences during the DEPRESSION caused her to question the values and the expectations that had shaped her early life. As a relief volunteer for the Junior League, she witnessed the extreme deprivation that was the lot of miners and workers in and around Birmingham. The poverty and accumulated misery that had long been invisible, she recalled, "gave me my first and ineradicable lesson on the injustice and inequalities of our society."

Virginia and her husband Clifford Durr, a young Rhodes scholar and lawyer whom she married in 1926, moved to Washington, D.C., in 1933, where Clifford took a job with the Reconstruction Finance Corporation. The democratic activism and political initiatives of the NEW DEAL provided Durr with a framework for understanding what could be done to meet the challenges raised by the Depression. Both she and her husband became avid supporters of Franklin ROOSEVELT and the pioneering reform efforts of the New Deal.

Through her work with the Women's Division of the Democratic National Committee, Durr became active in efforts to expand VOTING RIGHTS for women in the South. Her interests led her to black educator and civil rights leader Mary McLeod BETHUNE, who advised Durr of the efforts being made by the NATIONAL ASSOCIATION FOR THE ADVANCEMENT OF COLORED PEOPLE (NAACP) and other groups to expand voting rights in the South. Durr also became acquainted with fellow Southerners, white and black, who were committed to building a broad base of support for New Deal reforms. She worked closely with Clark FOREMAN in planning an interracial meeting in Birmingham, Alabama, in 1938, dedicated to confronting the economic inequities that undermined the development of the South's resources and people. Circumstances also caused the historic gathering to take a stand against racial segregation, a new departure for Southern LIBERALISM. The meeting culminated with the founding of the SOUTHERN CONFERENCE FOR HUMAN WELFARE (SCHW).

Durr became a leading organizer of the SCHW's campaign to secure congressional legislation to abolish the poll tax in federal elections and a director of the NATIONAL COMMITTEE TO ABOLISH THE POLL TAX. During WORLD WAR II, she worked with Eleanor ROOSEVELT to expand and protect the voting rights of black and white soldiers serving in the armed forces. During the 1940s, Durr was active in efforts to register black and white voters in Virginia, working closely with Luther Porter JACKSON, head of the Virginia Voters League.

Virginia and Clifford Durr were both vocal critics of the TRUMAN administration's cold war policies, particularly the loyalty program aimed at ridding the government of COMMUNIST sympathizers. Durr's experiences in the civil rights movement made her especially wary of the abuses inherent in such a program. She wrote: "My position on communists is what it has always been—that they represent the extreme left of the political circuit, and I often disagree with their program and methods, but I see so clearly that when one group of people is made untouchable the liberties of all suffer, and our Democracy is on the way to ruin. I see and feel so clearly how it has crippled the lives and hopes of both the Negro and the white people of the South."

In 1948, Durr supported the third party presidential candidacy of Henry WALLACE and ran for the U.S. Senate in Virginia on Wallace's PROGRESSIVE PARTY ticket. In the South, Wallace's campaign built on the inroads that the SCHW, NAACP chapters, and CIO unions had made during the 1940s by promoting voter registration, holding integrated public meetings, and running black and white candidates for office on the Progressive Party ticket. Wallace toured the South from VIRGINIA to MISSISSIPPI in the fall of 1948, and spoke only to nonsegregated groups, a first for a major presidential candidate. The tour generated violent protests, as well as impressive showings of support. Harry Truman did not tour the South during his presidential campaign.

Their unwillingness to accommodate the cold war orthodoxy made it increasingly difficult for the Durrs to remain in Washington. In 1951, after a brief stay in Denver, where Clifford's support of Virginia's political liberalism (expressed by her opposition to the Korean War) cost him his job, they returned to Alabama, settling in Montgomery. In 1954, Virginia Durr was subpoenaed to appear before a special hearing of Senator James EASTLAND's Internal Security Subcommittee in New Orleans. Durr submitted a statement saying that she was not a Communist and declaring her "utter and complete contempt of this committee." Upon appearing before the committee, she refused to answer any questions. Sitting there, silently, she occasionally took out her compact and powdered her nose. In large part because of the intervention of her friend Senate Majority Leader Lyndon JOHNSON, Eastland's committee did not hold Durr in contempt.

In Montgomery, the Durrs joined the local chapter of the NAACP and became acquainted with E. D. NIXON, Rosa PARKS, and other civil rights activists. When Parks was arrested in December 1955 for refusing to give up her seat on a city bus to a white man, Cliff and Virginia Durr accompanied Nixon to bail Parks out of jail. Clifford Durr advised young African-American attorney Fred GRAY on making a legal challenge to bus segregation in Montgomery, which culminated in a SUPREME COURT ruling that ordered desegregation of the buses. Meanwhile, Virginia Durr had aided the boycotters, often driving them home from work, and helped raise Northern financial support.

Durr chronicled the movement in Montgomery and throughout the South in an outpouring of letters to friends in other parts of the country. Her letters convey the power of the mass black protests that nurtured the early leadership of Martin Luther KING, JR., as well as the vicious determination of white Southern resistance and the indifference of the federal government and Northern public opinion. Durr embraced the student movement sparked by the SIT-IN protests in 1960, and housed and fed many of the young people traveling South during the 1960s. However, she challenged Northerners who viewed race as exclusively a "Southern" problem, and predicted that the despair and poverty that circumscribed the lives and opportunities of blacks in Northern cities would erupt in violence.

The fall of legalized segregation in the South raised new challenges in the struggle for economic and racial justice. During the 1970s and 1980s, Durr remained active in local and state politics, and was a popular speaker on college campuses and at historical conventions. In 1994, she received an honorary doctorate from the University of Alabama. Never content to dwell on the past, Durr continued to speak out against economic inequalities, and remained a passionate advocate of racial INTEGRATION. She frequently asked young people, often somewhat impatiently, "Well, what are *you* going to do?"

BIBLIOGRAPHY

Barnard, Hollinger F., ed. *Outside the Magic Circle: The Autobiography of Virginia Foster Durr.* 1985.

Salmond, John A. *The Conscience of a Lawyer: Clifford J. Durr and American Civil Liberties, 1899–1975.* 1990.

Sullivan, Patricia. *Days of Hope: Race and Democracy in the New Deal Era.* 1996.

Patricia Sullivan

E

Eastland, James O.

(1905–1986), senator.

James O. Eastland, a native of Doddsville, Mississippi, served in the U.S. Senate from 1942 until 1978. During the last six years of his senatorial career, he was president pro tem. He was a member of Mississippi's plantation elite and espoused notions of paternalism and black inferiority.

Eastland's first significant senatorial speech was an ill-informed proclamation of black inferiority. Near the end of World War II, Eastland pronounced the performance of African-American soldiers as unsatisfactory. Eastland said they were lazy, ignorant, and inclined toward sexual violence. Efforts to incorporate such inferior beings into American life, he said, would lead to social equality and interracial marriage.

Predictably, when the Supreme Court ruled in the BROWN v. BOARD OF EDUCATION (1954) case, Eastland called for a restoration of "Americanism" and massive resistance. He quickly joined forces with the WHITE CITIZENS' COUNCIL. Like other leading Citizens' Council supporters, he consistently portrayed black and white advocates of civil rights reform as communists.

Throughout the 1960s, he used his position as chair of the powerful Senate Judiciary Committee to block civil rights legislation. Consequently, Eastland became a lightening rod for advocates of civil rights reform. His sharpest critic was Fannie Lou HAMER, who like Eastland resided in Sunflower County. Until his retirement in 1978, African-American activists in the Delta made unseating Eastland their primary goal.

Realizing that federal legislation and Mississippi demographics made appeals to African Americans necessary for statewide political candidates, Eastland sought (but failed to receive) support from the state

Three Southern Democratic senators meet on March 21, 1964, to discuss the tactics of their opposition to the Civil Rights Bill of 1964. From left to right: Harry F. Byrd, Sr., of Virginia; Allen Ellender of Louisiana; and James O. Eastland of Mississippi. (CORBIS/ Bettmann)

NAACP. Stunned by the shunning of representatives of a race he professed to love, Eastland resigned from the Senate. He lived out his retirement on his 5,800-acre cotton plantation.

BIBLIOGRAPHY

Dittmer, John. *Local People: The Struggle for Civil Rights in Mississippi.* 1994.
Marsh, George. *God's Long Summer: Stories of Faith and Civil Rights.* 1997.
Mills, Kay. *This Little Light of Mine: The Life of Fannie Lou Hamer.* 1993.

Bradley G. Bond

Eastman, Charles Alexander

(1858–1939), Native American physician, author.

Charles Eastman was a leader who explained Native American values and hardships. At the same time, he personified the confusion in Native American societies during their period of greatest peril early in the twentieth century. He was born near the Lower Agency jurisdiction in Minnesota in 1858 as a Santee Dakota, who endured upheaval surrounding the Sioux War of 1862. Through encouragement from his father Many Lightnings, Charles began a formal education at age 15, graduated from Dartmouth College in 1887, and from Boston University School of Medicine in 1890. Thereafter he pursued a career in federal service as a physician at Pine Ridge Agency, 1890–1893; Carlisle Indian School as an "outing agent" to observe its graduates, 1899; Crow Creek Agency as a physician, 1900–1903; and investigator of tribal rolls, 1903–1909, especially as preparation for the federal claims payment due Dakota people for losses following the 1862 war.

With many books Eastman explained tribal cultures and circumstances to outsiders. His *Indian Boyhood* (1902) and *From the Deep Woods to Civilization* (1916) were autobiographical. *The Soul of the Indian* (1911) was an expression of spiritual traditions. As a founder and leader in the pioneering Pan-Indian Society of American Indians (founded 1911) and a recipient of the Chicago Indian Council File award, he defended Indian rights and exemplified tribal accomplishments.

In several ways he personified confusion in the lives of his Native American contemporaries. A tribal legend indicated that the young Eastman missed Dakota exile because relatives who headed for Canada after the 1862 war left him in the care of a white settler in exchange for food. Soon he joined Santee relatives who renounced tribalism to become Flandreau Santee homesteaders, and entered his name on a tribal roll that transferred to the federal Flandreau Indian Boarding School. Due to resulting confusion coupled with changes of residence during federal service, he received benefits from three jurisdictions. As a former Santee of Nebraska, Eastman received an 80-acre allotment on the Santee Reservation. As a Flandreau Santee, he used the 1889 Lakota Sioux Agreement to claim $160 instead of 160 acres on Lakota land or ceded acreage. As a Flandreau Santee in federal service at Pine Ridge, he accepted the issue of four head of livestock for himself plus two head for his daughter. During 1905, an audit turned Eastman (and his half-brother Demas) into a test case for tribal members who without fraudulent intent received benefits at several jurisdictions. Charles requested a deduction of $160 from his salary and the return of his 80-acre Santee allotment in order to exercise his right under the 1889 Agreement to take 160 acres on Lakota land or the Rosebud ceded acreage in Gregory County as a suitable settlement.

Among Native Americans, Eastman exemplified professional achievement, opposition to federal mismanagement, and devotion to cultural preservation as well as legal rights among American Indians.

BIBLIOGRAPHY

Wilson, Raymond. *Ohiyesa: Charles Eastman, Santee Sioux.* 1983.

Herbert T. Hoover

East St. Louis Race Riot of 1917

American participation in WORLD WAR I, with the avowed objective of making the world safe for democ-

National Guardsmen escort a frightened black man to safety during the East St. Louis Race Riot on June 6, 1917. (CORBIS/Bettmann)

racy, led at home to a contradictory series of racial conflicts in the nation's industrial cities. East St. Louis (1917), Houston (1919), Knoxville (1919), Chicago (1919), and TULSA (1921) produced explosions of murder, arson, and massive assaults on the civil rights of African Americans. These riots tightened the grip of segregation in American cities and worsened the already dismal relations between white and black citizens.

East St. Louis, Illinois, was an industrial poor sister to its wealthier namesake across the Mississippi River. Its fully segregated population was principally blue-collar labor which increased rapidly with the outbreak of European war in 1914. Black and white southerners left their rural backgrounds to compete for employment, housing, and social satisfaction in rapidly changing East St. Louis. When the Aluminum Ore Company fired two hundred white workers and recruited four hundred black workers, where there had been none a few years earlier, tensions escalated and white workers went out on strike. Democratic politicians blamed Republican industrialists for importing black strikers and Republican voters. Wartime enthusiasm led to white perceptions of black invaders seeking to take over the community. For black residents the martial perception focused on the need to fight back to protect their lives and property.

The riot was sparked July 1, 1917, when a Ford sedan with four white men in it drove through the black section of the city firing racial slurs and revolvers. Minutes later, four plainclothes police responding to the drive-by shootings drove their unmarked Ford police car to the scene of the disturbance. There they were met by a barrage of fire from black gunners who confused them with the earlier white raiders. Two police in the car were killed, and the other two were wounded. The story quickly spread into white East St. Louis where white workers combined by the thousands to retaliate. Rioters powered their way across black neighborhoods burning three hundred homes and killing black victims. Officially, the death count was declared to be 39 blacks and 9 whites with 750 wounded. Credible witnesses, including the police, however, estimated the deaths at over one hundred in this first battle in America's war at home.

BIBLIOGRAPHY

Rudwick, Elliot. *Race Riot at East St. Louis July 2, 1917.* 1964.

Rudwick, Elliot, editor. *The East St. Louis Race Riot of 1917* (Film). University Publications of America, Frederick, Md. 1985.

Clifford H. Scott

Edelman, Marian Wright

(1939–), activist and attorney.

Marian Wright Edelman, an acclaimed "crusading" attorney for disadvantaged children, was the founding president of the CHILDREN'S DEFENSE FUND (CDF) and is a civil rights movement activist. Wright, an African American, was born on June 6, 1939, in the rural town of Bennettesville, South Carolina, to Arthur Jerome Wright (a minister) and Maggie Leola Bowen Wright (a housewife). Although blacks and whites in and around Bennettesville had separate neighborhoods, schools, and churches, Marian's parents expected their five children to become educated and serve their community in spite of SEGREGATION.

Wright attended Marlboro Training High School and pursued a degree at Spelman College in Atlanta, Georgia. Her outstanding academic record won her a Charles Merrill Grant for study abroad in her junior year. Participating in a liberating experience abroad lessened Wright's desire to return to the segregated South of the late 1950s. However, she returned to Spelman for her senior year to encounter college student protests. In Atlanta, she participated in a sit-in in which she was among fourteen students arrested (see SIT-INS). This experience led her to forego a plan for graduate studies in Russia in order to attend Yale University Law School. Graduating as valedictorian from Spelman entitled her to become John Hay Whitney Fellow at Yale.

During her final year at Yale in 1963, Wright traveled to MISSISSIPPI to work on voter registration campaigns there. After completing her Yale law degree, Wright returned to Mississippi to work as one of the first two Legal Defense and Education interns of the NATIONAL ASSOCIATION FOR THE ADVANCEMENT OF COLORED PEOPLE (NAACP). She also opened a law office after becoming the first African-American woman to pass the bar examination in Mississippi. As Bernice McNair Barnett illustrates in *Sisters in Struggle*, Wright and other black women lawyers performed key leadership roles in the black civil rights struggle as they worked behind-the-scenes on legal briefs, bail bonds, and school DESEGREGATION. One of Wright's most significant functions was her profound commitment to getting youth demonstrators out of jail. She continued her civil rights activism in Mississippi by heading the NAACP Legal Defense and Education Fund there until 1968.

While in Mississippi, Wright met and married Peter Edelman, a Harvard Law School graduate and one of Robert F. Kennedy's legislative assistants. Their interracial union produced three children, Joshua, Jonah, and Ezra. During her Mississippi civil rights work,

Marian Wright Edelman, the president of the Children's Defense Fund, addresses a Call to Renewal luncheon in Washington, D.C., on September 14, 1996. The Call to Renewal group was formed to attempt to counter the effects of the religious right. (AP/Wide World Photos)

Marian realized that in order to change the situation there she needed to change federal policies. She received a Field Foundation Grant to research how to make laws that would help disadvantaged individuals. Thus, she moved to Washington, D.C., in March 1968 and helped develop the Washington Research Project; its goal was to make new laws and existing laws better to help poor people. In 1973, she created and became president of the CHILDREN'S DEFENSE FUND.

Marian Wright Edelman is the author of *Children Out of School in America* (1974); *Portrait of Inequality: Black and White Children in America* (1980); *School Suspensions: Are They Helping Children?* (1980); and *Families in Peril: An Agenda for Social Change* (1987).

BIBLIOGRAPHY

Barnett, Bernice McNair. *Sisters in Struggle: Invisible Black Women Leaders of the Civil Rights Movement, 1945–1975.* (Forthcoming).

Guy-Sheftall, Beverly. "Marian Wright Edelman." In *Notable Black American Women*, edited by Jessie Carney Smith. 1992.

Morris, Aldon. *The Origins of the Civil Rights Movement.* 1984.

Otfinoski, Steve. *Marian Wright Edelman: Defender of Children's Rights.* 1991.

Thompson, Kathleen. "Marian Wright Edelman." In *Black Women in America*, edited by Darlene Clark Hine. 1993.

Shaunda Partida

Education

The modern civil rights movement cannot be understood apart from the conditions of social inequality that characterized American society at the beginning of the twentieth century. This earlier period was characterized by a legacy of institutional RACISM and discrimination rooted in the perceived threat that white America was to lose its dominance of post–Civil War political and economic institutions. This period was also a formative period for American civil rights, witnessing the elevation of education for black and Latino Americans as a central component of demands for social justice that would climax in the 1950s and 1960s.

Black public education after the Civil War became a preeminent national concern after the passage of the three RECONSTRUCTION amendments to the U.S. Constitution, including the THIRTEENTH AMENDMENT (1865), outlawing slavery; the FOURTEENTH AMENDMENT (1867), defining citizenship; and the FIFTEENTH AMENDMENT (1870), providing the right to vote for all males, regardless of race. Prior to the Civil War, blacks had been incorporated into the nation's economy as property and into its social life as a separate community whose participation in public life was highly limited and controlled. The end of the Civil War demanded that a community of previously marginalized American citizens be incorporated as full-fledged participants in American society. Providing black Americans with the opportunity for an education was an important way to accomplish this goal, but one that would require large-scale changes.

While philanthropic investment from the American North funded the first schools for a small number of blacks after the Civil War, Reconstruction administrations in the South organized the first public school systems available to large numbers of black students between 1865 and 1877. Those efforts were short-lived, however. Former Confederate officials regained political control of Southern state governments following a political compromise in 1877 between Republican President Rutherford B. Hayes and Southern Democrats. Fueled by antiblack sentiment and a disdain for the civil rights legislation of "carpetbagger" regimes, these reactionary state officials began a systematic assault on newly won black liberties that would continue through the end of the century, including limits on their access to public privileges and services. By 1890, poll taxes, grandfather clauses (exempting whites from literacy-test requirements demanded of minorities), labor restrictions, and impediments to travel had eroded the rights won by blacks during Reconstruction. State officials were aided in their dismissal of black civil rights by state and federal courts, whose legal decisions turned the new restrictions into law. In a landmark case that seemed to exemplify the reaction against black freedom, the Supreme Court of the United States in 1896 announced its monumental PLESSY V. FERGUSON decision. In *Plessy*, the Supreme Court declared that the U.S. Constitution permitted state governments to separate blacks and whites in "separate-but-equal" public accommodations through state law, a practice known as JIM CROW style SEGREGATION. Protected by the separate-but-equal doctrine announced in *Plessy*, Jim Crow created a new system of social relations in the American South that tightly regulated the conduct of black Americans in public until the beginning of the modern civil rights movement. If the Civil War had ended with the promise of social equality for black Americans, by 1896 that promise had been wholly abandoned by the American political system.

The formation of the NATIONAL ASSOCIATION FOR THE ADVANCEMENT OF COLORED PEOPLE (NAACP) in 1909 signaled the beginning of an organized attempt to stop the discriminatory and often violent results of Jim Crow segregation. Founded by a group of social activists that included black intellectual W. E. B. DU BOIS and wealthy white philanthropists committed to the cause of black rights, the NAACP fought the continued erosion of black civil rights and the absence of black participation in public life. Financial difficulties, the beginning of WORLD WAR I, and organizational questions made early success difficult. Nonetheless, in these early years and continuing through the 1920s, the NAACP commissioned exploratory legal cases designed to reestablish black civil rights in education, transportation, housing, and employment.

With the support of local chapters of the NAACP, these early cases expanded into an organized legal campaign in the 1930s. Charles Hamilton Houston, former dean of Howard Law School, was hired to direct the NAACP's Legal Committee starting in 1934 and became the chief architect of the NAACP's legal effort against segregated education. Directing a group of talented young lawyers trained in American constitutional law, many of whom (including U.S. Supreme Court Justice Thurgood MARSHALL) would go on to distinguished careers in the American legal establishment, Houston outlined a methodical legal campaign aimed at destroying Jim Crow. Under Houston's guidance, the NAACP lawyers filed strategic lawsuits in federal court against Southern state governments to increase funding for black schools, to establish university and postgraduate programs for blacks where none existed, and to erode the legal principles upon which *Plessy* rested. Notable cases included *Missouri ex rel. Gaines v. Canada* (Missouri, 1938), *Sipuel v. Oklahoma* (Oklahoma, 1948), *Sweatt v. Painter* (Texas, 1950), and *McLaurin v. Oklahoma* (Oklahoma, 1950). By 1952 the success of the NAACP attorneys in the area of education had established new legal principles upon which it could challenge the separate-but-equal doctrine itself. In BROWN V. BOARD OF EDUCATION (1954), a lawsuit argued by the NAACP attorneys that ranks among the most important cases in U.S. history, the U.S. Supreme Court unanimously declared the *Plessy v. Ferguson* decision of 1896 to be unconstitutional. Abandoning the rationale it had used to enshrine Jim Crow into law in 1896, the Supreme Court declared that the Fourteenth Amendment of the U.S. Constitution did not permit the segregation of blacks and whites in public accommodations, ordering the end of more than fifty years of state-supported segregation of blacks and whites in public facilities and ushering in the modern civil rights era. *Brown v. Board of Education* was also an important moment in American legal history, one which showed the ways in which law could be used to direct dramatic transformations in America's racial hierarchy. The NAACP's use of social-science research to show the detrimental effects of segregation on black pupils also generated wide debate among legal scholars that has continued through the present day.

Though less known than the efforts to establish black civil rights in public education, efforts by Latino citizens of the United States to desegregate public schools in the American Southwest are also of historical importance to the American civil rights movement. Beginning in 1930 and continuing over the next decade, Mexican-American plaintiffs initiated a series of sporadic legal actions in state courts to stop the segregation of Mexican-American schoolchildren in Southern California and south-central Texas. Early lawsuits included *Alvarez v. Lemon Grove* (San Diego, California, 1930) and *Salvatierra v. Independent School District* (Del Rio, Texas, 1930). While fear of black freedom in the years after Reconstruction had fueled the creation of a uniform system of segregated black schools in the former Confederate South, segregation of Mexican Americans was a more gradual and uneven response by school officials who became threatened by a rapid increase in the number of Mexican-American students in the Southwest after 1910.

Two reasons explained this rapid growth. First, the Mexican Revolution of 1910 uprooted millions of peasants from the Mexican countryside, thousands of whom fled permanently to the United States in search of work, land, and political stability. Second, increasing industrial, manufacturing, and agricultural capacity provided new employment opportunities for Mexican Americans in growing communities of the Southwest. While a pattern of discrimination against Mexican Americans had prevailed in many parts of the Southwest after the Mexican War (1846–1848), including segregation in some public school systems organized after 1850, only after 1910 did school officials begin to perceive and react to increased Mexican migration as a systematic threat to the racial composition of the Southwest's predominantly white school systems.

Seeking to expand on their earlier cases amid the growing civil rights activism of WORLD WAR II in America, Mexican-American plaintiffs renewed their legal effort against segregated public schools in 1944. Acting through a variety of Latin American civil rights organizations, including the LEAGUE OF UNITED LATIN AMERICAN CITIZENS (LULAC), the Alianza Hispana-Americana, and the AMERICAN GI FORUM, they won a series of related federal court cases in the same years that the NAACP attorneys were waging their attack on Jim Crow education in the American South. In *Mendez v. Westminster* (California, 1946), *Delgado v. Bastrop* (Texas, 1948), and *Gonzalez v. Sheely* (Arizona, 1952), attorneys used the federal courts to stop the arbitrary segregation of Mexican Americans near Los Angeles, San Antonio, and Phoenix. Using the same social-science arguments in court that the NAACP would later use in *Brown v. Board of Education* to attack the *Plessy* doctrine, these attorneys helped to reveal some of the systemic similarities between structures of segregation in the American Southwest and the American South.

While the Mexican-American legal effort against segregated schools in the American Southwest was a distinct movement that was smaller and less organized than the NAACP's legal campaign in the American South, the Mexican-American and black legal efforts can be understood as parallel and complementary components of the modern civil rights movement; one designed to establish the civil rights of minority citizens on a national level. While the organizational support of the respective black and Mexican-American communities was significant, American civil rights organizations—including the AMERICAN CIVIL LIBERTIES UNION, the American Jewish Congress, the NATIONAL LAWYERS GUILD, the Julius Rosenwald Fund, and the Marshall Civil Liberties Trust—simultaneously engaged in the American civil rights movement.

Legal efforts in the Mexican-American community against segregated schools slowed after 1955. Attorneys were increasingly stymied by legal nomenclature defining Latin Americans as "white" or "Caucasian," a legal technicality that made claims of segregation more difficult to establish. Meanwhile, recalcitrant school boards continued to justify segregation on the basis of language difficulties, claiming that pupils whose native language was often Spanish were ill-prepared to attend school alongside English-speaking whites. Finally, the absence of a unified legal attack made Mexican-American lawsuits more difficult to organize and sustain. Not until 1970, in *Cisneros v. Corpus Christi Independent School District* (Texas, 1970), did civil rights attorneys representing the MEXICAN AMERICAN LEGAL DEFENSE AND EDUCATION FUND (MALDEF) succeed in extending the legal protections established in *Brown v. Board of Education* to Mexican Americans.

BIBLIOGRAPHY

Greenberg, Jack. *Crusaders in the Courts: How a Dedicated Band of Lawyers Fought for the Civil Rights Revolution.* 1994.

Kibbe, Pauline. *Latin Americans in Texas.* 1946.

Kluger, Richard. *Simple Justice: The History of Brown v. Board of Education and Black America's Struggle for Equality.* 1977.

Martin, Waldo, Jr., ed. *Brown v. Board of Education: A Brief History with Documents.* 1998.

McPherson, James. *The Abolitionist Legacy: From Reconstruction to the NAACP.* 1975.

Montejano, David. *Anglos and Mexicans in the Making of Texas, 1836–1986.* 1987.

San Miguel, Guadalupe. *"Let All of Them Take Heed": Mexican Americans and the Campaign for Educational Equality in Texas, 1910–1981.* 1987.

Tushnet, Mark. *The NAACP's Legal Strategy Against Segregated Education, 1925–1950.* 1987.

Woodward, C. Vann. *Origins of the New South, 1877–1913.* 1951.

Ruben Flores

Eisenhower, Dwight David ("Ike")

(1890–1969), U.S. president, 1953–1961.

Dwight D. Eisenhower was supreme commander of Allied Forces in Europe, 1942–1945, and Republican president of the United States, 1953–1961. Eisenhower's background in the Army, whose JIM CROW traditions he upheld as wartime commander, did not prepare him for the African-American freedom struggle. Historians are generally critical of his civil rights record as president. Eisenhower's strongest actions were in areas where federal jurisdiction was clearcut. In

President Dwight D. Eisenhower poses in his office on June 23, 1958, during a meeting to discuss civil rights issues. On the left are Lester B. Granger, executive secretary of the National Urban League; Martin Luther King, Jr., president of the Southern Christian Leadership Congress; and E. Frederic Morrow, a White House official. On the right are A. Philip Randolph, AFL-CIO vice president and head of the International Brotherhood of Sleeping Car Porters; William Rogers, the U.S. attorney general; and Roy Wilkins, executive secretary of the NAACP.

1953–1954, he oversaw completion of the military desegregation decreed by President Harry S. TRUMAN's 1948 executive order, including integration of Southern naval bases. His administration also used its influence to end segregation of public facilities in the District of Columbia in 1953. In other areas Eisenhower's activism was limited, particularly when measured against the progressive positions adopted by Eisenhower appointees Chief Justice Earl Warren and Attorney General Herbert BROWNELL. Significantly, he kept his distance from the emergent civil rights movement and only once invited its leaders, on June 23, 1958, to the White House.

Eisenhower wished to remain neutral on the constitutionality of segregation, but the Supreme Court's BROWN V. TOPEKA BOARD OF EDUCATION judgments of 1954–55 made this impossible. Nevertheless he refrained from committing the moral authority of the presidency in support of integration by his refusal to endorse publically the *Brown* decisions. Eisenhower also tolerated violations by Southern state authorities, notably in Texas and Alabama, of federal-court integration orders in 1956. Convinced that only gradual racial change was possible, he commented privately, "The fellow who tries to tell me that you can do these things by force is just plain nuts." To Earl Warren and other critics, however, his reticence encouraged the South's massive resistance to school integration. Eventually, Eisenhower did resort to compulsion: in September 1957, he federalized the Arkansas National Guard and despatched a thousand U.S. Army paratroopers to protect the first black pupils entering Central High School, Little Rock, from white mob violence. This intervention signaled that segregationists could not use force to maintain separate schools but resolved little else. Governor Orval Faubus closed Little Rock schools for the 1958–1959 school year, a tactic copied by certain Virginia cities and counties to prevent integration. Significantly only 49 school districts carried out any desegregation in 1958–1960, compared with 712 in 1955–1957.

Eisenhower also signed the first CIVIL RIGHTS ACTS since RECONSTRUCTION, but their significance was largely symbolic. The 1957 legislation enhanced federal power to promote equal voting rights. Thanks partly to Eisenhower's limp leadership, however, provisions authorizing Justice Department enforcement of integration were stripped from the bill in Congress. The 1960 legislation appointed federal referees to counter widespread Southern violation of black suffrage rights, but its enforcement powers were weak.

Whatever the limitations of his actions, Eisenhower's civil rights legacy was significant and complex. He created precedents for greater federal activism in the 1960s, but also laid the foundations for a new civil rights conservatism. His philosophy merged support for the general principle of civil rights and for the limitation of federal enforcement powers, a position to which many former champions of white supremacy would later adhere in the 1970s.

BIBLIOGRAPHY

Ambrose, Stephen E. *Eisenhower the President, 1952–1969.* 1984.

Burk, Robert F. *The Eisenhower Administration and Black Civil Rights.* 1984.

Dalfiume, Richard M. *Desegregation of U.S. Armed Forces: Fighting on Two Fronts, 1939–1953.* 1969.

Lawson, Stephen. *Black Ballots: Voting Rights in the South, 1944–1969.* 1976.

Morrow, E. Frederic. *Black Man in the White House.* 1963.

Iwan Morgan

El Comité

See Comité, El.

Elementary and Secondary Education Act of 1965

The Elementary and Secondary Education Act (ESEA) of 1965 was the first authorization of expansive federal spending in the arena of public EDUCATION, a responsibility traditionally viewed to rest totally at the state and local level. The legislation reflected the assumptions of 1960s liberals that an upgraded educational system would compensate for poverty within homes and communities of children, serving as an outside force that would lead ultimately to greater economic opportunity for the affected students. A compensatory education proposal, the ESEA, was therefore a centerpiece of President Lyndon JOHNSON'S WAR ON POVERTY.

One of the first components of Johnson's 1965 legislative package, introduced following his landslide victory in 1964, the ESEA was signed by the president on April 11 after passing both houses of CONGRESS comfortably. After the bill's passage, Johnson claimed:

"I worked harder and longer on this measure than on any . . . since I came to Washington in 1931." Johnson's hands-on engagement in lobbying for the measure was confirmed by administration officials.

Previous efforts to develop a federal role in funding education had been defeated in Congress by a combination of Republicans, Southern Democrats worried about an alteration of Southern race relations by proposals that would have limited funding to desegregated schools, and Roman Catholics concerned that students being educated in parochial schools would be denied the benefits of the funding. The Democratic landslide of 1964 reduced the number of Republicans in Congress. And, the CIVIL RIGHTS ACT OF 1964, with its ban on federal funding to segregated educational institutions, lessened the issue of race.

Most important, the role of religion was lessened as the Johnson administration assuaged the two key interest groups active in the arena of federal school funding, the National Catholic Welfare Conference and the NATIONAL EDUCATION ASSOCIATION, in advance of the bill's introduction. A compromise, expressed in Title I of the act, created a funding formula based on the number of poor children in local districts, whether they were attending sectarian or nonsectarian schools.

Moreover, special educational services funded under the act would explicitly be available to private school students. The ESEA's Title II, aspects of which were determined to be unconstitutional in *Flast* v. *Cohen* (1968), authorized federal funds to be used for the purchase of library materials and textbooks for public and private school students. Similar provisions were made for the innovative educational programs funded under Title III.

Implementation of the ESEA was hampered by a reorganization of the Office of Education that slowed the preparation of operational guidelines for the program, and by Congress's delay in passing the appropriations measure that contained the actual funding for the program (just at $1 billion under Title I in the first year). Despite the presence of 20,000 operational Title I projects by the end of the Johnson administration, only about half of the severely disadvantaged elementary schoolchildren were benefited. More problematic in terms of the original antipoverty assumptions of the legislation, local school boards and administrators were able to redirect funds so that, according to one federal study, by the mid-1970s nearly two-thirds of the beneficiaries of Title I funds were not poor.

BIBLIOGRAPHY

Califano, Joseph A., Jr., *The Triumph and Tragedy of Lyndon Johnson: The White House Years.* 1991.

Congressional Quarterly, Inc. *Congress and the Nation, Volume II, 1965–1968.* 1969.

Jeffrey, Julie Roy. *Education for Children of the Poor: A Study of the Origins and Implementation of the Elementary and Secondary Education Act of 1965.* 1978.

Matusow, Allen J. "Statement." In *The Great Society: A Twenty-Year Critique,* edited by Barbara C. Jordan and Elspeth D. Rostow. 1986.

Jay Barth

Emancipation

In a civil rights context, emancipation means liberation from slavery. In the United States emancipation was an aspect of public policy. Though it is usually depicted as the freeing of black slaves by the EMANCIPATION PROCLAMATION or by the THIRTEENTH AMENDMENT, emancipation was a series of actions taken by states and the federal government to end African-American slavery. The Emancipation Proclamation and the Thirteenth Amendment completed the erasure of slavery from the American nation. Both the enslaved and their semifree kin had initiated and maintained the prolonged struggle for freedom. The efforts of slaves themselves were crucial to emancipation. This was especially the case as increasing numbers of slaves ran away to the Union lines, giving their labor and support to the Union cause in a significant blow for continued enslavement. The focus here, however, is on the role of institutional and government action in emancipation.

Antislavery organizations contributed to the campaign and were a major influence on emancipation policies. Between the appearance of the first such group in 1775, in Pennsylvania, and the establishment of one in Virginia in 1792, each state had at least one active antislavery or manumission society. By 1805, every Northern state had provided for eventual emancipation. Such antislavery actions and organizations typified the first emancipation. From the effort's first significant success in 1777 when Vermont abolished slavery through its culmination on July 4, 1827, when New York's decree for general emancipation became effective, the first emancipation ended legal slavery in the North.

New York's actions were illustrative of early manumission efforts. According to the 1790 census, New York, with more than 21,000 slaves, held more people in bondage than all the other Northern states combined. In 1799, the state passed an emancipation act. Because of the intense opposition of slave owners and of others opposed to a nonslave black population, like the majority of other slavery-terminating statutes of the first emancipation, New York's initial act was a

A nineteenth-century poster advocating emancipation, emphasizing its benefits to blacks and whites alike. At the center is Abraham Lincoln, surrounded by members of both races. (Archive Photos)

compromise: gradual emancipation with compensation for owners. Generally, those laws proclaimed that all blacks born after the date of passage or on a date specified in the bill (July 4 was a favorite date) were free but owed service to their mothers' owners until some such age as twenty-one or twenty-five. Therefore, freedom was a promise to a future generation to be born with financial obligations.

The disappearance of legal slavery from the North only altered the geographic scope of the institution. Slavery continued to grow numerically and territorially; the slave population more than doubled between the first emancipation and the end of the Civil War, from approximately 1.8 million in 1827 to over four million in 1865.

The Civil War accelerated emancipation. In the First Confiscation Act of August 1861, Congress mandated freedom for slaves used in support of the Confederate military. Then in a series of actions in 1862, Congress abolished slavery in the District of Columbia, prohibited it in the territories, and, in the Second

Confiscation Act, declared free any rebel-owned slave who fled to Union lines. The Thirteenth Amendment, ratified in 1865, brought universal emancipation across the country.

Emancipation had been problematic for many whites. Diverse individuals, including abolitionists and slave owners, struggled with the property rights of slave owners. Many believed that owners deserved to be compensated for their investment in slaves but disagreed on the nature of the compensation. The continually increasing number of nonslave blacks, the expansion of abolitionism, and RACISM stimulated calls for colonization of blacks. Especially in the South, colonization was premised largely on the belief in the inability of blacks and whites to live together harmoniously. Men as varied as Thomas Jefferson, author of the first significant proposal to deport nonslave blacks, and Abraham Lincoln insisted on the expulsion of manumitted blacks as a prerequisite for emancipation.

Colonization was attempted only on a meager scale, but discrimination and SEGREGATION became commonplace in all aspects of American society. States eliminated slavery without providing civil rights for freedmen. Some practices associated with slavery, such as antimiscegenation laws and laws prohibiting black testimony against whites in courts, were strengthened. Before they abolished slavery, Northern states had no statutory barriers to voting by blacks, but blacks were rarely permitted to vote. Beginning with Ohio in 1802, Northern states formally removed or severely restricted blacks' right to vote so that by 1840 fewer than 7 percent of Northern free blacks still had access to the franchise. The exceptions tended to be in New England. The pattern was repeated in EDUCATION, EMPLOYMENT, HOUSING, justice, religion, transportation, and social relations. Except in voting, the New England states kept company with other Northern states. Thus, in many ways, the pre–Civil War North foreshadowed the post–Civil War South.

The freeing of the slaves in the South simultaneously disrupted the old regime of the region and directed the nation along a new course. Emancipation in the ex-Confederacy accompanied the military defeat of the world's most powerful slaveholding class. The ostensible need to protect the newly freed from their former masters provided the victors with a disguise for their more pressing desire to prevent or delay the reemergence of the defeated class and region. Protection of the freed Negro also furnished Northern congressmen, assisted by compliant states, with the means to enhance the power of the federal government radically and to establish the constitutional and philosophical bases and precedents for post–WORLD WAR II civil rights legislation.

The response of former slaves to emancipation was fairly uniform across the long march to freedom. On manumission, blacks strove individually and collectively to make real their emancipation. Most remained in the locale of their enslavement. They initiated searches in pursuit of separated family members. They discarded slave names in favor of names that identified aspects of their new status or that were indistinguishable from those of whites. Names such as Cato, Smiley, and Gallitin's Joe gave way to James Carpenter, Miriam Freeman, and Tyler Washington. Ex-slaves created or expanded churches and denominations, social groups such as masonic lodges, literary circles, and mutual aid and benefit societies. They vigorously pursued EDUCATION, as they entered existing institutions or attended newly created segregated schools when they were excluded. Notwithstanding the negative circumstances ex-slaves had to endure, emancipation was a major development in the drive of African Americans for full inclusion in American society.

BIBLIOGRAPHY

Belz, Herman. *Emancipation and Equal Rights: Politics and Constitutionalism in the Civil War Era.* 1978.

Berlin, Ira. *Slaves Without Masters: The Free Negro in the Antebellum South.* 1974.

Berlin, Ira, Barbara J. Fields, et al., eds. *Slaves No More: Three Essays on Emancipation and the Civil War.* 1992.

Berlin, Ira, and Ronald Hoffman. *Slavery and Freedom in the Age of the American Revolution.* 1983.

Boles, John B., ed. *Masters and Slaves in the House of the Lord: Race and Religion in the American South.* 1988.

Conniff, Michael L., and Thomas J. Davis, eds. *Africans in the Americas: A History of the Black Diaspora.* 1994.

Du Bois, W. E. B. *Black Reconstruction in America: An Essay Toward a History of the Part Which Black Folk Played in the Attempt to Reconstruct Democracy in America, 1860–1880.* 1966.

Foner, Eric. *Politics and Ideology in the Age of the Civil War.* 1980.

Foner, Eric. *Reconstruction: America's Unfinished Revolution, 1863–1877.* 1988.

Gerteis, Louis S. *From Contraband to Freedman: Federal Policy Toward Southern Blacks 1861–1865.* 1973.

Harding, Vincent. *There Is a River: The Black Struggle for Freedom in America.* 1981.

Jordan, Winthrop D. *White Over Black: American Attitudes Toward the Negro, 1550–1812.* 1968.

Levine, Bruce C. *Half Slave and Half Free: The Roots of Civil War.* 1992.

MacLeod, Duncan J. *Slavery, Race and the American Revolution.* 1975.

Nash, Gary B. *Race, Class, and Politics: Essays in American Colonial and Revolutionary Society.* 1986.

Wood, Forrest G. *Black Scare: The Racist Response to Emancipation and Reconstruction.* 1969.

Ashton Wesley Welch

Emancipation Proclamation

On September 22, 1862, President Abraham Lincoln issued the "preliminary" EMANCIPATION PROCLAMATION, which stated that as of January 1, 1863, slaves living in areas under Confederate control would be "forever free." The official proclamation of January 1863 differed philosophically from the preliminary proclamation by omitting mention of compensated emancipation and colonization of freed slaves outside U.S. boundaries.

Reflecting Lincoln's political limitations, the proclamation only applied to states or parts of states in active rebellion against the United States: territory outside his authority. Lincoln worried that extending emancipation to loyal border states would push them to join the Confederacy. Thus, the proclamation specifically excluded Delaware, Maryland, Missouri, Tennessee, and Union-occupied counties in Louisiana and Virginia. In reality, the proclamation itself freed few slaves. By committing the United States to freeing the slaves, however, the proclamation introduced a moral component that changed the context of the war. Furthermore, many slaves aware of the proclamation ignored its enforcement boundaries, and considered themselves free nonetheless.

Lincoln issued the proclamation as Commander-in-Chief, perceiving emancipation as a military necessity by which to deny the Confederacy a valuable source of manual labor. In addition, the significant numbers of slaves escaping to the protection of Union lines demanded that the issue of freedom be addressed. The proclamation also authorized enrollment of black men into the United States armed forces, thus allowing almost 200,000 African Americans to fight for the freedom of their race.

The THIRTEENTH AMENDMENT, ratified in December 1865, secured the intent behind the proclamation by constitutionally outlawing slavery.

By the President of the United States of America:

A Proclamation.

Whereas, on the twenty-second day of September, in the year of our Lord one thousand eight hundred and sixty-two, a proclamation was issued by the President of the United States, containing, among other things, the following, to wit:

"That on the first day of January, in the year of our Lord one thousand eight hundred and sixty-three, all persons held as slaves within any State or designated part of a State, the people whereof shall then be in rebellion against the United States, shall be then, thenceforward, and forever free; and the Executive Government of the United States, including the military and naval authority thereof, will recognize and maintain the freedom of such persons, and will do no act or acts to repress such persons, or any of them, in any efforts they may make for their actual freedom.

"That the Executive will, on the first day of January aforesaid, by proclamation, designate the States and parts of States, if any, in which the people thereof, respectively, shall then be in rebellion against the United States; and the fact that any State, or the people thereof, shall on that day be, in good faith, represented in the Congress of the United States by members chosen thereto at elections wherein a majority of the qualified voters of such State shall have participated, shall, in the absence of strong countervailing testimony, be deemed conclusive evidence that such State, and the people thereof, are not then in rebellion against the United States."

Now, therefore I, Abraham Lincoln, President of the United States, by virtue of the power in me vested as Commander-in-Chief, of the Army and Navy of the United States in time of actual armed rebellion against the authority and government of the United States, and as a fit and necessary war measure for suppressing said rebellion, do, on this first day of January, in the year of our Lord one thousand eight hundred and sixty-three, and in accordance with my purpose so to do publicly proclaimed for the full period of one hundred days, from the day first above mentioned, order and designate as the States and parts of States wherein the people thereof respectively, are this day in rebellion against the United States, the following, to wit:

Arkansas, Texas, Louisiana (except the Parishes of St. Bernard, Plaquemines, Jefferson, St. John, St. Charles, St. James Ascension, Assumption, Terrebonne, Lafourche, St. Mary, St. Martin, and Orleans, including the City of New Orleans), Mississippi, Alabama, Florida, Georgia, South Carolina, North Carolina, and Virginia, (except the forty-eight counties designated as West Virginia, and also the counties of Berkley, Accomac, Northampton, Elizabeth City, York, Princess Ann, and Norfolk, including the cities of Norfolk and Portsmouth), and which excepted parts, are for the present, left precisely as if this proclamation were not issued.

And by virtue of the power, and for the purpose aforesaid, I do order and declare that all persons held as slaves within said designated States, and parts of States, are, and henceforward shall be free; and that the Executive government of the United States, including the military and naval authorities thereof, will recognize and maintain the freedom of said persons.

And I hereby enjoin upon the people so declared to be free to abstain from all violence, unless in necessary self-defence; and I recommend to them that, in all cases when allowed, they labor faithfully for reasonable wages.

And I further declare and make known, that such persons of suitable condition, will be received into the armed service of the United States to garrison forts, positions, stations, and other places, and to man vessels of all sorts in said service.

And upon this act, sincerely believed to be an act of justice, warranted by the Constitution, upon military necessity, I invoke the considerate judgment of mankind, and the gracious favor of Almighty God.

In witness whereof, I have hereunto set my hand and caused the seal of the United States to be affixed.

Done at the City of Washington, this first day of January, in the year of our Lord one thousand eight hundred and sixty three, and of the Independence of the United States of America the eighty-seventh.

ABRAHAM LINCOLN

By the President:

WILLIAM H. SEWARD
Secretary of State

BIBLIOGRAPHY

Berlin, Ira, et al., eds. *Freedom: A Documentary History of Emancipation, 1861–1867.* 1982–1993.
Franklin, John Hope. *The Emancipation Proclamation.* 1963.
Franklin, John Hope. "The Emancipation Proclamation: An Act of Justice," *Prologue* 25 (1993): 148–155.
Quarles, Benjamin. *Lincoln and the Negro.* 1962.

Michelle A. Krowl

Emergency School Aid Act

In 1970, President Richard NIXON, concerned that Southern states were financially unable to meet court-ordered DESEGREGATION mandates, recommended that CONGRESS pass legislation providing them with federal assistance. The president's bill (HR 17846) sought funds exclusively for Southern states to promote remedial programs for minority schools and general aid to Southern districts. Several key senators, however, disapproved of Nixon's bill and sponsored a competitor, the Quality Integrated Education Act (S 682), which would have provided nationwide aid explicitly targeted for INTEGRATION programs. Further controversy surrounded recipients of the targeted funds. Local Education Agencies (LEAs) and Non-Profit Organizations (NPOs) lobbied to obtain monies to accomplish their respective agendas. LEAs tended to favor remedial programs for segregated schools, whereas NPOs, usually religious and civil rights groups, tended to favor desegregation efforts.

The law that has become known as the Emergency School Aid Act of 1972 (Title VII of PL 92-318) (ESAA) was a compromise bill on both counts. The ESAA offered aid not only to Southern states but to the entire nation, and it explicitly designated the funds both for desegregation efforts and for remedial programs in schools with a minority population greater than 50 percent. The funds were to be administered by LEAs, but NPOs were encouraged to submit integration proposals for such initiatives as bilingual education, educational television, magnet schools (schools whose special curriculum would attract students from a variety of racial backgrounds), and neutral-site schools (schools located so as to be accessible to students of various races).

Expenditures averaged $230 million annually between 1973 and 1977, with 92 percent of the funds going to LEAs and 8 percent to NPOs. Though the intent of the bill was centered around desegregation and integration, its monies were often used simply for compensatory programs for minority children in segregated schools. In 1978 CONGRESS sought to rectify this situation and amended the ESAA to focus more directly on newly desegregating districts (PL 95-561). But in 1981 the ESAA was subsumed under the Chapter Two block grant of the Omnibus Budget Reconciliation Act of 1981 (PL 97-35), causing many schools to lose as much as 85 to 90 percent of their integration funding. New York, for example, spent more than $20 million in 1981 on integration efforts but in 1982 spent less than $3 million. An attempt, fronted by New York Senator Daniel Patrick Moynihan, was made in 1983 to extend the ESAA; but that bill (S 1256) as well as a similar House bill (HR 2207) failed in the Senate, largely because of popular backlash against busing policies that had long been associated with the Emergency School Aid Act.

BIBLIOGRAPHY

Crocker, Stephen. *An Evaluation of the Emergency School Aid Act Nonprofit Organization Program,* 4 vols. 1978.
Department of Health, Education, and Welfare. *A Summary of Federal Aid Under the Emergency School Aid Act.* 1978.
Henderson, Anne T. "Chapter 2: For Better or Worse?" *Phi Delta Kappan* 67 (8) (April 1986): 597–602.
United States Congress House Committee on Education and Labor. *Emergency School Aid Act: Report Together with Individual and Dissenting Views.* 1983.
United States Congress House Committee on Education and Labor. *To Reinstate the Emergency School Aid Act: Hearing before the . . . Ninety-eighth Congress, First Session, on H.R. 2207.* 1983.
United States Congress Senate Committee on Labor and Human Resources. *Emergency School Aid Extension Act of 1983: Hearing Before the . . . Ninety-eighth Congress, First Session on S. 1256.* 1984.

Milton Gaither

Employment

The term "employment" has ironic resonance for Americans of African descent, who were "employed" as slaves for over two centuries. It is easily forgotten that slavery was primarily a system of labor that served rational economic purposes. Indeed, if it had not been for the scarcity of labor in the New World, it is doubtful that colonial settlers and planters would have gone all the way to Africa to import workers, and to compel them to work under a ruthless system that contradicted the noble principles on which the nation was founded. Nor did slavery redound to the benefit of slaveholders alone. Not only was the regional economy of the South dependent on black labor, but even as late as 1860 cotton accounted for 60 percent of American exports. Cotton was the raw material for textile manufacturing in both Britain and the United States, and textiles were the linchpin of the industrial revolution. In *The Philosophy of Poverty* (1934), Karl Marx summed up the relationship between slavery, cotton, and industrial development in a single epigrammatic sentence: "Without slavery there is no cotton; without cotton there is no modern industry."

As the British economist Brinley Thomas wrote in *Migration and Economic Growth* (1973), " . . . after the Civil War the best thing that could have happened to the black workers of the United States would have been a fair opportunity to contribute to satisfying the great demand for labour in the growing cities of the North and West." This did not happen, however. There was an invisible color line across Northern industry that barred blacks categorically from employment in the vast manufacturing sector, except for a few menial or low-paying jobs that white workers spurned. Instead, the North relied on immigrants from Europe for its burgeoning industries. In effect, the industrial revolution in the United States was "for whites only," and, as David Roediger shows in *The Wages of Whiteness* (1991), white workers and their unions played an active role in constructing an identity that equated industrial labor with whiteness.

If black labor was superfluous in the North, it was indispensable in the South. In the aftermath of slavery most black men and women continued to work in agriculture as sharecroppers, tenant farmers, and contract laborers. Instead of integrating blacks into the industrial mainstream, the nation forged a system of occupational apartheid whereby immigrants provided the necessary labor for Northern industry and blacks provided the necessary labor for Southern agriculture. This regional and racial division of labor cast the mold for generations more of racial inequality and conflict. As Robert Blauner argued in *Racial Oppression in America* (1972), blacks were relegated to work in the poorest and most exploitative sectors of the national economy, made all the worse by a system of racial oppression that was violent and dehumanizing. Immigrants, too, were exploited, but they worked in industries close to the dynamic center of an expanding industrial economy, and with time were able to escape poverty and provide their children with opportunities for social and economic mobility.

The first breach in the wall of occupational apartheid occurred during the First World War, when immigration was reduced to a trickle. The opening up of opportunities in Northern industry triggered a mass movement of blacks to Northern cities. The "great migration," as it was called, led to the development of large black communities in Chicago, New York, and other cities in the North, and represented the first major advance in the economic and social condition of the nation's black population.

The next advance occurred during the Second World War. Initially, blacks reaped little gain from the rebounding economy since whites, left unemployed by the Depression, were given preference in hiring. This is what prompted A. Philip RANDOLPH to threaten a march on Washington, which he called off only after President FRANKLIN D. ROOSEVELT agreed to issue an executive order banning discrimination in federal employment and defense industries. Eventually, deepening labor shortages triggered another mass migration of Southern blacks, and by the end of the war 1.5 million blacks were part of the war-production work force. This represented another breach in the nation's system of occupational apartheid—one that set the stage for future change as well. As Frances Piven and Richard Cloward observed in *Poor People's Movements* (1979), in Northern cities blacks were able "to construct the occupational and institutional foundation from which to mount resistance to white oppression."

Still, as recently as 1950, two-thirds of African Americans lived in the South, half of them in rural areas. This was to change with the introduction of labor-saving technology that drastically reduced the need for black agricultural labor. As the mechanization of agriculture accelerated in the 1960s, Southern blacks migrated to cities all across the nation. To some contemporary observers it appeared that at last blacks would follow in the footsteps of immigrants.

However, when blacks arrived in Northern cities, they encountered a far less favorable structure of opportunity than had existed for immigrants decades earlier. For one thing, these labor markets had been captured by immigrant groups who engaged in a combination of ethnic nepotism and unabashed RACISM. For another, the occupational structures were themselves changing. Not only were droves of manufacturing jobs wiped out by automation, but a reorganization of the global economy resulted in the export of millions of manufacturing jobs to less developed parts of the world. Jobs lost to de-industrialization were eventually replaced by jobs in expanding service sectors, but here again employment discrimination was pervasive even when blacks had the requisite education and skills.

Leaders of the civil rights movement optimistically believed that once the walls of SEGREGATION came tumbling down, blacks would be free to assume their rightful place in American society. However, it soon became apparent that Title VII of the CIVIL RIGHTS ACT OF 1964 proscribing discrimination in employment was doing little to alter entrenched racism in the workplace. A good example is the American Telephone and Telegraph Company (AT&T), which was the nation's largest employer and a major government contractor. In 1973, nine years after passage of the 1964 Civil Rights Act, AT&T was an archetypal example of caste segregation in the workplace. Of the 351,000 Americans in low-paying operator or clerical categories, 95 percent were women. Of 234,000 higher-paid craft workers, 95 percent were male and only 6 percent were black. Virtually no women or blacks were in management positions, and even supervisory personnel in "female" departments were male. With President Richard NIXON's backing, the Federal Communications Commission held up an AT&T rate increase until the company entered into a landmark consent decree, agreeing to change its employment policies and meet employment targets for women and minorities.

Another crucial policy initiative of the Nixon administration was the Philadelphia Plan, which required that all contractors working on large, federally funded projects adopt "numerical goals and timetables" to assure the DESEGREGATION of their work force. This policy was originally developed during the Johnson administration, but encountered vehement opposition then from organized labor and contractors alike, and was rescinded shortly after Hubert Humphrey's defeat in 1968. Why Nixon—who got elected on the basis of a "Southern strategy" that appealed to the white backlash—revived the Philadelphia Plan has been the subject of much speculation. The unsung hero was Arthur Fletcher, the black Assistant Secretary of Labor. This was a period when black militancy was on the rise, and memories were still fresh of the "riots" that followed the assassination of Martin Luther KING, JR. Then too, in the summer of 1969, came a series of strident job protests at construction sites in Philadelphia, Chicago, and numerous other cities that put pressure on the Nixon administration to defuse the conflict. This was the context in which Fletcher maneuvered to resurrect the Philadelphia Plan. Though originally aimed at building trades controlled by Democratic unions, after the Plan survived court challenges, "goals and timetables" were extended to cover all government contractors, including colleges and universities. This marked the birth of AFFIRMATIVE ACTION as we know it today.

Although affirmative action has been the subject of much ideological contention, there can be little question that it achieved its main policy objective: the rapid integration of blacks into occupational sectors from which they had been excluded through all of American history. The occupational spheres where blacks have made the most progress—in government service,

the professions, corporate management, and major blue-collar occupations—are all areas in which vigorous affirmative action programs have been in place for over two decades. On the other hand, insofar as progress has depended upon governmental intervention, it does not reflect an autonomous and self-sustaining deracialization of labor markets. Now that the scope of affirmative action has been cut back by a series of SUPREME COURT decisions and political referenda, there is little to prevent employers and universities from reverting to old ways of doing business. Blacks also have been negatively impacted by the recent downsizing of government, especially in the social service branches, which have been the staple of the black middle class. As happened when RECONSTRUCTION was ended more than a century ago, there is real danger that many of the gains wrung out of white society during "the Second Reconstruction" will undergo a slow but steady erosion.

Nor should we forget that even during the buoyant economy of the 1990s, 28 percent of blacks remained mired in poverty. Tight labor markets recently have reduced levels of black unemployment, especially for young males, but the rates of unemployment for blacks still far exceed those for comparable groups of whites. In any particular occupational category—whether blue-collar or white-collar, whether in the professions or in the service sector—blacks continue to be substantially underrepresented in the more desirable and lucrative jobs. Hence, the existence of a small black elite and a precarious middle class should not obscure the fact that occupational apartheid is far from a thing of the past.

BIBLIOGRAPHY

Baron, Harold. "The Demand for Black Labor." In *Radical America* (March–April 1971).

Blauner, Robert. *Racial Oppression in America.* 1972.

Freeman Richard B., and William M. Rogers III. "Area Economic Conditions and the Labor Market Outcomes of Young Men in the 1990s Expansion." In *National Bureau of Economic Research*, 1999.

Hill, Herbert. "Black Workers, Organized Labor, and Title VII of the 1964 Civil Rights Act: Legislative History and Litigation." In Herbert Hill and James E. Jones, *Race in America.* 1993.

Jones, Jacqueline. *Labor of Love, Labor of Sorrow: Black Women, Work, and the Family from Slavery to the Present.* 1985.

Jones, Jacqueline. *American Work: Four Centuries of Black and White Labor.* 1998.

Moss, Philip, and Chris Tilly. "Why Black Men Are Doing Worse in the Labor Market." Social Science Research Council, 1991.

Oliver, Melvin L., and Thomas M. Shapiro. *Black Wealth/White Wealth.* 1995.

Roediger, David R. *The Wages of Whiteness.* 1991.

Skrentny, John David. *The Ironies of Affirmative Action.* 1996.

Steinberg, Stephen. *Turning Back: The Retreat from Racial Justice in American Thought and Policy.* 1995.

Wilson, William Julius. *When Work Disappears.* 1996.

Stephen Steinberg

Equal Employment Opportunities Commission

The Equal Employment Opportunities Commission (EEOC) was created as an independent federal executive agency charged with hearing specific complaints of EMPLOYMENT discrimination and developing policies to end discriminatory employment practices in public and private employment. It is responsible for enforcing TITLE VII OF THE 1964 CIVIL RIGHTS ACT, which prohibits employment discrimination on the basis of race, color, national origin, religion, or sex. The EEOC consists of a five-member commission and a supporting bureaucracy with headquarters in Washington, D.C., and field offices throughout the United States.

In order to secure the votes of moderate Republicans that were needed to pass the 1964 Civil Rights bill, President Lyndon B. JOHNSON agreed to a series of compromises that initially left the new EEOC without its own enforcement powers. It was only given the power to conciliate discrimination disputes. Where conciliation proved unsuccessful, the EEOC could only recommend to the U.S. Attorney General that a lawsuit be filed by the Department of Justice. If the Justice Department was persuaded that a "pattern or practice of resistance" to fair employment existed, it could then initiate a suit on behalf of the plaintiff(s). The EEOC thus became the only federal regulatory agency without its own enforcement mechanism. At first, the EEOC's investigatory powers could only be initiated after a specific complaint was filed with it. Unlike the National Labor Relations Board, the Federal Trade Commission, and the Securities and Exchange Commission, the EEOC could not issue cease-and-desist orders to bring discriminatory practices to an immediate halt or to initiate legal action in the federal courts. The legal framework established by Title VII was much weaker than the one established to remedy school SEGREGATION that was a part of the same 1964 Civil Rights Act. The lack of EEOC enforcement powers placed much of the early burden of enforcement on individual workers, who, in most cases, had to seek help from a civil rights organization or public-interest law center to pursue their case in the courts. Yet, only the federal government possessed the vast resources required to eliminate the extensive patterns of discrimination that still existed throughout the U.S. economy.

Congressional supporters of equal employment legislation had downplayed the widespread existence of racial discrimination in the workplace, predicting that the EEOC would address a relatively small number of egregious cases. The DEMOCRATIC PARTY's leadership believed that the law would mainly affect the South, treating racial discrimination elsewhere as isolated incidents of wrongdoing, not systemic patterns of injustice. From the onset, congressional opponents used the appropriations process as a second chance to restrict the EEOC's full effectiveness. Throughout its history, the EEOC has been plagued by budget limitations, inadequate staffing, and frequent leadership turnover.

Upon going into operation in 1965, the EEOC was deluged with complaints. Within its first year, the EEOC received four times the number that had been estimated during the congressional hearings. The unanticipated high volume of complaints, coupled with the commission's perennial lack of funding and staff shortages, quickly led to a severe backlog of cases. By the end of 1972 only half of the 80,000 cases the EEOC had recommended for action had even been investigated. In its first years of operations the EEOC prioritized complaints of racial discrimination against private employers. From the onset it adopted a bias toward handling individual complaints of discrimination, even though it recognized that proceeding on a case-by-case basis would never eliminate job discrimination on a broader scale.

Congressional amendments enacted in 1972 finally granted the EEOC the right to sue in court. Title VII coverage was significantly expanded to include state and local public employees, and there were a number of other improvements to the statute. However, the EEOC has made relatively little use of these new powers; the majority of pathbreaking class-action suits that have implemented broad antidiscrimination remedies were won through the federal courts, not through the intervention of the EEOC.

Opposition to civil rights enforcement during the REAGAN and BUSH administrations led to severe cuts in EEOC funding and sharp declines in staff. Under the chairmanship of Clarence Thomas (later appointed to the U.S. Supreme Court), the EEOC came out in opposition to the use of goals, timetables, and quotas for minorities in the workforce. In early 1986, the EEOC announced that it was abandoning AFFIRMATIVE ACTION hiring goals and timetables in its settlements with private employers. After the Supreme Court upheld their use, the EEOC reluctantly agreed to drop its opposition. Reflecting President Reagan's policy of only pursuing the claims of identifiable victims, the EEOC showed a sharp decline in the number of class-action lawsuits it initiated. By 1992, systemic cases constituted a mere 8.6 percent of cases filed by the agency. This came at a time when few private attorneys possessed the resources needed to take on a class-action suit because of the high costs of preparing such cases.

During the 1990s the agency was given additional responsibilities without any additional funding. It now also has jurisdiction over the Age Discrimination and Employment Act (see AGE DISCRIMINATION); the Equal Pay Act; Sections 501 and 504 of the REHABILITATION ACT, which prohibit discrimination against people with disabilities in federal employment; sections of the CIVIL RIGHTS ACT OF 1991; and Title I of the AMERICANS WITH DISABILITIES ACT (ADA), which prohibits discrimination against people with disabilities in private and state and local governments. These added responsibilities have resulted in increased caseloads, the Commission received 95,000 new cases in 1995.

During the Clinton administration, the EEOC has been revitalized. Beginning in 1995, the commission implemented a series of administrative changes that succeeded in reducing the number of pending cases by 40,000. The commission remains understaffed and continues to wrestle with whether to focus on individual cases or larger, class-action suits. While the bulk of its cases remain smaller individual ones, it is the larger cases that result in more sweeping improvements in the workplace. The expansion of the EEOC's authority has led it into new regulatory arenas, such as determining the extent to which religious expression should be allowed in the workplace and the scope of disabilities protected from discrimination under the ADA.

BIBLIOGRAPHY

Amaker, Norman. *Civil Rights and the Reagan Administration.* 1988.

Benokratis, Nicole, and Joseph Feagin. *Affirmative Action and Employment Opportunities: Action, Inaction, and Reaction* 1978.

Bullock, Charles III and Lamb, Charles; *The Implementation of Civil Rights Policy.* 1984.

Gould, William. *Black Workers in White Unions: Job Discrimination in the United States.* 1977.

Hill, Herbert. "The Equal Employment Opportunity Acts of 1964 and 1972: A Critical Analysis of the Legislative history and Administration of the Law." *Industrial Relations Law Journal* 2, no. 1 (Spring 1977).

Hill, Herbert. *Black Labor and the American Legal System.* 1985.

Nathan, Richard. *Jobs and Civil Rights.* 1969.

Slessarev, Helene. *The Betrayal of the Urban Poor.* 1997.

Sovern, Michael. *The Legal Restraints on Racial Discrimination.* 1966.

U.S. Civil Rights Commission. *Federal Civil Rights Enforcement Efforts.* 1970.

Whalen, Charles, and Barbara Whalen. *The Longest Debate: A Legislative History of the 1964 Civil Rights Act.* 1985.

Helene Slessarev

Equal Opportunity

During the peak of civil rights activity in 1964, President Lyndon B. JOHNSON issued Executive Order 11246, which required employers to consider qualified minority persons as serious candidates. This measure marked the onset of equal opportunity AFFIRMATIVE ACTION programs which, by definition, included efforts to increase the numbers of minorities and women in employment and higher education. In part these policies were a response to the excessive unemployment rates of African Americans.

In the 1990s, opponents of affirmative action have charged that the program practices racial discrimination against white males through the use of quotas and preferences. Merit, in their view, is overlooked in favor of placing representative numbers of minorities in employment and in college and university slots; anger and division result, along with a lowering of initiative among those who receive the benefits. Still other opponents maintain that the program has achieved its goal of lowering barriers and is no longer needed. Proponents, on the other hand, insist that the program serves to aid in eliminating the effects of past discrimination while addressing ongoing unfairness. That equal opportunity emphasizes color generates these positions of reform and resistance.

In 1941, President Franklin D. ROOSEVELT made an early effort toward equal opportunity through Executive Order 8802. This action proscribed discrimination based on race or national origin in the defense industries. Post–World War II America saw other early indicators that major institutions, both public and private, would be subject to trends of equal opportunity as well as assaults on discrimination. President Harry S. TRUMAN in 1947 issued an executive order that ended the racial SEGREGATION of the United States military (see also ARMED FORCES) Jackie ROBINSON's incursion into major league baseball was epochal, a precursor of things to come. The well-publicized BROWN V. BOARD OF EDUCATION decision (1954), which reversed PLESSY V. FERGUSON (1896), directly addressed equal opportunity in EDUCATION and indirectly supported it in areas where education might lead. These events foreshadowed the public upheaval that would lead to legislation.

Popular participation in efforts to end discrimination became known as the civil rights movement or, as historians Winfred Kelly and Albert Harbison suggested, the "Negro Revolution." In 1955, the Reverend Dr. Martin Luther KING, JR., led a successful bus boycott in Montgomery, Alabama (see MONTGOMERY BUS BOYCOTT). The bus campaign was followed by other attempts at ending discrimination through large-scale participation. FREEDOM RIDES, SIT-INS, demonstrations, and other activist approaches were numerous through the 1960s. On August 27, 1963, the MARCH ON WASHINGTON, D.C., with an estimated crowd of 200,000 persons, took place and generated worldwide publicity. These activities, which at times aroused disruptive and violent reaction, stirred the federal government toward long-term solutions.

Two major federal laws form the foundation for equal opportunity programs and expectations in the 1990s: The CIVIL RIGHTS ACT OF 1964 under TITLE VII, which pertains to employers of more than twenty-five persons, outlaws discrimination in hiring based on race, color, sex, religion, or national origin. The EQUAL EMPLOYMENT OPPORTUNITY COMMISSION (EEOC) was authorized to investigate complaints and to enforce the fair employment provisions of this law. The Equal Employment Opportunity Act of 1972 was enacted to expand the range of Title VII and to grant more authority to the EEOC.

Other official acts, both before and after passage of these federal laws, contributed to equal opportunity. In 1960, then Vice President Richard M. NIXON, who chaired the Committee on Government Contracts, presented to President Dwight D. EISENHOWER a report that cited employer indifference to discrimination as an obstacle to hiring and promoting qualified applicants. The very next year, President John F. KENNEDY issued Executive Order 10925, which required government contractors to take "affirmative action" to counteract discrimination. In 1965, President Johnson issued Executive Order 11246, which required a nondiscrimination clause in government contracts. These and other measures promoted equal opportunity through the 1960s and 1970s.

Statutes passed by Congress during the 1970s supported equal opportunity and affirmative action. In 1973, the REHABILITATION ACT was passed to include qualified handicapped persons. The Readjustment Assistance Act (1974) extended the same benefits to Vietnam-era and disabled veterans as well.

Controversy has surfaced, often in relation to affirmative action initiatives and reverse discrimination claims; such challenges frequently concern the application and interpretation of Title VII. In order to clarify its position on such issues, the EEOC has published guidelines for affirmative action. These provisions constitute an account and an opinion of Title VII.

First, EEOC supports voluntary action under certain conditions. This action is warranted if existing or expected employment practices have an adverse impact on the subject. Such action is also warranted to correct past discrimination. If a labor pool is "artificially limited" as a result of past discrimination, steps may be taken to produce qualified candidates. This provision encourages initiative by the employers.

The EEOC also requires that affirmative action plans consist of three distinct components: (1) a reasonable self-analysis; (2) a reasonable basis; and (3) reasonable action. Self-analysis examines employment practices to determine the effects of prior discrimination as well as the possible presence of current ills in hiring. In the event that discrimination or related problems are identified, a "reasonable basis" has thus been established for taking action under the guidelines. Action pursued under the guidelines must bear a "reasonable relationship" to the problem(s) disclosed. This reasonable action could include schedules for change, new practices, goals, timetables and other steps that would end discrimination and its effects.

Equal opportunity efforts, along with affirmative action, have many supporters and detractors. There are those who denounce the objections to affirmative actions. The Reverend Jesse JACKSON, for example, cites data to support his contention that most endeavors that involve power, authority, and wealth are dominated by the white male segment of the population, with equal opportunity ventures making only small inroads. William Bowen and Derek Bok, in *Shape of the River*, observe that black students admitted to prestigious universities through affirmative action have the highest rate of Ph.D. completion of any group. This outcome clearly contradicts the position that such candidates are marginal, if not unworthy of entry into the apex of academe. Other supporters maintain that "old boy" networks are norms of long duration that exclude minorities and women. They argue further that affirmative action simply provides some with what is an even opportunity rather than an unfair advantage.

Those who attack equal opportunity and affirmative action are just as vehement as those who praise them. The demise of merit is offered as a major criticism. Unfair appointments have the potential to cause the collapse of a society in which achievement and quality have been synonymous. If unqualified individuals are consistently promoted at the expense of those who are better, eventually a serious decline in incentive could become widespread, and this might well cause the best and brightest to lose productivity. In some instances, recipients of equal opportunity benefits have complained of being labeled as ill-qualified holders of sinecures. This image of incompetence has caused them to oppose the continued existence of the program. Critics such as Thomas Sowell and Dinesh D'Souza maintain that lethargic performance, racial tensions, and lowered academic outcomes are inevitable results of preferential treatment.

Prior to the equal opportunity and affirmative action efforts, dismal performance in schools and racial tensions existed in abundance. Inner city and rural conditions of poverty prevailed as well. Additionally, as Seymour Martin Lipset observed early in the 1990s, the majority of the emerging middle-class African Americans made their gains without federal sponsorship in any form. The claims and counterclaims on this subject continue.

BIBLIOGRAPHY

Bacchi, Carol Lee. *The Politics of Affirmative Action.* 1996.
Benokraitis, Nijole, and Joe R. Feacin. *Affirmative Action and Equal Opportunity: Action, Inaction, Reaction.* 1978.
Bowen, William, and Derek Bok. *Shape of the River: The Long-Term Consequences of Considering Race in College and University Admissions.* 1998.
Cahn, Steven. *The Affirmative Action Debate.* 1995.
Cose, Ellis. *Color Blind.* 1997.
Drake, W. Avon. *Affirmative Action and the Stalled Quest for Black Progress.* 1996.
Glazer, Nathan. *Affirmative Discrimination.* 1975.
Lawrence, Charles R., III. *We Won't Go Back.* 1997.
McWhirter, Daven. *The End of Affirmative Action.* 1996.
Mills, Nicolaus. *Debating Affirmative Action.* 1994.
Post, Robert. *Race and Representation.* 1998.
Reed, Merl E. *Seedtime for the Modern Civil Rights Movement.* 1991.
Sadler, A. E. *Affirmative Action.* 1996.
Turner, Ronald. *The Past and Future of Affirmative Action.* 1990.

Stanley W. Johnson

Equal Rights Amendment, Movement for

The quest for full constitutional equality for women began in 1923 soon after the ratification of the NINETEENTH AMENDMENT, the amendment that guaranteed woman suffrage. A newly proposed equal rights amendment, the brainchild of the National Woman's Party (NWP), the confrontational wing of the suffrage movement, immediately generated controversy because its adoption would spell the end of special labor laws for women. Despite the opposition of progressive women, the NWP, under the leadership of Alice Paul,

Supporters of the Equal Rights Amendment march in Chicago, Illinois, on May 10, 1980. At the front of the march stand Betty Friedan of New York City, Addie Wyatt of Washington, D.C., and Jean Stapleton of Hollywood, California, among others. At the extreme left are television talkshow host and producer Phil Donahue and actress Marlo Thomas. (CORBIS/Bettmann)

had the amendment introduced into Congress by Senator Charles Curtis and Rep. Daniel R. Anthony (both Republicans from Kansas); it read: "Men and women shall have equal rights throughout the United States and every place subject to its jurisdiction."

The split in the women's movement hampered other concerted action for women's rights, but WORLD WAR II generated some support for the amendment. In 1943, the House Judiciary Committee reworded the amendment to read: "Equality of rights under the law shall not be denied or abridged by the United States or by any state on account of sex." In 1946, having been endorsed by both major political parties, the Equal Rights Amendment (ERA) won a majority in a floor vote in the Senate (38–35), although not the two-thirds required for further action. This small success generated an active opposition from progressive women and their supporters. Senator Carl Hayden (D-Ariz.) succeeded in adding a rider to the ERA when it was voted on in 1950, 1953, and 1960, that preserved "any rights, benefits, or exemptions" conferred by law upon women. ERA supporters then killed this "compromise" resolution. The resulting political configuration had conservative Republicans and Southern Democrats largely in support of the ERA and liberals in both parties opposed.

In 1963, the PRESIDENT'S COMMISSION ON THE STATUS OF WOMEN attempted to forge a compromise over the ERA. In its report, the Commission endorsed constitutional equality for women through a Supreme Court case, following the model of BROWN V. BOARD

OF EDUCATION, a strategy suggested by civil rights advocate Pauli Murray. However, the addition of "sex" to the employment title of the CIVIL RIGHTS ACT OF 1964 (proposed by Howard Smith (D-Va.), a supporter of the ERA) soon doomed sex-specific labor laws and thus removed the chief obstacle to unified support for the ERA.

The appearance of a new women's movement led Congress on March 22, 1972, to recommend ratification of the amendment, with a now-customary seven-year time limit. Ratification appeared certain; twenty-two states ratified by the end of the year, with eight states following in 1973. However, identification of the ERA with a new feminist movement inspired Phyllis Schlafly, a Republican activist, to mobilize conservatives against the amendment, citing connections to movements for abortion and gay rights as well as the prospect that women would be subjected to the draft. By 1978, thirty-five states, three states shy of the requisite number, had ratified (and four states attempted to rescind ratifications). In October, with ratification now uncertain, Congress extended the period for 39 months to June 30, 1982. By that date, however, no additional states had ratified. Since its defeat, feminists have had the amendment introduced repeatedly in Congress but without success.

The ERA proved to be a valuable tool first for mobilizing feminists and then for organizing the radical right as well. Its defeat bespoke a genuine lack of consensus, particularly in the South, about how extensively changes should occur in gender roles. However, SUPREME COURT decisions since 1971 have brought women under the cover of the equal protection clause of the FOURTEENTH AMENDMENT, barring distinctions in the law based on sex except where the state could offer an "exceedingly persuasive" justification that the distinction was "substantially related" to an "important governmental objective." (See, for example, *United States v. Virginia* [1996].) Both state and federal codes now also prohibit sex discrimination in many areas. The legal status of women at the end of the century thus differs dramatically from the moment in 1923 when the amendment was first imagined.

BIBLIOGRAPHY

Becker, Susan D. *The Origins of the Equal Rights Amendment: American Feminism Between the Wars.* 1981.

Berry, Mary Frances. *Why ERA Failed: Women's Rights and the Amending Process of the Constitution.* 1986.

Brown, Barbara A., et al. "The Equal Rights Amendment: A Constitutional Basis for Equal Rights for Women." *Yale Law Journal* 80 (April 1971): 871–985.

Harrison, Cynthia. *On Account of Sex: The Politics of Women's Issues, 1945–1968.* 1988.

Mathews, Donald, and Jane Sherron De Hart. *Sex, Gender, and the Politics of ERA: A State and the Nation.* 1990.

Cynthia Harrison

Ethnicity and Race

Discrimination can be based on many factors, including RACE, religion, gender, CLASS, and ethnicity. Ethnic discrimination, such as was exhibited in the United States against the Irish in the nineteenth century and Italians and Russian Jews in the early part of the twentieth century, has much in common with racial discrimination. Ethnic prejudice, like race prejudice, is grounded on stereotypes that have little or no basis in reality. However, ethnic whites have for the most part been able to escape these stereotypes over time and achieve full inclusion in U.S. society faster than have blacks. In addition, members of white ethnic groups have sometimes exhibited strong racial prejudice.

The United States, as a nation of immigrants, has both welcomed newcomers and worried about "alien" groups that brought with them different languages, religions, and folkways. Historians have documented the rise of NATIVISM in the nineteenth century. Nativism is both a policy that favors native inhabitants over immigrants and an ideology that seeks to perpetuate the indigenous culture. With the beginning of large-scale immigration by the Irish in the 1820s and 1830s, native-born Protestant leaders raised concerns about the Irish and their allegiance to the Roman Catholic Church. Irish immigrants were subjected to discrimination and characterized as unreliable. Further, the rise of ethnic discrimination in the nineteenth century was stimulated by biological theories that equated ethnicity with race. Ethnic groups that today are categorized as Caucasian were given distinct racial identities. Thus, Swedes and Danes were part of the Scandinavian races, while Arabs, Mexicans, Germans, and Jews were each accorded a separate racial identity. Stereotypes, both good and bad, abounded for each "race," just as more obvious racial stereotypes existed for Africans and Asians. Moreover, racial theorists argued for the superiority of white, northern European races.

American nativism intensified with the influx of immigrants between the 1880s and the beginning of World War I in 1914. Millions of immigrants from southern and eastern Europe—who were Jewish and Catholic—frightened many white Anglo-Saxon Protestants (WASPs). WASPS believed that these ethnic groups brought with them crime, vice, and cultural values opposed to long-standing American beliefs. Moreover, the growing urbanization of the country attracted African Americans from the South as well as the new immigrants, leading to complex mixes of both ethnic and racial discrimination. (see IMMIGRATION AND IMMIGRANTS).

The U.S. Immigration Commission issued a report in 1909 that played on these nativist fears, helping to pave the way for drastic restrictions on immigration in the 1920s (see IMMIGRATION ACT OF 1924). The linkage between ethnic and racial prejudice became more noticeable in the Roaring Twenties when the KU KLUX KLAN (KKK) enjoyed a revival that went beyond the states of the former confederacy. The KKK attacked African Americans, Catholics, Jews, and immigrants, arguing that a national revival was needed to "rescue" the white race. Though the KKK soon experienced a decline in membership, its message has remained unchanged.

The rise of Nazism in the 1930s showed the dangerousness of nineteenth-century racial theories. Adolf Hitler and his followers justified the extermination of Jews and the conquest of other countries in order to support and purify the Germanic peoples, who were supposedly members of an exalted Aryan race. The 1945 Nuremberg war trials of Nazi leaders discredited these ideas.

The American civil rights movement of the 1950s and 1960s focused primarily on racial discrimination. Yet when it came time for Congress to enact major legislation, it inserted language into the CIVIL RIGHTS ACT OF 1964 that barred discrimination in public accommodations and EMPLOYMENT based on national origin. The EQUAL EMPLOYMENT OPPORTUNITY COMMISSION has defined national-origin discrimination broadly. It includes, but is not limited to, the denial of equal opportunity because of birthplace, ancestry, culture, or linguistic characteristics common to a specific ethnic group. Equal employment opportunity cannot be denied because of marriage or association with persons of a national origin group; membership or association with specific ethnic promotion groups; attendance or participation in schools, churches, temples, or mosques generally associated with a national origin group; or a surname associated with a national origin group.

The U.S. courts have defined "national origin" as meaning the country from which a person or a person's forebears came. Therefore, employment discrimination against a person or persons because of Russian, Portuguese, or Italian heritage is proscribed. Moreover, favoring a person of an ethnic minority over a person of Anglo-Saxon heritage violates the law. The courts have also read "national origin" to include a distinct cultural heritage or geographical place, even if no current nation exists. Under this reading, employment discrimination against Cajuns, Gypsies, or Puerto Ricans is proscribed by the Civil Rights Act of 1964. A rule requiring employees to speak only En-

glish at all times on the job may violate the Act unless an employer shows it to be necessary for conducting business. In addition, an employer must show a legitimate nondiscriminatory reason for the denial of employment opportunity because of an individual's accent or manner of speaking.

Despite the similarities between ethnic and racial prejudice, generations of immigrants have been assimilated into American society. Although social scientists have challenged the idea of the American "melting pot," where ethnic values are replaced with American values, ethnic whites have had the opportunity to blend into the dominant culture and avoid discrimination. EDUCATION has been a key factor in this process, as ethnic whites learned English and set out to shed their parents' ethnic heritage. In contrast, racial discrimination has proved more difficult to escape because of skin color and other racially identifiable characteristics. Moreover, white ethnic communities tend to assimilate the dominant culture's attitudes towards race. In the 1960s and 1970s, the so-called "white backlash" against African Americans and civil rights came in part from assimilated ethnic white communities.

In the 1990s the growing population and power of Hispanic Americans started a new debate involving ethnicity. Some people contend that unlike previous ethnic groups, Hispanic Americans do not wish to assimilate into the dominant U.S. culture but rather want to "Hispanicize" parts of the country. Such fears have led state governments, such as Arizona and California, to enact laws that make English the official language of government. Although courts have struck down these laws, it is clear that ethnicity, like race, will remain a source of friction in U.S. society.

BIBLIOGRAPHY

Baltzell, E. Digby. *The Protestant Establishment.* 1964.

Bennett, David H. *The Party of Fear: The American Far Right from Nativism to the Militia Movement.* 1995.

Grittner, Frederick K. *White Slavery: Myth, Ideology and American Law.* 1990.

Handlin, Oscar. *Race and Nationality in American Life.* 1957.

Higham, John. *Strangers in the Land: Patterns of American Nativism 1860–1925.* 1966.

Frederick K. Grittner

Ethnic Studies

Ethnic studies is a multidisciplinary analysis of the origins, history, identity, culture, symbols, values, norms, institutions, and experiences of individual ethnic groups (i.e., groups who share a subjective sense of common identity, ancestry, history, peoplehood, language, and culture). Generally, the term "ethnic studies" refers to postsecondary-school courses and programs, whereas "multicultural education" connotes k–12 schooling. A popular misconception is that ethnic studies is the study of people of color or racial minorities only. However, while the area emerged out of the larger African-American, Chicano/Latino-American, Asian-American, and Native American civil rights struggles for racial justice in the 1960s and 1970s, Ethnic Studies also includes the study of European Americans, such as Jewish and Italian Americans.

Ethnic studies first developed in colleges and universities in the late 1960s. Black students, many of whom had organized SIT-INS, FREEDOM RIDES, and FREEDOM SCHOOLS to end racial segregation, initiated a movement to have higher education infused with "relevance" to their lives and made "accessible" to their communities. Soon, Latino, Asian, and Native American students joined African Americans in multiethnic campus coalitions to demand "self-determination," control over educational agenda, and "ethnic studies" content and courses. They emphasized the need for ethnic "inclusion," cultural "relevance," social "action," and "education for liberation." In critiques of the traditional cannon (i.e., commonly accepted and taken-for-granted general truths, models, and standards of evaluation), Chicano, Asian, and Native American activists charged that the content and process of higher education were racist, European-centered, and exclusionary, and that they marginalized the experiences and lifestyles of racial minorities as well as of women, gays, and lesbians. (See WOMEN AND CIVIL RIGHTS STRUGGLES; GAY AND LESBIAN RIGHTS.) The activists argued that traditional academic theories, methods, and assumptions validated white, Anglo, European, male, elite dominance over other groups. Thus activists fought for the creation of *new* theories, methods, and curricula that included and recognized the experiences of people with a history of enslavement, labor exploitation, racially motivated violence, and discrimination in the United States.

From 1967 to 1970, struggles for ethnic studies exploded as students occupied school and other buildings and waged strikes. In 1968, the longest and most violent student strike in U.S. history occurred at San Francisco State, where coalitions of Latino-American, Native-American, Asian-American, and African-American students demanded ethnic studies courses and faculty. By the end of the strike in 1969, the first School of Ethnic Studies and department of African-American Studies were established at San Francisco State University. California State at Northridge established the first Chicano Studies department and the University of California at Los Angeles initi-

ated Asian-American Studies. American-Indian Studies expanded at tribal colleges and spread to public universities. Throughout the 1970s, ethnic studies progressed from experimental courses to established minors, majors, certificates, and degrees offered by new programs, centers, institutes, and departments. Ethnic studies associations such as the National Council of Black Studies, the Association for Asian-American Studies, the National Association of Chicano Studies, and the National Indian Education Association were founded. Research conferences and publications proliferated and promoted "legitimacy" of such studies.

During the 1980s and 1990s, ethnic studies evolved in the wake of political backlash, internal and external critiques, and several significant controversies: Should the true purpose of education be training and organizing *inside* ethnic communities? How can internal gender hierarchies and the marginalization of women of color be resolved? Is racial separatism promoted by ethnic studies? Is there a need for "ethnic studies" in the light of curriculum "multiculturalization" and "internationalization?" Are the theories, research methods, curricula, teaching, and scholarship in ethnic studies of high quality? What terminology is appropriate and "politically correct"? Should there be a common curriculum for ethnic studies?

In the 1980s, critiques by women of color forced the gender question in ethnic studies (which was male-centered) and the race question in Women's Studies (which was white, European, and middle-class centered). Out of their critiques of exclusionary practices, African-American, Chicana, Asian-American, Native American, and other women of color transformed ethnic studies into a new field involving "integrative race, gender, class intersection studies," which recognized and analyzed "multiple" oppressions and privileges.

In the 1990s, although not as institutionalized as Women's Studies and African-American Studies, Latino, Asian, Native American, and gay/lesbian studies remain viable. However, all ethnic studies programs face an uncertain future as their autonomy and funding base are eroded by changing administrative commitments, loss of some public and legislative support, internal divisions, and academic competition for students, scholars, and resources.

See also AFROCENTRISM; BLACK STUDIES.

BIBLIOGRAPHY

Banks, James A. *Teaching Strategies for Ethnic Studies.* 1997.
Barnett, Bernice McNair, Rose M. Brewer, and M. Bahati Kuumba, eds. "New Directions in Race, Gender, and Class: African American Perspectives." Special issue of *Race, Gender, Class* 6 (2). 1999.

Belkhir, Jean, and Bernice McNair Barnett, eds. *Race, Gender and Class in Sociology: Towards an Inclusive Curriculum.* 1997.

Butler, Jonnella E. and John C. Walter, eds. *Transforming the Curriculum: Ethnic Studies and Women's Studies.* 1991.

Cordova, Teresa, ed. *Chicano Studies: Critical Connections Between Research and Community.* 1992.

Hull, Gloria T., Patricia Bell Scott, and Barbara Smith, eds. *All the Women Are White, All the Blacks Are Men, but Some of Us Are Brave: Black Women's Studies.* 1982.

Bernice McNair Barnett

Evers, James Charles

(1922–), politician, businessman, and civil rights leader.

Charles Evers was born on September 11, 1922 in Decatur, Mississippi. He served in World War II, graduated from Alcorn College, and eventually journeyed to Chicago after being threatened and bankrupted for advocating black voter registration. Hardworking and ambitious, Evers had a knack for business (both legal and illegal). His memoir, *Evers*, is filled with money-making schemes: food sales, moneylending, gambling, petty thievery, bootlegging, and numbers running. He also taught school and owned or worked in restaurants, motels, liquor stores, and radio stations.

Evers returned to MISSISSIPPI and civil rights activities in 1963 when his younger brother Medgar, then state field secretary for the NATIONAL ASSOCIATION FOR THE ADVANCEMENT OF COLORED PEOPLE (NAACP), was assassinated. (See MEDGAR EVERS.) After the funeral, Charles announced he would be taking over as state field secretary in his brother's place. Brash and fearless, Evers claimed the position without consulting NAACP leaders and without apparent concern for his personal safety.

From 1963 to 1965, Evers spent much of his time battling others within the civil rights movement, particularly the Mississippi COUNCIL OF FEDERATED ORGANIZATIONS (COFO) coalition. Like many NAACP officials, Evers believed in hierarchical and dictatorial leadership, and had little use for COFO's slow, ground-up efforts to organize communities and develop indigenous leadership. He undermined COFO's work and accused the activists of being outside agitators. But he argued just as fiercely with his bosses at the NAACP and narrowly escaped being fired for his unwillingness to take direction.

Yet among black Mississippians, Evers was a wildly popular folk hero. Brother to the martyred Medgar and a charismatic and powerful speaker, Evers exuded hope and confidence. Through his bold actions and public challenges, Evers inspired many African Americans, helping to weaken decades of white supremacy. In late 1965, with COFO's influence declining, Evers mobilized communities throughout southwest Mississippi. Working for political power and economic opportunity, he used the passage of the VOTING RIGHTS ACT (CIVIL RIGHTS ACT OF 1965) to precipitate massive voter registration drives. Simultaneously, he called for boycotts, using the collective economic power of African Americans to demand immediate changes in black–white relations.

Supported by this power base, Evers emerged as a politician and national spokesperson for the Mississippi movement. He is best known for being the first black mayor of an integrated Mississippi town since RECONSTRUCTION. In addition to serving as mayor of Fayette from 1969 to 1981 and from 1985 to 1989, he ran highly publicized campaigns, for the U.S. House of Representatives in 1968, governor of Mississippi in 1971, and U.S. Senate in 1978. Briefly prominent in national Democratic party politics, Evers followed the trend of national political power and became a supporter of Ronald Reagan and the Republican party. This switch cost him his first mayoral election after twelve years in office.

James Charles Evers gives a typically low-key speech, ca. 1965. (CORBIS)

Evers has been criticized for using intimidation to enforce boycotts; for his self-promotion and profit-seeking; for his pragmatic approach to politics and civil rights work; and for making deals with powerful whites. Caring little about such criticism, Evers defends his actions with characteristic confidence and defiance. Willing to stand on his record, he says, "Maybe I did snitch, tom, and kiss ass, but look at the results" (*New Orleans Times-Picayune*, April 19, 1998).

BIBLIOGRAPHY

Dittmer, John. *Local People: The Struggle for Civil Rights in Mississippi.* 1995.
Evers, Charles. *Evers*, edited by Grace Halsell. 1971.
"Images of State's Worst Era Available." *New Orleans Times-Picayune.* April 19, 1998.
Payne, Charles. *I've Got the Light of Freedom: The Organizing Tradition and the Mississippi Freedom Struggle.* 1995.

Emilye Crosby

Evers, Medgar

(1925–1963), civil rights activist, NAACP field secretary for Mississippi.

Born in Decatur, Mississippi, Medgar Wylie Evers served in France during World War II, and after the war enrolled at Alcorn College. There he met Myrlie Beasley; they were married during his senior year. Upon graduation the young couple moved to the all-black town of Mound Bayou in the Mississippi Delta, where Medgar worked as an insurance salesman. Distressed by the abject poverty of Delta blacks, Evers felt guilty about selling policies to people who could barely put food on their tables. After unsuccessfully applying for admission to the University of Mississippi law school, Evers accepted the NATIONAL ASSOCIATION FOR THE ADVANCEMENT OF COLORED PEOPLE (NAACP's) offer to become the state's first field secretary.

During the late 1950s Mississippi whites launched a reign of terror against blacks who fought for their civil rights. After the white Citizens' Council crushed attempts by the NAACP to desegregate public schools in 1955, Evers and other black leaders fought a holding action for the remainder of the decade. Evers spent much of his time investigating racially motivated homicides, including the murder of young Emmett TILL and the lynching of Mack Charles Parker. With school desegregation and voting rights efforts stopped in their tracks, Evers crisscrossed the state delivering "Pep Talks" at local NAACP meetings, attempting to help blacks break through the cycle of fear.

Evers's efforts began to pay off in 1961, when local youths inspired by his example launched the first di-

Medgar Evers in his office at NAACP state headquarters in Jackson, Mississippi, August 9, 1955. (AP/Wide World Photos)

rect action campaigns in Mississippi, including a well-publicized sit-in by Tougaloo College students at the Jackson public library. There followed the Freedom Rides, which brought organizers from the STUDENT NONVIOLENT COORDINATING COMMITTEE (SNCC) and CONGRESS OF RACIAL EQUALITY (CORE) into the state. Originally ambivalent about outsiders poaching on what had been NAACP turf, Evers developed a good working relationship with these militant young activists as the racial climate in Mississippi heated up.

Nineteen sixty-three was a critical year for the black freedom struggle in Mississippi, with SNCC's voter registration drive in Greenwood, Aaron Henry's movement in Clarksdale, and the local NAACP-led campaign in Jackson all attempting to crack open the "Closed Society." As the Jackson movement gained national attention as a result of police brutality and mass arrests, Evers became the man in the middle, attempting to bridge the gap between the young activists and the more conservative NAACP national leaders, who had come down to redirect the movement from the streets to a less dangerous voter registration campaign.

At 12:20 A.M. on June 12, Evers pulled into his driveway after attending a mass meeting. As he got out of his car he was hit in the back by a rifle shot fired by Byron De La Beckwith, a Citizens' Council member. Evers died on the way to the hospital.

In death Medgar Evers became a heroic symbol of the civil rights movement, cut down at the very moment he was in the forefront of the struggle. In the lonely days of the 1950s he and a handful of black men and women had kept the spirit of protest alive in Mississippi. Evers had laid the groundwork, and those who fought the successful battles against JIM CROW in the mid-1960s stood in the shadow of this courageous and dedicated leader.

BIBLIOGRAPHY

Dittmer, John. *Local People: The Struggle for Civil Rights in Mississippi.* 1994.

Evers, Mrs. Myrlie (with William Peters). *For Us, the Living.* 1967; 2d ed. 1997.

Payne, Charles. *I've Got the Light of Freedom: The Organizing Tradition and the Mississippi Freedom Struggle.* 1995.

Salter, John R. *Jackson, Mississippi: An American Chronicle of Struggle and Schism.* 1987.

John Dittmer

Exodusters

A dramatic manifestation of the abolition of racial slavery was the freedpeople's ability to travel from place to place without fear of reprisal. The tradition of Southern blacks choosing to migrate North predated their emancipation from bondage. But the numbers increased dramatically after the war when 20,000 Southern African Americans, in what was termed the Exodus to Kansas, migrated to Kansas from Mississippi, Louisiana, Texas, Kentucky, and Tennessee in the spring of 1879. Beginning around 1915 and continuing through World War II, in an era known as the Great Migration, the number of migrants exploded. These migrants were often termed exodusters, providing a biblical reference to their search for a new promised land.

Nearly 500,000 African Americans chose to leave the South in the first few years of the movement. Increased production for the war in Europe and a drastic reduction in immigrant labor created economic opportunity in the urban North, and dissatisfied blacks faced with limited employment prospects and a society which labeled them inferior raced north to fill the job openings. Unequal justice, racial violence, and JIM CROW segregation contributed as much if not more to the decision to migrate as economic incentives.

The migration influenced civil rights protests in the North and South. In the North, access to the franchise and better educational facilities nurtured an increasingly politicized group of African Americans. In the South, white opposition to the black migration allowed those who remained to use the threat of exodus to call for improved economic and social conditions. Not only was the act of migration itself a form of social

protest, but the communities resulting from this demographic shift provided the contexts for continued demands for civil rights among African Americans.

BIBLIOGRAPHY

Grossman, James R. *Land of Hope: Chicago, Black Southerners, and the Great Migration.* 1989.

Harris, Alferdteen, ed. *Black Exodus: The Great Migration from the American South.* 1991.

Marks, Carole. *Farewell—We're Good and Gone: The Black Migration.* 1989.

Woodson, Carter G. *A Century of Negro Migration.* 1918.

Elizabeth Gessel

Eyes on the Prize

In 1986 a multipart documentary presentation of the civil rights movement called "Eyes on the Prize" was aired by PBS. The series, created and produced in part under contract to the Civil Rights Project, Inc., a nonprofit organization established in 1985 to research, develop, produce, and archive material relating to American civil rights, was the brainchild of Blackside, Incorporated's executive producer, Henry Hampton. Hampton said that he created "Eyes on the Prize" to chronicle the emotional urgency and reality of extraordinary times, 1954–1985, that were the key years of the movement. He and the Blackside staff were committed to assuring that this critical moment in American history was available and preserved for those who did not experience it and so that it might be taught to the children of tomorrow. Since 1989 "Eyes on the Prize" has become part of an educational package that includes two sets of videotape documentaries with companion books, a proposed tele-course, and a volume of narratives from many movement participants.

This important contribution to movement historiography is informed through the lens of the television and newsreel cameras as well as the voices and memories of many of the movement's participants. *Eyes on the Prize* is not the most comprehensive chronicle of the civil rights movement. Perhaps its greatest contribution—true to its creator's intent—is that this chronicle is an instructive, inspiring, and enlightening package that can be used to offer a perspective of the movement to people of all ages and educational levels.

BIBLIOGRAPHY

Carson, Clayborne, et al. *The Eyes on the Prize: Civil Rights Reader: Documents, Speeches, and Firsthand Accounts from the Black Freedom Struggle, 1954–1990.* 1991.

Eyes on the Prize [videocassette]. *America's Civil Rights Years.* Blackside, Inc. PBS Video. 1986.

Eyes on the Prize [videocassette]. *America at the Racial Crossroads.* Blackside, Inc. PBS Video. 1990.

Eyes on the Prize [videorecording]: *Teacher In-Service Video.* New Learning Project, Inc. PBS Video. 1993.

Hampton, Henry, and Steve Fayer, with Sarah Flynn.

Voices of Freedom: An Oral History of the Civil Rights Movement from the 1950s through the 1980s. 1990.

Williams, Juan. *Eyes on the Prize: America's Civil Rights Years, 1954–1965.* 1987.

Homer Douglass Hill

F

Fair Employment Practice Committee

Shortages of workers and the need for national unity during WORLD WAR II encouraged federal intervention on behalf of African Americans in the labor market. BROTHERHOOD OF SLEEPING CAR PORTERS (BSCP) President A. Philip RANDOLPH threatened a march of 100,000 African Americans on Washington, D.C. to protest both racial discrimination in defense EMPLOYMENT and a JIM CROW U.S Army. Fearing disruption of the war effort and ideological embarrassment in the fight against Nazism, President Franklin D. ROOSEVELT issued Executive Order 8802 on June 25, 1941, to end discrimination "in the employment of workers in defense industries or government because of race, creed, color, or national origin." The order created the President's Committee on Fair Employment Practice, known as the "Fair Employment Practice Committee" or FEPC.

After a series of public hearings over the next year that embarrassed major defense contractors and exposed the extent of discrimination, Roosevelt curtailed the FEPC's workings by placing it under the jurisdiction of the War Manpower Commission (WMC) on July 30, 1942. A subsequent Executive Order, 9346, reconstituted the committee (then known as the "Second Committee") as an independent agency on May 27, 1943, in the Office of Emergency Management. Despite lack of resources and limited powers, FEPC became a beachhead for civil rights within the federal government. It legitimized black protest by channeling agitation into administrative procedures, even though these procedures mostly proved inadequate to

dismantle the structural impediments to economic advancement.

For five years, FEPC investigated discrimination in hiring and upgrading of workers by private employers, government agencies, and unions alike. It held more than fifteen public hearings in major cities, including Chicago, New York, Birmingham, and Los Angeles, and settled five thousand cases, stopping over forty strikes that derived from racial animosity. It was most successful in areas hampered by a "manpower" shortage, such as Cleveland and Detroit, where it settled 40 percent of cases. It handled discrimination against Jews in New York and Chicanos in the Southwest.

Working mainly by individual complaint—brought by laboring people directly or by way of a race-advancement organization such as the NATIONAL ASSOCIATION FOR THE ADVANCEMENT OF COLORED PEOPLE (NAACP)—FEPC proceeded through conferences and negotiations. It established regional offices throughout the country, and the Atlanta office challenged local mores by having white and black women use the same toilet facilities. Nearly 90 percent of complaints came from African Americans. The FEPC provided no remedy for discrimination on account of "sex," but women from the covered groups filed 30.8 percent of the cases docketed. Sometimes discriminatory acts against African-American women, based on cultural stereotypes and exacerbated by their tending to family responsibilities, stemmed from their being black and female and not merely from their race.

High-profile cases in which employers and unions rejected or ignored FEPC directives—involving the railways and the West Coast shipyards—proved impervious to its chief tactics of public exposure and moral suasion. Its cease and desist orders were unenforceable because it could not bring offenders to court. FEPC could recommend withdrawal of a government contract, but no wartime president ever withdrew one. President Harry TRUMAN's failure to implement an FEPC directive against Capital Transit, even after military seizure of the Washington, D.C., firm during a November 1945 strike, led Commissioner Charles H. HOUSTON to resign in angry protest.

All along FEPC had lacked power to counter political pressure. Paul McNutt of the WMC, for example, canceled hearings against Southern railways and the railroad brotherhoods. After the FEPC finally proceeded with these in September 1943, Roosevelt responded by appointing another fact-finding committee rather than enforcing its finding and risking a disruption of rail service. These hearings, in turn, provided an excuse for Virginia Democrat Howard W. SMITH to conduct a hostile congressional hearing in which the railroad's attorney charged FEPC with being "a doctrinaire and starry-eyed, bureaucratic agency." Other Southern members of CONGRESS claimed that FEPC was "more concerned in tearing down the existing social order" than with fighting employment discrimination or winning the war. Northern Republican conservatives, who objected to government interference in labor relations, joined the attack by associating its restrictions on employers with Communism. FEPC succumbed to such opposition when Congress first defunded the wartime agency and then blocked bills for a permanent FEPC. After more than a decade of congressional failure to revive FEPC, TITLE VII OF THE 1964 CIVIL RIGHTS ACT passed with "sex" added to its mandate, ironically in part due to FEPC's old nemesis Howard W. Smith.

The politics of race shaped the composition of the committee. White men held the chairmanship, including the moderate Southerner Mark Ethridge of the Louisville *Courier-Journal*, the labor priest Msgr. Francis K. Haas, and New Dealer Malcom Ross; a black man, George M. Johnson of Howard Law School, was deputy chairman and head of the legal division. The commissioners represented unions, employers, and the black community, including Milton P. WEBSTER of the BSCP and black Chicago alderman Earl Dickerson. Nonetheless, FEPC was too multiracial for the likes of Dixiecrat Representative Richard RUSSELL of Georgia, who tried to scandalize the nation by charging that black male executives had white female secretaries and earned too-high salaries. The agency indeed possessed a dedicated multiracial staff, many of whom would continue to fight for civil rights in subsequent years, such as Clarence M. MITCHELL of the NAACP and Will Maslow of the American Jewish Congress.

Agency field staff attempted to persuade reluctant employers and unions to advance African-American workers and not merely to settle individual complaints. Through its local efforts, FEPC proved to be a precursor to AFFIRMATIVE ACTION. It encouraged employers to send racially mixed crews out to sea and on the road (despite complaints that black and white men could not share sleeping quarters or truck booths), and to upgrade black workers into skilled jobs. In spite of eliminating many racial designations on employment applications, advertisements, and U.S. Employment Service referrals, it still would ask for overall employment by race and monitor an employer's overall racial patterns. In the context of World War II, its promotion of fair employment, that is, nondiscrimination, constituted positive action. The FEPC experience taught the impossibility of ignoring group bias when individuals suffered discrimination based on their classification as members of that group.

BIBLIOGRAPHY

Boris, Eileen. "Fair Employment and the Origins of Affirmative Action in the 1940s." *NWSA Journal* 10 (1998): 142–151.

Boris, Eileen. "'You Wouldn't Want One of 'Em Dancing With Your Wife': Racialized Bodies on the Job in WWII." *American Quarterly* 50 (1998): 77–108.

Daniel, Cletus E. *Chicano Workers and the Politics of Fairness: The FEOC in the Southwest, 1941–1946.* 1990.

Graham, Hugh Davis. *The Civil Rights Era: Origin and Development of National Policy.* 1990.

Harris, William H. "Federal Intervention in Union Discrimination: FEPC and West Coast Shipyards During World War II." *Labor History* 22 (1981): 325–347.

Kersten, Andrew E. *Fighting for Fair Employment: The FEPC in the Midwest, 1941–1946.* In press.

Moreno, Paul. *From Direct Action to Affirmative Action: Fair Employment Law and Policy in America, 1933–1972.* 1997.

Reed, Merl E. *Seedtime for the Modern Civil Rights Movement: The President's Committee on Fair Employment Practice 1941–1946.* 1991.

Ross, Malcom. *All Manner of Men.* 1948.

Ruchames, Louis. *Race, Jobs, and Politics: The Story of the FEPC.* 1953.

Records of the Fair Employment Practice Committee, housed in the National Archives as Record Group 228, are available on microfilm. They consist of office and field records, including hearing transcripts, board minutes, correspondence, and closed and unresolved case files.

Eileen Boris

Fair Housing Act (Civil Rights Act of 1968)

The Fair Housing Act of 1968 banned racial discrimination in the sale or rental of housing, though exclusions of certain types of owner-occupied properties reduced its coverage to about 80 percent of the nation's housing. In June 1968, the SUPREME COURT found, in *Jones v. Mayer*, that the CIVIL RIGHTS ACT OF 1866 had banned racial discrimination in all residential real estate, thereby extending coverage to virtually all housing. Nevertheless, legislative compromises in the Fair Housing Act so weakened its enforcement provisions that it could have little impact. The primary responsibility to enforce the law fell on the shoulders of individuals who could file civil suits if they believed they had suffered discrimination. Indeed, in the years since its passage, few American cities have reduced racial residential segregation substantially.

Racial residential segregation had long concerned civil rights activists. Housing discrimination confined most African Americans to the least desirable housing, and the high prices and short supply worsened by discrimination led to endemic overcrowding and unsafe conditions. Moreover, de facto segregation in schools outside the South was based in large part on residential segregation. The NATIONAL ASSOCIATION FOR THE ADVANCEMENT OF COLORED PEOPLE (NAACP) had early waged a successful Supreme Court challenge to racial residential zoning laws (*Buchanan v. Warley* 1917). And it successfully petitioned the court (*Shelly v. Kramer*, 1947) to ban enforcement of restrictive covenants—private agreements among white property owners that excluded African Americans and others from white neighborhoods. Also, activists had pressured President John F. KENNEDY to fulfill a campaign promise and issue Executive Order 11063, banning discrimination in housing where federal government funds were involved.

But none of these measures were sufficient to lessen the ubiquitous and overt racial segregation that plagued the nation's cities. And the passage of the CIVIL RIGHTS ACT OF 1964 and the VOTING RIGHTS ACT (CIVIL RIGHTS ACT OF 1965) left housing discrimination unaddressed. Moreover, urban riots during the mid-1960s pointed to potential grave difficulties if the nation were to fail to address racial residential segregation. Indeed, Martin Luther KING, JR. had attempted, though without much success, to turn the nation's attention to the problem. During 1966, Dr. King's Chicago Freedom Movement attempted to open that city's white neighborhoods to African Americans and to force the city to prosecute slum landlords violating health and safety codes.

For his part, President Lyndon B. JOHNSON offered fair housing legislation in both 1966 and 1967, but intense opposition from Southern senators and waning support for civil rights resulted in defeat. Fair housing legislation returned to the Senate in 1968 as an amendment to a bill to protect civil rights workers.

This time, supporters worked out compromises to gain the crucial support of Senator Everett Dirkson, the Republican leader from Illinois. The bill passed the Senate, seventy-one to twenty, in early March after the Kerner Commission issued its report implicating housing discrimination as a central factor in ghetto poverty and black anger. The assassination of Dr. King undermined the bill's opposition in the House of Representatives and on April 10, the House passed it, 229 to 195, with significant support from liberal Republicans.

BIBLIOGRAPHY

Casey-Leininger, Charles F. *Creating Democracy in Housing: Civil Rights and Housing Policy in Cincinnati, 1945–1980.* 1993.

Graham, Hugh Davis. *The Civil Rights Era: The Origins and Development of National Policy, 1960–1872.* 1990.

Grier, George, and Eunice Grier. *Equality and Beyond: Housing Segregation and the Goals of the Great Society.* 1966.

Lewis, David L. *King: A Biography.* 1978.

Massey, Douglas S., and Nancy A. Denton. *American Apartheid: Segregation and the Making of the Underclass.* 1993.

Vose, Clement. *Caucasians Only: The Supreme Court, the NAACP, and the Restrictive Covenant Cases.* 1959.

Charles F. Casey-Leininger

Farmer, James

(1920– 1999), civil rights leader, union organizer.

James Farmer was born in Marshall, Texas, on January 12, 1920, the son of James Leonard and Pearl Farmer. James Farmer is one of the major heroes of the civil rights movement, a living legacy who continues to inspire us. At the age of three and a half years, he first experienced racism in Holly Springs, Mississippi. In his *Lay Bare the Heart: An Autobiography of the Civil Rights Movement* (1985), he related a story of an experience that he and his mother shared on a hot summer day while walking home from shopping. Young James wanted a soda pop as they approached a drugstore; however, his mother suggested that he wait until they arrived home because there were drinks in the refrigerator. In the meantime, he watched another young boy go into the drugstore, sit at the counter, and drink a soft drink through a straw. This further convinced him that he could get a soft drink from the drugstore. His mother shared with him the reality of conditions in the South under JIM CROW, simply by telling him that the other person was white and he was colored; therefore, he could not be served at the drugstore counter. This single event would follow him for the remainder of his life, causing him to have recurring

James Farmer, executive director of the Congress for Racial Equality (CORE) from 1960 to 1966, sits in his office at CORE headquarters in New York City, June 20, 1964. (CORBIS/Bettmann)

nightmares. His dreams reflected the reality of growing up living under racist conditions in Mississippi.

Farmer began his formal education at the age of four, and he graduated from Wiley College at the age of eighteen. From Wiley, he went to Howard University's School of Religion, where he earned a Bachelor of Divinity in 1941. His civil rights career began in 1942, when he led a group of fellow activists and civil rights advocates in a passive SIT-IN at the Jack Spratt Coffee Shop in Chicago, Illinois, because their interracial group had been refused service. They returned repeatedly for several days until everyone was served. He helped to found the CONGRESS OF RACIAL EQUALITY (CORE) in April 1942. As its most impressive leader, he was a pioneer of the successful FREEDOM RIDES of the early 1960s: the most important of the nonviolent demonstrations to challenge segregated public accommodations in interstate travel. He was a very significant proponent of civil disobedience as well as of nonviolent direct action as strategies for the civil rights struggle.

Married twice and with two children, Farmer led a varied, interesting life. He entered the political arena in 1968, when he ran on the Republican ticket against black Democrat Shirley CHISHOLM to represent the Twelfth Congressional District of Brooklyn. Farmer has been the recipient of numerous honorary doctoral degrees and awards. The most prestigious of these was the Presidential Medal of Freedom, the nation's high-

est civilian honor. Other awards he has received include numerous honorary doctoral degrees and awards such as the American Veterans Award, the John Dewey Award from the League for Industrial Democracy, and the Lifetime Achievement Award at the Black Image Awards ceremony in 1997. In honor of his seventy-third birthday in 1993, Omega Psi Phi created the James Farmer Civil Rights Trailblazer Award. James Farmer Day was declared in the District of Columbia in 1993.

James Farmer's contributions to the civil rights movement owed greatly to his commitment, dedication, organizational skill, and leadership. His contributions are appreciated by those who have been inspired by his words and booming voice, and who have been mentored or taught by following his example. He continues to share his personal stories and life by teaching younger generations about the importance of civil rights activism. Farmer was a crucial part of the mainstream civil rights leadership, which included Whitney YOUNG of the URBAN LEAGUE; Roy WILKINS of the NATIONAL ASSOCIATION FOR THE ADVANCEMENT OF COLORED PEOPLE (NAACP); and Martin Luther KING, JR. of the SOUTHERN CHRISTIAN LEADERSHIP CONFERENCE.

BIBLIOGRAPHY

Chappell, Kevin. "'Where Are the Civil Rights Icons of the '60s': What Black Activists Are Doing in the 90s?" *Ebony* 51, 10 (1996): 10.
"Civil Rights Veteran James Farmer Awarded Medal of Freedom." *Jet* 93, 10 (1998): 4.
Farmer, James. *Freedom—When?* 1965.
Farmer, James. *Lay Bare the Heart: An Autobiography of the Civil Rights Movement.* 1985.

Dorothy A. Smith-Akubue

Farm Labor Organizing Committee

The Farm Labor Organizing Committee (FLOC), with a membership made up of seasonal and migrant farm workers, was founded in the Midwest as a small, independent union in 1967 by Baldemar Velázquez, who has continued to serve as the organization's president through the end of the twentieth century and beyond. Velázquez recalls how the FLOC in its early days marched with the Black Panthers in Toledo and Lima, Ohio, during the late 1960s and 1970s in protest against civil rights violations and police abuse. The union refused to advocate acts of violence but otherwise was supportive of the Panthers' positions on social issues. Confronting similar civil rights violations and police abuse in Florida and Texas, the union also subsequently marched in unity with organizations like the

RAZA UNIDA PARTY and took part in the growing Latino political consciousness that resulted in the election of more Latino officials in the Rio Grande Valley and elsewhere (see also Rodolfo "Corky" GONZALES).

FLOC, which originated in the Midwest but soon attracted members in the South and Southwest as well, is perhaps best known for its seven-year boycott (1979–1986) against the Campbell Soup Company. In 1984, in the midst of that boycott, FLOC organizers became involved in Jesse JACKSON's presidential campaign. They won votes for Jackson and participated in a spirited floor demonstration on behalf of the Campbell Soup boycott at the Democratic National Convention, though the full resolution of that dispute was still two years away. After a protracted struggle, the union was ultimately victorious, and far-reaching multiparty agreements were finally made with Campbell Soup and its affiliate Vlasic in 1986. Beneficiaries of those agreements were FLOC members: the seasonal, migrant tomato and pickle growers employed by Campbell Soup and Vlasic in Ohio and Michigan. In the years that followed, FLOC negotiated and signed similar agreements with Heinz and other corporations operating in the same areas.

Partly out of a need for allies and partly because it represents Mexican-American citizens and undocumented immigrants, this small union has also immersed itself in the mainstream of the nation's civil rights movement and the LABOR MOVEMENT (see also UNIONS) as well, especially through its charter of affiliation in 1994 with the AFL/CIO.

In the late 1990s, the FLOC was involved in an ongoing campaign to organize farmworkers employed by the Mt. Olive Pickle Company of Mt. Olive, North Carolina. At the dawn of the twenty-first century, President Velázquez speculates that there will soon come a further day of reckoning for these migrant workers: "Many in the first generation are undocumented. But within a few years of living here they will have children, and those children will be citizens. These new citizens will not accept the conditions and treatment endured by their parents. I can see them combining with middle class Latino citizens who benefited from affirmative action and now want to know why government is failing their people. Sooner or later this will become a force to be reckoned with."

BIBLIOGRAPHY

Barger, W. K., and Ernesto M. Reza. *The Farm Labor Movement in the Midwest: Social Change and Adaptation Among Migrant Farmworkers.* 1994.

Farm Labor Organizing Committee Web Site: http://www.iupui.edu/~floc

Michael Ferner

Farrakhan, Louis

(1933–), religious leader.

Minister Louis Abdul Haleem Farrakhan is the highly controversial leader of the NATION OF ISLAM, a radical, separatist black religious movement. Born on May 17, 1933 in the Bronx, New York, Louis Eugene Walcott was raised in Boston by his West Indian mother. Deeply religious, Louis became an altar boy at the Episcopalian church in his Roxbury neighborhood. He graduated with honors from the prestigious Boston English High School, where he also participated on the track team and played the violin in the school orchestra. After attending the Winston-Salem Teachers College from 1951 to 1953, he dropped out to pursue his favorite avocation of music and intended to make it his career. An accomplished musician, Walcott performed professionally on the Boston nightclub circuit as a singer of calypso and country songs. In 1955 at the age of twenty-two, Louis Walcott was recruited by Minister MALCOLM X of the Nation of Islam. Following the custom of the Nation, he dropped his surname and took an "X," which meant "undetermined," ex-slave, ex-Christian, ex-smoker, ex-drinker, ex-mainstream American. After Louis X proved himself in the movement for a number of years, the Honorable Elijah MUHAMMAD, the supreme leader of the Nation of Islam, gave him his Muslim name of "Abdul Haleem Farrakhan." He was appointed to be the head minister of Boston Temple No. 11. As a rising star within the Nation, Minister Farrakhan also wrote the only song, "A White Man's Heaven Is A Black Man's Hell," and dramatic play, "Orgena," or "A Negro" spelled backwards, officially sanctioned by Mr. Muhammad.

Through leaders such as the Honorable Elijah Muhammad and Ministers Malcolm X and Louis Farrakhan, the Nation of Islam became a major foil and critic of the American civil rights movement led by Dr. Martin Luther KING, JR. in the 1950s and 1960s. They criticized the goal of integration with the American mainstream, citing the pervasive racism, and they opted for racial separation and the creation of a separate black nation somewhere in the United States or in the world. They also criticized King's stance of nonviolence and replaced it with a strategy of self-defense "by any means necessary." One of the most significant accomplishments of the Nation of Islam was to help change the self-perception and ethnic definition of black Americans, from a stance of self-hatred, identity confusion, and inferiority to one of self-affirmation, ethnic pride, and dignity. With the speeches of leaders such as Malcolm X and Louis Farrakhan, the Black Consciousness and BLACK POWER movement of the late 1960s and 1970s helped to change the elements of culture of an entire country, reflected in the change from "Negro" to "black." Through its message and discipline, the Nation also helped to rehabilitate the lives of thousands of poor black people who were either in prison or trapped by drugs, alcohol, and crime.

After Malcolm X's assassination on February 23, 1965, Minister Farrakhan replaced Malcolm as the head minister of Harlem's Temple No. 7 and as the National Representative of the Nation, the second in command. Like his predecessor, Louis Farrakhan is a dynamic, charismatic leader and a powerful speaker with the ability to appeal to the masses of black people.

When Elijah Muhammad died on February 25, 1975, the Nation of Islam experienced several large schisms. Wallace Muhammad, the fifth of Elijah's six sons, was surprisingly chosen as the Supreme Minister by the leadership hierarchy. Disappointed that he was not chosen as Elijah's successor, Minister Louis Farrakhan led a breakaway group and began rebuilding his own Nation in November 1977. Farrakhan disagreed with Wallace Muhammad's attempts to move the Nation to orthodox Sunni Islam and Muhammad's rejection of his father's separatist teachings and radical black nationalism.

Minister Farrakhan became known to the American public through a series of controversies that were stirred up when he first supported Rev. Jesse JACKSON's 1984 presidential campaign. During the campaign, his Fruit of Islam guards provided security for Jackson. There were excited hopes of finally uniting the civil rights supporters, represented by Jackson, with Farrakhan's black nationalists. However, Louis Farrakhan exacerbated the "Hymietown" controversy of the Jackson campaign by threatening to censure *Washington Post* reporter Milton Coleman in the black community. Coleman, a black journalist, had reported Jackson's off-the-record use of the offensive reference to Jewish influence in New York City. Minister Farrakhan has also become embroiled in a continuing controversy with the American Jewish community by making allegedly anti-Semitic statements. Claiming that his statements have been taken out of context unfairly, Farrakhan has denied being anti-Semitic. Furthermore, he contends that a distorted media focus on this issue has not adequately covered the achievements of his movement.

Farrakhan's Nation of Islam has been successful in getting rid of drug dealers in a number of public housing projects and private apartment buildings. It has established a clinic for the treatment of acquired immunodeficiency syndrome (AIDS) patients in Washington, D.C. A cosmetics company, Clean and Fresh, has marketed its products in the black community. The group's weekly newspaper is *The Final Call*. Farrakhan has allowed his members to participate in elec-

toral politics and has appointed five women ministers, both of which were forbidden under Elijah Muhammad.

On October 16, 1995, the Honorable Louis Farrakhan's MILLION MAN MARCH was held in Washington, D.C., drawing a crowd of largely black men, estimated between 800,000 to over 1 million. It was the largest black gathering in history, surpassing the 250,000 people at the March on Washington rally led by Dr. Martin Luther King, Jr., in August, 1963. (See MARCH ON WASHINGTON.) Although the core of Farrakhan's Nation of Islam is estimated to be between 50,000 to 100,000 members, his influence is much greater. His speeches across the country have attracted crowds of more than 40,000 in large cities. His group is the fastest growing of the various Muslim movements—perhaps helped by the influence of rap groups such as Public Enemy and Prince Akeem. International branches of the Nation have been formed in Ghana, London, Paris, South Africa, and the Caribbean Islands.

Minister Louis Farrakhan and his wife, Khadijah, have eleven children, several of whom serve in the Nation's hierarchy.

BIBLIOGRAPHY

Eure, Joseph D., and Richard Jerome. *Back Where We Belong: Selected Speeches by Minister Louis Farrakhan*, 1989.

Evanier, David, and Alan M. Schwartz. "Louis Farrakhan: The Campaign to Manipulate Public Opinion." *ADL Research Report*, 1989.

Farrakhan, Louis. *Seven Speeches by Minister Louis Farrakhan*, 1974.

Farrakhan, Louis. *A Torchlight for America*, 1990.

Farrakhan, Louis. *The Convention of the Oppressed*, 1998.

Gardell, Mattias. *In the Name of Elijah Muhammad: Louis Farrakhan and the Nation of Islam*, 1996.

Lincoln, C. Eric. *The Black Muslims in America*, 1960.

Mamiya, Lawrence H. "From Black Muslim to Bilalian: The Evolution of a Movement." *Journal for the Scientific Study of Religion* 17, 2 (1982): 138–151.

Mamiya, Lawrence H. "Minister Louis Farrakhan and the Final Call: Schism in the Muslim Movement." In *The Muslim Community in North America*, edited by Earle Waugh, Baha Abu-Laban, and Regula Querishi. 1983.

Mamiya, Lawrence H. "Minister Louis Farrakhan." *Contemporary Black Leaders*, edited by David DeLeon. 1994.

Muhammad, Elijah. *Message to the Black Man*. 1965.

Lawrence H. Mamiya

Father Divine (George Baker)

(1879–1965), religious and civil rights leader.

Born George Baker to a poor African-American family in Rockville, Maryland, the man who would become

The charismatic religious leader and founder of the Peace Mission Movement, Father Divine, at the peak of his popularity, surrounded by his followers in 1937. (Archive Photos)

renowned as Father Divine began his career as an itinerant Baptist preacher. Deeply influenced by the positive thinking of New Thought, he was present in 1906 at the Azusa Street Revival in Los Angeles, the religious phenomenon that initiated the modern Pentecostal Movement. Father Divine was an ardent advocate of civil rights and a serious practitioner of racial INTEGRATION, taking unpopular and illegal positions in that day, but in a stance not unrelated to his role as a charismatic and messianic religious leader whose followers believed he was God incarnate. In establishing his communal Kingdom on earth, Father (as he was known to his flock) not only presided over a perfectionistic interracial community but removed the very mechanics of RACISM.

In Father's Peace Mission Movement, he eliminated distinctions of race by eliminating the vocabulary that made racial distinctions possible. The words "Negro," "Colored," and "Black" were expunged from speech

and replaced by the value-free terms "light-complected" and "dark-complected." Also, the Movement's communal single-sex hotels required roommates to be racially mixed. At the triumphalist nightly communion banquets presided over by Father, seating was called "Enacting the Bill." This meant that chairs were assigned alternately to light-complected and dark-complected people. "Enacting the Bill's" seating arrangement was perceived as actualizing the U.S. CONSTITUTION's Bill of Rights. Father articulated a flag-waving American patriotism, which was an expression of his conviction that basic U.S. law was itself not racially biased.

In the world, Peace Mission followers participated in "Don't buy where you can't work" campaigns, and Father flirted with political action by founding the Righteous Government Platform in 1936. Father's spiritual marriage to Edna Mae Ritchings, a white Canadian follower, was heralded as a profound symbol of the interracialism of the Kingdom. Toward the end of his life, Father stated that he himself had personally transcended race.

BIBLIOGRAPHY

Watts, Jill M. *God, Harlem U.S.A.* 1992.
Weisbrot, Robert. *Father Divine and the Struggle for Racial Equality.* 1983.

Richard Newman

Faubus, Orval Eugene

(1910–1994), Arkansas governor, 1955–1967.

Orval Faubus made news headlines on September 3, 1957, with reports that he had dispatched National Guardsmen to Central High School in Little Rock, Arkansas, to prevent the implementation of a court-ordered desegregation plan. By interposing his authority as head of a sovereign state between federal government and the carrying out of an unpopular order at a local level, Faubus precipitated a constitutional crisis. This crisis was was resolved when President Dwight D. EISENHOWER federalized the National Guard and sent in soldiers from the 101st Airborne Division to escort nine African-American students into classes. Faubus's actions were all the more surprising given his reputation as a racial moderate, who cut his political teeth in the liberal 1948 Sid McMath state administration, and had avoided extremist pronouncements on school desegregation immediately after the 1954 BROWN V. BOARD OF EDUCATION decision. However, pressure from Jim Johnson, head of the state's WHITE CITIZENS' COUNCILS and challenger for the governorship in 1956, pushed Faubus into an increasingly extremist position. When Faubus was hailed

Governor Orval Faubus of Arkansas called the National Guard to block school integration in Little Rock, Arkansas. On September 25, 1957, President Dwight D. Eisenhower ordered federal troops to force the integration of Little Rock's Central High School. Faubus is shown here smiling on his way out of a meeting with President Eisenhower at the White House. (AP/Wide World Photos)

as a hero by southern conservatives for his stand in 1957, his actions grew increasingly reckless, and in 1958 he closed all of Little Rock's schools to prevent integration. Although eventually overruled by the United States Supreme Court, this further show of defiance earned Faubus an unprecedented six consecutive terms in office. Faubus's legacy is not that of a virulent race baiter in the Deep South political tradition, but of a southern moderate who ignored moral and legal responsibilities in favor of electoral success.

BIBLIOGRAPHY

Freyer, Tony. *The Little Rock Crisis: A Constitutional Interpretation*. 1984.
Reed, Roy. *Faubus: The Life and Times of an American Prodigal*. 1997.

John A. Kirk

Federal Bureau of Investigation (FBI)

For nearly the entirety of the twentieth century, the FBI and the civil rights movement have been bound tight. The nation's federal police had a *de jure* mandate to probe such civil rights violations as police brutality and a *de facto* mandate to spy on anyone committed to the struggle for racial justice. For this century's greater part, bureau officials had to be forced to enforce civil rights law. On the surveillance front, they needed scarcely a nudge.

Civil rights played a small part in Attorney General Charles J. Bonaparte's decision in 1908 to create a Bureau of Investigation (the word "Federal" came in 1935). Bonaparte's concern, which President Theodore Roosevelt shared, was with the rise of PEONAGE (involuntary slavery and servitude) in the turpentine camps of FLORIDA and elsewhere across the South. Overall, however, government policy followed the lead of Bonaparte's successor, who announced, in response to a wave of LYNCHING, that the Justice Department had "no authority . . . to protect citizens of African descent in the enjoyment of civil rights generally."

However reluctant to protect those citizens, the FBI proved quite willing to protect what J. Edgar Hoover would later call "the hard-working, tax-paying, law-abiding people." That "real America," in the view of the man who served as director under eight presidents (1924–1972), needed protection from an imagined black menace. The bureau's first two mega-cases along the color line involved the Mann (or White Slave Traffic) Act pursuit of boxing champion Jack Johnson and the mail-fraud crusade against Marcus GARVEY. In between those cases, the bureau surveyed black America in its entirety. Its WORLD WAR I probe began with a rumor that Mexico and "the colored element" in the United States would form an alliance and enter the war on Kaiser Wilhelm's behalf. During the next great war, in the summer of 1942, the FBI surveyed "un-American ideologies" in "colored neighborhoods." Again, the bureau found time to focus on individuals as well—ranging from Olympic champion Jesse Owens to A. Philip RANDOLPH's all-black MARCH ON WASHINGTON MOVEMENT. The latter, which led to President Franklin D. ROOSEVELT's executive order establishing a FAIR EMPLOYMENT PRACTICE COMMITTEE, rated a wiretap.

With Hitler abroad and lynching somewhat rampant at home, FDR's NEW DEAL and WORLD WAR II years also witnessed the first measurable pressure on the FBI to investigate civil rights abuses. Additional pressure came after the war when Harry S. TRUMAN, enraged upon learning that several black veterans had been lynched with their uniforms on, appointed a PRESIDENT'S COMMITTEE ON CIVIL RIGHTS. Still, this pressure was at best nominal. FBI investigations remained episodic and generally limited to highly technical violations of two RECONSTRUCTION era statutes, the CIVIL RIGHTS ACT OF 1866 and the Enforcement Act of 1870.

Hoover always made the case that his bureau lacked constitutional authority to jump into civil rights enforcement. That there was no constitutional basis whatsoever for moving on the other front failed to deter him. His agents leaked derogatory information on Paul ROBESON to, among others, Illinois Senator Everett Dirksen; opened Robeson's mail; tapped his telephone; and sought to document a rumored affair with Lord Louis Mountbatten's wife. The director seemed especially interested in a report "that Lady Mountbatten has a huge naked statue of Paul Robeson in her home."

FBI success in avoiding or minimizing civil rights enforcement came slowly to an end in the 1960s, following BROWN V. BOARD OF EDUCATION (1954), the MONTGOMERY BUS BOYCOTT (1955–1956), the student SIT-INS (1960), and the ever-present crush thereafter of an onrushing civil rights movement. Under the CIVIL RIGHTS ACT OF 1957 and the CIVIL RIGHTS ACT OF 1960, Attorney General Robert F. KENNEDY ordered the FBI to gather voter registration statistics as part of a strategy to ensure black voting by filing suit against registrars. The attorney general next took a page from the director's book by authorizing an FBI wiretap on the movement's recognized leader, Martin Luther KING, JR. In regard to the other major legislation (the CIVIL RIGHTS ACT OF 1964 and the VOTING RIGHTS ACT OF 1965) and events of the 1960s (FREEDOM RIDES; INTEGRATION crises at the University of Alabama and Ole Miss; the Birmingham demonstrations; the 1963 MARCH ON WASHINGTON; Selma; and then riots in Watts, Newark, and Detroit), the FBI was always present—always unwilling to enforce civil rights law but quite willing to open a file on anyone.

By the late 1960s FBI intelligence work slipped completely over the line into counterintelligence. Having opened a formal counterintelligence program known as COINTELPRO–White Hate Group against the KU KLUX KLAN and other "white hate groups" in the midst of the FREEDOM SUMMER murders (1964), bureau officials opened a COINTELPRO–Black Hate Group three years later in response to urban riots. Even after the assassinations of that decade, Hoover's agents targeted the image of the prince of nonviolence (King) and the prince of violence (MALCOLM X) alike. The overall purpose of COINTELPRO–Black Hate Group was "to expose, disrupt, misdirect, discredit, or otherwise neutralize the activities of black nationalist . . . leadership, spokesmen, membership, and supporters." Several targets ended up dead, including Chicago Black Panther Fred Hampton—shot sleeping in his bed during a police raid. The Panther-cum-

informant who helped the bureau organize that raid received a cash bonus. (See BLACK PANTHER PARTY.)

A formal push into counterintelligence did not mean that the FBI neglected community surveillance. A sampling of those efforts includes: rabble rouser, agitator, and ADEX Indices; a key black extremist portfolio; a black nationalist photograph album; a racial calendar; and brigades of ghetto and BLACPRO informants. By the summer of 1968 the bureau had 3,248 ghetto informants alone, all promised up to $400 for a single juicy tidbit and charged with monitoring "the attitude of the Negro community towards the white community."

With Hoover's death in 1972 and fallout from Vietnam and Watergate, as well as congressional investigations of the intelligence community, the FBI began to change. Over the past quarter-century there has been less foot-dragging on either the routine or the spectacular civil rights case. The bureau still gets its share of the latter—notably, the Rodney King police beating in California and the siege of a religious compound in Waco, Texas. Unfortunately, rumors of continuing intelligence and counterintelligence activities abound. A supposed program called *Frühmenschen* (primitive man) was the most outlandish. According to a former bureau informant who submitted an affidavit in a bribery case against a black county commissioner in Atlanta, this nationwide sting targeted elected and appointed black officials. It is perhaps more unfortunate that the FBI's history, on what it once called "Racial Matters," is such that virtually any charge, whether ill-founded or not, can find a loud and large constituency.

BIBLIOGRAPHY

Garrow, David J. *The FBI and Martin Luther King, Jr.: From "SOLO" to Memphis.* 1981.
Hill, Robert A., ed. *The FBI's RACON: Racial Conditions in the United States during World War II.* 1995.
O'Reilly, Kenneth. *"Racial Matters:" The FBI's Secret File on Black America, 1960–1972.* 1989.
O'Reilly, Kenneth. *Black Americans: The FBI Files.* 1994.

Kenneth O'Reilly

Federal Election Bill of 1890

The Federal Election Bill of 1890 resulted from two simultaneous developments in the post-Reconstruction era: black disfranchisement in the Democratic-controlled South and widespread balloting frauds nationwide. Both developments stemmed in part from the ineffectiveness of the federal enforcement acts (known as "force acts"), which the Republican Congress had implemented in the early 1870s primarily to protect Southern blacks' voting rights constitutionalized by the FIFTEENTH AMENDMENT in 1870. The Democratic recapture of the House in 1875 and the consequent stalemate in the national government between the two parties throughout most of the 1880s made it impossible for the Republicans either to enforce or to remove these "force acts." In 1888, when the Republicans won both houses of the Congress and the presidency, the party saw its opportunity to renew efforts to enforce the Fifteenth Amendment.

Generally known as the "Lodge Bill," the Federal Election Bill was first introduced into the House in July 1889 by Henry Cabot Lodge of Massachusetts. The original intent of the Lodge Bill was twofold: to stop the Southern Democratic suppression of the black votes, which consisted of the bulk of Republican supporters in the South, and to eliminate the election frauds that were rampant throughout the nation's major cities and that were normally associated with the Democratic bosses. The remedy provided by the Lodge Bill was the establishment of a powerful and comprehensive federal mechanism of election supervision. The bill, among other things, ordered the installation for each judicial circuit of a chief federal election supervisor empowered to challenge any fraudulent practice in federal elections. In addition, the bill proposed to establish a board of canvassers to examine the returns and to arbitrate controversial returns. Citing the recent Supreme Court decisions in *Ex parte Siebold* (1880) and *Ex parte Yarbrough* (1884) cases, Lodge stated that, in part, the bill meant to restore suffrage to blacks, who "deserved some better reward" for the part they had played in the Civil War.

On July 2, 1889, the House passed the Lodge Bill 155–149, with no Democrat voting for it; but the Senate, in which the Republicans had a majority of 14 over the 37 Democrats, made the bill secondary to a protariff bill, arguing that the latter was vital to attract Northern voters in the upcoming elections of 1890. At the insistence and urging of George F. Hoar of Massachusetts, who was in charge of the bill, the Senate began, on December 2, 1890, to debate a modified version of the original Lodge Bill. The Democrats strongly opposed the bill, charging that the Republicans were interfering with STATES' RIGHTS and creating federal patronage. The Democrats were joined by the Republican senators from the Western states, who wanted to get rid of the election bill in exchange for Southern support of a bill amending the Sherman Silver Purchase Act. If the silver bill became law, the Western mining states would benefit from increased governmental purchase of silver. Unable to pass the election bill, the Senate voted 34–29 on January 5, 1890, to put it aside, making way for the silver bill, which was passed by the Senate but eventually defeated in the House. When Hoar brought up the elec-

tion bill for another discussion shortly after the Senate finished with the silver bill, the Senate voted 35–34 to terminate any further discussion of it. Six Republicans, all from the Western states, joined 29 Democrats in this final vote. The bill was never again brought up for discussion. The defeat of the election bill symbolized the inability of the REPUBLICAN PARTY to revive the Radical Reconstruction, which finally ended in 1894, when a Democratic Congress repealed most of the provisions of the Republican-made enforcement acts.

BIBLIOGRAPHY

Garraty, John. *Henry Cabot Lodge: A Biography.* 1953.

Hirshson, Stanley P. *Farewell to the Bloody Shirt: Northern Republicans and the Southern Negro, 1877–1893.* 1962.

Socolofsky, Homer E., and Allen B. Spetter. *The Presidency of Benjamin Harrison.* 1987.

Wang, Xi. *The Trial of Democracy: Black Suffrage and Northern Republicans, 1860–1910.* 1997.

Welch, Richard E., Jr. *George Frisbie Hoar and the Half-Breed Republicans.* 1971.

Welch, Richard E., Jr. "The Federal Election Bill of 1890: Postscripts and Prelude." *Journal of American History* 52 (December 1965): 511–526.

Wellborn, Fred. "The Influence of the Silver-Republican Senators, 1889–1891," *Mississippi Valley Historical Review* 14 (1927–1928): 462–480.

Xi Wang

Fellowship of Reconciliation (FOR)

In the words of Coretta Scott King, "FOR has been in the forefront of the nonviolent struggle for peace with justice. What is important about FOR is what it stands for. And that is a courageous dedication to the the liberation of humanity to the triple evils of poverty, racism and violence."

Founded in the United States in 1915, as part of the international religious antiwar movement, the Fellowship of Reconciliation (FOR) became active in defending the rights of conscientious objectors during WORLD WAR I and helped organize the National Civil Liberties Bureau, a precursor of the AMERICAN CIVIL LIBERTIES UNION (ACLU). A center for Christian socialists and pacifists, FOR helped organize the National Conference of Christians and Jews and actively opposed the U.S. Marine intervention in Nicaragua in the 1920s, sending a peace delegation to the rebel leader, Augusto Sandino.

In the 1930s it aligned itself with labor and launched its "Ambassadors for Peace" program to resist militarization and war. FOR also attracted Reverend A. J. Muste, a Christian socialist who was to become its most important leader. During WORLD WAR II, it actively opposed the internment of Japanese

Americans and the persecution of Jews and European anti-Fascists. (See JAPANESE AMERICAN INTERNMENT CASES; JAPANESE AMERICAN REDRESS AND REPARATIONS MOVEMENT.)

In the postwar era FOR under Muste's leadership campaigned against both racial segregation and conscription. FOR staff members played an important support role in the MONTGOMERY BUS BOYCOTT and FOR helped to popularize Martin Luther KING, JR.'s philosophy of nonviolence.

From the 1960s on FOR has played a significant role in a variety of peace and social justice campaigns, building homeless shelters in the early 1960s when the government was advocating nuclear fallout shelters, working with Vietnamese Buddhist pacifists in seeking peace in Vietnam, playing an important role in initiating the Nuclear Freeze campaign of the 1980s, and sending over a million dollars in medical supplies to the victims of the Gulf War. (See VIETNAM WAR.)

A target of both governmental and vigilante attacks since the 1920s, FOR has outlived most of its detractors, campaigning today against handgun-related violence in the United States and, through its Bosnia Student Project, helping student victims of the fighting from all sides to safety. As such, it and FOR groups abroad continue to show both the vitality and the necessity of social activism in the struggles for peace, civil rights, and social justice.

BIBLIOGRAPHY
Robinson, Jo Ann Ooiman. *Abraham Went Out: A Biography of A. J. Muste.* 1981.

Records of the FOR, the most valuable source for scholars, are at Swarthmore College.

Norman Markowitz

Feminism

Feminism is the theory that women should have economic, political, and social rights equal to those of men. The movement for women's rights has had a long association with the civil rights movement. As a political ideology and movement, feminism emerged with the revolutions in the United States (1777–1783) and in France (1789–1799). The first major feminist theorist was Mary Wollstonecraft, who, inspired by the ideals of "the rights of man," wrote *A Vindication of the Rights of Women* in 1792.

The feminist movement in the United States largely came out of the abolitionist movement. Angelina Grimké, Sarah Grimké, Lucretia Mott, Susan B. ANTHONY, Elizabeth Cady STANTON, and Lucy STONE, early pioneers of the women's rights movement, began their political activity as anti-slavery activists, or abolitionists. In 1848, almost two hundred people met in Seneca Falls, New York, at the first feminist or women's rights conference. Elizabeth Cady Stanton wrote "The Declaration of Sentiments," modeled on the Declaration of Independence, which outlined women's grievances and listed women's rights demands. The most contentious issue, supported by abolitionist and feminist Frederick DOUGLASS, was the demand for women's suffrage. From the 1830s through the end of the Civil War, feminists and abolitionists worked side by side. This alliance was broken in the wake of RECONSTRUCTION.

From the 1870s through the 1950s, the civil rights and women's movements were not very visible and disconnected. A second wave of activism, the reemergence of feminism, came in the late 1960s; and like their abolitionist forebears, a large majority of the feminist pioneers, in particular, came from the civil rights movement. Betty FRIEDAN's book *The Feminine Mystique* was published in 1963. Although this book spoke to concerns and needs of white, middle-class urban and suburban women, Friedan's roots were in the radical and civil rights movements of the 1940s and 1950s. In 1966, along with Pauli MURRAY, an African-American Episcopalian minister and lawyer, and Dorothy Haener from the United Automobile Workers, Friedan founded the NATIONAL ORGANIZATION FOR WOMEN (NOW). The organization was conceived in the context of the civil rights movement, and much of the civil rights legislation of the period, such as the CIVIL RIGHTS ACT OF 1964, encompassed women. NOW is the largest feminist organization in the United States.

Sara Evans wrote in *Personal Politics: The Roots of Women's Liberation in the Civil Rights Movement and the New Left* (1980) that the younger women who organized the early radical women's liberation groups came out of the civil rights movement and began the process of redefining feminism with a radical critique of sexual or gender politics. Later years have seen many critiques and redefinitions of feminism, in particular bringing in an analysis of CLASS, RACE, and sexuality. Alice Walker, a Pulitzer Prize–winning author, developed the concept of "womanist," which referred to the independence and strength of African-American women without embracing what Walker believed to be the white-middle-class concept of feminism. The second-wave feminist movement was not all-white and not all-middle-class. Organizations such as the Third World Women's Alliance, the National Black Feminist Organization, Women of la Raza, and the Union Women's Alliance to Gain Equality attest to feminist diversity. Other manifestations of feminism include liberal feminism, radical feminism, cultural feminism, black feminism, lesbian feminism, socialist feminism, and revolutionary feminism. Some journalists speak of power feminism, some Republicans refer to conservative feminism, and one even finds postfeminism and anti-feminism. Rush Limbaugh, a right-wing radio broadcaster, derided feminists as "feminazis"—a term that may indicate how threatening strong women appear to their detractors.

Since the 1960s the feminist movement has been one of the largest and most sustained of all the social protest movements. Many women do not define themselves as feminists, yet every poll indicates overwhelming support for the feminist agenda: equal pay for comparable work, equal access into all jobs and professions, expansion of child care, reproductive rights, and an end to violence against women. The women's movement has brought about vast social, economic, political, and sexual progress for women, ranging from the legalization of abortion to the entrance of large numbers of women into politics, business, the labor movement, the professions, and SPORTS. There is greater cultural visibility of women acting in their own right, and women have made a lasting impact on issues of EDUCATION, RELIGION, and sexuality. The feminist movement has profoundly changed the way that many women and men view themselves. The women's movement's major defeat was its inability to pass the EQUAL RIGHTS AMENDMENT. Yet in spite of progress there is a continuing ambivalence about feminism. Members of the media regularly ask, "Is there a future for feminism?" or "Is feminism dead?"

Internationally, feminism reached a major milestone at the 1996 United Nations–sponsored Women's Conference in Beijing, China, where for the first time a UN conference declared women's rights to be fundamental human rights.

BIBLIOGRAPHY

Evans, Sara. *Personal Politics: The Roots of Women's Liberation in the Civil Rights Movement and the New Left.* 1980.

Flexner, Eleanor. *A Century of Struggle.* 1980.

Friedan, Betty. *The Feminine Mystique.* 1963.

Millett, Kate. *Sexual Politics.* 1970.

O'Neill, William L. *Feminism in America: A History.* 1989.

Rowbotham, Sheila. *Threads Through Time.* 1999.

Barbara Winslow

Fierro de Bright, Josefina

(1920–1998), political activist.

Josefina Fierro de Bright emerged during the 1930s as an influential grassroots political leader and executive secretary of El Congreso del Pueblo de Habla Española (CONGRESS OF SPANISH-SPEAKING PEOPLE), a Mexican-American working-class political movement based in Los Angeles, California. Josefina Fierro was born in 1920 in Mexicali, Mexico, to parents who were active in the Mexican Revolution. During childhood, she moved with her mother to Los Angeles, and later settled in Madera, California. In about 1938, Fierro enrolled at the University of California, Los Angeles, where she planned to study medicine. Soon afterward, she met and married John Bright, a radical Hollywood screenwriter. With Bright, Fierro built her life upon the radical foundation her revolutionary parents had laid.

In 1938 Fierro de Bright joined El Congreso and quickly became its executive secretary. The leftist, working-class organization—founded in Los Angeles in 1938 by labor organizer Luisa Moreno—pursued a broad agenda of social reform. It defended the rights and dignity of both Mexican Americans and Mexican nationals, and lobbied for government initiatives to provide HOUSING, EMPLOYMENT, EDUCATION, relief, and medical care. In Los Angeles, during World War II, Fierro de Bright helped to organize the Sleepy Lagoon Defense Committee. (Several Mexican-American youths were convicted of a murder committed in an area of L.A. known as Sleepy Lagoon. The trial violated the defendants' civil rights and the Defense Committee eventually succeeded in getting the convictions overturned on appeal.) Fierro de Bright helped call for U.S. federal intervention to halt the 1943 ZOOT SUIT RIOTS in the city.

Following World War II, Fierro de Bright organized Henry WALLACE's 1948 presidential campaign in California. During the anti-communist hysteria of the late 1940s, Fierro de Bright feared that her past radicalism and noncitizen immigration status would make her a target for harassment and investigation. Labeled a "subversive alien" by the federal government, she returned permanently to Mexico rather than testify before the HOUSE UN-AMERICAN ACTIVITIES COMMITTEE. She died in Mexico in 1998.

BIBLIOGRAPHY

Corona, Bert, and Martio T. García. *Memories of Chicano History: The Life and Narrative of Bert Corona.* 1994.

García, Mario T. *Mexican Americans: Leadership, Ideology, and Identity, 1930–1960.* 1989.

Douglas W. Dodd

Fifteenth Amendment

The final Reconstruction Amendment to the United States Constitution, ratified on March 30, 1870, declared, "The right of citizens of the United States to vote shall not be denied or abridged by the United States or by any State on account of race, color, or

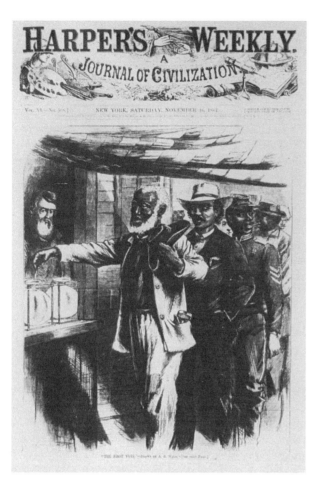

Freed African Americans stand in line to cast their votes. Cover illustration headed "The First Vote" in Harper's Weekly, *November 1867 issue.* (National Archives and Records Administration)

previous condition of servitude." By the end of the nineteenth century, the limitations of protections afforded by this amendment were apparent. However, by the centennial of its adoption, the Fifteenth Amendment was invigorated by congressional action and SUPREME COURT interpretation. Thus strengthened, the amendment stands as a bulwark of political rights for all Americans.

Before the Civil War there was not widespread political support for the enfranchisement of African Americans, even in northern states. Many state constitutions explicitly excluded blacks from voting. In 1864, for example, Nevada was admitted as the thirty-sixth state, although its constitution confined the vote to white male citizens.

In January 1866, as members of Congress framed the FOURTEENTH AMENDMENT, Representative James G. Blaine of Maine proposed that states disenfranchising persons "on account of race or color" be punished by a corresponding reduction in congressional rep-

resentation. The ensuing debate demonstrated serious divisions over the advisability of black suffrage, and the final version spoke only of the denial of the vote to "male inhabitants," a change that alienated many women's suffrage activists.

Black suffrage supporters were heartened when, on January 8, 1867, Congress overrode President Andrew Johnson's veto of a statute providing for enfranchisement in the District of Columbia. Soon thereafter, congressional Republicans claimed three more legislative victories: requiring black suffrage in federal territories; conditioning Nebraska's admission as a state on black enfranchisement (again over Johnson's veto); and mandating, under the First Reconstruction Act of March 2, 1867, that southern states seeking readmission to the Union must grant the vote to African Americans.

Meanwhile, several northern states rejected black suffrage measures. Only Minnesota and Iowa bucked the national trend. The results of the 1868 presidential and congressional elections set the stage for a Republican push for what became the Fifteenth Amendment. The party in power was concerned about Ulysses S. Grant's slim majority in the popular vote and about lost House seats in the incoming Forty-first Congress. A constitutional amendment would serve two important purposes: (1) providing new black voters to help maintain Republican control in northern and border states, and (2) ensuring that voting requirements imposed on southern states could not be repealed by a later Congress. Radical and moderate Republican newspapers endorsed this blatantly partisan strategy that simultaneously furthered the goal of equal justice.

Shepherded by Representative George S. Boutwell (Republican of Massachusetts), the first attempt during the lame-duck session emerged from the House Judiciary Committee on January 11, 1869. The proposal would have outlawed the government's denial of the right to vote "by reason of race, color, or previous condition of slavery of any citizen or class of citizens of the United States." On January 30, the House defeated two competing proposals and passed Boutwell's joint resolution by the requisite two-thirds majority (150 to 42).

In the Senate, meanwhile, William M. Stewart's (Republican from Nevada) proposal of January 28, 1869, which additionally protected the right to "hold office," garnered the most attention. The Stewart version's chief rivals were both more radical. One (Jacob Howard's) would have affirmatively granted the right to vote and hold office to American citizens of "African descent." The second (Henry Wilson's) even outlawed voting restrictions based on "nativity, property, education, or religious belief." What followed was a series of often-inconsistent compromises, alliances, and realliances among radical Republicans, who opposed qualifications restricting black voting and office-holding; moderate Republicans, whose overriding concern was for additional black voters; and Democrats, who switched allegiances in order to sabotage voting rights initiatives.

Proposals moved from chamber to chamber, and on February 24, 1869, a conference committee convened to reconcile the Senate offering (which protected voting and office-holding) and the House version (which added bans on most suffrage tests). The amendment that emerged, basically Stewart's original language without the reference to office-holding, was stripped of the more radical provisions. The next day the House approved; the Senate followed on February 26.

Six days later, in his first inaugural address, President Grant endorsed the Fifteenth Amendment. Over the succeeding twelve months, debate was predictably partisan. Southern passage was virtually assured by Republican control of state legislatures and by a congressional act, in April 1869, that required Mississippi, Texas, and Virginia to ratify the amendment as a condition to readmission to the Union. The trouble spot was the Midwest. In Indiana, for example, dozens of Democratic legislators resigned their offices in an effort to thwart ratification. Parliamentary maneuvering by the Republican Speaker of the House neutralized the Democratic strategy, however, and the Hoosier State was counted among the three-fourths needed for adoption.

Soon after ratification, Congress provided legislative protection for black voters through three "Enforcement Acts" (1870). By the time military Reconstruction ended, however, prosecution rates had declined dramatically, and African-American suffrage was under attack by unfriendly legislatures in the Southern and border states. The United States Supreme Court was largely unsympathetic to the plight of blacks who attempted to exercise their Fifteenth Amendment rights. In *United States v. Reese* (1876) and *United States v. Cruikshank* (1876), Congress's powers effectively to enforce the Fifteenth Amendment in state elections were severely restricted. During the late nineteenth and early twentieth centuries, poll taxes, grandfather clauses, and literacy and property qualifications withstood court challenges.

In SMITH V. ALLWRIGHT (1944), the Supreme Court breathed new life into the Fifteenth Amendment, holding that white primaries were illegal state actions in violation of constitutionally protected voting rights. Then, with the enactment of the VOTING RIGHTS ACT (CIVIL RIGHTS ACT OF 1965), Congress at last fulfilled the promise made nearly a century before to persons of color who yearned to exercise their most fundamental political right and duty.

BIBLIOGRAPHY

Braxton, A. Caperton. *The Fifteenth Amendment: An Account of Its Enactment.* 1934.

Elliott, Ward E. Y. *The Rise of Guardian Democracy: The Supreme Court's Role in Voting Rights Disputes, 1845–1969.* 1975.

Gillette, William. *The Right to Vote: Politics and the Passage of the Fifteenth Amendment.* 1965.

Gillette, William. *Retreat from Reconstruction: 1869–1879.* 1979.

Kousser, J. Morgan. *The Shaping of Southern Politics: Suffrage Restriction and the Establishment of the One-party South, 1880–1910.* 1974.

Michael Allan Wolf
Daniel A. Wolf

Fifth Circuit, United States Court of Appeals for the

The Fifth Circuit Court of Appeals stood in the eye of the civil rights storm of the 1960s, adjudicating cases originating in seventeen federal district courts that served six states of the Deep South—Georgia, Florida, Alabama, Mississippi, Louisiana, and Texas—and the Canal Zone. One of nine intermediate appeals courts established by the 1891 Judiciary Act, the Court first convened on June 16 that same year at the Customs House in New Orleans. The Supreme Court Justice who was allotted to the Circuit, Lucius Quintus Cincinnatus Lamar, presided, flanked by the solo Fifth Circuit Judge appointed under the 1869 Judiciary Act, Don Albert Pardee, of Louisiana, and veteran District Judge Robert Andrew Hill of Mississippi. As authorized by the 1891 act, President Benjamin Harrison appointed a second circuit judge in 1892. Thereafter the Court's membership expanded to three (1899), four (1930), five (1938), six (1942), seven (1954), nine (1961), and fifteen (1968) as its caseload gradually increased (docketed: 131 [1900], 318 [1930], 408 [1950], 577 [1960]) before exploding to 874 in 1963 and 1,033 in 1964.

The caseload crisis, generated in part by civil rights litigation, was an administrative crisis transformed into a political one when, in 1964, the Judicial Conference of the United States proposed splitting the circuit, the boundaries of which had been fixed since 1866. Realignment was perceived as changing substantive civil rights law by redistributing judges of a Court riven by ideological conflict. On one side stood "The Four," composed of leader Elbert P. TUTTLE, energetic John R. BROWN, culturally attuned Richard T. RIVES, and scholarly John Minor WISDOM. At some personal cost, they challenged prevailing regional racial practices and disturbed district judge decisions by enforcing and harmonizing national law on suffrage and civil rights as laid down by the Earl WARREN—led Supreme Court and Congress. Their peer antagonist was Mississippi's Old South patrician Benjamin Franklin Cameron. His sensational 1961 charge—that the Court's panels were "stacked" in civil rights cases to produce social change outcomes that were anathema to community norms and corrosive of state power—illuminated the stakes involved in realignment. The ebbing of passions and changing Court membership, including the first black member, Jimmy CARTER-appointee Joseph W. Hatchett, permitted circuit reorganization in 1980. Congress then divided the twenty-six-judge old Fifth, which in 1981 reported 4,907 case filings. Louisiana, Mississippi, Texas and, to 1982, the Canal Zone constituted the new Fifth, headquartered at New Orleans with ten districts and fourteen circuit judges increased to sixteen in 1984 and seventeen in 1990—to process 8,086 cases docketed in 1998. Georgia, Florida, and Alabama constituted the new Eleventh Circuit, headquartered at Atlanta with nine districts and twelve judges.

Landmark civil rights cases emerged from the Fifth Circuit from its inception. Decades before establishment of the court of appeals, the Circuit Court for Louisiana's Eastern District in the *Slaughterhouse Cases* (1870) expansively interpreted the FOURTEENTH AMENDMENT's "privilege or immunities" clause to accord national protection to a broad spectrum of fundamental rights—an interpretation later roundly rejected by the Supreme Court. The impact of the seminal 1873 decision influenced a conservative Fifth Circuit appeals court from the 1930s through the 1950s. The Fifth suffered Supreme Court reversals when it hesitated to find the requisite Fourteenth Amendment "state action" in Texas Democratic "white" primary cases and, over an influential dissent by Judge Brown, deferred to state power in the Tuskegee racial gerrymandering case. As early as 1944, however, the Court broadly construed a RECONSTRUCTION-era federal criminal statute's "color of [state] law" stipulation to reach a Georgia sheriff who had unlawfully killed a black youth in his custody, and it provided relief for a death-sentenced black defendant who had unwittingly waived objections to a jury from which blacks were systematically excluded.

The Court of the 1960s responded favorably to VOTING RIGHTS claims, fashioning creative procedures to expedite such cases and ordering drastic remedies that were erosive of traditional state power. Meanwhile, the Supreme Court's historic 1954–1955 *Brown* decisions generated high-conflict school integration cases (see BROWN V. BOARD OF EDUCATION). Spawned

too were collateral cases challenging racially and, in a 1981 case contesting Mississippi University for Women's admission policy, sexually segregated higher education as well as other racially segregated public facilities, particularly municipal golf courses and swimming pools. The Court initially interpreted *Brown*, as did its counterparts in the Fourth and Eighth circuits, to forbid state segregation, not to require integration. Abandonment of that less interpretation in *Singleton v. Jackson Municipal Separate School District* (1965) was amplified the next year by the John Minor Wisdom pioneering opinion in *United States v. Jefferson County Board of Education*. Holding that school boards had a duty to integrate, he ordered prompt conversion of existing dual systems to unitary nonracial systems, a position adopted by the Supreme Court in 1968–1969 and applied by it in 1992 to reverse a determination by the reconstituted Fifth that Mississippi had disestablished its formerly segregated higher education system. In the mid-1990s the Court eased the burden of proof needed to validate the existence of a "unitary" educational system, while it waffled on majority–minority districts under the VOTING RIGHTS ACT OF 1965 as amended in 1982.

James MEREDITH's denial of admission to the University of Mississippi in 1961 sparked a major constitutional crisis. Wisdom's admission order in *Meredith v. Fair* (1962) survived repeated Cameron-instigated "stays," only to confront popular insurrectionary manifestations and outright defiance from Governor Ross Barnett and his lieutenant governor. Having held both officials in contempt for their states' rights interposition, the Court delayed hearings pending suppression by the federalized National Guard of related riots. Divided 4–4 over demands for a jury trial, the Court certified the case to the Supreme Court, which narrowly denied a jury trial right. "Changed circumstances" subsequently enabled the Fifth to avoid criminal contempt proceedings altogether.

AFFIRMATIVE ACTION programs in employment and later in higher education became a quintessential civil rights focus. Such cases arising in the 1970s typically pitted the imperative of EQUAL OPPORTUNITY against that of seniority based on prior racially discriminatory practices. Kaiser Aluminum's voluntary plan, founded on past societal racial discrimination, met rebuff in the Fifth in 1977 but received subsequent Supreme Court approval. So, too, racially preferential admissions programs in higher education received a cool reception in the new Fifth when it considered that adopted by the University of Texas Law School. Applying the strict scrutiny used in evaluating racial classifications under a "color-blind" fourteenth Amendment's equal protection clause and finding no narrowly tailored compelling state interest, the Court held such racial preferences unconstitutional in HOPWOOD V. STATE OF TEXAS (1996).

Since the 1930s, the old and new Fifth Circuit has served as a vital forum for aggrieved litigants alleging deprivations of their civil rights. Its law-molding role and the wielding of its equity powers in the 1960s have reshaped regional social relations as it reflected and influenced national law. By the 1990s, however, different circuit configurations, different judges, and different issues have suggested different outcomes in civil rights cases.

BIBLIOGRAPHY

Barrow, Deborah J. *A Court Divided: The Fifth Circuit Court of Appeals and the Politics of Judicial Reform.* 1988.

Bass, Jack. *Unlikely Heroes.* 1981.

Couch, Harvey C. *A History of the Fifth Circuit: 1891–1981.* 1984.

Hamilton, Charles V. *The Bench and the Ballot: Southern Federal Judges and Black Voters.* 1973.

Harrington, James C. "Civil Rights." *Texas Tech Law Review* 26–29 (1995–1999): 447–515, 615–653, 367–448, 433–526.

Howard, J. Woodford, Jr. *Courts of Appeals in the Federal Judicial System: A Study of the Second, Fifth, and District of Columbia Circuits.* 1981.

Peltason, Jack W. *Fifty-Eight Lonely Men: Southern Federal Judges and School Desegregation.* 1961.

Read, Frank T., and Lucy S. McGough. *Let Them Be Judged: The Integration of the Deep South.* 1978.

Peter G. Fish

Filipino Labor Union

The formation of the Filipino Labor Union (FLU) in 1933 represented the emergence of organized labor militancy among mainland Filipino farm workers. These workers unionized with the expectation that labor activism would improve their wages and working conditions and offer protection from violence and discrimination. Filipino labor contractors provided leadership, but rank-and-file workers influenced the selection of strike committees and union officers.

In August 1933, the union led seven hundred lettuce pickers in California's Salinas Valley on a one-day strike to protest low wages. The walkout failed after growers brought in Mexican, South Asian, and Japanese replacement workers. Salinas business interests then tried to undermine unionization by forming the Filipino Labor Supply Association, an organization composed of rival labor contractors opposed to the FLU.

Together with the Vegetable Packers Association (VPA), the FLU went on strike again the following year. Its strike goals included its recognition as a legit-imate union and the doubling of hourly wages to forty cents. In addition to replacing striking workers with FLSA laborers and Mexican immigrants, growers responded by shooting two Filipino strikers and using the police to harass many others. When the violent atmosphere led to mediation, the VPA accepted arbitration despite its prior agreement not to bargain without the FLU.

Although it received criticism in the press and lacked the full support of the Filipino community, the FLU remained on strike. Vigilantes and law enforcement officers continued a campaign of violence and coercion. After vigilantes burned down a camp housing hundreds of workers, the union decided to end the strike. In a negotiated settlement, the FLU secured union recognition and the forty-cent hourly wage. Including another strike in 1936, FLU activities demonstrated the potential of ethnic labor unionism and persuaded the American Federation of Labor to charter a combined Mexican–Filipino agricultural union.

BIBLIOGRAPHY

Chan, Sucheng. *Asian Americans: An Interpretive History.* 1991.

DeWitt, Howard A. "The Filipino Labor Union: The Salinas Lettuce Strike of 1934." *Amerasia Journal* 5 (1978): 1–22.

Takaki, Ronald. *Strangers from a Different Shore: A History of Asian Americans.* 1989.

S. H. Tang

Film

Cinema in the twentieth century provides an invaluable key to understanding the changing climate of race relations in America. As in the political and social arenas, African Americans have had to struggle for equality on screen and off. Their battle with Hollywood has been a struggle against shallow, exaggerated, or underdeveloped characterizations.

At the turn of the twentieth century, common motifs of "movies" were black or white minstrels, already widely popular in vaudeville. Over the next two decades, black characters began to fall into various crude categories: popeyed, chicken-stealing "coons"; doomed mixed-race "mulattoes"; gentle, loyal "toms" or "sambos"; the obese, devoted but tyrannical "mammy"; and the menacing black male "buck."

D. W. Griffith united all these stereotypes in his epic *Birth of a Nation* (1915), in which RECONSTRUCTION was portrayed as a dark age overrun by robbing and raping freed slaves. The film was a huge box office success and won critical acclaim although its racial hatred did not go unnoticed. The embryonic NATIONAL

ASSOCIATION FOR THE ADVANCEMENT OF COLORED PEOPLE (NAACP) tried to have it banned—and failed.

From 1913, a handful of African Americans, including Oscar Micheaux and the actor Noble Johnson, established independent production companies, but they could not compete with the large budgets of Hollywood pictures. Besides, the impact of the "talkies" during the late 1920s encouraged the major studios to use black talent in the new "musicals" instead of white actors in blackface, which had been established practice since the days of vaudeville. By 1929 the film industry was ready to test the marketability of "Negro movies" with the first all black productions, *Hearts in Dixie* and *Hallelujah.*

During the 1930s, Hollywood found roles for black actors as numerous jittery black manservants and jolly maids providing comedy for Depression-era audiences. Although most of the 1930s movies kept African Americans clowning in the background, a few productions began to probe issues of RACE and RACISM. The most significant of these was *Imitation of Life* (1934), which directly compared and contrasted the lives of two women—one white, one black—but treated each woman's story with sympathy and dignity. The film signified an increasingly liberal consciousness in America. It was also a box office hit, and its star, Louise Beavers, briefly became the most successful black actress in Hollywood. Another "progressive" picture, Mervyn LeRoy's much underrated *They Won't Forget* (1937) was ruthless in its portrayal of the victimization of an innocent black janitor by a white district attorney ambitious for political power.

One of the first black "principals," Paul ROBESON, with his powerful voice and charismatic presence, was cast as an exotic savage, albeit a dignified one, in films like *The Emperor Jones* (1933) and the British production *Sanders of the River* (1935). Deeply unhappy with the one-dimensional, conforming images of blacks on screen, Robeson sought better parts in Europe but failed to find them. In 1936, he took on the role of Joe in *Showboat*—ironically, a character who became one of the best-known symbols of the oppressed but enduring black man in cinematic history.

Roles were limiting and often patronizing, but the skill with which many actors—such as Stepin Fetchit, Butterfly McQueen, Louise Beavers, Bill Robinson, and Paul Robeson—transcended these stereotypes was impressive and moving. In the controversial *Gone with the Wind* (1939), Hattie McDaniel imbued the role of Mammy with such dignity and strength that she became the first African American to be nominated for—and win—an Oscar.

Louis Armstrong and Ella Fitzgerald were household names in the 1940s, and increasingly black screen characters emerged as performers. Entertainers like Lena Horne, Ethel Waters, and Hazel Scott became musical heroines, providing diverting interludes in mainstream pictures.

At the same time, Hollywood felt that its patriotic duty was to portray a nation united during wartime, not one severed by race divisions. War movies inevitably featured soldiers from all ethnic backgrounds, including blacks, and the taboo of keeping black actors from playing significant dramatic roles was broken. Postwar films were able to deal more freely with issues, and the black characters took on a new self-sacrificing dignity in films like *Home of the Brave* (1949) and *Intruder in the Dust* (1949). *Pinky* (1949) even dealt with interracial romance although its mulatto heroine was played by a white actress.

The 1950s were the first years to give rise to real black "stars." Ethel Waters was the first African-American actress to carry a major studio production with *The Member of the Wedding* and Dorothy Dandridge graced the cover of *Life* magazine after a string of significant roles in pictures such as *Island in the Sun* (1957), *Porgy and Bess* (1959), and *Carmen Jones* (1954), for which she received an Academy Award nomination. But with the paucity of decent parts, Dandridge went to Europe, as Paul Robeson had done, only to encounter similar discrimination abroad.

Meanwhile, INTEGRATION became the 1950s buzzword, and Sidney Poitier was its hero. Hollywood recognized his universal appeal, and in such movies as *No Way Out* (1950) and *The Defiant Ones* (1958), Poitier's upstanding, educated, and intelligent characters came to epitomize the "colorless black." By 1967, although wildly out of step with a more sophisticated, contemporary society, Hollywood even cast this "acceptable" black man as worthy of being brought home by Katharine Houghton to meet the family in *Guess Who's Coming to Dinner.*

Over the following turbulent decade, rioting and violent protests forced a radical change in Hollywood. Early 1960s movies such as *A Raisin in the Sun* (1961) and *Lilies of the Field* (1963) were motivated by integrationist-fueled optimism, but by the end of the decade, the disparity between Hollywood's self-martyring Tom heroes and the age of black pride and MALCOLM X was too extreme for the studios to ignore. The gentle protagonists Poitier and Harry Belafonte were replaced with America's first BLACK POWER sexual icon, Jim Brown, in movies like *Rio Conchos* (1964) and *The Dirty Dozen* (1967).

By the 1970s black writers and directors such as Melvin Van Peebles and Ossie Davis were not only writing about the black community but also aiming to please a black audience. *Sweet Sweetback's Baadasssss Song* (1971), *Shaft* (1971), and *Superfly* (1972) became so successful that the studios copied the formula in a number of mediocre "blaxploitation" pictures. Hollywood was waking up to the realization that black audiences constituted a lucrative untapped market.

At the same time a young black comedian was fast becoming a superstar, with films like *Silver Streak* (1976) and *Which Way Is Up?* (1977). Richard Pryor as the crazy, wisecracking black brother was safely entrenched as Gene Wilder's sidekick, and the Wilder–Pryor partnership was to prove the rebirth of the "buddy" films of the 1950s in which race was just ignored.

The decade ended with a flop. *The Wiz* (1978) boasted a glittering cast, including Richard Pryor, Diana Ross, and Michael Jackson. It received poor reviews and convinced Hollywood once more that all-black movies held no box office appeal.

By the 1980s, formulaic comedies like *Beverly Hills Cop* (1984) and *Jumping Jack Flash* (1987), and their "coon"-gestured stars, Eddie Murphy and Whoopi Goldberg, were the key ingredients in Hollywood's steady output of mainstream hits. The strong ethnic identity of black performers of the 1970s was replaced by a series of culturally bereft oddballs.

In these early years of the decade, black actors were kept mainly in supporting roles: Danny Glover to Mel Gibson in the *Lethal Weapon* trilogy; Murphy to both Nick Nolte in *48 Hours* (1982) and Dan Akroyd in *Changing Places*. Apart from Spielberg's *The Color Purple* in 1985, black women were limited mostly to a variety of "exotic" and mulatto roles.

Then, in 1986, Spike Lee's shoestring-budget, independent *She's Gotta Have It* became an overnight hit. It was a film about black life with a true black aesthetic, but it also appealed to mass white audiences and, once again, studio executives began to take notice.

The Rodney King riots in 1992 made the black ghetto voice painfully significant. John Singleton captured the anger of south central Los Angeles in his directorial debut, *Boyz N the Hood* (1991), and was rewarded with the first Academy Award nomination for a black director. In the same year, Melvin's son, Mario Van Peebles's *New Jack City* fused the bleak New York ghetto with the power of Gangsta Rap in a galvanizing combination.

Meanwhile Spike Lee was receiving acclaim for his successful movie trio—*Do the Right Thing* (1989), *Mo' Better Blues* (1990), and *Jungle Fever* (1991). Warner Brothers was sufficiently impressed by Lee to take the gamble on financing his next movie, a dramatic film biography of black fundamentalist Malcolm X. Hollywood had never before invested such big money in a film dedicated to a polemical black figure in the belief that, despite its antiwhite politics, the movie would still hold appeal for a mixed-race audience.

Although Warner Brothers probably had more faith in the cult status of Lee than the box office draw of the film's subject matter, this partnership between black and white Hollywood signified a new opportunity for black filmmakers. Black pressure groups were concerned. They feared that studio interference might distort the politics. But the film was a success, and its star, Denzel Washington, received an Oscar nomination.

In the late 1990s, there was progress in subverting the stereotypes. Literally turning the tables on the white actors in blackface of the beginning of the century, the choice of Will Smith to play the white cowboy James West in *Wild Wild West* (1999) suggests that some taboos for black performers may have been broken permanently. Black women have also had a chance to play intelligent, sympathetic characters in movies like *Waiting to Exhale* (1995) and *Down in the Delta* (1998).

Yet two slave epics were commercial flops. Spielberg's "liberating" *Amistad* (1997) marginalized its black characters, and *Beloved* (1998) floundered in a confused storyline. The long-awaited *Star Wars: Episode I–The Phantom Menace* (1999) revealed how unable Hollywood is to detect its own subconscious negative imagery, personified by the misjudged and archaic "coon" character Jar Jar Binks.

Perhaps it is still difficult for major studio executives, who have grown up with a limited perception of black screen characters and who remain constantly scared of alienating the majority white audience, to shake off the legacy of a century of black pigeonholing. Attainment of equality at the movies now seems to lie in the hands of the increasingly popular black independent filmmakers. The onus on these actors, directors, writers, and producers now is to take the action beyond the pathological scenarios of 1990s ghettoland, to paint a true reflection of black individuals from all social strata, and to reflect the full range of African-American life.

Filmography

1915	*The Nigger*	1933	*International House*
1915	*Birth of a Nation*	1934	*Imitation of Life*
1916	*Birth of a Race*	1935	*The Little Colonel*
1919	*The Homesteader*	1936	*Showboat*
1922	*Sunshine Sammy* (from the "Our Gang" movies)	1937	*They Won't Forget*
		1939	*Gone with the Wind*
1923	*The House behind the Cedars*	1940	*Of Mice and Men*
		1942	*In This Our Life*
1927	*Uncle Tom's Cabin*	1943	*Cabin in the Sky*
1927	*The Jazz Singer*	1943	*Stormy Weather*
1929	*Hearts in Dixie*	1944	*Since You Went Away*
1929	*Hallelujah*	1945	*Rhapsody in Blue*
1931	*Arrowsmith*	1946	*Song of the South*
1932	*I Am a Fugitive from a Chain Gang*	1949	*Lost Boundaries*
		1949	*Home of the Brave*

1949	*Pinky*	1976	*Silver Streak*
1949	*Intruder in the Dust*	1977	*Which Way Is Up?*
1950	*No Way Out*	1978	*The Wiz*
1952	*Cry, the Beloved Country*	1982	*48 Hours*
1954	*Carmen Jones*	1987	*Lethal Weapon*
1955	*The Blackboard Jungle*	1983	*Trading Places*
1957	*Island in the Sun*	1984	*Beverly Hills Cop*
1957	*Edge of the City*	1984	*A Soldier's Story*
1958	*The Defiant Ones*	1985	*The Color Purple*
1959	*Porgy and Bess*	1986	*She's Gotta Have It*
1961	*A Raisin in the Sun*	1987	*Mississippi Burning*
1963	*The Cool World*	1989	*Glory*
1963	*Lilies of the Field*	1989	*Driving Miss Daisy*
1964	*Nothing but a Man*	1989	*Do the Right Thing*
1964	*One Potato, Two Potato*	1990	*Daughters of the Dust*
1964	*Black like Me*	1990	*House Party*
1964	*Rio Conchos*	1990	*Mo' Better Blues*
1967	*The Dirty Dozen*	1990	*The Long Walk Home*
1967	*Guess Who's Coming*	1991	*Jungle Fever*
	to Dinner	1991	*Boyz N the Hood*
1967	*Hurry Sundown*	1991	*New Jack City*
1969	*Slaves*	1992	*Malcolm X*
1969	*The Learning Tree*	1993	*Made in America*
1969	*Putney Swope*	1994	*The Shawshank*
1970	*They Call Me*		*Redemption*
	MISTER Tibbs	1995	*Waiting to Exhale*
1970	*Cotton Comes to Harlem*	1996	*Once Upon a Time . . .*
1971	*Sweet Sweetback's*		*When We Were Colored*
	Baadasssss Song	1996	*Get On the Bus*
1971	*Shaft*	1997	*A Time to Kill*
1972	*Superfly*	1997	*Amistad*
1972	*Sounder*	1998	*Beloved*
1972	*Buck and the Preacher*	1998	*Down in the Delta*
1973	*Cleopatra Jones*	1999	*Wild Wild West*
1974	*Three the Hard Way*	1999	*The Phantom Menace*

BIBLIOGRAPHY

Bogle, Donald. *Toms, Coons, Mulattoes, Mammies and Bucks—An Interpretative History of Blacks in American Films.* 1994.

Bona, Damien, and Mason Wiley. *The Unofficial History of the Academy Awards.* 1993.

Campbell, Edward D. C., Jr. *The Celluloid South: Hollywood and the Southern Myth.* 1983.

Cripps, Thomas. *Slow Fade to Black: The Negro in American Film, 1900–1942.* 1977.

Diawara, Manthia. *Black American Cinema.* 1993.

Ellison, Mary. "Blacks in American Film." In *Cinema, Politics and Society in America,* edited by Philip Davies and Brian Neve. 1981.

Fredrickson, George M. *The Black Image in the White Mind: The Debate on Afro-American Character and Destiny 1817–1914.* 1971.

Guerrero, Ed. *Framing Blackness: The African-American Image in Film.* 1993.

Kirby, Jack Temple. *Media-Made Dixie: The South in the American Imagination.* 1986.

Leab, Daniel J. *From Sambo to Superspade—The Black Experience in Motion Pictures.* 1975.

Powers, Anne, ed. *Blacks in American Movies—A Selected Bibliography.* 1974.

Amy Shindler

First Amenia Conference

See Amenia Conferences.

First World War

See World War I.

Flores Magón, Ricardo, and Enrique Flores Magón

Anarchists, Mexican-American civil rights activists.

Ricardo Flores Magón (1873–1922) is recognized as the principal precursor of Mexico's epic Revolution of 1910, and a forerunner of the Mexican-American civil rights movement.

Born in the southern Mexican state of Oaxaca, Flores Magón studied in Mexico City and launched his

Ricardo Flores Magón is recognized as the principal precursor of Mexico's revolution of 1910. Younger brother and fellow anarchist Enrique accompanied his brother in a number of his activities. (Los Angeles Times)

career as a journalist for the political opposition in that city in 1900. After repeated arrests he left Mexico, crossing into Texas in 1904. Harassed in Texas, Missouri, and California by Mexican agents and cooperative United States authorities, Flores Magón still managed to publish his newspaper, *Regeneración*; to form the Mexican Liberal Party and issue a call for revolution with a program for the future; and to try to initiate armed revolts in 1906 and 1908.

In the evolution of his social and political thought, Flores Magón came to be a committed anarchist, alienating many liberal and socialist supporters in both the United States and Mexico. He was arrested and imprisoned repeatedly in the United States, beginning in 1907, with the usual charge being violations of United States neutrality laws. As time went on, he became more and more concerned with international issues. His voluminous writings are extremely important in the development of anarchist thought. His years in the United States also led to increasing concern for the problems of Mexicans in the United States. Living principally in the American Southwest, he experienced the racism and discrimination against Mexicans common in that area. He reacted against the situation in many of his later writings and is today cited often by modern Mexican-American civil rights leaders. Running afoul of the World War I antiradical laws, his final arrest led to a 20-year sentence in the federal penitentiaries. He died in Leavenworth, Kansas, in 1922 and his body was returned to a hero's welcome in Mexico by railroad union workers. Younger brother Enrique (1877–1954) accompanied Ricardo in a number of his activities, served time in United States prisons, and ultimately returned to Mexico to write and lecture on the struggles for many years.

BIBLIOGRAPHY

Albro, Ward S. *Always a Rebel: Ricardo Flores Magón and the Mexican Revolution.* 1992.

MacLachlan, Colin M. *Anarchism and the Mexican Revolution: The Political Trials of Ricardo Flores Magón in the United States.* 1991.

Raat, W. Dirk. *Revoltosos: Mexico's Rebels in the United States, 1903–1923.* 1981.

Ward S. Albro

Florida

"We're a Southern state and damn proud of it," a resident of north Florida commented as he sat in his pickup truck with the decal of a confederate flag on the back window, but three hundred miles to the south, a resident of Miami looked thoroughly bewildered when asked what it meant to be a Southerner.

For much of its recent history, Florida has been essentially two states—one that extends south from the Georgia border to Ocala and is identified with the South and its social, political, and racial traditions. And the other that extends north from Key West to Orlando, with a heritage that has little connection to the South, that has a diverse ethnic and racial population, and with a population that has viewed the state as part of a national and international community.

Florida's Southern heritage took root in the early nineteenth century and dominated the state for much of the nineteenth and twentieth centuries. The decision to secede from the Union in January 1861 and the subsequent experience of the Civil War and RECONSTRUCTION seared this heritage into the Florida soul. In the aftermath of the war, Florida stood isolated from the national mainstream and mired in rural poverty.

During the period from 1885 to 1923, native whites reasserted their leadership and imposed a political ideology that would shape the state for most of the twentieth century. The Constitution of 1885 was but the first step in reestablishing rule by whites and constructing a racial caste system that would ensure preservation of the state's Southern heritage. By 1900, these men effectively eliminated black and independent, rural white voters from the political process with the adoption of a poll tax and a host of voting restrictions. For the next sixty-five years, state elections were effectively decided within the Democratic primary, to such an extent that candidates typically did not campaign in the general election.

Race relations remained in ferment throughout this formative period. The economic fluctuations in Florida, the migration of black citizens northward in search of freedom and opportunity, the democratic ideology surrounding WORLD WAR I, and the social uncertainty of the war years threatened the social and racial fabric that whites had so diligently constructed. In this climate of racial uncertainty, violence escalated and 40,000 black Floridians departed. When the exodus threatened the labor supply, especially in the citrus, lumber, and turpentine industries, Governor Sidney Catts, one of the most outspoken racists of his day, called for unity and harmony among the races. Few black citizens trusted Catts, however, and when lynchings surged and wholesale attacks took place against the black communities of Ocoee, Perry, and Rosewood, the exodus continued as a silent protest against conditions in Florida. By 1924, in the aftermath of the destruction of Rosewood, black hopes for freedom had been extinguished.

The profoundly racist and antidemocratic excesses of this era in Florida also impeded the efforts of women to participate in the political process. White leaders did not support submission of the NINE-

TEENTH AMENDMENT to the United States Constitution to voters, nor did they ratify women's suffrage until 1969, and then only in recognition of the fiftieth anniversary of the Florida League of Women Voters. As in other Southern states, white men in Florida had white women serving another function for the world that they had designed. These women were meant to be the social and genetic glue that maintained white supremacy.

As soon as the Nineteenth Amendment was adopted in 1921, many women in Florida evidenced their contempt for the male construction of society by going to the polls to vote. Two women immediately campaigned for state office and, although defeated, they and other women made clear their opposition to the political and social ideology of the state. The leading women activists during this period were May Mann Jennings, wife of former progressive Governor William S. Jennings, and the women who made up the Florida State League of Women Voters. Jennings and the League championed such reforms as the right of women to serve on juries and the right of women to manage their own property. Despite their efforts, the intensely white, male culture of the state made it exceedingly difficult for women to participate in the political process and to have their voices taken seriously prior to 1945.

On the eve of WORLD WAR II, the political scientist V. O. Key, Jr., observed that Florida was different from other Southern states because of its extended geography and the large influx of newcomers from the North. Key reasoned that because of these conditions, and the fact that Florida had a relatively small black population, it would be the first Southern state to develop a viable two-party system and to abandon segregation. While race had never had the same impact in many areas of Florida that it had in such states as Mississippi, Georgia, Alabama, and South Carolina, race was every bit as central to daily life in areas north of Ocala. For these northern Floridians, control of the state Democratic Party and therefore state politics remained crucial during this (prewar) era.

The racial battle lines in Florida really formed during World War II and during the immediate postwar period, as the state enjoyed a dramatic economic and population boom and as black citizens tried to capitalize on the rhetoric of war and the social changes accompanying the war to end segregation. Also, the broad-based commitment to economic development in Florida steadily eroded its racial and social traditions. The companies and new residents who had migrated from the Northeast and Midwest had no intention of having their interests jeopardized by a commitment to a Southern past.

In this context, the two issues of race and reapportionment were inextricably linked in the 1950s. Rural, north Florida legislators "took a blood oath to stick together" to maintain control of state politics. When the U.S. Supreme Court announced its BROWN V. BOARD OF EDUCATION OF TOPEKA decision on May 17, 1954, these legislators used the decision to reassert their political dominance, denouncing the Court and drafting proposals calling for massive resistance. They also created a special committee, chaired by former Governor Charley Johns, in 1956, to investigate the NATIONAL ASSOCIATION FOR THE ADVANCEMENT OF COLORED PEOPLE (NAACP) and to ensure conformity of thought in the state's public schools and universities through the removal of dissidents. The committee sanctioned burning books that were considered offensive to state values.

Efforts by white leaders to stymie desegregation persisted into the 1960s, but numerous local demonstrations and a national campaign conducted in St. Augustine by the Reverend Martin Luther KING, JR., in 1964 sapped the will of these Floridians. The demonstrations underscored former Governor LeRoy Collins's contention that racism would only polarize Floridians and hurt its economic development. Ironically, as Collins's successors fought to block school desegregation in the 1960s, they led efforts to recruit new businesses, all of which demanded a stable economic and political environment to conduct their enterprises.

Although Florida's economic development steadily eroded its commitment to segregation, federal government intervention was an essential ingredient in changing the political culture. In 1964 Congress adopted the CIVIL RIGHTS ACT OF 1964 and the VOTING RIGHTS ACT (CIVIL RIGHTS ACT OF 1965). Two years later, the U.S. Supreme Court ended the domination of state politics by north Florida politicians when it ordered the implementation of one person/one vote in Florida.

The actions of the federal government helped the high-growth areas of south and central Florida to assume leadership of the state. Ironically, in this new political milieu, black Floridians found that their interests (like those of north Floridians) were being neglected in favor of the needs of south Floridians. The massive migration of Cuban Americans, who relocated to Dade County beginning in 1959, shifted the political discourse from race to ethnicity and immigration. As the state's Southern heritage was abandoned, so was concern about racial matters.

Other issues that came to dominate state politics were those focusing on the environment and education. Women headed these efforts, in large measure because they were considered nonthreatening and socially acceptable by the "good old boy" world of Florida politics. But women gave these issues an urgency that men did not want or expect. Led by May Mann

288   Ford, Gerald Rudolph

Jennings, Marjory Stoneman Douglas, and Marjorie Carr, women denounced the depredation of Florida's environment by commercial interests in the postwar era. Their leadership paved the way for the emergence of a new generation of women leaders in the 1970s, including Gwen Margolis and Toni Jennings, both of whom served as presidents of the Florida Senate, and Betty Castor, who became the first woman elected to the state cabinet, as commissioner of education.

The new politics of diversity and gender opened up other avenues of political discourse in the state. Gays and lesbians entered the political fray, seeking legal protection from discrimination. In local battles, gays and lesbians secured antidiscrimination protection in seven cities, six of which are in south Florida. But at the state level, opponents generally prevailed by building a coalition across regional lines to stymie issues such as same-sex marriage.

Despite the shift in political culture, issues of diversity and civil rights continue to generate sharp divisions and have created coalitions that extend across regional lines. North and south Floridians, for example, have joined together to block the EQUAL RIGHTS AMENDMENT and to regulate other forms of social behavior. The legacy of nineteenth-century Florida continues to influence the mentality of its citizens at the dawn of the new millennium.

BIBLIOGRAPHY
Colburn, David R., and Jane L. Landers, eds. *The African American Heritage of Florida.* 1995.
Colburn, David R., and Lance deHaven-Smith. *Government in the Sunshine State.* 1999.
Gannon, Michael V., ed. *The New History of Florida.* 1996.
Mohl, Raymond A. "Race and Space in the Modern City: Interstate-95 and the Black Community in Miami." In *Urban Policy in Twentieth Century America,* edited by Arnold R. Hirsch and Raymond A. Mohl. 1993.
Mormino, Gary R., and George E. Pozzetta. *The Immigrant World of Ybor City: Italians and Their Latin Neighbors in Tampa, 1885–1985.* 1987.

David R. Colburn

Ford, Gerald Rudolph

(1913–), U.S. President, 1974–1977.

Gerald R. Ford, a Republican, served as thirty-eighth President of the United States, from August 9, 1974 to January 20, 1977. He had previously served as a congressman from Michigan (1949–1973), and as President Richard NIXON's vice president (1973–1974).

Ford's most noteworthy action concerning civil rights was to oppose the decision of federal district court judge Arthur Garrity, Jr., to order busing to in-

In this 1976 photograph, President Gerald Ford shakes hands with Senator Daniel Inouye of Hawaii, prior to officially revoking the presidential order that set up detention camps for Japanese Americans during World War II. (AP/Wide World Photos)

tegrate Boston's public schools. Ford supported neighborhood schools and believed busing should be used only to end *de jure* segregation, not the *de facto* segregation produced by Boston's ethnic neighborhood settlement patterns.

After there was violent opposition to Garrity's order taking place in the fall of 1974, Ford called on Boston's citizens "to respect the law," but his announced opposition to busing provoked Boston Mayor Kevin White to claim Ford had "fanned the flames of resistance."

Ford rejected Massachusetts Governor Francis Sargent's request for federal troops to help quell the violence, saying that Sargent must first use "the full resources of the state" to maintain order. However, Ford ordered federal troops to prepare to intervene "as a last resort," but state and local authorities restored order without federal assistance.

During the 1976 presidential election campaign, Ford, seeking a full term, fired his Agriculture Secretary, Earl Butz, following politically embarrassing published reports that Butz had told a racist joke. President Ford lost the 1976 election, winning 49 percent of the two-party vote to Democratic opponent Jimmy Carter's 51 percent. Among African-American voters, Ford won 17 percent to Carter's 83 percent.

BIBLIOGRAPHY

Ford, Gerald R. *A Time to Heal.* 1980.
Greene, John Robert. *The Presidency of Gerald R. Ford.* 1995.
Koenig, Louis W. *The Chief Executive,* 6th ed. 1996.
Pomper, Gerald M., and colleagues. *The Election of 1976: Reports and Interpretations.* 1977.
Witcover, Jules. *Marathon: The Pursuit of the Presidency 1972–1976.* 1978.

Malcolm Lee Cross

Foreman, Clark Howell

(1901–1977), New Deal official, civil rights and civil liberties activist.

Clark Foreman was born to white Southern privilege in Atlanta, Georgia, at the turn of the century; his grandfather, Clark Howell, was editor of the *Atlanta Constitution.* While a student at the University of Georgia, Foreman witnessed a LYNCHING, which, as a contemporary recalled, "burned a hole in his head." This experience led to Foreman's ultimate rejection of the SEGREGATION system in the South and his commitment to the struggle for racial justice.

After college, Foreman did graduate work at Harvard University, and then traveled and studied in Europe. During his time away from the South, he struggled with the "race question" and became increasingly critical of the assumptions and traditions that bol-

stered white supremacy. He returned to Atlanta only after learning about the work of the COMMISSION ON INTERRACIAL COOPERATION (CIC), and went to work as secretary of the CIC's Georgia Committee. Foreman soon became frustrated by the Committee's weak effort to challenge white racial attitudes and practices. That effort, Foreman recalled, "was so pitifully small compared to the total job that had to be done. We were treating symptoms on the assumption that eventually the disease would be cured."

Foreman left Atlanta and pursued graduate studies at Columbia University in New York while working for the Phelps–Stokes Foundation and the Rosenwald Fund. He continued to focus his attention on the racial situation in the South. From 1929 to 1931, as part of his dissertation research, Foreman and African-American sociologist Horace Mann BOND conducted a Rosenwald-sponsored study of black education in the South, documenting the close correlation between environmental factors and black educational achievement. Foreman's work attracted the attention of Harold ICKES, Interior Secretary of the Roosevelt administration, who hired him as Special Advisor on Negro Affairs. Foreman and his associate, Robert C. WEAVER, a young black intellectual with a doctorate in economics, inserted no-discrimination clauses into the programs of the Public Works Administration (PWA); they also devised a "quota system" to provide a tangible way to measure compliance. In 1935, Ickes named Foreman director of the power division of the PWA; five years later, he became director of defense housing for the Federal Works Administration. Controversy erupted around Foreman when he refused to bow to congressional pressure to bar blacks from the Sojourner Truth housing project in Detroit, federal housing originally intended for black occupancy. He became the target of a successful effort by Southern congressional opponents to oust him from government.

While in Washington, Foreman became part of a loose network of young Southern white liberals and black civil rights activists who challenged the insular structures that had dominated Southern life since the turn of the century. In 1938, Foreman advised President Roosevelt on his ill-fated effort to "purge" Southern conservative opponents of New Deal reform. As part of that effort, Foreman, Clifford Durr, and several other Southerners wrote "The Report on Economic Conditions of the South," which emphasized the essential role of the federal government in promoting the economic development of the region. In response to the report, more than 1,000 black and white Southerners met in Birmingham, ALABAMA, in November 1938, in support of a liberal program of economic and political reform. At that meeting they formed the Southern Conference for Human Welfare (SCHW).

Foreman, who became president of SCHW in 1942, played a leading role in shaping the agenda and program of the organization. SCHW sponsored a biracial program focusing on the expansion of Voting Rights and voter registration as central to the liberalization of regional and national politics. SCHW worked with the National Association for the Advancement of Colored People (NAACP), CIO unions, the CIO Political Action Committee, and various civic groups at local, state, and national levels, promoting political and economic democracy in the South and sponsoring challenges to the segregation system.

In 1948, Foreman served as national treasurer of Henry Wallace's Progressive Party. In the South, the Wallace campaign built on inroads made by SCHW during the 1940s, expanding voter registration efforts and running both black and white candidates for state and local office. Wallace attacked the segregation system during a tour through the South and drew national press attention with his refusal to address segregated audiences. Foreman accompanied Wallace on these tours, where they met with violent protests but also drew large audiences of black and white supporters. Foreman took pride in the fact that Wallace was the first major presidential candidate to refuse to address segregated audiences in the South. Harry Truman ducked the issue by not visiting the South during his campaign tours.

As the Cold War intensified at home and abroad, Foreman devoted his energies to the fight to protect basic civil liberties. He served as director of the National Emergency Civil Liberties Committee (NECLC) from 1951 to 1968, during which time the NECLC won several major cases that reversed the "anti-subversive" legislation of the 1950s.

Bibliography

Foreman, Clark. "The Decade of Hope." *Phylon* 12 (1951): 137–50.
Sullivan, Patricia. *Days of Hope: Race and Democracy in the New Deal Era.* 1986.

Patricia Sullivan

Forman, James

(1928–   ), civil rights leader.

James Forman was born in Chicago, spent much of his early life with his grandmother in Marshall County, Mississippi, and graduated from Englewood High School in Chicago. He joined the Air Force in 1947 and was discharged in 1951. After briefly attending the

James Forman, former executive secretary of the Student Nonviolent Coordinating Committee, shown here in 1969, the year he organized the National Black Development Conference. (AP/Wide World Photos)

University of Southern California, he graduated from Roosevelt University in California in 1957, where he was influenced by well-known academics such as Walter Weisskopf and St. Clair Drake. Besides teaching school and trying his hand at writing fiction, Forman covered school integration efforts in Little Rock, Arkansas, in 1958 (the year that Governor Orval Faubus closed Little Rock's Central High School) for the Chicago *Defender*. But what really brought him into the orbit of the fledgling civil rights movement was the mass eviction of black sharecroppers from their land in Fayette County, Tennessee, in the fall of 1960. The evictions attracted national attention, and Forman moved back and forth between Chicago and West Tennessee, raising money for and helping to organize the evicted farmers.

In 1961 Forman became executive secretary for the Student Nonviolent Coordinating Committee (SNCC) and took on the responsibility for bringing some degree of organization to a disparate group of young men and women of both races. Forman worked primarily in the Atlanta office but was often deeply involved in campaigns across the Deep South, especially in Alabama. He also organized fund-raising efforts, primarily in the North, and established an effective publicity department for SNCC. By the late 1960s, with SNCC in disarray and exhausted by the stress of his position, Forman resigned. Aside from some contacts with the BLACK PANTHER PARTY and radical union groups in Michigan, Forman largely disappeared from public view, though his "Black Manifesto" did attract national attention in the spring of 1969 when he called for America's churches to give $500 million in reparations to African Americans.

In the aftermath of the movement, Forman gained an M.A. from Cornell University and a Ph.D. from the Union of Experimental Colleges and Universities in Washington, D.C., in the early 1980s. This advanced study and research focused on a historical analysis of the "Black Belt Thesis" of the COMMUNIST PARTY USA. Forman essentially agreed with their position that African Americans were a "nation," not just a "minority." As a result, they should work toward autonomy within the United States and eventually aim for self-determination on the model of the various ethnic republics of the (then) Soviet Union.

In many ways Forman was the intellectual leader of the more radical sector of the civil rights movement. His *The Making of Black Revolutionaries* (1972) is perhaps the single most interesting book produced by a participant in the civil rights movement. The theory of political organizing articulated there emphasizes the need both for a mass base and centralized coordination, but rejects charismatic leadership as essential to the success of a political movement. In this, Forman typified the SNCC suspicion of Martin Luther KING, JR.'s SOUTHERN CHRISTIAN LEADERSHIP CONFERENCE (SCLC), while also rejecting King's philosophical commitment to nonviolence. Nonviolence, for Forman, was an organizing tool, useful only as long as it was effective. Yet by stressing centralized coordination, Forman also came into conflict with those in SNCC who felt that the organization should be a loosely structured group of freelance organizers, who always deferred to local communities—an attitude that Forman called, "local people-itis."

Central to Forman's vision was the necessity of political education. A wide reader, his general views were considerably influenced by the writings of Kwame Nkrumah, Mao Zedong, and especially Franz Fanon. In his capacity as International Affairs Director of SNCC between 1967 and 1969, Forman sought to establish links between the civil rights movement in the United States and movements for human rights and self-determination—in South Africa particularly and in the Third World more generally.

It is difficult to overestimate James Forman's contribution to the effectiveness of SNCC and the civil rights movement—despite, or perhaps because of, the fact that he was somewhat older than most of his compatriots. He was the voice of realism among idealists, and he saw concrete self-interest rather than abstract morality as the crucial component in political behavior. In comparison with better-known contemporaries in the movement, then and since, Forman generally assumed a background position. In this respect, his importance for SNCC was similar to that of Bayard RUSTIN for SCLC and the mainstream of the civil rights movement. Overall, the intellectual as political organizer and tactician, the role which Forman so importantly played, has been a more familiar figure in revolutionary struggles in Europe and the Third World than in the United States.

James Forman now lives in Washington, D.C., where he is the president of the Unemployed and Poverty Action Council Legal Defense, Education and Research Fund, Inc. (UPAC).

BIBLIOGRAPHY

Branch, Taylor. *Parting the Waters: America in the King Years, 1953–64.* 1988.

Branch, Taylor. *Pillars of Fire: America in the King Years, 1963–65.* 1998.

Carson, Clayborne. *In Struggle: SNCC and the Black Awakening of the 1960s.* 1981.

Forman, James. *Sammy Younge, Jr.: The First Black College Student to Die in the Black Liberation Movement.* 1968.

Forman, James. *The Making of Black Revolutionaries.* 1972.

Forman, James. *Self-Determination: An Examination of the Question and Its Application to the African-American People.* 1984.

Forman, James. *High Tide of Black Resistance and Other Political and Literary Writings.* 1994.

Richard H. King

Fortune, Timothy Thomas

(1856–1928), journalist and civil rights leader.

Born in Marianna, Florida, T. Thomas Fortune received limited education in Florida, sponsored by the Freedmen's Bureau (see BUREAU OF REFUGEES, FREEDMEN, AND ABANDONED LANDS). In Jacksonville he learned the printer's trade and became an expert compositor. He entered the Preparatory Department at Howard University, but lack of money forced him to abandon his plans. Returning to Florida, he began work on a black newspaper, *The Peoples' Advocate,* and married. From this union five children were born before Fortune and his wife separated in 1906.

After he moved to New York City in 1879, Fortune's career in printing and journalism made significant gains. He became part owner of various newspapers, including *The Rumors*, a weekly tabloid that became the *Globe* with Fortune as editor. After its failure, he published the *New York Freeman* before it became the *New York Age*, with Fortune and Jerome B. Peterson as joint owners. The *Age's* greatest contributions were Fortune's editorial condemning all forms of racial discrimination and demanding full equality for blacks. Disliked by whites, Fortune expressed views in favor of progress for blacks in the areas of education, vocational training, and land purchase, among others, that were similar to those of Booker T. WASHINGTON, whom he supported. However, the two men had contrasting images in the public eye. Fortune's editorials were valuable to Washington in answering Washington black critics. Moreover, Fortune helped ghost-write many of Washington's speeches and several books published under Washington's name. Their relationship changed because of Washington's conciliatory views and his refusal to help Fortune to obtain a governmental appointment.

Fortune would be the major force in the founding of the NATIONAL AFRO-AMERICAN LEAGUE in 1890. A forerunner of the NIAGARA MOVEMENT and other civil rights organizations of the twentieth century, it failed because of a lack of funds and its inability to recruit other black leaders. In 1893, Fortune responded to an appeal by black leaders and a few whites for a conference in Rochester, New York, in September 1898, at which the National Afro-American Council was organized. At the opening session, Fortune voiced concern for the fate of Cubans, Filipinos, and Puerto Ricans after the U.S. defeat of Spain in the Spanish-American War. Doubtful that this organization would succeed, Fortune resigned as president, but the Council expressed the same objectives as the Afro-American League. When the Niagara Movement in 1905 expressed a similar "Declaration of Principles"—suffrage and civil rights—Fortune accused W. E. B. DU BOIS of copying his platform. Fortune also felt that the attack by Du Bois and William Monroe TROTTER on Booker T. Washington was unfair. Strife and controversies in the Council over supporters of either Du Bois or Washington weakened the organization after the last meeting in 1906. Similarly, the Niagara Movement ceased to function effectively after 1911. The objectives and goals of these organizations were incorporated into an early platform of the NATIONAL ASSOCIATION FOR THE ADVANCEMENT OF COLORED PEOPLE (NAACP). Fortune had resigned from the Council in March 1904, but one of his most significant legacies was that the

goals and objectives of the League and Council shaped many of the goals of the NAACP.

His various newspaper ownership ventures were never total financial successes. He was forced to supplement his income by writing articles for various black newspapers and by depending on friends. Fortune became an alcoholic during these years, suffering a mental breakdown in 1907, soon after separating from his wife, and was practically destitute. After regaining his health during the last decade of his life, he wrote editorials and special columns for the *Norfolk Journal and Guide* (1919–1928) and was editor of the *Negro World* (1919–1928), a publication of Marcus GARVEY's UNIVERSAL NEGRO IMPROVEMENT ASSOCIATION, before Fortune's death in April 1928.

BIBLIOGRAPHY

Fortune, T. Thomas. *Black and White: Life and Labor in the South.* 1886.
Fortune, T. Thomas. *The Negro in Politics.* 1886.
Fortune, T. Thomas. *Dreams of Life.* 1905.
Thornbrough, Emma Lou. *Thomas Fortune: Militant Journalist.* 1970.
Thornbrough, Emma Lou. "T. Thomas Fortune: Militant Editor in the Age of Accommodation." In *Black Leaders of the Twentieth Century*, edited by John Hope Franklin and August Meier. 1982.

Charles Vincent

Foster, Autherine Lucy

See Lucy Foster, Autherine.

Fourteenth Amendment

Ratified in 1868, the Fourteenth Amendment was adopted to protect the rights and liberties of former slaves and to settle issues of congressional representation in the wake of the Civil War. Written in broad language, the amendment has become the driving engine of civil rights litigation. It has also been the primary vehicle for applying the BILL OF RIGHTS to the states.

The amendment contains five sections. Sections 2–4 dealt with reconstituting Congress, the political rights of former Confederate leaders, and the disposition of Confederate debt in the aftermath of the Civil War. Section 4 also prohibited any person from making "any claim for the loss or emancipation of any slave." Section 5 gives Congress the power to enforce the amendment "by appropriate legislation." Whereas all the sections affected the status of blacks after the Civil War, Section 1 has been the most important for the development of civil rights in the United States. Section 1 reads:

> All persons born or naturalized in the United States and subject to the jurisdiction thereof, are citizens of the United States and of the State wherein they reside. No State shall make or enforce any law which shall abridge the privileges or immunities of citizens of the United States; nor shall any State deprive any person of life, liberty, or property without due process of law; nor deny to any person within its jurisdiction the equal protection of the laws.

This section was specifically designed to reverse the holding in DRED SCOTT V. SANDFORD (1857) that blacks were not citizens of the United States. Numerous Supreme Court cases, many debates in Congress, and an enormous amount of scholarship have been devoted to elucidating what else this section was meant to accomplish.

Background and Adoption

During the Civil War, Congress passed, and sent on to the states, the THIRTEENTH AMENDMENT, which abolished slavery in the United States. By the end of the war, slavery was a dead institution in much of the South, and the remnants ended with the ratification of the amendment on December 6, 1865. Many Northerners naively thought that the adoption of the amendment and the total abolition of slavery would lead to inclusion of former slaves, the freedmen as they were known, in the political structure of the South. This did not happen, because former Confederates, who retained political power in the postwar South, passed a series of restrictive laws, known as BLACK CODES, to repress blacks. The black codes denied all but the most basic rights to former slaves while creating various criminal and civil sanctions designed to keep blacks tied to the land in a system that resembled serfdom.

Congress responded to the black codes with the CIVIL RIGHTS ACT OF 1866, which passed over President Andrew Johnson's veto. This act declared that all former slaves were citizens of the United States and guaranteed these new citizens many substantive rights as citizens, including the rights to own property, sign contracts, and travel at will. The law also declared that the former slaves were to have the "full and equal benefit of all laws . . . as is enjoyed by white citizens."

Congress claimed power to pass this unprecedented bill under its authority to enforce the newly adopted Thirteenth Amendment. While overwhelmingly supported by the Republican majority in Congress, some Republicans, including the influential Representative John Bingham of Ohio, had reservations about the constitutionality of the Civil Rights Act

of 1866. They doubted that Congress could pass such a law under the Thirteenth Amendment. To ensure that the new civil rights legislation would pass constitutional muster, in 1866, Congress passed the Fourteenth Amendment, which the states ratified in 1868.

Most scholars believe that the framers of the Fourteenth Amendment intended to radically alter the structure of the American government by giving the national government the power to compel the states to provide equal treatment to all citizens. In addition, most scholars believe that the clause "No State shall make or enforce any law which shall abridge the privileges or immunities of citizens of the United States" meant that the states had to respect the limitations on government found in the national Bill of Rights. Scholars have been more divided on whether the framers of the Fourteenth Amendment intended to give the national government the power to regulate voting in the states although the arguments of supporters of the amendment in Congress seem to support the notion that the phrases "equal protection of the laws" and "privileges and immunities of citizens" included VOTING RIGHTS.

In 1871, Congress passed the KU KLUX KLAN ACT (also called the Enforcement Act) to prohibit private action by terrorists such as members of the KU KLUX KLAN who attempted to prevent blacks from voting or exercising their civil rights. In the CIVIL RIGHTS ACT OF 1875, Congress further expanded on the meaning of the amendment to prohibit discrimination in privately owned "inns, public conveyances . . . theaters, and other places of public amusement."

Early Interpretations

The Supreme Court read the new amendment in the narrowest ways possible and thus undercut attempts by Congress to give substance to the freedom of the recently emancipated slaves. In only a few cases, the Court supported the civil rights claims of minorities under the amendment.

Where racial discrimination was blatant and obvious, the Court sometimes struck down state acts for denying blacks either the "equal protection of the laws" or "due process of law." For example, in *Strauder v. West Virginia* (1880), the Court reversed the conviction of a black because West Virginia law limited jury service to whites. In *Ex parte Virginia* (1880) and *Neal v. Delaware* (1880), the Court reversed convictions of blacks where there was clear evidence that blacks had been deliberately excluded from juries even though no statute required such an exclusion. Similarly, in YICK WO V. HOPKINS (1886), the Court struck down a San Francisco ordinance requiring that laundries be housed in brick structures. While racially neutral on its face, the Court found that, in fact, it had been applied only against Chinese laundry owners while virtually all white laundry owners had been granted an exemption from the law.

Such civil rights victories were rare, however, in the years following the adoption of the amendment. In the *Slaughterhouse Cases* (1873) the Supreme Court substantially limited the meaning of the new amendment by denying that its privileges and immunities clause made the Bill of Rights applicable to the states. In *Virginia v. Rives* (1880), the Court held that the regular, persistent, and pervasive absence of blacks from juries, unless caused by statute or by the direct and blatant action of the state, did not constitute discrimination or the denial of due process of black defendants. In the *Civil Rights Cases* (1883), the Court held that the amendment did not give Congress the power to regulate private action. Thus the Court struck down most of the Civil Rights Act of 1875, holding here that private acts of discrimination by the owners of theaters or restaurants were not within the jurisdiction of Congress under the Fourteenth Amendment. Instead, the Court asserted that the amendment allowed only the national government to limit what is called "state action."

The Court also used the state action argument in *United States v. Harris* (1883). In this case, the Court reversed the convictions of Klansmen convicted under the Ku Klux Klan Act of 1871 because their acts of terror were "private" and, according to the Court, the Fourteenth Amendment prohibited only state action. The Court refused to accept the argument that Congress could protect the liberties of the former slaves if the states refused to act. This line of cases culminated with PLESSY V. FERGUSON (1896), in which the Court held that statutes requiring segregation did not violate the equal protection clause of the Fourteenth Amendment as long as the state required that the separate facilities be "equal." Until the 1940s, however, the federal courts refused actually to consider whether there was any substance to the "equal" aspect of the doctrine of "separate but equal."

The Rebirth of Equal Protection

With a few minor exceptions, from 1896 until the Great Depression, the Fourteenth Amendment was of little use to minorities seeking "equal protection of the laws." In *Gitlow v. New York* (1925), which did not involve race, the Supreme Court accepted the idea that freedom of speech was a fundamental liberty protected by the Fourteenth Amendment. In the next four decades, the Court gradually incorporated most of the Bill of Rights to protect the liberties of Americans from infringement by the states.

In the 1930s, the Court used the Fourteenth Amendment to free Angelo Herndon, a black Communist sentenced to a Georgia chain gang for his advocacy of black rights as well as for his communist beliefs. The court applied the due process clause to order new trials for some of the Scottsboro boys who, in sham trials in Alabama, had been convicted of raping two white females. These decisions did not strike at segregation or racism but did begin to reinvigorate the Fourteenth Amendment as a tool for racial justice.

Starting with *Gaines v. Canada* (1938), the Court began to require the integration of southern graduate and professional schools in which there were no separate facilities for blacks. In *Sweatt v. Painter* (1950), the Court ordered the integration of the University of Texas School of Law on the grounds that the separate law school for blacks was not, and never could be, "equal" to the University of Texas School of Law. Then, in 1954, in BROWN V. BOARD OF EDUCATION OF TOPEKA, KANSAS, the Court used the equal protection clause of the amendment to strike down segregation in all public schools. In the dozen years that followed, the Court dismantled the system of de jure segregation that had permeated the South. Buses, elevators, theaters, libraries, restaurants, municipal swimming pools, parks, and golf courses, and virtually all other public facilities went from segregated to integrated. This revitalization of the equal protection clause culminated with LOVING V. VIRGINIA (1967), in which the Court held that the Fourteenth Amendment barred the states from prohibiting interracial marriage. Ironically, a combination of stiff resistance from southern whites and residential housing patterns kept most public schools de facto segregated, even as laws requiring segregation disappeared.

Equal Protection and Race in the Modern Era

The end of legalized segregation did not end RACISM, discrimination, or inequality. Since the 1960s, courts and legislatures have tried various methods to increase minority participation in the economy. These have included AFFIRMATIVE ACTION programs to recruit more minorities to schools and jobs, quotas to guarantee the presence of more minorities in educational institutions and in some forms of employment, and minority "set-asides" in government-funded construction to facilitate the integration of the construction business. There have also been attempts to create "majority minority" congressional districts in which the election of minorities to Congress is guaranteed.

The courts have provided some support for these programs. In *United Steelworkers v. Weber* (1971), the Supreme Court upheld an employer's "voluntary, race-conscious efforts to abolish traditional patterns of racial segregation." In *Regents of the University of California v. Bakke* (1978; see BAKKE), the Court held that a quota system for minority admissions to a state medical school denied equal protection to white applicants but, at the same time, the Court held that RACE could be a factor in making decisions on admission to state colleges and universities.

In recent years, however, some lower federal courts have moved away from this position, arguing that the Constitution must be seen as "color-blind" with regard to race and affirmative action. The Supreme Court has struck down minority set-asides in *City of Richmond v. J. A. Croson Co.* (1989) on equal protection grounds. On those same grounds, in SHAW V. RENO (1993) and *Miller v. Johnson* (1995), the Court struck down reapportionment schemes designed to guarantee the election of blacks to Congress.

Over 130 years after its adoption, the Fourteenth Amendment remains one of the most important provisions of the Constitution. It has been the vehicle for ending discrimination against blacks and other minorities. Even noncitizens have turned to its protective umbrella in cases like *Plyler v. Doe* (1982), which established that states could not discriminate against the children of illegal aliens by barring them from the public schools. This case, which involved Mexican-American children, illustrates the racial and civil rights aspects of immigration (see IMMIGRATION AND IMMIGRANTS). But the Rehnquist Court (see William REHNQUIST) has also used the Fourteenth Amendment to prevent remedial legislation and programs designed to counter the historical effects of racism and the legacy of segregation.

BIBLIOGRAPHY

Curtis, Michael Kent. *"No State Shall Abridge": The Fourteenth Amendment and the Bill of Rights.* 1990.
Hyman, Harold M., and William M. Wiecek. *Equal Justice Under the Law.* 1982.
Kluger, Richard. *Simple Justice.* 1975.
Nieman, Donald. *Promises to Keep.* 1991.

Paul Finkelman

Fourth Circuit, United States Court of Appeals for the

As early as 1895 civil rights figured importantly in the work of the Fourth Circuit Court of Appeals. That court was one of a new tier created by the U.S. Congress in 1891 and was composed of nine intermediate appellate courts positioned between the federal district courts and the Supreme Court. Presiding at the Fourth's convening in Richmond, Virginia, on June 16, 1891, was Cleveland Democrat Chief Justice Mel-

ville W. Fuller. Like his predecessors and successors, he was allotted to the Circuit that since 1866 included federal trial courts in seven geographically described districts within five states of the mid-Atlantic South: Maryland, Virginia, West Virginia, and North and South Carolina. Joining Fuller was the lone Circuit Judge authorized by the 1869 Judiciary Act, Maryland Republican Hugh Lennox Bond. Bond had presided over the historic 1871 South Carolina Klan trials, had valiantly struggled in 1874 to breathe life into the Fourteenth Amendment's "privileges or immunities" clause, and had released from state incarceration South Carolina's Republican presidential electors in the critical 1876 Rutherford B. Hayes–Samuel J. Tilden race. Also present was the Circuit's senior district judge, West Virginian John J. Jackson, Jr., an ardent 1861 Virginia antisecessionist. A second circuit judge became Bond's associate in 1892; only in 1916 did Congress authorize a third judge for a tribunal that sat in three-judge panels. The Court's relatively low caseloads (docketed: 53 [1900], 106 [1920], 196 [1950], 224 [1960]) effectively capped the membership at three until 1961, after which caseloads increased dramatically in the developing region: to 1,166 in 1970, 2,206 in 1980, and 3,235 in 1990. Additional judgeships resulted in a bench of: five (1961), seven (1966), ten (1978), eleven (1984), fifteen (1990)—none of them filled by a black appointee. By 1998, the Court docketed 4,897 cases originating in nine districts within its five states with fifty-one authorized judgeships.

Early civil rights cases decided by the Fourth Circuit appellate court centered on political rights that were related to citizenship: voting and jury service. Outcomes disfavored black claimants. Chief Justice Fuller hastily mobilized the new bench in 1895 to dissolve an injunction against the enforcement of SOUTH CAROLINA's racially discriminatory voter-registration laws, which had been deemed unconstitutional by the lower court under the FOURTEENTH and FIFTEENTH AMENDMENTS. Improbably invoking the "political question" doctrine, in *Green v. Mills* (1890), Fuller's decision cleared the path for a state constitution modeled on that of Mississippi. Disfranchising the black electorate, it facilitated noncompetitive "white supremacy" party politics in the Palmetto State. Not until 1930 in *West v. Bliley* did the Fourth Circuit step ahead of the SUPREME COURT and favor a black claimant barred from voting in the Democratic primary election by Virginia law delegating voter qualifications to the party. Meanwhile, allegations of race-based exclusion from grand and petit juries confronted a stiff standard of proof based on the Supreme Court's *Virginia v. Rives* (1880) precedent, a federalism cause célèbre arising in the Fourth Circuit.

Led by presiding judge John J. PARKER, the Fourth issued far-reaching EMPLOYMENT and voting decisions in the 1940s. It ordered equalization of black and white teachers' salaries in the wake of arguments advanced by Thurgood MARSHALL and William H. HASTIE and, following arguments by Charles H. HOUSTON, restrained railway labor unions that barred black members from making collective bargaining agreements that sacrificed blacks' seniority and related promotion rights. Sternly rebuffed were South Carolina's attempts to insulate its "white" Democratic primary from attacks under the Fourteenth and Fifteenth Amendments by rendering the primary election a purely private affair and thereby severing that election's overt links with any constitutionally challengeable "state action" in the form of law or official practice. Greater caution greeted a challenge to Virginia's poll tax.

Application of the Fourteenth Amendment's equal protection clause to social relations vexed the Court. It nevertheless held, in 1945, that Baltimore's Enoch Pratt Free Library performed a state function and was constitutionally barred from excluding blacks. The reason-based *Plessy* doctrine still prevailing in 1950 (see PLESSY v. FERGUSON), supported Baltimore's racially segregated public parks, however. Reversal came in the wake of BROWN v. BOARD OF EDUCATION (1954), when the Fourth Circuit applied its rationale in *Dawson v. Mayor* (1955) and ordered DESEGREGATION of the city's pools—a decision affirmed by the Supreme Court. Similarly, in transportation cases, the appeals court in 1948 approved "reasonable" SEGREGATION of passengers by interstate bus companies. By 1955, segregated local public transportation and even private carriers acting "under color of [state] law" became subject to *Brown*'s repudiation of the "separate but equal" doctrine.

Black plaintiffs challenging Virginia's egregiously unequal educational facilities won favorable outcomes in 1949–1950 with application of the substantive equality standard. That *Plessy*-derived doctrine also undergirded two of the cases originating in the Fourth Circuit that were reversed in *Brown: Briggs v. Elliott* (1951) and *Davis v. County School Board of Prince Edward County, Virginia* (1952). *Brown*, as interpreted by John Parker, did not mandate federal judicial "takeover" of public schools, nor did it require schoolhouse race-mixing. It merely forbade official discrimination. Deference to traditional state powers, doubts about the capacity of the courts to effect social change, and concern for interracial peace encouraged judicial forbearance, including exhaustion of state-provided remedies. State defiance and delaying tactics induced the Supreme Court's reversal of Fourth Circuit decisions authored by Clement L. Haynsworth, Jr., in 1963 that

abstained from resolving the Prince Edward's school closing case and in 1965 treated Virginia's "freedom of choice" transfer plans favorably. Supreme Court rebuke of the Fourth in *Green v. New Kent County* (1968) imposed an affirmative duty on segregated dual school systems to convert to nonracial unitary systems. Chief Justice Warren Burger in *Swann v. Charlotte-Mecklenburg Board of Education* (1971) adumbrated the available remedial strategies while expanding the limited-relief approved by the Fourth in a case that had been argued at Richmond by Julius Chambers, Jack GREENBERG, and James M. Nabrit III.

Beginning in 1993, the Fourth Circuit held that the Equal Protection Clause barred sexual segregation at the state-supported Citadel and Virginia Military Institute. Parallel higher educational institutions of "substantive comparability" were deemed constitutional, but not by the Supreme Court under its "heightened scrutiny" test as used to evaluate gender-based classifications.

Expansion of federal protection against private racial discrimination emerged in *McCrary v. Runyon* (1975). Haynsworth, cued by precedent, held in a decision affirmed by the Supreme Court that a surviving portion of the CIVIL RIGHTS ACT of 1866 protecting the right to make and enforce contracts barred racially discriminatory admissions at private schools. The Fourth in *Patterson v. McLean Credit Union* (1986), affirmed by the Supreme Court, subsequently excepted on-the-job racial discrimination from its scope, but Congress in 1991 overruled that narrow statutory interpretation.

The Fourth acted cautiously in employment discrimination cases, approving in *Griggs v. Duke Power Co.* (1970) educational qualifications for promotion to a job that did not require them—only to suffer Supreme Court reversal. Years later, in *Croson v. City of Richmond* (1987), the appeals court looked to prevailing Supreme Court precedent in holding that past societal racial discrimination validated Richmond's ordinance requiring nonminority construction contractors to subcontract 30 percent of all city-awarded projects ("set-aside" quotas) to minority-owned business enterprises (MBEs). The William H. REHNQUIST–led Supreme Court's intervening adoption of a strict scrutiny test for such racial preference cases that were challenged on equal protection grounds reversed the outcome in a landmark AFFIRMATIVE ACTION decision.

With exceptions, in civil rights cases the Fourth Circuit Court of Appeals has manifested fidelity to Supreme Court commands interpreted in the light of regional cultural norms by restrained judicial interpreters of the law. Creative jurisprudence and innovative procedures to effect bold social change have been largely eschewed by the Fourth under Chief Judge J. Harvie Wilkinson and his predecessors.

BIBLIOGRAPHY

Burris, William C. *Duty and the Law: Judge John J. Parker and the Constitution.* 1987.

Fish, Peter G. "A New Court Opens: The United States Court of Appeals for the Fourth Circuit." *Georgia Journal of Southern Legal History* 2, Nos. 1 & 2 (1993).

Frank, John Paul. *Clement Haynsworth, the Senate, and the Supreme Court.* 1991.

Kluger, Richard. *Simple Justice: The History of* Brown v. Board of Education, *and Black America's Struggle for Equality.* 1975.

Peltason, Jack W. *Fifty-Eight Lonely Men: Southern Federal Judges and School Desegregation.* 1961.

Race Relations Law Reporter. 1956–1967.

Wilkinson, J. Harvie. *From Brown to Bakke: The Supreme Court and School Integration, 1954–1978.* 1979.

Peter G. Fish

Franklin, John Hope

(1915–), author, scholar, educator, historian.

"[T]he true scholar who is a Negro has no real choice but to remain in his field, to 'stick to his knitting,' to persevere," John Hope Franklin wrote in a 1963 article titled "The Dilemma of the American Negro Scholar" (Franklin, *Race and History*, p. 305). There were times, however, when the scholar should use his training, talents, and resources to defend equal rights, although it was extremely important to keep in mind the differences between scholarship and advocacy.

If most of his career was devoted to research, writing, lecturing, and teaching, at various junctures Franklin became involved in the struggle for civil rights. He had experienced racial segregation on a number of occasions in his native Oklahoma, and when his father's law offices were burned to the ground during the 1921 TULSA RACE RIOT, it left a deep mark on the family. He held a strong conviction that weak injustices done to African Americans must be corrected. In 1948, Franklin assisted Thurgood MARSHALL, of the NATIONAL ASSOCIATION FOR THE ADVANCEMENT OF COLORED PEOPLE (NAACP) Legal Defense Fund, in preparing background information in *Johnson v. Board of Trustees of University of Kentucky.* Louisville school teacher and civil rights activist Lyman T. Johnson argued that he had been deprived of due process and equal protection under the Constitution when the university provided "substitute facilities" rather than permit him to enter its graduate school. In 1949, the United States District Court ruled in Johnson's favor. In the summer of 1953, following the SUPREME COURT's deferred judgment of five cases

Historian and educator, Franklin, throughout his career, combined scholarship with social activism. In 1997, President Bill Clinton asked Prof. Franklin to lead a national dialogue on race issues. (AP/Wide World Photos)

challenging racial segregation in public schools, Franklin again assisted Marshall in preparing historical background information. Now he prepared a monograph on, as he put it, "the way in which the Southerners defied, ignored, and worked against every conception of equality laid down in the Fourteenth Amendment and subsequent legislation." It was used in the final NAACP brief in what became the landmark 1954 case of *Brown v. Board of Education of Topeka,* ending segregation in the schools. (See BROWN V. BOARD OF EDUCATION.) As the civil rights movement expanded, Franklin demonstrated his support in a number of ways, including participating with Martin Luther KING, Jr. and others in the 1965 march from Selma to Montgomery. Then, and later, he focused some of his historical studies on subjects directly related to equal rights. In 1974, for example, he wrote in *Prologue* on "The Enforcement of the Civil Rights Act of 1875" and in 1976 he delivered the Jefferson Lectures, later published as *Racial Equality in America*. His classic study *From Slavery to Freedom: A History of African Americans*, first published in 1947 and now co-authored in its seventh edition with Alfred Moss, examines many facets of the equal rights problem throughout American history.

During his career, Franklin experienced discrimination and segregation on numerous occasions. These encounters ranged from being kicked off a train with his mother because she refused to leave the section reserved for whites when he was seven years old; to being advised in 1943 by the president of St. Augustine's College in Raleigh, North Carolina, where he was a faculty member, that he might learn habits of neatness and cleanliness in the army; to being unable to buy a house in certain sections of Brooklyn, New York, in 1956, because of his color. In the mid-1990s, he continued to experience the discriminatory attitudes of whites. At the prestigious Cosmos Club in Washington, D.C., shortly before leaving to receive the Medal of Freedom at the White House, a woman approached him and asked him to get her coat from the cloak room. Such experiences have shaped Franklin's determination to achieve a colorblind society.

In 1997, Franklin was appointed to chair the Advisory Board to President CLINTON's Initiative on Race, working tirelessly in that capacity. During the year of the board's existence, Franklin pushed for increased federal funding to fight discrimination in jobs and housing. The board recommended, among other things, to increase the minimum wage, and to create a "Presidential Council" on race. While John Hope Franklin has persevered remarkably well as a historian, he has also lent his considerable talents and energy to solving racial problems. In so doing, he has demonstrated that he believes America will fulfill its destiny only when equality becomes the birthright of all Americans, regardless of race or national origin.

BIBLIOGRAPHY

Franklin, John Hope. "The Dilemma of the American Negro Scholar." In *Race and History: Selected Essays, 1938–1988*. 1989.

Franklin, John Hope. "The Enforcement of the Civil Rights Act of 1875." *Prologue* 6 (Winter 1974): 225–35.

Franklin, John Hope. *Racial Equality in America*. 1976.

Franklin, John Hope, and Moss, Alfred. *From Slavery to Freedom: A History of African Americans*, 7th ed. 1994.

Loren Schweninger

Freedmen's Bureau

See Bureau of Refugees, Freedmen, and Abandoned Lands.

Freedom (publication)

Freedom was a monthly publication produced by African Americans in tabloid newspaper format that championed the causes of civil liberties, labor unions, and rights of the working class from January 1951 to August 1955. Its publisher was listed as Freedom Associates, located on West 125th Street in New York City. For most of its nearly five-year existence *Freedom* was edited by Louis E. Burnham, with George B. Murphy, Jr., serving as general manager.

Perhaps the most eminent personality associated with the journal's editorial board was Paul Robeson, who was its chairman. Most issues ran to eight pages and included a column by Robeson entitled "Here's My Story," a black history feature for young readers entitled "Stories for Children," and a page devoted to "News of Colored Peoples in Other Lands: Africa, Asia, Caribbeans, Latin America." Another frequent feature was "News Around the Nation," listing items of interest reprinted by *Freedom* from other black newspapers.

Among the major campaigns waged by *Freedom* were efforts to restore Robeson's passport after his freedom to travel had been restricted by U.S. government officials and support for the legal challenges to school segregation that culminated in the *Brown v. Board of Education* decision by the U.S. Supreme Court in 1954. (*See* BROWN V. TOPEKA BOARD OF EDUCATION.)

Freedom attracted a distinguished coterie of contributing writers, including W. E. B. Du Bois, John Henrik Clarke, Herbert Aptheker, and Lorraine Hansberry. Hansberry served as the publication's Associate Editor, a post she held when the publication folded with the July–August issue in 1955.

BIBLIOGRAPHY

Freedom, vol. I, no. 1 through vol. I, no. 6.

Clint C. Wilson II

Freedom Democratic Party, Mississippi

See Mississippi Freedom Democratic Party.

Freedom Rides

What is traditionally called the Freedom Ride Movement began on May 4, 1961. It was sponsored by the

On May 14, 1961, Freedom Riders stand next to their bus after the vehicle was set on fire by a mob that had followed it out of Anniston, Alabama. (CORBIS/ Bettmann)

CONGRESS OF RACIAL EQUALITY (CORE) and involved national director James FARMER and, at the start, thirteen other Freedom Riders traveling by bus from Washington, D.C., to New Orleans, Louisiana. Many more joined later. Their objective was to test the enforcement of a recent Supreme Court decision, the *Boynton v. Virginia* case. The 1960 *Boynton* decision declared that segregated interstate transportation facilities were unconstitutional. Its legal precedents were the MORGAN V. VIRGINIA Supreme Court decision of 1946 and the *Keys v. Carolina Coach Company* ruling by the Interstate Commerce Commission in 1955.

James Farmer and CORE members had also assessed the enforcement of the *Morgan* decision in 1947 when they participated in a "Journey of Reconciliation" through four states in the upper South. What they found was that the ruling was being ignored, and they were arrested for their efforts.

In May 1961, Farmer and another group of nonviolent activists set out in hopes that they would have better luck in the enforcement of the *Boynton* decision. The passengers were a diverse group of men and women of different races. The many problems that attended this Freedom Ride varied, from fistfights at terminals to the firebombing of a bus to unbridled mob violence in Birmingham and Montgomery, Alabama. The Freedom Riders themselves were assaulted and arrested, and some were permanently injured. Po-

lice protection tended to be sporadic at best, with an occasional conspiracy between policemen and members of the mob that allowed the mob to have a free rein in committing a wide range of outrages.

The Birmingham mob violence was especially brutal, to such an extent that Farmer considered ending the project. What changed his mind was a new influx of civil rights devotees from the Nashville Student Movement. In workshops held on the campus of Fisk University in Nashville, Tennessee, these young people had been carefully trained in the philosophy and tactics of nonviolence. It was this group that led the Freedom Ride from Birmingham to Montgomery, where mob violence again erupted.

In Montgomery, the Freedom Riders took some time to recuperate and attend strategy meetings. At this point, a different type of social activist joined the movement. Less committed to the principles of nonviolence than previous Freedom Riders had been, these activists had the courage and determination that made terminating the Freedom Ride, as some had suggested, unthinkable.

It was this reinvigorated group of Freedom Riders that traveled on to Jackson, Mississippi. As soon as they were identified as Freedom Riders by the authorities in Jackson, they were arrested. And yet their spirits and their numbers were unabated. New busloads of Freedom Riders continued to arrive. By this time, there was no single group or philosophy behind the Freedom Rides. Whites felt that they belonged in this movement as much as blacks, and women as much as men. The Freedom Riders were fined $200 and sentenced to sixty days in Mississippi's PARCHMAN FARM prison, notorious for its mistreatment of its inmates.

Despite the abuses they received, the Freedom Riders eventually served out their terms and returned to their homes. The Freedom Rides did not end with this, however. Americans sympathetic to the cause of freedom continued to engage in such enterprises throughout the summer of 1961. Ultimately, the obstacles to interstate travel that had so harried blacks were overcome, and the chief beneficiary was the nation.

BIBLIOGRAPHY

Barnes, Catherine A. *Journey from Jim Crow: the Desegregation of Southern Transit*. 1983.

Farmer, James. *Lay Bare the Heart: An Autobiography of the Civil Rights Movement*. 1998.

Forman, James. *The Making of Black Revolutionaries*. 1985.

Garrow, David. *Bearing the Cross*. 1986.

Lewis, John. *Walking with the Wind, a Memoir of the Movement*. 1998.

Meier, August, and Elliott Rudwick. "The First Freedom Ride," *Phylon* XXX (Fall 1969): 213–222.

O'Reilley, Kenneth. "The FBI and the Civil Rights Movement," *Journal of Southern History* LIV (May, 1988): 201–232.

Stoper, Emily. *The Student Nonviolent Coordinating Committee*. 1968.

A. D. Simmons

Freedom Schools

Freedom schools, also known as "community schools," were alternative, informal, community-based schools organized to prepare students for liberation from oppressive forces and for sociopolitical empowerment. Different types of freedom schools were organized by various racial and ethnic groups during the social movements of the 1960s and 1970s; however, the black freedom schools in MISSISSIPPI are best known for contributions to the civil rights struggle and racial integration.

Mississippi freedom schools were organized by Charles Cobb, Robert MOSES, and Staughton Lynd during the FREEDOM SUMMER of 1964, when thousands of black and white college students, many from outside Mississippi, risked their lives by engaging in interracial community organizing throughout the racially segregated state. Whereas the CITIZENSHIP SCHOOLS founded by Septima Clark were specifically designed to teach adult literacy for voter registration and citizenship, the Mississippi freedom schools were designed to teach a range of skills and activities promoting individual freedom and interracial contact for children and youth as well as adults, usually black, who lived in fear and isolation. Freedom schools as organizing tools had a broader scope but less longevity and geographical coverage than citizenship schools. They concentrated on local people in rural areas of Mississippi, such as Philadelphia, McComb, Jackson, Tougaloo, Ruleville, Meridian, Indianola, Natchez, Vicksburg, Biloxi, Greenville, Greenwood, and Canton.

Although there was not a great deal of uniformity in their structure, most freedom schools were placed in or near black neighborhoods, had average-size classes of fifteen to twenty students in churches or outdoors, involved the active participation of students, parents, and local people in key decision making, taught remedial and basic curricula, and exposed students to African-American history, heroes, and heroines. Freedom school teachers, among them Bob Moses, Ruby Doris Smith ROBINSON, Doris Derby, Casey HAYDEN, and Joyce Ladner, included white and black college students as instructors, and encouraged black Mississippians to question their government and its Europe-centered history. The schools did not operate freely and peacefully at all times; rather they (often) encountered virulent opposition from white segregationists, which even took the form of late night bullets and fire bombs.

Through mass meetings, voter registration campaigns, Freedom Singers, newspapers, plays, freedom libraries, and communal living, teachers exposed black children and adults to positive interracial interactions for the first times in their lives, taught subjects relevant to their everyday experiences, and widened the horizons of poor blacks living in racial isolation.

BIBLIOGRAPHY

Barnett, Bernice McNair. "Sisters in Struggle: Invisible Black Women Leaders of the Civil Rights Movement, 1940–1975." Forthcoming.

Dittmer, John. *Local People*. 1995.

Payne, Charles. *I've Got the Light of Freedom: The Organizing Tradition in Mississippi*. 1995.

McAdam, Doug. *Freedom Summer*. 1988.

Zinn, Howard. *SNCC: The 1960s Freedom Struggle*. 1969.

Bernice McNair Barnett

Freedom's People

"Freedom's People," a radio program featuring prominent black Americans of the World War II era, debuted in September 1941 on NBC's Red network. The U.S. Office of Education sponsored and produced the show to promote national unity and improve race relations. The series of monthly educational shows strove to portray the contributions blacks have made to American culture and civilization. It featured music, dramatic presentations, and interviews to advance its message of racial equality. It was the brainchild of Ambrose Caliver, the highest ranking black in the education office. NBC resisted the idea at first, calling it "propaganda" for blacks. It relented on the condition that the show be primarily entertainment-oriented.

The first show dealt with black contributions to American music, showing the origins of Negro spirituals, ballads and blues. Renowned singer and actor Paul ROBESON, whom *Time* magazine in 1943 called "the most famous living Negro," hosted the inaugural show. The program showcased some of the premier black musicians of the time. Performers included jazzman Noble Sissle and his orchestra, renowned blues composer W. C. Handy, and balladeer Joshua White. But the rich, towering voice of Robeson singing the Negro spirituals, "Swing Low, Sweet Chariot," and "No More" highlighted the truly extraordinary show.

The next three shows dealt with arts and literature, science, and sports. The science show featured a narrative on black explorer Matthew Henson, who accompanied Robert Peary to the North Pole. It closed with a live narrative of agricultural scientist George Washington CARVER. Live interviews also highlighted the segment on sports, with appearances by Olympic gold medallist Jesse Owens and boxing great Joe Louis. Musical performances by such legendary black artists as Cab Calloway and Count Basie punctuated the broadcasts.

Other shows centered on blacks in education, the military, and the workplace. The military episode aired just two weeks after the Japanese attack on Pearl Harbor. IT featured short dramatizations of black participation in past wars. In the next program, about achievements by black workers, African-American labor activist A. Philip RANDOLPH spoke live about discrimination in defense plants. In the final episode of "Freedom's People," Caliver linked Christianity and democracy with racial equality. The show featured a speech by Rev. W. H. Jernagin, president of the Fraternal Council of Negro Churches. Jernagin said churches must take an active role in promoting equality in economic, social and public institutions.

The original episodes, which are held at the National Archives' motion picture, sound and video branch in College Park, Maryland, remain a somewhat obscure but landmark event in the civil rights struggle. For the first time, a major radio network series dealt exclusively with black contributions to American society. Critics argue that the show dealt with racial equality in a limited and indirect way, using entertainment as the medium for the message. Yet a more direct approach likely would have made the series unacceptable to the radio networks and Office of Education. It also might have alienated a substantial portion of the show's white listeners. Caliver proposed a second series of ten to twelve "Freedom's People" shows but neither NBC nor the Office of Education pursued the idea.

BIBLIOGRAPHY

Barlow, William. "Radio." In *Encyclopedia of African-American Culture and History,* edited by Jack Salzman, David Lionel Smith, and Cornel West. 1996.

Savage, Barbara Dianne. *Broadcasting Freedom: Radio, War, and the Politics of Race 1938–1948.* 1999.

"For Native Sons," *Time Magazine* (September 29, 1941): 38.

"Freedom's People, New Radio Series," *School Life* 27 (November 1941): 38

Ken R. Wells

Freedom Summer (1964)

Initiated by the COUNCIL OF FEDERATED ORGANIZATIONS, the Freedom Summer project attempted the reformation of Mississippi politics and society. Approximately 1,000 volunteers, mostly white college students, established Freedom Schools and voter registration projects to accomplish that goal.

FREEDOM SCHOOLS combined instruction in academic subjects, cultural studies, and leadership development. Nearly half of the student volunteers taught an estimated 3,500 black Mississippians in the schools.

The cornerstone of Freedom Summer was a statewide voter registration project. Volunteers attempted to register African Americans to vote in the November 1964 presidential election and in a mock election for alternative delegates to the Democratic national convention.

Thousands of blacks registered in their homes for the mock election. The MISSISSIPPI FREEDOM DEMOCRATIC PARTY (MFDP) delegation they elected to the Democratic convention, however, was not fully recognized or allowed seats. White resistance hindered registration for the presidential election. Of the 17,000 African Americans who attempted to register, only 1,600 succeeded.

Freedom Summer was the pinnacle of the mass movement for civil rights reform in Mississippi. It was also the pinnacle of massive resistance. By the end of the summer, four black Mississippians were killed. Scores of volunteers and participants were beaten; more than 1,000 arrests were made; and nearly seventy churches, homes, and businesses (two-thirds of them in McComb) were burned or bombed.

While the immediate results of Freedom Schools and the voter registration project might be considered minimal, their long-term impact was impressive. The MFDP struggle at the Democratic convention attracted powerful supporters to its cause and to the VOTING RIGHTS ACT OF 1965. Freedom Schools and the voter registration project functioned as cornerstones for community projects, voter education, and voter registration projects.

BIBLIOGRAPHY

Belfrage, Sally. *Freedom Summer* 1965.
McAdam, Doug. *Freedom Summer.* 1988.
Mills, Nicolaus. *Like a Holy Crusade: Mississippi, 1964—The Turning of the Civil Rights Movement in America.* 1992.

Bradley G. Bond

Freedomways

Freedomways was a quarterly literary and social commentary magazine embracing issues of civil rights and PAN-AFRICANISM that began publication in 1961 and continued until 1985. Its subtitle was "A Quarterly Review of the Negro Freedom Movement." The salutatory article in the inaugural issue of May 1, 1961, described the journal's editorial objective as "a public forum for the review, examination, and debate of all problems confronting Negroes in the United States." It also sought to furnish "*accurate* information on the liberation movements in Africa itself." During its second year, it began to include poetry and short stories by black authors.

Although the magazine listed its publisher as Freedomways Associates, Inc., of New York City, its first editor was Shirley Graham, wife of the noted historian and sociologist W. E. B. DU BOIS. Over the years *Freedomways* published numerous articles by and about Du Bois and his philosophies. Graham served on the editorial staff until her death in 1977. Other contributors included Kwame Nkrumah, Jesse JACKSON, Ossie Davis, Lorraine HANSBERRY, and Jomo Kenyatta.

Never a financially stable enterprise during its twenty-four-year existence, *Freedomways* contained little advertising and depended upon private donations and various fund-raising events for support. Circulation peaked at approximately 7,000, although the actual number was usually under that figure. In 1975 *Freedomways* reported its paid circulation as 5,700. By that time it had survived a near-disastrous fire in 1970 in which its uninsured building suffered heavy damage. Throughout its history, *Freedomways* stayed true to its original mission of reporting on the African-American freedom struggle and related freedom struggles worldwide.

BIBLIOGRAPHY

Kaiser, Ernest, ed. *A Freedomways Reader.* 1977.
Wolseley, Roland E. *The Black Press U.S.A.* 1990.

Clint C. Wilson II

Free Speech Movement

What is known as the Free Speech Movement is best described by a series of events that took place at the University of California at Berkeley in late 1964. These events commenced a decade of unrest and protest on American college campuses which began over civil rights and political free speech, and culminated in massive anti-war protests over U.S. involvement in VIET NAM.

The beginning of the Free Speech Movement occurred at the Republican National Convention in June of 1964. Barry GOLDWATER was nominated for president, and his supporters accused his opponents of illegally recruiting student volunteers from the Berkeley campus. On September 4, 1964, the Ad Hoc Committee to End Discrimination picketed the *Oakland Tribune* newspaper offices with recruits from the Berkeley campus.

Ten days later, the university administration decided to enforce campus rules against the collection of funds and the use of university facilities for the planning and implementation of off-campus political and social action. Citing interference with the flow of traffic, posters, easels, and tables used to solicit political activism were banned.

On September 17 and 18, twenty diverse campus organizations came together to form a coalition called the United Front. These organizations covered the spectrum of political philosophy at Berkeley, ranging from the left-leaning STUDENTS FOR A DEMOCRATIC SOCIETY and the CONGRESS OF RACIAL EQUALITY to more conservative groups such as Youth for Goldwater and the Young Republicans. The United Front also counted religious organizations such as the Inter-Faith Council among its ranks.

The United Front announced its opposition to the ban on political activism on campus. In response, the university administration qualified its position by proclaiming that while informational activity was allowed, advocacy of action was not. The United Front viewed this stance as an unconstitutional abridgement of their freedom of speech and held a protest rally on the steps of Sproul Hall, the Berkeley administration building.

Mario Savio leading a Free Speech demonstration at the University of California at Berkeley in 1964. (AP/Wide World Photos)

The tense situation escalated when the university took disciplinary action against five students. On October 1, over 3,000 demonstrators blocked a police car holding activist Jack Weinberg. The next day, 450 police assembled on campus to free the police car, while negotiations between the administration and protest leaders led to the dispersal of the protesters, the release of Weinberg, and an agreement for the two sides to discuss differences.

On October 3–4, 1964, the United Front evolved into the Free Speech Movement (FSM), and it was in this vein that the protest leaders participated in discussions with the administration over campus political issues. Negotiations continued into November (as did on-campus protests and demonstrations) until the chancellor of the university suspended negotiations on November 9.

The Berkeley administration then softened its regulations to allow for the demanded political activities, but with restrictions on where they could be performed. Protests continued over disciplinary actions against student leaders with a rally of 4,000 at Sproul Hall on November 20, culminating with a rally of 6,000 on December 2. About a thousand of those demonstrators took over Sproul Hall and occupied it for the

night, before the police arrived to clear the hall and arrest the demonstrators. At this point, the Academic Senate became involved, and the school faculty raised $8,500 towards bail for students and sent resolutions to the school administration urging compromise.

On December 8, 1964, the demonstrations and protests ended with the Academic Senate's approval of free speech reforms and appeal procedures for students facing disciplinary actions. However, a significant period of campus protest and upheaval had begun in the United States.

BIBLIOGRAPHY

Free Speech Movement Web Site. http://www.straw. com/fsm-a/

Robinson, Greg. "San Francisco and Oakland." In *Encyclopedia of African-American Culture and History*, edited by Jack Salzman, David Lionel Smith, and Cornel West. 1996.

Rossman, Michael. "Looking Back at the Free Speech Movement [1974]." *California Monthly* (December 1974).

Sigler, Jay A., ed. "Freedom of Speech." *Civil Rights in America: 1500 to the Present.* 1998.

Weinberg, Jack. "The Free Speech Movement and Civil Rights." *University of California, Campus CORElator.* (January 1965).

Michael Dawson

Friedan, Betty

(1921–), feminist, founded National Organization of Women.

Sometimes called the "mother of the modern women's movement," Betty Friedan with her critique of women's subordination in the domestic sphere helped galvanize the second feminist movement. Raised in New Jersey, she became a journalist after her graduation from Smith in 1942, but abandoned her career after marrying and starting a family. Questioning her classmates at their fifteenth reunion, Friedan discov-ered that many women's lives did not match the picture of domestic bliss depicted in the media. In *The Feminine Mystique* (1963), Friedan argued that there was a conspiracy on the part of the media, advertisers, and psychologists to convince women they could find fulfillment only in their domestic role. Yet, Friedan claimed, women were dissatisfied with their lives as suburban housewives and needed to regain a sense of their identity through opportunities for work outside the home. Her analysis resonated with many middle-class American women; the book sold over a million copies and is credited with reviving feminism. In 1966, Friedan founded the NATIONAL ORGANIZATION OF WOMEN to help women take advantage of the protection against employment discrimination written into the 1964 Civil Rights Act. She served as NOW's president until 1970, and campaigned for the EQUAL RIGHTS AMENDMENT and for abortion rights. Yet Friedan, a liberal feminist who sought women's integration into existing social and political structures, was soon challenged by radical feminists who developed critiques of capitalism and of patriarchy. Friedan criticized radical feminists for being antimale and for focusing too much on "bedroom" issues and sexual politics; she was criticized for her white, middle-class outlook and her disapproval of lesbianism. By the early 1980s, Friedan was arguing that feminism had become too woman-centered, and that in "the second stage" of the movement, women and men would have to learn to work together to come up with new ways to reconcile work and family life. In recent years, Friedan has written about aging, arguing that aging should be seen as an opportunity rather than a threat.

American feminist writer Betty Friedan. The button she is wearing says, "August 26/Women's Strike for Equality." (Archive Photos)

BIBLIOGRAPHY

Friedan, Betty. *It Changed My Life: Writings on the Women's Movement.* 1976.
Friedan, Betty. *The Second Stage.* 1981.
Friedan, Betty. *The Fountain of Age.* 1993.
Reynolds, Moira Davison. *Women Champions of Human Rights.* 1991.

Renee Romano

G

Galarza, Ernesto

(1905–1984), Latino civil rights and labor leader.

Ernesto Galarza was one of the most prominent Latino labor and civil rights leaders of the twentieth century. During World War II he played a leading role for the Pan American Union (today known as the Organization of American States, or OAS). The government of Bolivia awarded Galarza the "Order of the Condor Medal," the highest honor given to a noncitizen of Bolivia, for promoting human rights and democracy in the Americas. He led the first farmworker union (the National Farm Labor Union) created in the United States in 1947 and dissolved only in 1960 and cofounded the nation's most prominent Latino civil rights organization, the National Council of La Raza, in 1967.

Galarza was also a Renaissance man. His over one hundred published works are wide-ranging and diverse. He was a poet, a writer of children's literature, and a social scientist and historian who transcended rigid disciplinary boundaries. His collective works contributed to laying the foundation for Chicano and Chicana studies as a new interdisciplinary field of critical scholarship in higher education. In 1979, Galarza became the first Mexican American to be nominated for the Nobel Prize in Literature.

Galarza was born in a small, isolated mountain village called Jalcocotán near Nayarit, Mexico, a village founded by the indigenous Huichol people of that region. He came to the United States with his mother at the age of eight during the 1910 Mexican Revolution

and settled in Sacramento, California. Graduating Phi Beta Kappa from Occidental College in 1927, Galarza earned his M.A. in Latin American history from Stanford University in 1929 and his Ph.D. in political science and history from Columbia University in 1944.

Galarza and his wife, Mae, founded a private elementary school in Long Island, New York, in 1932. They named it the "Year-Long School" and developed a curriculum that promoted the ideals and objectives of progressive public education. During World War II, Galarza created and headed the Division of Labor and Social Information on Latin America for the Pan American Union, for which he traveled throughout the Americas promoting and advocating the rights of workers to organize labor unions. Galarza resigned in 1947 because of his public opposition to U.S. foreign policy and in particular because of U.S. support for military dictatorships in Latin America.

In 1948, Galarza became a key organizer and leader of the National Farm Labor Union (NFLU), which had evolved from the SOUTHERN TENANT FARMERS' UNION, a forerunner of the civil rights movement in the South. He was assigned the task of building the first farmworkers' union in CALIFORNIA. Galarza led numerous strikes against major agri-business corporations and confronted their political allies in state and federal governments. Galarza's farmworkers' union set the foundation for the later emergence of the UNITED FARM WORKERS under the leadership of César CHÁVEZ in the 1960s.

Galarza retired from the LABOR MOVEMENT in 1960 but did not end his activism. He became part of President Lyndon B. Johnson's WAR ON POVERTY as a

305

member of the Federal Economic and Youth Opportunities Agency and labor counsel to the Committee on Education and Labor of the U.S. House of Representatives, chaired at the time by Adam Clayton POW-ELL, Jr. Galarza became a community organizer in San Jose, California, and fought hard for the survival of a Latino *barrio* called "Alviso," whose extinction was imminent as a consequence of urban renewal. In 1967, he co-founded the Southwest Council of La Raza, which evolved into the national civil rights organization the National Council of La Raza.

Galarza's published academic writings collectively contribute to the critical understanding of the exploitative conditions faced by American farmworkers. Several of his books were benchmarks. His *Merchants of Labor: The Bracero Story* exposed the Mexican "guest" worker program created by the U.S. Congress during World War II and contributed to the termination of that program. In *Spiders in the House and Workers in the Fields*, Dr. Galarza showed how laws, government regulations, and government agencies were manipulated to undermine the struggle to unionize farmworkers. His last major work, *Farm Workers and Agri-Business in California*, captures in dramatic fashion the rise of agricultural corporate power. His autobiography, *Barrio Boy*, was praised by the *New York Times* for "redefining the American experience."

BIBLIOGRAPHY

"Activism and Struggle in the Life of Ernesto Galarza." *Hispanic Journal of Behavioral Sciences* 7, no. 2 (June 1985): 135–152.

Galarza, Ernesto. *Barrio Boy: The Story of a Boy's Acculturation.* 1971.

Carlos Muñoz, Jr.

Gandhi, Mohandas Karamchand ("Mahatma")

(1869–1948), Indian independence leader.

As spiritual and tactical leader of the movement for Indian independence from British rule, former lawyer Mahatma Gandhi led the effort to rid India of its caste system and was a key negotiator in 1947 as British India was divided into the independent nations of India and Pakistan. He was felled by a fanatic's bullet in 1948.

The African-American civil rights movement owes much to the teachings of Mahatma Gandhi and his nonviolent campaign for Indian independence. From the 1920s on, the African-American press followed events in India closely, hailing Gandhi as an inspirational, saintly figure, debating the applicability of Gan-

Indian leader Mahatma Gandhi stands in a traditional sari, ca. 1940. (Archive Photos)

dhian tactics to the African-American predicament, and appealing for a "Black Gandhi" to rise up in America to lead the freedom struggle.

Gandhian ideas were further disseminated as a result of personal contacts with Gandhi and his followers. Krishnalal Shridharani, for example, visited America in 1934. His guide to the use of Gandhian ideas in the United States, *War Without Violence*, greatly influenced the CONGRESS OF RACIAL EQUALITY (CORE) and informed its 1947 Journey of Reconciliation. A. Philip RANDOLPH's canceled March on Washington in 1941—one of the earliest black campaigns to employ Gandhian notions of nonviolent pressure—was similarly influenced by Shridharani's work.

Several African-American preachers, scholars, and teachers also met Gandhi or his disciples in India, returning to educate others about the philosophy and practice of nonviolent protest. Influential visitors included three successive deans of Howard University, Howard Thurman in 1935, Benjamin MAYS in 1936, and Mordecai Johnson in 1949, a year after Gandhi's assassination, as well as James Lawson, who became leader of the Nashville civil rights movement, William Stuart Nelson of the AMERICAN FRIENDS SERVICE COMMITTEE, and Bayard RUSTIN, a founding member of CORE. These individuals served as important interpreters of Gandhian tactics for the generation of African-American activists who spearheaded the nonviolent direct action campaigns of the 1950s and 1960s, most notably Martin Luther KING, JR.

By the time King himself visited India in 1959, he was already celebrated as the leading proponent of Gandhian tactics in the African-American freedom struggle. During the early stages of the MONTGOMERY BUS BOYCOTT he had received considerable strategic advice and moral encouragement from the likes of Thurman, Mays, Johnson, and Nelson, who quickly saw him as their long-awaited "Black Gandhi"—rather more quickly, it should be noted, than King saw himself in that role. Nevertheless, under the close tutelage of Rustin and Glenn Smiley of the FELLOWSHIP OF RECONCILIATION, King eventually embraced nonviolence as both the most effective and the most morally sound tactic for black deliverance, and as a way of life.

Eclectic innovators rather than doctrinaire purists, African-American activists such as King did not borrow Gandhi's teachings wholesale. Instead, they selected those aspects of his philosophy that were particularly appropriate to the American context, adapting them to fit the needs of an oppressed minority, rather than the oppressed majority that Gandhi had led. Certainly, the Mahatma's idea of *satyagraha* (love force), whereby the oppressed would win freedom, and ultimately the hearts of their enemies, by their capacity to suffer and love was retained; but it was recast in terms of a Christian vision of redemptive love in order to appeal to the Southern black masses who formed the vanguard of the freedom struggle.

BIBLIOGRAPHY

Anderson, Jervis. *Bayard Rustin: Troubles I've Seen, A Biography.* 1997.
Branch, Taylor. *Parting the Waters: America in the King Years, 1954–1963.* 1988.
Kapur, Sudarshan. *Raising Up a Prophet: The African-American Encounter with Gandhi.* 1992.
Miller, Keith D. *Voice of Deliverance: The Language of Martin Luther King, Jr. and Its Sources.* 1992.
"Mohandas Karamchand Gandhi." In *The Concise Columbia Encyclopedia*, 2nd ed., edited by Barbara A. Chernow and George A. Vallasi. 1989.
Shridharani, Krishnalal. *War Without Violence: A Study of Gandhi's Method and Its Accomplishments.* 1939.

Jenny Walker

Garvey, Marcus Mosiah

(1887–1940), Pan-Africanist, journalist, and black nationalist.

Marcus Garvey, the founder of the UNIVERSAL NEGRO IMPROVEMENT ASSOCIATION (UNIA), was a charismatic orator who organized the first black mass protest movement in the history of the United States. Garvey's black nationalist movement in the 1920s was a forerunner of the BLACK POWER phase of the civil rights movement in the 1960s. (See also PAN-AFRICANISM.) He promoted Garveyism, an ideology that advocated black nationalism at the economic, religious, cultural, territorial, and social levels; black self-determination; and African redemption. With the central focus on the goodness of blackness, Garveyism preached the power of the black race, the evil doings of the white race, and

Within a decade of founding the Universal Negro Improvement Association (UNIA) in Jamaica in 1914, Marcus Garvey built the UNIA into the largest independent African-American political association in the United States. (Prints and Photographs Division, Library of Congress)

the need for all blacks to "return to Africa." Garveyism was predicated on the belief that blacks could achieve equality only by becoming independent of whites and by establishing their own businesses, governments, and nation-states.

Marcus Garvey was born August 17, 1887, in St. Ann's Bay, Jamaica, British West Indies, to Marcus and Sarah Garvey. As the youngest of eleven children born to parents of maroon descent (pure African heritage), Garvey developed a strong sense of racial pride. He completed a few years of elementary school, became an apprentice to a printer in Kingston, Jamaica, and dropped out of school at the age of fourteen. However, by the age of twenty Garvey had educated himself, especially about the experiences and hardships suffered by the poor, and had begun to oppose British colonial rule in Jamaica. In 1910, Garvey traveled to South and Central America, where he was repulsed by the exploitation of blacks. This later reinforced his philosophy of black independence and equality with whites. Garvey reasoned that the only way to aid black people in "uplifting" themselves would be to instill in them a sense of self-esteem and pride and to encourage them to celebrate their African past. For the problems blacks faced, Garvey proposed a twofold nationalist solution: (1) blacks should achieve economic security by the building of their own enterprises and banding together; and (2) blacks should create a great new African empire.

To implement his vision, Garvey founded the United Negro Improvement Association (UNIA) in Jamaica in 1911. Garvey led the UNIA in its promotion of racial pride, unity, and international commerce. In 1916 Garvey traveled to the United States and formed another branch of the UNIA in Harlem, New York City, where he promoted his commercial ventures and "Back to Africa" programs. Gaining considerable interest from black city dwellers, whose suffering from racial violence and economic discrimination was perhaps greatest, Garvey recruited thousands into the UNIA. He used his skills as a journalist and created the UNIA's weekly newspaper *The Negro World*, which began publication in New York in 1919 and had a weekly circulation of over 200,000.

With considerable economic support from his constituents, Garvey established branches of the UNIA throughout the United States. Having been positively impressed by Booker T. WASHINGTON's emphasis on black self-help and vocational education at Tuskegee Institute, Garvey started the Black Star Line (an African-American steamship company). Garvey provided loans and technical assistance to blacks who wanted to start their own businesses and sold stock in his own business at $5.00 a share. After this, there were talks between Garvey and the government of Liberia con-

cerning the transportation of American blacks "back to Africa." However, fearing that Garvey would seize power once an African-American colony was established, advocates of Garvey's "Back to Africa" campaign withdrew their support from the plan. This was not the first time Garvey encountered opposition from black contemporaries. An early admirer of Booker T. Washington's advocacy of the self-help approach to racial uplift and accommodation to racial segregation, Garvey had tense relationships with W. E. B. Du Bois and other leaders of the NATIONAL ORGANIZATION FOR THE ADVANCEMENT OF COLORED PEOPLE (NAACP), which emphasized racial integration and civil rights over economic self-determination. Moreover, Garvey's support of white segregationists' opposition to racial mixing and his endorsement of the Ku Klux Klan belief in racial purity and racial separatism outraged Du Bois and other black integrationists.

Garvey's cooperative business ventures began to tumble. Overwhelmed with legal and financial difficulties and the distancing of his "supporters," Garvey traveled abroad in an attempt to raise funds for his foundering company and dwindling dreams of racial uplift. At the same time, the U.S. government was building a case against him. Charging him with the misuse of the U.S. mail service and the misappropriation of funds from Black Star Line investors, Garvey was convicted of mail fraud and sentenced to prison in 1925. After serving two years of a five-year sentence, Garvey was released and deported back to his homeland of Jamaica in 1927. While in Jamaica, he attempted to construct a political base for the rebuilding and reconstruction of his dream. In 1935, Garvey and his second wife Amy Jacques Garvey went to London, England, where he died in 1940.

BIBLIOGRAPHY

Cronon, Edmund David. *Black Moses: The Story of Marcus Garvey and the Universal Negro Improvement Association*, 1962.

Garvey, Amy Jacques. *Garvey and Garveyism*, 1963.

Hill, Robert, ed. *The Marcus Garvey and Universal Negro Improvement Papers*, 1983–1990.

Donny C. Barnett

Gay Activists Alliance

Founded in New York City in December 1969, a few months after the STONEWALL RIOTS in Greenwich Village spawned a gay liberation movement, an organization that took the name Gay Activists Alliance (GAA) began direct-action protests in quest of civil rights and protection for homosexuals. Made up in part of drop-outs from an earlier alliance—the anarchic and leftist Gay Liberation Front (GLF)—as well as previously non-aligned gay males and lesbians, in the following months GAA established itself as an energetic programmer of marches, picket lines, sit-ins, political lobbying, educational pamphleteering, and "zaps"—confrontations that embarrassed or befuddled persons or organizations who denigrated homosexuals or who hounded or criminally entrapped them.

In its weekly general meetings, Gay Activists Alliance was also a promoter of gay self-respect and self-affirmation; thousands of "closeted" homosexual men and women soon either joined or supported the Alliance. Modeling itself to some extent on the African-American civil rights movement, which proclaimed that "Black Is Beautiful," GAA declared that "Gay Is Good" and encouraged "Gay Pride." The Greek letter *lambda*, used by chemists and physicists to symbolize an exchange of energy, was adopted by the very energetic GAA; on flags and banners it was yellow-gold on a blue background. By the late 1970s, there were dozens of GAA branches across the country.

In 1973, GAA Washington (D.C.) succeeded in securing passage of the D.C. Human Rights Law, one of the first legislative attempts to ban discrimination against gays and lesbians. Among GAA New York's challenges were: a sit-in at the offices of Governor Nelson Rockefeller on behalf of state civil rights legislation for homosexuals; a face-to-face protest with editors of the New York *Daily News*, as well as at *Harper's* magazine, in response to the publication of anti-gay articles; confrontations with both CBS and ABC News men and women whose reportage had disparaged the homosexual lifestyle (the "Dick Cavett Show" was obliged to grant show time nationally to GAA spokespersons); occupation of the district attorneys' offices in Hauppauge, Long Island, and Bridgeport, Connecticut, to protest police harassment and the beating of several Alliance members; a meeting with a representative of the Archdiocese of New York to denounce the Catholic Church's continuing opposition to homosexual civil rights; and the lobbying of the American Psychiatric Association in a successful effort to remove homosexuality from the APA's list of psychiatric disorders. The passing of New York City's Gay Civil Rights Bill—long a goal of GAA—took place in 1986; it affirmed another GAA objective: "a fair employment act to outlaw discrimination on the basis of sexual orientation."

BIBLIOGRAPHY

Alwood, Edward. *Straight News: Gays, Lesbians and the News Media.* 1996.
Fisher, Peter. *The Gay Mystique.* 1972.
Hogan, Steve, and Lee Hudson. *Completely Queer: The Gay and Lesbian Encyclopedia.* 1998.
Kaiser, Charles. *The Gay Metropolis 1940–1996.* 1997.
Loughery, John. *The Other Side of Silence: Men's Lives and Gay Identities—A Twentieth-Century History.* 1998.
Marotta, Toby. *The Politics of Homosexuality.* 1981.
Teal, Donn. *The Gay Militants: How Gay Liberation Began in America, 1969–1971.* 2nd ed. 1995.
Tobin (Lahusen), Kay, and Randy Wicker. *The Gay Crusaders.* 1975.

Marc Rubin
Donn Teal

Gay and Lesbian Rights

Although the first decades of the twentieth century were a period of visibility in some urban settings for gay men and lesbians, the end of Prohibition corresponded with the end of this openness and the start of an era in which a nearly absolute denial of social and political rights for gays and lesbians who expressed their sexual orientation existed across the United States. The Red Scare era marked the height of public animosity against gay men and lesbians during the century, with "perverts" in government linked with communists as the key threats to American national autonomy (see MCCARTHYISM). American media coverage of gay life continually reinforced negative stereotypes about gays and lesbians and the notion that homosexuality was a mental illness. (See HOMOPHOBIA.)

Out of this deep suppression, a disorganized HOMOPHILE MOVEMENT did arise in the United States. In 1951, the MATTACHINE SOCIETY was founded in Los Angeles; led by Harry HAY and committed to both social and political advances for gays, the male-dominated organization grew in urban settings during the decade. The first postwar lesbian organization, the DAUGHTERS OF BILITIS, was founded in San Francisco in 1955. Although later East Coast branches of the organizations were more aggressive in their stances, the members of the organizations, in general, emphasized the meaninglessness of the difference between homosexuals and heterosexuals ("straights") and argued for their right to assimilate into straight-dominated society. Orderly protests—such as those at the White House in 1965—tended to focus on issues such as employment discrimination within the federal government.

The STONEWALL RIOTS of June 1969 in New York's Greenwich Village and the flurry of activities in their immediate aftermath helped to create a dramatic increase in visible activism by gay men and lesbians and a split within the movement between assimilationists and those espousing a more radical "Gay Is Good"

Participants in the Gay Rights March in Washington, D.C., in October 1987, hold a street-wide cloth placard proclaiming the kinship of their movement with the civil rights movement. (CORBIS/Lee Snider)

ideology, such as the members of the New York City-based Gay Liberation Front (GLF). Of these new organizations, the most stable was the GAY ACTIVISTS ALLIANCE, which steered an ideological middle path between the Mattachine Society and GLF.

During the 1970s, the battle for gay and lesbian rights remained primarily localized, with significant successes. By early 1974, seven American cities had adopted ordinances that provided some level of protection from discrimination against gays and lesbians in employment and housing. Gays and lesbians also began to play a greater role in local electoral politics, including the historic election of Harvey Milk to the San Francisco Board of Supervisors in 1977. Late in the decade, however, conservative forces began to overturn a number of local antidiscrimination ordinances; most prominent was a successful campaign, led by entertainer Anita Bryant, to repeal through referendum the Dade County (Florida) ordinance. On the other hand, just before his death by assassination, Milk led a surprisingly successful campaign to defeat a California state proposition, the Briggs Amendment, that would have barred gay public school teachers in the state.

At the national level, the most significant victory for the gay rights movement during the decade was not at the ballot box: A campaign to remove homosexuality from the official list of mental disorders maintained by the American Psychiatric Association succeeded in late 1973. In addition, the first explicitly national gay civil rights organization, The National Gay Task Force, was formed in 1973, and a gay and lesbian newsmagazine founded in 1967, *The Advocate*, expanded its national audience significantly.

The incursion of Acquired Immune Deficiency Syndrome (AIDS) into the gay community had innumerable effects on gay and lesbian civil rights in the 1980s. First, the crisis helped to reunite the movement as gay men and lesbians came together in response. In their work, traditional civil rights issues became secondary to new issues, such as health care access, emanating out of the pandemic. While male leaders of the movement in communities throughout the country were struck down by AIDS, the awareness of many men's homosexuality that came from their deaths—including that of actor Rock Hudson—did have the indirect impact of making many Americans aware of the presence of gays in all spheres of society. Finally, especially early on, fears about the spread of AIDS provided a vital rhetorical weapon for conservative opponents of gay political advances.

Just as consciousness of the devastating impact of AIDS was developing, the United States Supreme Court asserted that state laws criminalizing sodomy were constitutional. In a 5–4 vote, a divided Court rejected the argument that a constitutional right to privacy extended to homosexual behavior within one's home in *Bowers* v. *Hardwick* (1986).

The Court's upholding of the sodomy statute and the reality of AIDS rejuvenated radicalism within the movement with the founding of organizations—typically decentralized, locally controlled, and often short-lived—such as the AIDS Coalition to Unleash Power (ACT-UP) and Queer Nation. Some groups began to engage in the "outing" of prominent gay men and lesbians, arguing that public awareness of gays' prominent roles in society took precedence over the privacy rights of the individuals.

Simultaneously, however, gays and lesbians began to play an unprecedented role in mainstream electoral politics at all levels of American politics, and the issue of gay and lesbian rights became central in the national political debate. In 1992, Democrat Bill CLINTON became the first successful presidential nominee to reach out actively to gay voters and financial contributors, promising to end discrimination against homosexuals throughout the federal government, including the ARMED FORCES. Conversely, opposition to the expansion of gay and lesbian civil rights became a centerpiece of Christian conservatives' political rhetoric, a view consistently reflected in the national REPUBLICAN PARTY platforms in the 1990s.

Soon after Clinton's 1993 inauguration, his plan to end the ban on homosexuals in the military led to a firestorm of criticism by military and congressional leaders. The result of the controversy was the development of a new policy, nicknamed "Don't ask, don't tell, don't pursue," which allowed gay men and lesbians to serve as long as they did not acknowledge their sexuality. Contrary to the Clinton Administration's original goal, however, Pentagon records showed that more service members were being discharged for homosexuality after the implementation of the new policy—later codified by Congress—than under the previous ban.

Congress also acted to limit states' recognition of same-sex marriages through passage of the Defense of Marriage Act of 1996. If legally sanctioned same-sex marriages were performed in any individual state, the Act gave other states the explicit right to refuse to recognize those marriages and denied any marital benefits under federal law to legally married same-sex couples.

Still, despite these national defeats, as of 1999, ten states and dozens of localities had put laws in place protecting the rights of gays and lesbians in the workplace and in housing. Legal battles remain active over the application of such antidiscrimination statutes to private organizations operating in those locales, such as the Boy Scouts of America. In 1996, the Supreme Court, in *Romer* v. *Evans*, disallowed the voiding of local antidiscrimination ordinances through a Colorado state constitutional amendment. Justice Anthony Kennedy, writing for the Court's 6–3 majority, wrote that the amendment violated the Equal Protections clause in that only "animosity" on the part of the voters led to an act that classified gay men and lesbians "not to further a proper legislative end but to make them unequal to everyone else."

As shown through public opinion polling and the media, dramatic cultural change on issues related to homosexuality had occurred by the end of the twentieth century. However, the gay and lesbian rights movement, lacking clear national leadership, remained distinctly fractured along lines of gender, class, ideology, and strategy, thus limiting the political gains of the movement.

BIBLIOGRAPHY

Adam, Barry D. *The Rise of a Gay and Lesbian Movement,* Rev. ed. 1995.

Bull, Chris, and John Gallagher. *Perfect Enemies: The Religious Right, the Gay Movement, and the Politics of the 1990s.* 1996.

Bull, Chris, ed. *Witness to Revolution: The Advocate Reports on Gay and Lesbian Politics, 1967–1999.* 1999.

Chauncey, George. *Gay New York: Gender, Urban Culture and the Making of the Gay Male World, 1890–1940.* 1994.

Cleninen, Dudley, and Adam Nagourney. *Out for Good: The Struggle to Build a Gay Rights Movement in America.* 1999.

Duberman, Martin. *Stonewall.* 1994.

Gallagher, John. "Are We Really Asking for Special Rights?" *The Advocate* (April 14, 1998): 24–37.

Loughery, John. *The Other Side of Silence: Men's Lives and Gay Identities—A Twentieth-Century History.* 1998.

Mixner, David *Stranger Among Friends.* 1996.

Sears, James T. *Lonely Hunters: An Oral History of Lesbian and Gay Southern Life, 1948–1968.* 1997.

Shilts, Randy. *And the Band Played On: Politics, People, and the AIDS Epidemic.* 1987.

Shilts, Randy. *Conduct Unbecoming: Gays & Lesbians in the U.S. Military.* 1993.

Shilts, Randy. *The Mayor of Castro Street: The Life and Times of Harvey Milk.* 1982.

Signorile, Michelangelo. *Queer in America: Sex, the Media, and the Closets of Power.* 1994.

Vaid, Urvashi. *Virtual Equality: The Mainstreaming of Gay and Lesbian Liberation.* 1995.

Welch, Paul. "Homosexuality in America." *Life* (June 26, 1964): 66–80.

Jay Barth

Gelders, Joseph

(1899–1950), labor and civil liberties activist.

Joseph Gelders served as a critical link among Southern liberals, such as those in the SOUTHERN CONFERENCE FOR HUMAN WELFARE (SCHW), labor organizations, and the Communist Party, during the 1930s and 1940s. Born in Birmingham, ALABAMA, to a prominent Jewish family, he confronted social ostracism because of his heritage. Gelders pursued undergraduate degrees at the University of Alabama and the Massachusetts Institute of Technology, leaving school to serve in the U.S. Army during World War I. After his war service, Gelders married Esther Frank, a Montgomery native; the couple eventually had one daughter, Marge Gelders Frantz.

Between 1919 and 1929 Gelders held several jobs, from steel worker to automobile salesman. In 1929 he returned to college, earning a master's degree in physics from the University of Alabama in 1931. That same year, the university hired him as assistant professor of physics. As was true of so many Americans, the Great Depression prompted Gelders to seek solutions to America's economic woes through readings in socialism. By 1935 he had become a member of the Communist Party, continuing to work without identifying his membership (see COMMUNIST PARTY USA).

In 1936 Gelders was kidnapped, savagely beaten, and left for dead on a deserted road in Birmingham as he sought to organize UNIONS in the area. This incident became the focus of the U.S. Senate's La Follette Committee Hearings on Violations of Free Speech and the Rights of Labor. In 1938 Gelders and Congress of Industrial Organizations (CIO) organizer Lucy Randolph MASON met with President FRANKLIN D. ROOSEVELT to seek his support for a conference on CIVIL LIBERTIES in the South. With Roosevelt's encouragement, Gelders and Mason joined with Clark FOREMAN and other Southern New Dealers and organized the founding meeting of the Southern Conference for Human Welfare (SCHW), an interracial organization dedicated to the expansion and protection of VOTING RIGHTS in the South. Gelders became executive secretary of SCHW's Committee on Civil Rights and played an active role in the creation of the National Committee to Abolish the Poll Tax.

Joseph Gelders died in 1950 at the age of fifty-one. His death was attributed in part to the injuries he sustained from his beating in 1936. Upon his death, the SOUTHERN CONFERENCE EDUCATIONAL FUND (SCEF), the successor to SCHW, created a Joseph Gelders Memorial Fund.

BIBLIOGRAPHY

Kelley, Robin D. G. *Hammer and Hoe: Alabama Communists During the Great Depression.* 1990.

Reed, Linda. *Simple Decency and Common Sense: The Southern Conference Movement, 1938–1963.* 1991.

Linda Reed

Gentlemen's Agreement (1907–1908)

The Gentleman's Agreement of 1907–1908 was one in a long line of anti-Asian measures taken by various agencies of local, state, and federal government. In 1882, after many years of anti-Chinese agitation and violence, the U.S. Congress outlawed immigration by Chinese working people. After 1900, the drive to renew the Chinese exclusion act spilled over into a movement to ban immigration from all of Asia. One manifestation of this anti-Asian hostility was a crisis in the San Francisco schools. That city's school board voted on October 11, 1906 to put Japanese- and Korean-American youngsters into the city's segregated schools for Chinese children. The local Japanese community complained to Tokyo, and the Japanese government lodged a furious protest with President Theodore Roosevelt. Roosevelt shared the exclusionists' anti-Asian prejudices, but he was reluctant to offend the rulers of Japan, which had emerged as Asia's strongest military power. He and Elihu Root, Secretary of State, persuaded the school board by March 13, 1907 to reverse their segregation order. In return, Roosevelt got the Japanese government to tighten exit restrictions on male labor migration, beginning in 1908. However, despite this Gentlemen's Agreement, Japanese women continued to come to the United States to join their husbands, and opponents of Japanese immigration continued to press for outright exclusion. California passed a law in 1912 forbidding Japanese (and other immigrants who were ineligible for citizenship on account of their race) to own land. Congress passed the IMMIGRATION ACT OF 1924 that excluded Japanese labor immigration formally and completely. And in 1942 the U.S. government took perhaps the ultimate anti-Japanese step when it imprisoned all the Japanese Americans on the West Coast under Executive Order 9066.

BIBLIOGRAPHY

Daniels, Roger. *The Politics of Prejudice: The Anti-Japanese Movement in California and the Struggle for Japanese Exclusion.* 1966.

Paul Spickard

Georgia

RECONSTRUCTION ended in Georgia in 1871 when white Democrats returned to power; six years later the Constitution of 1877 repudiated many of the gains made by African Americans in the Reconstruction Constitution of 1868. This reactionary document attacked black political power by establishing a cumulative poll tax and reducing the number of elective offices; it limited black educational opportunity by approving a segregated system of public primary schools with a three-month term; and it ensured white planter domination with an apportionment system that guaranteed rural control of the state legislature.

The policy of public separation of the races began to be codified in 1891 with the passage of Georgia's first JIM CROW law, segregating the railroads and streetcars. African Americans protested the new legislation and local ordinances in Atlanta, Augusta, Rome, and Savannah. In many cases they were able to delay implementation, but by 1910 segregated public transportation was the law and practice throughout the state. Eventually most aspects of public life in Georgia were segregated, including convict lease camps.

In an effort to "reform" voting, Georgia Progressive leaders effectively disenfranchised black men through adoption of a white primary (1900) and a literacy test, property qualifications, and a grandfather clause (1908).

State laws and local ordinances reflected a hardening of white attitudes on race that was also manifested in an explosion of violence and terror. Between 1890 and 1940, Georgia often led the nation in LYNCHING with at least 450 recorded lynchings during that period. Twenty-five blacks were killed and hundreds wounded in the Atlanta race riot of 1906, and in the countryside "whitecappers" terrorized rural blacks and in some cases succeeded in forcing almost every African American out of certain counties.

State support of public EDUCATION was minimal and even worse for black schools. State funds were distributed by local school boards, which gave a disproportionate share of the funds to white schools. Black teachers had less training than whites; black students had shorter terms each year; and many black schoolhouses were dilapidated. The earliest black colleges were established by Northern philanthropic groups, but in 1890 the state created the Georgia State Industrial College for Colored Youth (later Savannah State University).

Many of the black colleges followed Booker T. WASHINGTON's Tuskegee model and offered a curriculum to train students in manual labor. Washington's accommodationist philosophy was challenged by Atlanta University professor W. E. B. DU BOIS, who argued in *The Souls of Black Folk* that a standard university education should be available to African Americans who wanted to be the next generation's teachers and professionals. Du Bois also opposed disenfranchisement and became a founding member of the NATIONAL ASSOCIATION FOR THE ADVANCEMENT OF COLORED PEOPLE (NAACP). Other Afro-Georgians turned to emigration as a response to adversity in the state. Followers of CME Bishop Lucius H. Holsey sought a separate state in the Western United States, whereas others looked to AME Bishop Henry McNeal TURNER and Marcus GARVEY and their Back to Africa movements.

The KU KLUX KLAN, reborn in Georgia in 1915, expanded significantly in the 1920s with national membership peaking at five million before declining in the 1930s. Although blacks were targeted by Klan violence, Catholics and Jews were also victimized. The lynching of Jewish Atlanta businessman Leo Frank in 1915 was a major factor in the Klan's revival. Former Populist leader Tom Watson promoted anti-Semitism and anti-Catholicism in *Tom Watson's Maga-*

Black and white passengers are seen still segregated on an Atlanta Transit Company trolley on April 23, 1956, following the Supreme Court decision outlawing segregation on all public buses. (AP/Wide World Photos)

zine. Catholics responded to a Watson-supported convent inspection law by organizing the Catholic Laymen's Association.

The WOMAN SUFFRAGE MOVEMENT was not popular among Georgians, and in 1919 Georgia became the first state to reject the NINETEENTH AMENDMENT. The next year, however, white women in Georgia voted for the first time when enough of the other states ratified the amendment for it to become the law of the land.

In the 1930s, the quality of education for black Georgians improved significantly. As late as 1914, there had been only one four-year public high school in Georgia for blacks; but the 1920s witnessed a 73 percent increase in black students attending public schools. By 1940, African Americans in 48 of Georgia's 159 counties had four-year public high school available to them. The turning point in Georgia public education came in 1937 when Governor Eurith D. Rivers persuaded the legislature to provide seven-month school terms and free textbooks to all students. Still the disparity between black and white public schools remained, with the state's investment in black schools amounting to $35 per child and in white schools $142 per child. The state also increased its involvement in black higher education. Many of the black colleges, which had offered mostly elementary and high school courses, began replacing their offerings with college-level courses. In 1943, Georgia Normal and Agricultural College, whose curriculum had included high school agricultural and industrial training, was transformed into a four-year teacher institution, Albany State College.

During the DEPRESSION Era, Georgia began a transformation from an economy based on rural agriculture to one based on urban industry. Depressed prices, the onslaught of the boll weevil, and the labor demands of Northern industry led many black Georgians to depart the countryside and the state. By 1970, blacks comprised a little over a quarter of the state's population. For those who remained, rural and urban black family income was less than half that of white families.

Georgia's black bourgeoisie and returning WORLD WAR II veterans led the efforts to overturn disenfranchisement in Georgia. The U.S. SUPREME COURT declared the white primary unconstitutional in 1944, and efforts were made to increase black voter registration. By the 1946 primary election, 100,000 black Georgians had registered. The NAACP, a leader in the voter registration drive, had increased its membership to 13,000 in forty branches throughout the state.

Some whites were also actively involved in promoting African-American civil rights. Lillian SMITH challenged Southern mores in her writing (her 1944 novel *Strange Fruit* portrayed an interracial romance) and her involvement in the civil rights movement. In 1942 Baptist clergyman Clarence Jordan established an interracial religious community, Koinonia, near Americus in southwest Georgia, which eventually became a haven for civil rights workers in the region.

As the NAACP continued its legal campaign against segregated schools in the federal courts by demonstrating the inequality of the so-called separate but equal schools, Georgia politicians made efforts in the early 1950s to "equalize" the state's schools and thus defuse the NAACP argument. Fearing these efforts would not stem the tide toward DESEGREGATION, the state legislature passed a constitutional amendment in 1953 that would allow the state to end support to public schools by providing parents tuition grants for private schools.

The Georgia legislature responded to BROWN V. BOARD OF EDUCATION (1954) by nullifying it and passing a series of laws designed to prevent the federally imposed desegregation of the public schools. State law provided for the closing of any desegregated school, the suspension of compulsory attendance laws, and the punishment of any peace officer who did not enforce the state's SEGREGATION statutes.

In 1956, the legislature continued its massive resistance to the federal court order by incorporating the Confederate battle flag onto the state flag. That same year three thousand members of a revived Ku Klux Klan attended a cross burning on Stone Mountain. Middle-class businessmen around the state who opposed desegregation were attracted to the newly organized WHITE CITIZENS COUNCILS. Although their methods differed, both the Klan and citizens councils had the same objective, to prevent desegregation and maintain the "Georgia way of life."

Although most white Georgians opposed desegregation, not all were willing to close their schools to maintain segregation. Atlanta business leaders, with much out-of-state business at stake, were the most prominent segregationists willing to accept school desegregation. In 1960, the state legislature appointed a Committee on Schools, chaired by John A. Sibley, to reexamine the school issue. The Sibley Committee recommended that the massive resistance laws be repealed and that individual communities be allowed to decide the issue of local school desegregation.

As white Georgians attempted to prevent or delay desegregation, black Georgians grew impatient. Martin Luther KING, JR., having successfully led the MONTGOMERY BUS BOYCOTT and formed the SOUTHERN CHRISTIAN LEADERSHIP CONFERENCE (SCLC), returned to Atlanta in 1960. That year a number of younger black leaders, many of them students inspired by the Greensboro, North Carolina, SIT-INS in February, began a series of sit-ins in Atlanta. The newly

The Ebenezer Baptist Church stands at an intersection of Auburn Avenue, the center of Atlanta's African-American community. Martin Luther King, Sr., and Martin Luther King, Jr., each ministered from this church's pulpit. (CORBIS/Flip Schulke)

organized STUDENT NONVIOLENT COORDINATING COMMITTEE (SNCC) made Atlanta its headquarters, where it joined the headquarters of other civil rights organizations including the SCLC and the SOUTHERN REGIONAL COUNCIL.

In December 1960, a federal court ordered that two black students, Charlayne Hunter and Hamilton Holmes, who had been denied admission to the University of Georgia, be admitted in January 1961. Rather than close the university as state law required, the legislature finally agreed to accept the Sibley Committee recommendations and allow local jurisdictions to make their own decisions regarding desegregation. The rural segregationist majority in the state legislature was dealt another major blow when the U.S. Supreme Court in 1962 declared unconstitutional the county unit system of apportionment that gave rural (and more rabidly segregationist) counties a disproportionately high representation.

Student sit-ins occurred in Augusta, Americus, Savannah, and Albany. In Albany, SNCC workers joined local organizers to form the ALBANY MOVEMENT in November 1961 and to petition and demonstrate for the city's desegregation. Mass meetings, characterized by unique a capella singing derived from the southwest Georgia African-American church, led to marches and mass arrests. Over seven hundred had been jailed when Albany Movement President William G. Anderson asked his friend Martin Luther King, Jr., to revive the flagging spirit of the black Albanians. King came to Albany, reinvigorated the movement, and was himself arrested and jailed. When King left the following summer after a second arrest and jailing, he admitted his failure in bringing about Albany's de-

segregation. Although King failed in Albany, the movement did not. Emboldened by a new spirit that led them to challenge the status quo, Albany's African Americans significantly increased the number of black registered voters; and, in 1963, one year before the CIVIL RIGHTS ACT OF 1964 required it, the city commission put an end to legal segregation.

Although schools in Atlanta, Savannah, Brunswick, and Athens were integrated in the early 1960s, most rural counties delayed the process until forced to act by the threatened denial of federal aid in the late 1960s. As public schools integrated, many white parents moved to "whiter" counties while others joined people like themselves to create private academies to keep their children from mixing with African Americans. The result was mostly black urban school systems surrounded by predominantly white suburban schools.

As the barriers of segregation dropped, many African Americans seized the opportunities offered by improved education, and the black middle class grew significantly. Atlanta became a magnet for middle-class African Americans from around the state and the nation. As they moved up the ladder, many of these blacks also moved out to the suburbs, leaving an increasingly poor and desperate black underclass in the inner cities.

AFFIRMATIVE ACTION policies in the 1970s and 1980s made it possible for a substantial number of African Americans to climb into the middle class. However, as more blacks succeeded, a growing number of whites spoke out against affirmative action, calling it reverse discrimination. Many of these whites joined the REPUBLICAN PARTY, making Georgia a truly two-party state for the first time in a century. In 1994, a Georgia Republican, Newt Gingrich, led his party in a midterm congressional election upset that resulted in his election as Speaker of the U.S. House of Representatives. In the meantime a growing number of African Americans entered the political arena. In 1971, Jimmy CARTER became the first governor since Reconstruction to advocate racial EQUALITY in the state. The following year Andrew YOUNG was elected the first black member of CONGRESS from Georgia in modern times, and in 1973 Maynard Jackson became Atlanta's first black mayor. By the late 1990s, three members of Georgia's congressional delegation were black.

Women, too, suffered defeats, but, reflecting national trends, they also have made advances since 1965. The Georgia legislature refused to ratify the EQUAL RIGHTS AMENDMENT. As more women were being employed outside the home in Georgia, in 1970 over half of white women in the workplace were either clerical workers or factory workers, and over half of black women were in service occupations. Like African

Americans, Georgia women of all races in 1970 earned an average of 55 to 60 percent of white male income. Since 1970, women's wages have increased, but a significant disparity between male and female income remains.

From the 1970s on there has been a substantial increase in the number of Latinos, mostly Mexican, in Georgia. As south Georgia farmers increased the production of vegetables, the demand for migrant labor rose, and poor Latin Americans responded to meet that need. In some places, Latinos have replaced African Americans as the major victims of discrimination.

The most recent group of Georgians to struggle for their civil rights are gays and lesbians. Both public attitudes and Georgia's 1816 statute outlawing sodomy made it difficult for gay Georgians to achieve equality with the state's heterosexual majority. In 1982, Michael Hardwick was arrested in his own home for engaging in sodomy. Although the charges were dropped, Hardwick decided to challenge the sodomy law in a case that went to the U.S. Supreme Court (*Bowers v. Hardwick*), which upheld the Georgia statute in 1986. Finally in 1998, the Georgia Supreme Court declared the sodomy statute unconstitutional (*Powell v. The State*) because it violated the state-guaranteed right of privacy. Anti-gay public attitudes, however, make the lives of openly gay Georgians, particularly those outside metropolitan Atlanta, difficult and insecure. With the 1997 bombing of an Atlanta lesbian and gay nightclub, gays realized that even in the more cosmopolitan state capital they were not always safe.

BIBLIOGRAPHY

Anderson, William G. "Reflections on the Origins of the Albany Movement." *Journal of Southwest Georgia History* 9 (1994): 1–14.

Bartley, Numan V. *The Creation of Modern Georgia*, 2nd ed. 1990.

Branch, Taylor. *Parting the Waters: America in the King Years, 1954–63*. 1988.

Branch, Taylor. *Pillar of Fire: America in the King Years, 1963–65*. 1998.

Brundage, W. Fitzhugh. *Lynching in the New South: Georgia and Virginia, 1880–1930*. 1993.

Chalfen, Michael. "Rev. Samuel B. Wells and Black Protest in Albany, 1945–1965." *Journal of Southwest Georgia History* 9 (1994): 37–64.

Clendinen, Dudley, and Adam Nagourney. *Out for Good: The Struggle to Build A Gay Rights Movement in America*. 1999.

Coleman, Kenneth, ed. *A History of Georgia*. 1977.

Davis, John Walker. "An Air of Defiance: Georgia's State Flag Change of 1956." *Georgia Historical Quarterly* 82 (1998): 305–330.

Dittmer, John. *Black Georgia in the Progressive Era, 1900–1920*. 1977.

Inscoe, John C., ed. *Georgia in Black and White: Explorations in the Race Relations of a Southern State, 1865–1950*. 1994.

K'Meyer, Tracy Elaine. *Interracialism and Christian Community in the Postwar South: The Story of Koinonia Farm*. 1997.

Litwack, Leon F. *Trouble in Mind: Black Southerners in the Age of Jim Crow*. 1998.

Lyon, Danny. *Memories of the Southern Civil Rights Movement*. 1992.

MacLean, Nancy. *Behind the Mask of Chivalry: The Making of the Second Ku Klux Klan*. 1994.

McGrath, Susan M. "From Tokenism to Community Control: Political Symbolism in the Desegregation of Atlanta's Public Schools, 1961–1973." *Georgia Historical Quarterly* 79 (1995): 842–872.

McRae, Elizabeth Gillespie. "Caretakers of Southern Civilization: Georgia Women and the Anti-Suffrage Campaign, 1914–1920." *Georgia Historical Quarterly* 82 (1998): 801–828.

Myers, Martha A. *Race, Labor & Punishment in the New South*. 1998.

Ricks, John A., III. "'De Lawd' Descends and Is Crucified: Martin Luther King, Jr. in Albany, Georgia." *Journal of Southwest Georgia History* 2 (1984): 3–14.

Tuck, Stephen. "A City Too Dignified to Hate: Civic Pride, Civil Rights, and Savannah in Comparative Perspective." *Georgia Historical Quarterly* 79 (1995): 539–559.

Lee W. Formwalt

Gomillion, Charles

(1900–1995), voting rights activist.

Charles Gomillion spearheaded voting rights efforts in Tuskegee, Alabama, which culminated in the landmark case of *Gomillion v. Lightfoot* (1960).

Born in South Carolina and educated at Paine College, Gomillion joined the faculty of Tuskegee Institute in 1928. After further study in sociology at Fisk University in 1934, Gomillion led efforts to register black voters and obtain tangible improvements for black sections of Tuskegee. Under his leadership the Tuskegee Men's Club was transformed into the Tuskegee Civic Association (TCA) in 1941 and became the organizational headquarters of efforts to encourage civic democracy. Gomillion believed that civic democracy involved all citizens, regardless of race, sharing the opportunities to vote, run for office, and assume responsibility for the community's well-being. As the number of registered black voters increased during the 1940s and 1950s, Gomillion and his supporters faced ongoing opposition from conservative whites fearful of losing their control to the black majority of Tuskegee and adjoining Macon County.

In 1957, State Representative Samuel Engelhardt convinced the Alabama legislature to redraw the boundaries of Tuskegee so that all but a handful of registered black voters were excluded from the city. Gomillion and the TCA challenged this gerrymander in the courts, and the Supreme Court in 1960 ordered a lower federal court to restore the original boundary. The decision in *Gomillion v. Lightfoot* opened the way not only for greater black voter participation in Tuskegee but also for increased federal inspection of voting registration procedures and practices throughout the South. Gomillion retired from public life in 1970 and from Tuskegee University in 1974.

BIBLIOGRAPHY

Norrell, Robert J. *Reaping the Whirlwind: The Civil Rights Movement in Tuskegee.* 1985.

Taper, Bernard. *Gomillion versus Lightfoot: The Tuskegee Gerrymander Case.* 1962.

Stephen C. Messer

Gonzales, Rodolfo "Corky"

(1928–   ), Chicano activist, boxer, poet.

A major activist—and poet—of the Chicano civil rights movement, Rodolfo "Corky" Gonzales sought justice for the Mexican-American people in COLORADO and throughout the Southwest by advocating decent HOUSING, EDUCATION, and EMPLOYMENT opportunities. Gonzales organized many conferences and protests; his two most notable civic rights contributions are his founding of the Denver-based CRUSADE FOR JUSTICE in 1966 and his ideological insistence on self-determination within the American political system.

Gonzales was an effective civil rights leader in part because his own background made him sensitive to labor conditions in the fields, the growing number of youth in the cities and, on a larger scale, the drafting and front-lining of Latinos in the KOREAN and VIETNAM wars. The son of a migrant worker, Gonzales struggled against the odds of his class to gain economic independence. As a youth in the 1940s, he worked in sugar beet fields while intermittently studying; he graduated from high school at the age of sixteen. Gonzales then trained as a featherweight boxer and won both the National Amateur Championship and the International Championship. In fact, he became popular with white sports fans and a hero in his barrio. Gonzales's difficult but triumphant youth inspired his autobiographical and epic poem *Yo soy Joaquín* (*I Am Joaquín*) (1967). Reflecting on his escape from poverty and relative success in the "white world," he wrote: "I bleed as the vicious gloves of hunger / Cut my face and eyes / As I fight my way from stinking

Rodolfo "Corky" Gonzales delivers a forceful speech on behalf of the rights of Chicanos. (The Denver Post)

barrios / To the glamour of the ring." *I Am Joaquín* is a fundamental, almost archetypal Chicano literary text in its expression of self and history; it surveys two thousands years of struggle and the Mexican-American inheritance of Spanish, indigenous, and "Anglo" cultures. Widely quoted by teachers, students, and fellow activists, this poem placed Gonzales in a strategic position as the voice of Chicano identity.

After he quit boxing and had worked at a number of manual jobs, he became District Captain of the Denver Democratic Party in 1957, and by 1959, Gonzales had owned and managed a bond business that helped Chicanos who were, justly or unjustly, imprisoned and who would not otherwise have the resources to post bail. His political and activist career really seemed to take shape by 1960, when he was appointed co-coordinator of the "Viva Kennedy" presidential campaign—a campaign securing substantial votes for John KENNEDY in Denver and, importantly, associating the Latino electorate with the DEMOCRATIC PARTY. Gonzales's allegiance to the Democrats was soon challenged, however, by a new cultural consciousness. Indeed, Rodolfo Gonzales began to find the two-party system oblivious to the needs of the CHICANO MOVEMENT, as Democrats and Republicans alike shared "from the same trough." Rising crime, the draft, substandard education, and the government's denial of land petitions became major concerns not only for Mexican Americans, but for other ethnic groups as well.

In 1968, Gonzales assembled with diverse activists in Washington, DC, to protest the treatment of Native Americans in Washington state. The Poor People's March, also known as the POOR PEOPLE'S CAMPAIGN, led by African-American activist Reverend Ralph ABERNATHY, mobilized to strike down fishing restrictions imposed on Native Americans. Here, Gonzales presented "The Plan of the Barrio," which demanded from the United States a recognition and valorization of Mexican-American culture, including the teaching of Spanish in schools. But for Gonzales, white society was slow to act. Back in Denver, Gonzales's CRUSADE FOR JUSTICE began to provide its own basic services to area Mexican Americans without governmental aid. Gonzales also began to share with Mexican Americans a sense of purpose that reached beyond city limits. In 1969, the Crusade for Justice sponsored the First National Chicano Youth Conference, a meeting of 1,500 representatives from a hundred organizations in the American Southwest. Here, members adopted *El Plan de Aztlán*, an outline for achieving Chicano liberation. Within the context of the freedom movements of the 1960s, it is important to note that the National Chicano Youth Conference paralleled (and shared members with) the black civil rights group, the STUDENT NONVIOLENT COORDINATING COMMITTEE (SNCC). Indeed, Chicana activist Elizabeth ("Betita") MARTÍNEZ coordinated the SNCC office in New York City.

During the 1960s and 1970s, Gonzales traveled throughout the Southwest to advocate the platform of La RAZA UNIDA, a platform that emphasized self-determination and posed an alternative to mainstream political organizations. However, in 1972 José Angel GUTIÉRREZ, the original founder of the party in Texas, defeated Gonzales in the election for national chairman. Debates over agenda turned Gonzales away from La Raza Unida, but not away from activism and outreach. Tireless in his commitment to civil rights and a pragmatist on how to achieve them, Gonzales in 1969 established the Escuela Tlatelolco in Denver, a private school for Chicanos. This institution continues to flourish and to prepare Mexican Americans for college; equally important, Mexican-American arts and culture are taught, for, in Gonzales's words, "there are no revolutions without poets."

BIBLIOGRAPHY

Gonzales, Rodolfo. *I Am Joaquín/Yo soy Joaquín.* Bilingual edition. 1975.

Hammerback, John C., Richard J. Jensen, and José Angel Gutiérrez. *A War of Words: Chicano Protest in the 1960s and 1970s.* 1985.

Larralde, Carlos. *Mexican American Movements and Leaders.* 1976.

Marín, Christine. *A Spokesman of the Mexican American Movement: Rodolfo "Corky" Gonzales and the Fight for Chicano Liberation, 1966–1972.* 1977.

Martínez Sutherland, Elizabeth, and Enriqueta Longeaux y Vasquez. *Viva la Raza!: The Struggle of the Mexican American People.* 1974.

Luz Elena Ramirez

González, Pedro J.

(1895–1995), broadcaster, musician, and political commentator.

Pedro J. Gonzáles migrated to the United States after a dramatic life in Mexico and eventually became perhaps the most important voice for Mexicans suffering the abuses of Depression-era Los Angeles. As a teenager, he served in the forces of Pancho Villa during the Mexican Revolution. According to popular accounts, in 1919, due to his support of the revolutionary leader Pasqual Orozco, Gonzáles faced a firing squad, only to have his life spared as a fourteen-year-old girl stepped in front of him. Three months later, he married the girl. After the couple migrated with their child in 1923, he found work in Los Angeles as a longshoreman. His habit of singing while on the job is said to have led him to a fledgling radio career by 1932.

Beginning as a Spanish-language radio announcer, González soon had his own show from four to six A.M. on KELW out of Burbank. Using recorded music to cater to the working-class Mexican laborer preparing for work, González also sang live with a group called Los Madrugadores (The Early Risers). He soon became the most popular Spanish-language musician in Los Angeles. His songs took the form of the folk ballad, or *corrido*, a kind of through-composed musical storytelling popular among the lower classes. The author of many *corridos* himself, González used these songs to discuss issues ranging from the plight of migrant labor to the evils of the 1930s deportation drives of Mexicans and Mexican Americans. González's show became the news source and a political tool for an entire community, many of whom could neither speak English nor read Spanish. His outspoken nature led to conflicts with the Anglo power establishment in the Los Angeles city government. District Attorney Buron Fitts first attempted to revoke González's broadcasting license. After failing, he had González arrested in 1934 on trumped-up charges of raping a young girl. Sentenced to fifty years in prison, González insisted on his innocence until the frame-up was exposed six years later. Never formally pardoned and cleared of the charges, he was deported to Mexico, where he resumed his broadcasting career. He returned to the United States in 1971 and became an American citizen in 1985. His life and career was the basis of the 1988 film *Break of Dawn* as well as of an earlier documentary, *Ballad of an Unsung Hero.* He died in 1995 at the age of ninety-nine.

BIBLIOGRAPHY

Sanchez, George. *Becoming Mexican American.* 1993.

Tomas Sandoval

Goodman, Andrew

See the entry at Chaney, James.

Gorras Blancas, Las

Las Gorras Blancas (White Caps) were rural Hispanic night riders from the Territory of New Mexico who resisted Anglo settlement on their community land grant during the late nineteenth century. The grant, a 500,000-acre tract conferred by the Mexican government in 1821, was known as the Las Vegas Community Grant. For over a half century Hispanic farmers and sheepherders had the grant to themselves—until the Atchison, Topeka and Santa Fe Railroad brought large numbers of Anglo farmers and cattle ranchers to the Las Vegas area in 1879. Widespread encroachment on the grant by these newcomers was met by approximately seven hundred *Gorras Blancas*, who pulled white caps over their heads to avoid detection, cut barbed-wire fences, and burned barns, haystacks, and homes in order to repel the intruders. They won at least a partial victory in 1903, when the federal Court of Private Land Claims granted a patent of ownership to the town of Las Vegas.

The *Gorras* were in fact part of the White Cap movement, which originated in Indiana in 1888 and spread to such states as Georgia, Mississippi, New Mexico, and Texas. The catalyst for *Las Gorras Blancas* was Juan José Herrera, a native New Mexican who, along with his two brothers, Pablo and Nicanor, infiltrated and radicalized the KNIGHTS OF LABOR in New Mexico. The *Gorras* also became involved in politics in 1890, joining a party that became associated with the Populist movement (see POPULIST PARTY).

BIBLIOGRAPHY

Larson, Robert W. "The White Caps of New Mexico: A Study of Ethnic Militancy in the Southwest." *Pacific Historical Review* 44 (1975): 171–185.

Rosenbaum, Robert J. *Mexicano Resistance in the Southwest: "The Sacred Right of Self-Preservation."* 1981.

Schlesinger, Andrew Bancroft. "Las Gorras Blancas, 1889–1891." *Journal of Mexican American History* 1 (1971): 87–143.

Robert W. Larson

Gray, Fred D.

(1930–   ), lawyer.

Fred Gray, lawyer, state legislator, and minister, has been an activist in the modern civil rights struggle. Gray provided legal representation for well-known civil rights activists, such as Rosa PARKS and Martin Luther KING, JR., and helped formulate the strategies for the successful MONTGOMERY BUS BOYCOTT in 1955. In addition, Gray provided legal counsel for subjects of the TUSKEGEE syphilis study, the DESEGREGATION of ALABAMA schools, and the 1965 Selma voting rights marches.

Born in Montgomery, Alabama, on December 14, 1930, Fred Gray received a B.A. degree from Alabama State College in Montgomery in 1951 and an LL.B. degree from Case Western Reserve University in Cleveland, Ohio, in 1954. After Gray was admitted to the Ohio state bar in 1954, he returned to Alabama and soon after focused his attention on the growing legal battles faced by civil rights workers in the racially segregated South. Immediately, Gray began work on the historic *City of Montgomery v. Rosa Parks*, a lawsuit that was based on a black woman's arrest for refusing to relinquish her seat on a public city bus to a white passenger in 1955. He was aided by his friend and mentor Clifford Durr, a white attorney, who assisted in getting Rosa Parks out of jail and helped with the legal research. Durr also played a crucial role in assisting Gray when the latter represented the NATIONAL ASSOCIATION FOR THE ADVANCEMENT OF COLORED PEOPLE (NAACP) in its lawsuit *NAACP v. Alabama*, a case contesting the unconstitutional banning of the NAACP in the state.

Fred Gray has worked as a lawyer for educational institutions, for the City of Tuskegee, Alabama, and for the NAACP. In 1970 he was elected to the Alabama State Legislature. Gray completed his memoir *Bus Ride to Justice* in 1995.

BIBLIOGRAPHY

Gray, Fred. *Bus Ride to Justice.* 1995.

Gray, Fred. *The Tuskegee Syphilis Experiment.* 1998.

Morris, Aldon. *Origins of the Civil Rights Movement.* 1984.

Donny C. Barnett

Great Depression

See New Deal and Depression.

Great Migration

See Migration.

Great Society

See War on Poverty.

Greenberg, Jack

(1924–   ), attorney.

Jack Greenberg was the civil rights attorney with the NATIONAL ASSOCIATION FOR THE ADVANCEMENT OF COLORED PEOPLE (NAACP) Legal Defense and Educational Fund, Inc. (LDF). After graduating from Columbia University Law School, Greenberg joined the LDF in 1949 as a staff attorney. In his first years with the LDF Greenberg worked on an important criminal trial in Florida, in which police officers beat confessions out of the African-American suspects, and on a college desegregation case in Delaware. He was the chief LDF attorney in the Delaware elementary and secondary school desegregation case, decided by the Supreme Court in 1954 along with *Brown v. Board of Education*. (See BROWN V. BOARD OF EDUCATION.) He became Thurgood MARSHALL's chief assistant in the 1950s, and was named director-counsel of the LDF in 1961 when Marshall was appointed to the federal bench. His appointment generated some controversy within the organization, with some arguing that the position should have gone to Robert Carter, a more senior African-American lawyer who had been general counsel of the NAACP since 1956. During his years as director-counsel, Greenberg led the LDF's efforts to implement desegregation in the Deep South after the Civil Rights Acts of 1964 and 1965. (See CIVIL RIGHTS ACT OF 1964.) He also coordinated the LDF's challenge to capital punishment, which began with a focus on the racially biased way in which the death penalty was meted out. The LDF also began a substantial campaign against employment discrimination, invoking Title VII of the CIVIL RIGHTS ACT OF 1964. He retired from the LDF in 1984 to teach law at Columbia.

BIBLIOGRAPHY
Greenberg, Jack. *Race Relations and American Law.* 1959.
Greenberg, Jack. *Crusaders in the Courts.* 1994.

Mark Tushnet

The defense team at the trial of Walter Lee Irvin, a black man who was accused of kidnapping and raping a white Florida housewife and was sentenced to die in the electric chair. Seated at the defense table in the foreground, from left to right are: Paul C. Perkins; Jack Greenberg; and Thurgood Marshall, chief counsel for the NAACP. (CORBIS/Bettmann)

Griffin, John A.

(1913–1997), sociologist, educator.

John A. Griffin, educator, associate director of the U.S. Community Relations Service in the 1960s, and executive director of the Southern Education Foundation from 1965 to 1978, devoted most of his adult life in his native GEORGIA to the struggle for civil rights. Modest and self-effacing, Griffin worked tirelessly behind the scenes in an effort to improve the quality of life for African Americans.

Griffin, a white Southerner from the small town of Monroe, Georgia, credited his early interest in civil rights to Southern sociologist Arthur Raper. In the summer of 1931, Raper, the author of a number of seminal works on Southern race relations, hired the seventeen-year-old student Griffin to collect materials for the book *Preface to Peasantry*, a study of the collapse of farm ownership in the rural South. After receiving B.A. and M.A. degrees in English from Emory University, Griffin eventually obtained a Ph.D. in sociology from the University of Wisconsin.

During the 1930s, Griffin joined Georgia Tech Professor Glenn Rainey in forming the Georgia Association for the Repeal of the Poll Tax and a larger group, the Southern Society Against the Poll Tax. He also hosted a weekly Atlanta radio interview show that dealt boldly with such controversial issues as the poll tax, black disfranchisement, and the abysmal state of race relations in the region. While teaching at Georgia Tech and Emory University, Griffin (with fellow sociologist Ernst Swanson) published *The Negro and the Schools* (1955), a critical look at the Southern states' inadequate support for African-American EDUCATION.

Griffin's most active involvement in the cause of civil rights came in 1964 and 1965, when he became associate director of the U.S. Community Relations Service under former Florida governor Leroy Collins. At considerable personal risk, Griffin traveled to some of the most intransigent white-controlled communities in the deep South in an effort to try to persuade white community leaders to accept the inevitability of change in racial relations.

From 1965 until his retirement in 1978, Griffin headed the Southern Education Foundation, which had been established in 1867 to improve educational opportunities for disadvantaged Southerners. Under Griffin's quiet but effective leadership, the Foundation exposed racial and economic inequities in the region's education system and struggled to enhance educational opportunities for all low-income students in the region, particularly African Americans. The John A. Griffin Award for Advancing Entity Equity in Educa-

tion has been given annually since 1990 to deserving recipients by the Southern Education Foundation. Among its recipients have been Congressman John LEWIS and lawyer Jack GREENBERG.

BIBLIOGRAPHY

Griffin, John A., and Ernst Swanson. *The Negro and the Schools*. 1955.

Southern Education Foundation Web Site: http://www.sefatl.org.

Dan T. Carter

Gutiérrez, José Angel

(1944–   ), Chicano leader, lawyer.

José Angel Gutiérrez was born and grew up in Crystal City, Texas. In 1963 he entered the political arena, helping to elect five Mexican Americans to the city council of Crystal City. In 1967, while a graduate student in political science at St. Mary's University in San Antonio, Texas, he helped found the Mexican American Youth Organization (MAYO), a group of activists dedicated to social change and to the development of young Chicanos as community leaders (see MEXICAN AMERICAN STUDENT ORGANIZATIONS). He obtained his master's degree in 1968 and then returned to Crystal City, eager to put MAYO's principles into practice in his hometown. With a population that was 80 percent Mexican American, Crystal City provided a unique opportunity to harness politics to achieve social and economic goals. In 1970 Gutiérrez led the effort to organize a local Chicano political party, La RAZA UNIDA (The United People). La Raza Unida helped elect additional Mexican Americans to the city council as well as to the school board. (See also CRYSTAL CITY ELECTORAL REVOLT.) Gutiérrez himself was elected as school board chairman. Sweeping changes were made in the municipal infrastructure to meet the needs of Chicano citizens, and Crystal City was soon hailed as an example of what group solidarity could accomplish.

La Raza Unida became a national party in 1972 and elected Gutiérrez as its chairman, but he was unable to repeat his successes in Crystal City at the national level. He served in this capacity until 1979 and in the meantime obtained a Ph.D. degree in political science from the University of Texas at Austin and a law degree from the University of Houston. Now practicing law in Dallas, he has remained in the forefront of the fight for Chicano rights, serving as a county judge and as the executive director of the Greater Texas Legal Foundation, a nonprofit organization that serves the legal needs of poor people.

BIBLIOGRAPHY

Gutiérrez, José Angel. *The Making of a Chicano Militant: Lessons from Crystal.* 1998.

"José Angel Gutiérrez." In *Leaders from the 1960s: A Biographical Sourcebook of American Activism,* edited by David DeLeon. 1994.

Rochelle C. Hayes

Guzmán, Pablo Yoruba

(1950–   ), Puerto Rican civil rights leader.

Born in New York City, Pablo Guzmán grew up in the predominantly Latino community of Harlem known as El Barrio. He began attending the State University of New York at Old Westbury and studied abroad in Mexico in 1969. Returning with a heightened sense of political awareness, he joined the Sociedad de Albizu Campos, named for the leader of the old Nationalist Party of Puerto Rico. In June 1969, the Sociedad merged with another group of politically active youths and, borrowing the name of a converted Chicago gang, called themselves the Young Lords Organization.

As an original member of the Central Committee of the organization, Guzmán figured prominently in the events of the limited yet effective political movement the Lords directed at the community of Boricua (i.e., Puerto Rican) youths and their families. Young Lords led creative "offensives" designed to bring attention to issues such as the lack of sanitation and health services, prison abuse, and the noninvolvement of Puerto Ricans in politics and education. As they fought for these issues, they also served their community directly by operating clinics, free breakfast programs, and general political and cultural education events designed to expand the El Barrio community's knowledge of the culture and history of Puerto Ricans.

After the group's demise, Guzmán became a constant presence in the Boricua community, acting as an occasional columnist for the *Village Voice* and becoming the first New York-born Latino radio personality in the city. Still a resident of New York City, Guzmán continues his advocacy.

BIBLIOGRAPHY

Guzmán, Pablo Yoruba. "La Vida Pura: A Lord of the Barrio." In *The Puerto Rican Movement: Voices from the Diaspora,* edited by Andrés Torres and José E. Velásquez. 1996.

Tomas Sandoval

Guzmán, Ralph C.

(1924–1985), political scientist, author, and civil rights activist.

A staunch advocate of issues of concern to Mexicans and Mexican Americans in the Southwest United States, Ralph Guzman helped legitimize them as a subject of academic study. Born Rafael Guzmán in Guanajuato, Mexico, Guzmán migrated to the United States as a child and attended schools in Arizona and California before leaving high school to serve in WORLD WAR II. In 1944, the year he also became a U.S. citizen, Guzmán was inducted into the Navy and finished the war as a radio operator. Returning home, he utilized the G.I. Bill to continue his education, receiving an A.A. in 1949 from East Los Angeles Community College and a B.A. in 1958 and M.A. in 1960, both from Los Angeles State College (California State University, Los Angeles). In 1970 he obtained his Ph.D. in political science from the University of California, Los Angeles.

As one of only a handful of Ph.D. recipients of Mexican descent in the nation, Guzmán used his status to help correct the omissions of Mexican Americans from academic study. In 1964, before the end of his formal education, he became the director of the Mexican-American Study Project at UCLA. His work there culminated with the publication of his first book, *The Mexican American People: The Nation's Second Largest Minority* (1970). This groundbreaking work provided an in-depth study of Chicanos at a sociological and political level and, as such, is considered one of the first to bring the topic into mainstream academic discourse. Guzmán's work continued through the next two decades as he served as a professor in colleges and universities throughout California.

At the same time, Guzmán actively participated in the causes of civil rights affecting Mexicans and through that example did much to further the notion of the Chicano professor/activist. As a columnist for the local Los Angeles alternative newspaper, *Eastside Sun,* he championed the issue of police brutality against Mexican youths. Through his role as the director of the civil rights department of the Alianza Hispano-Americana, he helped litigate against the educational segregation of Mexican youth. He was a prominent member of the COMMUNITY SERVICE ORGANIZATION (CSO), one of the earliest and more active associations representing the causes of civil rights for Mexican Americans in the Southwest. In recognition of his tireless advocacy, the AMERICAN CIVIL LIBERTIES UNION (ACLU) appointed him to their board of directors. He was the first Mexican American ever to hold that position.

By most accounts, Guzmán's most significant research dealt with the disproportionate numbers of Chicano deaths in the war in Vietnam. His findings suggest that they died at a rate more than twice their numbers in the general population. This helped to spawn antiwar sentiment within the Mexican communities of the Southwest, culminating in mass protests and teach-ins throughout Los Angeles in the early 1970s.

After serving as a deputy assistant secretary of state under President Jimmy Carter, Guzmán returned to academia. He died in 1985 while serving as a professor at the University of California, Santa Cruz.

BIBLIOGRAPHY

Grebler, Leo, Joan W. Moore, and Ralph C. Guzmán. *The Mexican American People: The Nation's Second Largest Minority.* 1970.

Guzmán, Ralph C. "Chicano Control of Chicano History—A Review of Selected Literature." *California Historical Quarterly* 52, no. 2 (1973): 170–175.

Tomas Sandoval

H

Hamer, Fannie Lou

(1917–1977), civil rights leader.

Mississippian Fannie Lou Hamer followed the activist examples set by other leading black women of the 1950s—Rosa PARKS, Septima CLARK, Daisy BATES, and Ella BAKER. Born Fannie Lou Townsend to Jim and Ella Townsend on October 6, 1917 in rural Montgomery County, the civil rights leader shared a birth year with John F. KENNEDY, and the two would coincidentally gain national prominence in the 1960s. Ella and Jim, sharecropper and minister, moved to Sunflower County when Fannie Lou was two years old, and the child received her six to eight years of education there. School years for sharecroppers averaged only about four months, and Hamer missed many of those because she had very poor clothing. At the age of six, Fannie Lou began working in the cotton field, and she labored many long years chopping and picking cotton until the plantation owner, W. D. Marlow, learned that she could read and write.

In 1944, she became the time and record keeper for Marlow; and in 1945, she married Perry Hamer, a tractor driver on the Marlow Plantation. For the next eighteen years of her adult life, Fannie Lou Hamer worked as sharecropper and time keeper on the plantation, some four miles east of Ruleville, Mississippi, the place where she and Perry made their home. On August 31, 1962, she suffered economic reprisal after an unsuccessful attempt to vote in the county seat of Indianola. Marlow appeared at the Hamers' home the very day of her unsuccessful voter registration effort to demand that she stop her attempts to vote. Familiar with the physical violence that would often follow economic reprisals and having received threats, Fannie Lou Hamer left her family to stay nearby with friends. However, the move did not stay the violence, and Fannie Lou Hamer and her friends miraculously escaped rounds of gunshots fired into the friends' home when a person or persons yet unknown discovered her presence there.

Fannie Lou Hamer became an active member of the STUDENT NONVIOLENT COORDINATING COMMITTEE (SNCC), founded in North Carolina in 1960, with encouragement and support from Ella Baker. Economic reprisals, a long-time sure way to put an end to concerted efforts by blacks who demanded equality, did not deter Hamer. She took the literacy test several times, and in 1963 she became a field secretary for SNCC and a registered voter. Hamer was beaten while in jail for attempting to integrate the bus station in Winona, Mississippi, and for her work with SNCC in voter registration. After 1963, Hamer worked with voter registration drives and with programs designed to assist economically deprived black families in Mississippi, circumstances with which she said she felt especially familiar.

The youngest of twenty siblings whose parents seldom were able to provide them adequate food and clothing, Hamer saw a link between lack of access to the political process and the poor economic status of blacks. She was instrumental in starting Delta Ministry, an extensive community development program, in 1963. On April 24, 1964, she took part in the founding of the MISSISSIPPI FREEDOM DEMOCRATIC PARTY

Fannie Lou Hamer, a representative of the Mississippi Freedom Democratic Party, was one of the highlights of the 1964 Democratic National Convention. She strides toward the convention hall entrance. August 25, 1964. (CORBIS/Bettmann)

(MFDP), becoming vice chairperson and a member of its delegation to the Democratic National Convention in Atlantic City, New Jersey, which challenged the seating of the regular all-white Mississippi delegation. In this capacity she made a televised address to the convention's Credentials Committee. The 1964 challenge failed despite a compromise offered through Hubert Humphrey and Walter Mondale that would have seated two nonvoting MFDP members selected by Humphrey (African-American Aaron HENRY, president of Mississippi NAACP chapters, and white American Ed King, chaplain at historically black Tougaloo College). Still the MFDP's actions resulted in an unprecedented pledge from the national DEMOCRATIC PARTY *not* to seat delegate groups that excluded blacks at the next convention, in 1968. Also in 1964 Hamer unsuccessfully attempted to run for the U.S. CONGRESS. As the regular Democratic Party disallowed her

name on the ballot, the MFDP conceived a "Freedom Ballot," which included all the candidates' names, black and white. Hamer defeated her white opponent, Congressman Jamie Whitten (33,099 to 41), in this nonbinding vote.

In 1965, Fannie Lou Hamer, Victoria Gray of Hattiesburg, and Annie Devine of Canton appealed to Congress, arguing that it was wrong to seat Mississippi's representatives, who were all white, when the state's population was 50 percent black. The three women watched as members of the House voted against their challenge, 228 to 143.

Hamer remained active in civic affairs in Mississippi for the remainder of her life, becoming a delegate to the Democratic National Convention in 1968 in Chicago. Her founding in 1969 of the Freedom Farms Corporation (FFC), a nonprofit venture designed to help needy families raise food and livestock, showed her concern for the economic plight of blacks in Mississippi. FFC also provided social services, minority business opportunities, scholarships, and grants for EDUCATION. When the NATIONAL COUNCIL OF NEGRO WOMEN started the Fannie Lou Hamer Day Care Center in Doddsville, Mississippi in 1970, Hamer became chairperson of its board. As late as 1976, even as she struggled to survive cancer, Hamer served as a member of the state executive committee of the Democratic Party of Mississippi.

Fannie Lou Hamer received wide recognition for her part in bringing about a major political transition in the Democratic Party and in raising significant questions that addressed basic human needs. In 1963, the Fifth Avenue Baptist Church in Nashville, Tennessee presented her one of her first awards, appropriately given for "Voter Registration and Hamer's Fight for Freedom for Mankind." Among her numerous other awards, the National Association of Business and Professional Women's Club presented Hamer its National Sojourner Truth Meritorious Service Award as a tribute to her strong defense of human dignity and fearless promotion of civil rights. Delta Sigma Theta Sorority awarded her a life membership. Many colleges and universities honored her with honorary degrees, including her neighboring institution, Tougaloo College, in 1969.

Fannie Lou Hamer gave numerous speeches across the country into the 1970s. She had grown weary by this time because of her struggle with cancer, but she continued to accept invitations to speak about what she held most dear, basic human rights for all Americans. She died on March 14, 1977 at the Mound Bayou Community Hospital.

Hamer's activism shows that at a time when women, especially white women, were just beginning to be concerned with FEMINISM, many black women were being forced to struggle for racial equality. Frederick Douglass spoke eloquently of the division that black men felt in terms of being American *and* black and trying to maintain a balance between the two. Black women spoke of being pulled in three directions—having to come to terms with being American, African American, and female. Some chose to work against RACISM first, recognizing that SEXISM could be addressed later; others chose to address sexism on a personal level even as they battled racism.

From Rosa Parks of the MONTGOMERY BUS BOYCOTT in 1955 to Fannie Lou Hamer in the 1960s, black women leaders courageously took the initiative, hoping that their individual efforts would make a difference for their people, their region, and indeed the nation. It was Hamer who emphatically stated that the problems in Mississippi were America's as well.

Fannie Lou Hamer's significance is to be seen in her dialogue with all Americans; she spoke not only for African Americans, but for all the country's citizens. She believed in social change, and she believed in crossing social boundaries to solve the problems that change would bring.

BIBLIOGRAPHY

Carson, Clayborne. *In Struggle: SNCC and the Black Awakening of the 1960s.* 1981.
Grant, Joanne. *Ella Baker: Freedom Bound.* 1998.
Mills, Kay. *This Little Light of Mine: The Life of Fannie Lou Hamer.* 1993.
Payne, Charles M. *I've Got the Light of Freedom: The Organizing Tradition and the Mississippi Freedom Struggle.* 1995.

Linda Reed

Hancock, Gordon Blaine

(1884–1970), educator and social activist.

Gordon Blaine Hancock (the "Gloomy Dean") was one of three organizers of the all-black Southern Conference on Race Relations that in December 1942 issued the DURHAM MANIFESTO, a comprehensive declaration by Southern blacks indicating what they wanted from whites. Published during the height of American involvement in WORLD WAR II, the Manifesto was intended as a point of departure for a meaningful dialogue between liberal whites and blacks. It served as the foundation upon which the SOUTHERN REGIONAL COUNCIL, a coalition of Southern black and white leaders committed to addressing solutions to the South's social, political, and racial problems, was formed in 1944.

Hancock was born June 13, 1884, in Ninety-Six township, Greenwood, South Carolina, to a former slave and a free black minister. A trained sociologist and ordained Baptist minister, Hancock acquired degrees from Benedict College, in South Carolina, and Colgate University, in New York, and then attended Harvard University prior to joining the faculty of Virginia Union University in 1921. From his base in Richmond, Hancock distinguished himself as both an educator and a social activist, maintaining that racial PREJUDICE and SEGREGATION threatened black social and economic survival.

For three decades Hancock worked through the pulpit, the black press, and organizations, including the Southern Regional Council, to promote racial pluralism, incorporating a social gospel based on economic self-reliance, black solidarity, interracial cooperation, full citizenship for African Americans, and opposition to segregation. Hancock's biographer, Raymond Gavins, described him as "probably the most articulate and popular champion of his race in Virginia for over a quarter century preceding the *Brown* decision of 1954."

BIBLIOGRAPHY

Gavins, Raymond. *The Perils and Prospects of Southern Black Leadership: Gordon Blaine Hancock, 1884–1970.* 1977.
Gavins, Raymond. "Gordon Blaine Hancock: A Black Profile from the New South." *Journal of Negro History* 54, no. 3 (July 1974): 207–227.
Gordon Blaine Hancock Papers. Rare Book, Manuscript, and Special Collections Library, Duke University.

Homer Douglass Hill

Hansberry, Lorraine

(1930–1965), playwright.

Playwright Lorraine Hansberry was born in Chicago into a family deeply committed to social change. Determined to support the voice of black protest through her writing, she drew upon her family's history of activism as well as her own experiences as a black female in America when crafting her works. Her first and best-known play, *A Raisin in the Sun,* was loosely based on her father's fight against Chicago's restrictive HOUSING covenants. *Raisin* was the first drama by a black woman to be produced on Broadway. The New York Drama Critics' Circle named it best dramatic play of the 1958–59 season, making Hansberry both the first black woman and the youngest playwright to win the honor. The great acclaim Hansberry received from the theater world was echoed by that of the black community, which applauded her sensitive articulation of many of the struggles blacks faced in contemporary America.

*The 28-year-old playwright Lorraine Hansberry.
March 25, 1959.* (CORBIS/Bettmann)

Hansberry used her newfound fame to lend further assistance to the civil rights movement. In speeches, interviews, essays, and letters to the editor, Hansberry challenged others to join the fight for equality and wrote many articles stressing the connection between art and social change. An ardent supporter of the STUDENT NONVIOLENT COORDINATING COMMITTEE (SNCC), Hansberry helped sponsor its fundraising events and contributed the text for a book of photos documenting the organization's work. Hansberry continued to work on her own creative projects as her activism blossomed, completing several more dramas before cancer claimed her at age thirty-four. Following her death, her former husband, Robert B. Nemiroff, whom she had married in 1953, compiled and edited her writings and published two volumes: *To Be Young, Gifted, and Black* (1969) and *Les Blancs: The Collected Last Plays of Lorraine Hansberry* (1972).

BIBLIOGRAPHY

Cheney, Ann. *Lorraine Hansberry.* 1984.
Nemiroff, Robert. *To Be Young, Gifted, and Black: Lorraine Hansberry in Her Own Words.* 1969.

Rochelle C. Hayes

Harding, Vincent

(1931–   ), civil rights activist, radical historian, and theologian.

Vincent Harding was born in Harlem in 1931 to West Indian immigrants, and was nurtured in the strong community of his Seventh-Day Adventist church. He graduated from the City College of New York in 1952, and received an M.S. degree from Columbia University in 1953 and a Ph.D. from the University of Chicago in 1965. In Chicago, Harding pastored an interracial Mennonite church and married Rosemarie Freeney. Freeney had grown up in Chicago, but her family was rooted in the Southern black experience, and her influence led to Harding's first connections with the civil rights movement. The movement combined the two major factors of Harding's early life, his pacifist Christian heritage (reawakened by grueling experience with the Army during the mid-1950s), and his black consciousness. In 1961, the Hardings moved to Atlanta and founded the Mennonite House, which served as an interracial movement headquarters and haven for freedom workers such as Martin Luther KING, JR., who lived around the corner. Harding was arrested in Albany, Georgia during the massive jail-ins there, and he performed critical mediation work at Birmingham in 1963. As with many others, the limited gains of the nonviolence crusade led him by the mid-1960s to become increasingly swayed by calls for black empowerment and violent revolution. Harding's relationship with Martin Luther King, Jr., was instrumental in the more radical turn the great civil rights leader took in the final year of his life, especially regarding public criticism of the VIETNAM WAR.

In 1965 Harding became chair of the history and sociology department at Spelman College in Atlanta, and in 1968 he became director of the Martin Luther King, Jr., Memorial Center and chair of the CBS "Black Heritage" television series. Though his increasingly radical leanings led to a separation from the King Center, he helped organize and was first director (1969–1974) of the Institute of the Black World (IBW), a pivotal organization in directing the emerging field of black studies along a path blazed by and for black people themselves. These commitments were reflected in Harding's influential historical writings, which sought to turn the field away from "Negro History," with its acceptance of the canonical understanding of a progressive American past, to "Black History," whose unflinching attention to the distinctive history of black Americans suggested a general American history of RACISM and oppression as well as a powerful history of black agency and resistance. Through the IBW, Harding and his colleagues sought to preach and practice the integration of scholarship and activism in a communal environment, often advocating black-led moral, political, and spiritual revolution.

By 1981, Harding's persistent goal of writing relevant scholarship and maintaining a connection to activist organizations found him increasingly uncomfortable in traditional academic settings, and he accepted a position at the Iliff School of Theology at the University of Denver as Professor of Religion and Social Transformation. This position has allowed him to continue his work, grounded in a spiritual understanding of the human condition and in close collaboration with his wife, Rosemarie. Together the Hardings continue to study and organize for liberation on all fronts for all people. Prominent in this effort has been the use of history to keep the memory of the civil rights movement alive in the present day. To this end, Harding has served as senior adviser to the celebrated *Eyes on the Prize: America's Civil Rights Years* public television series; and he has written several popular books on black radicalism throughout American history and especially the civil rights era, highlighting its continuing relevance to today's political struggles.

BIBLIOGRAPHY

Abelove, Henry, et al., *Visions of History: Interviews.* 1983.

Harding, Rachel E. "Biography, Democracy and Spirit: An Interview with Vincent Harding." *Callaloo* 20, no. 3 (Summer 1997): 682–699.

Harding, Vincent. *Beyond Chaos: Black History and the Search for the New Land.* 1970.

Harding, Vincent. *The Other American Revolution.* 1980.

Harding, Vincent. *There Is a River: The Black Struggle for Freedom in America.* 1981.

Harding, Vincent. *Hope and History: Why We Must Share the Story of the Movement.* 1990.

Harding, Vincent. *Martin Luther King: The Inconvenient Hero.* 1996.

Meier, August, and Elliot Rudwick. *Black History and the Historical Profession.* 1986.

Milton Gaither

Jamaican-born Claude McKay (1890–1948) was a poet and novelist whose powerful literary voice is a symbol of the Harlem Renaissance. His novels include Home to Harlem *(1928) and* Banjo *(1929). Photo ca. 1923.* (CORBIS)

Harlem Renaissance

The Harlem Renaissance was a seminal period of African-American activism and achievement in politics, intellectual thought, literature, music, visual arts, theater, and dance from approximately 1919 to 1932. It has been most commonly associated with an outpouring of literature, music, visual art, dance, and theater by African-American artists. However, much of the impetus for the Renaissance came from the emergence of political institutions and a new black political activism in the period immediately before, during, and after WORLD WAR I. This era featured a huge upsurge in racist violence. It was also marked by the increasing and often patronizing fascination of white Americans and Europeans with African Americans and their culture.

The political institutions of the Renaissance included the integrationists of the NATIONAL ASSOCIATION FOR THE ADVANCEMENT OF COLORED PEOPLE (NAACP) and the NATIONAL URBAN LEAGUE, the nationalists of Marcus GARVEY's UNIVERSAL NEGRO IMPROVEMENT ASSOCIATION, the nationalistic communists of the AFRICAN BLOOD BROTHERHOOD, the socialists of the circle around A. PHILIP RANDOLPH, and Chandler Owen's influential journal, *The Messen-*

Poet, novelist, and playwright Countee Cullen, ca. 1932. The precocious successes of Countee Cullen (1903–1946) are often regarded as the starting point of the Harlem Renaissance. (CORBIS/Bettmann)

ger. While these groups were often in conflict with each other, they generally projected a sense of African-American political dynamism and self-assertion that found its expression in the revitalized notion of a "New Negro."

The chief social change that made the Renaissance possible was the migration of millions of African Americans from the Southern United States and the Caribbean to the urban centers of the North—African Americans who wanted to escape the JIM CROW South and to take advantage of job opportunities that opened up in northern industries during World War I. This allowed for the birth, or relocation and growth, of African-American-oriented institutions, such as the NAACP and its journal *The* CRISIS, the Urban League and its journal *Opportunity*, and *The Messenger*, which all played important roles in promoting the Renaissance.

Harlem became preeminently linked to the Renaissance for four basic reasons. First, there was the sheer size of the black population in Harlem, rivaled only by the "Black Belt" of Chicago's South Side. Second, Har-

lem's location in New York City, the center of most American culture industries, permitted easier interaction between black artists and intellectuals and these industries (and among black and white artists and intellectuals) than was possible elsewhere. Third, because Harlem was in large part an attractive neighborhood that had become available to African Americans due to over-building, it became a living symbol of African-American potential and optimism. Finally, Harlem was one of the most important centers of gay activity in the United States. This was significant because it was largely gay networks of black and white intellectuals and artists who promoted the work of black artists and writers (many of whom were themselves gay or bisexual) to mainstream publishers of books and magazines, foundations, and so on.

The Renaissance slowly disintegrated under the economic pressures of the Great Depression in the early 1930s. These pressures limited the interest and ability of "mainstream" cultural institutions in supporting black artists and intellectuals and eliminated or weakened many black institutions. This relatively gradual change tended to move black artists and intellectuals closer to the political Left, particularly the Communist Party (see COMMUNIST PARTY USA).

In many respects, the different and often contradictory aspects of the Harlem Renaissance comprised a declaration of African-American independence. As with the original Declaration, this assertion of independence did not immediately bring independence, either politically or culturally. Nonetheless, it left a legacy of achievement and possibility that inspired and informed later African-American cultural and political movements.

BIBLIOGRAPHY

Anderson, Jervis. *This Was Harlem*. 1982.
Huggins, Nathan. *Harlem Renaissance*. 1971.
Hutchinson, George. *The Harlem Renaissance in Black and White*. 1995.
Lewis, David Levering. *When Harlem Was in Vogue*. 1979.

James Smethurst

Harper, Frances Watkins

(1825–1911), writer.

Frances Ellen Watkins Harper, who came to be regarded as one of the most talented African-American women of her generation, was born in 1825 in Baltimore, Maryland, to a free family. She experienced considerable discrimination in her childhood, as Baltimore was still a slave-holding area. After the death of her mother when Frances was only two years old, the child, who had no siblings, was raised by her aunt and uncle, the latter an abolitionist minister and educator. Her love of learning and literary ability were clear at an early age, although she had to abandon her formal education at her uncle's school to undertake work as a housekeeper at the age of thirteen. Self-educated thereafter, she managed to satisfy her thirst for knowledge by reading books in an employer's bookstore.

At twenty-five, Frances Watkins moved to Ohio to teach vocational education at Union Seminary, an organization affiliated with the African Methodist Episcopal Church and later a part of Wilberforce University. She became the school's first African-American woman to teach in her field. A move to Pennsylvania for a new job two years later was not so successful. She abandoned the new position, but—though homesick for it—could not return to Maryland because of a prohibition there against the return of free blacks.

Ever since her years at her uncle's school, Frances had been imbued with a sense of the cruelty of slavery, and this awareness was strengthened as she increasingly witnessed the evils of the practice. By her late twenties, Harper was producing anti-slavery essays, and she had become very active in assisting slaves seeking to escape their condition. She spent time at the Philadelphia station of the Underground Railroad and worked for the abolitionist cause from Boston and other locations. At twenty-nine she began lecturing, principally on the topic of slavery, sometimes integrating poetry into the lectures. Her success as a lecturer for the Maine Anti-Slavery Society led to a similar role with the Pennsylvania Anti-Slavery Society. She lectured throughout the Northeastern states and Ohio, and offered financial support as well to abolition and other causes she endorsed.

Frances Watkins's reform activities were interrupted for four years by her marriage to Fenton Harper, a widower with whom she established a home on a farm in Ohio, and with whom she had a daughter, Mary. His premature death in 1864 enabled her to resume her political work, turning her attention to the advancement of manumitted African Americans.

Known as the "Bronze Muse," Frances Harper traveled throughout the postwar South from 1867 through 1871. She spoke to church groups, women's organizations, and other bodies about the importance of African-American rights, social responsibility, ethical conduct, learning, and, increasingly, FEMINISM. Her growing visibility in feminist circles coincided with the growth of the women's movement. Her agenda included many causes that feminists typically embraced, such as temperance, a field in which she was particularly active from the mid-1870s through the early 1890s, serving in leadership roles in prominent temperance organizations. Harper participated in two women's suffrage conventions and was a member of the AMERICAN WOMAN SUFFRAGE ASSOCIATION and the National Council of Women. Although she cared deeply about women's issues and foresaw an imminent era of female liberation, Harper became too dismayed by the RACISM of some white feminists to put great faith in their efforts, and joined other African-American women in condemning the situation and urging the creation of black feminist organizations. Accordingly, Harper was a force in the birth of the NATIONAL ASSOCIATION OF COLORED WOMEN, in 1896.

Frances Harper's chief legacy is the large body of writing she produced over her approximately six-decade literary career, portions of which are only now being fully appreciated by scholars. She helped African Americans of her day to redefine their self-image. Beginning mainly as a poet, by age twenty-six she had published a collection of poems entitled *Forest Leaves* (*Autumn Leaves*). She gained fame, however, through the 1854 publication of *Poems on Miscellaneous Subjects* (with a preface by abolitionist William Lloyd Garrison). The book enjoyed astonishing success and was reprinted four times. For a poet of her generation Harper was uncharacteristically political and serious-minded, using her poetry to communicate the injustices facing African-Americans and women in particular, in such poems as "The Slave Mother." Highly acclaimed in its own day and often reprinted today, it portrays the horrors of slavery, specifically the anguish of a mother and a child being taken away from each other. Harper again broke new ground five years later with her short story "The Two Offers" (1859), whose publication likely made her the first African-American woman to publish a short story. The piece, which appeared in the *Anglo-African*, challenged traditional ideas about societal roles for women and the value of marriage.

Harper's greatest literary achievement was her 1892 novel *Iola Leroy, or Shadows Uplifted* (once mistakenly believed to be the first novel produced by a female African American). It sought to correct disparaging stereotypes of African Americans and to promote harmony between the races, as many whites had become disparaging of blacks who continued to express frustration with their condition. *Iola Leroy* provided a valuable glimpse into the post–Civil War experience of African Americans and the discrimination and hardships that persisted after they became free. It also interwove themes concerning the difficulties facing all women and African-American women in particular. The purpose of *Iola Leroy* was to teach people about the problems African Americans faced in the aftermath of slavery; it reminded them that it was unfair to condemn blacks, who had not had long to experience freedom and often had been denied adequate resources to make their lives successful. The book provided an optimistic view of whether blacks could stop experiencing the aftereffects of slavery. The heroine's partially African-American background is revealed to her upon the death of her white father. She loses and then regains her freedom and does not conceal her African-American heritage, even at some personal cost. Iola discovers her mulatto mother and her brother, and rejects a number of marriage proposals in favor of establishing her own independence, waiting until she finds a mate who embraces her values. Loosely structured like many other contemporary women's novels, *Iola Leroy* retained its artistic individuality. Although it was widely read and praised upon its publication, by the end of Harper's life opinion had changed about the book's merits, its popularity having been affected by shifts in literary fashion. Still it has always been regarded as a cultural barometer of its time. Since its 1987 reprinting, it has become a staple of many university classes dealing with women's issues and literature, partly because of its relevance to present-day feminist issues.

Francis Watkins Harper continued to express her concern about social issues until her death, in Philadelphia in February 1911.

BIBLIOGRAPHY

Baym, Nina. *Woman's Fiction: A Guide to Novels by and About Women in America 1820–1870.* 1978.
Brown, Hallie Q. *Homespun Heroines and Other Women of Distinction.* 1926.
Harper, Frances E. W. *Iola Leroy, or Shadows Uplifted.* 1893. Reprint, 1987.
Sherman, Joan R. *Invisible Poets: Afro-Americans of the Nineteenth Century.* 1989.
Shockley, Ann Allen. *Afro-American Women Writers 1746–1933.* 1988.
Smith, Jessie Carney, ed. *Notable Black American Women.* 1992.

Sarah Kurian

Hastie, William Henry

(1904–1976), federal judge and legal activist.

Born in Knoxville, Tennessee, William H. Hastie received his early education there and later in Washington, D.C. After graduating as president of Phi Beta Kappa and first in his class at Amherst College in 1925, Hastie entered Harvard Law School in 1927, where he served on the *Harvard Law Review* and graduated with an L.L.B. degree in 1930. Two years later he received the degree of Doctor of Juridical Science, also from Harvard.

Hastie played a major role in the civil rights struggles of his era. Following the 1932 election of Franklin D. ROOSEVELT, Hastie achieved high visibility as a race relations advisor to the new president. In 1937, Roosevelt appointed him judge for the federal district of the Virgin Islands, making him the first African-American federal magistrate. He returned in 1939 to Howard University Law School as dean and professor of law and became chair of the National Legal Committee of the NATIONAL ASSOCIATION FOR THE ADVANCEMENT OF COLORED PEOPLE (NAACP), a post that allowed him to shape the course of civil rights litigation. Along with Thurgood MARSHALL, he argued successfully in *Smith v. Allwright* (1941) that a Texas all-white primary election law violated the FIFTEENTH AMENDMENT. He also joined with Marshall in arguing the landmark case of *Morgan v. Virginia* (1946). Hastie and Marshall persuaded the SUPREME COURT that a Virginia statute that required segregated seating by race on interstate buses imposed an improper burden on the flow of national commerce. Taken together, the victories in *Smith* and *Morgan* were crucial in the NAACP's attack on the South's dual system of race accommodations. The Court's decision in *Smith* leveled a significant barrier to black voting; its holding in *Morgan* underscored, even as informal SEGREGATION continued, that such practices on interstate buses would not survive legal challenge.

Hastie gained national attention for the civil rights effort in other ways. In early 1943, for example, he resigned as Secretary of War Henry L. Stimson's civilian aide to protest the government's racial policies of discrimination in the armed forces. That same year the NAACP awarded Hastie its prestigious Spingarn Medal as an "uncompromising champion of equal justice." A year later Hastie threw his support behind the NATIONAL COMMITTEE TO ABOLISH THE POLL TAX.

Hastie served for three years as governor of the Virgin Islands (1946–1949), after which President Harry S. TRUMAN appointed him to the Court of Appeals for the Third United States Circuit, the highest judicial position then attained by an African American. Despite his twenty-one years of service in the judiciary, only two dozen of his 486 opinions dealt with civil rights issues. The most important of these reveal a Madisonian commitment to constitutional law rooted in judicial restraint. In *Lynch v. Torquato* (1965), for example, Hastie declined an opportunity to expand the state action theories he had advanced as counsel in *Smith*. He held that the FOURTEENTH AMENDMENT's equal protection clause did not extend to the internal operations of the DEMOCRATIC PARTY. In his off-the-bench writings, Hastie also warned that AFFIRMATIVE ACTION programs based on race alone violated the CONSTITUTION.

BIBLIOGRAPHY

Rusch, Jonathan J. "William H. Hastie and the Vindication of Civil Rights." *Howard Law Review* 27 (1978): 749–820.

Ware, Gilbert. *William Hastie; Grace under Fire.* 1984.

Kermit L. Hall

Hawai'i

The overriding civil rights issue in Hawai'i is sovereignty. In January 1893, American businessmen in Hawai'i with the help of marines and sailors from the *U.S.S. Boston* illegally overthrew the Hawaiian monarchy, established early in the century by Kamehameha I, the Great. During the nineteenth century foreign powers, including Britain, France, and the United States, and Russia, had vied for control of the Hawaiian Islands, first sighted by Europeans when Captain James Cook, on his third voyage to the Pacific, stumbled upon them in 1778.

The Hawaiians, sailing from the Marquesas, had discovered these islands circa 400 A.D. and settled them, creating a unique culture left intact until 1778. The murder of Cook by Hawaiians the next year did not deter other Europeans from landing and establishing agriculture and industry beginning with whaling and the sandalwood trade, then moving to sugar and pineapple plantations later. From the beginning, U.S. missionaries, who conveniently arrived in Hawai'i in 1820 just when the monarchy was abolishing the *kapu* (taboo) system, allied themselves with the *ali'i*, the ruling families. From this alliance came the increasing influence of missionary descendants, many of whom had married ali'i Hawaiians and acquired considerable land and governmental power in the process. The oft-repeated saying about those New England missionaries is, "They came to Hawai'i to do good and ended up doing well."

When the last monarchs—King David Kalakaua followed by Queen Liliuokalani, who ascended the throne in 1891—were becoming increasingly independent of and recalcitrant to U.S. business interests, a self-proclaimed Annexation Committee, which had been formed in 1892, called a meeting in the armory and formed a Committee of Public Safety consisting of U.S. businessmen living in Hawai'i. This group denounced the queen and gave itself the power to take whatever steps it deemed necessary to secure what it called the protection of liberty, life, and property in Hawai'i. The Committee of Public Safety asked American Minister Plenipotentiary and commander of all U.S. forces in Hawai'i, John L. Stevens, to land troops there because of unrest in the community. He agreed. On January 17, 1893, a force of 162 heavily armed troops came ashore, marched through Honolulu, and spent the night amid government buildings. The Provisional Government (PG) took control and immediately ordered that all arms be surrendered and the country be ruled by martial law. Habeas corpus was suspended, and the queen was arrested and imprisoned in her home. The Provisional Government asked that the American minister assume a quasi-protectorate over the Islands. Two weeks after the revolution, the American flag was raised over the government building, and people were required to take an oath of allegiance to the new government. Hawaiians declared they would eat stones rather than sign the "loathsome oath" and be disloyal to their queen. From this protest the famous Stone Eating Song, "Mele 'ai' Pohaku," was born.

Meanwhile Grover Cleveland was elected president in the United States. He sent James Blount to Hawai'i to look into the conditions under which the monarchy had been overthrown. In his report Blount charged that the revolution was the result of a conspiracy between Minister Stevens and the revolutionary leaders. Despite the finding of the Blount Report, the Republic of Hawaii was established in 1894, with Sanford Dole named president. In 1898, Hawai'i was annexed to the United States; and in 1900, the Organic Act established the Territory of Hawaii. Hawai'i became the fiftieth U.S. state in 1959.

After the overthrow, haole (white) business interests thrived. Plantation laborers—first from China in 1852, then from Portugal, Japan, Puerto Rico, Korea, and the Phillipines—had been brought in to supplant the Hawaiian labor force, decimated by Western diseases such as measles and syphilis, for which the workers had no immunity. Although the first trade union was formed in 1884, the plantation system of divide and conquer kept ethnic groups apart until the great strike of 1920. This was the longest strike ever conducted in the territory. It was also the first economic action taken by more than one national group of laborers, successfully joining together Japanese and Filipinos.

Between the world wars, two famous criminal cases brought national attention to Hawai'i and revealed a dual system of justice for whites and minorities. In 1928, a disturbed teenager, Myles Fukunaga, kidnapped ten-year-old Gill Jamieson from Punahou School while posing as a hospital orderly. He murdered the boy and demanded a ransom, an act that shook Honolulu and the Japanese-American community to their foundations. On November 19, 1929, Fukunaga was executed.

In 1931, the Massie case hit Hawai'i and seriously threatened the Territory's Organic Act. One night in September 1931, Thalia Massie, wife of Lieutenant

Thomas H. Massie, was found badly beaten and wandering about Ala Moana Road in Honolulu. At about the same time, five local men—two Hawaiians, two Japanese, and a Chinese-Hawaiian, known to many as the Kalihi Gang—were arrested in another part of town for assault and battery. Mrs. Massie framed the men, saying they had attacked and raped her although she had been seen that night with a stranger. A mistrial was declared in this case. Then Thalia Massie's mother, Grace Fortescue, came to Hawai'i, and, together with Lieutenant Massie and two U.S. sailors, kidnapped, shot, and killed Joe Kahahawai, one of the falsely accused. Now a case of kidnap and murder was prosecuted against those four participants. The trial, in which Clarence Darrow defended the four, made national headlines and focused attention on Hawai'i's system of law enforcement. The jury found the four guilty of manslaughter and recommended leniency. The judge sentenced them to ten years in prison, but public furor on the mainland was intense. Several bills were introduced in CONGRESS to amend the Organic Act in such a way that the Territory of Hawai'i would no longer have self-government. Consequently, Governor Judd of Hawai'i commuted the sentence of the four to one hour of incarceration in his office. The Massie case left bitter feelings in its wake for many years. The outcomes of the Fukunaga and Massie cases clearly pointed to a dual system of justice in Hawai'i, based on race.

On December 7, 1941, Pearl Harbor was attacked by Japan, forcing the United States to enter WORLD WAR II. In Hawai'i martial law was declared, suspending the civil rights and liberties of the citizens. Two cases protesting this martial law reached the SUPREME COURT in 1945. In an interesting 6–2 decision, the Court held that the phrase "martial law" in the Hawaiian Organic Act was intended to give the military the necessary power to act in case of threatened invasion but not to the point of taking over the civil courts. Such an action, the Court declared, was contrary to the BILL OF RIGHTS in the Constitution. But by 1945 this ruling was moot; the war was over.

The most egregious suspension of civil rights was the internment of Japanese Americans in concentration camps for the duration of the war. The islands' Japanese Americans were persecuted, and 1,400 from Hawai'i were sent to the camps, both in Hawai'i and on the mainland. The absurdity of the U.S. internment policy is revealed by the fact that Japanese Americans from Hawai'i were only very selectively sent to camps, but Japanese Americans from the entire Pacific Coast area were sent inland en masse. If Japanese Americans were a threat to U.S. security, surely those living in Hawai'i, only a territory and much closer to Japan than was the mainland, would be the greatest threat. Here the economics of war took precedence over the hysteria. Hawai'i would have collapsed as a staging ground for the war if all of Hawai'i's Japanese Americans had been removed and interned.

During World War II in Hawai'i, General Order #38 established formal military control over labor. Workers were frozen in their jobs and salaries. After the war, the American Federation of Labor (AFL) and the Congress of Industrial Organizations (CIO) became active again. In 1951, there occurred the celebrated trial of the "Hawaii seven." Seven residents of Hawai'i were arrested by the FEDERAL BUREAU OF INVESTIGATION (FBI) and convicted of having violated the Smith Act. (A circuit court of appeals later reversed the verdict.) A Commission on Subversive Activities was established to watch the activities of the supposed Communists.

To many Americans of Japanese Ancestry (AJA) veterans of World War II, the road to social reform and greater equality was politics. By 1954, most of the AJA veterans were back in Hawai'i from college or law school and settled into their jobs, ready to run for public office. The Democrats swept the elections of 1954 and 1956 for the first time in Hawai'i's history, placing many AJAs in the Territorial Legislature. Among those elected were Spark Matsunaga and Daniel Inouye, who later became U.S. senators.

Hawai'i became the fiftieth state on March 12, 1959, by a vote of the U.S. Congress; President Dwight EISENHOWER signed the proclamation on August 12, 1959. Since 1959 there has been a reversal of the postwar assimilationist trend in favor of Hawaiian nationalism and sovereignty, at least on the part of Hawaiians and part-Hawaiians, who compose approximately 20 percent of the population. Increasing wealth in the state has led Hawaiians to demand a portion of it. Between 1959 and 1989, defense spending in Hawai'i continued to increase, but soon tourism became the largest income producer with the decline of the pineapple and sugar industries. Today Hawai'i relies largely on tourism, creating a conflict for residents who depend on jobs in this industry but also may resent the packaging of their culture as paradise, as well as the colonial nature of tourism. As a consequence, the Hawaiian Renaissance, which began around 1970, blossomed into a sovereignty movement so strong that Governor John Waihee, Hawai'i's first governor of Hawaiian ancestry, lowered the U.S. flag to half mast for five days during the January 1993 centennial of the overthrow of the monarchy.

On November 23, 1993, President William CLINTON signed a resolution passed by the U.S. House of Representatives and the U.S. Senate formally apologizing for the overthrow of the Hawaiian nation that had taken place a century before. The resolution expressed a commitment to reconciliation between the

United States and native Hawaiians, but a disclaimer stated that this resolution was not meant to serve as a settlement of any claims against the United States. The U.S. government has determined that native Hawaiians are not considered aboriginal Americans and do not have a separate governmental structure as Native American tribes do. This places native Hawaiians in a separate and indeterminate category apart from other native Americans and creates many legal questions. By approving this resolution, Congress does admit that native Hawaiians never directly gave up their claims to their sovereignty as a people or their land, but does not intend for the resolution to serve as a settlement of claims. Hawaiian leaders both applauded and scoffed at this apology.

Although there are many similarities between the colonized histories of other Native Americans and native Hawaiians, the U.S. government will not grant claims to native Hawaiians even to the extent that Japanese Americans were monetarily compensated ($20,000 per person) for their unlawful internment during World War II. Hawaiians finally won their first major victory in the movement to recover Hawaiian land when the island of Kahoolawe was formally turned over from the federal government to the Kahoolawe Island Reserve Commission on May 7, 1994, a first step toward Hawaiian sovereignty. This law provided for further transfer of management to a "sovereign, native Hawaiian entity" after ten years of control by the U.S. Navy (1994–2004), during which period the Navy would spend $400 million to clean up unexploded bombs and shells, the island having been used for target practice by the U.S. military from 1941 to 1990. Since the 1970s Hawaiian activists had been making "illegal" trips to Kahoolawe for religious and political purposes despite the dangers from ordnance.

Because of Hawai'i's designation as a territory for much of its modern political life, the civil rights of its citizens have not always paralleled those of U.S. mainlanders. Although there was never official legal SEGREGATION, or Jim CROW, in Hawai'i, minorities were marginalized politically and legally by the policies of a conservative and largely white ruling class until after World War II. At this point martial law was lifted, and Japanese Americans, who today hold substantial power in the state government and public education system, were first elected to political office in large numbers. Today, Hawaiians seeking sovereignty have labeled all ethnic and white non-Hawaiians as "neocolonialists," further complicating valid arguments for redress from the illegal overthrow in 1893. At the millennium it appears that some form of sovereignty for Hawaiians will take place; but the specific model is contested by various activist groups, and the terrain is uncertain. University of Hawai'i Law School Professor Williamson

Chang summarizes the situtation by explaining that "civil rights" applies to those seeking equal justice and rights as citizens of a government they not only belong to but want to be part of. The sovereignty issue is about the rights of a nation, not the demands of citizens of an entity (the United States) that they actually oppose being part of and subject to. At present the idea of "nation" refers to those of native Hawaiian ancestry, but it could be broadened to include other citizens of Hawai'i; the issue of who would belong to or be allowed to be part of a sovereign Hawaiian nation is unresolved.

BIBLIOGRAPHY
Beechert, Edward D. *Honolulu: Crossroads of the Pacific.* 1992.
Fuchs, Lawrence. *Hawaii Pono.* 1993.
Kukendall, Ralph S, and A. Grove Day. *Hawaii: A History from Polynesian Kingdom to American Statehood.* 1976.
Liliuokalani, Lydia. *Hawaii's Story by Hawaii's Queen.* 1898.
Mackenzie, Melody Kapilialoha. *Native Hawaiian Rights Handbook.* 1991.
Rayson, Ann. *Modern Hawaiian History.* 1994.

Ann Rayson

Hay, Harry

(1912–   ), gay movement founder.

Harry Hay founded the MATTACHINE SOCIETY, the first organization of homosexuals in the United States, and was one of the first scholars of lesbian and gay studies. Hay spent most of his youth in southern California and attended Stanford University. Seeking work as an actor, he immersed himself in the artistic world of Los Angeles in the 1930s and soon found his political consciousness awakened by radical friends and colleagues. He joined the COMMUNIST PARTY and spent fifteen years as a member, teaching Marxist theory and music and working with educational theater groups.

The idea of an organization of gays first came to him in 1948 when he was teaching and working for the Communist Party in support of Henry WALLACE's bid for president. Imagining the possibility of mobilizing the support of his growing gay social circle for the campaign, he proposed the formation of "Bachelors for Wallace." Though nothing came of the idea at the time, two years later he decided to try to put the idea of a gay political group into action. Hay, Rudi Gernreich, who was his lover at the time, and three friends joined together to form the Mattachine Society.

Hay's background in Marxist theory influenced his conception of a political agenda for homosexuals. Just as workers needed to recognize their shared consciousness as a class in order to bring about change, homosexuals, Hay and his allies believed, needed to reject society's view of them as aberrant and take pride in their community and culture. Then, they could fight to end their own oppression.

The Mattachine Society grew rapidly, but within a few years internal divisions, largely revolving around the founders' ties to the Communist Party, led to the resignation of Hay and the other founders from its leadership. In 1955, the HOUSE UN-AMERICAN ACTIVITIES COMMITTEE summoned Hay to testify about his involvement in the party, from which he had resigned a few years earlier.

After his work with Mattachine and the Communist Party ended, Hay devoted much of his time to researching and writing about homosexuality. He elaborated on his long-held belief that gays and lesbians constitute a cultural minority that crosses national boundaries and shares language, values, and behaviors. Using extensive anthropological and historical research, he argued that homosexuals have always existed and have held valuable social roles in many cultures. He focused in particular on Native Americans, documenting the existence of people, sometimes called "berdaches," who were neither male nor female and held important spiritual positions.

Hay has continued his involvement with politics and human rights issues, particularly gay and lesbian organizing, throughout his life. In 1969, he helped start the Gay Liberation Front of Los Angeles. In the early 1980s, he and his long-time lover, John Burnside, joined the Radical Faeries and have maintained close ties with that movement since then.

BIBLIOGRAPHY

D'Emilio, John. *Sexual Politics, Sexual Communities: The Making of a Homosexual Minority in the United States, 1940–1970.* 1983.

Hay, Harry. *Radically Gay: Gay Liberation in the Words of Its Founder,* edited by Will Roscoe. 1996.

Timmons, Stuart. *The Trouble with Harry Hay: Founder of the Modern Gay Movement.* 1990.

Pippa Holloway

Hayden, Sandra ("Casey") Cason

(1937–   ), student movement founder, activist.

Born in Texas, Sandra "Casey" Cason Hayden was one of the most influential white activists in student-based organizaions in the 1960s, particularly the STUDENT NONVIOLENT COORDINATING COMMITTEE (SNCC) and STUDENTS FOR A DEMOCRATIC SOCIETY (SDS). As a student at the University of Texas, her strong spiri-

tuality led her to the YWCA and the Christian Faith and Life Community, where she resided in the only integrated housing on campus. She lived in what she called the "beloved community" of SNCC from 1960 to 1966, and helped organize the 1964 FREEDOM SUMMER voter registration project. Her 1960 speech to the NATIONAL STUDENT ASSOCIATION congress brought national student support to the Southern SIT-IN movement and introduced her to future SDS president Tom HAYDEN, whom she married in 1961. Casey Hayden influenced the writing of SDS's New Left manifesto, the Port Huron Statement (1962).

While Hayden's activities on behalf of civil rights encompassed issues such as poverty, unionism, racial discrimination, and political participation, she is perhaps best known for her contribution to women's rights. The "Women's Memo," submitted by Hayden and Mary King to SNCC's 1964 Waveland Staff Retreat, highlighted the bias felt by women in SNCC and encouraged the organization to consider gender equality as worthy a goal as racial equality. In 1965 Hayden and King distributed "Sex and Caste," a revised version of their Waveland memo, to other women they knew in the social justice movement, many of whom credited the Hayden–King paper with inspiring the second wave of the women's movement.

BIBLIOGRAPHY

Evans, Sara. *Personal Politics: The Roots of Women's Liberation in the Civil Rights Movement and the New Left.* 1979.

Hayden, Casey. "A Nurturing Movement: Nonviolence, SNCC, and Feminism." *Southern Exposure* 16 (1988): 48–53.

Hayden, Casey. "Fields of Blue." In *Deep in Our Hearts: Nine White Women in the Freedom Movement.* (Forthcoming.)

Michelle A. Krowl

Head Start

Project Head Start began in 1965 under the directive of President Lyndon JOHNSON as an umbrella term for a panoply of federally funded initiatives to counter poverty, illiteracy, under-education, and health problems among poor children in the United States. As the embodiment of diverse forces in public policy, social science research, and the political struggles of the time, Head Start represented the theories, aspirations, and ideals of various sectors of U.S. society. Head Start emerged out of the context of the civil rights movement and the WAR ON POVERTY as a growing concern for the nation's poor. It spurred a number of reformist, though often rushed, state interventions. In this

Teacher Royce Lawson leads her group of four-year-old pre-kindergarteners during "circle time" as part of the Clark Atlanta University Head Start Program. April 26, 1995. (AP/Wide World Photos)

view, education was thought to be the virtual panacea to poverty, mechanistically launching disadvantaged children into the ranks of the middle class. In the academy, support for Head Start programs was buttressed by a firm, if overzealous, reinvigoration of environmentalist theories of child development and intelligence. Scholars such as Benjamin Bloom and J. McVicker Hunt countered claims made by social scientists of the 1950s that intelligence was overwhelmingly inherited from one's biological parents. Additionally, applied researchers working in the fields of early education and child development across the nation were producing examples of enhanced IQ scores and academic achievement among mentally retarded children at institutions with special education programs. The findings from these studies were often referenced as evidence for the effectiveness of early intervention initiatives for the poor as well. National leaders seized the effort as a productive means to stem the shrinking ranks of personnel suitable for military service and lower-level industrial labor. The convergence of these three major influences produced a context in which serious and, eventually, sustained efforts would be made to break the "cycle of poverty" that had devastated the lives of over 40 million Americans (12

million children) by the 1960s. In attempts to embody a comprehensive child development program, Head Start comprised a series of related services including preschool and early elementary education and curriculum development, nutrition and dietary programs, immunizations and general health care, parent-teacher-student workshops, career development plans, and family skills training.

In its early years, Head Start was quickly overwhelmed with applicants across the country, receiving at points five times as many applications as planned. At its early height in the late 1960s, Project Head Start served over half a million impoverished young people and families across the country. Local programs strove to involve target families at all levels of decision making and planning, while its national level coordination remained in Washington, D.C. Extensive parent involvement in early education efforts marked an extremely novel aspect of Project Head Start where educators up to that point had focused almost exclusively on the school as an institution and the classroom as the space for learning. Moreover, the emphasis on the "whole child" approach to intervention—encompassing academic and intellectual stimulus, home environment, community support systems, health and nutrition concerns—signaled a radical break with past efforts at liberal social welfare reform. Head Start underwent significant ebbs and tides alongside frequent reconfigurations at all levels. Its peak levels of operation and funding occurred during the Democratic presidencies of Lyndon Johnson and Jimmy CARTER. Conversely, it suffered its most drastic fiscal reductions during the general social service cutbacks of the Republican NIXON and REAGAN administrations. Today, Head Start persists as a tenuous federal program with over two thousand local affiliates that receive sporadic government funding amid a continually growing organizational structure and participant base. As a result, the recently founded National Head Start Association has taken to formulating joint public/private funding schemes to support the continuation of its diversified services.

Timeline

1962 President Kennedy's Panel on Mental Retardation issues its first proposal for a public compensatory educational program for "economically disadvantaged children."

1964 Head Start national planning and steering committee is formed.

1965 Project Head Start is launched as an eight-week summer program.

1966 Head Start programs are expanded to year-long programs with a more comprehensive scope and wider participant base.

1969 The Westinghouse Report is released, allegedly demonstrating the wholesale failure of Head Start.

1970 The Kirschner Report is released. It compares health and education services for children in nearly fifty communities served by Head Start programs, indicating the reported success and usefulness of Head Start initiatives.

1973 The Head Start National Directors Association is founded at a conference in Kansas City, Missouri. The new group emerges as a collective effort to battle President Nixon's cutbacks in community action agencies nationwide.

1974 The Head Start Parents Association is founded in Washington, D.C.

1975 The Head Start Staff Association is formed at an organizational meeting in Los Angeles, CA.

1976 The Friends of Head Start national affiliation is created.

1990 The four national affiliates of Project Head Start votes to merge into one association on June 7, the twenty-fifth anniversary of the initiative. The new organization is called the National Head Start Association.

BIBLIOGRAPHY

Zigler, Edward, and Jeanette Valentine, eds. *Project Head Start: A Legacy of the War on Poverty.* 1979.

Zigler, Edward, and Susan Muenchow. *Head Start: The Inside Story of America's Most Successful Educational Experiment.* 1992.

                                            Jared Sexton

Hedgeman, Anna Arnold

(1899–1990), civil rights advocate, public servant, author, and educator.

Anna Arnold grew up in Anoka, Minnesota, and attended Hamline University, a Methodist College, in St. Paul, Minnesota. In 1933, she married Merritt A. Hedgeman, a musician. She first encountered segregation in 1922 at her first teaching job at Rust College in Holly Springs, Mississippi. In 1924, she accepted a position with a YWCA in Springfield, Ohio, beginning a relationship which lasted on and off for twelve years and wherein she helped to develop a variety of international programs in education. In her varied career she lost three bids for elected office at the national and local levels.

Hedgeman began working for the Emergency Relief Bureau as New York City's first consultant on racial problems in 1934. In 1941 she joined A. Philip RANDOLPH's MARCH ON WASHINGTON MOVEMENT, which was designed to fight segregation and discrimination against African Americans in defense industries and the military. In 1944, Hedgeman became executive director of Randolph's National Council for a Permanent FAIR EMPLOYMENT PRACTICE COMMITTEE, but was forced to resign when the major legislative drive of 1946 failed. Hedgeman then became Dean of Women at Howard University. She was appointed assistant to the administrator of the Federal Security Agency (later Health, Education and Welfare), in 1948, becoming the first black to hold office at the administrative level. Hedgeman became a mayoral assistant to New York City Mayor Robert F. Wagner, Jr. in 1954. She was responsible for eight city departments, acting as their liaison with the mayor, and remained in the post until 1958. In 1958 she became a public relations consultant to S. B. Fuller's cosmetics firm and an associate editor and columnist for his *New York Age*, until he discontinued the publication in 1960. Hedgeman also had her own radio program, "One Woman's Opinion," on a local station.

At her suggestion, Randolph's call for a March on Washington to pressure for job opportunities became amalgamated with Martin Luther KING, JR.'s planned march to pressure for a strong civil rights bill, becoming the March on Washington for Jobs and Freedom in August 1963. The only woman on the organizing committee of the March, Hedgeman protested the slighting of women. As Coordinator of Special Events for the newly formed Commission on Religion and Race of the National Council of Churches, her assignment was to relate the March to the new commitment of Protestant churches to justice for all. Hedgeman deserves some credit for the fact that about a third of the 250,000 marchers were white.

After mandatory retirement from the National Council of Churches in 1967, she and her husband established Hedgeman Consultant Services in 1968, while she continued her efforts to improve conditions for the people of Harlem. Hedgeman published her autobiography and study of black leadership, *The Trumpet Sounds*, in 1964, following it in 1977 with an assessment of the civil rights movement, *The Gift of Chaos*. Merritt Hedgeman died in 1988; Anna Hedgeman died two years later at the age of ninety, the recipient of many honors and awards for her work in race relations.

She devoted her life to black advancement and made important contributions to the civil rights cause, but partly because of her gender, partly because of her desire to better her situation, and partly forced by circumstances, she constantly changed jobs, never remaining in one sufficiently long to achieve the recognition she deserved. Anna Arnold Hedgeman earned the right to be acknowledged as an important role model in a field where traditionally there have been far too few black women.

BIBLIOGRAPHY

Amsterdam News. February 10, 1990.

Hedgeman papers. Schomburg Center for Research in Black Culture, New York.

Obituary. *New York Times.* January 26, 1990.

Pfeffer, Paula F. "Anna Arnold Hedgeman." In *Black Women in the United States: An Historical Encyclopedia,* edited by Darlene Clark Hine. 1993.

Paula F. Pfeffer

Height, Dorothy

(1912–   ), club woman and civil rights activist.

For more than sixty years, Dorothy Height has been a leader in the struggle for civil rights while pushing black women's issues to the forefront of the movement. Through her participation in a variety of women's organizations, including the Young Women's Christian Association (YWCA)—see YOUNG MEN'S CHRISTIAN ASSOCIATION AND YOUNG WOMEN'S CHRISTIAN ASSOCIATION—and the NATIONAL COUNCIL OF NEGRO WOMEN (NCNW), Height has worked to im-

Dorothy Height, a part-time activist at age 85. She has just resigned the presidency of the National Council of Negro Women. Washington, DC, December 5, 1997. (AP/Wide World Photos)

prove job opportunities for African-American women and has addressed the issue of sexual discrimination as well as inequalities in EMPLOYMENT and HOUSING.

Dorothy Height was born in Richmond, Virginia, and at the age of four moved with her family to the coal-mining town of Rankin, Pennsylvania. The daughter of a coal miner and a private duty nurse, Height excelled in school and was recognized as a leader in her local community. At a young age, she participated in a local YWCA branch and became president of the Pennsylvania State Federation of Girls' Clubs. After three years of study, Height graduated from New York University in 1932 and attained a master's degree in educational psychology the following year. Height worked at various odd jobs after college until finding work as a caseworker for the New York City Department of Welfare and later as an administrator at Harlem's YWCA.

From 1937 to 1939 Height served as assistant director of the YWCA's Emma Ransome House in Harlem. She later served as executive director of the Phillis Wheatley YWCA in Washington, D.C. During her time there, Height spoke out on New York's domestic worker "slave" markets and the limited housing available to single black women in Washington, D.C. Height's outspokenness on issues of equality placed her at the center of the YWCA's movement to integrate its chapters (see INTEGRATION). After becoming a member of the YWCA's national board in 1944, Height played a pivotal role in writing the association's first interracial charter, introduced at a YWCA national convention in 1947. In 1965, Height was named director of the YWCA's Center for Racial Justice.

Dorothy Height's service for the YWCA and her tenure as president of the Delta Sigma Theta Sorority from 1947 to 1956 prepared her for her role as president of the NCNW. Height had been involved with the NCNW since meeting with founder Mary McLeod BETHUNE in the 1930s during her service with the YWCA. Height's appointment to the office of president in 1957 represented a shift in the council's strategy toward greater political involvement. With onset of the civil rights movement in the late 1950s, Height geared the council to develop grassroots efforts toward improving living and working conditions for black women. Programs such as Women in Community Service (WICS) and the Wednesdays in Mississippi (WIMS) program brought together women of different faiths and racial backgrounds to spearhead voter registrations campaigns and to educate other women on the importance of DESEGREGATION and VOTING RIGHTS.

In her efforts to ensure that women's issues (see WOMEN AND CIVIL RIGHTS STRUGGLES) remained at the forefront of the civil rights movement, Height was often the lone woman among men organizing civil rights campaigns. Height was, in fact, the only woman to attend organizing sessions for the 1963 MARCH ON WASHINGTON.

Many women, including members of the NCNW, criticized Height's emphasis on civil rights, arguing that the council's focus on desegregation and voting rights was at the expense of issues such as sexual discrimination, job opportunities, and poverty. Yet Height saw involvement in the civil rights movement as uplifting the status of black people and, thus, as uplifting the status of black women.

In 1997, Height retired as president of the NCNW and was named president emerita of the organization. Described as one of the leading civil rights figures of the twentieth century, Height has received numerous awards and honors for her commitment to improving the quality of life for African-American women, including several honorary doctoral degrees. Her role as an advocate of human rights and equality has shaped the many organizations with which she has been involved.

BIBLIOGRAPHY

Giddings, Paula. *In Search of Sisterhood: Delta Sigma Theta.* 1988.

Hill, Ruth Edmonds. *The Black Women Oral History Project.* 1991.

Weisenfeld, Judith. *African American Women and Christian Activism.* 1997.

White, Deborah Gray. *Too Heavy a Load: Black Women in Defense of Themselves.* 1999.

Kori Kelley

Henry, Aaron

(1922–1997), Mississippi NAACP president.

Born into poverty on a Delta plantation in 1922, Aaron Henry first worked as a porter and shoeshine boy in a Clarksdale hotel, and later served for three years in the Pacific during World War II. He then took a degree in pharmacy at Xavier University in New Orleans. Back home in Clarksdale in 1950, he managed a drugstore (which he soon bought) and married Noelle Michael.

Henry was one of those World War II veterans—like Medgar EVERS and Amzie MOORE—who returned home fighting, vowing to destroy JIM CROW and everything it symbolized. A charter member of the delta-based Regional Council of Negro Leadership, Henry founded the Coahoma County branch of the NATIONAL ASSOCIATION FOR THE ADVANCEMENT OF COLORED PEOPLE (NAACP) in 1953. Elected state NAACP president in 1960, the Clarksdale pharmacist called for a new militancy: "Our actions will probably result in many of us being guests in the jails of the state. We will make these jails Temples of Freedom."

For the next four years Henry was at the center of movement activity. Elected president of the COUNCIL OF FEDERATED ORGANIZATIONS (COFO) at its founding in 1962, Henry also ran as COFO's candidate for governor in the 1963 Freedom Vote, a mock election held to demonstrate to the nation that Mississippi blacks were denied the franchise. Henry's major activity during this time was his leadership of a boycott and direct action campaign in Clarksdale, which sustained itself for more than two years against intractable white opposition. In the spring of 1963 two white men fire-bombed the Henrys' home. Later that month an explosion ripped a hole through the roof of his drugstore. Arrested and jailed after defying a court injunction prohibiting picketing, Henry was assigned to a garbage truck work detail, an attempt at humiliation that only increased his prestige.

He was active in the FREEDOM SUMMER project in 1964, when nearly a thousand volunteers came into the state to work on a variety of projects, including the

Aaron Henry, leader of the Mississippi Freedom Democratic Party, at a meeting of the credentials committee of the 1964 Democratic National Convention. He is arguing that his representatives be seated in place of the all-white delegation from Mississippi. August 22, 1964. (AP/Wide World Photos)

formation of the MISSISSIPPI FREEDOM DEMOCRATIC PARTY (MFDP). Henry chaired the MFDP delegation that challenged the white supremacist "regular" delegation at the 1964 national Democratic convention. The MFDP lost its challenge, and thereafter Henry began to drift away from his early movement allies, put off by their new black nationalist agenda.

In the late 1960s Henry was a founder of Mississippi Action for Progress (MAP), a Head Start program that competed with the more militant Child Development Group of Mississippi (CDGM). He headed the Mississippi NAACP from 1960 to 1994. Henry was also part of a coalition that successfully challenged the relicensing of Jackson's major television station, WLBT, which had a long history of antiblack programming and policy. He helped rebuild the state's Democratic Party in the late 1970s, serving as cochairman, and in 1979 won election to the state legislature, a position he held until 1995. Still an activist well into his seventies, Henry publicly protested the state's plan to close two historically black colleges, and lobbied for the reopening of the 1960s cases of those accused of murdering civil

rights activists Medgar EVERS and Vernon Dahmer. Henry died of congestive heart failure May 19, 1997.

BIBLIOGRAPHY

Dittmer, John. *Local People: The Struggle for Civil Rights in Mississippi.* 1994.
Silver, James W. *Mississippi: The Closed Society.* 1964.

John Dittmer

Highlander Folk School

Highlander Folk School opened in November 1932, largely as the brainchild of Savannah, Tennessee, native Myles HORTON. The Cumberland University and Union Theological Seminary graduate saw adult education and political organization as solutions for Southern Appalachia's poor population. Influenced by Christian socialism, espoused at Union as well as at successful rural folk schools in Denmark, Horton established Highlander with fellow socialist educator

Don West on property donated by long-time social activist Lillian Johnson, near Monteagle, Tennessee.

Despite frequent financial troubles, Highlander's staff began to help Tennessee workers in 1933, when coal miners around nearby Wilder went on an unsuccessful strike. Staff members such as James DOMBROWSKI and Mary Lawrance established several union locals and pressured the Works Progress Administration (WPA) to raise wages nationally. Envisioning self-supporting, democratic organizations, Highlander's faculty offered labor history, economics, and sociology courses for union representatives (see UNIONS). In 1937, Highlander joined the Congress of Industrial Organization's (CIO's) campaign to organize Southern textile workers (see AFL-CIO). In 1947 the union severed ties to Highlander because of rumored communist influence there. These charges frequently plagued Highlander.

Highlander's faculty supported integrated education as early as the 1940s. Black speakers, such as Fisk University sociologist Charles S. Johnson, appeared there. In 1944 Highlander created the South's first integrated union school with its United Auto Workers Summer School. Horton required integrated workshops despite the CIO's resistance.

Anticipating the Supreme Court's BROWN V. BOARD OF EDUCATION decision, Highlander began workshops in 1953 for teachers and civic leaders concerning peaceful approaches to school DESEGREGATION. Attending the 1955 workshop was Montgomery, Alabama, seamstress and NATIONAL ASSOCIATION FOR THE ADVANCEMENT OF COLORED PEOPLE (NAACP) secretary Rosa PARKS, whom Highlander assisted financially later that year after she sparked the MONTGOMERY BUS BOYCOTT. Black student leaders, such as John LEWIS and Marion Barry, planned strategies at Highlander in the early 1960s for SIT-IN demonstrations at segregated eating establishments. The STUDENT NONVIOLENT COORDINATING COMMITTEE (SNCC) was born two weeks after one 1960 Highlander workshop.

CITIZENSHIP SCHOOLS represented another successful Highlander project. Instructors trained African-American adults to read, write, and pass literacy requirements for voter registration (see VOTING RIGHTS). The most successful schools were located in South Carolina. From 1954 to 1964, the estimated number of blacks registered to vote in Charleston County rose from 5,000 to 14,000. Registered black voters on Johns Island increased from 200 to 700 from 1956 to 1960, by virtue of the leadership of local businessman Esau Jenkins and teachers Septima CLARK and Bernice ROBINSON.

Although Tennessee's legislature revoked Highlander Folk School's charter in 1961, over a questionable ceding of property to Myles Horton and political

objections, Horton soon (that same year) opened the Highlander Education and Training Center in Knoxville with a new charter. Highlander hosted additional workshops for SNCC leaders, aided voter registration in the 1964 Mississippi FREEDOM SUMMER project, and sponsored campaign workshops for black political candidates. Determining that civil rights leaders no longer needed organizational support, Highlander's staff shifted emphasis in the mid-1960s. Highlander Center, which relocated to New Market, Tennessee, in 1972, has since refocused on Appalachian workers' needs, such as environmental preservation and health care.

BIBLIOGRAPHY

Adams, Frank. *Unearthing Seeds of Fire: The Idea of Highlander.* 1975.
Glen, John M. *Highlander: No Ordinary School,* 2nd ed. 1996.
Horton, Aimee I. *The Highlander Folk School: A History of Its Major Programs, 1932–1961.* 1989.
Horton, Myles. *The Long Haul: An Autobiography.* 1990.
Horton, Myles, and Paulo Freire. *We Make the Road by Walking: Conversations on Education and Social Change.* 1990.

Wesley Brian Borucki

Hill, Herbert

(1924–), civil rights activist and scholar.

Herbert Hill served the civil rights movement as both activist and scholar, exposing and combating racial discrimination in the workplace. As national labor secretary of the NATIONAL ASSOCIATION FOR THE ADVANCEMENT OF COLORED PEOPLE (NAACP) for more than twenty years and as a distinguished scholar, Hill insisted that race remained the central problem in American life and labor.

Born in New York City in 1924, Hill became fascinated with black culture as a young man. During WORLD WAR II, he was active in union politics, where he became a friend of C. L. R. James and other anti-Stalinist radicals. Hill raised the issue of racial discrimination in the labor movement and clashed with Stalinists, who believed that the defense of the Soviet Union must take precedence over racial issues.

After the war, Hill was elected to the board of the Harlem branch of the NAACP and organized demonstrations against police brutality and racial segregation. Hill joined the national staff of the NAACP in 1948. Soon becoming its national labor secretary, Hill sought to recruit black industrial workers to the NAACP and challenged the labor movement to live up to its racially egalitarian rhetoric. He also served as special consultant to the United Nations and the U.S. EQUAL EMPLOYMENT OPPORTUNITY COMMISSION and testified many times in federal court about racial discrimination in industry.

Throughout his NAACP career, Hill labored as a scholar. In 1977, he became professor of Afro-American studies and industrial relations at the University of Wisconsin-Madison. His many books and articles highlighted the discrimination African Americans confronted both as workers and in the labor movement. He also edited two early collections of black literature. His debate with Herbert Gutman, the most prominent labor historian of his generation, reconfigured the world of American labor history. Hill established "the unifying role of racism among white workers" historically and proved that many labor historians downplayed white racism. The emergence of a new generation of scholars examining the central role of "whiteness" in the American working class testifies to Hill's enduring influence.

BIBLIOGRAPHY

"The Communist Party: Enemy of Negro Equality." *The Crisis* (June–July 1951).

Hill, Herbert. *Employment, Race and Poverty*, edited by Arthur M. Ross and Herbert Hill. 1967.

Hill, Herbert. *Black Labor and the American Legal System.* 1977.

Hill, Herbert. "Myth-Making as Labor History: Herbert Gutman and the United Mine Workers of America." *International Journal of Politics, Culture, and Society* 2, no. 2 (Winter 1988).

Hill, Herbert. *Race in America and the Struggle for Equality*, edited by Herbert Hill and James E. Jones, Jr. 1993.

Hill, Herbert. "The Problem of Race in American Labor History." *Reviews in American History* 24, no. 2 (June 1996).

Oral history interview with Timothy B. Tyson, Madison, Wisconsin, February 22, 1999. Audiotapes in the possession of the author.

Timothy B. Tyson

Hill, Oliver W.

(1907–   ), civil rights lawyer.

Born in 1907 in Richmond, Virginia, Hill grew up in Roanoke and attended Dunbar High School in Washington, D.C. He graduated from Howard University in 1931 and subsequently entered Howard Law School, graduating in 1933. Hill received his legal education from Charles H. HOUSTON, who instructed his students to play a leading role in the African-American struggle to gain full equality under the law. Upon graduation, Hill entered private practice in Roanoke, Virginia, where he also investigated the conditions of

NAACP attorneys Spottswood Robinson (center) and Oliver W. Hill (right), both of Richmond, Virginia, are interviewed outside federal court in Alexandria, Virginia, after closing arguments for a court battle challenging Virginia's "massive resistance" policy toward school integration. September 12, 1957. (CORBIS/Bettmann)

black public schools for the NATIONAL ASSOCIATION FOR THE ADVANCEMENT OF COLORED PEOPLE (NAACP). He moved to Richmond in 1939 to practice law, and served as chairman of the Legal Committee of the Virginia State Conference of the NAACP from 1940 to 1961.

Hill fought inequality and discrimination on a number of fronts—in education, transportation, and housing. The most notable case Hill litigated was *Davis v. County School Board of Prince Edward County, Virginia*, one of the five cases the Supreme Court heard under the name BROWN V. BOARD OF EDUCATION in 1954. In addition to his legal activities, Hill ran for political office, hoping to inspire African Americans to pay their poll taxes, register, and vote. In 1947, he campaigned to become one of the Democratic primary candidates for delegate to the Virginia General Assembly. Although Hill failed to win the nomination, his campaign greatly increased the number of registered black voters in Richmond. In 1948, Hill ran for the Richmond City Council and won, becoming the first African American to serve on the City Council since 1898.

From 1961 to 1966, Hill was assistant to the commissioner in the Federal Housing Administration. Since 1966, Hill has been a senior partner of the Hill, Tucker, and Marsh law firm in Richmond, Virginia.

BIBLIOGRAPHY

Higginbotham, A. Leon, Jr. "Conversations with Civil Rights Crusaders." *Virginia Lawyer* 37 (1989): 11–16.

Kluger, Richard. *Simple Justice: The History of Brown v. Board of Education and Black America's Struggle for Equality.* 1977.

Shirelle, Phillips, ed. *Who's Who Among African Americans,* 10th ed. 1997.

Larissa M. Smith

Homeless Rights

Homeless persons lack many of the civil rights enjoyed by Americans fortunate enough to have property or a permanent address. The onerous nineteenth-century proscriptions against the indigent poor have largely been replaced by more subtle means of control. Nonetheless, at the end of the twentieth century, the legal and social status of the hundreds of thousands of people who live on America's streets remain a critical civil rights battleground.

In the decades after the Civil War, industrial progress left in its wake swelling numbers of homeless and wandering "tramps." Tramps were mainly American-born and English-speaking white men, yet most Americans viewed them as moral outcasts and a menace to orderly society. States and localities passed laws against sleeping out, begging, and other vagrancy crimes. Tramps were hunted for bounties, tried without the benifit of jury or counsel, and summarily sentenced to hard labor. In 1894, in the midst of an economic depression that left millions without work or shelter, unemployed workers organized "industrial armies" in cities and towns across the country—the most bizarre and famous of which was known as "Coxey's army," led by Jacob S. Coxey of Ohio—in a national march on Washington. The "industrial armies" sympathized with the then-current Populist reform movement (see POPULIST PARTY), but their demands focused on federal funding for jobs and for equal treatment as American citizens. Although the march itself failed, it raised the country's awareness that unemployment and homelessness had social causes beyond individual moral deficiency, and of the injustice of the vagrancy laws.

In the early twentieth century, the protests of the homeless poor—or hoboes, as they were called—took a more radical turn. Linking up with the INDUSTRIAL WORKERS OF THE WORLD, hoboes protested vagrancy laws as part of the IWW's "free speech" campaigns. WORLD WAR I unleashed a wave of repression from which the IWW, with its anarcho-syndicalist visions and its radical hobo following, never recovered.

The fight for homeless rights rebounded with the onset of the Depression in 1929, as homeless encampments known as "Hoovervilles" became symbolic of a failed economic policy and of social injustice. In Harlem and other urban centers, unemployment councils

Homeless advocate Mitch Snyder, who nearly died during a 51-day fast in 1984 protesting the Reagan administration's delaying tactics and equivocations toward an allotment of money for the homeless. March 1987. (Kenneth Jarecke/Contact Press Images/PNI)

took up the fight against evictions, for the first time bringing African Americans into the organized struggle for housing rights. Led by communists and other leftists, these councils worked largely within the framework of the NEW DEAL promise that housing, jobs, and social security were fundamental American rights.

Since the 1970s, and especially in the wake of the 1980s recession, American cities have experienced the appearance of the "new homeless": manual workers displaced in the service economy; women and children and the mentally ill turned into the streets by welfare, housing, and health care cutbacks; and employed as well as retired men and women unable to afford the cost of housing. In the 1980s, homeless activist Mitch Snyder and the Washington, D.C.–based Community for Creative Non-Violence launched hunger strikes, seized buildings, and engaged in other acts of civil disobedience and direct action, including a march on the nation's capital, on October 7, 1989. Although Mitch Snyder took his own life in 1991, his pioneering tactics successfully inserted homeless rights into national politics.

Presently, a web of homeless rights organizations gives voice to this otherwise marginalized and disfranchised population. Local groups combining both homeless persons and committed activists, often affiliated with the National Coalition for the Homeless (NCH), focus on problems of emergency food and shelter, evictions, welfare, health care, veterans' rights, living wage laws, and other needs of the homeless poor. Some of these organizations, such as Food Not Bombs, address global questions of peace and social justice. Homeless activists have also launched over fifty street newspapers to "combat poverty through freedom of speech."

The homeless movement has put special emphasis on equality before the law. Local governments have responded to the new homeless with new repressive measures, as the old vagrancy laws were overturned by U.S. courts in the 1960s and early 1970s. Cities have adopted laws restricting begging, sleeping, and loitering in public places, and police have conducted sweeps to clear neighborhoods of the undesirable poor. In many cases, a lack of permanent address means loss of VOTING RIGHTS, loss of protection from unreasonable search and seizure and, for homeless parents, loss of custody of their children. The National Law Center on Homelessness and Poverty (NLCHP) and other advocacy groups have challenged antihomeless ordinances as violations of the right to free speech, to travel, and to equal treatment under the law.

BIBLIOGRAPHY

Monkkonen, Eric H., ed. *Walking to Work: Tramps in America, 1790–1935.* 1984.

Piven, Frances Fox, and Richard A. Cloward. *Poor People's Movements: Why They Succeed, How They Fail.* 1979.

Rossi, Peter H. *Down and Out in America: The Origins of Homelessness.* 1989.

Schwantes, Carlos A. *Coxey's Army: An American Odyssey.* 1985.

Stoner, Madeleine R. *The Civil Rights of Homeless People: Law, Social Policy, and Social Works Practice.* 1995.

Wright, Talmage. *Out of Place: Homeless Mobilizations, Subcities, and Contested Landscapes.* 1997.

Resources: National Coalition for the Homeless; Community for Creative Non-Violence; National Law Center on Homelessness and Poverty; and North American Street Newspaper Association.

Charles Postel

Home Rule for Washington, D.C.

Because the U.S. Constitution assures Congress's "exclusive jurisdiction" over the federal district, residents of Washington, D.C., have lacked traditional powers of self-governance. During RECONSTRUCTION, the RADICAL REPUBLICANS in Congress implemented a number of civil rights measures, including the enfranchisement of black men. A shift of power in Congress, however, resulted in 1874 in the elimination of elected government in favor of a presidentially appointed commission, an act District of Columbia resident Frederick DOUGLASS declared was intended to eliminate the rights of Freedmen.

The U.S. Senate approved home rule bills five times between 1949 and 1960, but the House District Com-

mittee, dominated by Southern conservatives, prevented the bills from ever reaching a vote on the House floor. It took the power of a national civil rights movement and the defeat of House district chairman John McMillan in 1972 to finally break the impasse. A year later Congress approved a home rule bill establishing an elected mayor and city council.

Critics of the home rule bill who warned that Congress retained too many powers over the DISTRICT OF COLUMBIA sought to make Washington an independent state and secured local approval for a new constitution in 1982. Congress refused to act on the measure until 1993, when the House of Representatives rejected it by a wide margin. Two years later Congress created a control board that took its mandate beyond repairing District finances to assume direction of public schools and other key departments. Many local residents objected to these restrictions on local governance, describing them as further blows to the ongoing civil rights struggle in the nation's capital.

BIBLIOGRAPHY

Diner, Stephen J. *Democracy, Federalism and the Governance of the Nation's Capital.* 1987.

Melder, Keith. *City of Magnificent Intentions: A History of the District of Columbia,* rev. ed. 1998.

Howard Gillette, Jr.

Homophile Movement

The homophile movement of the 1950s and 1960s was the first organized movement for gay and lesbian rights in the United States. Several nationwide organizations comprised the movement: the MATTACHINE SOCIETY, the first such group and one with a primarily male membership; the DAUGHTERS OF BILITIS, organized by and for women; ONE Inc, which published the magazine *ONE;* and the Society for Individual Rights, formed about a decade after the others. In addition, a number of locally based groups joined the movement, especially following the dissolution of the national Mattachine organization. In the 1960s many of the most politically active local organizations were on the East Coast and in 1963, four of them formed a coalition named ECHO, short for East Coast Homophile Organizations.

Individuals in the homophile movement shared the goal of improving the status of gays and lesbians in society, but they often disagreed on the means of accomplishing this. Two basic approaches emerged, one more radical and one more accommodationist.

The origins of the radical perspective are usually first attributed to a man named Harry HAY, a former

COMMUNIST PARTY member who founded the Mattachine Society. Rejecting the idea that homosexuality was a pathology or moral weakness, Hay argued that gays were uniquely special and unfairly persecuted by the dominant society's heterosexually biased definitions of sex roles. Borrowing from Marxist ideas about class consciousness, Mattachine's founders believed that gays should develop their own culture, community, and sense of pride in themselves from which they could stage a challenge to society's oppression.

Other gays and lesbians soon countered with a more conservative and assimilationist perspective. At the Mattachine Society's 1953 convention a group of individuals challenged the ideas of Hay and other leaders, as well as their right to lead. They said that gays and lesbians were just like heterosexuals, except in their choice of sexual partners. In order to gain equality in society, homosexuals had to prove they were the same as everyone else. They also pushed for the dissolution of Mattachine's association with the Communist Party through the election of new leaders who did not have Communist backgrounds.

This second faction dominated the leadership of the homophile movement for much of the 1950s, shaping the movement in a variety of ways. Rather than working to build the gay community as Mattachine's founders had suggested, homophile organizations now began working to convince professionals and leaders in the wider society that homosexuality was an inconsequential difference. In practice, this meant a rejection of the earlier strategy of protests and movements for legal reform in favor of participating in charity fund-raising drives, and other civic activities. Another manifestation of this philosophy can be found in the homophile movement's ideas about gender identity. Assimilationists hoped to dispel the stereotype of masculine women and feminine men, and the Daughters of Bilitis in particular instructed lesbians to avoid male dress.

The members of the homophile movement represented just a fraction of all homosexuals in the United States in this period. The majority of its members were white, middle-class, urban residents who often had little in common with the many individuals nationwide who engaged in same-sex sexual behavior.

In the late 1960s and early 1970s a radical gay liberation movement emerged, and many believed this new movement to be a rejection of an earlier homophile movement that was more conservative and accommodationist. Historical scholarship in the 1980s, particularly the work of John D'Emilio, has served as a reminder, however, that a radical gay political movement had not only existed previously, but had been conceived of and born in the 1950s, one of the decades in U.S. history most hostile to homosexuality.

BIBLIOGRAPHY

D'Emilio, John. *Sexual Politics, Sexual Communities: The Making of a Homosexual Minority in the United States, 1940–70.* 1983.

Katz, Jonathan. *Gay American History: Lesbians and Gay Men in the U.S.A.: A Documentary History,* rev. ed. 1992.

Sears, James T. *Lonely Hunters: An Oral History of Lesbian and Gay Southern Life, 1948–68.* 1997.

Timmons, Stuart. *The Trouble with Harry Hay: Founder of the Modern Gay Movement.* 1990.

Pippa Holloway

Homophobia

The term "homophobia" describes several attitudes and behaviors about social life that involve gender and sexuality. In general, homophobia refers to the unfounded fear of homosexual individuals, of their sexual behavior, and of gay and lesbian communities. This fear often turns to discrimination and deep-seated hatred, including violence against individuals and groups who may be lesbian, gay (male homosexual), or transgender (involving an identity change that includes changing from one gender to the other, not necessarily through surgical procedures). Closely associated with the women's rights movement and struggles for sexual liberation, the word "homophobia" has been widely used since the 1970s. It has been used especially since the STONEWALL Inn rebellion, June 28 and 29, 1969, in New York City, when hundreds of men and women rioted against police harassment and extortion of the patrons of the Stonewall Inn gay bar in Greenwich Village. The events of these two nights are considered by many to be the birth of the modern gay rights movement in the United States (see also GAY AND LESBIAN RIGHTS).

Homophobia can function on several levels. At the *individual, interpersonal level,* homophobia involves an individual's fear of someone else's presumed gay, lesbian, or transgender sexuality and may also include people's fear that they may come to be attracted to their own gender. In this sense, homophobia is related to heterosexism, or the idea that all social and sexual life is, by nature, heterosexual—the social and sexual relations between a woman and a man. Heterosexism assumes that there is only one "right" way to function as a man and only one "right" way to function as a woman. Heterosexism further assumes that all women and all men are heterosexual in their erotic attraction. Homophobia at this interpersonal level sometimes leads to name-calling in the playground, at school, at home, in the streets, or at work. Homophobic names—for example, "faggot," "dyke," "sissy"—are meant to ridicule, to insult, and to hurt someone be-

October 19, 1998. In New York City, a man holds a candle and a placard during a vigil for Matthew Shepard. Thousands of people attended the "political funeral" to protest his murder. Shepard was twenty-two when he was beaten to death in Wyoming. (Rommel Pecson/Impact Visuals/PNI)

cause his or her sexual behavior is not (or is not believed to be) heterosexual.

Homophobic name-calling often leads to "gay bashing"—acts of violence against homosexual individuals or those thought to be homosexual. Such violent acts are as much "hate crimes" as are those targeted at individuals because of their race, religion, ethnicity, mental or physical disability, or gender. Since the 1970s, gay rights groups such as the National Gay and Lesbian Task Force and Lambda Legal Defense and Education Fund have recorded an increasing number of violent attacks against gay, lesbian, and transgender communities in the United States. In October 1998, for example, a twenty-one-year-old white, gay University of Wyoming student, Matthew Shepard, was beaten to death. The case caught national attention and raised indignation about the risks many gay, lesbian, and transgender individuals face. The FEDERAL BUREAU OF INVESTIGATION reported 4,558 hate crimes in 1991, 7,587 in 1993, and almost 9,000 in 1996; and it is believed that a majority of hate crimes remain unreported. By the end of 1998, only eleven states included sexual orientation in their anti-hate crimes laws.

At the *institutional level*, homophobia refers to how institutions, employers, and organizations discriminate on the basis of sexuality. Most state and federal laws, for example, do not include sexuality or sexual orientation as a basis for protection against discrimination in EMPLOYMENT and attacks of violence. In March 1999, for example, a Bakersfield school district in California was ordered by the state's Labor Commission to apologize to an award-winning science teacher for removing fifteen students from his class because some parents did not want their children in a gay teacher's class. It was the teacher's sexuality, not his ability to carry out his work, that became the object for parental scrutiny. Two decades earlier, in 1978, California State Senator John Briggs placed Proposition 6 on the ballot to ban gays and lesbians from teaching in the state's public school system. Although the initiative failed, it symbolized conservative efforts to legally prevent gays and lesbians from participating as full members of society.

At the *cultural and social level*, homophobia helps create collective negative attitudes and beliefs against lesbian, gay, and transgender communities. In their advertisement and programming, the media have portrayed heterosexuality as the only possible norm, and have by and large underreported and ridiculed all other forms of sexual or erotic expression. "Effeminate" and "ineffectual" men in television and motion pictures often bring ridicule to gays by portraying them with exaggerated or what are believed to be stereotypical manners.

Civil rights for gay and lesbian individuals, families, and communities have focused on creating spaces where they can socialize and organize safely, without fear of harm by homophobic individuals or groups. Activists have emphasized that guaranteeing legal protection and rights for gays and lesbians must be part of a tradition of civil rights for all, and that these should not be considered "special rights." Even though discrimination against gays and lesbians has different origins from the discrimination that racial minorities experience, hate crimes plague almost all minorities. Violent attacks against one member of a minority group are meant to send a message of hatred against that entire community. For this reason, national and state mobilizations with rallies, town meetings, school presentations, and religious events have focused on making the public aware that sexuality and sexual orientation must not be targets for discrimination.

BIBLIOGRAPHY

Blumenfeld, Warren, J., ed. *Homophobia: How We All Pay the Price.* 1992.
Hemphill, Essex, and Joseph Beam, eds. *Brother to Brother.* 1991.
Leong, Russell, ed. *Asian American Sexualities: Dimensions of the Gay and Lesbian Experience.* 1996.
Lorde, Audre. *Zami: A New Spelling of My Name.* 1982.
MIT Video Productions. "Homophobia in the Media and Society: One Life to Live and Beyond." April 20, 1993.
Moraga, Cherríe, and Gloria Anzaldúa, eds. *This Bridge Called My Back: Writings by Radical Women of Color.* 1983.
Ramos, Juanita, ed. *Compañeras: Latina Lesbians.* 1994.
Smith, Barbara. "Homophobia: Why Bring It Up?" In *The Gay and Lesbian Studies Reader,* edited by H. Abelove, M. A. Barale, and D. M. Halperin, 1993.

Horacio N. Roque Ramírez

Hope, John

(1868–1936), educator.

John Hope, president of Morehouse College, Atlanta, and black leader, was born in Augusta, Georgia, the son of a free black mother and a white Scottish father. After attending Worcester Academy in Massachusetts, Hope entered Brown University, in Providence, Rhode Island, where he graduated in 1894. Although light-skinned enough to pass as white, Hope accepted a position as Professor of Classics at the all-black Roger Williams College in Nashville, Tennessee. In 1898, he accepted a position at Atlanta Baptist College; eight years later, he became the first African-American president of the college (renamed Morehouse College in 1913). In 1929, when Morehouse united with Spelman College and Atlanta University, Hope was named president of the "new" Atlanta University.

Hope's civil rights activities were manifold. Even before he joined Morehouse, Hope was a prominent activist who courteously but firmly challenged BOOKER T. WASHINGTON's accommodationist policies. In 1896, he made a public speech demanding "social equality"—the nightmare of white racists. In 1905, Hope joined his close friend and collaborator, W. E. B. DU BOIS, in organizing the NIAGARA MOVEMENT to lobby for equal rights. Four years later, Hope attended the founding conference of the NATIONAL ASSOCIATION FOR THE ADVANCEMENT OF COLORED PEOPLE (NAACP), and he remained a strong supporter (in 1915, he was offered but declined the post of NAACP Field Secretary). During World War I, Hope worked with the YOUNG MEN'S CHRISTIAN ASSOCIATION (YMCA) to secure fair treatment for black soldiers. In later years, Hope was active with the COMMISSION ON INTERRACIAL COOPERATION, a liberal Southern organization, and served as its president in 1932.

BIBLIOGRAPHY

Lewis, David Levering. *W. E. B. DuBois: Biography of a Race, 1868–1919.* 1993.
Torrence, Ridgely. *The Story of John Hope.* 1948.

Greg Robinson

Hopwood v. State of Texas

Originating from a lawsuit filed by four white applicants to the University of Texas School of Law in 1992, *Hopwood v. Texas* (1996) challenged the use of race as an admissions criteria by public universities and graduate schools. In March 1996, a three-judge panel ruled that the University of Texas School of Law could not use race as a factor in admissions in order to (1) diversify their student body, (2) change a perceived hostile environment, (3) challenge their poor reputation in the local community, or (4) eliminate any effects of past discrimination by agents other than themselves. In July 1996, the Supreme Court refused to hear this case; as a result, the lower court decision remains in place without the authority of the Supreme Court. As a federal appellate court decision, *Hopwood v. Texas* serves as a precedent only for state schools in the FIFTH CIRCUIT: Texas, Louisiana, and Mississippi.

Much of the controversy around the appellate court's decision has centered around the fact that a federal appellate panel determined that the SUPREME COURT's ruling in *Regents of the University of California v. Bakke* (see BAKKE), which held that creating a diverse student body is a compelling governmental interest, is no longer a binding precedent. This is especially significant because the Supreme Court has not overturned *Bakke*. This case has been seen as a great challenge to race-based affirmative action programs in higher education and has immediately resulted in markedly less diverse student bodies in programs that have followed the *Hopwood* ruling.

BIBLIOGRAPHY

Caplan, Lincoln, with Dorian Friedman and Julian E. Barnes. "The *Hopwood* Effect Kicks In on Campus." *U.S. News and World Report* (December 23, 1996): 26–28.

Cheryl J. Hopwood v. State of Texas 861 F.Supp 551 (W.D. Tex 1994), 78 F.3d 932 (5th Cir, 1996), rehearing denied 84 F.3d 720 (5th Cir), cert denied, 116 S.Ct 2581 (1996).

Graglia, Lino A. "*Hopwood* v. *Texas*: Racial Preferences in Higher Education Upheld and Endorsed." *Journal of Legal Education* 45 (March 1995): 79–93.

Jaschik, Scott and Douglas Lederman, "Appeals Court Bars Racial Preference in College Admissions." *Chronicle of Higher Education* (March 29, 1996): A26–A27.

Wright, Victor V. "*Hopwood* v. *Texas*: The Fifth Circuit Engages in Suspect Compelling Interest Analysis in Striking Down an Affirmative Action Admissions Program." *Houston Law Review* 34 (Fall 1997): 871–907.

Michelle Donaldson Deardorff

Horton, Myles and Zilphia Mae

(1905–1990 and 1913–1956), social activists and educators.

Born in 1905 in Savannah, Tennessee, Myles Horton spent his life seeking ways to empower ordinary people to act against the problems and injustices they faced. A poor white boy himself from Appalachia, he harbored a permanent antipathy to any "missionary" approach to education that condescendingly undertook to uplift the ignorant. After studies with prominent theologian Reinhold Niebuhr at New York's Union Theological Seminary in 1929 and with sociologist Robert Park at the University of Chicago in 1930, Horton undertook a tour of Danish folk schools in 1931. The communal living, peer learning, and nonvocational but purposeful style of these schools were central to the HIGHLANDER FOLK SCHOOL, established by Horton in 1932 in Monteagle, Tennessee. Another key feature—group singing—became an in-

tegral part of Highlander's curriculum with the arrival of Zilphia Mae Johnson.

The daughter of a mine owner, Johnson had left the family home because of her pro-labor views and was directed to Monteagle by Howard Kester of the FELLOWSHIP OF RECONCILIATION. After a whirlwind romance, she married Horton in March 1935. Aided by musician Ralph Tefferteller, she encouraged students to share the songs of their home communities and to adapt the lyrics to contemporary situations. Until her sudden death in 1956, she collected songs and mimeographed song sheets for picket lines and protest marches. The most famous song she uncovered was a hymn, "I Will Overcome," that striking tobacco workers adapted as "We Will Overcome" on picket lines in Charleston, South Carolina in 1945. At Highlander, it became the anthem of the civil rights movement: WE SHALL OVERCOME. Zilphia's untimely death was due to the aggravation of an undiagnosed kidney ailment by swallowing either moonshine deliberately or office-cleaning fluid accidentally.

Frank Adams, in his biography of Myles Horton's Highlander colleague, James DOMBROWSKI, suggests that the latter's resignation in 1942 was partly spurred by his colleagues' reluctance to confront the race issue. However, Horton himself had already embraced the need for blacks and whites to unite and fight together in his own union-organizing efforts, and the CIO's Southern campaigns in the 1940s soon established Highlander as the region's premier interracial labor education center (see AFL–CIO). As a Southern progressive after 1948 (see PROGRESSIVE PARTY), Horton refused to sever his ties with the COMMUNIST PARTY and his school lost CIO support. Smeared as "a Communist training center" after HUAC investigations in 1954, Highlander was eventually raided by Tennessee state authorities in 1959. The Red Scare probably made Highlander freer to pursue racial issues, however, as Horton secured liberal foundation support for rural leadership development schemes and for programs to prepare the South for school DESEGREGATION. Both initiatives brought a succession of African-American activists to Monteagle, including Rosa PARKS, Martin Luther KING, JR., James FORMAN, and John LEWIS.

Highlander's integrated living and Horton's insistence that education should empower people to act and not wait for others to act on their behalf was profoundly liberating for black Southerners. Via the CITIZENSHIP SCHOOLS and numerous workshops, Horton's philosophy enabled Highlander to aid in the development of the civil rights movement without intruding on indigenous African-American leadership. Having helped nurture black activism, Horton seemed the readiest among white liberals to accept that by

1966 whites should focus on a complementary agenda of organizing the white poor. Ultimately, this returned Highlander to its Appalachian starting point after Horton's retirement in 1970, as he encouraged his successors to tackle issues of human rights and environmental degradation. He died in January 1990.

BIBLIOGRAPHY

Horton, Aimee I. *The Highlander Folk School: A History of Its Major Programs, 1932–1961.* 1989.

Horton, Myles, and Paolo Freire. *We Make the Road by Walking: Conversations on Education and Social Change,* edited by Brenda Bell, John Gaventa, and John Peters. 1990.

Horton, Myles, with Judith Kohl and Herbert Kohl. *The Long Haul: An Autobiography.* 1990.

Peter J. Ling

House Un-American Activities Committee

In the dozen years after 1945, the House Un-American Activities Committee (HUAC) acquired its lasting notoriety, although it had been spawned in 1938 during an anti–New Deal spasm of the House of Representatives. In the COLD WAR's early harrowing days HUAC was eager to seek out the enemy within: the communist sympathizers who were held to be plotting to deliver the United States to the Soviet Union. The Committee's definition of the communist conspiracy was vague, however, so that progressives of many kinds could find themselves under scrutiny. Empowered to issue subpoenas, HUAC summoned hundreds of citizens to interrogate them on their political beliefs. At state level about a dozen "little HUACs" sprang up to ape its activities, and by the 1950s Senate committees (such as that chaired by Senator Joseph McCarthy; see MCCARTHYISM) were also joining the red-hunting game. These inquisitions served to stifle dissent, eroding those freedoms of speech, press, and assembly promised by the Constitution's First Amendment.

In its early, anti-Roosevelt days HUAC had made only a modest impact, but the Cold War resuscitated it, and the election of a highly conservative Congress in 1946 gave it license to roam. Its credibility was boosted when the redoubtable FBI chief, J. Edgar Hoover, deigned to appear before it early in 1947; thereafter, the FBI provided HUAC with much covert assistance, helping to guide its inquisitorial impulses. HUAC's 1947 hearings on communist influence in Hollywood made it a household name, and precipitated the studios' notorious blacklist. The Committee's intimidatory capacity was enhanced when uncooperative witnesses went to prison for contempt of

Senator Joseph McCarthy, in a gesture that betokens self-promotion and a touch of macabre humor, holds a broom in the vicinity of the Capitol and threatens to "sweep out" communists from the U.S. military. 1951. (Archive Photos/PNI)

Congress. HUAC also investigated a host of educational, cultural, civil rights, and labor organizations.

By the 1950s, HUAC had perfected the techniques of exposure. Friendly witnesses supplied the names of their suspect associates, who were then summoned. Mindful that contempt citations could lead to prison, such witnesses frequently resorted to the Fifth Amendment, declining to answer questions lest they incriminate themselves. But this did not protect them in their jobs, and HUAC summoned many witnesses in order to get them fired by their employers. HUAC sometimes appeared also at the scene of labor disputes, collaborating in attacks on labor militants; and civil rights activists were also harassed. In 1956 HUAC's citations of several African-American leaders were read into the *Congressional Record*, and in that year too the Committee interrogated Paul ROBESON, who scorned it for wanting to "shut up every Negro who has the courage to stand up and fight for the rights of his people."

By the more liberal 1960s, support grew for HUAC's abolition. In 1965, in a case involving Louisiana's "little HUAC," the Supreme Court ruled against governmental action that had "a chilling effect upon the exercise of First Amendment rights," and this doctrine was used to challenge the constitutionality of HUAC itself. HUAC escaped a full legal test, but in 1969 its name was changed to the Committee on Internal Security and it ceased issuing subpoenas. In 1975 the House of Representatives finally resolved the issue of the Committee's constitutionality by abolishing it.

BIBLIOGRAPHY

Carr, Robert K. *The House Committee on Un-American Activities, 1945–1950.* 1952.
Caute, David. *The Great Fear: The Anti-Communist Purge Under Truman and Eisenhower.* 1978.
Goodman, Walter. *The Committee: The Extraordinary Career of the House Committee on Un-American Activities.* 1968.
Heale, M. J. *American Anticommunism: Combating the Enemy Within, 1935–1965.* 1990.
Schrecker, Ellen. *Many Choices: McCarthyism in America.* 1998.

M. J. Heale

Housing

During the twentieth century, job discrimination limited the ability of most African Americans to obtain desirable housing and housing discrimination limited their choices to the least desirable neighborhoods. Prior to the beginning of the twentieth century, however, housing discrimination was less important than poverty in determining where blacks lived. But the "Great Migration" of the first three decades of the twentieth century combined with the decline of the walking city to alter old black-white urban residential patterns. Nearly one and a half million blacks left the South during the 1910s and 1920s for the cities of the North and West; at the same time, new transportation technologies, particularly the automobile, were giving whites greater residential choices.

As black newcomers began competing with working-class whites for housing, whites developed various weapons to force blacks into racially defined neighborhoods. They erected legal barriers, including residential zoning and racially restrictive real estate covenants and deed restrictions. Real estate agents and individual owners in white neighborhoods largely refused to sell or rent to blacks. And, starting in the 1930s, a federally sponsored neighborhood mortgage risk rating system helped systematize existing discriminatory lending practices.

Violence, too, proved to be an important exclusionary tool. Whites initiated a number of riots during this period, culminating in the bloody RED SUMMER OF 1919—in Chicago, East St. Louis, and other cities.

Whites also engaged in individual acts of violence, which even included the dynamiting of black homes. This pattern of violence confined most African Americans to the relative safety of the ghetto.

With severely limited housing choices, African Americans found themselves competing with each other for a restricted supply of the least desirable housing, often at inflated prices. Families were forced to double and triple up in cramped apartments, and pay as much as double the rent that whites paid for similar housing elsewhere.

The NATIONAL ASSOCIATION FOR THE ADVANCEMENT OF COLORED PEOPLE (NAACP) began to wage a campaign against enforced residential segregation. Its efforts led to a successful SUPREME COURT challenge to municipal racial residential zoning ordinances (*Buchanan v. Warley*, 1917). But the organization suffered a major loss when the Court found that private racially restrictive covenants were legally enforceable contracts (*Corrigan v. Buckley*, 1926). Housing discrimination was also given a boost by way of zoning ordinances that segregated low-cost, high-density housing from more expensive, lower-density homes. Although race-neutral on their face, these ordinances effectively restricted blacks, whose incomes averaged far lower than whites, to the least desirable neighborhoods and made explicitly racial zoning unnecessary.

Planners and housing reformers, alarmed by decaying neighborhoods in the core of America's older cities, sought to improve housing conditions through slum clearance and the construction of racially segregated low-income housing projects. Insufficient funding, however, meant that too few units were ever built to meet the housing needs of low-income blacks. Enough of these plans were carried out so that they helped to exacerbate racial segregation. The builders feared the blighting effects of racial violence; more important, they believed that racially and economically mixed neighborhoods would cut some residents adrift from their cultural roots. The residents thus alienated would neglect their neighborhoods.

Although the Great Depression slowed the migration of African Americans to cities, WORLD WAR II and postwar prosperity accelerated migration to unprecedented levels. Moreover, the Depression and the war had so slowed housing construction that overcrowding increased dramatically in the immediate postwar period. Families lived in basements, garages, cramped apartments, wherever they could find shelter—and most of this housing was old and worn to begin with.

Aside from restrictive covenants, whose enforcement the NAACP persuaded the Supreme Court to ban (*Shelly v. Kramer*, 1947), most prewar forms of racial residential discrimination, including violence, persisted. At this juncture federal policy took on added importance. Federally financed superhighway construction opened up the urban fringe to development and federal mortgage insurance programs made mortgages available on an unprecedented scale. At the same time, federal mortgage risk assessment policies favored the construction of new suburban housing, which discrimination of various kinds closed to most African Americans.

Local business interests also used highway construction and urban renewal to level slums adjacent to central business districts. In some cities, old slums were replaced with vast tracts of poorly maintained public housing, such as the high-rise apartment buildings that warehoused African-American families on Chicago's Southside. Other displaced black families crowded into older housing being abandoned by the white middle classes as they fled to the suburbs.

The first black residents of these formerly white middle-class neighborhoods were often middle-class families. However, discrimination had the effect of inflating purchase prices and mortgage rates. Black homeowners strapped for cash found it difficult to maintain their homes, and financial institutions were reluctant to make home improvement loans in African-American neighborhoods. Landlords also found that the restricted housing market meant that they could charge high rents and not maintain the properties. These conditions accelerated the decay of older housing that the black middle class had inherited. To make matters worse, middle-class African-American families were followed by those with lower incomes, to whom slumlords rented subdivided, overcrowded, and poorly maintained housing. Thus genteel middle-class neighborhoods soon decayed into slums from which few black families could escape.

With the ban on the enforcement of restrictive covenants, civil rights activists turned their attention to bans on other forms of racial housing discrimination. Supported now by many planners and housing reformers, civil rights activists argued that a racially restricted housing market forced housing prices up for African Americans and quality down. They argued that part of the solution to poor housing would come when blacks could compete freely with whites on location, quality, and price. Landlords and sellers of residential property would then be forced, the argument went, to treat blacks and whites equally, and blacks with the requisite income could escape from the worst housing in the least desirable neighborhoods.

Civil rights activism resulted in a number of state and local fair housing ordinances during the 1950s and 1960s: the federal FAIR HOUSING ACT (CIVIL RIGHTS ACT OF 1968), and a Supreme Court decision (*Jones v. Mayer*, 1968), which ruled that the CIVIL RIGHTS ACT OF 1866 banned racial discrimination in all residential real estate. Enforcement, however, fell largely on those who had been harmed, whom the law required to bring complaints of discrimination as private civil actions. Such actions have had little effect in the face of widespread, persistent, albeit now largely covert, discrimination.

Housing reform and civil rights activism also resulted in attempts, starting as early as the immediate postwar years, to develop scatter-site low-income housing to disperse the ghetto. Federal court decisions like that against the Chicago Metropolitan Housing Authority (*Gautreaux v. the Chicago Housing Authority*, 1969, 1976) have assisted these efforts, by requiring some housing authorities to assist blacks in obtaining subsidized housing outside African-American neighborhoods. Nevertheless, Congress has kept the funding for this subsidized low-income housing limited. And, where funding has been available, suburban white communities have often resisted such programs.

The failure of fair housing legislation and scatter-site housing programs have meant uniformly high rates of residential racial segregation in the nation's metropolitan areas and growing poverty in inner-city black neighborhoods. Residents of these slum ghettos live in racial isolation and concentrated poverty on an unprecedented scale.

The causes of the formation and persistence of these vast decaying ghettos remain under debate. Conservative theoreticians like Charles Murray have argued that a culture of poverty exists in poor neighborhoods, in part, because of disincentives to responsible behavior created by a too generous, poorly conceived welfare state. Liberal theorists have sought other answers. William Julius Wilson argues for the increasing importance of class over race in the persistence and deepening of ghetto poverty. As the manufacturing economy has declined and jobs have moved to suburban locations, the ability of city residents to support their families and maintain their neighborhoods has declined dramatically and a declining tax base has undermined the ability of central cities to assist them. This situation has fallen disproportionately on the shoulders of black families as a result of earlier ghettoization and lack of access to education and good jobs. Poverty has further concentrated in inner-city black neighborhoods, he argues, as middle-class blacks, assisted by the civil rights revolution, have moved out of the worst inner-city neighborhoods.

Douglas S. Massey and Nancy A. Denton agree with Wilson that structural dislocations in the economy are implicated in the persistence of decaying, black, inner-city slums. But, they argue that ongoing housing discrimination has combined with the changing economy to create vast poor black neighborhoods where welfare dependence has been necessary to survival for multiple generations. The dearth of role models consisting of those engaged in legitimate paid work in these neighborhoods has tended to perpetuate the poverty of their residents. Rather than a culture of poverty, Massey and Denton argue, the United States has a culture of apartheid that perpetuates poverty in inner-city black neighborhoods.

BIBLIOGRAPHY

Casey-Leininger, Charles F. *Creating Democracy in Housing: Civil Rights and Housing Policy in Cincinnati, 1945–1980.* 1993.

Fairbanks, Robert B. *Making Better Citizens: Housing Reform and the Community Movement Strategy in Cincinnati, 1890–1960.* 1988.

Grossman, James R. *Land of Hope: Chicago, Black Southerners, and the Great Migration.* 1989.

Helper, Rose. *Racial Policies and Practices of Real Estate Brokers.* 1969.

Hirsch, Arnold R. *Making the Second Ghetto: Race and Housing in Chicago, 1940–1960.* 1983.

Jackson, Kenneth. *The Crabgrass Frontier: The Suburbanization of the United States.* 1985.

Kerner Commission. *Report of the National Advisory Commission on Civil Disorders.* 1968.

Kusmer, Kenneth L. "African Americans in the City Since World War II: From the Industrial to the Postindustrial Era." In *The New African American Urban History,* edited by Kenneth W. Goings and Raymond A. Mohl. 1996.

Lemann, Nicholas. *The Promised Land: The Great Black Migration and How It Changed America.* 1991.

Massey, Douglas S., and Nancy A. Denton. *American Apartheid: Segregation and the Making of the Underclass.* 1993.

Murray, Charles A. *Losing Ground: American Social Policy, 1950–1980.* 1984.

Myrdal, Gunnar. *An American Dilemma: The Negro Problem and Modern Democracy,* 5th ed. 1944.

Sugrue, Thomas J. *Origins of the Urban Crisis: Race and Inequality in Postwar Detroit.* 1996.

Taeuber, Karl, and Alma Taeuber. *Negroes in Cities: Residential Segregation and Neighborhood Change.* 1965.

Taylor, Henry Louis, Jr. "The Black Residential Experience and Community Formation in Antebellum Cincinnati." In *Race and the City: Work, Community, and Protest in Cincinnati, 1820–1970,* edited by Henry Louis Taylor, Jr. 1993.

Vose, Clement. *Caucasians Only: The Supreme Court, the NAACP, and the Restrictive Covenant Cases.* 1959.

Wilson, William Julius. *The Declining Significance of Race: Blacks and Changing American Institutions,* 2nd ed. 1980.

Wilson, William Julius. *The Truly Disadvantaged: The Inner City, the Underclass, and Public Policy.* 1987.

Charles F. Casey-Leininger

Houston, Charles Hamilton

(1895–1950), civil rights attorney and legal educator.

Charles Hamilton Houston, the son of a Washington attorney, attended Amherst College, graduating in

Charles H. Houston in his law office in 1939, shortly after leaving the legal staff of the NAACP. Houston was the mentor to a generation of civil rights attorneys, including Thurgood Marshall. (CORBIS/ Bettmann)

1915. He served in the armed forces in Europe during the First World War, where he was outraged by the racism he found in the U.S. Army. He also contracted a mild case of tuberculosis, which affected him throughout his life.

On returning to civilian life, Houston enrolled in the class of 1922 at Harvard Law School, where he was the first African-American member elected, on the basis of his grades, to the prestigious *Harvard Law Review.* After receiving an academic fellowship sponsored by Harvard law professor Felix Frankfurter, which allowed him to travel and study in Spain, Houston returned to Washington and joined his father's law practice.

Houston also joined the faculty of the Howard University Law School, where he served as academic dean from 1929 to 1935. Relying in part on the results of a survey of African-American lawyers he prepared for a New York foundation, Houston led the transformation of Howard from a night law school primarily for federal government employees to a nationally accredited law school dedicated to training, in Houston's words, "social engineers," who would help bring about a revolutionary change in race relations through the development of civil rights law. Revered as a teacher who insisted on academic rigor, Houston became the mentor to a generation of civil rights attorneys, including Oliver HILL, Spottswood Robinson, and, most notably,

Thurgood MARSHALL, who assisted Houston in defending George Crawford, an African-American accused of murdering a prominent Virginia socialite in 1932.

Houston left Howard in 1935 to join the staff of the NATIONAL ASSOCIATION FOR THE ADVANCEMENT OF COLORED PEOPLE (NAACP) in New York, becoming the first full-time lawyer on the organization's staff. He reshaped an existing plan prepared by Nathan Margold for a sustained and systematic litigation challenge to racial segregation, proposing to attack racial segregation in Southern universities and professional schools, and to challenge the lesser salaries paid to African-American teachers in segregated school systems. Houston traveled throughout the South preparing a film showing the unequal facilities in segregated schools, and devoted most of his litigation efforts to developing strategies for attacks on the failure of Southern universities to provide professional education for African Americans. Those attacks culminated in the Supreme Court's decision in *Missouri ex rel. Gaines v. Canada* (1938), which required Missouri to create a law school for its African-American citizens instead of supporting them with scholarships in other states' law schools. Houston also insisted that the NAACP hire Marshall as his assistant, with an eye to guaranteeing that the NAACP legal staff would have a talented, hard-working, and dedicated successor when Houston left the staff.

Houston left the NAACP in 1939, largely for health reasons. He rejoined his law firm and continued to represent African-American interests. Important clients included African-American railway workers who were barred from membership in railway unions. Houston persuaded the Supreme Court that white-only unions had a "duty of fair representation" to all railway workers, even those excluded from membership (*Steele v. Louisville & Nashville Railroad Co.*, 1944). He also served briefly as a presidential appointee to the wartime FAIR EMPLOYMENT PRACTICE COMMITTEE. Houston was a member of the team of lawyers who argued against the constitutionally of enforcing contractual provisions known as restrictive covenants, which barred white homeowners from selling their property to African-American buyers (*Hurd v. Hodge*, decided together with the better-known *Shelley v. Kramer* in 1948).

During the 1940s Houston began to develop lawsuits challenging racial segregation in the District of Columbia's public schools. His strategy, in some tension with the one then under consideration at the NAACP's national office, sought to increase the appropriations to African-American schools so that, while they remained separate from white schools, they would at least be equal in material endowments. The litigation was in the process of being reshaped into a broader attack on segregation when Houston suffered the first of a series of heart attacks that forced him to withdraw from law practice and, finally, led to his death in 1950.

Houston was an inspirational figure to his students, including Marshall, who repeatedly invoked his name and his vision of lawyers as instruments for social change in explaining the importance of the NAACP's legal program.

BIBLIOGRAPHY

McNeil, Genna Rae. *Groundwork: Charles Hamilton Houston and the Struggle for Civil Rights*. 1983.
Tushnet, Mark V. *The NAACP's Legal Strategy Against Segregated Education, 1925–1950*. 1987.

Mark V. Tushnet

Huerta, Dolores

(1930–   ), labor leader and civil rights activist.

Dolores Huerta was vice president of the UNITED FARM WORKERS OF AMERICA (UFW) and is a social activist whose lifelong commitment to the rights of farm workers places her in the forefront of Chicano labor unionism and community organizing. Born on April 10, 1930, in Dawson, New Mexico, Huerta was raised by her divorced mother in Stockton, California, who owned a small hotel patronized primarily by farm workers and working-class *mexicanos*. Huerta's father, a coal miner, became involved in labor organization during the Great Depression and served as the secretary-treasurer for the Congress of Industrial Organizations (CIO) local in Las Vegas, New Mexico. (See AFL-CIO.) In 1938 he also served as a representative in the New Mexico state legislature.

In the mid 1950s Huerta became an organizer in Fred Ross Sr.'s COMMUNITY SERVICE ORGANIZATION (CSO) and in 1962 she and her second husband, Ventura Huerta, a fellow organizer, were sent to Sacramento, where she first met Cesar CHAVEZ. Like Chavez, Huerta became convinced that organizing agricultural workers was possible, and this shared conviction led to the founding of the National Farm Workers Association (NFWA), headquartered in Delano, California. In 1965, Filipino workers from the AGRICULTURAL WORKERS ORGANIZING COMMITTEE (AWOC) requested the support of the NFWA in striking against grape growers. The following year the two organizations combined to form the UFW and together staged the five-year-long "Delano Grape Strike."

As the UFW's chief contract negotiator, Huerta succeeded in gaining the right to bargain collectively, established the first health and benefits plan for farm workers, and helped to bring about the banning of pesticides DDT and parathyon, which posed dangerous health threats to the farm worker, the consumer, and the environment. Philosophically, the two UFW leaders, Huerta and Chavez, were often at odds with each other, but Huerta's organizational and rhetorical skills proved indispensable. In 1968–1969, and later in the 1970s, she directed the Manhattan table grape boycott and also coordinated the East Coast table grape, lettuce, and Gallo wine boycotts. During this time she was exposed to the feminist movement, which only strengthened her views on the need for social justice for all people (see FEMINISM). Based largely on her labor activity and championing of civil rights she was elected co-chair of the 1972 California delegation to the Democratic National Convention. Furthermore, throughout the 1970s she directed the Citizenship Participation Day Department (CPD), which attempted to protect such union victories as the federal Agricultural Labor Relations Act, which recognized for the first time the collective bargaining rights of farm workers in California.

During the 1980s and 1990s, long legal battles stymied the growth and gains made by the farm workers movement, but Huerta continued to champion the civil and human rights of all who toiled in the fields, including undocumented workers. In the 1980s she spearheaded the organizational drive to defend the right of migrant and immigrant children to receive needed social services, as well as a successfully lobbying effort for the eventual passage of the 1985 Rodino amnesty legislation program that granted amnesty for undocumented workers who had lived, worked, and paid taxes in the United States. Because of her labor and civil rights struggles, Huerta has received numerous honors, including the Outstanding Labor Leader Award in 1984; in 1993 she was inducted into the National Women's Hall of Fame, received the AMERICAN CIVIL LIBERTIES UNION Roger Baldwin Medal of Liberty Award, the Eugene V. Debs Foundation Outstanding American Award, and the Ellis Island Medal of Freedom Award.

Since Cesar Chavez's death in 1993, Dolores Huerta has promoted female political leadership and increased her involvement in feminist organizations. Currently she serves as the secretary-treasurer of the United Farm Workers, vice president of the Coalition for Labor Union Women, vice president of the California AFL-CIO, and is a board member of The Feminist Majority.

BIBLIOGRAPHY

Coburn, Judith. "Dolores Huerta: La Pasionaria of the Farmworkers." *Ms.* (November 1976): 11–16.

Day, Mark. *Forty Acres: César Chávez and the Farm Workers.* 1971.

Garcia, Richard A. "Dolores Huerta: Woman, Organizer, and Symbol." In *California History* (Spring 1993): 57–71.

Huerta, Dolores. "Dolores Huerta Talks About Republicans, César, Children, and Her Home Town." In *Awakened Minority: The Mexican-Americans.* 2nd ed., edited by Manuel Servin. 1974.

Huerta, Dolores. "Reflections on the UFW Experience." *Center Magazine* (July–August 1985).

Griswold del Castillo, Richard, and Richard A. Garcia. *César Chávez: A Triumph of Spirit.* 1995.

Meier, Matt S. *Notable Latino Americans: A Bibliographic Dictionary.* 1997.

Mirandé, Alfredo, and Evangelina Enríquez. *La Chicana: The Mexican-American Woman.* 1979.

Rose, Margaret. "Traditional and Nontraditional Patterns of Female Activism in the United Farm Workers of America, 1962 to 1980." *Frontiers* 11, no. 1 (1990): 26–32.

Maria Raquel Casas

Hughes, James Langston

(1902–1967), writer.

James Langston Hughes was born in Joplin, Missouri, in 1902, but spent the first thirteen years of his life with his grandmother in Lawrence, Kansas, before moving with his mother to Detroit and Cleveland. He lived briefly with his father in Mexico City, but returned to New York City in 1921 to attend Columbia University, which he left after one year. He wrote "The Negro Speaks of Rivers" while crossing the Mississippi to visit his father. The river reminded him of the role of other big rivers in black history and of Abraham Lincoln, who it was said decided to end slavery after traveling south on the Mississippi.

In 1923, Hughes sailed with a merchant steamer to Africa. His poem "The White Ones" is a critique of African colonization by Europeans, and Africa would become an important theme in his writing. While traveling in Africa and, later, in Europe, he wrote poems that were published in *The* CRISIS, the magazine of the NATIONAL ASSOCIATION FOR THE ADVANCEMENT OF COLORED PEOPLE (NAACP). In 1925, Hughes enrolled at Lincoln University, in Pennsylvania, graduating in 1929. During this period, he met Charlotte Osgood Mason, who was his literary patron until 1931.

A poet for over thirty years, Hughes wrote in all literary forms. For many, his name is synonymous with the HARLEM RENAISSANCE. In the words of Henry Louis Gates, Jr., "he helped to define the spirit of the age, from a literary point of view." According to Arnold Rampersad, Hughes was prepared for his role as

A beaming Langston Hughes. 1935. (© Archive Photos)

a "spokes person" for his race. His heritage can be traced to several key figures in the African-American civil rights struggle, including an ancestor who died with John Brown at Harper's Ferry and an uncle, John Mercer Langston, a famous black American of the nineteenth century. Hughes's life was also influenced by the Great Migration, World War I, and his father, James Nathaniel Hughes (whom he hated).

Hughes wrote primarily about the experiences of ordinary black people, especially in urban settings, "people up today and down tomorrow." These experiences are represented by the character and exploits of Simple, his comic Harlemite. Hughes bore witness to the Great Migration in "One Way Ticket." In "Harlem" and "Mother to Son," he explored the harsh realities of black urban life. While "The Weary Blues" and "Jazzonia" evoke the spirit of jazz and the blues, they also celebrate the muted cries, vibrant soul, and resilience of black Americans in hostile urban environments. Hughes, ironically, saw Harlem as such a setting, representing, simultaneously, a Mecca of black cultural production, a spiritual haven, and the place where African-American dreams were deferred.

At his death in 1967, Hughes's career had spanned over four decades. He had taught in several U.S. universities, had collaborated with several writers of the Harlem Renaissance, including Arna Bontemps and Zora Neale Hurston, and had written several volumes of poetry, works of fiction and nonfiction, plays, works for children, and two autobiographies, *The Big Sea* (1940) and *I Wonder as I Wander* (1956). Two impor-

tant biographies on Hughes are Arnold Rampersad's *The Life of Langston Hughes,* Vol. I (1986) and Vol. II (1988), and Faith Berry's *Langston Hughes: Before and Beyond Harlem* (1983).

BIBLIOGRAPHY

Berry, Faith. *Langston Hughes: Before and Beyond Harlem.* 1983.

Gates, Henry Louis, Jr., and Kwame Anthony Appiah, eds. *Langston Hughes: Critical Perspectives Past and Present.* 1993.

Hughes, Langston. *The Big Sea.* 1940.

Hughes, Langston. *I Wonder as I Wander.* 1956.

O'Daniel, Therman B. *Langston Hughes: Black Genius.* 1971.

Rampersad, Arnold. *The Life of Langston Hughes,* Vols. I and II. 1986, 1988.

Maureen N. Eke

Humphrey, Hubert Horatio

(1911–1978), U.S. senator and vice president.

Hubert H. Humphrey maintained a strong interest in civil rights issues while serving as mayor of Minneapolis (1945–1948), senator from Minnesota (1949–1964, 1971–1978), and vice president of the United States (1965–1968). Few other members of the DEMOCRATIC PARTY were so closely identified with the quest for racial justice during the thirty years after World War II.

Humphrey's commitment to civil rights was a bit ironic given that he had almost no contact with African Americans while growing up in South Dakota during the Great Depression. Yet as a youth he developed strong convictions about the dignity of each person, took to heart Christian teachings about the equality of all before God, and acquired empathy for the economically disadvantaged. Humphrey witnessed many of the evils of racism while attending graduate school at Louisiana State University. Like other liberals during the 1940s, Humphrey was deeply influenced by the horrors of Nazi Germany and by Gunnar Myrdal's *An American Dilemma*. Indeed, throughout his life Humphrey remained convinced of the basic goodness of most people and viewed racism as a serious problem but also an anomaly. He saw himself as mobilizing the public to live up to its democratic ideals.

Humphrey made race a central issue during his term as mayor of Minneapolis. He created a Mayor's Council on Human Relations that, with the help of noted Fisk University sociologist Charles Johnson, oversaw an extensive Community Self-Survey of racial attitudes and minority living conditions. Humphrey and the Council, moreover, led a successful fight for the nation's first municipal Fair Employment Practice Committee and implemented a program to improve police-minority relations. Significant problems remained when Humphrey left office, but he could justly claim that his administration had made important beginnings in several areas.

These activities raised Humphrey's profile among liberal leaders around the country, but his efforts at the 1948 Democratic National Convention led many Americans to associate him with the civil rights issue. Humphrey rallied delegates to support a strong civil rights plank through an electrifying speech that urged the party to "get out of the shadow of state's rights and walk forthrightly into the bright sunshine of human rights." The approval of the plank signaled a redefinition of LIBERALISM. Whereas most liberal Democrats had downplayed racial matters during the 1930s, now being a liberal meant being for civil rights. The plank also deepened divisions between the Northern and Southern wings of the Democratic Party.

Humphrey would not enjoy another significant civil rights triumph for fifteen years. As a senator during the 1950s, he regularly introduced civil rights legislation dealing with VOTING RIGHTS, EMPLOYMENT, LYNCHING, and SEGREGATION in interstate transportation, among other matters, but vehement opposition from Southern Democrats and indifference from many Republicans prevented any strong measure from becoming law. The logjam broke in 1964 when, taking advantage of public outcry over the violence Southern law officers had used against peaceful demonstrators,

Humphrey played the leading role in guiding the CIVIL RIGHTS ACT OF 1964 through the Senate. Among the most important laws passed in the twentieth century, the 1964 Civil Rights Act outlawed segregation in public accommodations, discrimination in employment, and discrimination in programs receiving federal money.

Humphrey's pro-civil rights reputation, however, became tarnished a few months later at the Democratic convention in Atlantic City. Eager to become Lyndon JOHNSON's running mate, he favored a compromise solution, devised by the Johnson administration, to a seating dispute involving the MISSISSIPPI FREEDOM DEMOCRATIC PARTY (MFDP) and the regular delegation from the Magnolia State. Humphrey's failure to back fully the MFDP, whose members had been beaten and intimidated by Mississippi authorities in their struggle to vote, caused some civil rights activists to see him and other liberals as untrustworthy individuals who would sell out the movement for personal gain.

With JIM CROW legally dead and the civil rights movement concentrating on the urban North, Humphrey focused increasingly on issues of economic opportunity. As vice president under Johnson, he oversaw largely unsuccessful annual efforts to find summer jobs and recreational opportunities for inner city residents. He also defended anti-poverty programs against growing opposition on the Left and the Right. As the Democratic nominee for president in 1968, he responded to mounting cries for "law and order" by urging the nation to stand for "order and justice." Humphrey returned to the Senate in 1971 and, with unemployment surging among African Americans, joined forces with the CONGRESSIONAL BLACK CAUCUS and several civil rights organizations to sponsor the Humphrey–Hawkins full employment bill. Early versions of the controversial measure defined employment as a civil right and provided for the creation of public-service jobs as a last resort for the unemployed. President Jimmy CARTER signed a largely toothless version of the bill in 1978 that contained neither of these provisions. Many African Americans responded to Humphrey's death that year by fondly recalling his commitment to racial equality.

BIBLIOGRAPHY

Humphrey, Hubert H. *Beyond Civil Rights*. 1968.

Loevy, Robert. *To End All Segregation: The Politics of the Passage of the 1964 Civil Rights Act*. 1990.

Solberg, Carl. *Hubert H. Humphrey: A Biography*. 1984.

Thurber, Timothy N. *The Politics of Equality: Hubert H. Humphrey and the African American Freedom Struggle*. 1998.

Whalen, Charles and Barbara Whalen. *The Longest Debate: A Legislative History of the 1964 Civil Rights Act.* 1985.

Timothy N. Thurber

Hurley, Ruby

(ca. 1910–1980), NAACP leader.

Ruby Hurley is best known for her work with the NATIONAL ASSOCIATION FOR THE ADVANCEMENT OF COLORED PEOPLE (NAACP), where she was a staff member for thirty-nine years. A native of Washington, D.C., she graduated from Dunbar High School in 1926 and attended Miner Teachers College and the Robert H. Terrell Law School. Little else is known about her personal life except that she was married to Lieutenant William L. Hurley, who worked with the U.S. Army Corps of Engineers. In 1939, she helped to reorganize the Washington, D.C. NAACP branch, where her work with young people prompted the national office to appoint her national youth secretary in 1943. Under her leadership the number of NAACP youth councils and college chapters expanded more than threefold by 1950, and youth membership increased from fifteen thousand to twenty-five thousand.

In 1951, Hurley opened an NAACP office in Birmingham, Alabama, and the following year she became NAACP regional director of the Southeast Region, which included North and South Carolina, Tennessee, Georgia, Mississippi, Alabama, and Florida. During the 1950s, she often traveled alone throughout the Deep South, investigating the brutal LYNCHING of African Americans, including the highly publicized 1955 MISSISSIPPI murder of teenager Emmett TILL. A year later, she accompanied Autherine LUCY in an unsuccessful effort to desegrate the University of Alabama. In retaliation for her activism, Hurley's home was firebombed and she received death threats. When the NAACP was legally banned in ALABAMA following the MONTGOMERY BUS BOYCOTT (1955–1956), Hurley moved her office to Atlanta.

As she was forced to travel on segregated buses throughout the South but refused to eat in segregated restaurants, the work took a toll on Hurley's health. She developed situational stress disorder, common among combat veterans and many civil rights activists operating in extreme danger. She finally retired from the NAACP in 1978 and died two years later after a prolonged illness. Somewhat bitter about the public focus of the 1960s' civil rights activities, Hurley understood what scholars only later have begun to recognize—that from the 1930s through the 1950s thousands of courageous and mostly anonymous Southern blacks laid the foundation for the more celebrated protests of the 1960s.

BIBLIOGRAPHY

Dunbar, Ernest. "Ruby Hurley's South," *Look* (August 1957).
NAACP Papers. Library of Congress, Washington, D.C.
Pierson, William D. "Ruby Hurley." In *Notable Black American Women,* edited by Jessie Carney Smith. 1992.
Raines, Howell. *My Soul is Rested: Movement Days in the Deep South Remembered.* 1977.
Thompson, Kathleen. "Ruby Hurley." In *Black Women in America: An Historical Encyclopedia.* Vol I, edited by Darlene Clark Hine. 1993.

Christina Greene

I

Ickes, Harold

(1874–1952), government official.

Born in Frankstown Township, Pennsylvania, Harold Ickes used his leadership as Secretary of the Interior from 1933 to 1946 and as head of the Public Works Administration (PWA) to construct policies that protected the civil rights of minorities and facilitated growth in African-American job opportunities within the federal government during the New Deal era (see NEW DEAL AND DEPRESSION). Appointed by President Franklin D. ROOSEVELT, Ickes was committed to including African Americans in the reform policies of the New Deal.

Ickes's willingness to hire African-American professionals and clerical workers at the Interior Department and the PWA set a trend followed by many government agencies thereafter. Ickes received much criticism from the African-American community for his appointment of a white man, Clark FOREMAN, to the position of Special Assistant on the Economic Status of Negroes. However, he then regained much of the respect he had lost by adding the Harvard-educated African American, Robert WEAVER, to work with Foreman. After the appointment of Weaver, the appointment of black advisers became a widely accepted practice.

Perhaps Ickes's most notable accomplishment was his September 1, 1933, order that prohibited discrimination on all PWA projects, including every PWA-financed contract. In 1934 Foreman and Weaver established a labor quota system to ensure the enforcement

As Secretary of the Interior in Franklin D. Roosevelt's administration, Harold Ickes granted singer Marian Anderson use of the Lincoln Memorial for a 1939 Easter Sunday concert, after the Daughters of the American Revolution had denied her the right to use Constitution Hall. (CORBIS)

of this law by requiring local contractors to employ a fixed number of black workers. This significant act shifted the burden of proof from the PWA to the contractors.

Under Ickes, several gains were made for the social status of African Americans. By his orders, the cafeteria and restrooms of the Interior Department were desegregated, eventually leading to the DESEGREGATION of all government agencies. He also worked to obtain permission from President Roosevelt for singer Marian Anderson to perform at the Lincoln Memorial in 1939 after she, and all other black performers, were restricted from Constitution Hall in Washington, D.C., by the Daughters of the American Revolution. This gesture is said to have helped catalyze a slowly mounting intolerance of discrimination on the part of the federal government during the 1930s.

Harold Ickes's use of government to facilitate racial justice opened up several opportunities for African Americans. His commitment to equality is discussed in his many publications on the Roosevelt era and is also expressed in the diary published after his death, *The Secret Diary of Harold L. Ickes* (1953–1954).

BIBLIOGRAPHY

Ickes, Harold. *The Secret Diary of Harold L. Ickes.* 3 vols. 1953–1954.
Kirby, John. *Black Americans in the Roosevelt Era: Liberalism and Race.* 1980.
Sitkoff, Harvard. *A New Deal for Blacks: The Emergence of Civil Rights as a National Issue.* Vol 1: *The Depression Decade.* 1978.
Sullivan, Patricia. *Days of Hope: Race and Democracy in the New Deal Era.* 1996.

Kori Kelley

Idaho

Whereas it is true that, both historically and currently, the population of Idaho is overwhelmingly white, a surprising variety of peoples have lived in and influenced the history of this mountain state. Because of the small number of African Americans in Idaho, there was no mass movement there for black equality in the post–World War II era. Nevertheless, there has been a consistent push by peoples of color for the rights that all Americans expect.

By the time Idaho achieved statehood in 1890, the Native American population had dwindled precipitously from disease, warfare, and forced relocation to reservations outside of Idaho. However, the Nez Perce, Coeur d'Alene, Bannock, and Shoshone nations all continue to maintain a presence in the state. As with tribes in other states, Idaho's Native Americans have struggled to survive and to carve out a niche in a state that did not welcome or appreciate their presence.

The struggle for civil rights in Idaho began not with African Americans but with Asian immigrants and Asian Americans. During the territorial and early statehood period, tens of thousands of people moved to Idaho to mine for gold and silver. When mining was at its height, close to one-third of Idaho's population was Chinese. Chinese immigrants played an important role in the economic development of the region, in agriculture as well as in mining. Nevertheless, the constitution of Idaho explicitly denied citizenship status to all "Asiatics"; although largely symbolic at that point, it was not until 1962 that the state constitution was amended. As sites were mined out and the national CHINESE EXCLUSION ACT of 1882 took effect, Idaho's Chinese population diminished by the early 1900s.

Japanese and Japanese Americans also suffered the onus of living in a state that was both overwhelmingly white and racist (see RACISM). In 1923, the state passed the Alien Land Law that, while not referring explicitly to Japanese, effectively denied Issei the right to own property in the state; the law would not be repealed for more than thirty years. During WORLD WAR II, one of the "relocation," or internment, camps for West Coast Issei and Nissei was established in southern Idaho (see JAPANESE-AMERICAN INTERNMENT CASES). Despite the vocal and racist objections of the state's governor, Camp Minidoka housed several thousand Japanese people, who provided essential labor for the state's farmers during the war.

African Americans, although few in number, were present in Idaho even in territorial days. Because of the remoteness of the state from the South and because of its economic base—farming, logging, and ranching, in addition to mining—not many blacks moved to Idaho in the twentieth century. Some of those who did relocate there took up farming, but most blacks moved to Idaho's cities—Boise and especially Pocatello. An important depot in the Union Pacific network, Pocatello was the heart of Idaho's black community into the 1970s. Blacks rarely experienced the trauma of legal SEGREGATION (a few municipalities had laws that singled out blacks for discriminatory treatment, such as a 7 P.M. curfew in Coeur d'Alene), in part at least because there were so few blacks in the state—in 1999 still below 1 percent of the population. What blacks did suffer from was isolation from fellow African Americans, a host of extralegal forms of discrimination, and limited job opportunities. As early as the 1910s, Idaho blacks organized themselves into chapters of the NATIONAL ASSOCIATION FOR THE ADVANCEMENT OF COLORED PEOPLE (NAACP) and other groups in order to fight racism. During the modern civil rights era, the paucity of blacks, the general lack of explicitly racist laws to challenge, and the political conservatism of white Idahoans meant that few protests occurred. In the aftermath of Martin Luther KING, JR.'s assassination, hundreds of Boiseans, black and white, gathered at the steps of the state capitol building to mourn America's loss.

The largest minority population in Idaho for much of the twentieth century has been Hispanic. Like other ethnic groups considered nonwhite by white Idahoans, Hispanics have experienced ongoing discrimination on the job, in school, and in housing. Most Hispanics arrived in Idaho as migratory farmworkers, and so they have struggled with the difficulties involved with a somewhat nomadic existence in a low-paid, irregular line of work. As the population has grown and started to exert some economic and political influence, issues affecting the Hispanic community have slowly received more consideration. For instance, ongoing efforts to push through a minimum wage bill for farmworkers indicates both increasing awareness of, and white resistance to, Hispanic Idahoans' quest for economic justice.

To this day, Idaho remains surprisingly white. The numbers of African Americans, Hispanics, and Asian Americans continue to grow, but the conservative white majority population has been somewhat uncomfortable with these changes. Indeed, many recent white migrants to Idaho have moved there to escape the diversity of their home states, especially California. Despite these problems, Idaho's population is becoming more diverse as its people slowly come to grips with the reality of a multicultural America.

BIBLIOGRAPHY

Mercier, Laurie, and Carole Simon Smolinski. *Idaho's Ethnic Heritage.* 1990.

Savage, W. Sherman. *Blacks in the West.* 1976.

Peter Cole

Illinois

Illinois statehood in 1818 was organized under the stipulations of the 1787 Northwest Ordinance, which prohibited slavery. Slaves and indentured servants of early French settlers were exempt from the prohibition, as were slaves working at the saline mines near Shawneetown. Attempts by proslavery forces in 1822 through 1824 to call for a new constitutional convention making slavery legal in Illinois failed. Illinois Supreme Court cases such as *Bailey v. Cromwell* (1841)

and abolitionist activism provided legal and moral safeguards against establishing slavery in Illinois. A new state constitution, ratified in 1848, prohibited free persons of color from settling in Illinois and prevented slave owners from bringing slaves into the state for the purposes of EMANCIPATION. The state legislature passed harsher measures in 1853, making it a crime to bring free blacks into Illinois. Of the 1.7 million people who lived in Illinois when the Civil War began, fewer than eight thousand were black.

The Civil War transformed the national discussion from slavery to emancipation. John Jones, a wealthy black Chicago abolitionist, pushed for the successful repeal of Illinois black laws (all legislation regulating the behavior of blacks). Governor Richard Yates lobbied the legislature to ratify the THIRTEENTH AMENDMENT, making Illinois the first state to do so. Between 1870 and 1890, the legislature took steps to advance black civil rights. In 1874, the Illinois General Assembly passed a law forbidding SEGREGATION in public schools. This was followed by a Civil Rights Act in 1885 that forbade racial discrimination in restaurants, hotels, theaters, streetcars, and other places of public accommodation and amusement. Blacks such as John W. E. Thomas, a state representative, E. H. Wright, a railroad incorporation clerk for Illinois, and Franklin A. Denison, an assistant prosecuting attorney for Chicago, increasingly assumed elected and appointed positions within state and municipal government.

RACISM remained the underlying factor in day-to-day interactions. Illinois blacks commonly experienced violence and discrimination in EMPLOYMENT, HOUSING, and the use of public facilities. Efforts to prevent the segregation of public schools in Edwardsville (*People v. Scott Bibb*) were undermined by the U.S. SUPREME COURT ruling in PLESSY V. FERGUSON (1896). Attacks on black coal miners at Spring Valley (1895) and the use of black strikebreakers in the Pana and Virden strikes of 1898 further fueled white resentment. Between 1900 and 1915, twelve black men were lynched in Illinois. Mob violence against blacks was further manifested in major race riots. The 1908 Springfield, Illinois, riot left seven dead. The nation was outraged that something so heinous could occur in Abraham Lincoln's hometown; the riot stimulated like-minded blacks and whites to form the NATIONAL ASSOCIATION FOR THE ADVANCEMENT OF COLORED PEOPLE in 1909. Unfortunately, race riots continued, with major upheavals at East St. Louis in 1917 and Chicago in 1919. In East St. Louis, fifty people were killed, hundreds more were injured, and more than sixteen acres of the city were ravaged. The toll in Chicago was equally frightening; thirty-eight people were killed, another 537 were injured, and more than a thousand were left homeless because of the destruction of property.

Various legislative initiatives prohibited racial discrimination on state contracts for public works buildings (1933) and prohibited racial discrimination in all defense contracts (1941). In 1943, commissions on race relations were established at the state level and in Chicago to deal with problems relating to housing, employment, and EDUCATION. So little progress was made that, by 1966, Martin Luther KING, JR., turned his attention to Chicago to rectify discriminatory practices in these areas. He was met with stones, bottles, and empty promises. Jesse Louis JACKSON, selected by King to head the labor and economic affairs department of the Southern Christian Leadership Conference, moved to Chicago after King's assassination to continue the fight for "civil economics" and educational reforms through People United to Save Humanity (Operation PUSH). Farther south, in Cairo, Illinois, blacks organized to protest the 1967 lynching of Robert L. Hunt, a black soldier. In the two decades that followed, Cairo blacks secured federal protection against the unlawful search and seizure of homes, got the right to lawful assembly and protest, and were able to change local government from commission form to aldermanic, thus ensuring the representation of blacks on the city council. A similar challenge by Springfield blacks to the commission form of government was successful in establishing an aldermanic system, providing black representation on the city council for the first time.

Illinois women strove to establish control of their own lives and property, to have equal guardianship of children, and to be given the right to vote. In the celebrated case of *Packard v. Packard* (1864), Elizabeth Parsons Ware Packard, confined to an insane asylum because she did not share her husband's strict Calvinist beliefs, was declared by the courts to be sane. She successfully lobbied for the Personal Liberty Bill (1867), which established medical and legal procedures to protect women from forced incarceration by their husbands. Similarly, the Illinois legislature passed laws in 1872 and 1874 prohibiting discrimination in employment based on sex, making fathers and mothers equal in inheritance from a child, and provided that both spouses' interests in real estate constituted dower rights. Women were eligible to run for elective school posts in 1873. The following year, ten county superintendents of schools in Illinois were women.

The battle for woman suffrage was hard fought. Women who had served in homefront leadership roles during the Civil War had refined the skills necessary to advance the suffrage question. On February 12, 1869, the Illinois Woman Suffrage Association (later renamed the Illinois Equal Suffrage Association) was established in Chicago. This group, led by Mary Livermore, abolitionist and codirector of the United States Sanitary Commission, became the major institutional force advancing woman suffrage. In 1891, the Illinois legislature passed a bill allowing women to vote in school official elections. By 1913, Illinois allowed women to vote in elections for statutory offices and referenda. When CONGRESS passed the NINETEENTH AMENDMENT, Illinois was the first state to ratify it. Encouraged by this victory, the legislature introduced the Illinois Equal Rights Bill to guarantee legal equality for women, but it failed. Decades later, the 1970 Illinois Constitution not only guaranteed citizens the traditional freedoms enumerated in the U.S. Bill of Rights, but extended them to include freedom from discrimination on the basis of race, color, creed, national ancestry, and sex in the hiring and promotion practices of an employer or in the sale or rental of property. It also granted women equal protection of the law and prohibited discrimination based solely on physical or mental disabilities. This broad language coupled with a determined opposition stymied efforts to support the federal Equal Rights Amendment, and it was never ratified in Illinois.

Jayne Byrne stunned political pundits in 1979 when she became the first elected female mayor of Chicago. Similarly, Carol Moseley-Braun, who defeated Democratic incumbent Alan Dixon in the 1992 primary, went on to become the first African-American female elected to the U.S. Senate. Finally, attempts to amend the Illinois Human Rights Act to prohibit discrimination in state hiring based on a person's sexual orientation have failed to pass the legislature. Only eight of 102 counties in Illinois specifically ban discrimination against gays and lesbians, and Chicago remains one of the few U.S. cities that offer domestic partner benefits to city employees.

BIBLIOGRAPHY

Abernathy, Ralph David. *And the Walls Came Tumbling Down.* 1990.

Bridges, Roger D. "Equality Deferred: Civil Rights for Illinois Blacks, 1865–1885." *Journal of the Illinois State Historical Society* 74 (1981): 82–108.

Ewing, Preston, Jr., and Jan Peterson Roddy. *Let My People Go: Cairo, Illinois, 1967–1973.* 1996.

Grimshaw, William J. *Bitter Fruit.* 1992.

Harris, N. Dwight. *The History of Negro Servitude in Illinois and of the Slavery Agitation in That State, 1719–1864.* 1904.

Mansbridge, Jane J. *Why We Lost the ERA.* 1986.

Portwood, Shirley J. "The Alton School Case and African American Community Consciousness, 1897–1908." *Illinois Historical Journal* 91 (Spring): 2–20.

Rudwick, Elliott M. *Race Riot at East St. Louis, July 2, 1917.* 1964.

Sapinsley, Barbara. *The Private War of Mrs. Packard.* 1991.

Senechal, Roberta. *The Sociogensis of a Race Riot: Springfield, Illinois, in 1908.* 1990.

Trout, Grace Wilbur. "Side Lights on Illinois Suffrage History." *Journal of the Illinois State Historical Society* 13 (1920–1921): 145–179.

Tuttle, William M., Jr. *Race Riot: Chicago in the Red Summer of 1919.* 1970.

Thomas F. Schwartz

Immigration Act of 1924

Sponsored by Sen. David Reed (R-Pa.) and Rep. Albert Johnson (R-Wash.), the Immigration Act of 1924 (43 Stat. 153), also known as the National Origins Quota Act, ended the era of open immigration from Europe and completed Asiatic exclusion. Its passage marked a fundamental change in American immigration policy by placing numerical restrictions on entry and by establishing a system of quotas that discriminated on the basis on nationality and race.

Political Background and Context

Popular support for immigration restriction grew after World War I, in large part fueled by the nationalism and "100 percent Americanism" generated during the war. Increasingly, Americans rejected the ideal of the melting pot and blamed immigrants for social problems associated with urbanization and industrialization. Scientific race theories, which deemed "Nordics" superior to the "Alpine and Mediterranean races" of southern and eastern Europe, allowed native-born Americans who descended from previous generations of immigrants to oppose new immigrants, while redeeming themselves. Moreover, the need for large-scale importation of unskilled labor, which had fueled the extraordinary economic growth of the late nineteenth and early twentieth century, had ebbed. In the atmosphere of postwar reaction, NATIVISM, and antiradicalism, few in Congress were willing to oppose the demands for immigration restriction made by patriotic orders, eugenicists, and organized labor.

Major Provisions of the Law

First, the law restricted immigration to 155,000 a year, or 15 percent of the average of one million a year that had prevailed during the decade before the war. It allotted quotas to European countries in the same proportion that the American people traced their ancestry to those countries, through immigration or the immigration of their forebears. Supporters of the concept argued that proportional quotas would preserve the composition of the American population. Northern and western European countries received more

than two-thirds of the quotas and eastern and southern European countries received less than one-third, based on calculations made by the Bureau of Census.

Second, the law excluded from immigration "persons ineligible to citizenship," a reference to the natives of all Asian countries. The United States Supreme Court ruled that Asians were racially ineligible to citizenship (*Ozawa v. United States*, 160 US 178 [1922] and *United States v. Thind*, 261 US 204 [1923]), according to its interpretation of naturalization law, which granted the right to citizenship to "white persons" (1790) and "persons of African nativity and descent" (1870). (See also OZAWA V. UNITED STATES and THIND, UNITED STATES V.) The exclusion of persons ineligible to citizenship achieved statutory Japanese exclusion, completed Asiatic exclusion, and introduced racial barriers to entry into the main body of immigration law.

Third, the quota system did not apply to the Western Hemisphere, in deference to American agricultural interests in the Southwest and diplomatic and business interests in Mexico and Canada. However, Mexican immigration was adversely affected by the law's harsh sanctions against unlawful entry. It made entry without inspection or without a valid passport a deportable offense; eliminated the statute of limitation on deportation; and created a land Border Patrol. The number of people deported or expelled from the country rose from approximately 2,500 in 1920 to 39,000 in 1930. By 1930 Mexicans comprised the majority of people expelled from the country.

After World War II, the national origins quota system became increasingly repugnant to Americans' liberal sensibilities. The racial requirement to naturalization was abolished in 1952. The growing influence of Euro-American ethnic groups in urban politics and civil rights legislation in 1964 paved the way for the abolition of national origins quotas in 1965.

BIBLIOGRAPHY

Daniels, Roger. *The Politics of Prejudice: The Anti-Japanese Movement in California and the Struggle for Japanese Exclusion.* 1977 (1962).

Gossett, Thomas. *Race: The History of an Idea in America.* 1997 (1963).

Haney-Lopez, Ian. *White by Law. The Legal Construction of Race.* 1995.

Higham, John. *Strangers in the Land, Patterns of US Nativism, 1850–1924.* 1985 (1955).

Ngai, Mae M. "The Architecture of Race in American Immigration Law: a Reexamination of the Reed Johnson Act of 1924." *Journal of American History.* In press.

Sanchez, George. *Becoming Mexican American: Ethnicity, Culture, and Identity in Chicago Los Angeles.* 1993.

Mae M. Ngai

Immigration Act of 1965

The Immigration and Nationality Act of 1965 (or Hart-Celler Act), which repealed the national origins quota system and formulated a preference system for immigrants, was a major revision in U.S. immigration law. Ironically, its long-range significance was not recognized when it was passed. Technically, it was merely a series of amendments to the Immigration and Nationality Act of 1952 (also known as the McCarran-Walter Act). Many of its proponents did not envision an increase in immigration because the act actually put a ceiling on immigrants moving from countries in the Western Hemisphere. Yet by removing previous discrimination aimed at potential immigrants from Asia and by legally encoding an emphasis on family reunification, the act is a watershed in enabling the resurgence of immigration to the United States in the decades to follow.

The Immigration and Nationality Act was a response to the increasingly cumbersome immigration policy stemming from the national quotas prescribed in the Immigration Acts of 1921 and 1924 (see IMMIGRATION ACT OF 1924). In the thirteen years before the 1965 act, only 61 percent of the available visas were used, while thousands of potential immigrants were denied admission because they were from countries with small quotas. The short-term solution was admission through temporary laws regarding refugees, displaced persons, and war brides. But pressure for a systematic change in immigration policy grew especially in the 1960s due to the civil rights movement which was used to point out the racial inequities of the present immigration system. After the 1964 Democratic landslide gave the Democratic Party a large majority in Congress, President Lyndon JOHNSON sent a reform proposal to Congress in early 1965, which was introduced by Rep. Emmanuel Celler and Senator Philip Hart and sponsored by thirty-two others. Those who were concerned that the bill would increase dramatically the immigration from Latin America, such as Senators Sam Ervin and Everett Dirksen, demanded an overall ceiling on immigration within the Western Hemisphere. Once that compromise was reached, the bill passed easily, 76 to 18 in the Senate and 320 to 69 in the House.

The provisions of the Immigration and Nationality Act contained major innovations. First, it voided national origins quotas and replaced them with ceilings of immigration on each of the two hemispheres. Under its provisions, 170,000 visas were to be issued for immigrants from the Eastern Hemisphere and 120,000 from the Western Hemisphere, with a ceiling of 20,000 for every Eastern Hemisphere nation (no limit was placed initially on countries in the Western

Hemisphere). Importantly, this clause invalidated the discriminatory national origins quota which had previously severely limited immigration from Asian countries. Second, a preference category system was devised to determine preference for visas. This system emphasized family reunification giving preference to children, spouses, and siblings of American citizens and permanent residents (first, second, fourth, fifth preference categories). It also gave preference to those with special skills in short supply in the United States (third and sixth preference categories).

The impact and consequences of the Immigration and Nationality Act were many. Levels of immigration increased dramatically. First, an average legal immigration of 191,000 between 1924 until 1965 grew to a level of 435,000 between 1965 and 1981 (and it grew yet again thereafter due to new legislation). Second, the countries of origin of immigrants changed dramatically after 1965. Asian countries, such as the Philippines, Korea, China, India, and Vietnam, which previously had negligible immigration because of their small national quotas, became among the most significant nations of immigration to the United States. Finally, preference categories for skilled immigrants encouraged the migration of professionals, especially from Asia. By the late 1970s, for example, over 70,000 medical doctors alone had immigrated to the United States.

BIBLIOGRAPHY

Briggs, Vernon M., Jr. *Immigration Policy and the American Labor Force.* 1984.

Chin, Gabriel J. "The Civil Rights Revolution Comes to Immigration Law: A New Look at the Immigration and Nationality Act of 1965." *North Carolina Law Review* 75 (1996): 273–345.

LeMay, Michael C. *From Open Door to Dutch Door: An Analysis of U.S. Immigration Policy Since 1820.* 1987.

Reimers, David. "Recent Immigration Policy: An Analysis." In *The Gateway,* edited by Barry Chiswick. 1982.

Ueda, Reed. *Postwar Immigrant America: A Social History.* 1994.

Jon Gjerde

Immigration and Immigrants

There were few developments in federal immigration policy in early U.S. history. Indeed, an "open-door" policy characterized primarily by a lack of federal restrictions, rather than outright inducements, defined the U.S. attitude toward immigration throughout much of the nineteenth century. The Immigration Act of 1875, which prohibited the immigration of prostitutes and convicts, marked the beginning of direct federal regulation of immigration. This legislation also

An immigrant woman and her three children pose pensively shortly after arriving at Ellis Island, New York, in 1905. (Museum of the City of New York/ Archive Photos)

specified that no Asians could be brought into the country without their consent in an effort to suppress the "coolie trade," a term used to describe the exploitation of Chinese laborers, a practice which critics likened to slavery. This provision addressed the anti-Chinese sentiment of labor organizations, especially on the West Coast, which saw the Chinese as competitors for jobs during a period of economic decline.

Indeed, Chinese immigrants became the primary targets of anti-immigration sentiment at this time. Congress responded to this anti-immigration sentiment by passing several CHINESE EXCLUSION ACTS in the 1880s and 1890s. These acts suspended the immigration of any Chinese person, except government officials, teachers, students, merchants, or tourists. The numbers of legal Chinese immigrants dropped dramatically after Chinese exclusion legislation was passed. In 1917, an immigration act passed by Congress replaced these Chinese exclusion acts with an "Asiatic-barred zone" which prohibited immigration

for permanent residence from Asian countries in general.

Building on the "success" of the Chinese Exclusions Acts, proponents of restrictions on immigration turned their attention to the "new immigrants" from southern and eastern Europe that had come to dominate immigration flows to the United States by the turn of the century. Beginning in the late 1890s, anti-immigration groups advocated a literacy test as a means of restricting immigration because they presumed it would deter the immigration of "undesirable races" from southern and eastern Europe. Initially, proimmigration forces, including ethnic organizations and employer associations, were able to block Congressional efforts to adopt a literacy test. Nevertheless, Congress finally passed a literacy test in the Immigration Act of 1917. However, the literacy test did not meet its proponents' expectations as many immigrants from southern and eastern Europe passed the literacy test and gained legal entry to the United States.

In response to the failure of the literacy test to reduce unwanted immigration, Congressional proponents of new immigration restrictions initiated legislation for a quota system that would regulate immigration explicitly on the basis of national origin. Calls for racial exclusion were based not only on the view that these new immigrants were culturally different and more difficult to assimilate but also on the perception that they were racially inferior. This type of racial thinking led Congress to pass the Emergency Immigration Restriction Act in 1921. This legislation established annual immigration quotas based on national origin. Annual quotas for each nation were set at 3 percent of that nationality in the U.S. population according to the 1910 census. The IMMIGRATION ACT OF 1924 provided for a permanent quota system that created national quotas under an overall annual immigration ceiling of 150,000 based on the proportion of each nationality's population in the overall white population in 1920. This national origins system, which became operational in 1929, limited the entry of ethnic minorities from countries outside of northern and western Europe because proportionally few immigrants from these countries resided in the United States by this time.

Two political developments after WORLD WAR II led to growing support for the liberalization of U.S. immigration policy. First, growing public awareness of Nazi atrocities during World War II created unprecedented support for human rights, which was translated into growing political support for the admission of refugees and the elimination of the discriminatory national origins system. Second, the emerging Cold War with the Soviet Union also resulted in demands for the admission of refugees from communist countries and the liberalization of the quota system, which discriminated against several European allies.

In spite of growing support for the liberalization of U.S. immigration policy, the 1952 Immigration and Nationality Act did not radically alter the national origins system. This legislation did liberalize the criteria for entry by removing the racial barriers to naturalization, thus making individuals from Asia eligible for immigration and permanent residence. As a result, quotas were established for the countries within the Asia-Pacific triangle, formerly the Asiatic-barred zone. Aside from creating the Asia-Pacific triangle, however, the 1952 legislation essentially left the national origins system intact.

By the 1960s, however, the economic and political environment increasingly favored proimmigration forces. Economic prosperity led employers and politicians to call for an increase in legal immigration as a means of sustaining economic growth. Additionally, the civil rights movement generated unprecedented opposition to racial discrimination in U.S. immigration policy. In this political and economic environment, the 1965 amendments to the Immigration and Nationality Act eliminated the national origins system and its underlying racial criteria from U.S. immigration policy (see IMMIGRATION ACT OF 1965). In the place of the national origins system, the 1965 legislation created a new quota system, which provided for equal per-country limits under an overall ceiling on legal immigration. (Initially, this immigration ceiling and the per-country limits only applied to countries in the Eastern Hemisphere, though a further amendment in 1976 applied these criteria to the Western Hemisphere.) Preference within the per-country limits was given to relatives of citizens and legal residents and individuals with special occupational skills.

The quota system created under the 1965 legislation remains the basic foundation of U.S. immigration policy today. Each nation is allotted an equal number of quotas within an overall immigration ceiling, and eligibility for immigration is based on family reunification, personal qualifications, and order of application. The elimination of the national origins system from U.S. immigration policy has had dramatic effects, contributing both to an increase in overall immigration and to the increasing ethnic diversity of legal immigrants to this country.

In spite of the dramatic consequences of the 1965 amendments to the Immigration and Nationality Act, critics have argued that this legislation remains discriminatory in its effects. Civil rights advocates contend that the per-country limits under the 1965 legislation hinder family reunification, as well as immigration in

general, for individuals from countries where the demand for visas is high. While quotas are underutilized in some countries, especially in Europe, demand for visas exceeds quota allowances in many developing countries. Hence, family members of legal residents in countries where demand exceeds visa allowances frequently have to wait much longer to obtain visas than applicants within a lower preference category, such as skilled workers, from a European country with underutilized quotas. Therefore, many civil rights advocates continue to demand additional changes to U.S. immigration policy, including the elimination of per-country limits.

In fact, civil rights considerations have been one of the most important factors shaping U.S. immigration policy after 1965. Passage of the 1986 Immigration Reform and Control Act, designed to reduce illegal immigration through the use of employer sanctions, would not have been possible without provisions designed to protect the due process rights of employers; to prevent discrimination against ethnic minorities entitled to work in the United States; and to make illegal immigrants who had resided in this country for several years eligible for legalization. Similarly, in spite of widespread public support for a reduction in both legal and illegal immigration by the 1990s, the Immigration Act of 1990 increased annual allowances for legal immigration partly to facilitate family reunification and to promote diversity in immigration flows to this country.

In spite of the growing influence of civil rights norms in the debate over immigration, U.S. immigration policy continues to be marred by racial discrimination and civil rights violations. For example, critics have documented Immigration and Naturalization Service abuses of the basic rights of suspected illegal immigrants, and efforts to crack down on illegal immigration have sometimes led to discrimination against citizens and legal residents who are ethnic minorities. Moreover, the most recent changes to U.S. immigration policy represent retrenchment in the area of basic civil rights for immigrants. The welfare reform legislation passed by Congress in 1996 denies basic federal benefits to legal immigrants, who are required to pay the same taxes as citizens, as well as illegal immigrants. The Illegal Immigration Reform and Responsibility Act of 1996 introduced a variety of new methods designed to deter and punish illegal immigration, including new restrictions on judicial review of Immigration and Naturalization Service decisions and limitations on the ability of asylum-seekers who have been denied entry to bring class action suits. Civil rights advocates correctly view these new developments in immigration policy as setbacks in terms of basic rights for immigrants.

At the same time, anti-immigration groups such as the Federation for American Immigration Reform are equally disappointed that Congress has not yet been able to reduce immigration further by limiting family reunification, strengthening employer sanctions, or adopting a national identification requirement. Civil rights considerations have been influential in blocking legislation in these areas. In conclusion, the idea of civil rights remains central to the debate over U.S. immigration policy, even though elements of this policy are still unfair and discriminatory.

BIBLIOGRAPHY

Briggs, Vernon M., Jr. *Mass Immigration and the National Interest.* 1992.

Fuchs, Lawrence H. "Immigration, Pluralism and Public Policy: the Challenge of the *Pluribus* to the *Unum.*" In *U.S. Immigration and Refugee Policy,* edited by Mary M. Kritz. 1983.

Fuchs, Lawrence H. *The American Kaleidoscope: Race, Ethnicity, and the Civic Culture.* 1990.

Harwood, Edwin. *In Liberty's Shadow: Illegal Aliens and Immigration Law Enforcement.* 1986.

Higham, John. *Strangers in the Land: Patterns of American Nativism: 1860–1925,* 2nd. edition. 1988.

Hull, Elizabeth. *Without Justice for All: The Constitutional Rights of Aliens.* 1985.

Hutchinson, E. P. *Legislative History of American Immigration Policy: 1798–1965.* 1981.

Keely, Charles B. "The United States of America: Retaining a Fair Immigration Policy." In *The Politics of Migration Policies,* edited by Daniel Kubat. 1993.

Konvitz, Milton R. *Civil Rights in Immigration.* 1953.

LeMay, Michael C. *From Open Door to Dutch Door: An Analysis of U.S. Immigration Policy Since 1820.* 1987.

Loescher, Gil, and John A. Scanlan. *Calculated Kindness: Refugees and America's Half-Open Door, 1945 to the Present.* 1986.

Miller, Mark J. "Never Ending Story: the U.S. Debate over Illegal Immigration." In *Nations of Immigrants: Australia, the United States, and International Migration,* edited by Gary P. Freeman and James Jupp. 1992.

Reimers, David M. "An Unintended Reform: the 1965 Immigration Act and Third World Immigration to the United States." *Journal of American Ethnic History* 3, 1 (Fall 1983): 9–28.

Reimers, David M. *Still the Golden Rule: The Third World Comes to America,* 2nd ed. 1992.

U.S. Immigration and Naturalization Service, *Statistical Yearbook of the Immigration and Naturalization Service, 1992.* 1993.

Debra L. DeLaet

Immigration Restriction League

The Immigration Restriction League was a small, but influential, organization formed in 1894 in Boston to advocate legal reform of American immigration policy. Consisting mainly of Harvard-trained intellectuals, such as Prescott F. Hall and Charles Warren, the IRL expressed a concern about increasing numbers of immigrants from southern and eastern Europe who allegedly were prone to illiteracy and criminality. Arguing initially that it was free of racial prejudice toward immigrants, the IRL threw its support behind a test of literacy for immigrants, regardless of racial background. Tirelessly promoting the literacy test through publicity campaigns, it gained a hearing in Congress when Senator Henry Cabot Lodge in 1895 introduced a literacy bill drawn up by the IRL. The bill, in revised form, passed both houses of Congress by late 1896, but President Grover Cleveland's veto and waning interest within the Republican leadership temporarily ended the discussion. (It would eventually become law in 1917.) In the early twentieth century, the IRL moved toward restriction policies aimed at national and "racial" groups, allied itself with the eugenics movement, and became blatantly racialist. It could claim some success when immigration restriction acts, which curbed immigration especially from southern and eastern Europe, were enacted by Congress in 1921 and 1924. IRL membership, never large, declined in the 1920s, but the last remnants of the group sought even more restrictive immigration policies into the 1930s, including limiting Mexican immigration and prohibiting entry to Jews fleeing Nazi Germany.

BIBLIOGRAPHY

Higham, John. *Strangers in the Land: Patterns of American Nativism 1860–1925.* 1955.

Knobel, Dale T. *"America for the Americans": The Nativist Movement in the United States.* 1996.

Soloman, Barbara Miller. *Ancestors and Immigrants: A Changing New England Tradition.* 1956.

Jon Gjerde

Independent Living Centers

The Independent Living Movement (ILM), a wing of the larger DISABILITY RIGHTS Movement, has focused on ensuring people with significant disabilities the means to achieve self-directed community-based living. In the early 1970s the first independent living centers were organized in Berkeley, Houston, and Boston, by and for physically disabled young adults, most of them white and middle-class, many of them recent or current college students. By the 1990s the centers had expanded their clientele to include adults of all ages with sensory, developmental, and emotional disabilities, including various ethnic minorities, though most were still from the original constituency. The ILM

Members of a support group sit in wheelchairs discussing issues at an Independent Living Center in Boston in 1994. (Bob Daemmrich/Stock, Boston/PNI)

paralleled the deinstitutionalization movements for people with psychiatric and developmental disabilities and ultimately forged links with them.

As early as 1959, rehabilitation professionals had unsuccessfully lobbied Congress to fund independent living for individuals for whom employment was not a practical objective. By the late 1970s advances in medicine and rehabilitation technology and the computer revolution had made employment possible for significantly disabled people, thus rendering obsolete the dichotomy between independent living and work. In 1978 Congress authorized federal grants for independent living centers. By the 1990s the federal-state vocational rehabilitation system funded some four hundred independent living centers.

Borrowing from the civil rights, consumer, and self-help movements, the ILM ideology has espoused five basic principles:

1. While the medical/vocational rehabilitation system promotes physical self-sufficiency, independent mobility (e.g., walking), and paid employment, the ILM supports those goals if they are practical objectives for individuals, but regards consumer choice and control and independent-living support services as more important.
2. Disability is primarily a social, rather than a medical, issue. The limitations people with disabilities confront in social and vocational functioning are not the inevitable result of their dis-

abilities but are largely caused by inaccessibility in the existing environment, particularly as regards the construction of buildings, "disincentives" in public policies, domination of disabled people by bureaucrats and professionals, prejudice in the culture, and institutionalized discrimination.

3. People with disabilities have a right to the means necessary for them to participate in the community. These include: legal protection from discrimination; the right to refuse treatment and services; the right to receive quality treatment and services; due process in all professional or governmental decision-making affecting them; equal access to public transportation and accommodations; and, most central to the ILM's objectives, the rights to deinstitutionalization and to support services for independent living. The ILM has pursued two major policy goals: elimination of work disincentives from federal income-maintenance and health-insurance programs and federally mandated funding for independent living services. The ILM has identified Personal Assistance Services (PAS) as the key support, that is, one person assisting another with tasks the individual would ordinarily do for himself or herself if he or she did not have a disability. PAS may include: personal maintenance and hygiene, mobility assistance, household chores (cooking, cleaning, child care), cog-

nitive tasks (money-handling, budget-planning), and communications access (interpreting, reading). In the early 1990s an estimated 9.6 million Americans needed PAS, with 7.8 million of them already living in the community, but only 10 percent of those individuals were using paid PAS. Viewed from the standpoint of civil rights theory, these claims by the ILM combined civil rights with benefit entitlements. Thereby it redefined services and assistive devices as alternative modes of functioning, not the means of caring for those who are fundamentally dependent, and made them matters of right, not charity.

4. Professional/consumer relationships are often adversarial, with power tilted to the professionals' side. The ILM has criticized manufacturers, vendors, and service providers as often serving their own financial and status interests at the expense of disabled people's best interests. Thus, independent living centers established advocacy departments and have offered personal self-advocacy and systems-change advocacy.

5. Disabled people should have majority power in designing and running the programs that affect them. Medical and social service professionals initially had a limited role in the ILM, as independent living leaders challenged the dominant ideologies of the rehabilitation/social service system and contested professionals' power. But by the early 1980s nondisabled professionals were taking an increasingly prominent role in running the centers. This paralleled a shift from activism to service provision in response to criticism by political conservatives and threats to withdraw federal funding. In consequence, during the 1980s disability rights advocacy moved outside the centers. In the 1990s federal law came to require that 50 percent of independent living centers' boards of directors and staffs be people with disabilities. A growing number of centers began to return to systems-change advocacy and political activism.

BIBLIOGRAPHY

Crewe, Nancy, and Irving Kenneth Zola, eds. *Independent Living For Physically Disabled People*. 1983.
National Council on Disability. *Achieving Independence: The Challenge of the Twenty-First Century*. 1996.

Paul K. Longmore

Indiana

A middle western state in the Old Northwest Territory—where slavery was first prohibited by the U.S.

Congress—Indiana's civil rights history is intertwined with that of the larger struggle for equal rights in this country. Indeed, before the Civil War, prejudice ran to great extremes in Indiana. Discrimination was codified in state law, denying both African Americans and women basic civil rights protections. Indiana's 1851 constitution denied blacks the right to vote (see VOTING RIGHTS), due process of law in the courts, access to public schooling and in fact prohibited them from settling in the state. That constitution denied women the right to vote as well as hold property.

The Civil War and RECONSTRUCTION set forces in motion, however, that brought about significant changes in civil rights in Indiana. In 1865 the Indiana General Assembly partially repealed the ban against African-American testimony in courts of law. A far more important step was taken the following year, when the Indiana Supreme Court, in the case of *Smith v. Moody*, declared that Article XIII of the state constitution, barring African-American migration into the state, was null and void because African Americans were citizens of the United States. Shortly thereafter, the ratification of the FIFTEENTH AMENDMENT to the U.S. Constitution nullified parts of the 1851 Indiana constitution, which had limited the franchise to white males.

During the early 1880s the issue of women's rights surfaced briefly in the state legislature and then receded, despite the efforts of feminists such as Helen M. Cougar, May Wright Sewall, and Ida Husted Harper. African Americans fared somewhat better legislatively. In 1885 the Indiana legislature passed a state civil rights law after the U.S. SUPREME COURT ruled that the CIVIL RIGHTS ACT OF 1875 was unconstitutional; this 1885 state legislation declared that all persons were entitled to equal access to public facilities and the right to serve on juries. The law proved mostly ineffective in accomplishing its stated purpose, however: African Americans continued to be denied the use of public transportation and accommodations.

The most flagrant example of contempt for due process of law in Indiana at this time was that of LYNCHING. At least twenty African Americans were lynched in the state between 1865 and 1903 for alleged crimes. In fact, so notorious was the state's record in this area then that the governor of GEORGIA cited Indiana as a justification for lynching in his own state. It was not until 1899 that Indiana, at the urging of Governor James Mount, finally passed an ANTI-LYNCHING law. The law appears to have had the desired effect; afterward, the only other recorded instance of a lynching in Indiana was in the city of Marion in 1930.

The Progressive Era witnessed a renewal of interest in women's rights (see WOMAN SUFFRAGE). The Indiana Women's Suffrage Association, organized in 1869, was revived in 1906, and in 1911 suffragists organized the Women's Franchise League of Indiana, which soon grew to sixty branches throughout the state. In 1917 the state legislature responded favorably to women suffragists' lobbying efforts, but the difficulty of amending the state constitution and an adverse state supreme court decision delayed suffrage. In early 1920, however, the state legislature ratified the NINE-TEENTH AMENDMENT to the federal constitution, and the following year added a women's suffrage amendment to the state constitution.

The rise of the KU KLUX KLAN in Indiana in the 1920s posed the most serious threat to civil rights there during the twentieth century. Despite opposition by the NATIONAL ASSOCIATION FOR THE ADVANCEMENT OF COLORED PEOPLE (NAACP), Klan-supported racial SEGREGATION was either sanctioned by law or custom in public restaurants, accommodations, transportation, schools, recreational facilities, and HOUSING throughout the state. Some rural Indiana communities even prohibited African Americans from staying within community boundaries overnight. In the 1930s, Indianapolis African-American attorney and state legislator Henry J. Richardson sought to strengthen civil rights in Indiana. He proposed legislation prohibiting discrimination in state public works projects and opening the state militia to African Americans. Both bills passed, although significant barriers remained to blacks joining the National Guard until 1941. Richardson also proposed an "Anti-hate" bill to strengthen Indiana's 1885 civil rights law, and two years later co-sponsored a bill with six other legislators to prohibit racial discrimination and intimidation. Neither of these proposed civil rights initiatives was passed by the state legislature, however.

WORLD WAR II and later revelations about the Holocaust drew public attention to Indiana's abysmal civil rights record and heightened awareness of the murderous consequences and base injustice of discrimination there. As a result, civil rights activists scored their first major postwar success in 1945 with passage of the state's first Fair Employment Practices Act. Although weak in its provisions for enforcement, the law did authorize the State Labor Commission to work toward abolishing discrimination in the workplace. Four years later, activists scored their second major victory when the legislature prohibited segregation in public education. Civil rights activists also employed nonlegislative means in the immediate postwar years to end discrimination in public accommodations. Spearheaded by NAACP branches throughout the state, African-American social and fraternal organizations, the CIO (see AFL-CIO), the Jewish Community Relations Council, and church-related groups, negotiations began with public facilities that barred African-American

patronage to secure compliance with the state's 1885 law. When negotiations were unsuccessful, civil rights activists employed nonviolent direct action tactics to desegregate those establishments.

In the 1950s and 1960s several cities, such as Indianapolis, established civil rights commissions. The Indiana Civil Liberties Union, dedicated to the protection of BILL OF RIGHTS guarantees, was founded in 1953. In the mid-1960s, intense lobbying by the Indiana Conference on Civil Rights Legislation as well as public demonstrations led to the creation of the Indiana Civil Rights Commission, a stronger law against discrimination in public accommodations, fair housing legislation, and the repeal of Indiana's prohibition against interracial marriage.

While much progress has been made in civil rights in Indiana since 1965, vestiges of the state's discriminatory past linger. In 1968 the Indianapolis NAACP filed suit against the city's school board, resulting in a 1976 desegregation order by the federal courts that remained in effect until 1998. Recent studies of racial housing patterns find that Indianapolis ranks among the top ten U.S. cities of its size in residential segregation. Today, nonwhites and women still experience discrimination in public accommodations, restaurants, and EMPLOYMENT. The major difference today is that they can use the force of law to seek redress in the courts. That such is the case is due, in large part, to the tireless efforts of civil rights advocates during the past 134 years.

BIBLIOGRAPHY

Cameron, James. *A Time of Terror*. 1994.
Cohen, Ronald D. *Children of the Mill: Schooling and Society in Gary Indiana, 1906–1960*. 1990.
Madison, James. *The Indiana Way: A State History*. 1986.
Thornbrough, Emma Lou. *The History of Indiana*, Vol. 3. *Indiana in the Civil War Era, 1850–1880*. 1965.
Thornbrough, Emma Lou. *The Negro in Indiana Before 1900: A Study of a Minority*. 1957.
Thornbrough, Emma Lou. *Since Emancipation: A History of Indiana Negroes, 1863–1963*. 1964.

Monroe H. Little, Jr.

Indian Child Welfare Act (1978)

Informal adoptions of Indian children were a common practice during most of American history, apparently in the belief that an education would make Indians "acceptable." Some orphans found on battlefields were adopted by sympathetic U.S. Army officers, who raised them. As kinships ties eroded, Indian parents could not provide for their families, and church and state agencies began placing Indian children with white foster parents. By the 1960s the practice had become almost a confiscation of Indian children for placement in non-Indian homes.

In South Dakota, 40 percent of the state adoptees in 1967–1968 were Indian children although Indians represented only 7 percent of the population. In 1971–1972 in Minnesota, nearly 25 percent of the Indian children under one year of age were adopted by non-Indians. By the early 1970s, tribes were demanding an investigation of the situation and remedial legislation. After extensive and controversial congressional hearings, the Indian Child Welfare act was passed in 1978. Its basic premise was that Indian tribes as politically recognized sovereigns had a vital interest in actions that separated children from their extended families. Many senators and members of CONGRESS worked on the bill, but Morris Udall of the House and Henry Jackson of the Senate are usually credited with its passage. The Department of Justice and the BUREAU OF INDIAN AFFAIRS strongly opposed the act, but President Jimmy CARTER signed it nonetheless.

The act has generated more litigation than any other federal statute regarding Indians except the Allotment Act, but has proved beneficial in setting rigorous standards that must be met in the matter of child adoption. Under the act, Indian tribal courts have exclusive jurisdiction over custody proceedings when the child is residing on the reservation. Their decisions must be given full faith and credit in other jurisdictions. State courts must transfer their proceedings to the tribal court upon petition of the tribe or the parents. Either parent can veto this transfer. An indigent parent or an Indian custodian has the right to a court-appointed lawyer in involuntary custody proceedings. Anyone seeking foster care placement or the termination of parental rights must satisfy the court that efforts have been made to preserve the Indian family. Evidentiary standards require clear and convincing evidence of the likelihood of damage to the child in its present condition before adoption or placement is decided.

With the majority of Indians now living off the reservations, the act creates unusual situations for people who do not reside there. Divorces where at least one parent is Indian become complicated, as the act gives the Indian spouse leverage that would not otherwise exist. Many tribes are vigilant in monitoring placements and adoptions because they have a vital interest in maintaining enrollments and families. So children with small amounts of Indian blood are likely to be placed in a new home situation with blood relatives with whom they have little acquaintance. The act stands as a unique effort by Congress to resolve a perplexing and longstanding problem of maintaining the Indian population in spite of the pressures for Indians to assimilate into the larger society.

BIBLIOGRAPHY
Getches, David H., Charles F. Wilkinson, and Robert A. Williams. *Cases and Materials on Federal Indian Law*, 4th ed. 1998.
Norgren, Jill, and Petra T. Shattuck, eds. *Partial Justice: Federal Indian Law in a Liberal Constitutional System.* 1991.

Vine Deloria, Jr.

Indian Citizenship Act of 1924

See American Indian Citizenship Act of 1924.

Indian Civil Rights Act of 1968

See American Indian Civil Rights Act of 1968.

Indian Claims Commission Act

On August 13, 1946, the Congress of the United States passed the Indian Claims Commission Act (*US Statutes at Large* 60: 1049–1056). The law established the Indian Claims Commission (ICC) to enable Indian tribes to sue the federal government for resolution of past wrongs accumulated from the nineteenth century. The ICC operated as a quasi-judicial agency of CONGRESS to settle issues of Indian land title, land use, and occupancy. By law the agency was a commission but in its operations acted the part of a court much like the U.S. Court of Claims. Indian tribes became plaintiffs and the U.S. government, defendant, in the legal proceedings. A federal Court of Claims had been created in 1855 but Indians seeking redress of grievances were barred from its use. The U.S. government ceased making treaties with Indians in 1871 but treaties made before 1871 remained in force, since they had never been invalidated. Provisions in over 400 treaties made between 1778 and 1871 had never been enforced and money owed to Indian tribes never paid. Indian people had to make special requests to Congress about their grievances. These circumstances led to Congress' authorization of review of Indian claims and allowance of suits for treaty violations and illegal taking of their lands. Hundreds of cases had been presented to Congress and the Court of Claims from 1880 to 1945. While the 1946 legislation helped rekindle Indian hopes for justice and fair resolution of disputes, it was a triumph for those who wanted to end Indian land claims and terminate the federal relationship with Indian tribes.

In 1944 Indian tribal leaders organized the National Congress of American Indians (NCAI) to protect Indian rights and defend tribal lands. They

The Indian Claims Commission was established to rectify wrongs stemming from seizures of Indian property by the United States government. President Truman has just signed a bill creating the commission. Behind his chair are members of the Ute tribe. August 1946. (CORBIS/Bettmann)

organized to resist a developing conservative U.S. policy of termination. By 1945 President Truman and the Congress had rejected John Collier's Bureau of Indian Affairs' policies of self-sufficiency and autonomy for Indian tribes. New Deal legislation such as the INDIAN REORGANIZATION ACT (1934), the Johnson-O'Malley Act (1934), and the Indian Arts and Crafts Board Act (1936) came into question. Truman placed Dillon S. Myer in charge of BUREAU OF INDIAN AFFAIRS relocation plans. Myer had supervised Japanese-American internment camps during World War II. The Claims Commission Act of 1946 could help resolve longstanding land claims issues between the U.S. government and Indian people. Those who traditionally supported allotment and assimilation policies saw the 1946 law as a way to terminate Indian tribes as wards of the federal government. Other measures pursued by the government strengthen this view. In 1952 the Bureau of Indian Affairs established the Voluntary Relocation Program to fund training, moving expenses, and employment assistance off reservations. In 1953 Congress

passed House Concurrent Resolution 108 to end the special legal relationship between Indians and the federal government. The goal was to end the reservation system, assimilate Indians into U.S. society, and end Indian treaty rights and legal status as independent cultural communities. In 1953 Congress also passed Public Law 280 that gave some states jurisdiction over the administration of justice on reservations. From 1954 to 1962, Congress adopted the termination policy and ended more than 100 tribes' relationships with the federal government in matters of tribal sovereignty, health care, and U.S. treaty and legal obligations.

Before 1946, the U.S. compelled Indians to take their claims about land, water, or other concerns directly to Congress. Many problems remained unresolved as of 1946. Initially, authorities thought the Indian Claims Commission proceedings would end Indian land claims and resolve Indian suits against the government for treaty violations in a short time. Once settled the solutions to the Indians' claims were irrevocable. There was a right to appeal from the ICC to the U.S. Court of Claims and Supreme Court. Over the period of its operation from 1946 to 1978, the ICC reviewed hundreds of cases and awarded millions of dollars in settlements. Settlements were awarded in money only for the value of the lands in question at the time when wrongfully taken. In some cases, Congress has funded a few eastern tribes to assist them in their purchase of lands. The Penobscot and Passamaquoddy of Maine, for example, obtained about 300,000 acres of forest land in this manner. But the ICC could not order the return of lands to Indians as part of an award. Therefore, no land was given back to Indians and only very small monetary settlements were allotted to the claimants.

The workings of the U.S. Court of Claims, 1855 to 1946, helped establish a model for the Indian Claims Commission proceedings. Discovering the basis for jurisdiction embedded in treaty rights, establishing tribal identity and boundaries, fixing the amount claimed, calculating "offsets" action, and making final judgment and award became the pattern of proceedings in the ICC. The Commission examined the original geographic area settled and claimed by the Indian nation. The most important issues in this part of the claims process were to describe the "territory the Indians occupied exclusively" and determine the value of the land at "the time of taking." The Commission gathered claimants' petitions, briefs with main legal points, responses by the government, and other written submissions by plaintiff and defendant. The ICC also collected reports written by experts and took oral expert testimony. The Commission made its findings of fact and opinions, wrote its orders, and determined the final monetary award due to the claimant.

Congress passed the Indian Claims Commission Act in 1946 to provide Indians with an avenue for settling their land claims against the federal government for the illegal taking of their lands through error, duress, fraud, or other dishonorable dealings. In some ways the law gave Indians their "day in court." The methods of implementation are open to criticism. Tribes were usually compensated for the value of their lands at the time of taking. Many times this amounted to only one to two dollars per acre. The government never paid compensation at the land's modern, current market value. Authorities also deducted from the final award amount the value of funds spent by the government on behalf of the tribe over a period of many years. These "offsets," plus attorneys' fees, and witness expenses had to be subtracted from the ultimate total monetary award. The law did not provide for the return of land to tribes and it provided only for a delayed, insufficient monetary payment for the land. Tribes at first thought they would get back their land. The ICC interpreted its authority to make monetary payments rather than awards in land.

The 1946 Indian Claims Commission Act provided "exceptionally broad grounds for suit" but during its proceedings to 1978 the Claims Commission "favored narrow construals and parsimonious settlements." During the period of its work, the ICC received and considered 614 claims. The Commission dismissed 204 of these dockets as being without merit. Awards were granted by the ICC in 342 cases. It is of interest to compare the outcomes of Indian Claims heard by the U.S. Court of Claims, 1881–1946. Only 35 cases of 219 claims (15.9 percent) received money awards of $77 million. But between 1946 and 1978 the ICC granted money settlements in 342 of 546 cases resolved (62.6 percent) amounting to over $818 million. In the cases it decided, the ICC awarded tribes $2.4 million per claim. Overall, this amount usually was not more than about $1.25 per acre based on the market value of an acre "at the time of taking."

In the beginning, the ICC was created to operate for a ten-year period but its work was extended several times to the 1970s. Indian tribes were given five years to file claims and prove ownership of any lands in question. The ICC would review the case, determine the money value of the Indians' claim, and award a monetary settlement. By 1956 it became evident that the planned ten-year period of operation for the ICC was too brief. Only 80 cases had been completed. Congress renewed the ICC in 1956 and in 1961. By 1960 only 125 dockets had been completed. On March 20, 1967, Congress extended the ICC to 1972 and expanded its membership to five, in part, because the Commission had a backlog of 347 undecided cases to adjudicate. When the work of the Commission concluded in 1978, there remained 68 unresolved claims. They were turned over to the U.S. Court of Claims.

Many Indian nations accepted monetary settlements and awards by the ICC but even those who accepted the cash awards were very disappointed and often angered by the results of a process that was billed as the Indians' "day in court." In the 1969 "Alcatraz Island Declaration by Indians of All Tribes," the protesting Indians asked, "How did we lose our land?" They answered that through wars, massacres, fraudulent treaties, land allotments, and expropriation, the government, corporations, and settlers took their land. Indians of all tribes objected to accepting money in return for land taken in such ways. The 1969 Alcatraz Declaration concluded that "the historical, spiritual and material needs of the Indian people cannot be satisfied except by what we demand . . . the return of our land." (See ALCATRAZ OCCUPATION.)

Among some positive consequences of the work of the ICC was heightened legal knowledge and skills among Indians. Tribal governments brought more and more suits to the federal and state courts beginning in the 1950s. They achieved major victories in water, fishing, and mineral rights cases. As well, tribes successfully defended legal, treaty, and land rights and protected tribal sovereignty. While the Congress originally set out to compensate Indian land losses and terminate them from the federal fiduciary relationship, by 1978, the policy of termination had been abandoned. The whole ICC process revitalized tribal community life and mobilized Indians to research their histories, organize their cases, and thus build autonomous community spirit.

BIBLIOGRAPHY

Barsh, Russell L. "Indian Land Claims Policy in the United States." *North Dakota Law Review* 58 (1982): 7–82.

Fixico, Donald. *Termination and Relocation: Federal Indian Policy, 1945–1960.* 1986.

Horr, David Agee, ed. *American Indian Ethnohistory.* 1974.

LeDuc, Thomas. "The Work of the Indian Claims Commission Under the Act of 1946." *Pacific Historical Review* 26 (1957): 1–16.

Lurie, Nancy Oestreich. "The Indian Claims Commission." *Annals of the American Academy of Political and Social Science.* (March 1978): 97–110.

Prucha, Francis Paul. *Documents of United States Indian Policy,* 2nd ed. 1990.

Rosenthal, Harvey D. *Their Day in Court: A History of the Indian Claims Commission.* 1990.

U.S. Indian Claims Commission. *Final Report.* 1979.

Rodger C. Henderson

Indian Religious Freedom Act of 1978

See American Indian Religious Freedom Act of 1978

Indian Reorganization Act of 1934

During the 1920s a growing number of reformers became concerned about the effects of federal policies on Native Americans. Investigators found that the forced assimilation and allotment of Indian lands carried out under the auspices of the DAWES SEVERALTY ACT of 1887 had disastrous effects on Indian reservations. This allotment program had broken up communally held land, distributed small tracts to individual Indians, and in the process opened up more than ninety million acres of "surplus" reservation lands to white settlement. The 1928 Meriam Report, in particular, detailed the high mortality rates, poor education, malnutrition, and poverty among Native Americans. The Report placed the blame for these deplorable conditions squarely at the feet of the BUREAU OF INDIAN AFFAIRS (BIA) and its implementation of federal Indian policy.

Extolling the virtues of cultural pluralism, reformers sought a different approach to Indian policy. They argued that self-determination and greater autonomy would revitalize Indians both economically and spiritually. Promising an "Indian New Deal," John Collier became Commissioner of Indian Affairs in 1933. At the heart of the new policy was the Indian Reorganization Act (IRA), often known as the Wheeler-Howard Act for its congressional sponsors. Though the final version of the bill was not as comprehensive as Collier would have liked, when President Franklin Delano ROOSEVELT signed it on June 18, 1934, IRA advocates regarded it as "Indian Independence Day."

The IRA prohibited further allotments of tribal land, stipulated that remaining "surplus" lands could be returned to the tribes, and authorized the Secretary of the Interior to spend up to $2 million annually in buying additional land for reservations. Ending the government's efforts to extinguish traditional customs and authority, the IRA authorized annual spending of $250,000 to assist tribal governments in their organization. Approved tribal governments would have the status of federally chartered corporations and could hold elections, hire legal counsel, negotiate with other government entities, and create courts to deal with local affairs. Tribal corporations could draw from a $10 million loan fund set up to aid Indian businesses. Furthermore, the IRA helped to restore tribal integrity and identity by promoting traditional arts and permitting previously banned religious ceremonies.

Tribes had two years to accept or reject the IRA provisions, and ultimately 181 tribes accepted the act while 77 rejected it. Critics attacked the IRA from all sides. The experiences of many Indians left them suspicious of any BIA directive, and some Indians who had received allotments rejected what seemed to them a return to tribalism and SEGREGATION on reservations. Others argued that a tribal government was a foreign concept that did not reflect traditional Native American political organizations or methods of choosing leaders. Additionally, BIA officials and members of Congress attacked the IRA as socialist while Christian missionaries feared a return to paganism.

Although the IRA was a significant departure from traditional policy, it never achieved the renaissance envisioned by its supporters. World War II drastically reduced federal expenditures on reservations and after the war legislators wanted to end the government's relationship with Indians. This effort led to the 1953 policy known as "Termination."

BIBLIOGRAPHY

Deloria, Vine, and Clifford M. Lytle. *American Indians, American Justice.* 1983.
Gibson, Arrell Morgan. *The American Indian: Prehistory to the Present.* 1980.
Iverson, Peter. *"We Are Still Here": American Indians in the Twentieth Century.* 1998.
Prucha, Francis Paul. *The Great Father: The United States Government and the Indians.* 1984.
Taylor, Graham D. *The New Deal and American Indian Tribalism: The Administration of the Indian Reorganization Act, 1934–45.* 1980.

L. Patrick Goines

Indian Self-Determination and Education Assistance Act of 1975

Legislation passed during the "Indian New Deal" planted the seeds of reform in Indian education, but these efforts failed to bear fruit until Native American activists in the 1960s and 1970s began pressing their demands for greater self-determination. Indian activists wanted to increase Native control of the federal programs that affected them. Congress responded with several acts, including the Indian Self-Determination and Education Assistance Act.

Initially proposed by Senator Henry Jackson of Washington, the Indian Self-Determination and Education Assistance Act became law in January 1975 and promised a new era in federal–Indian relations. The governing concept was that the tribes best understood their specific needs and that if Indians created and administered their own programs they could end the long-standing pattern of federal dependency and paternalism. The act authorized tribal governments to design their own EDUCATION, health care, HOUSING, and other programs, and then directly contract with federal agencies for grants and technical support to further the delivery of these services. The tribes could decide for themselves if they wanted to participate in any given program. Furthermore, Indian parents gained more authority on local school boards and the government could make cash grants to tribes for training programs and the acquisition of land.

Critics argue that the 1975 act simply rehashed provisions found in the 1934 INDIAN REORGANIZATION ACT. They contend that as long as the BUREAU OF INDIAN AFFAIRS has extensive discretionary power to reject contract applications and disburse funds, the act only creates the illusion of Native American control, rather than true self-determination.

BIBLIOGRAPHY

DeJong, David H. *Promises of the Past: A History of Indian Education in the United States.* 1993.

Deloria, Vine, and Clifford M. Lytle. *American Indians, American Justice.* 1983.

Senese, Guy B. *Self-Determination and the Social Education of Native Americans.* 1991.

L. Patrick Goines

Industrial Workers of the World

Embracing Marxian socialism and industrial unionism, a 1905 Chicago convention of labor radicals formed the Industrial Workers of the World (IWW). The founders committed the organization to recruiting unskilled minority workers often ignored by existing craft-based unions. (See EMPLOYMENT.)

Founded by white socialists and unionists like Eugene Debs, Mother Jones, and Bill Heywood, the IWW preached "one big union" to tie the working class together. Basic was the opening of ranks to all workers, especially the growing cadre of blacks, men, and "new" immigrants who provided the unskilled work force for emerging mass-production factories. Subject to factionalism, the IWW foundered during its initial years—sporadic activism achieved some success but anchored the union's reputation as a militant group. In 1912, however, it achieved national recognition for its successful organization of multi-gender, multi-ethnic textile workers in the Eastern United States, where its direct-action strategy forced employers to capitulate to some worker demands.

The early 1910s witnessed the pinnacle of the IWW's successes; from then on, the union's bark was usually larger than its bite. While protesting free-speech restrictions in Western towns in 1917, the

President Calvin Coolidge meets with Mary "Mother" Jones, ca. 1923–1928. Jones helped found the Industrial Workers of the World. (CORBIS)

group substantiated its reputation as a subversive organization. In 1918, subject to the full brunt of the U.S. Justice Department, the IWW was effectively demolished by accusations of treason and the imprisonment of its officials. The post–World War I "Red Scare" did little to help it reclaim its reputation. Still existing, though with little impact, the IWW's greatest legacy is its direct-action strategies and its inclusion of non-white, unskilled, and often female workers—all of whom had been ignored by the earlier era's trade-based unions like the American Federation of Labor (see AFL-CIO).

BIBLIOGRAPHY

Dubofsky, Melvyn. *We Shall Be All.* 1969.
Salerno, Salvatore. *Red November, Black November: Culture and Community in the Industrial Workers of the World.* 1989.
Thompson, Fred, and Patrick Murfin. *The IWW: Its First Seventy Years—1905–1975.* 1976.

Gregory L. Parker

Innis, Roy

(1934–   ), civil rights leader.

Born in St. Croix, Virgin Islands, Roy Innis moved to New York City in his teens, and attended Stuyvesant

Roy Innis, civil rights activist, national director of the Congress of Racial Equality (CORE) since 1968, walks near a courthouse in New York City in 1990. (Lisa Quinones/Black Star)

High School. After a stint in the U.S. Army during the Korean War, Innis attended City College of New York, majoring in chemistry. He subsequently worked as a laboratory assistant and union steward at Montefiore Hospital. During this period, Innis became attracted to black nationalist theories.

In 1963, Innis joined the New York chapter of the nonviolent civil rights group the CONGRESS OF RACIAL EQUALITY (CORE). Although regarded as an extremist for his nationalist ideas, Innis soon was named to the chapter's education committee, where he championed tutoring programs for black students and devised strategies for implementing community-controlled education. After becoming head of New York CORE in 1965, Innis led an unsuccessful fight for an independent school board for Harlem's public schools. During the mid-1960s, as CORE altered its original multiracial and nonviolent program, Innis grew more powerful, and in 1968 he was named CORE's national director.

As director of CORE, and in the *Manhattan Tribune,* a newspaper he published, Innis denounced INTEGRATION and called for black control of ghetto social and economic institutions. Despite Innis's visibility, CORE shrank dramatically in funds and membership during the 1970s. By the 1980s, Innis had become an outspoken conservative, and was notable for his opposition to AFFIRMATIVE ACTION and gun control and his endorsement of right-wing theoretician Lyndon LaRouche. Innis ran for CONGRESS in 1986, and challenged New York's mayor David Dinkins in his race for reelection in 1993.

BIBLIOGRAPHY

Meier, August, and Elliott Rudwick. *CORE: A Study in the Civil Rights Movement, 1942–1968.* 1973.
"Roy Innis." *Current Biography.* June 1969.

Greg Robinson

In re Ah Yup

In re Ah Yup (1878) was a decision rendered by Judge Lorenzo Sawyer of the U.S. District Court for California in response to a petition filed by three Chinese residing in the United States—Ah Yup, Li Huang, and Leong Lan—for naturalized citizenship. This was a landmark decision because it required the court to decide whether Chinese, who were racially neither white nor black, had the right of naturalization. The Naturalization Act of 1790 had stated that only an alien who was a "free, white person" and who had resided in the United States for at least two years could petition to become a naturalized U.S. citizen. After the Civil War, the naturalization law was amended in 1870 to make "aliens of African nativity and persons of African descent" eligible (16 Stat. 256, paragraph 7). During the debates in Congress, Senator Charles Sumner urged that the Chinese likewise be made eligible, but to no avail. When all federal laws were codified in 1874, the phrase "being a free white person" was inadvertently left out of Section 2165 of the Revised Statutes, which stated simply that "an alien may be admitted to become a citizen." Until that omission was corrected in 1875 (in Section 2169 of the Revised Statutes of 1875), a number of Chinese on the East Coast managed to acquire naturalized citizenship.

When Ah Yup of San Francisco, "a native and citizen of the empire of China, of the Mongolian race," submitted his petition in 1878, his attorney, Benjamin S. Brooks, argued that "white" was a "very indefinite description" and could therefore include persons from "the lightest blonde to the most swarthy brunette." However, the circuit court decided that "white person" had a "well settled meaning in common popular speech" and that "white" did not include persons of the "Mongolian race." Though Ah Yup's petition was denied, Chinese elsewhere continued to petition for citizenship because the decision of one lower federal court was not binding upon other federal courts. Those efforts were ended in 1882 by a provision in the Chinese Exclusion Act of 1882, which forbade any court, state or federal, from granting citizenship to Chinese.

Chinese did not acquire the right of naturalization until 1943 when Congress rescinded all the Chinese exclusion laws and granted a token immigration quota of 105 persons a year, as well as the right of naturalization, to Chinese immigrants. These actions were taken in order to promote better relations with China, an ally of the United States during World War II.

The Ah Yup case is significant because it offers historical evidence that there *were* Chinese who wanted to become American citizens, the stereotypical view that they had come to the United States only as temporary sojourners to earn some money before returning home notwithstanding. It also demonstrates that though relatively few Chinese spoke English well, they were nevertheless knowledgeable about such American institutions as the judicial system, that they did not hesitate to hire well-known attorneys to represent them, and that they desired to obtain the same civil rights as those enjoyed by other immigrants and American citizens.

BIBLIOGRAPHY

In re Ah Yup, 1 Fed. Case 223 (1878) at 223.

Lesser, Jeff H. "Always 'Outsiders': Asians, Naturalization, and the Supreme Court," *Amerasia Journal* 2, 1 (1985–1986): 83–100.

McClain, Charles J. "Tortuous Path, Elusive Goal: The Asian Quest for American Citizenship," *Asian Law Journal* 2, 1 (May 1995): 33–60.

Sucheng Chan

Integration

Facilities such as schools and residential areas are said to be *integrated* when their racial composition matches that of some broader population. A school is integrated, for example, when the ratio of white to African-American students in the school is the same as the ratio in the school district (or perhaps the neighborhood). Integration is different from desegregation, which means only the elimination of racial barriers to entry into a facility and does not require an assessment of racial composition. A school that had been all white because of legally mandated segregation would be desegregated as soon as the school board opened the school up to all in the neighborhood, for example, but it might not be an integrated school if the neighborhood were nearly all white.

Although integration and desegregation can be distinguished in this way, the courts, civil rights activists,

Dr. and Mrs. Charles Atkins and their sons pause to glance at a segregation sign at the Atchison, Topeka, and Santa Fe Railroad Depot in Oklahoma City, Oklahoma, on November 25, 1955, after the Interstate Commerce Commission ordered an end to all separate seating on all interstate public carriers. (AP/Wide World Photos)

and their opponents all came to blur the line in the long aftermath of *Brown v. Board of Education.* (See BROWN V. TOPEKA BOARD OF EDUCATION.) Technically the SUPREME COURT in *Brown* required only desegregation, not integration. But resistance in the Deep South even to desegregation led the Court to insist on desegregation plans that, in its term, "worked." The only way to measure whether a plan worked was to see whether substantial integration had occurred. Some civil rights activists pursued a vision of a colorblind society, not one where only the law ignored race, but where African Americans (and other racial minorities) could be found in every important social institution in proportion to their presence in the population generally.

Achieving true integration called for more substantial social changes than desegregation alone would have. In the schools, it required the use of aggressive student assignment policies that meant that some students would be bused substantial distances to their schools. In higher education and in employment, it required the adoption of affirmative action programs. These measures in turn elicited substantial opposition, primarily from whites who thought they were being forced to accept an unfair burden, but sometimes from African Americans who either thought that the burdens of busing were too substantial or that the vision of a truly integrated society improperly minimized the internal strengths of minority communities.

Resistance to integration led the courts to reduce the pressure they placed on schools to develop remedies for legal segregation. It generated legal attacks on affirmative action as well. By the 1990s public schools in large urban areas were hardly integrated at all, even though all legally mandated segregation had been eliminated. The persistence of racial separation resulted from residential segregation and the economics of housing. Workplaces were significantly more integrated than they had been in the era of segregation, but residential segregation, sometimes the result of economics and sometimes the result of people's wishes to live near others with whom they were particularly comfortable, continued to characterize American society.

BIBLIOGRAPHY

Armor, David J. *Forced Justice: School Desegregation and the Law.* 1995.

Hacker, Andrew. *Two Nations: Black and White, Separate, Hostile, Unequal.* 1992.

Massey, Douglas S., and Nancy A. Denton. *American Apartheid: Segregation and the Making of the Underclass.* 1993.

Orfield, Gary. *Dismantling Desegregation: The Quiet Reversal of Brown v. Board of Education.* 1996.

Mark Tushnet

International Hotel Episode

On November 27, 1968, 150 elderly Filipino tenants from the Manilatown district of San Francisco began a nine-year-long antieviction campaign against financial district redevelopment interests. Widespread student and community grassroots support helped to make this event a milestone in Asian-American civil rights history. The campaign culminated in the deployment of over three hundred riot police, mounted patrols, antisniper units, and fire ladders in a 3 a.m. eviction raid. A three-thousand-person barricade was brutally cleared away by authorities before tenants were physically removed from the premises.

The International Hotel was located on the last remaining block of a once-thriving Filipino-American enclave. Formerly consisting of over ten square blocks and located near the edge of San Francisco's Chinatown, Manilatown was considered home to many Filipino farmworkers, merchant marines, and service workers. During the 1960s, the encroachment of an expanding financial district had slated much of the residential Manilatown community for "higher use" development.

The original intent of International Hotel owner Walter Shorenstein, president of Milton Meyer & Co., was to demolish the building in order to build a multilevel parking lot on the site. In protest, tenants, represented by the United Filipino Association (UFA), marched to Milton Meyer & Co. offices and were successful in obtaining a lease agreement to be signed on March 16, 1969. However, in the early morning hours of March 16, a fire swept through the north wing of the second floor of the International Hotel. Arson was suspected. Three tenants—Pio Rosete, Marcario Salermo, and Robert Knauff—were killed in the fire. Milton Meyer & Co. canceled the lease agreement and used the fire as justification for the demolition of an unsafe building.

Mounting opposition forced Shorenstein to sign a three-year lease scheduled to end on June 30, 1972. In the meantime, the building went through extensive renovation at the hands of hundreds of student and community volunteers. Abandoned street-level storefronts were replaced with community centers. Burned-out hotel rooms were rebuilt, plastered, and painted.

International Hotel storefronts such as the Asian Community Center, Chinese Progressive Association, and the Kearney Street Workshop became conduits for political, social, and cultural transformation of the San Francisco Chinatown–Manilatown area. Community center participants included student activists from the Third World Liberation Front strikes at San Francisco State College and the University of California at Berkeley. Veteran Chinese-American labor activists, whose involvement dated back to the 1930s, and individuals involved in the campaign to normalize relations between the United States and the People's Republic of China saw the International Hotel block as an alternative to the more conservative Chinese Six Companies establishment.

By March 1974, Shorenstein transferred property ownership to a Chinese-Thai liquor baron, Supasit Mahaguna, who held title to the property under the name Four Seas Investment Corporation. The property transfer had the effect of changing the target of the struggle from local big capital to foreign Asian capital. Negotiations with Mahaguna for lease extensions proved fruitless, and eventually a decision of the California Supreme Court forced Sheriff Richard Hongisto to carry out the eviction in 1977.

In this nine-year period, the key factor prompting the series of eviction postponements, numerous court stays, and intervention by local politicians was vigorous public support. The participation of volunteers and the organization of the tenants had built a new level of community solidarity and intense opposition to the eviction. A new tenant organization, the International Hotel Tenants Association (IHTA), was formed as a democratically elected representative organization for the tenants. Its daily functions involved caring for the general welfare needs of the mostly elderly Filipino and Chinese residents.

Following the tumultuous forced eviction, tenants and community members continued to lobby for low-income housing on the International Hotel site. With public support they were able to forestall Four Seas' development plans for twenty years. Finally, groundbreaking is scheduled in 1998 for a building, including a parochial school on the ground floors and 104 units of low-income housing on the upper floors. Also planned is a Manilatown museum and cultural center on the ground floor.

BIBLIOGRAPHY

Elliot, Marc. "Tenants Ousted from Hotel." *San Francisco Progress* 58:1 (1977): 1.

Habal, Estella. "International Hotel Remembered, 1977 Eviction of Manilatown, S.F., Chronology of the International Hotel Struggle 1968–97." 1997.

Habal, Estella. Meaning of the International Hotel. Speech at Chinese Historical Society. 1997.

IHTA. "The Fight for Low-Income Housing Is the Struggle of the International Hotel." 1977.

Moon, Etta. Meaning of the International Hotel. Speech at Chinese Historical Society. 1997.

Nee, Victor G., and Brett de Bary. *Longtime Californ': A Documentary Study of an American Chinatown.* 1972.

Workshop, Kearney Street. "We Won't Move." Kearny Street Workshop. 1977.

Harvey Dong

International Indian Treaty Council and Conferences

The first International Indian Treaty Conference was held in July 1974, on the Standing Rock Sioux Reservation in South Dakota. Organized by the AMERICAN INDIAN MOVEMENT (AIM) and hosted by the people of Standing Rock themselves, the conference had been requested by the Lakota Treaty Council, a group formed by Frank Fools Crow and other traditional chiefs. More than four thousand people representing ninety-eight indigenous nations attended the event. The purpose of the gathering was to create a mechanism through which Lakota treaty issues might be combined with those of other native peoples and presented within appropriate international forums. To this end, Fools Crow and his colleagues charged AIM leader Russell MEANS with the responsibility of creating a new organization, designated as the International Indian Treaty Council (IITC).

Means named Cherokee activist Jimmie Durham to direct "AIM's international diplomatic arm" and, in early 1975, an office was established on United Nations Plaza in New York. Over the next two years, Durham did a truly remarkable job of establishing relations with key U.N. staffers and sympathetic member-states. By 1977, IITC had been credentialed as the world's first indigenous NGO (non-governmental organization) with United Nations consultative status. The same year, IITC was asked to organize Native American participation in an NGO conference on discrimination scheduled for September, in Geneva, Switzerland. Durham again performed brilliantly, bringing delegations from sixty indigenous peoples throughout the Western Hemisphere to present their cases to the more than 400 U.N. officials, governmental representatives, and NGO delegates assembled for the event.

"Indian Summer in Geneva" had a lasting effect. A second NGO conference, devoted specifically to indigenous rights questions, was scheduled for 1981. This in turn led to the establishment of a Working Group on Indigenous Populations within the U.N. Economic and Social Council (ECOSOC). Among the tasks assigned the Working Group were provisioning of a regular forum in which native grievances could be recorded, a global survey of the material conditions imposed upon native peoples, a comprehensive study of indigenous treaty rights, and, most important, the drafting of a "Universal Declaration of the Rights of Indigenous Peoples" for submission to the U.N. General Assembly and ultimate incorporation into international law.

Unfortunately, having thus gotten the ball rolling, IITC itself underwent a process of rapid decline. By 1980, factional infighting had caused the resignations of Durham and several of the more capable staff members he had recruited. Their replacements were increasingly viewed as siding with leftist governments against the rights of native peoples within their borders. Attendance at IITC's annual treaty conferences plummeted, and most of the indigenous nations it claimed to represent formed their own delegations to the Working Group. In 1984, even Russell Means publicly distanced himself from the organization.

By 1990, the transformation was complete. Having incorporated itself under U.S. law and made itself accountable to a hand-picked advisory board rather than the traditional elders councils that had created it, IITC severed its last links to its original constituency. Although it continues to promote itself as a broadbased and "organic" entity, it exists today as a narrow, insular, and self-consciously professionalized clique considered by many activists to serve more as an obstruction to, than as a champion of, indigenous rights.

BIBLIOGRAPHY

Deloria, Vine, Jr. *Behind the Trail of Broken Treaties: An Indian Declaration of Independence*. 2nd ed., 1984.

Dunbar Ortiz, Roxanne. *Indians of the Americas: Human Rights and Self-Determination*. 1984.

Durham, Jimmie. *A Certain Lack of Coherence: Writings on Art and Cultural Politics*. 1993.

Means, Russell, with Marvin J. Wolf. *Where White Men Fear to Tread: The Autobiography of Russell Means*. 1995.

Ward Churchill

International Labor Defense

The International Labor Defense (ILD) was founded in the United States in 1925 by Communist Party, USA (CPUSA), activists and their allies "to defend all persons persecuted for their activity in the labor movement." As such the ILD was an expression of the world Communist movement's commitment both to mobilize the masses of the nonwhite world against COLONIALISM and for socialism, and to coordinate campaigns for civil liberties ("workers' democracy") with trade union struggles.

From its inception, the ILD sought to provide aid to minority activists and their families. It also adopted a strategy of "mass defense," which saw the courts as fixed against labor defendants and contended that courtroom action must be augmented with mass protests to mobilize public opinion.

Gaining early recognition in the campaign to save Sacco and Vanzetti and obtain the release of longtime labor prisoners Tom Mooney, Warren Billings, and James McNamara, the ILD, under the leadership of African-American attorney and CPUSA leader William Patterson, made its most important contribution to the struggle for civil rights and civil liberties by taking a leading role in the SCOTTSBORO CASE (1931). Besides acting swiftly to save the lives of the Scottsboro defendants, the ILD led the moderate NATIONAL ASSOCIATION FOR THE ADVANCEMENT OF COLORED PEOPLE (NAACP) to involve itself in a controversial rape case and broaden its activities generally.

For the first time since the international abolitionist movement, the ILD made the imprisonment of black Americans the source of protests throughout the world, from London to Shanghai. It also played a leading role in the national movement against LYNCHING and in the defense of Angelo Herndon in Georgia, Euel Lee in Maryland, and other black Americans, including Communists, radicals, and nonpolitical victims of lynch law.

In the late 1930s, under the leadership of radical New York Congressman Vito MARCANTONIO, the ILD defended CIO union organizers and organized a significant campaign against peonage on Southern plantations, which held many blacks in a form of feudal bondage.

Merged into the left-led CIVIL RIGHTS CONGRESS in 1946, the ILD, like other mass organizations of the Communist-led left, was segregated out of the political mainstream by anti-Communist legislation and extensive repression (trials of leaders, blacklists, etc.). Its traditions, however, of combining "inside" legal civil rights and civil liberties judicial actions with "outside" mass protests would live on in the civil rights movement, as would many of the black and white activists who had participated in its campaigns. Its spirit can still be seen in both legal and mass protests against police brutality in U.S. cities.

BIBLIOGRAPHY

Horne, Gerald. *Communist Front: The Civil Right Congress, 1946–1946*. 1987.

Martin, Charles. "The International Labor Defense and Black America." *Labor History* 26 (1985).

Papers of the International Labor Defense. 1988. University Publications of America (microfilm).

Norman Markowitz

Internet, Censorship and the

The Internet's origins lie in ARPANET, a computer network designed to withstand nuclear attack, established by the U.S. Department of Defense in 1969. Although fewer than three thousand computers were linked to the Net in 1981, by 1993, with the Internet having been termed the "information superhighway," the number was approximately one million. The Net's has grown exponentially, with some 200 million computers linked to the Net as the new millennium begins.

As a mode of communication, the Internet is unique in its instantaneous nature, its promotion of dialogue over one-way commentary, and its twenty-four–hour operation. Crippling governmental regulation of the Internet is its transcendence of national borders and the fact that it is an open network, absent an oversight agency with the capability of filtering material or creating zones on the Net.

Despite these regulatory difficulties, CONGRESS passed the Communications Decency Act (CDA) of 1996 as a response to the presence of sexual materials on the Internet deemed harmful to minors. The law criminalized the sending of "obscene or indecent" messages to minors and the transmission or display to underage persons of any material "that, in context, depicts or describes, in terms patently offensive as measured by contemporary community standards, sexual or excretory activities or organs."

The key components of the act, however, did not pass constitutional muster. In *Reno* v. *ACLU* (1997), the SUPREME COURT focused on the inherent vagueness of the CDA in striking down the act. Justice John Paul Stevens, writing for the Court majority, contended that the "ambiguous" CDA was likely to suppress legitimate, constitutionally protected speech among adults, resulting in an "obvious chilling effect on free speech" in general. Such "chilling" would be made more severe in the eyes of the Court by the significant criminal penalties that accompanied violations of the act. Although *Reno* established broad protection for Internet communication, court battles continue over issues such as the regulation of commercial sites with pornographic content and the blocking of Internet sites on public library computers.

In a lower federal court review of the CDA, the Internet was termed "the most participatory form of mass speech yet developed." Indeed, the mode of communication serves as an organizing tool for civil rights movements with significant potential. It is important to realize, however, the continuing relationship between socioeconomic status and access to the medium. Groups with disproportionately poorer and less educated members are limited in their use of the Internet as a way of activating mass movements. Cyberspace also remains a male-dominated world, with over 60 percent of users estimated to be men. The Internet, however, has been espoused by gay and lesbian activist groups as an effective tool in promoting their civil rights activities.

In thinking about the possible future implications of the Internet for civil rights, it is crucial to recognize that groups opposed to the interests of racial, ethnic, and sexual minorities have increasingly made use of the Internet in recruiting members and organizing activities. One watchdog organization identified the presence of over 1,400 sites created by "hate groups" at the end of the 1990s.

BIBLIOGRAPHY

Liberty (The National Council for Civil Liberties), ed. *Liberating Cyberspace: Civil Liberties, Human Rights and the Internet.* 1999.

Marriott, Michel. "Rising Tide: Sites Born of Hate," *New York Times,* March 18, 1999. Section G, p. 1.

Reno v. American Civil Liberties Union, 117 S. Ct. 2329 (1997).

Signorile, Michelangelo. *Queer in America: Sex, the Media, and the Closets of Power.* 1993.

U.S. Department of Commerce. *Falling Through the Net: Defining the Digital Divide.* 1999.

Jay Barth

Iowa

The territory of Iowa, a part of the 1803 Louisiana Purchase, was established as a "free" state in 1846. By 1845, Anglo-American settlers had permanently displaced seventeen American Indian groups. Over the next decade, the Meskwaki returned to Iowa from their federally assigned reservation in Kansas. In 1856, they bought back land on the Iowa River and established the "Meskwaki Settlement."

Prohibition of slavery and involuntary servitude were incorporated into the Iowa State Constitution under the Bill of Rights, Article I, Section 23. Despite the minuscule presence of blacks, the issue of their rights and privileges was central to contemporaneous political debates. Anxiety over a large migration of slaves from the South prompted the General Assembly to pass a series of laws restricting the entry of blacks.

Although concern for the civil rights of black Americans was not the prevailing sentiment, Iowan opposition to the institution of slavery within the state was reflected in the first Iowa Supreme Court ruling. In 1834, in the first case heard by the Iowa Supreme Court, it was ruled that a Missouri slave residing in the territory was neither fugitive nor slave. In 1857 the Iowa Supreme Court judgment in favor of Dred Scott's claim to freedom was overturned by the U.S. Supreme Court, which decided that Scott, a slave from Missouri living in the free state of Iowa, was not a citizen and therefore could not sue for his freedom.

The Iowa Constitution, ratified in 1857, opens with a "Bill of Rights." It is the cornerstone of human rights in Iowa and incorporates ideas from the U.S. Constitution and the French National Assembly's Declaration of the Rights of Man and Citizen. Uniquely, Iowa's Bill of Rights includes explicit sections on the rights and freedoms of all its residents, including the equal rights of foreign residents.

In 1868 the Iowa Constitution was amended by a popular referendum. The restrictive reference to white males in the State Constitution was voided, which effectively extended the franchise to black men. By 1880, black men could also be elected to public office.

The Iowa State Supreme Court ruled in favor of public school desegregation in 1869. This was followed in 1884 by the Civil Rights Act; however, several amendments were required before racial segregation was legally, if not always in practice, dismantled. The explicit language of the Iowa Bill of Rights supported the punishment of violations of civil rights.

Between 1870 and 1918, resolutions to amend the gender discriminatory provision restricting voter qualifications to "males" were debated in the General Assembly. Iowan Carrie Chapman CATT was elected president of the National Woman Suffrage Association. While Ms. Chapman Catt is celebrated as a champion of white women's rights, her prejudice against the rights of women of color continues to attract criticism. Although the General Assembly endorsed the woman suffrage amendment in 1915, it was subsequently defeated in a popular referendum.

Iowa's political, social, and economic order continues to be determined by an agricultural economy, although several urban areas have developed around an industrial sector. Most Iowans are of white European origin, however the small black population, many of whom migrated from the South after the Civil War, have made significant contributions to the state. Over the last few decades, immigrants from Southeast Asia, Africa, and Latin America have increased Iowa's demographic diversity.

The Iowa Department of Human Rights, under the authority of the governor, includes a division of Latino affairs, a division on the status of African Americans, and a division on the status of women, whose members are appointed by the governor. Each of these divisions contains a commission whose overall purpose is to study and address the particular needs of its group and to make programmatic and policy recommendations to the governor, as well as to provide services and information for the public and private sector.

BIBLIOGRAPHY

Battailee, Gretchen M., David M. Gradwohl, and Charles P. Silet, eds. *The World Between Two Rivers*. 1978.

Dykstra, Robert R. *Bright Radical Star: Black Freedom and White Supremacy on the Hawkeye Frontier*. 1993.

Foley, Douglas E. *The Heartland Chronicles*. 1995.

Hake, Herbert V. *Iowa Inside Out*. 1968.

Hawthorne, Frances E. *African Americans in Iowa: A Chronicle of Contributions 1830–1992*. 1992.

Iowa Constitution and Essays. n.d.

Schwieder, Dorothy. *Iowa: The Middle Land*. 1996.

Katya Gibel Azoulay

Islam, Nation of

See Nation of Islam

J

Jackson, Esther Cooper

(1917–), civil rights activist.

Esther Cooper Jackson was born into an activist family. Her mother, Esther I. Cooper, served prominently in the local P.T.A. and was president of the Arlington, Virginia, branch of the NATIONAL ASSOCIATION FOR THE ADVANCEMENT OF COLORED PEOPLE (NAACP) during the 1920s. Esther Jackson graduated from Washington, D.C.'s Dunbar High School in 1934 and Oberlin College in 1938. She earned her master's degree in sociology at Fisk University, where she wrote her master's thesis entitled, "Negro Domestic Workers in Relation to Trade Unionism," under the directorship of Dr. Charles S. Johnson.

While at Fisk, Jackson lived in a local settlement house and joined the Communist Party. (See COMMUNIST PARTY USA.) In 1939 she met James E. Jackson, Jr., a Communist Party member and leader of the recently formed SOUTHERN NEGRO YOUTH CONGRESS (SNYC). In the spring of 1940, at the urging of her mother, she turned down a scholarship from the University of Chicago and decided to join James Jackson and the SNYC in Birmingham, Alabama. The two married in 1941 and eventually raised two children, Harriet Dolores and Kathryn Alice. For a time she maintained her maiden name, Cooper, adopting Jackson at a later date.

As one of a number of important women members in the SNYC, Jackson brought an awareness of struggle to the organization that reflected her family's activist history and her commitment to a simultaneous campaign against racial, gender, and economic exploitation. Within the SNYC she agitated against sexism. She pushed the organization to battle on multiple fronts by tapping into an array of locally based networks of black organizations and institutions, from the church, to womens' clubs, to the NAACP. At the urging of some of the organization's male leadership she assumed a public leadership role for the SNYC. From 1941 to 1946 Jackson served as its executive secretary. She also represented the SNYC at a number of international events, including the Fifth Pan-African Congress and the World Youth Organization's effort to rebuild Stalingrad, U.S.S.R. Her work in the international arena helped to connect local struggles in the United States to struggles for justice around the world.

During the 1950s, as the executive secretary of the National Committee for Defense of Negro Leadership, Jackson dedicated a great part of her energies to the defense of her husband against charges of subversion levied by the House Un-American Activities Committee. In 1961, along with Shirley Graham Du Bois and W. E. B. DU BOIS, she helped found and then edit FREEDOMWAYS magazine, an important voice in the struggle for civil rights from 1961 through 1985. She has been a staff member of the Progressive Party of Michigan, the NATIONAL URBAN LEAGUE, and the Girl Scouts of America. She is coauthor of *Black Titan: W. E. B. Du Bois* and *Paul Robeson: The Great Forerunner.*

BIBLIOGRAPHY

Jackson, Esther Cooper. Interview with Peter F. Lau, March 13, 1997.

383

Kelley, Robin D. G. *Hammer and Hoe: Alabama Communists during the Great Depression.* 1990.

Papers of the Southern Negro Youth Congress. Moorland-Spingarn Library, Howard University, Washington, D.C.

Richards, Johnnetta. "The Southern Negro Youth Congress: A History." Doctoral dissertation, University of Cincinnati. 1987.

                                            Peter F. Lau

Jackson, George

(1942–1971), prison revolutionary.

George Lester Jackson was raised in the Chicago ghetto, then in Watts, Los Angeles. After numerous scrapes with the law, in 1961 nineteen-year-old Jackson pleaded guilty to second-degree armed robbery as an accessory in a $70 gas station holdup. His sentence was one year to life. Over ten years, Jackson joined in prison gang activity and assaults on guards, receiving disciplinary action forty-seven times. The result was numerous extensions of sentence.

In 1967 Jackson underwent a political transformation, becoming a master teacher of revolutionary ideology and guerilla tactics. Jackson saw prisoners as the vanguard of an emerging American people's revolution. At Soledad Prison in 1968 Jackson earned prisoners' admiration through his martial arts prowess. Then he recruited students, supplying them with contraband reading, including *The Communist Manifesto.* These books became the backbone of a secret political education.

Through this politicization process, many black convicts became ready to take action against racism in the prison. In 1970 when a fistfight broke out on the yard, three black prisoners were killed by guard gunrail fire. After the "Soledad Incident," black prisoners readied themselves to take extreme reprisals. George Jackson taught a doctrine he termed "selective retaliatory violence." Black prisoners would kill one guard for every black convict killed by guards.

Three days after the Soledad Incident, a white Soledad guard was thrown to his death from a prison tier. George Jackson, Fleeta Drumgo, and John Clutchette were charged in the death. They became known as "the Soledad Brothers." For Jackson, already serving one year to life, this meant the death penalty. The three defendants were moved to San Quentin to await trial in San Francisco.

Overnight, Jackson became a cause célèbre. He had been writing his first book, *Soledad Brother: The Prison Letters of George Jackson* and it was an instant bestseller when it was published in 1970. Chapters of the Sole-

dad Brothers Defense Committee appeared across the nation and in Europe. Donations poured in and Jackson's popular support became vast. Jackson was named BLACK PANTHER Party Field Marshal in 1970.

Within San Quentin's Adjustment Center, Jackson drew a group of revolutionaries about him. He spent long hours writing his next book, *Blood In My Eye,* a bitter polemic and practical handbook of guerrilla war. "The outlaw and the lumpen will make the revolution," he wrote. "The people, the workers, will adopt it." In a 1971 interview, he compared himself to Nat Turner and insisted that "resistance to unjust bonds, organized injustice, can never be interpreted as crime."

On August 21, 1971, a gun was introduced into the Adjustment Center. On the way back from a visit, Jackson drew the weapon. He released his fellow Adjustment Center inmates. Minutes later, three guards and two white convicts lay dead in Jackson's cell. Three other guards were wounded. George Jackson then made his final stand. Gun in hand, he bolted out of the Adjustment Center into the San Quentin "plaza," where he was killed by a marksman on the yard gunrail.

BIBLIOGRAPHY

Armstrong, Gregory. *The Dragon Has Come.* 1974.

Carr, James, with Dan Hammer and Isaac Cronin. *BAD: The Autobiography of James Carr.* 1975.

Cummins, Eric. *The Rise and Fall of California's Radical Prison Movement.* 1994.

Durden-Smith, Jo. *Who Killed George Jackson?* 1976.

Jackson, George. *Soledad Brother: The Prison Letters of George Jackson.* 1970.

Jackson, George. *Blood in My Eye.* 1972.

                                            Eric Cummins

Jackson, James E., Jr.

(1914–), civil rights activist and labor organizer.

James E. Jackson, Jr., was raised in an influential and activist family in the predominantly black Jackson Ward of Richmond, Virginia. His father, James Jackson, Sr., was a pharmacist and a NATIONAL ASSOCIATION FOR THE ADVANCEMENT OF COLORED PEOPLE (NAACP) leader during the 1920s. The family pharmacy served as a center of black Richmond's ongoing struggle for civil rights and it was in its back room that James Jackson, Jr., was schooled in the ethic of service to the community and in the importance of political struggle.

James Jackson, Jr.'s activism began early. In 1931 he fought to become the first black Eagle Scout in the

South. Ultimately, Jackson received Scouting's highest honor only to have Virginia's then-Governor, John Garland Pollard, refuse to pin the medal on his uniform. That same year Jackson entered Virginia Union University. He became active in a number of organizations, including the interracial Cooperative Independents Club, which he led onto the floor of the Virginia State Legislature demanding the abolition of segregation in education. While at Virginia Union he also joined the Communist Party and dedicated himself to the international struggle for full social, political, and economic justice. (See COMMUNIST PARTY USA.)

Jackson received a B.S. degree in 1934, and earned a degree in pharmacy from Howard University. For a time he worked with his father in Richmond. In 1937 he helped found the SOUTHERN NEGRO YOUTH CONGRESS (SNYC). The following year he helped lead the effort to organize Richmond's black tobacco workers who successfully struck the Export Leaf Tobacco Factory of the British American Tobacco Company for union recognition and better wages. As a research assistant for Gunnar Myrdal's AN AMERICAN DILEMMA, Jackson canvassed the South. On a research trip to Fisk University in Nashville, Tennessee, he met Esther Cooper, whom he married in 1941 and with whom he raised two children.

During the 1940s Jackson served as one of the SNYC's principal leaders. In 1943 he entered the U.S. Army and served eighteen months in the China-Burma-India theatre. In February 1946 he left the army with the rank of sergeant and returned to work with the SNYC. Following the SNYC's October 1946 gathering in Columbia, South Carolina, Jackson resigned from its staff to serve as the State Chairman of the Communist Party of Louisiana. In Louisiana he was subjected to constant harassment and arrested on charges of inciting a riot and threatening the security of the state. In 1947 he and his family fled to Detroit, Michigan, where he led organizing efforts in the Ford Motor Company plant. In 1949 he became Southern Regional Director of the Communist Party and later served as a member of the Party's National Committee. In 1951, Jackson was indicted under the Smith Act for alleged acts of subversion and advocating the overthrow of the government. Although Jackson was convicted of the charges in 1955, after a lengthy appeal the charges were overturned.

During the 1950s and beyond Jackson remained active. He served as editor of the Communist Party's paper, *The Worker*. He penned numerous articles and pamphlets and authored a number of books including *A View from Here* and *Revolutionary Tracings*.

BIBLIOGRAPHY

Jackson, Esther Cooper, and James E. Jackson, Jr. Interview with Peter F. Lau.

Kelley, Robin D. G. *Hammer and Hoe: Alabama Communists during the Great Depression.* 1990.

Papers of the Southern Negro Youth Congress. Moorland-Spingarn Library, Howard University, Washington, D.C.

Richards, Johnnetta. "The Southern Negro Youth Congress: A History." Doctoral dissertation, University of Cincinnati. 1987.

Sullivan, Patricia. *Days of Hope: Race and Democracy in the New Deal Era.* 1996.

Peter F. Lau

Jackson, Jesse L.

(1941–), minister, civil rights leader, politician.

Jesse Jackson was born October 8, 1941 in Greenville, South Carolina, to Helen Burns. Although his natural father was Noah Robinson, he was raised by his mother and Charles Henry Jackson, whom she married in 1943. He was educated at Sterling High School in Greenville and after graduation in 1959, won a football scholarship to the University of Illinois at Champaign-Urbana. Not allowed to play quarterback, he left the university and enrolled at North Carolina Agricultural & Technical State University, where he graduated in 1964 with a degree in sociology.

A charismatic and natural leader, Jackson was active in civil rights issues at North Carolina A&T and was becoming increasingly aware of the dynamic Dr. Martin Luther KING, JR., who headed the SOUTHERN CHRISTIAN LEADERSHIP CONFERENCE (SCLC). Jackson enrolled in the Chicago Theological Seminary in 1964. He was ordained by renowned ministers Rev. Clay Evans and Rev. C. L. Franklin in 1965. The following year, Jackson joined SCLC, being appointed to head the Chicago office of OPERATION BREADBASKET, SCLC's economic development arm, and becoming head of Breadbasket in 1967.

Through Operation Breadbasket, SCLC pressured merchants with large black consumer profiles to hire black Americans and contribute to their causes. This led to "fair share" agreements (pioneered by the NAACP) with major companies, who were encouraged to hire not only black individuals, but black firms as well, and to contribute to black-owned banks and other organizations.

On April 4, 1968, Martin Luther King, Jr., was assassinated at the Lorraine Hotel in Memphis, Tennessee, and Jesse Jackson, by this time a loyal staffer, was present. This moment provided a kind of notoriety

Clergyman and politician Jesse Jackson ran for the U.S. presidency in 1984 and 1988. (CORBIS/ Shelley Gazin)

that has followed Jackson: he rushed to King, cradled his head in his arms, then appeared at a press conference the following day in Chicago in the same clothes that he said contained King's blood. After the death of Dr. King, conflict arose at SCLC between Jackson and King's successor, Rev. Ralph David Abernathy, having to do primarily with Jackson's leadership of Operation Breadbasket. The lack of reconciliation led to a breach, with Jackson leaving SCLC to form a new organization in Chicago, PEOPLE UNITED TO SAVE HUMANITY (Operation PUSH), in 1971.

Operation PUSH adopted a civil rights posture, but focused on economic development activities similar to those of Operation Breadbasket; its focus also included political participation and urban education. In 1975, Jackson created the PUSH for Excellence (PUSH/Excel) program, as a mechanism to inspire black youth to achievement in education; by 1977 it became funded by the Department of Health Education and Welfare and expanded to cities such as Chi-

cago, Kansas City, and Los Angeles. Schools were given small grants to foster accountability by students and the involvement of parents and community, but in the end this attempt at reform was resisted.

Jackson had been a formidable figure in DEMOCRATIC PARTY politics since at least 1968. After the election of Ronald Reagan in 1980, Jackson organized 100 black ministers in Chicago to resist the introduction of Reagan's policies in Chicago by Mayor Jane Byrne. This resistance movement led many to conceive of Jackson as a viable force able to resist Reagan on a national level and the idea of a black presidential candidacy was germinating between 1981 and 1983. By the summer of 1983, the slogan "run Jesse run" emerged as a popular reflection of black opinion and in the fall, Rev. Jackson declared his candidacy for the Democratic party's nomination for president. His platform would be devoted to raising those "boats stuck on the bottom" of society.

His campaign was helped immeasurably by the heroic act of going to Syria and obtaining the release of captured black American pilot, Lt. Robert Goodman. This boosted the credibility of a campaign that was untraditional and unlikely to win in the eyes of a great number of voters. In primary elections Jackson won victories in Virginia, the District of Columbia, and Louisiana, and came in second in South Carolina, Arkansas, and Mississippi. Combined with his fair showing in other state primaries, this yielded 3.3 million votes (20 percent of those cast) and 384 delegates to the Democratic convention that year. Although Jackson established in this process a clear dominance of the black vote, winning 90 percent of those cast, he suffered with white voters who believed that he was unqualified to be president. Moreover it was discovered that he had used the term "Hymietown" to describe New York City, a comment many Jews regarded as anti-Semitic, and this unfortunate mistake cost Jackson the New York primary and greatly damaged his credibility. Nevertheless, his speech at the 1984 Democratic Convention, which connected with the downtrodden of all colors and proffered themes of personal redemption and unfinished expectations, was one of the most memorable in American political history.

Rev. Jackson ran again in 1988, this time winning the regional primary known as "Super Tuesday," later doubling his popular vote to nearly 7 million (close to one-third of all votes—2 million of which were white voters), and winning 1,200 convention delegates. This campaign marked Jackson not only as a black leader but also, with his proven exploits in both domestic and foreign affairs, as a genuine leader of the Democratic party. The campaign was also important for its eventual influence on public policy, as Jackson championed such issues as peace in the Middle East through mutual negotiations, equal pay for women, nuclear freeze, the use of pension funds to stimulate community development, and especially an anti-apartheid position for the U.S. government. Part of Jackson's political legacy is that many of these issues have subsequently become law.

Since the 1988 campaign, he has become the leading liberal political activist who does not hold elective office in the United States, and he is regularly called upon to interpret issues either through his own CNN television show or via other major national news media. He has also maintained his stature within the Democratic party, being regarded as a close confidant to President Bill Clinton, in matters such as his impeachment, and as his Personal Envoy to Africa for Democracy and Human Rights.

Through it all, he has continued to pursue the fulfillment of Martin Luther King's dream, by leading his reformulated organization, the Rainbow/PUSH Coalition, into traditional civil rights battles, such as demonstrations in opposition to the rollback of AFFIRMATIVE ACTION in the guise of California's proposition 209, passed in 1996. He has also launched a significant new thrust in the direction of economic parity, challenging corporations to invest in underserved neighborhoods with the "Wall Street Project" and speaking throughout the Black Belt South and Appalachia. Finally, he has achieved global recognition for his private statesmanship for peace, when in June of 1999, he strikingly negotiated the release of three American soldiers held in prison in Yugoslavia in the midst of a war that NATO had launched against Yugoslavia's ruthless leader, Slobodan Milosevic, for practicing "ethnic cleansing" in Kosovo. Jackson also participated in war settlement of the Sierra Leone conflict. Therefore, at the dawn of a new century, he has become the "drum major for justice" that his mentor Martin Luther King, Jr., was, and he is opening up new avenues in this struggle both at home and abroad.

BIBLIOGRAPHY

Barker, Lucius. *Our Time Has Come: A Delegate's Diary of Jesse Jackson's 1984 Presidential Campaign.* 1988.

Frady, Marshall. *Jesse: The Life and Pilgrimage of Jesse Jackson.* 1996.

Reynolds, Barbara A. *Jesse Jackson: America's David.* 1985.

Ronald W. Walters

Jackson, Luther Porter

(1892–1950), community activist and historian.

Born in 1892 in Lexington, Kentucky, Jackson earned his undergraduate and masters degrees from Fisk University. He received his Ph.D. in history from the University of Chicago in 1937. In 1922, he started teaching history at Virginia Normal and Industrial Institute, which was renamed Virginia State College in 1930. In 1929, Jackson was appointed chairman of the history and social science unit at Virginia State and served in this position until his death in 1950.

In 1941, Jackson organized the Virginia Voters League to educate blacks and others in how to pay their poll taxes, register, and vote. The Virginia Voters League coordinated the work of city and county voter leagues throughout the state. Writing in the *Journal of Negro Education* in 1945, Jackson credited the League with increasing the number of qualified black voters in Virginia from 25,000 in 1940 to 50,000 in 1945. Jackson promoted voter education and citizenship rights through several organizations, including the Virginia State Conference of the NATIONAL ASSOCIATION FOR THE ADVANCEMENT OF COLORED PEOPLE (NAACP), the Negro Organization Society of Virginia, the Virginia Teachers Association, and the SOUTHERN CONFERENCE FOR HUMAN WELFARE. In addition to his community activism, Jackson was a distinguished scholar and educator. He published several works on African Americans in Virginia, including his doctoral dissertation *Free Negro Labor and Property Holding in Virginia, 1830–1860* (1972), and *Negro Office Holders in Virginia, 1860–1895* (1945).

As president of the Virginia Voters League, Jackson compiled the annual publication, *The Voting Status of Negroes in Virginia*. From 1942 to 1948, he wrote a column called "Rights and Duties in a Democracy" for the *Norfolk Journal and Guide*.

BIBLIOGRAPHY

Gavins, Raymond. "Hancock, Jackson, and Young: Virginia's Black Triumverate, 1930–1945." *Virginia Magazine of History and Biography* 94 (1986): 470–486.

Johnston, J. H. "Luther Porter Jackson, 1892–1950." *Negro History Bulletin.* 13 (1950): 195–197.

Luther Porter Jackson Papers. Johnston Memorial Library, Virginia State University, Ettrick, Va.

Larissa M. Smith

Japanese American Citizens League

The Japanese American Citizens League (JACL) is the largest and one of the oldest national Asian-American civil rights organizations. It was established in 1929 as a response to discriminatory treatment and legislation against Japanese in the United States since the beginning of the twentieth century. Japan-born residents (Issei) were denied naturalization rights by the Supreme Court in OZAWA V. UNITED STATES in 1922, while further Japanese immigration was forbidden by

Congress in the Immigration Act of 1924. Relegated to a permanent alien status, they looked to their American-born citizens' children (Nisei) to secure the future for persons of Japanese descent in the United States. The JACL had some notable successes during the decade following its founding. It supported passage of the Lea-Nye bill granting citizenship to 500 World War I veterans of Asian ancestry and took part in the repeal of the Cable Act of 1922, which had revoked the citizenship of American women married to aliens.

The JACL, however, was controversial from the beginning, even among Japanese Americans. The professional background of its founders made many Nisei regard it as an elitist organization. In order to gain acceptance by the American public, as well as by the state and federal governments, the JACL adhered to a policy of 100 percent Americanism and discouraged anything that might cast doubt on the loyalty of Japanese Americans to the United States. The actions of the government were to be supported, even when these might prove harmful to the interests of the Japanese-American population.

With the growing prospects for a war between Japan and the United States in the late 1930s, members of the organization were recruited by the federal government to act as informers on their own community. When war came, JACL leaders felt it their duty to show their loyalty to the United States by cooperating with the curfew imposed on Japanese Americans, and the subsequent removal and incarceration of the hundred and twenty thousand persons of Japanese descent living in the Pacific coast states. During the war, the organization continued to endorse governmental and military actions which it believed would lead to acceptance of Japanese Americans following the end of hostilities. Its support for the creation of a military unit for Japanese Americans led to the formation of the 442nd Regiment, which became the most decorated unit in American history for its size and length of service. This same program unfortunately led the government to isolate approximately eighteen thousand mostly loyal Japanese Americans in Tule Lake Relocation Center, California, a segregated camp for purportedly disloyal persons. The suffering there was greater than in the other nine so-called relocation centers.

As a consequence of the JACL's progovernment actions, it became widely unpopular among the imprisoned Japanese-American community. Leaders were attacked in the camps and some had to be removed for their safety. According to Saburo Kido, a founder of the JACL and its wartime president, membership greatly declined and many believed that the organization was a thing to be shunned. In early 1945, with the closure of the camps imminent, the JACL continued to avoid even the appearances of disloyalty. When

more than five thousand Nisei, who had renounced their American citizenship because of wartime mistreatment and pressures within the camps, applied for aid in having it restored, the organization turned its back on them.

The policy of exaggerated loyalty that made the JACL subject to criticism during the war worked in its favor with the coming of peace in 1945, giving it the influence it needed with the national government to help better the lives of persons of Japanese descent. It supported court cases arising from the war, including *Ex parte Endo* (1944), which challenged the mass detention of Japanese Americans in the relocation centers, and ruled that the government could not incarcerate concededly loyal citizens against their will. The organization worked for passage of the Immigration and Naturalization Act of 1952, which removed the bar against the naturalization of the Issei, and advocated the CIVIL LIBERTIES ACT OF 1988, which provided redress of twenty thousand dollars for each of over 80,000 Japanese Americans who had been held in internment camps.

By the last decade of the twentieth century, the JACL had firmly established itself as the only recognized organization representing the political interests of Japanese Americans. With a membership of 23,000, it maintains a national headquarters in San Francisco, California, five regional offices, and 112 chapters located in twenty-six states and Japan. The *Pacific Citizen*, the organization's newspaper, was established in 1930, and has since that time kept Japanese Americans informed of news of interest to their community.

BIBLIOGRAPHY

Chuman, Frank F. *The Bamboo People: The Law and Japanese-Americans.* 1976.

Collins, Donald E. *Native American Aliens: Disloyalty and Renunciation of Citizenship by Japanese Americans During World War II.* 1985.

Daniels, Roger. *Prisoners Without Trial: Japanese Americans in World War II.* 1993.

Hosokawa, Bill. *JACL: The History of the Japanese American Citizens League.* 1982.

Japanese American Citizens League. http://jacl.org

Masaoka, Mike, and Bill Hosokawa. *They Call Me Moses Masaoka.* 1987.

Niiya, Brian, ed. *Japanese American History: An A-Z Reference from 1868 to the Present.* 1993.

Weglyn, Michi. *Years of Infamy; the Untold Story of America's Concentration Camps.* 1976.

Donald E. Collins

Japanese American Internment Cases

The evacuation and internment of 120,000 Japanese Americans, including 70,000 native-born American

A soldier escorts Japanese Americans in the back of a truck during their evacuation from Seattle, Washington, to a relocation center. 1942. (CORBIS)

citizens, by the United States government during World War II, resulted in four major cases being brought before the U.S. SUPREME COURT: *Hirabayashi v. the U.S.* (1943); *Yasui v. the U.S.* (1943); *Korematsu v. the U.S.* (1944); and *Ex parte Endo* (1944).

These cases were outgrowths of actions by the federal government against Japanese Americans following the December 7, 1941, attack on Pearl Harbor, Hawaii, which brought the United States into the war. Many in the general public and in the government believed that an invasion by the forces of Japan was not only possible, but imminent. This belief, combined with nearly a half century of social, economic, and political discrimination against the Japanese population on the West Coast, encouraged the government to act against Japanese-American residents. Additionally, the complete absence of a Japanese-American political power base made them subject to restrictive military orders and legislation not applied equally to resident German and Italian enemy aliens and their American-born children.

On February 14, 1942, Lieutenant General John L. DeWitt, commanding general of the Western Defense Command, submitted a report to the Secretary of War recommending that all persons of Japanese descent be evacuated from the Pacific coast. This report was noted for its blatant racism. Accusing American-born

citizens of Japanese descent of possessing the "undiluted" blood of an enemy race, DeWitt assured his superior that "112,000 (sic) potential enemies" were at large on the vital Pacific coast. The fact that no sabotage had yet occurred was explained as a confirming indication that it would take place.

Bowing to the judgment of the military, President Franklin D. ROOSEVELT issued Executive Order 9066, giving the Secretary of War and designated military commanders authority to prescribe restricted military areas and to exclude any or all persons from such places. On March 21, 1942, Congress enacted legislation providing penalties for violations of orders arising from the president's order. General DeWitt subsequently established Military Areas One and Two, consisting of California, Oregon, Washington, and part of Arizona. During the coming months, Japanese Americans alone would be subjected to curfew, exclusion from the Pacific coast states, and internment for up to three years based solely on racial characteristics rather than on individual tests of loyalty.

These restrictions on their liberty were challenged by four Nisei (American-born children of alien Japanese parents) in cases that would reach the Supreme Court during the war years. On March 12, 1942, Minoru Yasui, an Oregon attorney and second lieutenant in the U.S. Army Reserve, purposely violated a curfew ordering persons of Japanese descent to remain indoors between 8:00 P.M. and 6:00 A.M. In May 1942, Gordon Hirabayashi, a University of Washington student, was charged and convicted of a curfew violation and refusal to obey an evacuation order. The third Nisei, Fred Korematsu, did not openly challenge the exclusion orders, but tried to evade them by disguising his ethnic identity. Following his arrest, he was taken as a test case by the AMERICAN CIVIL LIBERTIES UNION, and assigned to attorney Wayne Collins. A fourth, Mitsuye Endo, was selected by Saburo Kido of the JAPANESE AMERICAN CITIZENS LEAGUE and attorney James Purcell to challenge the authority of the army to incarcerate persons whose loyalty to the United States was unquestionable. A petition of habeas corpus was filed against Milton Eisenhower, who headed the camps in which the evacuated Japanese population were being held, to show why Endo, an admittedly loyal person, was being detained. Each of the four cases was heard in federal district courts and forwarded to the U.S. SUPREME COURT for final adjudication.

The *Hirabayashi* and *Yasui* cases reached the Supreme Court on June 21, 1943. Because the sentences for Hirabayashi's two convictions ran concurrently, the Court was able to avoid an opinion on the more important issue of the government's evacuation program, and confine itself solely to the validity of the curfew order. The questions before the court in these two cases were whether the military commander's curfew order was an unconstitutional delegation by Congress of its legislative power, and whether it violated the Fifth Amendment by discriminating against only citizens of Japanese ancestry. Chief Justice Harlan F. Stone reasoned in his opinion that acts which may be unconstitutional in peacetime must give way to military necessity during times of war. Since the governmental and social actions against Japanese Americans might lead some of them to form an attachment to Japan, the curfew as applied was ruled to be an appropriate military measure against sabotage. A unanimous decision upheld the curfew violation convictions of both men.

The *Korematsu* and *Endo* cases reached the Supreme Court on December 18, 1944. By this time, Allied victory over Japan seemed assured and there were doubts regarding continued internment of Japanese Americans. Nevertheless, Korematsu's conviction for violating evacuation orders was upheld by a six to three vote. The benefit of hindsight, the Court ruled, did not allow it to overrule the judgment of the military that an unspecified number within the Japanese-American population were disloyal and could, under the circumstances of the military situation as it existed in 1942, be segregated from the loyal population. The evacuation was therefore constitutional. At the same time,

the Court overturned the District Court's *Endo* decision and ruled that an admittedly loyal American citizen could not be held in a relocation camp against his or her will. With this decision, the government began the process of closing the internment camps and resettling their inhabitants.

While the Supreme Court decisions stand today as the law of the land, the injustice of the decisions is accepted almost without opposition by historians and the public at large. The District Court convictions of Korematsu and Hirabayashi were finally reversed, however, thanks to historian and attorney Peter Irons who discovered that the government had suppressed evidence that, if it had been presented to the Supreme Court, could very well have resulted in different verdicts. An effort to reverse Yasui's conviction ceased upon his death in 1986. On January 12, 1988, Judge Donald S. Voohrees District Court opinion for Hirabayashi noted that "the sacrifices made by Gordon Hirabayashi, Fred Korematsu, and Minoru Yasui may, it is hoped, stay the hand of a government again tempted to imprison a defenseless minority without trial and for no offense."

BIBLIOGRAPHY

Irons, Peter. *Justice at War: The Story of the Japanese American Internment Cases.* 1983.
Irons, Peter, ed. *Justice Delayed: The Record of the Japanese American Internment Cases.* 1989.
Niiya, Brian, ed. *Japanese American History: An A-Z Reference from 1868 to the Present.* 1993.

Donald E. Collins

Japanese American Redress Movement

The movement for redress for the incarceration of Japanese Americans between 1942 and 1946 began in 1970, although some claim that protest statements made during the 1940s were its true roots. In 1970, a San Francisco activist, Edison Uno, introduced a motion calling for a campaign to achieve redress of wartime injustices at the biennial convention of the JAPANESE AMERICAN CITIZENS LEAGUE (JACL), the major organization of the Japanese-American community. The normal word, reparations, was avoided because of its monetary connotations. The JACL took no definitive action for eight years, although a committee to investigate redress had been established in 1974.

In 1978 the JACL agreed to pursue redress with the goal of a $25,000 government payment to each affected individual as well as the creation of a fund for community betterment and education. Shortly thereafter it decided to push for legislation creating a federal fact-finding commission. Within the Japanese-American community this proposal was attacked on two fronts. Conservatives, led by Senator S. I. Hayakawa (R-Ca), immediately attacked it as "absurd and ridiculous," while more radical groups called the commission aspect "a sign of weakness and confusion." They eventually created a National Council for Japanese American Redress led by William Hohri whose major activity became the prosecution of a complex and hopeless lawsuit asking for compensation of $210,000 per individual.

In 1980, after hearings in which representatives of the contending Japanese-American groups testified, Congress passed and President Jimmy CARTER signed a bill creating the Commission on the Wartime Relocation and Internment of Civilians (CWRIC) which was charged with investigating whether any wrong was done to Japanese Americans during WORLD WAR II. After completing a massive investigation and holding hearings across the country, the CWRIC concluded that the wartime incarceration of Japanese Americans "was not justified by military necessity. . . . [Its] broad historical causes were race prejudice, war hysteria, and a failure of political leadership." It recommended a formal apology, a one-time cash payment of $25,000 to surviving victims, and the creation of a $1.25 billion trust fund for appropriate public education.

Also in 1983 three of the "Japanese-American" SUPREME COURT cases of World War II which had convicted Gordon Hirabayashi, Fred Korematsu, and Minoru Yasui (see the "Chronology" sidebar) were unexpectedly reopened. These unusual proceedings were made possible because Professor Peter Irons had discovered archival documents showing that the Department of Justice had knowingly suppressed evidence and made misrepresentations to the Supreme Court. While the cases did not, as the plaintiffs hoped, lead to rehearings by the highest court, they did result in lower court reversals that provided further justification for redress.

A bill effecting the recommendations of the CWRIC was passed and signed into law in 1988, and, after two additional years of legislative struggle, the stipulated $20,000 payments were authorized. More than eighty thousand Japanese Americans have received payments totaling nearly $1.5 billion and a letter of apology signed by President George Bush. A result that had seemed an "impossible dream" twenty years before had become a reality.

See also JAPANESE AMERICAN INTERNMENT CASES.

Chronology

Jun. 28, 1940   Alien Registration Act of 1940 requires the annual registration of all aliens.

Dec. 7, 1941   Attack on Pearl Harbor by Imperial Japanese forces begins the war between the United States and Japan.

Dec. 7–8, 1941   The internment of selected Japanese nationals begins. After Germany and Italy declare war on the United States, selected German and Italian nationals are also interned. During the entire war perhaps 8,300 Japanese aliens were interned, along with some 2,300 German aliens and a few hundred Italian aliens. All were under the jurisdiction of the Immigration and Naturalization Service.

Feb. 19, 1942   Franklin D. Roosevelt signs Executive Order 9066 empowering military commanders within the United States to order civilians to move. It specifies no ethnic or racial group but its primary targets are Japanese Americans. Eventually more than 120,000 persons of Japanese birth or ancestry, more than two-thirds of them American citizens, were incarcerated in ten concentration camps, euphemistically called "Relocation Centers."

Mar. 18, 1942   Roosevelt issues Executive Order 9102 creating the War Relocation Authority, which will administer the "Relocation Centers."

Mar. 21, 1942   Statute enacted making it a crime for civilians to disobey a military order to leave a designated location.

Mar. 23, 1942   Civilian Exclusion Order No. 1 is issued by General John L. DeWitt, Western Defense Command, ordering all Japanese persons "alien and non-alien" to leave Bainbridge Island, near Seattle, by March 30. They are taken to the camp at Manzanar in Southern California. More than a hundred other such orders follow during the spring and summer.

Jun. 23, 1943   The United State Supreme Court, by a vote of 9-0, upholds the conviction of Gordon K. Hirabayashi for violating a curfew order by General DeWitt, *Hirabayashi v. U.S.* (320 *US* 81).

Dec. 18, 1944   The Supreme Court, by a vote of 6-3, upholds Fred T. Korematsu's conviction for violating one of DeWitt's civilian exclusion orders, *Korematsu v. U.S.* (323 *US* 214), and hands down, 9-0, *Ex parte Endo* (323 *US* 283) barring the continued detention and or restriction of "loyal" Japanese American citizens.

Sep. 4, 1945   Western Defense Command rescinds all its restrictive regulations affecting enemy aliens.

Jul. 2, 1948   The Japanese American Claims Act provides limited compensation for property losses only. The $38 million awarded covers only a small fraction of all losses.

Jun. 27, 1952   McCarran-Walter Act ends all racial/ethnic bars to naturalization.

Aug. 10, 1988   President Reagan signs bill effecting the recommendations of the CWRIC.

Oct. 9, 1990   First redress check goes to 107-year-old Rev. Matsumo Eto of Los Angeles.

BIBLIOGRAPHY

Daniels, Roger. *Prisoners Without Trial: Japanese Americans in World War II.* 1993.

Horii, William. *Repairing America: An Account of the Movement for Japanese American Redress.* 1988.

Maki, Mitchell, Harry H. L. Kitano, and S. Megan Bechtold. *The Impossible Dream: How Japanese Americans Obtained Redress.* 1999.

Roger Daniels

Jerry Lewis Telethon Controversy

Telethons have long been controversial in the disability community. Activists condemn them as demeaning; others argue that despite their indignities telethons have raised funds essential for services and equipment. The criticism attracted little public notice until 1981 when a newspaper essay by disabled lawyer Evan Kemp, whose parents had helped found the Muscular Dystrophy Association, castigated the MDA telethon's "pity approach." For the first time, donations fell below the previous year's. A decade later (1991–1994), disabled activists in many cities held Labor Day protests against the MDA telethon. Although they focused on that broadcast and its host, comic actor Jerry Lewis, the long-term criticism in the disability rights press applied as well to the telethons produced by the Arthritis Foundation, the National Easter Seal Society, and the United Cerebral Palsy Associations.

The criticism leveled three main charges: 1. Telethons define the problems of disabled people in almost exclusively medical terms, downplaying or ignoring discrimination, lack of accommodations, and inaccessibility. They define the necessary solutions as medical treatment rather than civil rights. Thus, unless cured or corrected, disabled people cannot establish valid social identities or become socially integrated. 2. Telethons depict disabled people as dependent objects of charity, rather than fellow citizens entitled to antidiscrimination protection and equal access. 3. By pervasively utilizing images of children, telethons infantilize disabled adults. Thus, no matter what their age, people with neuromuscular disabilities are labeled as "Jerry's Kids."

The irony is that by 1998 the changing economics of broadcasting had killed every telethon but Lewis's.

BIBLIOGRAPHY

Longmore, Paul K. "Conspicuous Contribution and American Cultural Dilemmas: Telethon Rituals of Cleansing and Renewal." *Discourses of Disability: The Body and Physical Difference in the Humanities,* edited by David Mitchell and Sharon Snyder. 1997.

Paul K. Longmore

Jim Crow

With origins in nineteenth-century popular culture, the term "Jim Crow" emerged as shorthand for racial segregation. More than a reference to the ubiquitous signs that designated "colored" and "white" public spaces across the twentieth-century South (water fountains, restrooms, waiting rooms, or theater entrances), Jim Crow defined the conspicuous and subtle practices of systematic racism.

Thomas "Daddy" Rice, a white minstrel performer, popularized the phrase in 1828 when he created a stage character based on a slave named Jim owned by a Mr. Crow. Mocking African Americans through his presentation, Rice blackened his face with burnt cork (blackface), donned a ragged costume, shuffled as he danced, and sang "ev'ry time I turn around I jump Jim Crow." Rice's popular ditty, "Jump Jim Crow," became an integral part of his routine, and by the 1830s his act propelled blackface minstrelsy into American culture and the term into American lexicon. Moving beyond its popular culture usage, Jim Crow came to refer to the practice of racial segregation in the antebellum North and to segregation laws passed in the postbellum South. Such law assigned racial designations to public conveyances, public accommodations, residential areas, schools, churches, cemeteries, and the like. These purportedly equal facilities were often as unequal, or nonexistent, as they were segregated.

In 1896, the SUPREME COURT upheld the doctrine of "separate but equal" in its decision, PLESSY V. FERGUSON. The laws, rules, and customs that evolved did not simply assign blacks to a fixed subordinate status, as historian C. Vann Woodward explains; rather, wrapped in racist rhetoric and rationalized by ideologies of black inferiority, they were used by whites to push blacks farther down. Jim Crow signified whites' control of virtually every aspect of public life. And the resulting black world included the inadequate, inferior, or indecent facilities that whites believed blacks deserved.

As used by African Americans, Jim Crow came to refer to all forms of trenchant racial bias. Notwithstanding the patterns of race relations identified with the South, Jim Crow appeared in other regions as de

In Oklahoma City, July 1939, a man drinks from a Jim Crow water fountain. (Prints and Photographs Division, Library of Congress)

facto segregation, informally restricting blacks to certain positions and places and excluding them from others. Similarly, although the term alluded to legal aspects of segregation, it also applied to culturally symbolic conventions or patterns of behavior that framed the social relations between blacks and whites. Blacks were supposed to defer to whites, for example, but whites were never to defer to backs. Because of the fluidity of its application, different groups of African Americans—women and men, and people of varying classes—"experienced" Jim Crow in different ways. Civil rights and women's movement activist Pauli MURRAY, for instance, coined the phrase "Jane Crow" to describe discrimination against women, especially black women.

Whether embodied by signs or symbols, laws or customs, Jim Crow's uses and abuses touched the lives of every African American without regard to class or gender. Enforced with or without formality, sanctioned by the Supreme Court, and reinforced by violence, Jim Crow allowed harsh discriminatory practices, validated racist conventions, and licensed biased racial

codes, and it was against these biases that civil rights activities focused.

BIBLIOGRAPHY

Litwack, Leon F. *Trouble in Mind: Black in the Age of Jim Crow.* 1998.

Murray, Pauli. "The Liberation of Black Women." In *Voices of the New Feminism*, ed. Mary Lou Thompson. pp. 76–102. 1970.

Toll, Robert C. *Blacking Up: The Minstrel Show in Nineteenth Century America.* 1974.

Van Deburg, William L. *Slavery and Race in Popular Culture.* 1984.

Woodward, C. Vann. *The Strange Career of Jim Crow.* 1974.

Leslie Brown

Johnson, Frank M.

(1918– 1999), judge.

Federal Judge Frank Johnson authored a series of crucial decisions supporting the civil rights movement.

Born in Winston County in northern ALABAMA, Johnson attended the University of Alabama and graduated from its law school in 1943. In 1953 Johnson, an active EISENHOWER supporter, was appointed United States Attorney for the Northern District of Alabama. Based on his impressive work in this position, he was elevated to the federal bench in 1955.

Johnson's civil rights decisions began immediately. In the midst of the MONTGOMERY BUS BOYCOTT in 1956, Johnson joined Judge Richard RIVES in declaring Montgomery's segregated bus seating ordinance unconstitutional (see SEGREGATION). When the SUPREME COURT upheld this decision in November, the bus boycott became the first nationally recognized successful direct-action campaign of the modern civil rights movement. In succeeding years, Johnson issued decisions that turned back an attempt to gerrymander black voters in Tuskegee, affirmed the right of black voters to register without duress in Macon County (see VOTING RIGHTS), supervised the integration of the Macon County public schools and eventually all public school districts in Alabama, and ordered protection for the Selma-to-Montgomery marchers in 1965.

Judge Johnson later authored landmark decisions mandating decent treatment of mental patients and prisoners in state facilities in Alabama and AFFIRMATIVE ACTION hiring of minorities by the Alabama State Police. After appointment to the Fifth Circuit Court of Appeals in 1979, Johnson took senior status in 1991. The federal courthouse in Montgomery was renamed the Frank M. Johnson, Jr., Federal Building and United States Courthouse in 1992.

BIBLIOGRAPHY

Bass, Jack. *Taming the Storm: The Life and Times of Judge Frank M. Johnson, Jr., and the South's Fight over Civil Rights.* 1993.

Stephen C. Messer

Johnson, James Weldon

(1871–1938), author, diplomat, and lawyer.

A native of Jacksonville, Florida, in 1900 James Weldon Johnson and his brother J. Rosamond Johnson wrote a song, "Lift Every Voice and Sing," which later became known as the "black national anthem."

After attending Atlanta University, Johnson returned to Jacksonville and became principal of the Stanton Grammar School, a school he had attended as a child. In 1901 he was the first African American admitted to the Florida State Bar Association. He later moved to New York with his brother and the two became part of the ragtime songwriting team, the Cole

and Johnson Brothers. While his brother participated in musical tours, Johnson studied literature at Columbia University and became involved in New York City politics. In 1905 he became the treasurer of the city's Colored Republican Club.

President Theodore Roosevelt appointed him U.S. consul to Venezuela in 1906 and he later held the same position in Nicaragua. Upon returning to New York, he became an editorial writer for the *New York Age*. In 1916, Joel Springarn, chairman of the NATIONAL ASSOCIATION FOR THE ADVANCEMENT OF COLORED PEOPLE (NAACP), asked Johnson to serve as a field secretary. By 1920, the NAACP membership had increased from nine thousand to ninety thousand. The same year, Johnson was appointed executive director and led the NAACP's fight for racial equality until 1930. Also during his tenure with the NAACP, Johnson was a recognized leader of the HARLEM RENAISSANCE, an important intellectual and artistic movement. He regularly contributed articles to *The Crisis*, a magazine published by the NAACP, and he encouraged younger writers to do the same.

Johnson was a prolific writer. He published a novel, *The Autobiography of an Ex-Colored Man* (1912), the historical work *Black Manhattan* (1930), several books of poetry including *God's Trombones: Seven Negro Sermons in Verse* (1927), and his autobiography, *Along This Way* (1933).

BIBLIOGRAPHY

Fleming, Robert E., editor. *James Weldon Johnson and Arna Wendell Bontemps: A Reference Guide.* 1978.

Levy, Eugene. *James Weldon Johnson: Black Leader, Black Voice.* 1973.

Shelly Eversley

Johnson, Lyndon Baines

(1908–1973), U.S. president.

Lyndon B. Johnson was President of the United States from 1963 to 1969. In civil rights, Johnson was essential as a legislative and executive leader. As Majority Leader of the U.S. Senate, Johnson led in the passage of a compromise CIVIL RIGHTS bill in 1957—the first passed since RECONSTRUCTION. But it was as president that Johnson exercised his most important leadership. Under him, the nation saw the passage of two of the most important pieces of legislation in U.S. history.

Johnson came to office in difficult times. The death of President Kennedy was a national tragedy, and Johnson was confronted with dealing with the mourning period, carrying on Kennedy's policy agenda, and making plans for the 1964 presidential campaign, all

President Lyndon B. Johnson meets with civil rights leaders in the White House, January 18, 1964. From left: Roy Wilkins, James Farmer, Dr. Martin Luther King, Jr., and Whitney Young. (AP/Wide World Photos)

simultaneously. He saw that to further those goals he must appeal to the American people to take the legacy of John Kennedy and apply it in the arena of civil rights. And getting Kennedy's civil rights bill passed would establish his credentials as president.

Johnson had almost unlimited energy and a predisposition for using any tactics necessary to succeed in pushing legislation through Congress. Bill Moyers, one of Johnson's closest aides, remembers him as a man of infinte practicality unencumbered with theory. That infinite practicality would be put to the test, for the stumbling blocks that had kept Kennedy from passing a civil rights act still remained in place. First, the president needed to do what he could to rally public opinion behind the cause. Second, he had to muster adequate votes in the House of Representatives to discharge the bill from the Rules Committee, which was chaired by Howard Smith of Virginia. Smith opposed strong national civil rights legislation. Finally, Johnson had to usher the legislation through the Senate, which had the stumbling block of its Judiciary

Committee, chaired by segregationist John Eastland of Mississippi; and there was the potential of a filibuster. THE CIVIL RIGHTS ACT OF 1964 demonstrated that Johnson was able, with effective legislative leadership, to accomplish all these tasks. The following year, Johnson pushed through Congress another sweeping civil rights action, the VOTING RIGHTS ACT OF 1965. Fittingly, the last major civil rights action of the Johnson administration, the passage of the CIVIL RIGHTS ACT OF 1968, came after he decided not to run for reelection. Poignantly, it was voted out of the Rules Committee on the day after Martin Luther King, Jr.'s, funeral.

Lyndon Johnson played a critical role in the passage of the 1964, 1965, and 1968 acts. His legacy, however, is that he was the first president who abandoned political expediency in the cause of civil rights and brought the entire prestige of his office into the battle. Johnson felt that he had the power and the obligation to do something in civil rights. There can be no question that the presidency of Lyndon Johnson exhibited in this field the greatest amount of sustained executive leadership in the nation's history.

BIBLIOGRAPHY

Graham, Hugh Davis. *Civil Rights and the Presidency.* 1992.

Jackson, Donald W., and James W. Riddlesperger, Jr. "The Eisenhower Administration and the 1957 Civil Rights Act." In *Reexamining the Eisenhower Presidency,* edited by Shirley Anne Warshaw. 1993.

Johnson, Lyndon B. *The Vantage Point.* 1971.

Loevy, Robert D. "The Presidency and Domestic Policy: The Civil Rights Act of 1964." In *The American Presidency,* edited by David C. Kozak and Kenneth N. Ciboski. 1985.

Stern, Mark. *Calculating Visions: Kennedy, Johnson, and Civil Rights.* 1992.

James W. Riddlesperger, Jr.

Jones, LeRoi

See Baraka, Amiri.

Jordan, Barbara Charlene

(1936–1996), U.S. congresswoman.

Barbara Jordan was born in the Fifth Ward of Houston, Texas to a black Baptist minister, Benjamin Jordan, and a domestic worker, Arlyne Jordan. She received her early education from Atherton Elementary and Phyllis Wheatley High schools. While a student at Wheatley, Jordan was a member of the Honors Society and excelled in debating. She graduated from high school in the upper 5 percent of her class. Jordan then went on to Texas Southern University where she majored in political science and history, and became a member of the Debate Team and Delta Sigma Theta Sorority. Graduating *magna cum laude* from Texas Southern University in 1956, she went on to earn a law degree from Boston University in 1959.

After leaving Boston University, Jordan taught political science for one year at Tuskegee Institute in Alabama. In 1960, she returned to her native Houston to take the bar examination and to set up private law practice. For four years, Jordan was very active in local and state Democratic politics and made two unsuccessful runs for the state legislature in 1962 and 1964. Her interest in politics was solidified in 1965 when she received her first appointive position as administrative assistant to the judge of Harris County. This appointment was followed by her election to the Texas Senate in 1966, which provided her the distinct honor of being the first of her race to serve in that body since

Barbara Jordan as a Texas state senator. March 1967. (AP/World Wide Photos)

1883. In 1972, she was elected president pro tempore of the Senate, and on June 10, 1972, served as Governor for a Day, making her the first black woman governor in the history of the United States.

Jordan's six-year record in the Senate shows a sensitivity to issues affecting the working class, the disabled, racial minorities, and women. She championed the cause of each group. Yet, it is the Worker's Compensation Act for which Jordan is most noted. This bill gave the state its first minimum wage law and increased worker's compensation coverage for on-the-job-injuries.

In 1976, it was the overwhelming mandate of the constituents of the newly created Congressional District of Texas that Barbara Jordan would be their representative. With this election, Jordan would go down in the record book again—first black Texan to serve in the United States Congress. As a member of the House, her reputation was that of a skilled politician and a forceful and dynamic individual. Probably the most important bill that she sponsored was one to extend the VOTING RIGHTS ACT (CIVIL RIGHTS ACT OF

1965) to Texas and other Western states in order to cover individuals with language barriers. This bill required bilingual or multilingual ballots in states where more than 5 percent of the voting age citizens spoke only a non-English language. Concomitant with the above bill were several other congressional acts cosponsored by Jordan which were helpful to older Americans, children, the environment, teachers, and the homeless. Equally important was Jordan's role in convincing the House Judiciary to extend the time allowed by Congress to win state ratification for the EQUAL RIGHTS AMENDMENT, a statute which would have placed equality of the sexes in the constitution. Also, Jordan gained national notoriety during the House Judiciary Committee hearings on the Watergate scandal on July 24, 1974, when she delivered an impassioned speech on the Constitution. "My faith in the Constitution is whole," said Jordan. "It is complete. It is total." Having been propelled into national stardom, Jordan was subsequently selected to deliver the keynote address at the 1976 Democratic Party Convention—the first black woman in the 144-year history of the organization.

During her lifetime, Jordan was the recipient of honorary doctorate degrees from twenty-five colleges and universities, including Texas Southern University, Tuskegee Institute, Princeton University, and Harvard University. Other honors included the selection of Jordan as Democratic Woman of the Year (1975) by Woman's National Democratic Club; Woman of the Year in Politics (1975) by the *Ladies Home Journal*; and one of Ten Women of the Year by *Time* magazine (January 5, 1976).

Barbara Jordan retired from public office in 1978. After donating her senatorial and congressional papers to her alma mater, Texas Southern University, Jordan went on to become a visiting professor at the Lyndon B. Johnson School of Public Affairs at the University of Texas at Austin. She held this post until her death on January 21, 1996. Her funeral was graced by attendance and tributes from dignitaries across the country, including President Bill CLINTON. Even in death Barbara Jordan gained another first, as she became the first black to be interred in the state cemetery in Austin, Texas.

BIBLIOGRAPHY

Barbara Jordan Papers. Manuscript Collection, Texas Southern University, Houston.
Bryant, Ira B. *Barbara Charlene Jordan: From the Ghetto to the Capitol.* 1977.
Jordan, Barbara, and Shelby Hearon. *Barbara Jordan: Self Portrait.* 1979.
Pitre, Merline. "Jordan, Barbara" In *Black Women in America: An Historical Encyclopedia,* edited by Darlene Hine. 1993.
Smith, Garland. *Black Texans of Distinction.* 1976.
Texas Legislature, Senate. *Senate Journal Legislatures.* 1967–1971.
Time Magazine. January 5, 1976.
United States Congress, House of Representatives. *House Journal Congress.* 1973–1977.

Merline Pitre

Jordan, Vernon Eulion, Jr.

(1935–   ), civil rights leader and lawyer.

A lawyer and civil rights activist, Vernon Jordan served as Georgia field secretary for the NATIONAL ASSOCIATION FOR THE ADVANCEMENT OF COLORED PEOPLE (NAACP) (1961–1963), director of the VOTER EDUCATION PROJECT of the SOUTHERN REGIONAL COUNCIL (1964–1968), executive director of the United Negro

Vernon Jordan after testifying before a grand jury investigating an alleged affair between President Bill Clinton and Monica Lewinsky. Jordan told reporters he would not comment on the grand jury proceedings. March 1998. (AP/Wide World Photos)

College Fund (1970–1971), and president of the NA-
TIONAL URBAN LEAGUE (1972–1981).

Born in Atlanta, the second of three sons of Vernon
Eulion Jordan, a postal supervisor at Fort McPherson,
and Mary Griggs Jordan, a caterer, Jordan grew up
in a federally funded public housing project and attended segregated schools in Atlanta. The only black
student in his graduating class at DePauw University
in Greencastle, Indiana, in 1957, he earned a law degree at Howard University in Washington, D.C., in
1960.

Jordan first practiced law as a clerk for the noted
civil rights lawyer Donald L. Hollowell in Atlanta,
where he worked on the suit to desegregate the University of Georgia. In 1961, he escorted Charlayne
Hunter through an angry white mob to enroll at the
university.

As Georgia field secretary for the NAACP, Jordan
led a successful boycott of Augusta stores that refused
to hire blacks. During his tenure as director of the
Voter Education Project, some two million blacks were
registered to vote, and the number of elected black
officials in the South increased almost eightfold.

After a year as a lawyer at the Office of Economic
Opportunity in Atlanta and a year's fellowship at
Harvard University, Jordan became executive director
of the United Negro College Fund, raising a record
$8 million for the thirty-six black colleges and univer-
sities supported by the Fund.

Succeeding Whitney M. Young, Jr., as president of
the National Urban League, Jordan emerged as one
of the most influential black leaders of the 1970s. Over
the next decade, the League grew from 99 to 118 affiliates, doubled its staff to 4,200 employees, and increased its annual budget from $40 million to $150
million. Jordan strengthened the links between the
civil rights movement and the corporate world. The
League became a major subcontractor for government employment and social welfare programs and
worked increasingly closely with CONGRESS, the executive departments, and the regulatory agencies as an
advocate of the interests of black Americans. It significantly expanded its research capacity, with new monographs and special studies, a policy research journal,
and a widely publicized annual report, *The State of
Black America*.

In May 1980, following a speech to the Fort Wayne,
Indiana, Urban League, Jordan was seriously wounded
by a sniper when he returned to his hotel late at night
in the company of a white woman. Stepping down
from the League presidency in December 1981, he
became a senior partner at the Washington law firm
Akin, Gump, Strauss, Hauer & Feld. Skilled at interpreting the ways of Washington to the nation's leading
corporations, Jordan himself served as a director of

American Express, Bankers Trust, Celanese, Dow
Jones, J. C. Penney, RJR Nabisco, Revlon, Sara Lee,
Union Carbide, and Xerox.

In 1992, an old friend, President-elect William
Jefferson Clinton, asked Jordan to serve as co-chair of
his transition team. Reportedly forgoing a cabinet
appointment, Jordan remained a confidante and
behind-the-scenes adviser of the president. Called to
testify in 1998 before the grand jury investigating the
president's relationship with White House intern
Monica Lewinsky, Jordan was one of three witnesses
deposed in February 1999 in Clinton's impeachment
trial in the U.S. Senate. Denying that his efforts to help
Lewinsky find a job were designed to buy her silence
in the Paula Corbin Jones lawsuit, Jordan traced his
efforts to assist young people in finding employment
to his own early experience, when his high school
bandmaster had interceded with Hollowell to get Jordan his first job.

BIBLIOGRAPHY

Contemporary Black Biography, vol. 3. 1993.
Current Biography Yearbook. 1993.
Luker, Ralph E. *Historical Dictionary of the Civil Rights Move-
    ment*. 1997.
Time, June 28, 1971, June 9, 1980, Feb. 2, 1998.
Washington Post. "Vernon Jordan, Urbane Leaguer," July
    28, 1977, p. B1; "Vernon Jordan: Battle Scars & Battle
    Hymns," Oct. 27, 1980, p. E1; "Jordan Crossing," Sept.
    10, 1981, p. A8; "The Man in Transition," Nov. 19,
    1992, p. D1; "First Friend," Jan. 27, 1998, p. E1; "A
    Powerful, Generous Mentor," Feb. 20, 1998, p. A8.
Who's Who in America, 53rd ed. 1999.

Nancy J. Weiss

Justice for Janitors

Justice for Janitors (JfJ) is an insurgent labor organizing movement within the Service Employees International Union (SEIU), noted for its success in using civil
rights strategies to organize private-sector custodial
workers. As most custodial workers in regions with a
strong JfJ presence are Mexican American, African
American, or immigrant, JfJ campaigns frame issues
of wages, benefits, and job security within the context
of civil rights for working people of color. In addition,
JfJ draws upon Mexican traditions of grass-roots organizing, and on models developed by César CHÁVEZ,
Dolores HUERTA, and the UNITED FARM WORKERS.

Originating in San Jose, California, in 1987, JfJ
started as a reaction among rank-and-file members of
SEIU to undemocratic union politics, falling wages,
poor working conditions, and the out-sourcing of custodial labor brought on by economic restructuring. JfJ

campaigns target corporations and government agencies that hire custodial firms, rather than the custodial firms themselves. Using street theater, guerrilla actions, corporate embarrassment campaigns, and nonviolent civil disobedience, JfJ has targeted employers such as Apple Computer, Hewlett-Packard, and NASA, pressuring them to sign contracts with union cleaning companies. JfJ campaigns have pioneered labor–community alliances, particularly between labor and church groups, civil rights organizations, and immigrant rights advocates, and have injected new life into the labor movement as a whole.

During the 1990s, the JfJ movement spread to cities such as San Diego, Los Angeles, Denver, St. Louis, Philadelphia, and Hartford. Amid general decline in organized labor, the JfJ movement managed to bring 25,000 new workers into unions during the period 1987–1991. In part due to the fact that AFL-CIO president John Sweeny comes out of the progressive wing of the SEIU, the JfJ model has influenced the direction of labor organizing in America.

BIBLIOGRAPHY

Howley, John. "Justice for Janitors: The Challenge of Organizing in Contract Services." *Labor Research Review* 9 (1990): 61–72.

Johnston, Paul. *Success While Others Fail; Social Movement Unionism and the Public Workplace.* 1994.

Joseph E. Heathcott

K

Kameny, Franklin

(1925–), gay activist.

Dr. Frank Kameny, a pioneering crusader for gay and lesbian civil rights, was born in New York in 1925. In 1956, after receiving a doctorate in astronomy from Harvard University, he moved to Washington, D.C., where he joined the faculty of Georgetown University; that same year, he accepted a position with the U.S. Army Map Service. In 1957, Kameny was summarily dismissed from the civil service, as a result of anonymous reports of his homosexuality. He unsuccessfully appealed the ruling, first to the Congressional Civil Service Committees, then through the federal court system, and eventually to the U.S. SUPREME COURT, which declined to hear the case.

In 1961, Kameny cofounded the Washington, D.C., chapter of the MATTACHINE SOCIETY, a homophile group. While Mattachine was a conservative organization whose members largely shared social perceptions of gays and lesbians as diseased, Kameny was a "radical activist" who advocated full civil rights for them. The Washington Mattachine chapter aided civil service workers threatened with dismissal, and Kameny edited a newsletter, the *Gazette*, which publicized acts of discrimination.

In 1965, Kameny organized a picket line at the offices of the U.S. Civil Service Commission—the first gay rights demonstration in American history. Three years later, at a meeting of the North American Conference of Homophile Organizations, an umbrella activist group, Kameny successfully sponsored a resolution to affirm the slogan "Gay Is Good." Although Kameny became less visible in the GAY AND LESBIAN RIGHTS movement after the Stonewall Riots of 1969, he remains an influential activist.

BIBLIOGRAPHY

Marcus, Eric. *Making History: The Struggle for Gay and Lesbian Equal Rights, 1945–1990.* 1992.
D'Emilio, John. *Sexual Politics, Sexual Communities.* 1986.

Greg Robinson

Kansas

Located in the geographical center of the United States, settled in the 1850s in roughly equal numbers by Yankee abolitionists, Southern sympathizers, and Midwestern farmers seeking economic opportunities, Kansas' legacy in the struggle for civil rights reflects the conflicting values of its people. Although it entered the Union as a free state—symbolic of the nation's struggle to abolish slavery—the reality for people of color, women, and other oppressed communities in Kansas did not always reach the promise of freedom and equality.

After the Civil War, perhaps 70,000 blacks migrated to Kansas, seeking land and escaping the poverty and violence of the South; few Kansans welcomed them. With the passage of the FIFTEENTH AMENDMENT, African-American men exercised their civil rights by voting and holding elected office, yet by 1900 all blacks were excluded from theaters, restaurants, and hotels, not by law but by custom (see SEGREGATION). Moreover, racially motivated violence against African Americans was not uncommon. Finally, restrictive housing clauses, limited educational and occupational opportunities (especially in the professions), and RACISM excluded blacks from the mainstream of Kansas life. African Americans quickly oganized to fight these conditions. For example, the annual Kansas State Colored Conventions first met in 1863 to demand an end to racial exclusion. African Americans also established their own businesses, churches, schools, fraternal organizations, and women's clubs (such as the Colored Women's Suffrage Association), all of which served as resources in their struggle for equality.

Women, black and white, also held an ambiguous place in Kansas civil society. They enjoyed property rights from the beginning of statehood, but white women could vote only in school elections. The first of two national campaigns for WOMAN SUFFRAGE was held in Kansas in 1867, led by Susan B. ANTHONY, Elizabeth Cady STANTON, and local activists. Republicans, who supported VOTING RIGHTS for African-American men, believed woman suffrage threatened black suffrage. They refused to support the movement for women and it failed. The campaign did, however, lead to the development of a national independent feminist movement, with woman suffrage as its primary goal. Another campaign in 1894 also failed, but in 1912 woman suffrage was adopted in Kansas, eight years before the NINETEENTH AMENDMENT, granting women the right to vote.

Mexican Americans migrated to Kansas early in the twentieth century, where they too experienced prejudice, especially from other immigrants with whom they competed for jobs. Classified as "colored persons," Mexican Americans were segregated in theaters, parks, restaurants, and even in some churches. As it did for African Americans, poverty and discrimination limited the INTEGRATION of Mexican Americans into the mainstream of Kansas life. Retaining a strong cultural identity with Mexico, few became citizens—which created strong ethnic communities but slowed acceptance by the dominant society.

Civil rights activists in Kansas helped bring about national change with the 1954 Supreme Court decision in *Brown v. Board of Education of Topeka* (see BROWN V. BOARD OF EDUCATION). An 1879 Kansas law had permitted separate black and white elementary schools in cities of more than 10,000. African Americans in Kansas had challenged the law through the courts since its passage, but not until 1951, when the Topeka branch of the NATIONAL ASSOCIATION FOR THE ADVANCEMENT OF COLORED PEOPLE (NAACP) filed the *Brown* suit, were they completely successful. The plaintiffs claimed that, although Topeka's black schools were the equal of white schools, segregated schools provided unequal EDUCATION by isolating black students from whites and this, sanctioned by law, imparted a feeling of inferiority to blacks. The SUPREME COURT agreed, paving the way for the complete dismantling of segregation in American society.

Brown inspired a nascent civil rights movement in Kansas, one that had its roots in WORLD WAR II and the fight for democracy. In Wichita, in 1958, an NAACP youth group successfully waged a two-week SIT-IN at Dockum's drugstore lunch counter and later integrated other businesses in the community. In the 1960s, direct action by students and civil rights organizations in Lawrence, Kansas City, Topeka, Wichita, and other cities led to the elimination of racial exclusion in public facilities as well as to the passage of a fair housing ordinance in 1967. At the same time, significant white resistance emerged to the civil rights movement and liberal legislation. Some Kansans rejected the intervention of the government in what they believed to be "legislating" equality, while others defended segregation by claiming that individuals had the right to do whatever they wanted with their property, including the excluding of people of color. Confronted with a recalcitrant white society, the BLACK POWER movement emerged as an alternative to traditional activism, promising to build and control black institutions. The movement frightened whites and led to a police crackdown on black activism. In 1970, in Kansas City, Lawrence, Topeka, and Wichita, racial violence erupted, and, in response, white vigilantes threatened retaliation.

Mexican Americans also fought for greater participation in Kansas society after World War II. Organized in 1948 by Mexican-American veterans, the AMERICAN G.I. FORUM lobbied for voting rights and job equity. Through newspapers, newsletters, and neighborhood action groups, such as the United Mexican American Voters of Kansas and the Mexican American Neighborhood Council, Hispanics fought for school curriculum reform, bilingual education, and vocational training and planning.

Since the 1960s, Kansas has continued (and continues) to have an ambiguous record in civil rights. For example, the Kansas Legislature approved the EQUAL RIGHTS AMENDMENT (ERA) in 1972, but a grassroots movement, led by conservative women and Christian fundamentalists, quickly organized to rescind the amendment. African Americans have gained greater political respresentation, serving in the state's House and Senate and as mayors of several smaller cities. Additionally, the black middle class has grown; between 1950 and 1990, the percentage of African Americans in the professions in Kansas increased from 4 to 16 percent. In 1979, however, African Americans in Topeka, including several of the original plaintiffs, reopened the *Brown* case, claiming that Topeka's schools were still segregated. Under court-ordered supervision to desegregate since 1994, Topeka finally achieved that goal in 1999, forty-five years after the original *Brown* decision.

BIBLIOGRAPHY

DuBois, Ellen Carol. *Feminism and Suffrage: The Emergence of an Independent Women's Movement in America, 1848–1869.* 1978.

Eick, Gretchen Cassel. "Lift Every Voice: The Civil Rights Movement and America's Heartland, Wichita, Kansas, 1954–1972." Doctoral dissertation, University of Kansas, 1997.

Kluger, Richard. *Simple Justice: The History of* Brown v. Board of Education: *Black America's Struggle for Equality.* 1976.

McCusker, Kristine M. "The Forgotten Years of America's Civil Rights Movement: The University of Kansas, 1939–1961." Master's thesis, University of Kansas, 1994.

Monhollon, Rusty. "'Away from the Dream': The Roots of Black Power in Lawrence, Kansas, 1960–1970." Master's thesis, University of Kansas, 1995.

Monhollon, Rusty. "Taking the Plunge: Race, Rights, and the Politics of Desegregation in Lawrence, Kansas, 1960." *Kansas History* 20 (Autumn 1997): 138–159.

Oppenheimer, Robert. "Acculturation or Assimilation: Mexican Immigrants in Kansas, 1900 to World War II." *Western Historical Quarterly* 16 (1985): 429–448.

Ortiz, Leonard David. "*La Voz de la Genie:* Chicano Activist Newspapers and Newsletters in the Kansas City Area, 1968–1989." *Kansas History* (1999).

Taylor, Quintard. *In Search of the Racial Frontier: African Americans in the American West. 1528–1990.* 1998.

Tuttle, William M., and Deborah Dandridge. "Kansas." In *Encyclopedia of African-American Culture and History,* edited by Jack Salzman, David Lionel Smith, and Cornel West. 1996.

Rusty L. Monhollon

Kennedy, John Fitzgerald

(1917–1963), U.S. president.

John F. Kennedy, a Democrat, served as thirty-fifth President of the United States, from January 20, 1961, to November 22, 1963. He had previously served as a U.S. representative (1946–1953) and then senator (1953–1960) from Massachusetts. As the Democratic nominee for president in 1960, Kennedy telephoned Coretta Scott King, wife of the Reverend Dr. Martin Luther King, Jr., to express his concern for the arrest and imprisonment of her husband by GEORGIA law enforcement authorities. His brother, campaign manager and future Attorney General Robert F. Kennedy, also telephoned a Georgia state judge to demand fair treatment for Dr. King. King was subsequently re-

leased, and Kennedy won 70 percent of the African-American vote in an election in which he won only 49.7 percent of the popular vote to Republican opponent Richard Nixon's 49.6 percent.

As president, Kennedy made unprecedented use of the federal bureaucracy to promote equal rights for African Americans. He ordered government agencies to recruit and promote more qualified African Americans, and used the Committee on Equal Employment Opportunity to monitor their compliance. Kennedy also directed the Interstate Commerce Commission to integrate the terminal facilities of interstate buses and the Justice Department, through appropriate legal action, to fight racial discrimination in voter registration (see VOTING RIGHTS) and promote the INTEGRATION of Southern public school systems, universities, and airports. He ordered an end to racial discrimination in federally financed housing programs. Kennedy personally negotiated with MISSISSIPPI governor Ross Barnett and ALABAMA governor George C. WALLACE in unsuccessful efforts to win their cooperation with federal efforts to integrate their states' major universities. He used U.S. marshals, the Army, and the federalized Mississippi National Guard to suppress violence that broke out in response to James MEREDITH's registration at the University of Mississippi, and federalized the Alabama National Guard to preserve peace in response to Wallace's opposition to African Americans' enrollment at the University of Alabama.

Kennedy regularly invited moderate Southern business, civic, and political leaders to the White House to urge them to promote voluntary integration and thereby forestall the rise of black militancy. He and his brother Robert also kept moderate black civil rights leaders informed of the administration's progress in promoting equal rights while at the same time soliciting their advice. The administration in fact collaborated with moderate black leaders to plan the 1963 MARCH ON WASHINGTON. On June 11, 1963, Kennedy gave a major televised address in which he defined racial equality as "a moral issue . . . as old as the Scriptures and . . . as clear as the American Constitution." Eight days later he sent to the Congress an ambitious bill that proposed to ban discrimination in hotels, restaurants, retail stores, and other areas of public accommodation and to give the Attorney General more authority to desegregate public schools (see DESEGREGATION). His proposal served as the basis for the CIVIL RIGHTS ACT OF 1964, passed after his death.

BIBLIOGRAPHY

Koenig, Louis W. *The Chief Executive,* 6th ed. 1996.

Schlesinger, Arthur M., Jr. *A Thousand Days: John F. Kennedy in the White House.* 1965.

President John Kennedy poses at the White House with a group of leaders of the March on Washington. From left: Whitney Young, Dr. Martin Luther King, John Lewis, Rabbi Joachim Prinz, Dr. Eugene P. Donnaly, A. Philip Randolph, Kennedy, Walter Reuther, Lyndon Johnson, and Roy Wilkins. August 28, 1963. (AP/Wide World Photos)

Sorensen, Theodore C. *Kennedy.* 1965.
White, Theodore, II. *The Making of the President, 1960.* 1961.

Malcolm Lee Cross

Kennedy, Robert Francis

(1925–1968), government official; politician.

Robert Francis Kennedy served as attorney general of the United States (1961–1964) and senator from New York (1965–1968). He was from a prominent Irish Catholic family, which encouraged public service and oriented him toward civil rights issues. During the 1950s he was an attorney in the Justice Department and served on the staffs of several Senate committees. After managing his brother's successful presidential campaign in 1960, he was appointed attorney general. (See KENNEDY, John F.)

While he substantially increased the number of African-American lawyers in the department and developed an active civil rights division, he was slow to grasp the urgency of the civil rights struggle. After local authorities permitted the 1961 Birmingham beating of the FREEDOM RIDERS, he increasingly supported the use of federal marshals and troops to protect civil rights activists. Kennedy believed that voting rights were essential if racial justice was to be achieved in the South; the Civil Rights Division was particularly active in this area. The efforts of the Justice Department ended segregation in interstate transportation and forced Southern public universities to admit qualified African-American students.

When Kennedy entered the Senate, he became an important spokesperson for political and economic

Senator Robert Kennedy visits a private home in the Mississippi Delta as part of an anti-poverty investigation. Marian Wright Edelman, second from right, conducted the investigation with Kennedy and other U.S. senators. April 11, 1967. (AP/Wide World Photos)

equality of opportunity. He pressed Northerners to meet their responsibilities to those who were disadvantaged as a result of past injustices. He repeatedly emphasized the interrelationship between poverty and racism. An example of this was his support of César CHÁVEZ's efforts to unionize migrant farm workers. These ideas were carried into his 1968 bid for the presidency. The assassination of Martin Luther KING, JR., intensified his commitment to the civil rights movement and the struggle for economic justice. As a result, he was heavily favored by the minority voters. He seemed the likely nominee of the Democratic Party at the time of his assassination in 1968.

BIBLIOGRAPHY

Kimball, Penn. *Bobby Kennedy and the New Politics*. 1968.

Lasky, Victor. *Robert F. Kennedy: The Myth and the Man*. 1968.

Schlesinger, Arthur M., Jr. *Robert Kennedy and His Times*. 1978.

Frank R. Martinie

Kentucky

Kentucky's first constitution, hastily drafted in 1792, discriminated against white women, Indians, free blacks, and those enslaved. During the antebellum period, a patriarchal society excluded most women from educational opportunities, the professions, and making a will. Upon marriage womens' property devolved to their husbands. In an unlikely divorce, women bore the burden of proof. Speaking tours throughout Kentucky by Frances Wright and Lucy Stone promoting womens' rights merely irked the male oligarchy. Only slaves experienced more limited opportunities.

Kentucky's constitutional guarantees for freedom of speech, press, religion, and for personal security were frequently violated as mobs of white Kentuckians periodically drove nonconformists from their midst. The December 1859 expulsion of the abolitionist community at Berea was typical.

Civil liberties declined during the Civil War. Legislation in 1861 restricted the civil rights of pro-Confederates, and soon members of the professional, legal, and political communities, threatened by martial law and *habeas corpus* suspension, took loyalty oaths. After 1862 election irregularities and newspaper censorship became routine.

In post-Civil War Kentucky anti-black and anti-women's rights attitudes predominated. The 1865–1866 legislature elevated new freedmen to roughly the status free blacks had held. The race code prevented blacks from giving court testimony against whites, sitting on juries, and voting, fastening second-class citizenship upon African Americans. Not until 1976 did Kentucky ratify the Civil War amendments.

State authorities refused to enforce the Civil Rights Acts of 1866 and 1875, thereby condoning on-going violence against blacks (see CIVIL RIGHTS ACT OF 1866; CIVIL RIGHTS ACT OF 1875). Beginning in 1866, statewide black conventions protested harassment, violence, and segregation. Adoption of the Fifteenth Amendment in 1870 enhanced their leverage. During 1870–1871 a boycott ended discriminatory policies on Louisville's streetcars, and in 1872 the legislature legalized black testimony against whites, though ten years passed before African Americans sat on juries. Repeated demonstrations led to a system of "equal" public education for blacks in 1874, though unequally funded until 1882.

These meager gains atrophied with the advent of JIM CROW legislation. In federal court an Anti-Separate Coach Committee led by William H. Steward successfully challenged an 1892 law segregating railway cars, only to lose in 1900 in a U.S. SUPREME COURT decision, *Chesapeake and Ohio Railroad Company v. Kentucky*. By the mid-1890s laws rigidly segregated the races in housing, recreation, and the marketplace. Racism reached a crescendo in the decade following the 1904 "Day Law," which quashed integrated education at Berea College, a private institution. A challenge in the U.S. Supreme Court, *Berea College v. Kentucky*, failed in 1908. A victory in *Buchanan v. Warley*, a 1917 U.S. Supreme Court reversal of a 1914 Louisville ordinance instituting *de jure* (legally approved) segregation in housing, was more significant nationally than in Kentucky.

Following the Civil War, most women remained tied to household duties, but those who worked outside the home were limited to a sixty-hour week after 1912. In 1888 widows and single-female taxpayers received the right to vote on education-related issues; in 1912 all women acquired the franchise on most educational matters.

Many women found an outlet through clubs, most of them segregated. Organizations such as the Kentucky Equal Rights Association, headed by Laura Clay and Madeline Breckinridge, led to increased employment in offices and factories. But married women could not own property before 1894, a wife's income remained her husband's property until 1900, and property acquired jointly belonged to husbands as late as the 1960s. Black women lived a world apart from white women. Many worked outside their homes but legal restrictions or local mores limited them to domestic or factory labor at discriminatory pay.

Differences between promise and achievement in civil rights have led critics to label twentieth-century Kentucky a "land of paradox"—a legacy of leadership among Southern states in civil rights legislation (at least with regard to women), raising unfulfilled hope. From the 1920s to the 1940s, the Commission on Interracial Cooperation headed by James Bond and the Commission on Negro Affairs proposed modest changes in education and employment, without notable success.

Two independent interracial organizations carried the burden of the civil rights movement in twentieth-century Kentucky: the NATIONAL ASSOCIATION FOR THE ADVANCEMENT OF COLORED PEOPLE (NAACP) and the Urban League. Though struggles between militants and accommodationists sometimes divided these organizations, new leaders such as attorney Charles Anderson and publisher Frank Stanley from the 1920s to the 1940s challenged economic discrimination and segregation. An early success came in 1920 when the legislature strengthened the 1897 anti-lynching law. (See ANTI-LYNCHING CAMPAIGN.)

During World War II defense jobs opened for black and white women. The wall of *de jure* (legally approved) segregation began to crumble when in 1949 Lyman T. Johnson became the first black to enter the University of Kentucky. *Brown v. Board of Education* finally opened the door for equal educational opportunities for African Americans, and by 1956 most of the state universities and 75 percent of the public schools had integrated. (See BROWN V. BOARD OF EDUCATION.) Failure to achieve more than token integration, however, resulted in repeated desegregation suits, busing to achieve equality, and changing residential patterns, climaxing in a wave of violence during the 1970s. A court-ordered desegregation plan implemented by the U.S. Civil Rights Office during the 1980s made Kentucky's schools by 1995 the most integrated in the nation.

Legal impediments also fell in other areas. In 1955 the Kentucky Court of Appeals struck down segregated public recreational facilities, and in 1960 the legislature created the Kentucky Commission on Human Rights, an integrated civil rights watchdog group that prompted state action against a patchwork of discriminatory mores, customs, and laws. In 1963 the governor issued a Fair Services Executive Order and a Code of Fair Practices, which ended discrimination in every area touched by state government.

Spurred by the federal Civil Rights Act of 1964, the legislature passed in 1966 a Kentucky Civil Rights Act which contained a wide-ranging public accommodations law that also prohibited employment discrimination. The next victory came in 1968 with the passage of a Fair Housing Act, climaxing a struggle begun in the 1950s by Anne and Carl BRADEN, white activists associated with the liberal Southern Conference Educational Fund. Racial discrimination in home buying and renting, unfortunately, remains a problem.

One of Kentucky's most significant achievements in recent years has been protecting the legal rights of minorities. A 1974 act which provided that victims of discrimination could seek financial compensation for actions that caused them humiliation survived a 1982 court challenge. With the Racial Justice Act passed in 1998, Kentucky became the first state to attack the troubling connection between racism and capital punishment. Defendants in potential death penalty cases may introduce evidence revealing patterns of racial bias in prosecutors' decisions to seek death sentences.

De jure discrimination has essentially ended in Kentucky, but the effects of two hundred years of discriminatory customs, mores, local restriction, and state laws remain.

BIBLIOGRAPHY

Hardin, John. *Fifty Years of Segregation: Black Higher Education in Kentucky, 1904–1954.* 1997.
Harrison, Lowell H., and James C. Klotter. *A New History of Kentucky.* 1997.
Kentucky Commission on Human Rights. *Kentucky's Black Heritage.* 1971.
Klotter, James C. *Kentucky: Portrait in Paradox, 1900–1950.* 1996.
Lucas, Marion B. *A History of Blacks in Kentucky.* Vol. I. *From Slavery to Segregation, 1760–1891.* 1992.
Wright, George C. *A History of Blacks in Kentucky.* Vol. II. *In Pursuit of Equality, 1890–1980.* 1992.

Marion B. Lucas

Kerner Commission Report

The National Advisory Commission on Civil Disorders, which outlined the racial divisions in American society, was appointed by President Lyndon JOHNSON on July 27, 1967, in the aftermath of a massive five-day uprising in the ghettos of Detroit. The Commission, popularly known as the Kerner Commission after its chairman, Illinois Governor Otto Kerner, was assigned

to report on the causes and prevention of urban riots. Johnson was initially criticized for limiting the membership of the eleven-member Commission to moderates—notably in his choice of African-American members, Senator Edward Brooke and NAACP Executive Director Roy WILKINS—and excluding representatives of inner-city communities.

The Commission held hearings between August 1 and November 7, 1967, during which time some 130 witnesses participated. The Commission also held a set of special hearings, at which it heard testimony from black movement leaders and elected officials, such as radical activist Stokely CARMICHAEL and Cleveland Mayor Carl Stokes.

In February 1968, the Commission announced its findings in a 500-page report, which was divided into profiles of different urban disorders, analysis of the causes of riots, and recommendations for action. The opening summary, drafted largely by the Commission's vice chairman, New York Mayor John Lindsay, expressed its conclusions in a notable (and widely quoted) phrase: "Our nation is moving toward two societies, one black, one white—separate and unequal." The report bluntly stated that ghetto uprisings, like the ghettos themselves, were fundamentally a product of white oppression: "What white Americans have never fully understood—but what the Negro can never forget—is that white society is deeply implicated in the ghetto. *White institutions created it, white institutions maintain it, and white society condones it.*" The report recommended an immediate $30 billion urban program, including open-housing legislation, aid to education, jobs programs for black youths, nationwide standardization of welfare benefits, and construction of public housing for the poor.

Despite the enormous publicity it received, the Commission's report was ineffective in bringing about urban reform. Although many blacks praised the Commission report for its description of ghetto conditions, they rejected its integrationist conclusions. Conversely, white liberals, including Vice President Herbert Humphrey, were distressed by the report's harsh criticism of white society, whereas conservatives such as Republican presidential candidate Richard NIXON argued that the report was a classic example of "liberal guilt," which blamed everything for urban riots except the rioters. President Johnson, who suspected that the uprisings were the product of a conspiracy by black radicals, was disappointed that the report failed to give him credit for the accomplishments of his Great Society program, and believed its recommendations to be politically and financially unrealistic. Thus, apart from the Commission's recommendation for open-housing legislation (which ultimately formed the basis of the FAIR HOUSING ACT (CIVIL

RIGHTS ACT OF 1968), the report was quickly shelved. Ironically, however, in April 1968, barely a month after the Committee's report was issued, the assassination of Dr. Martin Luther KING, Jr. set off the greatest wave of urban uprisings in U.S. history, providing eloquent testimony to the problems described in the report.

BIBLIOGRAPHY

Lemann, Nicholas. *The Promised Land.* 1991.
National Advisory Commission on Civil Disorders. *Report.* 1968.

Greg Robinson

King, Martin Luther, Jr.

(1929–1968), religious and civil rights leader.

Martin Luther King, Jr., (1929–1968), pastor and Nobel Laureate, was the single most influential American in the twentieth century and the single most important black leader in U.S. history. He was the leading interpreter of the civil rights movement and its most potent national symbol. His birthday was established as a federal holiday in 1986—the only American with such an honor in his name alone. He has been dubbed correctly the nation's moral conscience.

The roots of Martin King's leadership are found in his birthplace—Atlanta, Georgia, where he was born to Alberta Christine Williams and Martin Luther King, Sr., on January 15, 1929. His father was the pastor of the influential Ebenezer Baptist Church and was a prominent civil rights leader in the black community.

Home and church provided the spiritual values that shaped young Martin's life. He was taught that God created all persons of equal worth and that everyone should be treated with dignity and respect. Segregation, therefore, was not only undemocratic; it was morally wrong and sinful. This religious belief instilled in Martin an early desire to devote his life to the service of others.

Martin King entered Morehouse College at fifteen and came under the powerful influence of President Benjamin E. Mays and religion professor George D. Kelsey. Both taught him that faith and intellect together could serve as useful tools in the struggle for social justice.

The importance of faith and intellect in the struggle for justice was reinforced at Crozer Theological Seminary (Chester, Pennsylvania) and the Boston University School of Theology. Martin King studied the social gospel theology of Walter Rauschenbusch, E. S. Brightman's philosophy of personalism, the social ethics of Reinhold Niebuhr, and Mahatma GANDHI's teachings on nonviolence. These intellectual re-

In Montgomery, Alabama, police officers apply force in arresting the Reverend Martin Luther King, Jr., for loitering near a courtroom where one of his Southern Christian Leadership Conference (SCLC) officers was on the stand. September 4, 1958. (CORBIS/Bettmann)

sources deepened his belief in a personal God, the innate worth of the human person, the interrelatedness of life, and the ethical responsibility to establish justice in society.

In 1954, after completing his residential requirements for the Ph.D. degree in systematic theology at Boston University, Martin King accepted an invitation to become the pastor of Dexter Avenue Baptist Church in Montgomery, Alabama. As he immersed himself in his pastoral and civic duties, he also worked on his dissertation, which he finished in the spring of 1955.

On December 1, 1955, Rosa Parks was arrested for refusing to give up her seat on a city bus to a white male passenger. In response, blacks initiated a bus boycott (December 5) and asked twenty-six-year-old Martin King to serve as their spokesperson. With the support of other leaders, King inspired 50,000 African Americans to walk the streets with dignity rather than ride the buses in humiliation.

Black churches played a major role in the success of the boycott. Not only was the bulk of the leadership derived from the churches, but strategy sessions and biweekly inspirational meetings were also held in them. The Christian message of justice, love, and hope defined the spiritual focus of the boycott. In sermons and inspirational talks, Martin King and other leaders appealed to the people to "keep God in the forefront," follow faithfully Gandhi's teachings on nonviolence, and remember that "the great glory of American democracy is the right to protest for right."

The success of the yearlong boycott turned King into a national leader and inspired ordinary grassroots people to take a direct and meaningful hand in pursuing their own freedom. Soon after, King founded the SOUTHERN CHRISTIAN LEADERSHIP CONFERENCE (SCLC), which adopted as its motto, "to redeem the soul of America." He resigned as pastor of Dexter to become copastor with his father at Ebenezer in Atlanta in order to gain more time and freedom for the burgeoning mass-oriented civil rights movement.

The sit-ins began in 1960, followed by the FREEDOM RIDES in 1961 and a host of other mass actions against segregation throughout the South. Although Martin King was neither the chief initiator nor a major participant in any of these events, he was the primary interpreter of their meaning to the nation. It was not until the Birmingham Movement in 1963 that King would assume a major leadership role analogous to Montgomery. He demonstrated the power of nonviolence in his confrontation with police brutality, supported by the infamous Commissioner of Public Safety, Eugene "Bull" Connor. In his now-famous "Letter from Birmingham Jail," he also leveled a devastating critique of white moderate Southern clergy who called him an "outsider" and questioned the propriety of civil disobedience and the timing of the protest.

The success in Birmingham was followed by the great MARCH ON WASHINGTON (August 28, 1963), where King gave his "I Have A Dream" speech to an assembled audience of 250,000, challenging Americans to make real the promises of democracy. It was arguably the greatest address given by an American, and it belongs alongside Lincoln's "Gettysburg Address." Both Birmingham and the March contributed to the passage of the 1964 Civil Rights Bill. (See CIVIL RIGHTS ACT OF 1964.) *Time* magazine named King "Man of the Year" in 1963, and he was awarded the Nobel Peace Prize in 1964.

Awards and personal recognition deepened King's commitment to work harder for justice on behalf of the poor in the United States and throughout the world. After receiving the Nobel Prize, he went immediately to Selma, Alabama, to publicly demonstrate to the world via the media that America could never be the democracy it claimed to be as long as black people were systematically denied the right to vote.

Dr. King displays his 1964 Nobel Peace Prize medal in Oslo, Norway. December 10, 1964. (AP/Wide World Photos)

With the state of Alabama as the arena of confrontation, King once again showed the power of nonviolent direct action to conquer blatant injustice and state-sponsored terror.

The Selma-to-Montgomery March and the subsequent signing of the Voting Rights Bill by President Lyndon JOHNSON (August 6, 1965) represented a watershed in the black freedom struggle. (See VOTING RIGHTS ACT [CIVIL RIGHTS ACT OF 1965].) Many supporters felt that its goal had been achieved. Five days later, the WATTS RIOT in Los Angeles erupted, leaving thirty-four dead. King was greatly distressed by the violence and the poverty and despair that caused it. He soon realized that the success of the civil rights movement in abolishing legal segregation in the South did not improve the quality of black life in the North. It was one thing to get people the right to eat hamburgers in a restaurant and quite another to help them get the money to buy them.

King realized that the struggle for justice was far from over. Indeed, the most difficult days lay ahead. Achieving social and political equality did not cost America anything. But economic equality would cost plenty. King chose Chicago as the arena to expose the depth of economic exploitation in the Northern ghettoes of America. He called the ghetto "a system of internal colonialism." While white liberals supported his campaign against de jure segregation in the South, they opposed his fight against de facto segregation in the North. King focused on eradicating slums and marching for open housing. But white resistance prevented him from achieving little more than a paper victory.

The rise of BLACK POWER on the James Meredith March in Mississippi (June 1966) and the white backlash that soon followed revealed the depth of black anger and white liberal racism. King rejected extremism on both sides—the separatism of black militants and the cleverly disguised racism of white liberals.

While King continued to devote most of his time to the fight against racism and poverty, he found that as a Christian minister he could not remain silent about America's unjust war in VIETNAM. He joined the struggle against war with the fight against racism and poverty—viewing them as inextricably bound together and as the three great evils of our time.

Against the advice of his friends in government and the civil rights movement, King leveled a devastating critique of America's war policy in Vietnam—first in Los Angeles (February 25, 1967) and then at Riverside Church in New York City (April 4, 1967). He called America "the greatest purveyor of violence in the world today." King insisted that God's judgment was going to rain down on America if this nation failed to end racism, poverty, and violence at home and abroad.

King would not compromise his stand against violence. He was against both the violent rhetoric of Black Power advocates and the guns and bombs of the American military in Vietnam. King received a hail of criticisms for his views on Vietnam. His critics claimed he had no expertise in American foreign policy and should know better than to mix international peace issues and the domestic struggle for civil rights. King did not back down because his stand against war was derived from his vocation as a minister of God. It did not matter how many people disagreed with him. "One with God is the majority," King retorted. His stand on nonviolence was absolute.

The once-popular King found himself alienated from former supporters in government and the media as well as many colleagues in the civil rights movement. Alone, depressed, and against tremendous odds, he continued to fight for freedom and justice and against racism, poverty, and war, because he believed that "right defeated is stronger than evil triumphant."

Exactly one year after his "Beyond Vietnam" speech at Riverside Church, King was assassinated in Memphis, Tennessee, while fighting for the rights of striking sanitation workers. He was also organizing the Poor Peoples March to Washington to demand a "Bill of Rights for the Disadvantaged."

King's legacy lives on today in the lives of people fighting for justice around the world. He was America's greatest moral leader—a black prophet who demanded that this nation live up to its moral possibilities, matching deed with its creed. With his life and words, he showed America what it could become—indeed must become—if this nation is going to be a just society for all its people and a beacon of freedom for the oppressed throughout the world.

BIBLIOGRAPHY
Branch, Taylor. *Parting the Waters: America in the King Years 1954–63.* 1988.
Branch, Taylor. *Pillar of Fire: America in the King Years 1963–65.* 1998.
Cone, James H. *Martin & Malcolm & America: A Dream or a Nightmare.* 1991.
Garrow, David J. *Bearing the Cross: Martin Luther King, Jr., and the Southern Christian Leadership Conference.* 1986.
The Papers of Martin Luther King, Jr.: The Birth of a New Age, Vol. 3. 1997.
Washington, James M. *A Testament of Hope: The Essential Writings of Martin Luther King, Jr.* 1986.

James H. Cone

King, Martin Luther, Sr.

(1899–1984), religious and civic leader.

The second of ten children, Martin Luther King was born in Stockbridge, Georgia, on December 19, 1899, to Delia (née Lindsay) and James Albert King. His parents were poor sharecroppers. Although "Daddy King," as Martin Luther King, Sr., was affectionately known, is best remembered as the father of the civil rights leader Martin Luther King, Jr., he was, however, a champion of social change and DESEGREGATION in his own right, a fact illustrated by the leadership roles of Baptist minister and civic leader which he assumed in his community throughout the 1930s and '40s. He not only succeeded his father-in-law, the Reverend A. D. Williams, as minister of the historic Ebenezer Baptist church in Atlanta, Georgia, in the fall of 1931, he was also actively involved in opposing the racial politics of his time. In 1935 King organized a voter registration drive that culminated in a march by several hundred blacks to Atlanta's City Hall to register en masse. This religious and political activism was both part of his own theological belief and something he had learned from his father-in-law, himself an activist in the NATIONAL ASSOCIATION FOR THE ADVANCEMENT OF COLORED PEOPLE (NAACP) and in the Atlanta Civic

Martin Luther King, Sr., delivers his farewell sermon at the Ebenezer Baptist Church in Atlanta. July 27, 1975. (CORBIS/Bettmann)

League that was set up following the racial violence of 1906 (in which several blacks were murdered). In his autobiography, "Daddy King" suggests that it was during these years that were formed the seeds of the civil rights movement to be headed by his son half a century later.

BIBLIOGRAPHY

King, Martin Luther Sr., with Clayton Riley. *Daddy King: An Autobiography.* 1980.

Edward Phillip Zuzee Antonio

KKK

See Ku Klux Klan.

Knights of Labor

The largest labor organization in North America during the nineteenth century, the Knights of Labor (KoL) emerged as a reaction to the erosion of autonomy within crafts and trades amid the advance of industrial capitalism. Rather than the narrow and racially exclusive model of trade unionism adopted by the American Federation of Labor (AF of L), the KoL promoted a working-class cultural movement based on equality and fraternal brotherhood.

The KoL was established in 1869 in Philadelphia, with a small but growing membership shrouded in secrecy and ritual. Most early "Knights," led by Uriah Stephens, were Anglo-Protestant Freemasons in skilled trades such as garment cutting and shoemaking. However, following a successful strike against the Southwestern Railroad in 1885, the ranks of the KoL swelled with unskilled immigrant industrial workers. Led by Terence Powderly, an Irish Catholic machinist from Scranton, Pennsylvania, the KoL rejected ritual secrecy, adopted an organizing model of labor solidarity, and established an open and public organization with a million members by 1886. The KoL was the first major labor organization to welcome blacks (even while excluding Chinese workers), and employed many black organizers. The first all-black local was established by Ottumwa, Iowa coal miners in 1884, and both segregated and integrated locals sprang up across the United States with 100,000 black members.

The success of the KoL was short-lived. The national organization was weakened by local fragmentation, infighting among the leadership, incoherent policies, squabbles with trade unions, and religious differences. Having grown too rapidly to forge a strong organizational structure, the KoL was crushed by company owners in a series of strikes in the Midwest and New England. Though the KoL was defunct by the twentieth century, its members went on to be active in the POPULIST PARTY, the Farmer's Alliance, the AF of L, the Congress of Industrial Organizations, the INDUSTRIAL WORKERS OF THE WORLD and the WOMAN SUFFRAGE and civil rights movements.

BIBLIOGRAPHY

Fink, Leon. *Workingmen's Democracy: The Knights of Labor and American Politics.* 1983.
Ware, Norman J. *The Labor Movement in the United States, 1860–1895: A Study in Democracy.* 1929.
Weir, Robert. *Beyond Labor's Veil: The Culture of the Knights of Labor.* 1996.

Joseph Heathcott

Know-Nothing Party

Formally known as the American Party or the Supreme Order of the Star Spangled Banner, this short-lived organization was the only important nativist political party (see NATIVISM). The main goal of the party was to curtail foreign immigration, especially Catholic immigration. The party program required that immigrants live in the United States for twenty-one years before becoming citizens, that they not be allowed to hold public office, and, in an indirect attack of Catholic schools, that their children be denied political rights unless educated in public schools. At a time when many states allowed immigrants to vote even before attaining citizenship, the Know-Nothings demanded that no non-citizens be allowed to vote. The party first appeared in the wake of the disastrous defeat of the Whigs in 1852, which destroyed that party.

In 1854, Know-Nothing candidates won 347 of 350 seats in the Massachusetts Legislature, both the state's Senate seats, and all its seats in the U.S. Congress, as well as the state's governorship. In 1856, Know-Nothing Congressman Nathaniel Banks became speaker of the House of Representatives. In the 1856 presidential election the party nominated former president Millard Fillmore, running on the slogan "Americans Must Rule America." Fillmore carried no states, but won 874,534 popular votes (21.53 percent). Fillmore's support came primarily from Southern Whigs, who did not want to vote for a Democrat and could not consider voting for the anti-slavery Republicans, then led by John C. Frémont. By 1860 the Know-Nothing Party had disappeared, the vast majority of its Northern supporters voting for the Republicans. In the North the party was moderately antislavery and somewhat supportive of black rights. In the South it had been proslavery, like every other political party in that region.

BIBLIOGRAPHY

Bennett, David H. *The Party of Fear: From Nativist Movements to the New Right in American History.* 1988.
Gineapp, William. *Origins of the Republican Party, 1852–1856.* 1987.

Paul Finkelman

Korean War

The Korean War began June 25, 1950, when communist North Korea invaded American-supported South Korea. The United States rallied the United Nations to repel the aggression, and the success of the UN forces, which initially trounced North Korea and by December were approaching the Manchurian border, brought China into the war. Driven back by North Korean forces to the southernmost reaches of the Korean peninsula, the UN troops under General Douglas MacArthur ultimately rebounded and reached the vicinity of the 38th parallel, the pre-invasion boundary between the two Koreas, where American troops and

their allies stabilized the battle line until the fighting ended in a truce on July 27, 1953.

The invasion of South Korea lent credence to a growing American belief in a worldwide communist conspiracy in which Joseph Stalin could employ his proxies—whether nations like China and North Korea or individual spies and sympathizers—to do his bidding. Before the invasion of South Korea, federal, state, and even local authorities had begun eliminating communists from government employment. In this climate, citizens banded together to purge alleged communists from influential professions like teaching, the arts, entertainment, and politics (see COMMUNIST PARTY USA). The living symbol of this era of repression was Senator Joseph R. McCarthy, a Wisconsin Republican, whose undocumented charges stoked the fires of anticommunism without revealing further details of Stalin's espionage network. McCarthy's irresponsible behavior upset President Dwight D. EISENHOWER, alienated a U.S. Senate investigating committee, and finally resulted in censure of the senator, who ended his days in comparative obscurity. Other politicians, however, such as Richard M. NIXON, burst on the scene as dedicated anticommunists and launched long careers. Similarly, J. Edgar Hoover used the threat of communist subversion, verified by several highly publicized instances of spying, to enhance the power and prestige of his FEDERAL BUREAU OF INVESTIGATION.

Although American battle deaths in Korea surpassed 33,000, resistance to military service remained largely unorganized, even though a far greater percentage of potential draftees received deferment as conscientious objectors during the Korean conflict than during WORLD WAR II. The lack of unity among war resistors was due in part to tensions between anticommunists and former communists in groups like the Women's International League for Peace and Freedom. The presence of former communists in such groups raised suspicions about the motives and loyalty of these organizations and their members. In fact, the closest approach to organized resistance to military service occurred when some eight hundred Air Force Reserve officers, combat veterans of World War II, claimed fear of flying to avoid further fighting in Korea. The crisis passed when the Air Force realized that public opinion supported the fliers, dropped court-martial proceedings, and quietly released most of them from active duty.

As an example of communist aggression, the Korean War helped provide a convenient club to fend off demands for civil rights reform. Even an ordinarily sensible politician like Thomas E. Dewey of New York detected communism in welfare programs for impoverished families. The union movement lost ground, in part because some organizers and leaders had demonstrable ties to communism, but also because the Korean conflict conferred an overriding priority on military spending at the expense of union-supported social programs.

Because the American Communist Party had preached racial equality, segregationists were able to invoke anticommunism in attacking the civil rights movement. Ironically, the Korean War, which justified anticommunism, also forced the armed services to carry out the policy of racial integration that President Harry S. TRUMAN had established in 1948. Before the war, only the Air Corps had broken up its segregated units and scattered African Americans throughout the service. The need for manpower in Korea compelled the other armed forces, too, to use men where they were most needed, regardless of race. In the summer of 1951, the Army disbanded its last racially segregated combat unit (the 25th Infantry).

BIBLIOGRAPHY

Kohn, Stephen M. *Jailed for Peace: The History of American Draft Law Violators, 1658–1985.* 1986.

MacGregory, Morris J., Jr. *Defense Studies Series: Integration of the Armed Forces, 1940–1965.* 1981.

Mitchell, Vance O. *Air Force Officers: Personnel Policy Development, 1944–1974.* 1996.

Schrecker, Ellen. *Many Are the Crimes: McCarthyism in America.* 1998.

Bernard C. Nalty

Ku Klux Klan

The Ku Klux Klan was conceived during the RECONSTRUCTION Era (1865–1877), to address the fears of Southern whites resulting from rapid social and economic changes. The name Ku Klux Klan was derived from the Greek word *kuklos*, which means "circle of friends." From the beginning the goals of the Ku Klux Klan have always been controversial. Klansmen have claimed that the organization is a Christian, chivalrous, and patriotic society that has benefitted society in general by enforcing the law and through humanitarian efforts. While those committed to old Southern traditions maintained this favorable view, the Klan became most generally associated with the terror of hooded night riders who were responsible for LYNCHING campaigns directed against people of color.

Over the past one hundred and thirty years, the Ku Klux Klan has experienced periods of resurgence and decline. The first Klan was formed by six young Confederate soldiers in the winter of 1865–1866 in Pulaski, Tennessee. By 1867, the organization had grown large enough to hold its first unity convention in Nashville, Tennessee, and Confederate General Nathan Bedford

Forrest (1821–1877) was chosen as the first Imperial Wizard. Some suggest that he disbanded the organization two years later, in 1869, in response to public pressures, while others argue that Forrest wanted to distance himself so that he would not be held responsible for Klan violence. Congress passed four anti-Klan laws in 1870 and conducted congressional investigations in 1871. Forrest and others called to testify disavowed their involvement in Klan-related violence.

William Joseph Simmons founded the second Klan in 1915, which eventually became the largest in history. Its numbers swelled nationally to between four and five million members by 1925. In post-World War I America, the Klan was able to take advantage of a national political climate shaped by public fears and intolerance, which led to restricted immigration and other conservative measures. While the Reconstruction era Klan focused its wrath on blacks, the Klan of the 1920s broadened its ideology to oppose other ethnics such as Catholics, Jews, and immigrants, as well as the political left and proponents of unionization. During this period, the Ku Klux Klan was a powerful political force in state governments, with Grand Dragon D.C. Stephenson's influence in Indiana being perhaps the most noteworthy. The second Klan experienced a rapid decline in 1926, amidst internal disputes and in the wake of public outcry against Klan lynchings. Perhaps the coup de grace of this period was Klan participation in a highly publicized and unpopular pro-Nazi joint celebration with the German-American Bund in New Jersey in 1940. (See AMERICAN NAZI PARTY.)

Klan activity continued to ebb and flow in the period after World War II. A third Klan emerged immediately following the war, which remained a small and fragmented Southern phenomenon and whose activity led to the passage of "antimask" laws and a roundup of Klansmen in North Carolina in 1952. However, the Klan experienced another resurgence in response to the civil rights movement. During the late 1950s and 1960s, the Klan supported the political work of the WHITE CITIZENS COUNCILS, which originated in Mississippi and sought to maintain segregation. From the civil rights period to the present, the Ku Klux Klan has become increasingly fractionalized. Many Klan organizations have joined with splinter groups that are continually evolving. One of the most controversial and widely known Klansmen is David Duke (1950–   ), who has been credited with the "Nazification of the Klan." He led the Knights of the Ku Klux Klan (1973–1982), and went on to win a Louisiana congressional seat in 1989 after forming the National Association for the Advancement of White People (NAAWP). Since the 1980s, Klan organizations have divided into traditional groups, which adhere to the original Klan

Hooded members of the Ku Klux Klan at a cross burning in southwestern Michigan, as part of a rebirth of Klan activities in that area. October 24, 1937. (CORBIS/Bettmann)

rituals dating back to Forrest, while other Klan organizations, considered more militant, have incorporated neo-Nazi symbols and ideology along with a more open acceptance of skinheads. At the present, the Ku Klux Klan is one faction of what has been termed the "White Power Movement," which draws together divergent white supremacist ideologies and strategies for social change ranging from political mainstreaming to violence. (See WHITE SUPREMACY.)

BIBLIOGRAPHY

Bridges, Tyler. *The Rise of David Duke*. 1994.

Chalmers, David M. *Hooded Americanism: The History of the Ku Klux Klan*. 1965.

Dobratz, Betty A., and Stephanie L. Shanks-Meile. *"White Power, White Pride!" The White Separatist Movement in the United States*. 1997.

Forster, Arnold, and Benjamin R. Epstein. *Report on the Ku Klux Klan*. 1965.

Katz, William Loren. *The Invisible Empire: The Ku Klux Klan Impact on History*. 1986.

MacLean, Nancy. *Behind the Mask of Chivalry: The Making of the Second Ku Klux Klan*. 1994.

Smith, John David. *Anti-Black Thought: 1863–1925*. Volume 9: *The Negro Problem*. 1993.

Tourgee, Albion Winegar. *The Invisible Empire*. 1989.

Trelease, Allen W. *White Terror: The Ku Klux Klan Conspiracy and Southern Reconstruction*. 1971.

Turner, John. *The Ku Klux Klan: A History of Racism and Violence*. 1981.

Wade, Wyn Craig. *The Fiery Cross: The Ku Klux Klan in America*. 1987.

Stephanie Shanks-Miele

Ku Klux Klan Act of 1871

Although the first KU KLUX KLAN was formed by Nathan Bedford Forrest in 1868, it was disbanded a year later owing to public pressures calling for a halt to the terror and violence associated with the night-riders.

Prior to 1871, the military was the primary mechanism for prosecuting Klan violence, but it was ineffective because military commanders were reluctant to supercede state civil courts during peacetime. Ulysses S. Grant, serving first as the commanding general under President Andrew Johnson, and as president of the United States beginning in 1869, had personal reservations about utilizing military force because he feared being tagged a military despot. Following the passage of the FIFTEENTH AMENDMENT in 1870, which guaranteed "Negro" suffrage, much of the intimidation, assault, and lynching was, in defense of the DEMOCRATIC PARTY, aimed at potential REPUBLICAN PARTY voters, many of whom were black. The Enforcement Act of 1870 made bribery and intimidation of voters a felony, and section 6 made it illegal for groups to disguise themselves or conspire to deny individuals their civil rights, or to punish them after they exercised their constitutional rights and privileges. Although this legislation was the impetus for a handful of arrests, which were all discharged, the impact of the act boiled down to insignificant symbolism, as the federal government made little effort to prosecute the Klan.

Southern Republicans continued to report Klan terror to Northern officials, and the U.S. Senate formed an investigating committee in 1871 that focused on atrocities in NORTH CAROLINA, as the existing CONGRESS was about to expire. The committee filed its report on March 10 after interviewing over fifty racially diverse witnesses from both political parties. The report confirmed that several Klan organizations were engaging in violent activities directed toward Democratic Party electoral victory, and that the Klan had been able to prevent the prosecution of its members for the crimes that the organization required them to commit. In response to the Senate report and the continued frustration of Southern governors, Congress passed a KKK bill on March 29, 1871, which sought to enforce the FOURTEENTH AMENDMENT. The bill contained provisions for monetary penalties and prison sentences for violators (section 1), conspiracies and disguises used to deprive people of their civil rights were made illegal (section 2), President Grant was given permission to use military force and suspend the writ of habeas corpus to control Klan activity (sections 3 and 4), jurors were required to take an oath swearing no loyalty to the Klan (section 5), and people with prior knowledge of Klan violence who did not act to prevent it would be held liable for it (section 6).

In the wake of political dissent flowing from passage of the act, President Grant was still reluctant to utilize military force; so he thought that federal prosecutions provided an alternative. The secretary of war and the attorney general hired undercover detectives supervised by the Secret Service to infiltrate the Klan and collect evidence about activities and the individuals involved in the terror. In a climate of strict secrecy, the Justice Department issued orders to Southern states to begin prosecution of the Klan. Congressional hearings and investigations also continued during this time period, and included limited testimony from Klansmen such as Forrest, who portrayed the Klan as a self-defense organization formed to return law and order to the South. Attorney General Amos T. Akerman was sent to North Carolina to investigate KKK activity, which led President Grant to order the Klan to disburse and surrender their arms and disguises. Mass arrests by the U.S. marshal began on October 19, 1871, continuing throughout 1872. Investigations and arrests in some places revealed a high level of white involvement in Klan activities; in places such as York County, South Carolina, nearly two-thirds of whites had participated in the Klan to some degree. Whereas the number of indictments across the South was large, the number of cases leading to prosecution and sentencing was relatively small. The overloaded federal courts were not able to meet the demands of trying such a tremendous number of cases, a situation that led to selective pardoning. By late 1873 and 1874, most of the charges against Klansmen were dropped although new cases continued to be prosecuted for several more years. Most of those sentenced had either served their terms or been pardoned by 1875.

The U.S. SUPREME COURT eviscerated the Ku Klux Act in 1876 by ruling that the federal government could no longer prosecute individuals although states would be forced to comply with federal civil rights provisions. Republicans passed a second civil rights act (the CIVIL RIGHTS ACT OF 1875) to grant equal access to public facilities and other housing accommodations regardless of race. Ironically, the Klan during this period served to further Northern reconstruction efforts, as Ku Klux violence provided the political climate needed to pass civil rights protections for blacks. Although the Ku Klux Act of 1871 dismantled the first Klan, Southern whites formed other, similar groups that kept blacks away from the polls through intimidation and physical violence. RECONSTRUCTION ended with the election of President Rutherford B. Hayes, who suspended the federal military occupation of the South; yet blacks still found themselves without the basic civil liberties that the period had sought to secure.

BIBLIOGRAPHY

Chalmers, David M. *Hooded Americanism: The History of the Ku Klux Klan.* 1965.

Klanwatch. *The Ku Klux Klan: A History of Racism and Violence.* 1981.
Trelease, Allen W. *White Terror: The Ku Klux Klan Conspiracy and Southern Reconstruction.* 1971.
Wade, Wyn Craig. *The Fiery Cross.* 1987.

Stephanie Shanks-Meile

Kunstler, William Moses

(1919–1995), radical lawyer.

William Kunstler specialized in protecting the rights of political dissenters and other unpopular clients. Born into a middle-class Jewish home in New York

Attorney William Kunstler, representing American Indian activist Russell Means, answers questions at a news conference in Minneapolis. June 6, 1975. (CORBIS/Bettmann)

City, Kunstler attended Yale University, where he majored in French, and later the Columbia University School of Law. In WORLD WAR II he was a signal intelligence officer with the U.S. 8th Army in the Pacific, where he earned the Bronze Star. In 1948, Kunstler received his LL.B. degree and was admitted to the New York bar. He was associate professor of law at New York Law School from 1950 to 1992, and he also helped to found the Law Center for Constitutional Rights. Kunstler worked as a partner with his brother in the firm of Kunstler & Kunstler, practicing marriage and family law, early in his career. During this time he took some civil rights cases.

In 1961, when the CONGRESS OF RACIAL EQUALITY (CORE) sponsored the FREEDOM RIDES, Kunstler traveled to Mississippi to give legal support to Jack H. Young, an African-American CORE lawyer who was defending the riders. This was a radicalizing experience for Kunstler. Later in the 1960s, Kunstler served as counsel for Martin Luther KING, JR., and his SOUTHERN CHRISTIAN LEADERSHIP CONFERENCE, as well as for the STUDENT NONVIOLENT COORDINATING COMMITTEE. He defended Stokely CARMICHAEL when he was arrested for civil rights agitation in Selma, Alabama, and represented Adam Clayton POWELL in his fight against his exclusion from CONGRESS.

Over the course of his career Kunstler had as his clients such diverse figures as comedian Lenny Bruce (when he was charged with obscenity), the Berrigan brothers, members of the BLACK PANTHER PARTY prisoners charged in the 1971 revolt at New York's Attica prison, AMERICAN INDIAN MOVEMENT radical Leonard Peltier, flag burner Gregory Johnson, and both MALCOLM X and his daughter Qubilah Shabazz. Kunstler was known for boldness, creativity, and provocative presentations in court. His most notorious defense was that of the Chicago Seven, charged in Chicago in the 1968 Democratic National Convention melee with conspiracy to cross state lines to incite a riot. He wrote eleven books, including *The Case for Courage: The Stories of Ten Famous American Attorneys Who Risked Their Careers in the Cause of Justice* (1962), *Trials and Tribulations* (1985), and *My Life As a Radical Lawyer* (1994).

BIBLIOGRAPHY
Kunstler, William. *My Life As a Radical Lawyer.* 1994.
Obituary. *New York Times*, p. B6, September 5, 1995.

Eric Cummins